鄭聖洙.
Sung S. Chung
Tel. (517) 351-2918.

INTRODUCTION TO CRIMINAL JUSTICE:

Theory and Practice

Sing S. Chang

Tel. (514) 351-2418

INTRODUCTION TO CRIMINAL JUSTICE:

Theory and Practice

Edited by

Dae H. Chang
Criminal Justice
Hugo Wall School of Urban and Public Affairs
Wichita State University
Wichita, Kansas

and

Michael J. Palmiotto
Criminal Justice
Hugo Wall School of Urban and Public Affairs
Wichita State University
Wichita, Kansas

Published by

MidContinent Academic Press, L.L.C.
Wichita, Kansas

Copyright © 1997 MidContinent Academic Press, L.L.C.

ISBN 0-9659545-0-1

Cover design by Jennifer Yeoman.

Printed in the United States of America.

All rights reserved. No part of this publication
may be reproduced in any form or by any process,
electronic or mechanical, including photocopy,
recording, scanning, or any information and retrieval
system, without permission in writing from the
publisher.

Published by:

MidContinent Academic Press, L.L.C.
The Forum Building
2144 North Broadway
Wichita, Kansas 67214

99 98 97

10 9 8 7 6 5 4 3 2 1

TABLE OF CONTENTS

About the Authors

Donald Blazicek received his doctorate from the University of Michigan and joined the faculty of the Department of Administration of Justice at Wichita State University in 1976. His primary interests in teaching and research were research methods, forensic psychiatry, security, and environmental protection. He wrote the original draft of chapter four, before passing away in 1995.

Ken Braunstein is emeritus professor of criminal justice, University of Nevada, Reno, where he served as a faculty member for 30 years, including 14 years as department chair. Prior to his faculty position he had security, police, and investigative experience in both the private and public sectors. He is a licensed security consultant by the State of Nevada, and is founder, principal consultant, and president of Forensic Science Consultants in Reno. He has extensive experience in gaming, hotel, and resort security, and has testified in depositions and courts of several states throughout the country. He is a member of the standing committee on gaming security for the American Society for Industrial Security, and is a past president of the Western and Pacific Association of Criminal Justice Educators. He holds a master's degree in police science and administration from Washington State University, and a bachelor's in law enforcement administration from San Jose State University.

Rolando V. del Carmen is Distinguished Professor of Criminal Justice at Sam Houston State University. He has law degrees from the Philippines, Southern Methodist University, the University of California at Berkeley, and the University of Illinois. He has published extensively in law and criminal justice and is the recipient of several national awards. He teaches criminal procedure, corrections law, legal liabilities, and a law seminar on the legal aspects of the criminal justice system.

Dae H. Chang received his Ph.D. from Michigan State University. He is a former Chairman and currently a professor of Criminal Justice, in the Hugo Wall School, Wichita State University. His areas of specialization include law enforcement, comparative or cross-cultural perspectives on crime and delinquency, and the application of criminological theory. Currently he is Editor-in-Chief of the International Journal of Comparative and Applied Criminal Justice — a post he has held for the past 22 years. He has written a dozen books and over 50 journal articles, and is now concentrating on international organized crime.

Wayne W. Dunning received his doctorate in chemistry from Iowa State University and taught chemistry for 11 years at Wichita State University. During that time he was also a member of the Wichita Police Reserve, assigned to duties as a detective, crime scene technician, and consultant to the forensic laboratory. In 1972 he combined his education in chemistry and experience in police work and joined the Department of Administration of Justice at Wichita State. Until his retirement in 1994, he taught courses in investigation, criminalistics, forensic photography, criminal evidence, and firearms. During his teaching career he was also a consultant to government agencies, public defenders, private attorneys, and insurance companies. He has testified as an expert witness for the prosecution/plaintiff and defense sides in criminal and civil trials, in state and federal courts, in Kansas and Missouri.

Miles Erpelding is the lead instructor for the Administration of Justice Department at Butler County Community College in El Dorado, Kansas. He received his Masters and Bachelors degrees from Wichita State University in Administration of Justice and is a political science graduate of Butler County Community College. His career includes over 13 years of service within the Kansas Judicial Branch and the Thirteenth Judicial District in El Dorado, Kansas. He served as a Court Services Officer the five years and most recently, as the Chief Court Services Officer for over eight years.

James Fagin is a full-professor and Director of the Undergraduate Criminal Justice program, the Masters Criminal Justice Administration program, and Masters Public Administration Programs at Chaminade University. He received his Ph.D. and M.S. from Southern Illinois University at Carbondale (SIU-C), and his B.A. from University of Nevada, Las Vegas. Dr. Fagin has published several articles, a textbook, and presented numerous papers to professional conferences. He has served as consultant to numerous public and private agencies and companies. He served as Acting President of Kima Theological College in Kenya, East Africa in 1987. His specialty in conflict resolution is hostage and barricaded subject negotiations and he has conducted seminars for numerous law enforcement and correctional agencies on this subject. He was President of the America Society of Public Administration Hawaii Chapter, 1996-1997 and the Hawaii Criminal Justice Educator Association, 1995-1996.

Richard G. Frey is an Associate Professor of Criminal Justice at SUNY College at Brockport. He was educated in law and political science at Cornell University, the University of Texas, and the University of Oregon. He co-authored a book on the legislative process and has written articles and presented papers on many law subjects, most recently on the conflicts between a defendant's right to a fair trial and freedom of the press.

Ronald G. Iacovetta, Associate Professor in Criminal Justice in the Hugo Wall School, Wichita State University, obtained his B.A. and M.A. from the Colorado State University and the Ph.D. from the University of Connecticut. He has published in the areas of delinquency, youth and corrections and has served as co-editor of a book on Critical Issues in Criminal Justice, and has written articles and book chapters on the subject of organized crime and cor-

rections. He has taught courses on organized and white collar crime at Wichita State University for the past 12 years. He served 6 years as chair of the Department of Administration of Justice and 3 years as Assistant Dean of the Graduate School at Wichita State University. Currently, he is doing research on gambling and Organized and White Collar Crime. Since the Summer of 1996, he has been the Associate Director of Undergraduate Programs in the Hugo Wall School of Urban and Public Affairs and continues to teach criminal justice.

Galan M. Janeksela is a Professor in the School of Social and Community Services, and Dean of the College of Health and Human Services at The University of Tennessee at Chattanooga. He previously served as Director of the Administration of Justice Program at Wichita State University. Prior to serving as Director, he was Chairperson of the Department of Administration of Justice at the same institution. He holds a Ph.D. in Sociology from Iowa State University. He has served as Guest Editor for several Special Issues of the *International Journal of Comparative and Applied Criminal Justice*, covering the areas of Comparative Juvenile Delinquency, and Female Criminality, and is currently a co-editor of a forthcoming book entitled *Juvenile Delinquency and Juvenile Justice: Comparative and International Perspectives* to be published by The Acorn Press. He has over forty publications to his credit, many of which are in the field of juvenile justice.

Andra Katz is currently an assistant professor of Criminal Justice at Wichita State University. She is teaching a course in crime causation as well as one in research methods. She is a doctoral graduate in the criminal justice department from Michigan State University. She worked extensively under the tutelage of Dr. David Carter, the director for the National Center for Community Policing, and has worked on related grants and projects. In addition, she taught criminology, police administration as an instructor, and taught graduate level courses as a teaching assistant while at Michigan State University. She is a co-in-structor for the criminal justice overseas study program in England through Michigan State University. She has attended seminars on areas of interest offered to law enforcement officers. Her areas of research are computer crime, international organized crime and community policing and has been involved in police training overseas.

Ineke Haen Marshall is professor of Criminal Justice at the University of Nebraska at Omaha. She studied sociology at the Catholic University of Brabant (The Netherlands), and obtained her Ph.D. in sociology at Bowling Green State University (US). Her research interests include criminal careers, ethnicity and crime, comparative criminological theory, self-report methodology, and drug policy. She has published in scholarly journals such as *Criminology, Journal of Research in Crime and Delinquency, American Sociological Review, The European Journal of Criminal Policy and Research*, and *Justice Quarterly*. She co-edited *Between Prohibition and Legalization: The Dutch Experiment in Drug Policy* (1996 Kugler Publications). She also edited *Minorities, Migrants, and Crime: Diversity and Similarity Across Europe and the United States* (Sage, 1997).

Chris E. Marshall is associate professor of Criminal Justice at the University of Nebraska at Omaha. He obtained his Ph.D. in sociology at Iowa State University. His scholarly interests include social control, theory, general methodology. He has published in scholarly journals such as *Violence and Victims, Criminal Justice Policy Review, Crime and Justice.*

Jerome McKean received his Ph.D. from Florida State University. He is an Assistant Professor of Criminal Justice and Criminology at Ball State University in Muncie, Indiana. He is the author of several articles and book chapters, and the co-author, with James E. Hendricks, of *Crisis Intervention: Contemporary Issues for On-Site Interveners*. He is currently engaged in research on the police response to domestic violence, empirical tests of self-control theory, and public attitudes toward the police.

Michael J. Palmiotto, Ph.D. is an Associate Professor of the Criminal Justice Program with the Hugo Wall School of Urban and Public Affairs at Wichita State University. He worked as a police officer in New York State and is the past Director of Criminal Justice and Police Training at the Community College of Beaver County, Monaca. Pennsylvania. He holds a masters degree from the John Jay College of Criminal Justice and a doctorate from the University of Pittsburgh. His law enforcement interests include civil liabilities, drug enforcement, criminal investigation, and community policing. He has numerous articles and has published a text on policing and on criminal investigation.

Michael Joseph Palmiotto has a masters in Public Administration from Central Flordia University. He has been employed as a county correction officer and as a state probation officer in central Flordia for six years. As a probation officer he did pre-sentence investigation, supervision, training and supervised probationers in a drug rehabilitation program. Currently, he is employed as a federal probation officer in Fayetteville, Arkansas.

Ken Peak is professor and former chair of criminal justice at the University of Nevada, Reno, where he was named "Teacher of the Year" by the university's Honor Society, 1984-85. He is presently chairman of the Police Section of the Academy of Criminal Justice Sciences, and recently served as president of the Western and Pacific Association of Criminal Justice Educators. He has been a municipal police officer, nine-county criminal justice planner, director of a four-state technical assistance institute, assistant professor of administration of justice (Wichita State University), and director of public safety at two universities. He has authored six books on policing, community policing and problem solving, justice administration, and bootlegging history, as well as nearly 50 additional journal articles and book chapters. He holds a doctorate from the University of Kansas.

Philip L. Reichel is a Professor of Sociology at the University of Northern Colorado. His teaching and research interests are in all aspects of criminal justice studies. His major publications include a text book on comparative criminal justice (*Comparative Criminal Justice Systems: A Topical Approach*, 1994, Prentice Hall Publishers) and on the American correctional system (*Corrections*, 1997, West Publishers). He has also published over twenty articles in professional journals and is an active member of the Academy of Criminal Justice Sciences and the American Society of Criminology.

Robert Frank Scott, Jr., is presently the Director of the Justice Studies program at Fort Hays State University in Hays, Kansas. He received his doctorate from Sam Houston State University, and his masters degree from SUNY-Buffalo. He has published in a variety of venues, most recently on the subject of the treatment of psychologically disturbed inmates in state prison systems.

Michael R. Smith is an assistant professor of criminal justice at Sam Houston State University.

He is a former police officer and a graduate of the University of South Carolina School of Law. He also holds a Ph.D. in Justice Studies from Arizona State University. He teaches courses on courts, criminal procedure, and the police.

Craig D. Uchida received his Ph.D. in Criminal Justice from the State University of New York at Albany. He is the Assistant Director for Grants Administration at the Office of Community Oriented Policing Services, U.S. Department of Justice. Prior to this, he served as the Director for the Office of Criminal Justice Research and as the Director of the Evaluation Division at the National Institute of Justice, U.S. Department of Justice. Before coming to the Department of Justice, he was a member of the graduate faculty at the Institute of Criminal Justice and Criminology at the University of Maryland, where he conducted field research on search warrant policies and practices, local drug enforcement efforts, and police innovation. He has published numerous articles in criminal justice-related journals, has edited two books, and has written chapters for books on law enforcement issues.

PREFACE

Introduction to Criminal Justice: Theory and Practice has been developed to accompany an introductory course in criminal justice. Although the book has been written primarily for aspiring criminologists, students of law, political science, sociology and other social science related disciplines can benefit from reading through it as well.

Our current vision with the text remains the same as it did back in 1976, when the first edition was being used in classrooms across America. This book is designed to help students understand the basics of criminal justice by providing information in two interrelated, yet mutually exclusive, areas: (1) the theoretical and philosophical aspects of crime and delinquency, and (2) the practical, day-to-day operations of the police, courts and correctional sub-systems. Only by gleaning insights from both areas can a student be truly grounded in the fundamentals of criminology.

With literally hundreds of crime-related issues constantly vying for our attention, it is difficult to pinpoint the specific areas on which to place our focus. That said, is has been the overriding goal of all our contributors to offer a series of comprehensive overviews of the most prevalent and controversial issues facing humanity, everything from the death-penalty debate to terrorism. We owe an intellectual debt of gratitude to each of the professionals who have contributed to this work.

Since our first edition two decades ago, we have been witness to a sad irony. Our world has improved tremendously on technological, medical, educational and other fronts; and we enjoy a greater amount of freedom and liberty now than in any other time in history. Yet despite these advances, statistics reveal that murders, rapes, assaults, theft and a myriad of other acts of crime have tended to grow at an even faster rate than the population itself. Fortunately, in the last several years there has been a decline in most index offenses.

For the past thirty years our local, state, and federal governments have allocated record amounts of funding toward crime prevention and punishment. As we raise our governmental spending and take greater personal precautions against crime, however, we actually increase our odds of being victimized by criminals. Statistically, there is a positive correlation between crime intervention and actual crime rates — a baffling reality, to be sure.

As scholars of criminal justice we might ask: Is our current criminal justice system hopelessly inadequate against the new, more sophisticated forms of crime? Should our nation's courts run on a 24-hours-a-day to foster speedier trials and encourage productivity at the expense of thoroughness? Should the courts focus more on due process and human rights than on actual crime control? Will the "three strikes and you're out" scheme work on all offenders of society?

Throughout the course of this term, you will learn the true extent to which people's ideas about law and order differ. Heated debates rage on in homes and classrooms around the nation about how to maintain peace in society, handle repeat offenders, assist the innocent victims of crime and so on. Yet one reality remains virtually undebated: the fear of crime is real and is felt by everyone.

A recent tell-tale article called "Thief Targets Justice" was publicized in a November, 1996 issue of The Wichita Eagle newspaper. The article describes how Supreme Court Justice Ruth Bader Ginsburg was the victim of a purse snatching incident in northwest Washington DC, near the Watergate apartment complex where she happened to live. Indeed, even the most recognized and respected of criminologists cannot escape the inevitability of crime.

The natural reaction of the populace toward society's upsurge in criminal activity has been to all-but disregard the police and arm themselves with guns and other weapons for greater protection. Many argue that the fear of crime has led people to take precautions that are unnecessary in some cases (e.g. carrying loaded weapons) and counterproductive in others (e.g. vigilante justice). Unfortunately, the solutions to crime often become part of the problem. This is a dilemma that must be dealt with intelligently as well as practically.

Dozens of crime-related topics are covered in detail in this text. None of them, you will undoubtedly find, have any guaranteed answers or clear-cut solutions. The process of studying this complex discipline is what's most important at this stage. Criminals are a permanent part of society and crime prevention is thus a necessity of modern life. We would all do well to recognize this fact and learn the many aspects of crime and our current criminology system so that we may work to improve society in the future.

Dae H. Chang
Michael Palmiotto
Wichita, Kansas
July, 1997

SECTION I

INTRODUCTION:

A Look At The
CRIMINAL JUSTICE SYSTEM

INTRODUCTION

Criminal justice is a broad field involving many topics, philosophies, and institutions. There are the traditional criminal justice institutions such as courts, law enforcement agencies and corrections agencies; and there are other equally important, but less well known, institutions also. Thus the scope and depth of the criminal justice field presents a unique challenge in the making of an introductory criminology text. By definition, an introductory book is to cover in broad strokes most aspects of its respective realm. However, it is difficult to find any one author who has the comprehensive knowledge and ability necessary to write on all major aspects of criminology and criminal justice.

The approach taken in this project has been to solicit a number of professionals and have them contribute their expertise to the text. This approach has its disadvantages as well as its rewards. One disadvantage is that the text takes on many characteristics of a "reader" — which is a compilation of previously published writings on criminology. While many criminal justice experts have contributed to the text, this book is not a reader. Every contributor has furnished original manuscripts that have been tailor-made for this book, in accordance with the specifications set by the editors.

On the other hand, one distinct advantage of this approach is that each area of study has been assigned to, and covered by, a recognized professional with unquestionable expertise in that field. An arduous task of the editors has been to present the material in such a manner that it follows a sound, organized structure.

The text is divided into six sections. **Section I** is an introduction to the overall criminal justice system. The two chapters therein present the basic overview necessary to study the system in a more detailed fashion.

Section II focuses upon the various theories and research methods used to gather data in the criminology field. There are numerous theories that attempt to explain the causes of criminal behavior. As such, it has been necessary to limit the discussion of the causes of such behaviors to the major theories that students will most likely encounter in future studies. Each student should be reminded, however, that there are other theories and ideas regarding the causes of crime which are not presented in this text.

Section III examines the bases of the American criminal justice system — the law. In the United States the law is the foundation of criminology and criminal justice institutions. Thus these chapters look closely at legal institutions such as the courts, along with the process of making laws, and the laws themselves.

Section IV examines the American police. Collectively the police represent perhaps the most visible, as well as criticized, criminal justice institution. Many in-class opinions will surely be voiced from discussions of these chapters.

Section V delves into an area of criminal justice that has oftentimes been neglected by academics and other criminology experts — the jails and prisons of our country. This is a most intriguing area, one that is decidedly crucial to securing a society of law and order. Frequently the focus of criminal justice institutions is on the mere catching and punishing of people who have violated the law. Yet a higher purpose needs to be addressed and served: Our system must find a way to promote successful and enduring rehabilitation of criminal offenders while securing the safety of our society.

Section VI tackles a myriad of controversial issues that are, more often than not, overlooked in other criminology texts. The justice system has a greater impact upon society and individuals than most people realize. Many times this impact extends beyond the traditional lines of police, courts, and prisons. At the heart of our field are some basic abstractions that form the very foundation of our government and society. Criminology, then, must address such topics as justice, fairness, security and should promote a greater understanding of how the American justice system compares to other social systems.

Section VI has four enlightening chapters that serve to illustrate the ways in which the criminal justice system touches everyone — not just the police, lawyers, judges, and criminals.

Rounding out the text is an appendix that contains fifteen examinations, one for each of the chapters 2 through 16. These exams can be used by the student to check his or her comprehension of the material presented or by the instructor for the same purpose.

Chapter 1

An Introduction to the Study of Criminal Justice

By

Dae H. Chang and **Richard C. Newman**

RADIO ADDRESS OF PRESIDENT CLINTON TO THE NATION

"Good morning. Today I want to talk about how to build upon the progress we've made together in working against crime and violence, and especially how we can fight against youth crime.

Four years ago it seemed to any Americans is if the forces of crime and violence had gained an intractable hold over our country, and law-abiding Americans were afraid that from now on they would just have to put up with the insecurity and loss that goes with rampant crime. I was determined to turn that around, to give people the tools they need to take back their streets and schools and neighborhoods, to reestablish a sense of security and true freedom in our country, and to restore our people's faith in the power of law and order.

We had a comprehensive plan to fight crime — to put 100,000 new community police officers on the street and tough new penalties on the books; to keep guns away from criminals by passing the Brady Bill and banning assault weapons; to steer young people away from crime, gangs and drugs in the first place. This approach is working.

This week the FBI reported that serious crime dropped another three percent last year, dropping for the fifth year in a row, the longest decline in more than 25 years. This is great news — not because it gives us a chance to sit back and rest on our laurels, but because it does show all of us that if we work together we can make a difference.

Now that we've finally turned the crime on the run, we have to redouble our efforts. We have to drive the forces of violence further and further into retreat. And as we move forward we have to remember that we're not just fighting against crime, we're fighting for the kind of nation we want to build together for the 21st century. For an America where people feel safe when they walk around the block at night, and untroubled when they kiss their children good-bye in the morning; an America where nobody's grandmother lives across the street from a crackhouse and nobody's child walks to school through a neighborhood overrun by gangs. We're fighting for our children and for their future.

As I begin my second term as President, the next stage in our fight must center on keeping our children safe and attacking the scourge of juvenile crime and gangs. I want every police officer, prosecutor and citizen in America working together to keep our young people safe and young criminals off the streets. This should be America's top priority in the fight for law and order over the next four years. I pledge it will be mine.

We must help parents protect their children and bring order and discipline to their lives. That's why I support school uniforms and community-based curfews. That's why we made zero tolerance for guns in schools the law of the land, and passed Megan's Law to demand that states tell a community whenever a dangerous sexual predator enters its midst.

Now we must do more to give young people something to say 'yes' to — after school, on weekends and in the summer. And we must finish the job of putting 100,000 police on our streets.

At the same time, young people must understand that if they break the law they will be punished; and if they commit violent crimes they will be punished severely. I am determined to break the backs of criminal gangs that have ruined too many lives and stolen too many futures by bringing the full force of the law against them.

One of the most difficult problems facing law enforcement in this fight is the power of gang members to thwart the criminal justice system by threatening and intimidating the witnesses against them. Too many people in too many communities will not testify about gang crimes because they are afraid of violent reprisal. We must not allow the voice of justice to be frightened into silence by the violent threat of gangs.

Today the Justice Department is releasing a report called, 'Preventing Gang And Drug-Related Witness Intimidation.' This report is a handbook for police officers, prosecutors and judges, to help them overcome the dangerous obstacle witness intimidation poses to the steady march of justice. It details the problems they face and helps to provide a blueprint for them to follow that will significantly help state and local gang investigation and prosecution. Starting today, the Justice Department will distribute this report to thousands of police departments, prosecutors and judges across America.

In the coming weeks, I will submit to Congress comprehensive legislation to combat youth violence and drug abuse. Together with all our other efforts against youth violence, this will be the top crime fighting priority of my second term. I've asked the Attorney General to closely examine the growing threat of witness intimidation by gangs and to recommend strong measures to stop it that can be included in legislation. We must not allow the very gangs we're fighting to grind the wheels of justice to a halt.

Over the past four years we've shown that we can roll back crime and violence. Now is not time to let up. There is still too much of it. But if we continue to work together, to stand up for what is right, to work with our community police officers, to take responsibility for ourselves and our families and the other children in our communities who need a guiding hand and an encouraging word — if we'll do all these things, we can keep the crime rate coming down and we can build the future our children deserve. Thanks for listening."

—The White House, January 11, 1997

"The problems of crime bring us together. Even as we join in common action, we know there can be no instant victory. Ancient evils do not yield to easy conquest. We cannot limit our efforts to enemies we can see. We must, with equal resolve, seek out new knowledge, new techniques, and new understanding."

—Message from President Johnson to the Congress, March 9, 1966.

"Decency, security and liberty alike demand that government officials shall be subjected to the same rules of conduct that are commands to the citizens. In a government of laws, existence of the government will be imperiled if it fails to observe the law scrupulously. Our government is the potent, the omni-present teacher. For good or ill, it teaches the whole people by its example."

—Justice Louis Brandeis

"People despotically governed and kept in order by punishments may avoid infraction of law, but they will lose their moral sense. People virtuously governed and kept in order by the inner law of self-control will retain their moral sense, and moreover become good...If a country had none but good rules for a hundred years, crime might by stamped out and the death-penalty abolished."

—Confucius, 511-479 B.C.

GENERAL INTRODUCTION

Welcome to the field of criminal justice. You are about to begin a course of study in which you will acquire a basic understanding of the criminal justice process and the theories and critical issues confronting our justice system. Since the mid 1960's, when President Lyndon Johnson established a Commission to study the justice system, interest in criminal justice has grown substantially. Becoming educated in this area is challenging and frustrating — challenging because the issues are both complex and timely, and frustrating because our current knowledge of crime and justice remains relatively limited.

For over three decades, national surveys have consistently shown crime to be one of our most pressing social problems. This apprehension is not limited to those people who are affiliated with the justice system. Politicians, business leaders, and ordinary citizens have all been focusing more of their attention on crime and crime prevention. Moreover, the issue is not solely a concern in this country, but is an international problem.

The media frequently carries accounts of violent armed robberies, sensationalized murders, multiple killings, and violent rapes. An increase in property crime has caused considerable distress and ensuing debates over possible interventions. Attempts to circumvent crime have occurred with limited success. Most citizens tend to conclude that the world is becoming increasingly chaotic and that the level of crime is part of an unstoppable breakdown of human conscience, moral codes, humanity, and peace among men and women.

Crime in the United States and the fear it creates are illustrated in the following examples. Each year, approximately 6 billion dollars are spent to protect industrial, retail, residential properties. Americans spend about 20 million dollars per annum to secure their personal belongings. A record number of retail stores are installing closed-circuit TVs to detect shoplifting. Burglar alarms are extremely popular items for Christmas-time shoppers. Hotels and motels are revolutionizing ways to control room theft; since it is unfathomable to change the lock on a room each time a guest checks out, hotel managers have the option of utilizing highly sophisticated methods — known as ACT or "Card Guard" — which was developed by American District Telegraph.[1] Other defensive measures against criminals which are being utilized by the public are carrying concealed weapons and pepper sprays, and learning martial arts or other forms of self-defense.

These precautionary measures taken by the general public against criminal activity are only temporary. Eventually society must find more logical solutions to make communities safe. The current emphasis on criminal justice education is the beginning of a new era, a step in the right direction. Most practitioners hope the thrust of this venture will be directed at long-term solutions, and not simply short-term measures against the menacing problems of crime and delinquency.

As a society we have been able to make signif-icant advances in the resolution of several problems plaguing humanity. Unfortunately, though, crime has not been one of them. The United States alone registered over 13.8 million criminal acts in 1995. Despite a slight decrease in violent crimes (3.2 percent from 1994) juvenile crime remains an urgent problem, particularly among young girls. In fact, female criminality in general has been on the rise since the early 1960's. Criminal activity was once confined to large metropolitan regions, but is now plaguing the rural areas as well. The smaller communities, once regarded as being crime-free, are now experiencing their own crime waves.

The question remains, What can be done? While many laypersons feel hopeless in improving the crime situation, the authors of this text believe that enduring solutions can be found. Society's awareness of the crime problem and concern for definitive interventions indicates that future endeavors may prove fruitful.

Solutions to the crime problem must eventually be found within the criminal justice system which is composed of the police, courts, and correctional institutions. The justice system that exists today, however, is often viewed as ineffective. Some critics contend that police organizations are outdated and that reforms are inevitable if more offenders are to be arrested. Simultaneously, police officials have indicated that their powers have been systematically curtailed in a proverbial haze of bureaucracy, and that the courts and legislative bodies have made their functions virtually unworkable. Police are also charging that today's courts are overly lenient and that too many hardened criminals are being "turned loose" onto the streets, therefore making police work more difficult.

Not only are the courts feeling the force of the blame; so too are the correctional institutions (often called "Crime Colleges"). America is in essence engaging in a criminal justice game of politics, in which everyone blames everyone else for the problems associated with criminality. Consequently the justice system is labeled as a "revolving door," where criminals are constantly flowing in and out of police departments, courts, and prisons.

Despite the fact that the United States witnesses high crime rates and problems with the criminal justice system, this country does enjoy more liberties and freedom than any other in the world today. The American justice system is often universally regarded as superior to those of other countries. Although ecumenical superiority is indeed a worthwhile goal, slight and steady improvements within our justice system should not be overlooked either; for if they are, criminals will eventually become dominant and crime will be a controlling force in our daily lives.

This book is designed to initiate your inquiry and understanding of the structure, process, and critical issues confronting our justice system. Its purpose is twofold. For those students who are considering a career in criminology, the book offers a panoramic view of the total justice system; it enables you to focus on the particular components of the system in which you wish to specialize.

For those students who may not have career aspirations in this area but want to become better informed of our system, this text offers a host of valuable insights that can not be obtained elsewhere. Regardless of your endeavors, you will, for the rest of your life, be paying for the justice system with your tax dollars. You will also be directly electing people to positions in the system or electing government leaders who will appoint officials to key positions. As a consumer of information the print and video media will frequently bring to your attention critical issues confronting criminal justice. As a taxpayer, voter, and consumer you will surely want to make informed judgments about such concerns. This book offers you a concise point of reference to begin that often difficult task of forming an educated opinion.

WHAT IS CRIMINAL JUSTICE?

There are two primary schools of thought within the field of criminology. The first school, which has the greatest number of supporters, maintains the traditional academic role of attempt-ing to gain scientific knowledge of criminal behavior. In this quest for knowledge the criminologist builds theories, deduces workable hypotheses for empirical verification, employs methodological techniques, and develops certain principles necessary for the explanation of criminal phenomena. This position is known in academic circles as "pure criminology."

The second school of thought maintains that criminologists have already accumulated enough insight into criminological phenomena, and that the time has come for them to actively apply their principles to practical, real life situations. Frequently, this school is labeled either "criminal justice" or "administration of justice." As indicated previously, pure criminology is an attempt to answer the questions of "what," "why," and "how," whereas "applied criminology" seeks to answer "what for?" In one light then pure criminology relates to the past and present while applied criminology relates to the future.

On any university campus, one generally finds both groups — one that identifies itself as "criminologists," and the other as "criminal justice educators." The emerging discipline, criminal justice, is in response to a need for relevance within the academic institutions, as well as criminal justice agencies throughout the United States. It is obvious that both groups are necessary and should work together. The task of academic criminology involves not only teaching aspirants the discipline but also research and writing. Without field research, criminologists cannot reinforce or reconstruct theory. Similarly, criminal justice educators cannot teach or apply certain techniques in the field of law enforcement, for instance, without its foundation of theory.

In recent years, however, we have found an intensity of attacks and criticisms against each other. In some sense it is a sign of healthy tension, as almost all social and academic endeavors find themselves "resistant to change." Just how long it will take for criminologists and criminal justice educators to work cooperatively is hard to predict. There have been some indicators, through interdisciplinary approaches to teaching and collaborative research undertakings, that imply the discipline will homogenize in the near future.

The label "criminal justice" is composed of two words that are related, yet mutually exclusive. The word "criminal" implies that crime is relative to social phenomenon, whereas "justice" implies that crime is relative to legal and political phenomenon. Therefore, criminal justice is concerned with causal implications of deviant behavior within a society's political structure.

In dealing with causal aspects of deviant behavior, we tend to look toward theoretical explanations. These explanations are usually found in the field of criminology, a subconcentration of sociology or psychology.[2] This discipline concerns itself with the etiology of criminal behavior. Three categories of criminal justice exist today:

> Criminal behavior is often inherited from generation to generation; this theory takes into account the biological and anthropological aspects of criminal behavior.[3]

> Environmental factors and conditions are strongly associated with criminal behavior; this theory is generally the concern of sociologists.[4]

> Mental factors of conditions are the primary cause of criminal behavior; theories that stem from this generalization are dealt with by psychiatry and psychology.[5]

Besides the casual aspects of criminality, other facets of criminal behavior are also reviewed and considered. Such facets include the criminal role, societal response to crime and criminal behavior, and cultural norms.

Sociology, in general, and criminology, in particular, are searching for academic solutions to criminality. Sociology has enjoyed unprecedented autonomy in teaching and researching the phenomenon of crime. Traditionally, criminology as an academic discipline has been divided into three

sub-disciplines as a means of studying criminal behavior. These are:

1. The process of law making and enforcing.

2. The process of law breaking.

3. The manner in which offenders are treated by societal agencies.

During the past 30 years some progress has been made in terms of theory-construction and theory-testing, which has paved the way for a clearer understanding of the crime phenomenon. Also in this regard, criminology as a sub-discipline of sociology, has developed considerably. From the standpoint of theory utilization, however, a substantial amount of these theories cannot by used in crime prevention or criminal rehabilitation. Why have these theories been thrown out? We can attribute this outcome mainly to academic criminology, which has been geared toward the explanation of causation. Courses such as criminology, penology, juvenile delinquency, deviance, social problems and social disorganization have primarily focused upon theory, divorcing applicability. Therefore, little attention has been given to the application of theory to the crime problem.[6]

Although criminologists appear autonomous in their fields, the study of conflict itself is not confined only to criminologists. Marshall Clinard, co-author of *Criminal Behavior System* once mentioned, "Much sociological criminological writing has been devoted to revealing theoretical and methodological errors in psychiatrically and psychoanalytically oriented research. Psychiatrists and psychoanalysts, on the other hand, seldom refer to sociological research, either because they are unfamiliar with it or because they choose to ignore it."[7]

In recent years an increasing number of criminologists have attempted to make their research findings more relevant to real crime situations. Any significant degree of change in the present criminal justice system, together with citizens' participation and community involvement, is deemed essential. So far, three objectives have been identified: crime prevention, crime control, and criminal rehabilitation. To effectively reach these three objectives the following must be considered: (1) identification of early symptoms and causes of delinquency and criminal acts, (2) legal strategies of patented criminal operational surveillance, (3) early apprehension, (4) scientific criminal investigation, (5) speed trials, and (6) confinement of those guilty and dangerous to the community.

Even though some subject matter is beyond our control, the efforts of sociology, psychology, political science, economics, and other social science disciplines must be coordinated. To date, consolidation of academic disciplines into an interdisciplinary and unified framework has been an exceedingly difficult task. A pragmatic framework for criminology does conflict with the academic criminologist. While most criminal justice programs continually subscribe to academically oriented courses, the core requirements of such programs are based on realism rather than idealism. In addition to academic courses, newly established degree requirements in criminal justice usually include practically and experimentally oriented courses. This new degree of criminal justice is more in tune with professional requirements and qualifications. Such trends in this area will inevitably continue in the years to come. Furthermore, crime related courses will gradually be separated from either sociology, public administration, or psychology, thereby making criminal justice an autonomous field of study.

The legal phenomenon and its implication in criminal justice encompasses a wide range of agencies and offices, ranging from the city police department to the U.S. Supreme Court.[8] Thousands of people at state, local, and federal levels are involved in the criminal justice system. This system is primarily concerned with the decision process associated with crime control. As this system becomes more complex, educational requirements become upgraded to meet the various changes in social conditions.

As early as 1916, Chief August Vollmer of the Berkeley Police Department in California initiated one of the first police training schools in the United States. Later this school was expanded into the University of California at Berkeley, and by 1931 Vollmer developed the School of Criminology on that campus. In 1929 the University of Chicago started a Police Science program, and that same year, the University of Southern California established a graduate program in Public Administration with a specialization in Law Enforcement. Michigan State University initiated a Bachelor of Science degree program in Police Administration and Public Safety in 1935.

The establishment of degree programs in criminal justice at universities, colleges and community colleges has increased considerably over the past two decades. In 1966 there were only 184 programs offering criminology or criminal justice courses. That figure rose to over 1,000 in 1978.[9] In 1997 around 1300 institutions contribute to the study of criminology, and by the year 2000, 1500 are anticipated. Moreover, a survey conducted by the International Association of Chiefs of Police identified 121 programs offering a full master's degree while 21 had established doctorates in some area of criminology or criminal justice.[10] The increased number of degree granting institutions throughout the country is a sign that demands have been placed upon our nation's colleges to supply qualified manpower to fill positions in law enforcement agencies, courts, correctional facilities, and field service organizations. During this same period, the growth of federal and state funding for research and educational training increased dramatically.

The reason for this increased demand for degree-granting criminal justice programs, concurrent with governmental funding for these programs, is that crime has reached epidemic levels in many American cities. For the first time in our country's history, crime has become the preeminent social problem. Indeed, the problem is so serious that succeeding Presidents have declared that "crime is our number one enemy" and that the nation must declare an "all out war against the menacing crime problem." The need for well educated personnel within the justice system remains essential if dependable solutions are to be obtained.

11

For the past two hundred years, American policemen were recruited from the lower socioeconomic classes. Brute strength was the most important quality of a policeman and educational requirements were aptly kept to a minimum. As "professionalism" became the goal of many police departments, efforts were made to escalate educational requirements. Gradually, these requirements rose to the point where a high school diploma was imperative for minimum requirements for entry into law enforcement. In recent years, many large police departments have required their recruits to have not only a high school diploma, but a college degree as well.

In today's departments the formal education of policemen plays a vital role in job promotions and salary raises. Therefore, to improve his or her career standing the policeman is compelled to attend a college or university initially for an Associate of Arts degree and, eventually, a Bachelor's degree. The same trend can be witnessed in correctional agencies. Although higher education does promote professionalism, it also creates problems within the police department. For instance, police departments must rearrange duty assignments so that they do not conflict with the classes taken by the police officers.

Another problem is witnessed when administrators of a police department make imposing suggestions regarding which college level courses a given officer should attend. Perhaps the most serious problem in this area, though, is the police officer's dislike for and misconceptions about college or university campuses. Such disdain is oftentimes due to many students' apprehension toward, and overt ridicule of, police officers.

Aside from officers' educational requirements, correctional institutional personnel and security officers are badly in need of formal education and training. From the standpoint of inmates' rehabilitation process, the presence of security guards in prisons and their manner of handling inmates, constitutes a very important element in the inmates' success or failure upon release. In fact, numerous studies have shown that on the average, inmates' educational levels have been higher than those of the security guards themselves.[11]

Particularly in recent years, vast amounts of funding have been appropriated for the advancement of inmates' education, while security guards' educational requirements have remained virtually unchanged. Consequently, security guards and inmates find it difficult to communicate with each other on the same level; this subsequently results in friction and frequent misunderstandings. Some efforts have been made to encourage security personnel to attend colleges or universities, but these efforts have not been widespread.

Although formal education may by a key to professionalism within the criminal justice system, experience and appropriate training are also needed. Hundreds of law schools throughout the United States graduate thousands of students each year. Even though many of these graduates fill positions within the justice system, the majority have no experience and training. This results in premature and inadequate programs within the various agencies and departments which are associated with crime prevention.

This fact is vividly illustrated by an anonymous prisoner, "Joe Convict" printed in a prison newspaper.[12]

Dear Judge,

When I stood before you that day in court, you said some very stirring things to me. For one thing, you stated that I should be ashamed of myself for the way I had avoided my duties and obligations toward society. Later, you spoke of your interest in my possible rehabilitation, and you said something to the effect that the real purpose of punishment is to reform, rather than punish. Then you handed me the 10-year sentence I am now serving.

Sir, I have been in prison for over three years and I have kept hoping to see you, so I could tell you about the progress I am making. But I have never seen you around this prison at all, and from what I can learn, neither has anyone else. In fact, I have been advised that you have never set foot in here in your life! I was amazed to learn this. The way you spoke so earnestly of penology, rehabilitation and so on, I naturally figured you must have known what you were talking about. Otherwise, how could you have possibly known what was best for me or the community?

However, since it is rather obvious that you know nothing whatsoever about this prison except from what you read in the paper or through gossip, I am curious to learn just how you arrived at your sentence. How can you possibly know just how long it may take to reform a person here?

It's kind of funny, in a sad way. An auto-mechanic must know something about cars; a carpenter must know something about building things, etc. But it seems that a judge — a man who deals with the lives and fate of other human beings — doesn't have to know anything at all about the places to which he sends people to be reformed. I guess all a judge has to know is courtroom procedure, a few legal phrases, and the limits of sentences.

Begging your pardon, sir, but it's kind of hard for me to work up much respect for such apathy and indifference.

Sincerely yours,

Joe Convict

As previously suggested, criminals are not restricted to any socioeconomic class, nor are they bound by heredity. Criminals exist in every level of our economic system and they come from all walks of life, from custodians to government officials. The Watergate episode is an excellent example of high-level corruption. Newspapers frequently include stories of deception and embezzlement by lawyers, judges, governors, congressmen and doctors, as well as those stories of criminal acts committed by people from lower class status. If this is difficult to grasp, consider your own behavior. Have you, upon recollection of your prior events, participated in an activity that, if reported, would have labeled you a criminal?[13] Think about it.

In recent years the public has realized the true extent of criminal behavior. This awareness is primarily due to the increase in educational levels among the general public, wider publicity through mass media, fluctuating economic conditions, and the constant concern for basic human rights. These concerns are reflected in the demands for accountability of government officials, consumer protection agencies, and individual rights activists. The public's crime conscious behaviors have subsequently caused backlogs in many courts. Police departments are constantly being informed of criminal behavior by citizens. Clearly the justice system has become more complex, and issues have become more confusing. It should be apparent by now that criminology is not consumed with the causes of crime; it is concerned with all areas directly or indirectly associated with the crime phenomenon.

CURRICULUM

In the previous sections, criminology justice was identified as a most demanding and important area in our society. The success or failure of improving our understanding of justice rests, in part, with the continued support of criminology studies in our colleges and universities. Those who are planning to enter the field should be encouraged to pursue a formal education, which of course would be augmented by practical experience.

The student who enters this discipline will find many courses offered and have the option of obtaining an Associate, Bachelor, or Master's degree. At the Associate of Science level, most community or junior colleges do not offer the same level of course work. The following courses seem to be most universal, however: (1) Introduction to Law Enforcement, Police Administration, Police Fundamentals, or Law Operations & Procedures; (2) Introduction to the Administration of Justice; (3) Traffic Control & Highway Safety; (4) Criminal Investigation; (5) Criminal Law & Procedure; (6) Intern, Practicum in Criminal Justice Agencies; (7) Contract & Interview Techniques; (8) Basic Corrections: Theory & Practice; (9) Crime/Delinquency Prevention; (10) Security Administration; (11) Law Enforcement in the Community; (12) Juvenile/Criminal Justice Procedures; and (13) Personal Identification. Traditionally, theory focused courses such as Criminology, Juvenile Delinquency, Penology, Sociology of Law, Deviant Behavior, and Abnormal Psychology are supplemented by two-year colleges.

The bachelor's level is more extensive and generally offers the following courses: (1) Criminalistics & Scientific Crime Detection; (2) Women in the Administration of Justice; (3) Investigative Technology; (4) Special Investigation; (5) Minorities in the Administration of Justice; (6) Senior Seminar; (7) Independent Study; (8) Internship or Practicum; (9) Automated Data Processing; (10) Research Methods; (11) Security Staff Supervision; (12) Community Crime Prevention Program; (13) Security Technology Security Staff Prevention; (14) Conflict Resolution in the Administration of Justice; (15) Planning; (16) Forensic Science; (17) Field Corrections Techniques; and (18) Institutional Corrections Techniques. Some of the aforementioned courses are dual listed wherein students can claim either undergraduate or graduate credit toward their intended degree.

At the graduate level, degrees leading to Master of Arts, Master of Science, Master of Criminal Justice, Master of Public Administration, or Master of Public Safety are offered at many institutions around the country. In addition to a Master's degree, a Doctor of Philosophy (Ph.D) or equivalent can be pursued. To obtain a Ph.D., additional courses either in academic and/or professional disciplines (Sociology, Psychology, Political Science, Public Administration, Social Work, Education, and Communications) must be completed.

On a typical Master's degree track, a candidate can choose from several areas of specialization (e.g. General Administration of Justice, Investigation, Agency Administration, Prevention Program Development, and Security). In many colleges several of these areas may be combined to fit the student's specific interests. At the Doctoral level, more theory and research methodology are addressed in addition to the Master's requirements. Because admission policies and course requirements are not uniform throughout the United States, students interested in pursuing a degree should write the institution they are interested in attending for their particular course requirements and offerings.

THE EXTENT OF CRIME IN THE UNITED STATES[14]

Law enforcement does not purport to know the total volume of crime, because of the many criminal acts which are not reported to official sources. Estimates of the level of unreported crime can be developed through costly victim surveys, but the reluctance of many victims to report all criminal actions to law enforcement agencies leads to a lack of statistical reliability. In light of this situation the best sources for obtaining usable crime counts are those considered to be most consistently reported, those which provide the capability of computing meaningful crime trends and rates. Table 1 shows the recent trends within violent crimes as well as the eight index crimes with a percent change from 1993 to 1995.

As an aggregate representation of data provided by the Uniform Crime Report, the following statistics have been provided as of 1995:

- One Crime Index Offense every 2 seconds.
- One Violent Crime every 18 seconds.
- One Property Crime every 3 seconds.
- One Murder every 24 minutes.
- One Forcible Rape every 5 minutes.
- One Robbery every 54 seconds.
- One Aggravated Assault every 29 seconds.
- One Burglary every 12 seconds.
- One Larceny-Theft every 4 seconds.
- One Motor Vehicle Theft every 21 seconds.

For the student interested in conducting crime research there are numerous sources of statistical data available. Along with the previously mentioned Uniform Crime report, the National Criminal Justice Information Service publishes an annual *Sourcebook of Criminal Justice Statistics*, which provides data from all three segments of the justice system. Many local and state agencies also prepare monthly, quarterly or annual reports that summarize agency activity. Perhaps the best known among the private organizations that conducts research is the International Association of Chiefs of Police.

A SUMMARY REPORT OF THE PRESIDENT'S COMMISSION OF LAW ENFORCEMENT AND ADMINISTRATION OF JUSTICE[15]

This section offers a summary of the findings from the Report of the President's Commission on Law Enforcement and Administration of Justice. The Commission was comprised of 19 members who were appointed by President Lyndon B. Johnson to analyze the American criminal justice system. It focused on problem identification as well as intervention, and made professional recommendations to the President in an effort to curtail the rise in crime in the United States. The Commission utilized several hundred consultants, advisers and other professionals already in the field. Five national surveys and hundreds of interviews were conducted, along with innumerable conferences and seminars. The report, which took eighteen months to complete, is generally regarded as the most comprehensive study of crime, juvenile delinquency, corrections and law enforcement currently available.

Although the study is now some thirty years old it is helpful to review its findings and recommendations, and compare them to the data collected by the scholars who have contributed to the chapters in this text. This will enable you to assess the extent to which the justice system has improved or failed to enhance its efforts to reduce crime.

Many Americans take comfort in thinking that crime is the vice of only a handful of people. This view is highly inaccurate. In the United States today, one boy in every six is referred to a juvenile court. A Commission survey showed that in 1965 more than two million Americans were received in prisons or juvenile training schools, or placed on probation. Another Commission study suggested that about 40 percent of all male children living in the United States would be arrested for a non-traffic offense during their lives. An independent survey of 1,700 persons found that 91 percent of the sample admitted to having committed acts for which they might have received jail or prison sentences.

Many Americans also think of crime as a narrow range of behaviors. It is not. An enormous variety of acts makes up the scope of crime. Crime is not just the archetypal rebellious teenager snatching a lady's purse or driving drunk. It is also

Table 1

Index Crimes	Number of Offenses 1993	Number of Offenses 1994	Number of Offenses 1995	Percent Change from 93-95
Violent Crime	1,926,017	1,857,670	1,798,785	-6.6%
Murder	24,526	23,326	21,597	-11.9%
Forcible Rape	106,014	102,216	97,464	-8.1%
Robbery	659,870	618,949	580,545	-12.0%
Aggravated Assault	1,135,607	1,113,179	1,099,179	-3.2%
Property Crime	12,218,777	12,131,873	12,068,358	-1.2%
Burglary	2,834,808	2,712,774	2,594,995	-8.5%
Larceny-Theft	7,820,909	7,879,812	8,000,631	+2.3%
Motor Vehicle Theft	1,563,060	1,539,287	1,472,732	-5.8%
Arson	82,348	83,928	80,382	-2.4%

the thirteen year old professional stealing cars "on order"; it is the well-heeled loan shark taking over previously legitimate businesses for organized crime lords; it is the quiet, young woman who suddenly and inexplicably murders her children and husband; it is the corporate executive conspiring with competitors to keep prices high. No single formula, theory or generalization can possibly explain the vast range of criminal behaviors.

Finally, many Americans think controlling crime is solely the task of the police, courts, and correction agencies. In truth, as the Commission's report made clear, crime could not be controlled without the interest and participation of schools, businesses, social agencies, private groups and individual citizens.

What, then, has been America's experience with crime and how had this experience shaped the nation's way of living? New insights into these questions were provided by the Commission's National Survey of Criminal Victims. In this survey, the first of its kind conducted on such a scope, 10,000 representative American households were asked about their experiences with crime, whether they reported those experiences to the police, and how those experiences affected their lives.

An important finding of the survey was that for the nation as a whole, there was far more crime than was reported. Burglaries occurred about three times more than were on record with the police. Robberies, aggravated assaults and larcenies over $50 also occurred twice as often as were reported. In some areas only one-tenth of the total number of certain kinds of crimes were reported to the police. Seventy-four percent of the neighborhood commercial establishments surveyed did not report to police the thefts committed by their own employees. The existence of crime, the debates about crime, the reports of crime, and the fear of crime have eroded the basic quality of life of most Americans.

A further study conducted in high crime areas of two large cities found that:

➤ 43 percent of the respondents said they stayed off the streets at night because of their fear of crime.

➤ 35 percent said they did not speak to strangers anymore because of their fear of crime.

➤ 21 percent said they used cars and cabs at night because of their fear of crime.

➤ 21 percent said they would like to move to another neighborhood because of their fear of crime.

The findings of the Commission's national survey generally supported those of the local surveys. Fully one-third of a representative sample of all Americans said it was unsafe to walk alone at night in their neighborhoods. Slightly more than one-third said they kept firearms in the house for protection against criminals. Twenty-eight percent said they kept watchdogs for the same reason.

In virtually every circumstance, developing an effective response to the problem of crime in America was exceedingly difficult. Because of the changes expected in the population over the next decade it was assumed that reducing crime would be more painstaking in the years to come. Young people commit a disproportionate share of crime and the number of young people in our society will grow at a much faster rate than the total population. Although the 15 to 17 year old age group represent only 5.4 percent of the population, it accounted for 12.8 percent of all arrests. Fifteen and sixteen-year-olds had the highest arrest rate in the United States. The problem in the years ahead were dramatically foretold by the fact that 23 percent of the population was 10 or under.

Despite the seriousness of the problem and the increasing challenge in the years ahead, the central conclusion of the Commission was that a significant reduction in crime was possible if the following objectives were vigorously pursued.

First, society must seek to prevent crime before it happens by assuring all Americans a stake in the benefits and responsibilities of American life, by strengthening law enforcement, and by reducing criminal opportunities.

Second, society's aim at reducing crime will be better served if the system of criminal justice develops a broader range of techniques with which to deal with individual offenders.

Third, the system of criminal justice must eliminate existing injustices if it is to achieve its ideals and win the respect and cooperation of all citizens.

Fourth, the system of criminal justice must attract more people and better people — police, prosecutors, judges, defense attorneys, probation and parole officers, and correction officials with more knowledge, expertise, initiative, and integrity.

Fifth, there must be much more operational and basic research into problems of crime and criminal administration, by both those within and outside the system.

Sixth, the police, courts, and correctional agencies must be given substantially greater amounts of money if they are to improve their ability to control crime.

Seventh, individual citizens, civic and business organizations, religious institutions, and all levels of government must take responsibility for planning and implementing the changes that must be made in the justice system if crime is to be reduced.

In terms of specific recommendations, what did these seven objectives mean? We will explore this question in greater depth in the next section.

Preventing Crime

The prevention of crime covers a wide range of activities: eliminating social conditions closely associated with crime; improving the ability of the criminal justice system to detect, apprehend, judge and reintegrate into their communities those who commit crime; and reducing the situations in which crimes are most likely to occur.

It was proposed that every effort should be made to strengthen the family, now often shattered by the grinding pressures of urban slums. Schools in the slums should be given enough resources to make them as viable as other schools and enable them to compensate for the various handicaps suffered by "slum children" — in other words, to help rescue them from their environment.

Employment opportunities should be enlarged and young people provided with more effective vocational training and individual job counseling.

Programs to create new kinds of jobs — such as probation aides, medical assistants, and teacher helpers — seem particularly promising.

The problem of increasing the ability of the police to detect and apprehend criminals is complicated. In one effort to determine how this objective could be achieved the Commission conducted an analysis of 1,905 crimes reported to the Los Angeles Police Department. The study showed the importance of identifying the perpetrator at the scene of the crime. Eighty-six percent of the crimes with named suspects were solved but only 12 percent of those with unnamed suspects were solved.

Another finding of the study was that there was a relationship between the speed of response and certainty of apprehension. On the average, responses to emergency calls resulting in arrests were 50 percent faster than those to emergency calls not resulting in arrest. On the basis of this finding and a cost effectiveness study to discover the best means to reduce response time, the Commission recommended an experimental program to develop computer-aided command-and-control systems for large police departments.

To insure the maximum use of such a system, headquarters must have a direct link with every on-duty police officer. Because large scale production would result in a substantial reduction of the cost of miniature two-way radios, the Commission recommended that the Federal Government initiate a developmental program for the equipment and that it consider guaranteeing the sale of a first production lot of around 20,000 units.

Two other steps to reduce police response time were recommended:

➤ Police callboxes, which are locked and inconspicuous in most cities, should be left open, brightly marked, and designated "police emergency callboxes."

➤ The telephone company should develop a single police number for each metropolitan area, and eventually for the entire United States. (This has essentially been accomplished now with 911.)

Enhancing the effectiveness of law enforcement, however, was more than a simple matter of improving police response time. For example, a study in Washington, D.C. found that courtroom time for a felony defendant who pleaded guilty totaled less than 1 hour, while the median time from his initial appearance to his disposition was 4 months.

In an effort to discover how courts could best accelerate the process of criminal justice, the known facts about felony cases in Washington were placed in a computer and the operation of the system was thus stimulated. After a number of possible solutions to the problem of delay were tested it appeared that the addition of a second grand jury which, with supporting personnel would cost less than $50.00 per year, would result in a 25 percent reduction in the time required for the typical felony case to move from initial appearance to trial.

Criminologists hoped that the application of these analyses, when combined with the Commission's recommended timetable laying out timespans for each step in the criminal justice process, would help court systems ascertain their procedural bottlenecks and develop ways to eliminate them.

Another way to prevent crimes was simply to reduce the opportunities to commit them. Auto theft is a good example. According to FBI statistics, a key had been left in the ignition or the engine had been left running in 42 percent of all stolen cars. Even in those cars taken when the ignition was locked, at least 20 percent were stolen by shorting the ignition with common household items like paper clips and tinfoil. In one city the elimination of the unlocked "off" position on the 1965 Chevrolet resulted in 50 percent fewer of those models being stolen in 1965 than were stolen in 1964. Those findings proved that a striking reduction in auto theft could be achieved merely by installing an ignition system that automatically ejected the key when the engine was turned off.

Stricter gun control also would reduce many kinds of crime. Here the Commission recommended (1) a strengthening of the Federal law governing the inter-state shipment of firearms, (2) the enactment of state laws requiring the registration of all handguns, rifles and shot guns, and (3) prohibiting the sale or ownership of firearms by certain categories of persons — dangerous criminals, habitual drunkards, and drug addicts. After 5 years the Commission advocated that Congress pass a Federal registration law applying to those states that had not passed their own registration laws.

New Ways of Dealing With Offenders

The Commission's second objective — the development of a broader range of alternatives for dealing with offenders — was based on the belief that, while there are those who must be completely segregated from society, there are many instances where segregation does more harm than good. Furthermore, by concentrating the resources of the police, courts and correctional agencies on the smaller number of offenders who really need them, it would be possible to give offenders more effective treatment.

A specific and important example of this principle was the Commission's suggestion that every community consider establishing a Youth Services Bureau — a community-based center to which juveniles would be referred by police, the courts, parents, schools and social agencies for counseling, education, work or recreation programs.

The Youth Services Bureau was an agency established to handle many troubled and troublesome youngsters outside the criminal system. It was needed in part because society had failed to give the juvenile court the resources that would allow it to function fully independently, as its founders hoped it would. In a survey of juvenile court judges, for example, 83 percent said no psychologist or psychiatrist was available to their courts on a regular basis; one-third said they did not have probation officers or social workers. Even where there were probation officers, the Commission found the average officer supervised 76 probationers, more then double the recommended caseloads.

The California Youth Authority had been conducting a controlled experiment to determine the effectiveness of another kind of alternative treatment program for juveniles. After initial screening, convicted juvenile delinquents were assigned on a random basis to either an experimental group or a control group. Those in the experimental group were returned to the community and received intensive individual counseling, group counseling and therapy, and family counseling. Those in the control group were assigned to California's regular institutional treatment program. The study found that 28 percent of the experimental group had their paroles revoked, compared with 52 percent in the control group. Furthermore, the community treatment program was less expensive than institutional treatment.

To make community-based treatments possible for both adults and juveniles the Commission encouraged the development of an entirely new kind of correctional institution: located close to population centers; maintaining close relations with school, employers, and universities; housing as few as 50 inmates; serving as a classification center, as a center for various kinds of community programs, and as a part of reentry into the community for those difficult and dangerous offenders who had required treatment in facilities with tighter custody. Such institutions would be useful in the operation of programs that permit selected inmates to work or study in the community during the day and return to a controlled environment at night. These programs permit long-term inmates to acclimate to society gradually rather than being discharged from maximum security institutions directly to the streets.

Another aspect of the Commission's conviction that offenders with different problems should be treated in different ways, was its recommendation about the handling of public drunkenness, which in 1965 accounted for one out of every three arrests in America. The grand number of these arrests, around 2 million, placed a burden on the police, clogged the lower courts, and crowded the penal institutions. The Commission therefore recommended that communities develop civil detoxification units and comprehensive after-care programs, and that with development of such programs, drunkenness, not accompanied by other unlawful conduct, would not be a criminal offense. Similarly, the Commission endorsed the expanded use of civil commitment for drug addicts.

Eliminating Unfairness

The third objective was to eliminate injustices so that the justice system could win the respect and cooperation of all citizens. Our society and its various institutions must give the police, courts, and correctional agencies the resources as well as the mandate to provide fair and dignified treatment for all. Yet the Commission found overwhelming evidence of institutional shortcomings in almost every sector of the United States.

A survey of lower court operations in a number of large American cities found cramped and noisy courtrooms, undignified and perfunctory procedures, and badly trained personnel overwhelmed by enormous caseloads. In short, the Commission witnessed assembly line justice. In at least three states, for example, the justices of the peace were paid only if they convicted an offender; they then collected a fee from the defendant — a practice deemed unconstitutional by the Supreme Court over 40 years ago.

Approximately one-forth of the 400,000 children detained in 1965 were held in adult jails and lockups, often with hardened criminals. In addition to the creation of new kinds of institutions such as the Youth Service Bureau and community-based correctional centers, the Commission proposed several important procedural changes. It advocated counsel at various points in the criminal process. For juveniles, it recommended providing counsel wherever coercive action was a possibility.

For adults, the Commission suggested providing counsel to all criminal defendants who faced a significant penalty — excluding traffic and similar petty charges — if they could not afford to provide counsel for themselves. In connection with this recommendation the Commission requested that each state finance regular, statewide assigned counsel and defender systems for indigents.

Another recommended procedural change was that every state, county and local jurisdiction provide judicial officers with sufficient information about individual defendants to permit the release without bail of those who could be safely released. In addition to eliminating the injustice of holding persons charged with crime merely because they could not afford bail, this recommendation would be cost effective. New York City alone, for instance, spent approximately $10 million per year holding persons who had not yet been found guilty of any crime.

Besides institutional injustices, the Commission learned that while the great majority of criminal justice and law enforcement personnel perform their duties justly even under the most trying of circumstances, some took advantage of their official positions and acted in a callous, corrupt, or brutal manner. Injustices would not surrender to simple solutions. Overcoming this problem required a wide variety of remedies including improved methods of selecting personnel, a massive infusion of additional funds, a revamping of existing procedures, and an adoption of more effective internal and external controls.

The relationship between the police and the urban poor deserve special mention. Here the Commission believed every large department, particularly those in communities with a substantial minority population, should have community-based machinery consisting of a headquarters planning and supervision unit and precinct units to carry out recommended programs. Effective citizen advisory committees were to be established in minority group neighborhoods. All departments with substantial minority populations should make special efforts to recruit minority group officers, and deploy and promote them fairly. They should have rigorous internal investigation units examine complaints of misconduct. The Commission felt it was vital for complaints of unfair treatment to be handled fairly. Fair treatment of every individual was an essential element of justice and a principle objective of the American criminal justice system.

Personnel

The fourth objective was that higher levels of knowledge, expertise, initiative, and integrity be achieved by police, judges, prosecutors, defense attorneys, and correctional authorities so that the system could improve its ability to control crime. The Commission saw one obstacle in recruiting better police officers — namely that the standard requirement of all candidates, regardless of qualification, was to begin their careers at the lowest level and generally remain there for 2 to 5 years before being eligible for promotion. Thus, a college graduate would enter a department at the same rank and pay and perform the same tasks as a person who entered with only a high school diploma or less.

The Commission recommended that police departments give up "single entry" and establish three levels at which candidates may begin their police careers. These three levels were represented by positions as either "community service officers," "police officers," or "police agents." In addition to providing an entry place for the better educated, this strategy would also permit police departments to tap the special knowledge, skills, and understanding of those brought up in the slums.

"Community service officers" (CSOs) would be uniformed but unarmed members of the police department. Two of their major responsibilities included maintaining close relations with juveniles in the area where they worked and focusing on the crime-breeding conditions with which other city agencies had not dealt. Typically the CSOs might be under 21 years of age, may not be required to meet conventional education requirements, and might work out of a store-front office. Serving as apprentice policemen, a substitute for the police cadet, the CSOs would contribute as members of a team with police officers and police agents.

"Police officers" would respond to calls for service, perform routine patrol, render emergency services, conduct preliminary investigations, and enforce traffic regulations. In order to qualify as a police officer at that time, a candidate needed to possess a high school diploma and demonstrate capacity for college level work.

"Police agents" would do whatever police jobs were most complicated, sensitive, and otherwise demanding. They might be specialists in police community-relations or juvenile delinquency. They may be in uniform patrolling a high-crime neighborhood or may even carry out staff duties. To become a police agent would require at least 2 years of college work and preferably a baccalaureate degree in liberal arts of social sciences. While candidates could enter the service at any one of the three levels, they also could work their way up as they met the basic education and other requirements.

In many jurisdictions there was a critical need for additional police personnel. Studies by the Commission indicated a recruiting need of 50,000 policemen back in 1967 just to fill positions already authorized. In order to increase police effectiveness additional staff specialists would be required, and when community service officers were added, manpower needs would become even greater.

The Commission also recommended every state to establish a commission on police standards to (1) set minimum recruiting and training standards and (2) provide financial and technical assistance for local police departments.

In order to improve the quality of judges, prosecutors, and defense attorneys, the Commission advised the following variety of steps. Some included were: taking the selection of judges out of partisan politics; a more regular use of seminars, conferences, and institutes to train sitting judges; the establishment of a judicial commission to excuse physically or mentally incapacitated judges from their duties without public humiliation; the abolition of part-time district attorneys and assistant district attorneys; and a broad range of measures to develop an enlarged and better trained pool of defense attorneys.

In the correctional system there was a critical shortage of probation and parole officers, teachers, caseworkers, vocational instructors, and group workers. The need for manpower increases in these areas were made clear by the findings from the Commission's national corrections survey.

Less than 3 percent of all personnel working in jails and institutions devoted their time to treatment and training. Furthermore:

➤ Eleven states did not offer any kind of probation services for adult misdemeanors, six offered only the barest fragments of such services, and most states offered them only on a spotty basis.

➤ Two-thirds of all state adult felony probationers were in caseloads over 100 persons.

To meet the requirements of both the correctional agencies and the courts, the Commission found an immediate need to double the nation's pool of juvenile probation officers, triple the number of probation officers working with adult felons, and increase sevenfold the number of officers working with misdemeanors.

Another area with a critical need for large numbers of expert criminal justice officers was organized crime control. Here, the Commission recommended that prosecutors and police in every city and state where organized crime was known to exist develop special organized crime units.

Research

The fifth objective was that every segment of the system of criminal justice devote a significant portion of its resources towards research to insure the development of new and effective methods of controlling crime. The Commission found that little research was being conducted into such matters as the increasing or decreasing criminal sanctions; possible methods for improving the effectiveness of various procedures of the police, courts, and correctional agencies; and the impact of the economics of crime.

Organized crime was another area in which almost no research had been conducted. The Commission realized that the only people with any significant knowledge about this problem were law enforcement officials. Those in other disciplines — social scientists, economists, lawyers — had not, until recently, even considered the possibility of research projects on organized crime.

A small fraction of 1 percent of the justice system's total budget was spent on research. This figure could be multiplied many times without matching the 3 percent industry spent on research, much less the 15 percent spent by the Defense Department. The Commission believed research should be multiplied many times over.

Research is a powerful force for change in the field of criminology, a truism that can perhaps be best documented by the history of the Vera Institute in New York. Here the research of a small, nongovernment agency had in a short time led to major changes in the bail procedures of approximately 100 cities, several states, and even the Federal Government. Because of the importance of research the Commission recommended that major criminal justice agencies — such as state courts, correctional systems, and big-city police departments — organized operational research units as integral parts of their structure.

In addition, the criminal justice agencies should welcome the efforts of scholars and other independent experts who seek to understand their problems and operations. Those agencies could not undertake the necessary research on their own; they urgently needed the help of outsiders.

The Commission also promoted the establishment of several regional research institutes designed to concentrate on a number of different disciplines on the crime problem. It further recommended the establishment of an independent National Criminal Research Foundation to stimulate and coordinate research, and disseminate its results.

One essential requirement for research was more complete information about the operation of the criminal process. To meet this requirement the Commission recommended the creation of a National Criminal Justice Statistics Center. The Center's first responsibility would be to work with the FBI, the Children's Bureau, the Federal Bureau of Prisons, and other agencies to develop an integrated picture of the number of crimes reported to the police, the number of persons arrested, the number of accused persons prosecuted, and the number of offenders placed on probation, both in prison and on parole.

Another major responsibility of the Center would be to continue the Commission's initial effort to supplement the FBI's Uniform Crime Reports by developing a new yardstick to measure the extent of crime in our society. The Commission believed that the government should be able to plot the levels of different kinds of crime in a city or state as precisely as the Labor Department and the Census Bureau currently plot the rate of unemployment. Just as unemployment information is essential to sound economic planning, criminal information is essential to official planning in the justice system.

Money

Sixth, the police, courts, and correctional agencies would require greater funding in order to control crime more effectively. Almost all of the specific recommendations made by the Commission would involve increased budgets. Substantially higher salaries would be offered to attract top-flight candidates to the system. For example, the median annual salary for a patrolman in a large city was a mere $5,300. Typically, the maximum salary was something less than $1,000 above the starting salary. The Commission felt the most important change that could be made in police salary scales was to increase maximums sharply. An FBI agent, for instance, started at $8,421 per year and if he or she served long and well enough could reach $16,905 per year without even being promoted to a supervisory position. The Commission was aware that reaching such figures was not immediately feasible in many cities, but it believed that there should at least be an across-the-board larger range from minimum to maximum.

Also promoted were new kinds of measures that would require additional funds such as Youth Services Bureaus, greatly enlarged misdemeanant probation services, and increased levels of research.

The Commission believed some of the additional sources — especially those devoted to innovative programs, training, education, and research — should be contributed by the Federal Government. Yet the Federal Government was already conducting an ample amount of programs specifically designed to attack the social problems often associated with crime. Obtaining the extra, and arguably exorbitant, funding requested by the Commission was a difficult task indeed.

While the Commission was convinced state and local governments would continue to carry the major burden of criminal administration, it recommended a vastly enlarged program of Federal assistance to strengthen law enforcement, crime prevention, and the Administration of Justice.

The program of Federal support was directed at eight major needs:

1. State and local planning

2. Education and training of criminal justice personnel.

3. Surveys and advisory services concerning the organization of police departments, courts, prosecuting offices, and corrections agencies.

4. Development of a coordinated national information system for operational and research purposes.

5. Funding of limited numbers of demonstration programs in justice agencies.

6. Scientific and technological research and development.

7. Development of national and regional research centers.

8. Grants-in-aid for operational innovations.

The Commission was not in any position to request the exact amount of money that would be needed to carry out its proposed program. It hypothesized, however, that a Federal program totaling hundreds of millions of dollars a year during the next decade could be effectively utilized. The Commission also believed the major responsibility for administering this program should lie within the Department of Justice. The state, cities, and counties also would have to make substantial increases in their contributions to the system of criminal justice.

Responsibility of Change

Seventh, individual citizens, social-service agencies, universities, religious institutions, civic and business groups, and all kinds of governmental agencies at all levels would become involved in planning and executing changes in the criminal justice system. The Commission was convinced that the financial and technical assistance program it proposed should be only a small part of the national effort to develop a more effective and fair response to crime.

In March of 1966, President Johnson asked the Attorney General to invite each Governor to form a State Committee on criminal administration. The response to this request was encouraging, as more than two-thirds of the states already had such committees or indicated they intended to form them.

It was recommended that in every city and state there should be an agency of one or more officials, with specific responsibilities for planning improvements in criminal administration and encouraging various interventions.

Planning agencies played a key role in helping state legislatures and city councils decide where additional funds and manpower were most needed, which new programs should be adopted, and where and how existing agencies might pool their resources on either a metropolitan or regional basis.

Planning agencies would include both officials from the system and citizens from other professions. Plans to improve criminal administration would be impossible to enact unless those responsible for criminal administration helped initiate them. On the other hand, crime prevention should be the task of the community as a whole.

While this report concentrated on recommendations for action by governments, the Commission was convinced that governmental actions alone would not be enough. Crime was a social problem that was interwoven into almost every aspect of American life. Controlling it involved improving the quality of family life, the school system, city planning, employment processes, and so forth. Controlling crime became a priority for every American institution.

Universities would increase their research on the problems of crime; private social welfare organizations and religious institutions would continue to experiment with advanced techniques of helping slum children overcome their environments; labor unions and businesses could enlarge their programs to provide prisoners with vocational training; and professional and community organizations could help probation and parole workers with their work.

The responsibility of the individual citizen ran far deeper than merely cooperating with the police or accepting jury duty or insuring the safety of his or her family by utilizing various security devices. Ideally, the citizen should also respect the law, refuse to cut corners, and reject the machiavellian argument that "anything goes as long as you don't get caught."

Most important of all, the citizen should on his or her own take a sincere interest in the problems of crime and criminal justice, seek information, openly express personal views, vote wisely, and get involved in crime interventions.

In summary, the Commission was sure that America could control crime if it would commit itself wholeheartedly to that task. The subsequent chapters in this text will indicate the extent to which the Commission's recommendations were adopted.

CAREERS IN CRIMINAL JUSTICE

The criminal justice system is a large network of organizations ranging from complex federal, state, and city agencies to small rural departments. In most cases the system is divided into three sub-systems: enforcement, court, and corrections. In short, police enforce the law, courts safeguard judicial processes, and corrections provide a host of treatment and rehabilitation services.

Allowing for a variation of different states and communities, the following are some types of positions found in each sub-system:

Enforcement
Patrolman
Investigation Officer
Traffic Officer
Sheriff
Administrator
Highway Patrolman
Game Warden
Juvenile Officer
Training Instructor
Crime Lab Technician
Dispatcher
Community Relations Officer

Courts
Prosecuting Attorney
Defense Attorney
Judge
Court Administrator
Bailiff
Court Clerk
Court Reporter

Corrections
Probation Officer
Parole Officer
Jail and Prison Custodial Officer
Counselor
Case Worker
Administrator
Recreation Specialist

Psychologist
Psychiatrist
Vocational/Academic Teacher

Other aspects of the justice system also require qualified individuals to assure a smooth operation. Included in these areas might be: administration, personnel, accounting, and clerical services. Opportunities are also available in crime laboratories where scientific techniques are used in the study of criminal evidence.

Federal Agencies

Federal agencies provide positions in many of the same areas mentioned above. Similar positions can be found in the federal courts and prison systems, while some positions in the area of enforcement might include: FBI agent, Park Ranger, Border Patrol Agent, Customs Agent, U.S. Marshall, and Military Police Officer. Other positions related to research, education, and rehabilitation can also be found in federal agencies, many of which are partially supported by federal funds.

Private Agencies

Private agencies provide many opportunities for careers, which are most often related to security, investigation, or rehabilitation. Positions can be found in insurance companies, banks, hotels, detective agencies, security or protective services, railroad and aircraft security, individual security, collegiate institutions, and half-way houses.

Where to Begin

These listings are only a small sample of the types of careers that are available. Possibilities are capacious and encompass a wide variety of interests. To assist in making the selection of a career, try to obtain as much information as possible, explore all the possibilities that complement your value system, and especially do not overlook the sources of information within your own community. To obtain more details:

1. Inquire about a list of colleges or universities which offer criminal justice programs.

In many cases these institutions also provide a placement service for students enrolled in their programs.

2. Contact a local office of the Civil Service Commission. It should be able to provide information about positions with various federal agencies, including the Federal Bureau of Investigation, Drug Enforcement Administration, Treasury-Secret Service, Customs Service, and Bureau or Prisons.

3. Visit the criminal justice agencies in your community. Individuals working in the field can give you the best method of achieving your career goals.

4. Request information from the criminal justice employment agencies within your state. Separate agencies may be found for police, courts, and corrections at the state, county, and local levels of employment.

5. Peruse professional journals concerning the criminal justice system. This should familiarize you with the workings of the system and may direct you toward a better understanding of your own objectives.

6. Surf the Internet for employment opportunities related to criminal justice and engage in some on-line chat rooms which correlate with your area of interest.

Education

The standard requirement for entrance into the criminal justice system has been high school graduation supplemented by training through academics and/or various in-service programs. While this may continue to be the present standard in many agencies, it cannot be denied that a definite trend has developed toward the requirement for some college education prior to employment. Some agencies already require a baccalaureate or even a master's degree as a qualification for entry-level positions.

This trend has become most obvious in the reports of the National Advisory Committee on Criminal Justice Standards and Goals. Similar recommendations have been made for other segments of the system as well. This strongly suggests that the individual preparing to enter the criminal justice system for the first time should look to higher education as the best avenue of approach.

Educational Programs

An increasing number of colleges and universities are offering degrees in criminal justice. At present, more than seven hundred institutions offer undergraduate degrees while as many as one hundred offer graduate level courses; these numbers continue to grow each year. Every state in the nation is now represented by a number of bona fide institutions offering such programs.

Career Ladders

The availability of college trained personnel has created the need for criminal justice agencies to modify career ladders to include educational qualifications in all phases of employment, initial hiring, transfer, and promotion. The Standards and Goals reports assert that "you men and women with histories of academic achievement naturally are interested in a progressive career in which they can look forward to promotions based on ability rather than seniority." This provides a challenge for all factions of the justice system, as employers look to college campuses for prospective employees.

Affirmative Action

Previously untapped "human resource options" such as minorities, ex-offenders, students, and volunteers can be sources of valuable assistance, and practices which have previously discouraged these groups from seeking employment within the system are being eliminated.

Specific guidelines have been given concerning the employment of all minority groups. One example is the recommendation of the National Advisory Commission on Criminal Justice Standards and Goals that "every police agency immediately should insure that it presents no artificial or arbitrary barriers — cultural or institutional — to discourage qualified individuals from seeking employment." The same type of guideline has been given to other agencies within the justice system, and steps are being taken to change situations where minority groups are over-represented in the system as offenders and under-represented as staff. In many instances even physical requirements have been modified to eliminate arbitrary discrimination.

The changing role and status of women in the workforce has opened up many positions that have traditionally been male-dominated. The Commission has provided impetus to this movement by advising that agencies should "provide career paths for women allowing each individual to attain a position classification commensurate with her particular degree of experience, skill, and ability." At present, there is a shortage of qualified women within the system, and this will continue unless more women become interested in criminal justice as a career.

Surprisingly, new opportunities are also becoming available to the ex-offender. Many agencies are realizing that the special skills and experiences of ex-offenders are valuable additions to their programs. This is especially true in programs directed toward rehabilitation and crime deterrence.

Other groups being recognized for their resource potential are students working in internship or work-study programs, and civilian volunteers.

New Horizons

Increased national attention is currently being given to all facets of the criminal justice system. This has brought about many changes with innovative programs and movements toward reform; the field of corrections has been especially affected. New programs designed as an alternative to imprisonment — such as half-way houses, work release programs, and diagnostic and community treatment centers — are being designed to help

improve methods of dealing with offenders. All of these programs call for additional personnel and provide terrific opportunities for those with professional training.

Juvenile Justice and the Delinquency Prevention Act

Also affected by these demands for reform are agencies that deal with juveniles. The Juvenile Justice and Delinquency Prevention Act, passed in September of 1974, has paved the way for many new activities in this area. This act calls for the development of new techniques for working with juveniles, especially those who are considered "non-criminals" and have become a part of the justice system because of such acts as runaway, truancy, or incorrigibility. A mandate has been given to develop methods for helping such youth without introducing them to the standard criminal justice procedures. These programs, as well as those directed toward the criminal juvenile, will undoubtedly create further opportunities for employment.

Volunteer Organizations

Many opportunities to work with community volunteers are also available. Organizations such as sheriff's posses, volunteer probation officers, and police reserves provide a means for individuals to become familiar with the criminal justice system and gain valuable experience. In addition, candidates for full-time employment are often taken from the ranks of such volunteer organizations.

Private Organizations

Of particular interest has been the increased number of private agencies dedicated to social problems such as drug abuse, alcoholism, and pre-delinquent youth. These private agencies also offer career opportunities for those with criminology backgrounds.

New Areas

Positions requiring expertise from the academic discipline are also becoming an important part of the justice system. Chemistry, computer science, and communications are a few of the areas from which qualified individuals are needed. Also important are positions related to research, planning, and education. A need for more adequate research efforts has created a demand for employees trained in research methodology, while the establishment of a Criminal Justice Planning Agency in each state by the Law Enforcement Assistance Administration emphasizes the added attention being given to planning. Planners are especially sought after to help prepare and direct a series of procedural changes that constantly take place.

A demand for qualified educators is also being felt, as the number of institutions offering criminal justice programs and the emphasis on higher education continues to grow. Of course, such professions require individuals who are well educated.

These few points only touch upon the many new directions of the justice system and its unprecedented growth. The system is not static, and opportunities for fulfilling careers are readily available. There is always a place for the dedicated individual who is motivated toward improving the justice system.

Professional Organizations

Professional organizations and their affiliations are important not only to get acquainted with nationally and internationally known personnel but also to enable a person to attend annual meetings at which time he or she will be allowed to participate in discussions, present papers, or collaborate with colleagues for grant-seeking, research and publication activities. There are also many college campuses that have their own student organizations that welcome new membership.

There are many national, regional, and state organizations tailored to suit individual career objectives. Among the well known criminology organizations are: The American Society of Criminology, The Academic of Criminal Justice

Sciences, American Criminal Justice Association, and The United Nations Congresses on Prevention of Crime and Treatment of Offenders. A description of these four organizations follows and more details can be found on the Internet. Information concerning other Criminal Justice organizations can be obtained from faculty members of colleges throughout the country. Criminal justice agencies may also have accessible information concerning such organizations.

The American Society of Criminology

The American Society of Criminology (ASC) was founded in 1941. This multi-disciplinary society encourages participants to exchange their views and findings in an effort to understand and control crime more effectively. The ASC was created to foster scholarship, research, education, and training within academic and private institutions, as well as within divisions of the justice system. The Society seeks to encourage scholarly, scientific, and practical exchange and cooperation among those engaged in research and knowledge in the field.

The ASC publishes *Criminology: An Interdisciplinary Journal*. This journal is devoted to crime and deviant behavior as found in all aspects of society. The thrust of this journal is on empirical research and scientific methodology. Theoretical issues with an empirical base are also taken into consideration. Those who are particularly interested in pursuing a career in criminal justice may belong to this society. To become a member, contact your instructor to obtain a membership application form.

The Academy of Criminal Justice Sciences

In addition to the ASC there is another organization known as the Academic of Criminal Justice Sciences (ACJS). ACJS is an organization composed of individuals who are involved in the professional advancement of the justice system through education. These persons include teachers, administrators, researchers, students, and practitioners actively working toward this end.

The purposes of ACJS are to foster excellence in education and research in the field of criminal justice in institutions of higher education; to encourage understanding and cooperation among those engaged in teaching and research in justice agencies and related fields; to provide a forum for the exchange of information among persons involved with education and research in the criminology field; and to serve as a clearinghouse for the collection and dissemination of information related to or produced by educational criminology programs as well as in operation agencies and allied fields. Anyone who wishes to become affiliated with this organization, participate in its annual conferences, or obtain newsletters should contact a faculty member for further information and an application form.

American Criminal Justice Association

Lambda Alpha Epsilon (LAE), commonly called the American Criminal Justice Association, was founded in 1937. As a fraternal association, Lambda Alpha Epsilon is dedicated to the achievement of professionalism within the institutes associated with criminal justice. Membership is selective and restricted to those persons who are vigorously engaged in the criminal justice field or are enrolled in a college level program related to criminology. The membership of LAE encompasses a myriad of institutions within the justice system. Utilizing this membership, the Association sponsors public educational programs, seminary and promotional activities to encourage participation in representative from criminal justice agencies in local, state, and federal jurisdictions are called upon for their knowledge and expertise. This Association publishes "the LAE Journal," which reports the Association's activities, provides employment prospects, and presents articles written by concerned persons within the criminal justice system.

The goals of the Association are essentially concerned with elevating the standards of personnel in the field of criminal justice in the following ways: (1) by encouraging further educational achievement, (2) by offering incentives for outstanding work done in their field, and (3) by providing scholarships for deserving persons desiring further educational achievement. Those interested in obtaining further information, should write to LAMBDA ALPHA EPSILON, National Headquarters, P.O. Box 214776, Sacramento, California, 95821.

The United Nations Congress on Prevention of Crime and Treatment of Offenders

The United Nations Congress on Prevention of Crime and Treatment of Offenders is international in scope and concerned with trials, detention, and the treatment of offenders. The Congresses on Prevention of Crime and Treatment of Offenders replaced the International Penal and Penitentiary Commission. It was agreed by the participating members of the organization in The Hague in 1950, that the United Nations should hold the international congresses in five-year intervals.

The United National Congresses have not only drafted principles and guidelines for policies in the apprehension of offenders but also charted principles for trial and treatment of offenders in prison. Moreover, the Congress has addressed itself to "Social Defense," or crime prevention. For the first time the 1975 Congress entertained law enforcement components on its agenda. Numerous publications resulted from the meeting from which one can obtain its bibliography and other published materials through the United Nations Publication/Document section in New York; any interested party can consult his or her local library for the call-number to obtain specific documents or publications.

The remaining chapters of this book will introduce the different facets of criminal justice to promote a greater understanding of this field in modern day terms.

ENDNOTES

[1] The ACT works this way: when a guest checks into a hotel, the clerk selects a plastic coded card, which he or she feeds into an entry terminal machine. He then dials into the machine the guest's room number and instead of a key, gives the guest a coded card. The guest inserts the card into the slot for opening and once the door is closed, it cannot be opened from the outside. At check-out time, the guest's card is destroyed and the door slot reset for the next occupant's card.

[2] Henry, Stuart, and Dragan Milovanovic. *Constitutive Criminology: Beyond Postmodernism.* London: SAGE Publications, Ltd, 1996, pp. 122-151.

[3] Reckless, Walter C. *The Crime Problem* (4th Edition). New York: Appleton-Century-Crofts, 1973, pp. 677-683.

[4] Sutherland, Edwin, and Donald R. Cressey. *Criminology* (9th Edition). New York: J.B. Lippincott, 1974, pp. 93-112.

[5] Johnson, Elmer H. *Crime, Correction and Society* (3rd Edition). Homewood, IL: The Dorsey Press, 1974, pp. 217-227.

[6] Chang, Dae H. Sociology: *An Applied Approach.* Lake Geneva, WI: Paladin House Publishers, 1973, pp. 219-260.

[7] Clinard, Marshall. *Sociology Today.* New York: Basic Books, 1961, p. 509.

[8] For further information on police, courts and corrections, see <1> Task Force Report; <2> Task Force Report: The Courts; <3> Task Force Report: Corrections; and <4> Task Force Report: Juvenile Delinquency and Youth Crime, all by the President's Commission on Law Enforcement and Administration of Justice, Government Printing Office, Washington, 1967.

[9] Ibid.

[10] For further information see R.W. Kobetz, *Law Enforcement and Criminal Justice Education Directory: 1975-76.* Gaithersburg, MD: International Association of Chiefs of Police, and Richard R. Bennett and Ineke Haen Marshall, "Criminal Justice Education in the United States: a Profile," *Journal of Criminal Justice*, Vol.7, 1979, pp. 147-72.

[11] Chang, Dae H. and Warren B. Armstrong. *The Prison Voices From the Inside.* Cambridge: Schenkman Publishing Co., 1972.

[12] "A Sentencing Judge," originally published in *The Eye Opener*, a Columbus, Ohio penal publication, was reprinted in the *Pontiac Flag News*, a prison newspaper of the Illinois State Penitentiary, Pontiac.

[13] As an example, a report sponsored by the British government and supervised by Dr. William Belson of London School of Economics, revealed that in 1975, almost nine out of ten boys in London have stolen by the time they leave school. The report was based on interviews with 1400 London boys, aged 13 to 16, chosen from a cross-section of British society. The results of the report were: <1> one in four had stolen from a car or truck; <2> of every 100 questioned, 88 said they had stolen at school, 70 from a shop, and 33 from a stall: <3> one in six had stolen a letter or parcel from the mail, one in 20 had stolen a car or truck; and <4> Thirty percent had received money or goods via threats or blackmail.

[14] Statistics provided by the *Uniform Crime Report*, 1982, 1995, U.S. Department of Justice, U.S. Government Printing Office, Washington, DC, 1983, 1995.

[15] The summary is taken from "The Challenge of Crime in a Free Society: A Report by the President's Commission on Law Enforcement and Administration of Justice," U.S. Printing Office, Washington, DC, 1967, pp. V-XI.

REFERENCES

Barlow, Hugh D.
    1966   *Introduction to Criminology*, 7th Edition. New York: Harper Collins College Publishers.

Bernard, Thomas J., and Richard McCleary
    1996   *Life Without Parole: Living in Prison Today*. Los Angeles: Roxbury Publishing.

Clinard, Marshall, Richard Quinney, and John Wildman
    1995   *Criminal Behavior System: A Typology*. New York: Holt, Rinehart and Winston.

Clinard, Marshall, and Peter C. Yeager
    1980   Corporate Crime. New York: Free Press.

Cromwell, Paul
    1996   *In Their Own Words: Criminals on Crime*. Los Angeles: Roxbury Publishing.

Fields, Charles B., and Richter H. Moore, Jr.
    1996   *Comparative Criminal Justice: Traditional and Nontraditional Systems of Law and Control*. Prospect Heights: Waveland Press.

Geller, William A., and Hans Toch
    1996   *Police Violence: Understanding and Controlling Police Abuse of Force*. New Haven, CT: Yale University Press.

Latessa, Edward J., and Harry E. Allen
    1997   *Corrections in the Community*. Cincinnati: Anderson Publishing.

McShane, Marilyn, and Frank P. Williams III
    1997   *Victims of Crime and the Victimization Process*. New York: Garland Publishing.

Noaks, Lesley, Michael Levi, and Mike Maguire
    1995   *Contemporary Issues in Criminology*. Cardiff: The University of Whales Press, 1995.

O'Shea, Kathleen A., and Beverly R. Fletcher
    1997   *Female Offenders: An Annotated Bibliography*. Westport: Greenwood Press, 1997.

Radelet, Louis A., and David L. Carter
    1994   *The Police and the Community*. Englewood Cliffs, NJ: Prentice-Hall.

Schmalleger, Frank
    1997   *Criminal Justice Today*, 4th Edition. Upper Saddle River: Prentice-Hall.

Schwartz, Martin D., and Dragan Milovanovic
    1996   *Race, Gender, and Class in Criminology: The Intersection*. New York: Garland Publishing.

Siegal, Larry J., and Joseph J. Senna
    1994   *Juvenile Delinquency: Theory, Practice and Law*, 5th Edition. St. Paul, MN: West Publishing.

Wilson, James Q., and Joan Petersilia
    1995   *Crime*. Dunmore: ICS Press.

Chapter 2

The Processing Stages of The Criminal Justice System

By

Miles Erpelding and **Craig D. Uchida**

This chapter examines the procedures in the criminal justice system. For our discussion we employ the "systems" approach, an examination of the steps an individual takes while going through the process. This approach enables us to envision the various actors in the system, their interaction with the offender, with each other, and the way they function. The police, courts, and corrections are the three major components of the process and each is related to the others in varying degrees. Cooperation and interdependence are found at the daily operational level. The police, for example, must work with the prosecutor in order to develop a court case. The sentencing judge has a direct impact on probation, prison populations, and the parole board. These concepts will become clearer as we proceed into the system.

Initial Contact and Pre-Arrest Investigation

An individual will initially be introduced to the criminal justice process through contact with a law enforcement agency. Police involvement in a crime begins in a number of ways. More notably, a complaint from a citizen or victim, an observation of criminal activity while patrolling the streets and highways, or through information developed during surveillance or as a result of an informant's tip.

An important aspect of the initial contact stage that has been neglected is the willingness or reluctance of the citizen to call the police and initiate the criminal justice process. Through victimization surveys, particularly the National Crime Victimization Survey, researchers have found that only approximately 40% of all crimes occurring are actually reported.[1] As a result, official statistics on crime (e.g., the FBI's Uniform Crime Reports) which rely principally upon these reports underestimate the true occurrence of criminal activity in the country by about one-half.

Research has shown that the public is hesitant for a variety of reasons to call the police when a crime has occurred . The most common reasons include the belief that the offender was unsuccessful in perpetration of the crime, or that the incident was a private or personal matter. Other reasons cited are that the police would not want to be bothered, lack of proof of a crime, not important enough, fear of reprisal by the perpetrator, too time consuming, and a perception that the police are inefficient, ineffective, or biased.[2]

Once the victims or witnesses call the police,

the probability of apprehension of a suspect at the scene is quite low. Research conducted in Florida, Illinois, New York, and California showed that 75% of the calls to the police concerning serious crimes were "discovery crimes" — those crimes discovered after the fact. The remaining crimes were "involvement crimes" — crimes in which the victim and suspect confront each other. In the involvement crimes, quick response by the police could make a difference in whether an arrest was made. The key to an on-scene arrest was the speed, or lack thereof, on the part of the citizen to report the crime. The longer the delay, the greater the opportunity for the suspect to escape. A crime reported while in progress had a 35 percent chance of response-related arrest. A report made within one minute after the incident started added an additional 18 percent chance for an arrest. By contrast, crimes reported between one and five minutes after the crime resulted in only a seven percent chance of arrest. This meant a substantial reduction in apprehension capacity.[3]

Preventive patrol involves police in actively observing the streets, watching for criminal activity as they drive through neighborhoods and business sectors of cities or towns. Although this type of patrol technique has a rather minimal impact on crime in terms of suspect arrests and general crime deterrence, it remains the backbone of the police routine.[4] Contemporary strategies such as directed patrol, specialized patrol, and the concept of problem-oriented policing seem to hold promise for increasing patrol efficiency.

When police engage in investigative work prior to an arrest they might rely on a "tip" from an informant or use other surveillance techniques such as stakeouts, wiretapping, or undercover infiltration of criminal organizations. The ultimate goal of any pre-arrest investigation is to legally acquire information and evidence to identify the individual(s) responsible for the illegal activity.

Arrest

An arrest involves the action of a law enforcement officer taking an individual into custody for allegedly committing a criminal act. According to Oran's *Law Dictionary for Nonlawyers*, an arrest is defined as "the official taking of a person to answer to criminal charges which involves at least temporarily depriving the person of liberty and may involve the use of force."[5] In 1994, the U.S. Department of Justice estimates there were a total of 14,648,700 individuals arrested in the United States. Of these arrests, only approximately five percent were for violent felony crimes such as murder, manslaughter, forcible rape, robbery, and aggravated assault. Another 15% were for felony property crimes including burglary, larceny-theft, motor vehicle theft, and arson. The other 80% of arrests included crimes of a "less serious nature," according to the Uniform Crime Reports, ranging from simple assaults to sex offenses to drug and alcohol law violations. Additionally, approximately 81% of the total number of individuals arrested were adults with the remaining 19% comprised of juveniles under the age of 18.[6]

Some arrests are made on the basis of warrants issued to the police by the courts. A warrant is an order from the court that directs the police to take the person identified in the warrant into custody. The warrant is usually based upon a complaint by a victim, an affidavit from a law enforcement officer, or a combination of both. The prosecuting attorney then presents this evidence to the court. If the court determines there is probable cause (reasonable grounds) to believe both that a crime has been committed and that it was committed by the individual named in the complaint, then a warrant for the individual's arrest will be issued.

Typically though, most arrests are "warrantless" — that is, they are made without prior authorization from the courts. The police may make a warrantless arrest for felonies if there is probable cause to believe a person has committed a felony and generally, no time is available to obtain a warrant. In the case of misdemeanors, however, the law usually authorizes warrantless arrests only if they were committed in the presence of the officer. Other conditions may include that the person will not be apprehended or evidence of the crime will be lost, or the person may cause injury to another or damage property unless the person is immediately arrested.

Arresting officers commonly exercise considerable discretion in determining whether to make an arrest. Reiss found that when citizens called the police, in 43 percent of all felonies and 52 percent of all misdemeanor situations the police decided not to arrest even though they had probable cause to do so.[7]

When the police contemplate an arrest they consider a number of variables. The single most important factor influencing an officer's discretion is the seriousness of the offense. Other variables can be grouped into three general categories: (1) offender variables, (2) situational variables, and (3) system variables.

According to Gaines, et al., offender variables include age, race, socioeconomic status, and demeanor. With respect to age, an arrest is more likely if the victim is older and the offender younger.[8] African-Americans are arrested for a disproportionate number of crimes. Socioeconomically, individuals in the middle or upper income brackets are less likely to be arrested and the more disrespectful or uncooperative a person is, the more likely an arrest will take place.

Situational variables generally apply to the officer's involvement in the criminal event. Research indicates that officer initiated involvement in situations is more likely to result in an arrest than that of a citizen's complaint. Also the presence of large crowds and visibility of the event tend to sway officers decisions to arrest more frequently.

System variables may include such dimensions as capacities of the criminal justice system, officer's perception of the law, peer group influences, and prevailing community opinions. The officer's prior experiences and frustrations with the processing of offenders through the "system" may result in justification for discretion. If the officer perceives unfairness in the laws or if the community's standards or enforcement expectations are lowered, officers may also extend greater discretion. The influence of officer's peer groups and the police subculture may impact discretion in determining which actions are acceptable and unacceptable.[9]

Once a suspect is arrested and prior to questioning they are usually advised of their constitutional right against self-incrimination, more notably the Miranda warning:

1. "You have the right to remain silent when questioned."

2. "If you choose to answer questions, statements you make can be used against you in a Court of Law."

3. "You have the right to an attorney before and/or during questioning."

4. "If you are unable to afford an attorney, one will be appointed for you by the Court."

5. "Do you understand each of these rights?"[10]

Typically, advisement of these rights is necessary when a individual is in custody and being interrogated. In the U.S. Supreme Court case of *Oregon v. Mathiason* (1977), the Court defines custodial interrogation as questioning initiated by law enforcement officers after an individual has been taken into custody or otherwise deprived of his freedom in a significant manner.[11] The Miranda warning does not necessarily apply to voluntary or unsolicited statements, admissions or confessions, and officers are not required to interrupt the individual giving such.

The conclusion of the arrest process involves the booking of the suspect. Booking is essentially a clerical process initiated upon arrival of the suspect at the police station or detention facility. Booking includes the gathering of information such as the suspect's name, address, date of birth, Social Security Number, height, weight, the time of the arrest, the offense involved, etc. Also, the suspect is ordinarily fingerprinted and photographed. Subsequently, they might also be placed in a police lineup for identification by a witness or the victim and may be subjected to further interrogation.

Initial Or First Appearance

All jurisdictions requires that a suspect be brought before a judge or magistrate shortly after arrest. The time period is described in most states as "without unnecessary delay." According to the U.S. Supreme Court in the cases of *McNabb v. U.S.* (1943)[12] and *County of Riverside v. Mc-Laughlin* (1991),[13] the Court's interpretation of this time period is generally within 48 hours after arrest.

The initial or first appearance serves three primary purposes. First, to provide the suspect with notice of the tentative criminal charges. Second, to explain the suspect's right to counsel. Finally, bail or bond considerations are made.

When the suspect is brought before the judge or magistrate, he is informed of the nature of the charges and advised of his constitutional due process rights. In felony cases, the court may initiate the grand jury process or schedule a preliminary hearing and the suspect will usually enter a not guilty plea. In contrast, suspects charged with misdemeanors may enter a plea of guilty or nolo contendere (no contest) at the initial hearing and the case may be disposed of immediately. If the suspect chooses to enter a not guilty plea, the court will set the case for trial, as grand juries or preliminary hearings are not typically utilized in misdemeanor cases.

In explaining the right to counsel, the court will give the suspect the opportunity to obtain legal representation. According to U.S. Department of Justice statistics, only slightly over 20% of all incarcerated offenders have adequate financial resources to hire their own attorneys.[14] If they are indigent (poor) and unable to afford an attorney, the court will appoint a public defender or court-appointed attorney to represent them. This right is extended to felony suspects by virtue of the 1963 case of *Gideon v. Wainwright*[15] and for misdemeanor suspects in the 1972 case of *Argersinger v. Hamlin*.[16] Some states are now obligating the offenders to reimburse the state for a portion of the costs associated with indigent defense services.

Bail or bond involves the financial or nonfinancial conditions under which suspects may be released while awaiting further processing in the criminal justice system. The purpose of bail is to assure appearance at later proceedings. In a U.S. Department of Justice study of the 75 largest counties in the U.S., approximately 63% of all felony offenders were granted some form of release before case disposition.[17] In some jurisdictions bail is largely determined by a set schedule which varies in amount according to the crime charged (i.e., the more serious the offense, the higher the bond required). In other jurisdictions, the court will make some attempt to evaluate each case individually. Usually the judge will considers the seriousness of the offense, the prior record of the offender, and various personal characteristics including residence location, employment, flight risk, etc.

There are several popular categories of bail, including:

1. Release on Recognizance: The offender is released on his written promise to appear. Generally, no cash or property is required.

2. Surety Bond: The offender pays a percentage of the bond amount, normally 10%, as a fee to a bondsman or bonding agent. The bonding agent them assumes liability for the full amount of the bond should the defendant not appear for court.

3. Property Bond: The offender may post evidence of tangible property such as land, houses, automobiles, etc. in lieu of money.

4. Cash Bond: The offender pays the actual amount of the bond as ordered by the court. The bond is returned upon the offender's appearance in court.

Determination Of The Charges

The prosecutor or district attorney enters the criminal justice process when he is notified by the police that an individual has been arrested. A police report, in some jurisdictions referred to as a standard offense report and, in particular cases, items of evidence, are forwarded to the prosecuting attorney for consideration of potential charges.

The prosecutor is said to have the broadest discretion within the criminal justice system. The prosecutor must make the decision whether or not to file criminal charges against the suspect. The power to not charge, known as *nolle prosequi*, is the single most unreviewed exercise of power of the criminal law available to an individual in the American system of justice.[18] Factors influencing the decision making process include the weight of the evidence, the characteristic of the crime, the prior record of the accused, the attitude of the victim, the cost of prosecution to the criminal justice system, and the availability of alternative procedures, just to name a few. According to a study of case processing in 30 urban jurisdictions, approximately one-half of all arrests resulted in dismissal prior to reaching the trial stage of the proceedings.[19] U.S. Attorneys declined prosecution in over 30% of the cases referred to them in 1993.[20]

Should the prosecutor decide not to prefer formal charges against the suspect, a concept known as diversion might be utilized. Diversion programs are commonly reserved for first-time, non-violent offenders. Diversion participants may be required to enter into a contract with the prosecutor whereby the offender agrees to refrain from violating the law for a period of time in lieu of prosecution. Some structured diversion programs require participants to complete requirements similar to conditions of probation and/or report regularly to a supervision officer. Diversion programs can be quite beneficial to those individuals whose first involvement with the criminal justice system may truly be an aberration or indiscretion not deserving of a formal criminal record.

Once the prosecuting attorney decides to initiate prosecution, the next step is to formalize the charges. There are two ways this is accomplished, depending upon the practices in different jurisdictions. One way is to present an "information," a charging document to the court. The information states the facts for each charge. It includes a description of the crime committed, where it occurred, and when. The description of the crime must cover every element in the legal or statutory definition of that particular crime.

The second method of formalizing the charges involves a grand jury indictment. Today, grand juries are empaneled in the federal system and about half of the states. In principle, the grand jury is another screening device intended to protect citizens against unwarranted prosecutions. The grand jury's sole function is to hear the state's case against the suspect and to determine whether there is probable cause to formally charge the suspect with a crime. The size of grand juries varies by statute in different jurisdictions, ranging from six to 23 members. Most states require a minimum of 12 jurors voting for prosecution while others may require only a simple majority. Commonly, grand jury members are selected at random from voter registration rolls.

The grand jury hearing is a secret proceeding, with neither the suspect nor his counsel present. The prosecutor presents his case to the jury, asks questions of witnesses called to testify before the jury, and serves as the jury's general legal advisor. Grand jury hearings are not typically bound by the standard rules of evidence applicable at trial. If the grand jury decides the suspect should be brought to trial, a document called a "True Bill" of indictment is issued to the court.

In states which do not use a grand jury process, a preliminary hearing is required in felony cases. Ideally, the preliminary hearing also protects felony suspects against unwarranted prosecutions. The preliminary hearing is frequently referred to as a "mini-trial" without a jury. At the hearing, the prosecutor bears the burden of producing sufficient evidence to satisfy the judge or magistrate that:

1. A crime was committed.

2. It was committed by the suspect.

3. It was committed within the jurisdiction of the court.

The prosecutor calls witness to testify and otherwise offers evidence in support of his case. The prosecution need reveal only enough of their case to satisfy the judge that there is justification for a trial, not prove that the suspect is guilty beyond a reasonable doubt. The suspect and his attorney may cross-examine witnesses and introduce evidence on their own behalf, though very few go beyond cross-examination.

An advantage of the preliminary hearing to the suspect is that it serves as an informal discovery device. That is, the suspect and his attorney discover or learn something about the strength of the prosecutor's case and can use that knowledge in preparation for the trial.

If the judge finds that sufficient evidence exists to justify a trial, the suspect will be "bound over." If not, the court will order the defendant released.

Arraignment On Information Or Indictment

After the defendant is indicted by the grand jury or formally accused through an information and following a preliminary hearing, the arraignment takes place. The defendant is brought before the court, hears the charges read to him, and is asked to enter a plea.

Felony defendants may plead not guilty, guilty as charged, or nolo contendere (no contest) at the arraignment. They may also enter pleas of not guilty by reason of insanity or not guilty by reason of alibi at this stage, depending upon the jurisdiction. Nolo contendere is equivalent to a guilty plea; however, procedurally it requires the prosecution to provide the court with a rendition of the facts in the case should it have gone to trial. Also, a plea of nolo contendre protects defendants from having an admission of criminal guilt used against them in a civil court in the event they are subsequently sued by the victim, for example. If a defendant stands mute (no response to the judge's request for a plea), a not guilty plea is entered for them by the court.

A substantial percentage of all felony defendants (approximately 70-85 percent) will plead guilty at this point in the process. The guilty plea rate varies considerably with the seriousness of the offense charged. Hence, defendants charged with crimes against property are more likely to enter guilty pleas than those charged with crimes against persons.

Of those defendants pleading guilty, the majority do so as a result of a plea bargain. Plea bargaining is a process where the prosecuting attorney and the defense counsel forge an agreement for either reduced or modified charges and/or sentencing concessions. Many factors play a role in this process including the strength or weakness of the evidence in the case, victim considerations, prosecutorial workload pressures, etc.

Prior to accepting a guilty plea, the judge must be certain that the defendant's decision to plead guilty is "intelligent, voluntary, and informed." To ascertain whether the defendant knows the implications of a guilty plea, the judge will ask the individual a series of questions. The judge will officially notify him of his right to a trial and right to be represented by counsel. He will ask about the voluntary nature of the plea. And he will advise the defendant of the possible sentencing consequences of his admission. If the judge is satisfied that the defendant is competent, knows what he is doing and appreciates the potential consequences of his actions, he will accept the plea and schedule a sentencing date. If the court believes that the defendant's guilty plea is not freely and voluntarily given, the judge may refuse to accept the plea and enter a not guilty plea for the defendant.

When a not guilty plea is entered, either by the defendant or by the judge, the court will schedule a date for a trial.

Pretrial Motions

Prior to the trial, the defense counsel may raise various procedural objections and present them to the trial court. A hearing may be held by the court to determine the validity of the motions. At this proceeding the defense may enter motions to suppress illegally obtained evidence, to dismiss the case entirely, or to request a change in venue (to move the trial to another location). Resolving these kinds of procedural questions may reduce delays at trial or may allow the defense more time to prepare a case prior to trial. In addition, denial of motions may become the basis for appeal if the defendant is convicted at trial.

Trial

For felony defendants who enter not guilty pleas at the arraignment and misdemeanor offenders at the first appearance stage, the next step in the process is the criminal trial. Based upon state legislation regarding speedy trials, the trial phase must usually commence within 90 to 120 days after arraignment or the defendant may be entitled to discharge from further liability, unless the delay is the result of an application for continuance by the defendant.

The hallmark of the criminal justice system is the jury trial. In some circumstances, however, the defendant may choose to have his case tried by a judge sitting alone; that is, he may request a bench trial.

The right to a jury trial in felony cases is absolute, but when an offense less than a felony is charged, such as a misdemeanor or a traffic offense, the situation is more variable. The Supreme Court ruled in *Duncan v. Louisiana (1968)*[21] that the constitutional right to a jury applies only to crimes punishable by incarceration of six months or more. As a result, many jurisdictions do not extend the right of jury trials to cases involving petty offenses like public intoxication, disorderly conduct, public order crimes, and minor traffic offenses.

At trial, the defendant receives the greatest amount of due process within the criminal justice system. That is, legal formalities abound in a trial setting. The defendant and the prosecution have an opposing, adversarial relationship. The adversary method of justice is based on the belief that the best way to reach the truth is through a legal contest between two competent lawyers in a court of law presided over by a judge who sees that the rules of evidence and the defendant's constitutional rights are observed.

Procedures followed at a trial are circumscribed by constitutions, statutes, and court rules. The court assumes that the defendant is innocent until proven guilty. The proof of guilt required is "beyond a reasonable doubt," the highest level of proof in the criminal justice system. Convictions must be based on properly obtained, presented, and interpreted evidence. The judge and jury act as fair and neutral observers who listen to the arguments and the evidence presented by the prosecutor and by the defense counsel. The primary role of the judge and jury is one of fact-finding: to determine, within the guidelines of the law, whether the facts would cause a reasonable person to conclude that the defendant was guilty of the criminal charges. This involves weighing the evidence and deciding whether it meets the standard of proof beyond a reasonable doubt.

If a defendant decides to exercise his right to a jury trial, the process begins with the selection of a fair and impartial jury. First, a list of names of citizens from which jurors will be chosen is drawn up by the court. The master list, which constitutes the population of potential jurors, is the venire or jury array. Usually the master list is taken from voter registration lists or drivers license information. Second, a random selection of names from the venire is taken to identify those citizens who will be summoned to begin their jury service. The juror candidates constitute the jury pool. The third and final step in the jury composition is the *voir dire* examination. *Voir dire* is a screening process that attempts to eliminate potential jurors who might be biased or unfair in the course of their duties. The prospective jurors are questioned by the prosecutor, the defense attorney, and sometimes the judge to determine their fitness to serve as jurors in the trial. Jurors may be excused by challenges made by the attorneys. Two primary types of challenges are utilized by attorneys. The "challenge for cause" results in the removal of a potential juror who may be unable to be impartial and render a verdict based solely on the evidence. The "peremptory challenge" allows the attorneys to dismiss prospective jurors for no particular or stated reason. In most jurisdictions the jury is made up of 12 members. The Supreme Court, in *Williams v. Florida (1970)*[22] approved the principle of six member juries, allowing states to use smaller juries.

Once the jury is empaneled, the prosecution and defense present their opening statements. The purpose of the opening statements is for both sides to describe the facts they intend to prove during the course of the trial, either swaying the jury toward conviction or acquittal. The prosecution then usually begins with the presentation of their evidence and direct examination of witness testimony. At the conclusion of the direct examination of a witness, the other side may cross-examine the witness by following up on statements, asking other relevant questions or generally working to impeach the witness. Once the prosecution has presented its evidence and rested, the defense has the option of presenting witnesses on the behalf of the defendant. However, since the burden of proof lies with the prosecution, the defense is under no obligation to do so and in fact may present no evidence if they feel the prosecution has not proven their case. At the conclusion of the presentation of all the evidence, the prosecution and defense have an opportunity to present an oral summary of the case in the form of closing arguments. After closing arguments the judge will instruct or charge the jury regarding the principle of law to be used in guiding their decision of guilty or not guilty, or some other allowable verdict (e.g., not guilty because of insanity). Most state constitutions require that trial jury verdicts be unanimous. But this concept is changing based on two Supreme Court decisions in 1972. In *Johnson v. Louisiana*[23] and in *Apodaca v. Oregon*[24] the Court approved the principle of non-unanimous jury verdicts and ruled that the Sixth Amendment right to trial by jury does not necessarily include a unanimous verdict.

Overall, trials are rare events within the system. George Cole estimates that only about eight percent of criminal cases are decided in this manner.[25] Eisenstein and Jacob found that in Chicago, Detroit, and Baltimore, cases were disposed of through jury trials less than ten percent of the time.[26] But despite its rare usage within the system, the trial is regarded as the pinnacle of the adversary process.

Sentencing

After conviction by trial or guilty plea, the defendant is brought before the court for sentencing. Within the sentencing decision lies a number of complex and controversial issues. Competing philosophies of corrections pervade the choice of sentence. Ideological conflicts between punishment and treatment and the question of whether deterrence works are some of the problems faced by judges and other agents within this stage of the process. In the majority of jurisdictions, the judge's personality, attitudes toward criminals and types of crimes, and other nonlegal factors have some impact on sentence selection. Statutory variation among jurisdictions in penalties for the same crime, oddly constructed penal codes, and disparate recommendations from probation officers in presentence reports, contribute to sentencing differences.

There are basically four objectives of sentencing — retribution, incapacitation, deterrence, and rehabilitation.

Retribution is punishment of an individual for an act they have committed. It means that society inflicts punishment on criminals because they have infringed on the rights of others and thus deserve sanctioning. The severity of the sanction should fit the seriousness of the crime. Retribution embraces today's philosophy of the "just deserts" model of sentencing. The basic tenets of the just deserts model suggest that punishment should be in direct proportion to the type and severity of the crime. This philosophy has helped to fuel the current trend of guideline sentencing.

The incapacitation goal of sentencing is to remove offenders from society. The assumption of incapacitation is that a crime may be prevented if the criminals are physically restrained and isolated from society. Incarceration is the most typical form of incapacitation, although modern methods may include electronically monitored house arrest and use of medications to modify the individual's behavior and/or desires (e.g., chemical castration of sex offenders).

Deterrence involves the threat, or the actual imposition, of punishment. The function of deterrence is to prevent law-abiding citizens from turning to crime and to discourage punished offenders from returning to crime. Two types of deterrence, general and specific, are popular today. General deterrence is the idea that the general population will be dissuaded from criminal behavior by observing that punishment will necessarily follow the commission of a crime. Specific deterrence is concerned with changes in the behavior of the convicted person and is individualized in that the correct amount and kind of punishment must be prescribed so the criminal will not repeat the offense.

The fourth and final goal of sentencing involves rehabilitation. Rehabilitation signifies the efforts to change an offender from a law-breaker to a law-abider and a productive member of society through treatment rather than punishment. The treatment process attempts to make the offender's attitudes, values, and personality more compatible with that of society's.

Sentencing usually takes place several days or even weeks after the trial verdict is rendered. During this period, a presentence investigation is conducted by a probation or court services officer. The majority of jurisdictions require presentence investigations in felony cases. Misdemeanor presentence investigations are at the discretion of the judge.

Typically, the officer gathers information concerning the current offense. The information generally includes: the prosecuting attorney and defendant's version of the crime; a victim's impact statement; the defendant's prior criminal record; the defendant's family, educational, employment, martial, and substance abuse history; and any other pertinent information describing the defendant.

With many jurisdictions adopting sentencing guidelines, the focus of the presentence investigation has shifted primarily to reporting an accurate criminal history in conjunction with the severity of the current offense.

The presentence report is then submitted to the court. This report aids the judge in reaching a sentencing decision, for it includes pertinent details about the individual, evaluates the case, and recommends disposition.

In principle there are four types of sentences — fines, probation, incarceration, and the death penalty.

A fine simply requires the convicted person to pay a specific amount of money to the state for the offense. Fines may be levied in combination with probation or incarceration.

Probation is an alternative to incarceration. As of January 1, 1995, there were approximately three million offenders under probation supervision in the United States. According to data from the U.S. Department of Justice, approximately 40% of felony offenders are granted straight probation.[27] The judge grants the offender conditional freedom allowing him to live in the community under supervision. General conditions of probation ordered by the court will usually require the offender to: refrain from violating the law, seek and/or maintain employment, refrain from possessing firearms, remain in the jurisdiction of the court, report to the probation officer as directed, and allow the officer to visit their home and/or work. Specific conditions vary per individual and may include: refraining from the use of alcohol and drugs, attendance at substance-abuse intervention programs, submission to random alcohol and drug screening, mental-health counseling, payment of restitution to victims, and community work service. Violation of these rules may result in revocation of probation and further punitive measures by the court.

The probation officer assigned to the case decides whether an infraction is serious enough to return the probationer to court and begin revocation proceedings. The judge makes the final revocation decision. He may choose to use a form of intermediate sanction such as intensive supervised probation. This requires the offender to: report to an officer three to five times per week, abide by a mandatory curfew, a weekly check of local arrest records, frequent alcohol and drug testing, mandatory employment, etc. The judge may also choose incarceration (especially in the event of revocation from intensive supervised probation).

Incarceration in jails or prisons is more complicated than a statutory rule specifying a certain number of years based on the seriousness of the crime and the characteristics of the offender. Usually legislatures provide a range in the length of the term that the judge may prescribe. The legislature normally stipulates where the sentence is to be served: less than one year usually means a jail; longer terms, the state penitentiary. The offender convicted of more than one charge may be sentenced for each offense. The judge stipulates whether sentences are to be served concurrently (all at one time) or consecutively (one after the other).

State penal codes vary as to the structure of the sentences. Two sentencing practices are prominent — indeterminate and determinate. Each makes certain assumptions about the goals of criminal sanctions. Indeterminate sentences are consistent with rehabilitation. The indeterminate or indefinite sentence is a period set by a judge in which there is a measure of time between the minimum date for a decision on parole eligibility and a maximum date when the sentence has been completed. The offender knows only the range of his sentence (e.g., 1 to 5 years) and that parole eligibility will probably occur after the minimum term has been served. This allows correctional personnel the discretion to make a release decision on the grounds of successful treatment. It also gives the offender incentive to work for early release.

Determinate sentences are fixed periods of time for incarceration. This type of sentence is based on the "just deserts" model of imprisonment. In the purest sense, this means that at the end of the prison term (e.g., 10 years) the offender

is automatically freed back into society. In many jurisdictions, legislatures have created sentencing guidelines mandating specific terms for specific offenses. As of mid-1995, 13 States have adopted some form of determinate sentencing.[28] This fixed, flat sentencing structure is not tied to a parole board or participation in treatment programs. Many jurisdictions still make provision for "good time," allowing release of the offender after 80-85% of his term is served.

The re-institution of the death penalty in 1976 by the Supreme Court has given judges and juries another punitive option to consider. Between 1930 and 1967 the death penalty has been used extensively in the United States, with more than 3,800 men and women put to death during that period. But in 1967, the Supreme Court ordered a stay of executions pending a hearing on the issue and in 1972 ruled that the death penalty, as administered, constituted cruel and unusual punishment. In a landmark decision (*Furman v. Georgia*),[29] the Court said that judges and juries imposed the death penalty in such an arbitrary, capricious, and discriminatory manner that is constituted cruel and unusual punishment. By 1976, Georgia and 34 other states had enacted new legislation to correct the faults pointed out by the Court. The new laws were tested by the Court in 1976 in the case of *Gregg v. Georgia*.[30] The Court upheld the laws that required the sentencing judge or jury to take into account specific aggravating and mitigating factors in deciding which convicted murderers should be sentenced to death. As a result, the death penalty was re-instituted and from January 1, 1977 to December 31, 1995, 313 convicted felons have been put to death by firing squad, electrocution, gas, lethal injection, or hanging. In addition, approximately 3,054 prisoners sit on death row awaiting execution.[31]

Release From Incarceration

Release from incarceration may take place in a number of ways. For misdemeanants, release occurs after they have served the full sentence specified by the court. Normally, misdemeanant prisoners have flat sentences with no latitude between minimum and maximum time. For incarcerated felons, however, release could take place through *parole*, *mandatory release*, or a *pardon*.

Parole — Parole involves the release of an individual who has been confined in a correctional facility to the community under supervision. The legislative body in almost all jurisdictions sets out the criteria for parole eligibility in a statute. In most jurisdictions inmates given an indeterminate sentence (of the minimum-maximum variety) are eligible for parole after serving the minimum. Other areas allow eligibility at any time, when the inmate has served a proportion of the maximum (e.g., one-third of the maximum), or when the inmate has served a proportion of the minimum. "Good time" credits also pay a role in eligibility. The concept behind "good time" is to reward an inmate who complies with prison regulations with a certain amount of time credited toward the sentence they serve. This allows them to be eligible for early release. Good time credits vary depending upon the jurisdiction. The most common statutory pattern is a sliding scale that takes 2-5 days per month off the sentence for serving the first and second years and up to 10-15 days per month off the sentence after having served several years. Some states have a flat-rate statutory good time structure. In Maryland, for example, five days per month are taken off each inmates sentence.

The parole decision is made by the state parole authority or parole board. Most boards are comprised of three to five members appointed by the governor. Some states have moved toward merit selection of board members from recommendations made by other agencies or groups.[32]

The parole decision is made when the parole board visits each prison in the state and holds hearings. At the hearings, eligible inmates are interviewed and their files are examined. The board considers a number of factors including the criminal record, prison adjustment, attitude of the offender, and the parole plan of the inmate.

Inmates who are granted parole remain in the legal custody of the state and must serve the remainder of their unexpired maximum sentence (including the amount of good time accrued) under the supervision of a parole officer. The parolee must meet several conditions when released, including: obeying the law, supporting his dependents, avoiding association with criminals, remaining within a certain jurisdiction, and reporting to his parole officer on a regular basis. If any of the above conditions, among other stipulations, are not met, parole may be revoked and the individual sent back to an institution to finish serving his term.

A negative decision at the parole hearing results in a "set-off" date which is the time of the next opportunity for parole eligibility. This date is determined by statute or the parole board's policy.

Mandatory Release — Mandatory release means that inmates are automatically released from prison after serving their maximum term minus good time. Technically, the inmate's full sentence has not expired, so he is supervised as though he were on parole. The conditions of mandatory release are the same as regular parole conditions and a return to prison could occur if violations take place.

Pardon — Another method of obtaining release from an institution is the pardon. A pardon is an action taken by an executive officer (governor or President) pardoning an individual of a crime which he committed. Pardons may also be used to correct mistakes in criminal justice or to restore rights lost upon conviction.

Appeals And Post-Conviction Remedies

Defendants may appeal their convictions to higher courts. All states have appellate machinery that allows the defendant at least one chance to appeal. The appellate process may ultimately involve the entire hierarchy of state and federal courts, eventually rising to the U.S. Supreme Court. However, before appeals move from state to federal review, state remedies generally must be exhausted.

An appeal is usually made within a certain time (10 days, for example) after conviction. Depending upon the jurisdiction, an appeal will begin with the "intermediate" appellate court (23 states have these courts) and then ascend to the state supreme court (all 50 states have one). In states that do not have intermediate courts, the defendant will appeal directly to the state supreme court. If these attempts fail, the convicted felon then appeals to the U.S. Supreme Court. The defendant may base his appeal on almost anything that could have reasonably prevented him from receiving a fair trial and/or sentence. Police entrapment, illegal search and seizure, unethical conduct by the prosecutor, and charging the jury incorrectly are some of the bases for appeal that can be made.

Appellate courts do not conduct new trials. Instead, their function is to review the record of the lower court to determine whether there were errors of law associated with the defendant's conviction or sentence.

The convicted felon may appeal both his conviction and his sentence. A sentence can be appealed whenever the method used by the judge in selecting penalties violates the Fourteenth Amendment's provisions for due process. But, in practice, very few sentences are appealed, compared to the number of convictions appealed. Part of the reason for the small number is the lack of specific procedures that the court is required to follow at sentencing. Historically, the sentencing stage allows enormous discretion on the part of the judge. It is a somewhat "invisible" process, making violations of the process difficult to establish.

The percentage of felony defendants found guilty at trial who appeal their convictions varies from as low as 30 percent in some jurisdictions to over 80 percent in others. The rate of appeals tends to vary with the sentence. Defendants sentenced to prison are more likely to appeal than those placed on probation.[33] In the vast majority of cases, the appellate court finds that the trial court's conviction or sentence was proper. Cole (1983) estimates that roughly 20 percent of appeals are successful in that convictions are reversed.[34] But reversal does not always mean freedom. The appellate court will reverse and remand the case, meaning that a new trial must take place. A successful appeal is simply an opportunity for the defendant to start over from the beginning, or from the point at which the legal error occurred. Appellate reversal of a conviction or a sentence is not an automatic victory that turns a conviction into an acquittal or necessarily reduces the punishment.

Concluding Remarks

This chapter has presented an overview of the criminal justice system from the pre-arrest stage to release from incarceration. We have tried to take a systems approach to the overview to show the interaction of the various actors within the process. By virtue of this interaction, cooperation and interdependence are important facets of the criminal justice system.

✳ ✳ ✳ ✳ ✳

ENDNOTES

[1] Bureau of Justice Statistics, *Criminal Victimization in the United States, 1973-92 Trends* (Washington, DC: U.S. Department of Justice, 1994), p. 5.
[2] K. Maguire, and A. Pastore, eds., *Sourcebook of Criminal Justice Statistics 1995* (U.S. Department of Justice, Bureau of Justice Statistics. Washington, DC, 1996), p. 251.

[3] W. Spelman, and D. Brown, *Calling the Police: A Replication of the Citizen Reporting Component of the Kansas City Response Time Analysis* (Washington, DC: The Police Foundation, 1981)

[4] G. Cordner, and R. Trojanowicz, *What Works in Policing? Operations and Administration Examined* (Cincinnati, OH: Anderson Publishing Co., 1992) p. 6-7.

[5] D. Oran, *Law Dictionary for Nonlawyers,* 2d ed., (St. Paul, MN: West Publishing Co., 1985)

[6] U.S. Department of Justice, Federal Bureau of Investigation, *Crime in the United States, 1994* (Washington, DC: USGPO, 1995)

[7] A. Reiss, *The Police and the Public* (New Haven, CT: Yale University Press, 1971)

[8] L. Gaines, V. Kappeler, and J. Vaughn, *Policing in America* (Cincinnati, OH: Anderson Publishing Co., 1997) p. 190-194

[9] R.G. Dunham, and G.P. Alpert, *Critical Issues in Policing: Contemporary Readings* (Prospect Heights, IL: Waveland Press, 1989) p. 135-136.

[10] *Miranda v. Arizona*, 384 U.S. 436 (1966)

[11] *Oregon v. Mathiason*, 429 U.S. 492, 97 S.Ct. 711 (1977)

[12] *McNabb v. United States*, 318 U.S. 332 (1943)

[13] *County of Riverside v. McLaughlin*, 111 S.Ct. 1661 (1991)

[14] U.S. Department of Justice, Bureau of Justice Statistics, *Indigent Defense* (Washington, DC: U.S. Department of Justice, 1996) p. 3.

[15] *Gideon v. Wainwright*, 372 U.S. 335 (1963)

[16] *Argersinger v. Hamlin*, 407 U.S. 25 (1972)

[17] U.S. Department of Justice, Bureau of Justice Statistics, *Pretrial Release of Felony Defendants, 1992* (Washington, DC: U.S. Department of Justice, 1994) p. 2.

[18] M. Gottfredson, and D. Gottfredson, *Decisionmaking in Criminal Justice: Toward the Rational Exercise of Discretion* (Cambridge, MA: Ballinger Publishing Co., 1980)

[19] B. Boland, P. Mahanna, and R. Stones, *The Prosecution of Felony Arrests, 1988* (Washington, DC: Bureau of Justice Statistics, 1993) p. 3.

[20] U.S. Department of Justice, Bureau of Justice Statistics, *Federal Criminal Case Processing, 1982-93, With Preliminary Data for 1994* (Washington, DC: USGPO, 1996) p. 4-5.

[21] *Duncan v. Louisiana*, 391 U.S. 145 (1968)

[22] *Williams v. Florida*, 399 U.S. 78 (1970)

[23] *Johnson v. Louisianna*, 406 U.S. 356 (1972)

[24] *Apodaca v. Oregon*, 406 U.S. 404 (1972)

[25] G. Cole, *The American System of Criminal Justice*, 3rd ed., (Monterey, CA: Brooks/Cole Publishing Co., 1983)

[26] J. Eisenstein, and H. Jacob, *Felony Justice* (Boston, MA: Little, Brown and Co., 1977)

[27] U.S. Department of Justice, Bureau of Justice Statistics, *Felony Sentences in State Courts, 1992* (Washington, DC: U.S. Department of Justice, January, 1995) p. 2.

[28] D. Hunzeker, *State Sentencing Systems & Truth in Sentencing, State Legislative Report*, Vol. 20, No. 3 (Denver, CO: National Conference of State Legislatures, 1995)

[29] *Furman v. Georgia*, 408 U.S. 145 (1972)

[30] *Gregg v. Georgia*, 428 U.S. 153 (1976)

[31] U.S. Department of Justice, Bureau of Justice Statistics, *Capital Punishment 1995*, (Washington, DC: U.S. Department of Justice, December, 1996) p. 1.

[32] V. O'Leary, and K.J. Hanrahan, *Parole Systems in the United States*, (Hackensack, NJ: National Council on Crime and Delinquency, 1976)

[33] Administrative Office of the United States Courts, *Annual Report of the Director, 1995* (Washington, DC: Administrative Office of the United States Courts, 1995)

[34] G. Cole, *The American System of Criminal Justice*, 3rd ed., (Monterey, CA: Brooks/Cole Publishing Co., 1983)

SECTION II

STUDYING CRIME
and
CRIMINAL BEHAVIOR:
THEORIES AND METHODS

Chapter *3*

Criminological Theory

By

Jerome McKean

This chapter begins with the assumption that many of its readers have decided that they do not like theory. For them, theory is unreal, impractical, and unnecessary. A dim view of theory is especially common when it comes to theories of crime, for crime is an urgent social concern, and it seems silly to waste energy on theorizing instead of going out into the real world and doing something about crime. As one of the author's students put it, "Theory is for wonks, not for cops."

But theory is not merely the ideas of some professor in an ivory tower. When someone says, "That's just theoretical," or, "I'm too practical to care about theories," they reveal that they misunderstand what theory is all about. *A theory is a set of statements about the real world.* The statements in a theory are often called *propositions.* The following statements are examples of theoretical propositions:

Most cops are on the take.

A kick in the rear would straighten out most delinquents.

Poor people commit crimes to survive.

We would have fewer murders if we applied the death penalty more frequently.

Everyone uses theories. As the examples show, any time that someone acts on the belief that one event (a kick in the rear) is related to another event (straightening out a delinquent), or that things with one characteristic (being a cop) tend to have another characteristic (being on the take), they are acting on the basis of a theoretical proposition. Theorizing is a universal and indispensable human activity.

When we use theoretical propositions in everyday life, we (and "we" includes scientists and scholars of all sorts) often take their truth for granted. Our "truths" are based on our own experience, tradition, and statements that we take on faith by those with knowledge or power (Babbie, 1996). For instance, consider the examples of theoretical propositions given above. Despite their acceptance as truth by any number of people, not one of the propositions has been shown to be true.

49

SCIENTIFIC THEORIES

What is good enough for everyday life is not good enough for making criminal justice policy or designing criminal justice programs. Lives are at stake. *Science* is an attempt to avoid the errors made in everyday inquiry by applying strict rules to the construction and testing of propositions. The rules of inquiry are usually considered part of the study of research methods, but it is important to realize that theory and research are inseparable. By proposing that certain relationships exist among events and characteristics, theories provide an agenda for research: theory tells us which relationships may be important and therefore worthy of study.

In turn, research tells us whether a theory is correct by testing *hypotheses* derived from the theory's propositions. Hypotheses are very specific versions of the propositions which can be compared to observable events. For example, the proposition that "We would have fewer murders if we applied the death penalty more frequently" might lead one to hypothesize that states which have executed a large number of murderers have lower murder rates than states which have not.

To test this hypothesis, a researcher would collect data on the number of persons each state has executed for murder and the murder rates for each state. She would use the data to see if the hypothesis is true (by the way, it is not true as stated). If the hypothesis is not true, the proposition must either be modified or abandoned.

When research supports the claim that a theory conforms to empirical reality, researchers tentatively accept it as true. No theory is accepted as the complete and final truth, no matter how well it is supported by research, for it is never true that we have learned all there is to learn about a phenomenon.

A scientific theory is consciously constructed to fulfill several purposes. *The purposes of scientif-ic theory are description, explanation, prediction, and (sometimes) application* (Reynolds, 1971). These purposes of theory will be illustrated as we consider the specific content of the leading theories of crime and criminal behavior.

DEFINITIONS OF CRIME AND IMPLICATIONS FOR THEORY

The accurate description of the phenomena that a theory deals with is necessary to accomplish any of the other purposes of a theory. We cannot explain, predict or control something until we know what it is. The propositions of a theory contain *concepts*, which are the words or images we use to represent our mental images of phenomena (Maxfield and Babbie: 1995). Criminological theories use concepts such as "crime," "delinquency," and "deviance."

The definition of the concepts employed in a theory is of great importance. The theorist is obligated to tell us how to find and measure the phenomenon being studied. Unless the theorist tells us precisely what he or she means when such terms are used, there is no way to prove or disprove the theory.

The definition of concepts also goes hand-in-hand with their explanation. To paraphrase Hirschi (1969:47), crime cannot be usefully defined apart from an attempt to explain it (crime) as defined. And one cannot explain crime without at least implicitly defining crime.

One reason that there are so many theories of criminal behavior is that the concept of crime can be defined in many ways. Criminologists have used four major approaches to defining crime in building their theories:

1. Crime as *law-violating behavior*.
2. Crime as *deviant* or *abnormal behavior*.

3. Crime as a *status*.
4. Crime as *acts of force, fraud or stealth in pursuit of self-interest* (Gottfredson and Hirschi, 1990; Vila, 1994).

Crime as Law-Violating Behavior

Most criminologists would probably agree with the following definition of crime (Sutherland, Cressey, and Luckenbill, 1992:4):

> Crime is behavior in violation of the criminal law. No matter how immoral, reprehensible, or indecent an act may be, it is not a criminal act unless it is outlawed by the state. The criminal law is a list of specific forms of human conduct that have been outlawed by political authority, which applies uniformly to all persons living under that authority, and which is enforced by punishment administered by the state.

The legal definition of crime has the advantages of being more or less in accord with everyday understanding of what crime is, and pointing us toward the statute books to find definitions of specific offenses. Crime is what the political rulers of a society say it is.

There are also problems with a legal definition. One problem is that *legal descriptions of crime are relative to time and place.* Many of the laws which are presently on the books apply to situations unknown to earlier generations, such as laws prohibiting obscene telephone calls. Statutes are written or amended as a result of social, economic and political processes. For example, possession of cocaine was not outlawed in the United States until the early years of the twentieth century. Coca leaves (from which cocaine is derived) were used in the making of Coca-Cola until at least 1903 (Abadinsky, 1993:63)

Laws also vary widely from state to state and nation to nation. For example, the laws of the American states differ as to whether it is possible for a husband to rape his wife (Karmen, 1996). As this implies, the same behavior may or may not be classified legally as a crime, depending on when, where, and by whom the behavior is committed.

A second problem with the legal definition of crime is that it includes very diverse kinds of behavior. In a typical state, acts which violate the law include everything from murder to speeding to underage drinking. Sutherland and his associates have described the implications that this has for theory (Sutherland, et al., 1992:11):

> If we examine crime as a whole, we run the risk of being overly general and ignoring significant differences among crimes. At the same time, if we examine concrete cases of crime, we run the risk of being too specific, of losing sight of the larger picture while getting lost in a maze of particulars.

To deal with the heterogeneity of legally-defined crime, criminologists have attempted to classify crimes in a variety of ways. Most commonly, criminologists attempt to distinguish crimes by their seriousness and by offense type. Examples of each of these classification schemes are presented below.

Seriousness

What does it mean to say that one crime is more serious than another? There are several ways in which crime seriousness is determined.

One method is to examine the *severity of the penalties* for an offense. In American criminal law, crimes are divided into the categories of felony and misdemeanor. A *felony* is a crime punishable by incarceration for one year or longer in a state correctional facility; a *misdemeanor* is a crime punishable by incarceration for less than one year, usually in a local correctional facility.

Another method is to measure public *perceptions* as to the seriousness of crimes. Using sophisticated survey methods, Wolfgang, Figlio, Tracey and Singer (1985) asked a representative sample of Americans to rate the severity of descriptions of specific offenses and assigned a "severity score" to each offense description. The average scores ranged from 72.1 for planting a bomb in a public building and killing twenty people to 0.2 for playing hooky from school. This study, as well as earlier research, also demonstrated that there is a strong consensus among persons of various nationalities, class positions, and races as to the seriousness of offenses (Warr, 1995).

A third method of ascertaining the seriousness of offenses is to develop measures of the *harm* that they cause. The most obvious measures of harm are physical damage and economic loss to victims, but many offenses also produce grave psychological damage. There is also the idea of harm to society or the public order, produced by offenses which may not have a specific human victim, such as disorderly conduct, public drunkenness, or disturbing the peace.

Although these different ways of measuring seriousness may produce similar rankings, they will not be in complete agreement with one another. For example, members of the public may not perceive the use of marijuana for the relief of pain by a terminally ill person as a serious offense, and it would be hard to argue that any harm has resulted to the user (although it may be argued that public order is threatened). Nevertheless, possession of marijuana in even small quantities is a felony in many states.

More often, the different ways of measuring seriousness are in agreement with one another. To take an obvious example, murder is a crime which is punished severely, which virtually everyone would agree is serious, and which causes great harm to the victim. Thus it is possible to make an important generalization about criminal behavior: *minor offenses are committed far more frequently than serious offenses.* As Felson (1994) points out, nine out of ten major crimes (called Index Offenses) known to the police are property crimes as opposed to the more serious violent crimes. Felson also notes that, of the nine million arrests in 1990, four out of five were not for Index Offenses at all.

Classifying crimes by their seriousness may not be relevant to the causes of the crime. There are several aspects to this. First, the same offense may be committed for a variety of different reasons, as described in the next section. On the other hand, *it is not clear that causes of offending differ by the seriousness of the offense,* however seriousness is measured. Is it plausible to think that the causes of stealing fifty dollars differ from the causes of stealing ten thousand dollars? Are the causes of one person hitting another different from the causes of one person shooting another? Perhaps the only difference in these cases is one of opportunity, rather than motivation or other casual factor. It should not be *assumed* that there are fundamental differences between serious offenses and minor offenses (Gottfredson and Hirschi, 1990).

Offense Type

Another approach to classifying crimes is to simply assume that different kinds of offenses also differ significantly in their nature. Thus, criminologists have specialized in the study of violent offenses, predatory property offenses, drug offenses, white-collar crimes, sex crimes, and so on. The assumption is that crimes which fall under the same offense type, such as burglary, are similar to one another in some way. The similarity may be in the motivation of the offenders, the techniques used to commit the crime (*modus operandi* or *M.O.*), or the opportunities available to commit the crime. The classification of crimes by offense type is often combined with the classification of crimes by offender type, as discussed below.

Specializing in the study of a particular offense type can be a useful strategy. Criminologists can study in detail the opportunity factors which may make it more likely that the offense will occur. For example, it may be quite useful to identify the factors which lead to high rates of auto theft in a particular part of town in order to make recommendations designed to reduce the auto theft rate.

Crime as Deviant Behavior

Legal definitions of crime, as we have noted, are relative to time and place. Many sociologists have attempted to deal with this problem by characterizing criminal behavior as an example of a broader category which they term *deviant behavior,* or deviance. Deviance has been defined in a variety of ways. One prominent sociologist gives the following definition (Tittle, 1995:124-125, italics in original):

> *. . . any behavior that the majority of a given group regards as unacceptable or that typically evokes a collective response of a negative type.* In this definition, "unacceptable" means disapproved, wrong, shameful, pitiful, inappropriate, bad, abnormal, or loathsome — in short, behavior that a group evaluates negatively. "Majority" means that over one-half of the people in a specified, bounded group regard the behavior as unacceptable.

Tittle's definition combines two elements which characterize most definitions of deviant behavior. *First, it is behavior which violates norms* (Sellin, 1938). Norms are rules or expectations for behavior. Norms may be formalized in law, as is the case for many acts which are regarded as crimes. Norms may also be informal, like the unwritten rule against talking during a theater performance. Second, *deviant behavior is behavior which elicits a negative response.* We will consider this second aspect of deviance more thoroughly in discussing the concept of crime as a status.

Deviant behavior is not necessarily criminal behavior. Many behaviors are regarded as unacceptable or evoke negative responses but are not against the law. A popular collection of articles by sociologists on deviance (Kelly, 1993) contains articles on hyperkinesis (hyperactivity by children), epilepsy, alcoholism, lying, mental illness, being a mortician, and obesity. None of these behaviors are against the law, but all may be deviant in some contexts. Another excellent example of a behavior which has increasingly come to be regarded as deviant in recent years is smoking.

Criminal behavior is not necessarily deviant behavior. As Tittle points out (1995:126-127):

> Mere illegality is not a reliable guide to the deviantness of some behavior since law does not necessarily reflect public opinion and many laws are never enforced. Indeed, law often expresses the desires and interests of special power groups that are able to mobilize legislative support, sometimes in direct opposition to majority views.

Behaviors which are sometimes illegal but not deviant include gambling, speeding, oral sex between consenting adults, underage drinking and tobacco use, and the use of physical violence to control children (spanking).

Although these exceptions are important, *most criminal behavior is also deviant behavior.* Criminal laws often reflect widely-accepted norms. Sociologists sometimes prefer to speak of deviant behavior rather than criminal behavior because the latter category is, in their view, more homogeneous. The concept of deviance also applies to societies that do not have formal legal systems or which do not make a clear distinction between legal rules and moral rules. On the other hand, what is considered deviant behavior also varies in time and space, and it is not clear that deviance is any less arbitrary a category than crime (Gibbs, 1966). For criminologists, the concept of deviance is useful because it reminds us that not all criminal behaviors are necessarily disapproved of, and that what is regarded as crime is often as much a matter of political power as it is popular disapproval.

As this discussion indicates, sociologists and many criminologists would not accept the idea that criminal behavior indicates a mental disturbance or psychopathology. But it is important to note that many psychologists do consider criminal behavior as deviant in an absolute sense. That is, they regard criminal behavior as a symptom of identifiable mental illnesses, much as jaundice is a symptom of liver failure (Raine, 1993). This view of criminal behavior is examined further in the section on biological and psychological perspectives on crime.

Crime as a Status

So far, we have dealt with crime as a behavior. Under this sort of definition, it makes sense to construct theories to deal with such questions as why people commit crimes and why some persons tend to commit more crimes than others. Another approach is to define crime as a status or label. For example, Barlow defines crime as "a label that is attached to human conduct by those who create and administer the criminal law'' (1978:9). Barlow's definition is based on the assumption that *no act is inherently criminal*. Whether an act is regarded as a crime depends on the *reaction* of authorities — police officers, prosecutors, and judges. This understanding of crime derives from the work of certain sociologists of deviance, such as Howard S. Becker. Becker argues that definitions of crime and deviance which emphasize the infraction of rules ignore the fact that deviance is created by society (1963:9):

> [S]ocial groups create deviance by making the rules whose infractions constitute deviance, and by applying those rules to particular people and labeling them as outsiders. From this point of view, deviance is *not* a quality of the act the person commits, but rather a consequence of the application by others of rules and sanctions to an ''offender.'' The deviant is one to whom that label has successfully been applied; deviant behavior is behavior that people so label.

Not surprisingly, criminologists and sociologists who emphasize status definitions of crime and deviance are called *labeling theorists*. Under this sort of definition of crime or deviance, it makes little sense to tackle the questions mentioned above. Instead, labeling theorists want to know why some conduct is labeled as criminal behavior while apparently similar conduct is not, why some persons who commit an act are labeled as criminals, while others who commit similar acts are not, and the processes by which social groups decide what and who is criminal. Attention is focused on those who label conduct as criminal as much as on those whose conduct is so labeled (Reiman, 1990).

Crimes as Acts of Force, Fraud, and Stealth

The definitions of crime and deviance described above have all been criticized for including too many different kinds of behaviors, and for being relative to time and place. Michael R. Gottfredson and Travis Hirschi have attempted to overcome these problems by defining crimes as ''. . . acts of force or fraud undertaken in pursuit of

self-interest'' (1990:15). To this definition, Vila (1994) has added acts of stealth.

Based on this definition, Gottfredson and Hirschi describe criminal acts as having certain characteristics. They assume that the use of force and fraud are pleasurable to human beings. *Crimes are pleasurable acts whose pleasures may be enjoyed immediately, which are mentally and physically easy to perform, and which are risky and exciting* (Gottfredson and Hirschi, 1990:12). Criminal acts are similar to other shortsighted but pleasurable behaviors, such as reckless driving, smoking, overeating, promiscuous sex, and skipping school. Gottfredson and Hirschi emphasize the idea that, contrary to media portrayals of crime, the well-planned criminal act is very rare (1990:16).

Critics of Gottfredson and Hirschi's concept of crime note that it may exclude acts which are against the law or regarded as deviant, such as white-collar and corporate crimes (Steffensmeier, 1989). The concept may also include legal acts which involve an element of fraud, such as advertising, salesmanship, political campaigning, and courtship (Tittle, 1995:57). Under this definition, organized, well-planned activities instigated for long-term gain are excluded, as are actions which are illegal but which are undertaken in the service of religious and political ideals.

Gottfredson and Hirschi might reply that although their definition excludes some rare forms of illegal behavior, it includes the vast majority of acts which are commonly regarded as crimes, and it helps direct us to a straightforward explanation for criminal behavior. Their *self-control theory* of crime is described later in this chapter.

Criminality

So far, we have been looking at crime, either as an act or a status. Gottfredson and Hirschi have suggested a useful distinction between crime and *criminality*, which they define as ''the propensities of individuals committing criminal acts'' (1990: 85).

Criminologists use several criteria to differentiate offenders from each other and from non-offenders. Four of the most often used criteria are *frequency, seriousness, chronicity, and specialization*. Those who commit crimes with greater frequency, or over a longer period of their lives, or who commit serious crimes may be said to exhibit more criminality than less frequent, less serious offenders.

The Serious Chronic Offender. Ask yourself the following questions: Have you ever stolen anything? Have you ever threatened to harm someone (including a family member)? Have your ever intentionally hit someone? Have you used tobacco or alcohol before you were of legal age? Have you ever tried marijuana, cocaine, or prescription medications which were not prescribed for you? Have you ever pretended to be sick in order to skip work? Have you ever driven a car while under the influence of drugs or alcohol? As a high school student, did you ditch school?

If you can answer yes to any of these questions, you are one of the vast majority of persons who may be classified as a delinquent or a criminal offender. Based on surveys in which people are asked about their criminal behavior (called self-report surveys), *most persons are criminals*. But most persons commit crimes infrequently, and the crimes they commit are minor offenses.

An important research question in criminology is the extent to which it makes sense to speak of frequent, or "high rate" offenders as differing from infrequent offenders. Some background is helpful. Wolfgang, Figlio, and Sellin (1972) conducted a study of 9,945 males who were born in 1945 and lived in Philadelphia from ages 10 to 18. Such a sample is called a birth cohort. The most striking finding was that *chronic delinquents* — those with five or more police contacts — were only 6.3 percent of the boys in the cohort, but accounted for 51.9 percent of all police contacts. Boys who were stopped more than once were also found to have committed more serious offenses. The research did not merely confirm the existence of chronic offenders, but also specified the proportion of the population which falls into this category.

The findings of the Philadelphia study have been replicated by other researchers (Blumstein, Farrington, and Moitra, 1985; Shannon, 1988; Tillman, 1987; Tracy, Wolfgang, and Figlio, 1985). Follow-up studies of chronic delinquents have found that they are also more likely than other youths to become involved in crime as adults. The research also indicates that chronic offenders are more likely to commit serious offenses, although the evidence suggests that offenders do *not* progress from less serious to more serious offenses (Datesman and Aickin, 1984; Hamparian, 1985). In short, *persons who are frequent offenders as youths are more likely to be chronic offenders and serious offenders.*

The Specialized Offender. Although the evidence is persuasive that there is an identifiable group of serious, chronic offenders, the same research suggests that *only a very small proportion of offenders can be said to be specialists*, that is, to commit one kind of crime to the exclusion of other types (Blumstein and Cohen, 1980; Lab, 1984; Miller, Dinitz, and Conrad, 1982; Petersilia, Greenwood, and Lavin ,1977; Shelden, Horvath, and Tracy, 1989; Shover, 1973; Wolfgang, Figlio, and Sellin, 1972).

This finding is very important, because it contradicts an image of the criminal which is popular in the media and among law enforcement officials (Gottfredson and Hirschi, 1990). The "professional" criminal, although he may have played a large role in the past (see Sutherland, 1937), has been replaced by amateur criminals who take advantage of the countless opportunities to commit crimes which characterize modern urban areas (Felson, 1994). "Serial" offenders — offenders who commit a series of murders, rapes, or some other offense — are also quite rare. For example, between 1970 and 1993, only 125 cases of multiple homicides by one offender were identified in the United States (Adler, Mueller and Laufer, 1995:233), a nation in which over 20,000 murders are reported in the typical year.

Thus, if one wishes to learn more about the characteristics of offenders and the causes of crime, it is not always useful to describe offenders as murderers, rapists, burglars, or drug dealers. This common practice assumes a degree of specialization which does not occur.

TYPES OF THEORIES

Now that we have examined the many ways in which crime is described, we are in a position to consider the many ways in which criminologists try to explain and predict crime. There are dozens of theories of crime. Which one is best? As the preceding section implies, the answer depends in part on how crime is defined. A theory which does a good job of explaining who gets labeled as a criminal may not be very good at explaining why persons commit illegal acts. Theories also differ in the assumptions with which they start and the level of explanation which is emphasized.

A review of some of the ways in which theories are classified is worthwhile, because it illustrates the challenge of explaining crime. Theories have been classified by levels of explanation, by whether they adopt a general or typological approach, and by the school of thought that they represent.

Levels of Explanation

Sampson and Lauritsen (1994:2) identify three levels of explanation: *individual, situational, and community or macrosocial*. The individual level of explanation focuses on characteristics of individuals, such as race, age, sex, class level, intelligence, and personality characteristics, that may make some persons more likely to commit crimes than others. Criminologists who are primarily interested in individual characteristics are concerned with the question of *motivation*, "Why do persons commit crimes?" Some criminologists, called *control theorists*, turn the question around and ask, "Why *don't* persons commit crimes?" A primary con-cern of motivational studies is the explanation of criminality.

Just because someone is motivated to commit a crime does not mean that a crime will occur. The motivated offender must have the *opportunity* to commit a crime. Situational explanations deal with factors that may influence whether or not a crime occurs. Sampson and Lauritsen (1994) suggest that whether or not a weapon is present, drug or alcohol use by the victim or offender, the role of bystanders or third parties, and victim behaviors, such as resistance or retaliation, may be important in determining whether or not a crime occurs.

The macrosocial, or community level of explanation deals with differences in crime *rates*. Why do some countries, such as the United States, have very high rates of crime compared to other industrialized democracies, such as Japan and England? Within the United States, why do neighborhoods or cities or states vary so much in their rates of crime? In trying to account for variations in crime rates, criminologists try to identify population characteristics, features of the social structure, and physical characteristics of places which might be associated with crime. Population characteristics are usually expressed in terms of the percentage of the population which falls into a category, such as the percentage who are poor, the percentage of males, the percentage of unemployed or the percentage of high school dropouts.

Social structure refers to patterns in the relationships between social actors, which may be either persons or organizations (Hagan, 1989). Several aspects of social structure have been of particular interest to criminologists. Among the most important are inequality in resources among various groups (Bridges and Myers, 1994; Hagan and Peterson, 1995), related differences in power, and differences in the degree of organization, which has to do with networks of friends, family members, and organizational members (Sampson and Lauritsen, 1994). Another important aspect of social structure is heterogeneity, that is, the mix of different racial, ethnic, age, and class groups.

The *ecological or physical structure* of a

neighborhood or city has also been implicated in the explanation of variations in crime rates. Students of crime have examined population density, housing composition (single versus multiple-family dwellings), and availability of parking adjacent to residences (which can affect opportunities for auto theft) (Felson, 1994; Roncek, 1981; Sampson and Lauritsen, 1994).

To make matters even more complicated, there are certainly *cross-level effects* (Sampson and Lauritsen, 1994) among the various levels. For example, the presence of opportunities to commit crimes may itself help to motivate offenders. The characteristics of individuals help to determine the social structure and physical structure of a neighborhood, e.g., poor persons often must live in multiple-family dwellings and may lack the political power to compel authorities to provide adequate law enforcement in their neighborhoods. Features of the social structure may also affect individual characteristics. For instance, lack of power and resources typically mean that poor inner-city residents have poorly funded schools, and thus it is not surprising that high numbers of high school dropouts are found in such areas. The lack of resources may also make it difficult for parents (who are often single mothers working two or more jobs) to adequately supervise their children, which further complicates the task of socialization. All these cross-level effects may help to produce variations in rates of crime.

Control Versus Learning Theories

The wide variety of phenomena and levels of explanation which are studied by criminologists has yielded a bewildering array of theories. A partial list compiled by Pearson and Weiner (1985) lists thirteen major theories or types of theories which are often cited in the literature of criminology. A chapter in an introductory reader cannot do justice to them.

Instead, we will focus on two general types of criminological theory which may incorporate some other theories. Control and learning theories also present a sharp contrast to one another in their

basic approaches to explaining crime. Although these are not the only important theories in criminology, they will serve to give the reader an idea of the current state of the field and illustrate the processes of theory construction and evaluation. By presenting these families of theories in detail, I hope to improve the reader's comprehension even at the cost of comprehensiveness.

Criminologists generally agree that *socialization* is an important process in the explanation of individual criminal behavior. Socialization is a "process of social interaction through which people acquire personality and learn values, norms, beliefs, skills, and other patterns of thought and behavior" (Curran and Renzetti, 1994:183). Socialization begins at birth and continues throughout one's life.

Much of our socialization is not deliberate; that is, those with whom we are interacting are not consciously trying to influence our thoughts and actions. When a child witnesses her parents fighting, for example, it may inadvertently teach the child that fighting is an acceptable way for spouses to interact. As this implies, socialization is not the same thing as education, although educational experiences are often intended to socialize.

Criminological theories which aim to explain crime and criminality can be broadly grouped into *control theories* and *learning theories*. The difference between them has to do with the role of socialization. Control theories attribute criminal behavior to a lack of socialization. Learning theories attribute criminal behavior to socialization in deviant thought and behavior patterns. In control theories, the offender is poorly socialized; in learning theories, the offender has learned to become a criminal in the same way that a person learns to become a basketball player, a mother, a police officer, or a good student.

Control theories begin with the question, why do people *conform* to the law? In general, control theorists answer this question by looking to factors which *discourage* crime, such as fear of punishment, disapproval from one's family and friends, loss of employment, and internal feelings of guilt.

Learning theories begin by asking why people break the law. In general, learning theorists look to factors which *encourage* crime, such as approval from friends, monetary gain, and relief of frustration.

The two sorts of theories differ in their depiction of criminal behavior. Control theorists are more likely to describe criminal behavior as Gottfredson and Hirschi (1990) describe it, as essentially selfish, short-sighted behavior requiring little skill or learning. Control theorists emphasize the individual, anti-social nature of criminal behavior. The benefits of crime are automatic and obvious, such as getting money or getting one's way. Learning theorists tend to view criminal behavior as social behavior, committed to gain approval or to accomplish goals which are widely shared by all members of society. Learning theorists depict crime as a group phenomenon, and are especially interested in the role of gangs, criminal organizations, and deviant groups in the workplace in promoting criminal behavior.

Control theories and learning theories also differ in their depiction of criminal offenders. Control theories have been called "kinds of people" theories by Albert K. Cohen (1966) because they often characterize offenders as different from non-offenders. Some, but not all, control theorists see the differences as persistent and stable over the offender's lifetime. Thus many control theories suggest that persons are born with or develop traits very early in their lives that make them more likely than others to commit crimes for their entire lives. For example, some control theorists argue that criminals are less intelligent than noncriminals, and that this may be an important reason for their crimes.

Learning theorists see offenders and non-offenders as essentially similar to one another, differing only in the situations in which they find themselves. The offender's orientation to crime is learned, so it is not caused by inherited or early-developing traits. As this implies, the offender's tendency to crime can change dramatically over the lifespan, depending on the circumstances in which the offender is placed.

The next two sections of this chapter describe some major concepts in control and learning theories and summarize some of the leading examples of each sort of theory.

CONTROL THEORIES

Control theories begin by asking the question, why *don't* people commit crimes? "Deviance is taken for granted; conformity must be explained" (Hirschi, 1969:10). What prevents a person from committing a crime, when it may be in her interest (at least in the short term) to do so?

This way of thinking about crime has important implications. For one thing, it suggests that *no special motivation or process is necessary to account for criminal behavior*. Criminal behavior is often in the interests of the offender. Criminal acts are shortcuts to obvious goals.

A second feature of control theories is that, contrary to learning theories, *criminal behavior does not require learning special techniques, attitudes, or definitions of the situation* (Gottfredson and Hirschi, 1990:18):

> The skill required to complete the general run of crime is minimal. Consider crimes of personal violence, assault, rape, and homicide. The major requirement for successful completion of these crimes is the appearance of superior strength or the command of instruments of force. A gun, a club, or a knife is often sufficient. Property crimes may require physical strength or dexterity, but in most cases no more than is necessary for the ordinary activities of life.

In control theories, criminal behavior is not *specifically* learned, as is playing basketball or operating a computer. Instead, virtually anyone may engage in most kinds of criminal behavior, just as anyone can use the telephone, operate a doorknob or climb a ladder. Although some learning may be required, no special process of differential reinforcement or association is needed. As implied above, control theorists would especially emphasize that one need not learn specific motivations for criminal behavior: *everyone is motivated to commit crimes*.

Basic Concepts in Control Theories

Types of Controls

In control theories, *crime is due to a failure of controls*. A control is simply anything that prevents crimes from occurring. Although control theorists use different nomenclature to describe types of controls, most would recognize distinctions between *internal controls (self-control)* and *external controls (social control)* and between *formal and informal social controls*.

Internal controls, or self-control, are internalized in the individual through the socialization process. Gottfredson and Hirschi (1990) have described the characteristics of persons with high and low levels of self-control. Persons with strong internal controls feel a sense of guilt if they break the law or deviate from important norms. They also tend to defer gratification rather than demand it here and now, to be "cautious, cognitive and verbal," instead of "adventuresome, active, and physical" (Gottfredson and Hirschi, 1990:89). In contrast persons with low self-control are not interested in long-term careers, do not value either manual or academic skills, and are self-centered and indifferent to the suffering and needs of others, although they may be thought charming and generous. They will gladly buy you a beer, but they won't volunteer to drive you home if you drink too much.

External controls, as Nye (1958) has pointed out, may be direct or indirect. *Direct controls* involve consciously punishing misbehavior or rewarding desirable behavior. *Indirect control* occurs when one refrains from misbehaving to spare others pain and disappointment. As this suggests, a person who can be controlled by his or her concern for others should also have strong self-control.

External, or social controls, may also be divided into formal and informal controls. Formal controls are imposed through an organized and well-defined process. The most important formal controls on criminal behavior are those imposed by the criminal justice system, namely, criminal punishments. Informal controls are imposed by the family, friendship groups, churches, neighborhoods, and others (Akers, 1994:15).

Biological and Psychological Theories

Psychological theories of crime take two approaches. One approach is to treat crime as learned behavior, and seek to understand the processes by which it is learned. This approach is essentially the same as that adapted by learning theorists in social psychology and sociology, and it will be considered in the section on learning theories of crime.

The second approach is more compatible with control theory. In it, psychologists seek to identify *psychopathologies* which lead to criminal behavior. These psychopathologies may have a psychological, physiological or genetic basis (Pallone and Hennesey, 1996; Raine, 1993). Jeffery (1978) describes the human organism's makeup, including our brain structure, as a product of the interaction between the environment and genetic endowment. In turn, an organism interacts with the environment to produce behavior. From the point of view of control theory, psychopathologies serve to prevent or counteract the effective socialization of the individual.

Researchers have identified dozens of genetic, physiological, and psychological characteristics that may have some effect on criminal behavior. For the sake of brevity and clarity, we shall examine only one example in depth. Some studies suggest that *neurotransmitters*, such as dopamine, norepinephrine, and serotonin, are found at lower levels in the brains of chronic, serious offenders than in other persons. Neurotransmitters are chemicals stored in the brain which are essential for information processing and communication (Raine, 1993).

Lower levels of neurotransmitters may be associated with a reduced ability for the individual to inhibit behavior in response to punishment or frustration (Fowles, 1988). That is, such persons are less able to learn from their mistakes, and thus less able to control their impulses. Raine (1993) suggests that poor nutrition and alcohol abuse may play a role in producing low levels of *serotonin*, which is the neurotransmitter most strongly associated with antisocial behavior.

Evaluation of the Neurotransmitter Hypothesis

Research on neurotransmitters illustrates both the promise and limitations of attempts to find psychopathological sources of criminal behavior. The research is based on very small samples of special populations, such as incarcerated criminals. The levels of neurotransmitters in the brain are measured indirectly, by examining blood, urine, or cerebrospinal fluid levels. The research rarely considers the effects of such factors as diet, substance abuse, or environmental factors on neurotransmitter levels. This is an important limitation, because most research has focused on incarcerated offenders, whose neurotransmitter levels may be affected by their incarceration. Few studies examine noninstiutionalized, community samples or use unofficial measures of criminal behavior (Raine, 1993).

It is undoubtedly true that human behavior depends on the functioning of the brain and the total physiological state of the person. What is not clear is the extent to which variation in physiological states is associated with variations in criminal behavior. Although studies of brain chemistry (and other psycho-physiological factors) suggest that convicted offenders differ from the norm, they do not demonstrate that persons who have unusual neurotransmitter levels are more likely to commit crimes than persons who do not. Research underway in Chicago (Earls and Visher, 1996) in which the growth and development of 500 infants are being assessed, may eventually allow generalizations to be made about physiology and crime.

Self-Control Theory

Most criminologists explain individual behavior in terms of *social* psychology, which examines the impact on criminal behavior of social variables, such as child-rearing practices, education, and peer pressure. One of the foremost social-psychological control theories is self-control theory. Self-control theory is the work of Gottfredson and Hirschi (1990), who, as we have seen, have done a great deal to describe the characteristics of control theory in general.

Self-control theory proposes that, given the opportunity to do so, persons with low levels of self-control are more likely to commit crimes than persons with high levels of self-control. Self-control is equivalent to internal control, as described earlier in this chapter. Gottfredson and Hirschi attribute low self-control to ineffective child-rearing (1990:95):

> In order to teach the child self-control, someone must (1) monitor the child's behavior, (2) recognize deviant behavior when it occurs, and (3) punish such behavior . . . The person who cares for the child will watch his behavior, see him doing things he should not do, and correct him. The result will be a child more capable of delaying gratification, more sensitive to the interests and desires of others, more independent, more willing to accept restraints on his activity, and more unlikely to use force or violence to attain his ends.

High or low self-control is thus established in early childhood, and is a persistent characteristic throughout a person's life. Persons with low self-control will also be less susceptible to external controls, including those imposed by school, employers, and the criminal justice system.

Evaluation of Self-Control Theory

Although there have been few studies which directly assess self-control theory, the theory is in accord with many research findings. For example, the theory predicts that most crimes will not require any high degree of skill, that offenders will not specialize in a particular type of offense, and that offenders will also exhibit other behaviors indicative of low self-control, such as drug and alcohol abuse, low educational achievement, difficulty keeping a job, and difficulty in relationships with others.

On the other hand, self-control theory does not account for some of the most important aspects of crime. For one thing, the theory is specifically a theory of criminality, rather than crime. It focuses on differences in criminal behavior among individuals, but does not directly address the role of situational and environmental characteristics which might make criminal behavior more likely. Hirschi (1986) has suggested that rational choice theories of crime (described below) may compliment the self-control theory of criminality.

The most often-heard criticism of the theory is that it may attribute too much importance to low self-control (Tittle, 1995:57):

> If weak self-control explains all instances of force or fraud in pursuit of self-interest, then no "criminal" activity can be rationally organized and self-consciously planned for instrumental purposes. This flies in the face of logic, evidence, and experience.

Tittle also notes that the theory simply ignores or discounts any other individual, group or organizational factors which might affect the relationship between self-control, criminal opportunity, and criminal behavior. For example, cultural variations, race, gender, age, and type of offense make no difference in the casual process which produces crime (Tittle, 1995:59-60). The theory also discounts the effects of social controls and other factors that may affect self-control throughout the course of a person's life.

Social Control Theories

In contrast to self-control theories, the various social control theories place greater emphasis on external, or social controls. In his earlier work, Hirschi (1969) identified four factors that help to bond persons to conventional society: *attachment, commitment, involvement, and belief.* His description of these bonding factors is generally accepted by modern social control theorists.

Attachment refers to sensitivity to the opinion of others based on one's affection for them (Hirschi, 1969:18). The stronger a person's attachments to others, especially parents, the less likely the person is to do things that would disappoint them. Attachments to others are important both as a source of self-control and as a form of social control. Parents or other caretakers instill a feeling of conscience as well as monitoring and correcting behavior on an ongoing basis.

Commitment and involvement have to do with the time and effort invested in conventional lines of activities (Hirschi, 1969:20-22). Briefly, the more one invests in conventional activities, the more one has to lose by committing acts of delinquency or crime. Sampson and Laub (1993) have refined this idea by incorporating the concept of *social capital.* The idea is that our relationships with others gives a person both an investment in mutually beneficial activities and a resource he or she can use in moving through life. "Networking" is a deliberate attempt to build such mutually beneficial relationships.

Belief in the rightness of the laws and the values that the laws express is the fourth element of the bond to society. Control theorists argue that "there is *variation* in the extent to which people believe that they should obey the rules of society, and furthermore, . . . the less a person believe that he should obey the rules, the more likely he is to violate them" (Hirschi, 1969:26).

In self-control theory, social controls are important mainly for their effects on *opportunities* to commit crime. Because low self-control develops early in the life course and persists throughout it, it determines the extent to which a person is susceptible to external controls. A person with low self-control doesn't care very much about the negative consequences of getting caught.

Although social control theorists would not disagree with the assertion that early socialization experiences are important, they would also stress the role of social controls at later stages in life in changing levels of *criminality* (Sampson and Laub, 1993). As Laub (1996:248) states:

[S]alient life events and social ties in adulthood — especially *attachment to the labor force* and *cohesive marriage* (or cohabitation) — explain desistance from criminal behavior regardless of prior differences in criminal propensity. In other words, pathways to both crime and conformity are modified by key institutions of social control in the transition to adulthood (e.g., employment, military service, and marriage). For instance, late onset of criminal behavior can be accounted for by weak social bonds in adulthood, despite a background of nondelinquent behavior. Conversely, desistance from criminal behavior in adulthood can be explained by strong social bonds in adulthood, despite a background of criminal behavior.

Not all attempts at social control are successful. Control theorists usually find that informal controls are more effective than formal controls. In their research, Sampson and Laub (1993) find that incarceration for juvenile or adult offenses had a negative effect on later job stability, and low job stability is associated with criminal behavior.

Evaluation of Social Control Theories

Social control theories help to address some of the limitations of self-control theory described earlier. They emphasize the importance of both self-control and external controls, and can also account for dynamic processes in which the criminality of persons change over time. But social control theories are still theories of criminality. Rational choice and routine activities theories, which are described below, provide theories of crime which may compliment control theories of criminality.

Rational Choice Theories

Rational choice theories, like other control theories, assume that people are motivated to commit crimes. Unlike self-control theory, which attempts to explain variations in the willingness to resort to force and fraud (criminality), rational choice theories focus on environmental and situational features which make a criminal event more likely (crime).

Rational choice theories are the distant heirs of the *Classical School of Criminology*, which was in turn a product of the Enlightenment of the seventeenth and eighteenth centuries, a time of revolutionary changes in social and political systems which was accompanied by equally radical changes in the understanding of human behavior. Cesare Beccaria (1764) and Jeremy Bentham (1892), the two foremost classical theorists, were among the first to suggest that criminal behavior was based on the offender's attempt to balance the benefits of such behaviors against their costs. They argued that a criminal justice system which employed a system of swift, certain and severe punishment could deter individuals from committing crime.

Modern rational choice theorists (who are sometimes called neoclassical criminologists), maintain an interest in policies which might prevent crimes from occurring, and an image of the offender which Bentham and Beccaria would have no trouble recognizing. According to Cornish and Clarke (1986:1), rational choice theory begins with the assumption that:

> . . . offenders seek to benefit themselves by their criminal behavior; that this involves the making of decisions and of choices, however rudimentary on occasion these processes might be; and that these processes exhibit a measure of rationality, albeit constrained by limits of time and ability and the availability of relevant information.

With this assumption, rational choice theorists go on to focus on the decision to commit a crime, as opposed to choosing legal behaviors which might accomplish the same goal. Because the context in which crimes occur may differ a great deal depending on the type of offense, a *crime-specific* approach is often used (Cornish and Clarke, 1986:2). Thus a rational choice theorist might build an elaborate model to help predict the likelihood of burglary, shoplifting, robbery, or even murder.

Cornish and Clarke (1986) illustrate rational choice theories with their models of the decision to commit a burglary. The decision to commit a burglary is depicted as a function of "background factors," such as psychological and socio-economic characteristics; background factors in turn influence the needs of the offender and his learning experiences relevant to the ways in which solutions to a need for money are evaluated, reactions to chance events and readiness to commit a burglary. Once someone decides to commit a burglary, they select targets on the basis of accessibility, detectability, and presence or absence of police, security guards, or neighborhood watchers. Success in committing a burglary is in itself reinforcing, and may lead to further offenses.

Evaluation of Rational Choice Theories

The rational choice modeling process provides a valuable way of developing and integrating knowledge about the situational factors which serve to encourage or discourage criminal behavior. For this reason, rational choice provides a basis for *situational crime prevention*, which refers to attempts to reduce specific forms of criminal behavior at specific sites by modifying the environment and the behaviors of persons who use the site frequently. For example, theft of autos from a parking lot may be discouraged by carefully planned lighting, limiting the hours of use, or removing barriers which limit visual surveillance from the street or nearby buildings (Clarke, 1992).

Despite its practical applications, the theory does not make adequate provision for variation in the rationality of offenders or of offenses. The extent to which offenders consider costs and benefits before they act varies widely. Similarly, some forms of offending, like theft, are more rational than other forms, like vandalism (Tittle, 1995).

The Routine Activities Approach

The routine activities approach is an attempt to explain the distribution of opportunities to commit crime. Cohen and Felson (1979) state that three things must converge in time and space for a crime to occur: *a motivated offender, a suitable target (either a person or a piece of property), and an*

absence of capable guardians. Felson (1993) adds that an offender may be controlled by a *"handler"* — a person who knows how to exercise social control over the offender. Adults, particularly parents and teachers, are handlers who can sometimes control the actions of children or youths. Targets may be guarded by people, such as security officers, housewives, or friends, or by mechanical systems, such a burglar alarms or a good deadbolt lock.

Unlike the control theories described previously, Cohen and Felson's theory emphasizes the structure and amount of criminal opportunities (Felson, 1993):

> Crime can increase even when social bonds persist, parents care deeply, and offender motivation stands pat . . . What varies is the pattern of daily life and the structure of households, work, school, and transport, as these make it more or less possible for conventional parents to carry out their inclinations and keep their kids out of trouble . . . When people choose to drive a car, to let their children drive the family car or have their own, to live several miles away from work and relatives, to have smaller families, to divorce and remarry, to sent their children away to college, to purchase lightweight durable goods, to enjoy alcoholic beverages, or to go out at night, these choices set the stage for criminal events.

The choices made by offenders, consumers, potential victims and handlers produce interactions in time and space which make criminal events more or less likely (Felson, 1993):

> People and things stay put and move over space and time and are tied into relationships while doing so. Things belong to people who belong to each other, but these ties are not always reinforced by proximity. When those so tied move together, guardianship and handling are simple. When they diverge, guardianship and handling are impaired. One might envision daily life as an ebb and flow of routine activities, setting the stage for informal social control to succeed much of the time, but not always.

Cohen and Felson (1979) argue that *much of the increase in crime since World War II may not be due to a drastic increase in motivated offenders, but to increasing opportunities for crime.* For example, auto thefts have increased with the growing number of automobiles available to steal, and burglaries have increased as the number of detached, one-family houses has increased. As this implies, prosperity and technological innovations may be criminogenic (crime-causing), in that they affect the distribution and number of criminal opportunities. Thus the rapid increases in crime experienced by the United States since the 1960s may be due to the success of the American economy rather than the failure of American "moral fiber."

Evaluation of the Routine Activities Approach

The routine activities approach has produced extremely valuable insights into the structure of criminal opportunities. The approach compliments both self-control theory and rational choice theories of criminality and crime (Felson, 1993; 1994). The most important problem with the theory is its inability to specify *which* routine activities produce increases or decreases in crime rates. Felson (1993:127) notes that "Any set of decisions that assembles a handled offender and a suitable target, in the absence of a capable guardian and intimate handler, will tend to be criminogenic." This formulation is too vague to allow one to identify particular sets of decisions that might be hypothesized to produce crime. Identification is based on trial and error, rather than on deduction from general propositions (Tittle, 1995:14).

Recent work by Osgood, Wilson, O'Malley, Bachman and Johnston (1996) addresses this problem and applies routine activities concepts to the explanation of individual delinquent behavior. Osgood and his associates suggest time spent socializing with peers in unstructured, unsupervised activities ("hanging out") present greater opportunities for deviant behavior than other situations. Their research supports this hypothesis, and also indicates that the decline in criminal behavior as persons age may be due to the declining amount of time spent on unstructured socializing.

Social Disorganization Theory

Social disorganization theory attempts to describe the ways in which the features of the social structure may affect the motivation to commit crimes (criminality). Two sociologists at the University of Chicago, Clifford Shaw and Henry McKay, developed the theory during the 1930s and 1940s and continued to refine it in subsequent decades (Shaw and McKay, 1942, 1969). The theory has been refined by Kornhauser (1978) and Sampson and Groves (1989).

Social disorganization theory attempts to explain variation in the capacity of neighborhoods within a city to control the conduct of their inhabitants. Areas within a city can be thought of as having differing levels of ability to control conduct. Hillary Rodham Clinton has popularized the ancient African proverb, "It takes a village to raise a child." The proverb captures the idea of social organization: an organized community is one in which people work together to assure that shared values, such as safety and peace, are achieved.

According to the theory as expounded by Sampson and Groves (1989), communities must be able to control *teenage peer groups* which have the potential to become gangs. This is related to the existence of *local friendship networks* which allow members of the community to recognize one another as well as strangers, and to control deviant behavior by the pressure of each other's opinions ("what would the neighbors think?"). A third component of social organization is the rate of *participation in local formal and voluntary organizations*, such as the Parent-Teachers Association, churches, and service clubs. Such participation reinforces and extends friendship networks and provides the community with the ability to defend its local interests in the political and economic arenas.

The degree of social organization in communities is affected by *economic level, mobility, and heterogeneity* (Kornhauser, 1978). Communities with a high percentage of poor persons, a high percentage of newcomers, and a mix of persons from different ethnic backgrounds will have a harder time developing the informal and organizational bases of control described above. Sampson (1987) has also specified the related problem of family disruption — divorce, single-parent families, and families consisting of unmarried women and their children — as an additional problem which may impede social organization. Implicit in this is the idea that urbanization is also an important variable — neighborhoods in large cities may have more problems of disorganization than neighborhoods in smaller localities (Sampson and Groves, 1989).

Evaluation of Social Disorganization Theory

Social disorganization theory provides a plausible connection between social structure and criminal behavior, especially if we link it to individual-level theories of social control. Because the theory requires data at several levels — individual, organizational, neighborhood, and city — it is hard to test, and only a few studies have been able to assess.

The chief rival explanation of the relationships between crime and poverty, racial and ethnic composition, mobility, family disruption and urbanization is that such correlations reflect the individual characteristics of members of the neighborhood population. For example, self-control theories might argue that "poor neighborhoods" are really neighborhoods of persons with low self-control, who would be expected to have difficulty in keeping jobs, maintaining families, raising children, and refraining from criminal behavior (Gottfredson and Hirschi, 1990; see McKean, 1996). Further research is needed to assess the relative importance of social structure and individual characteristics in producing disorganized neighborhoods.

LEARNING THEORIES

Learning theories attribute crime to effective, rather than ineffective socialization. Unlike control theories, which depict criminal behavior as natural and spontaneous, learning theories assume that, "in addition to weak bonding and the absence of restraints, some positive motivation is necessary for sustained involvement in delinquent behavior" (Elliott, Ageton, and Cantor, 1979:15). As this statement implies, learning theorists see control theories as partial and incomplete explanations of criminal behavior. They recognize the salience of restraints on behavior, but do not regard the motivation to commit crimes as a given.

To learning theorists, "conformity and crime are two sides of the same coin" (Akers, 1994: 111). That is, *criminal behavior and conforming behavior have the same causes*, and learning theories thus explain both criminal and noncriminal behavior (Sutherland, et al., 1992:90).

Because learning theories are very general, their proponents claim that more specific theories of criminal behavior, including control theories, can be subsumed under learning theories (Akers, 1994; Pearson and Weiner, 1985). This claim will be examined further after we look at the basic components of learning theories.

Differential Reinforcement (Social Learning Theory)

Learning theory, in various manifestations, is important in psychology, social psychology, and sociology. In criminology, learning theorists, especially Ronald Akers (1994) developed learning theory as a reformulation of Edwin Sutherland's theory of *differential association*. Sutherland's theory is based on nine propositions (Sutherland, 1947:6-7):

1. Criminal behavior is learned.
2. Criminal behavior is learned in interaction with other persons in a process of communication.
3. The principal part of the learning of criminal behavior occurs within intimate personal groups.
4. When criminal behavior is learned, the learning includes (a) techniques of committing

the crime, which are sometimes very complicated, sometimes very simple and (b) the specific direction of motives, drives, rationalizations, and attitudes.

5. The specific direction of motives and drives is learned from the definition of the legal codes as favorable or unfavorable.

6. A person becomes delinquent because of an excess of definitions favorable to violation of the law over definitions unfavorable to the violation of the law. [Sutherland refers to this proposition as "the principle of differential association."]

7. Differential associations may vary in frequency, duration, priority, and intensity.

8. The process of learning criminal behavior by association with criminal and anti-criminal patterns involves all of the mechanisms that are involved in any other learning.

9. Although criminal behavior is an expression of general needs and values, it is not explained by those general needs and values, because noncriminal behavior is an expression of the same needs and values.

In studying Sutherland's propositions, note the contrast between his theory and control theories. Where control theories discount the need for offenders to learn specific techniques or motives or attitudes, differential association theory is based on this idea. Where control theories depict criminal behavior as a natural and universal tendency which must be inhibited, differential association theory denies that criminal behavior can be explained by "general needs and values."

In the years since Sutherland first stated his theory, several persons have tried to revise it to make it more specific and compatible with modern psychological learning theories. The most successful effort was that of Akers, originally in collaboration with Burgess (Burgess and Akers, 1966). Burgess and Akers identify the "learning mechanisms" referred to by Sutherland as those found in modern behavioral theory (Akers, 1994).

Behavioral theory begins with the assumption that most behavior is *"operant,"* that is, conditioned and shaped by the rewards and punishments it produces. Behavior that is rewarded (*reinforced*) tends to be repeated; behavior that is punished tends to be decreased or extinguished. Rewards included *social* reinforcers, such as approval from others or the achievement of symbolic goals such as religious salvation or a "bad rep." *Punishment* includes both attaching painful social and physical consequences to behavior or removing rewards or desirable consequences, as when a child loses his freedom (is "grounded") for breaking his parents' rules. The process of learning (inducing or extinguishing behaviors) is thus a process of *operant conditioning*.

Akers also incorporates Sutherland's concept of *definitions* into his theory (Akers, 1994:97):

Definitions are one's own attitudes or meaning that one attaches to given behavior. That is, they are orientations, rationalizations, definitions of the situation, and other evaluations and moral attitudes that define the commission of an act as right or wrong, good or bad, desirable or undesirable.

Persons with attitudes which are approving toward criminal behavior are more likely to engage in it. Approving attitudes may be *positive* — defining the behavior as permissible or desirable, or *neutralizing* — justifying, excusing, or rationalizing the behavior (Akers, 1994:97). The process by which one is exposed to and learns (through operant conditioning) definitions which favor criminal behavior is still called differential association (Akers, 1994:96):

The groups with which one is in differential association provide the major social contexts in which all the mechanisms of social learning operate. They not only expose one to definitions, they also present them with models to imitate and with differential reinforcement . . . for criminal or conforming behavior.

Family members and friends are the most important groups in this process, although a person is also influenced by neighbors, churches, school teachers, authority figures, and mass media celebrities.

Another useful idea in social learning theory is that of *learning history*. After a person commits a

66

delinquent act, the likelihood that the act will be repeated is affected by the extent to which it is reinforced or punished. Reinforcement and punishment also affect one's definitions, which in turn further affect the likelihood that one will repeat the act (Akers, 1994:99-100).

Typically, differential association precedes deviant behavior. The acquisition of definitions favorable to crime may begin with the family, that is, one may learn directly from one's parents to commit crimes, as may be the case when persons abused as children later abuse their own children. Criminal behavior is also learned in *peer groups*, especially in adolescence, when children are under less parental control. A child may be attracted to a group due to circumstances having little to do with delinquency, such as proximity or friendship with a member of the group. Such associations then lead to learning definitions favorable to law violation, deviant behavior, and the differential reinforcement of the behavior. The extent to which the behavior is reinforced or punished affects the continuation of old associations and the seeking of new associations (Akers, 1994:100). Aker's theory thus specifies the most common process by which a person becomes a delinquent as follows:

Differential Association $\longrightarrow$
Definitions $\longrightarrow$ Criminal Behavior $\longrightarrow$
$\longrightarrow$ Differential Reinforcement

Evaluation of Social Learning Theory

The theory of differential association and reinforcement, like self-control theory, is a general theory of behavior. Potentially, it is applicable to any action which arises from social sources and has punitive or reinforcing consequences. The process of operant conditioning which is at the heart of the theory has been demonstrated to be a fundamental method of learning by extensive psychological and educational research (Akers, 1994). Because operant conditioning is undoubtedly an important and universal learning process, learning theorists have made the claim that the features of society which may encourage criminal behavior, such as differences in norms and social control systems, operate through operant conditioning (Akers, 1994; Pearson and Weiner, 1985).

The great strength of social learning theories is their ability to account for the *group nature of delinquency*. Much criminological research literature suggests that most delinquent behavior occurs in a group context. That is, youths whose peers are delinquent are more likely to be delinquent, and delinquent acts themselves are often committed by youths as a part of a group activity, such as fights between gangs or parties involving binge drinking or drug use. Of course, the gang is the delinquent group that is of greatest interest to learning theorists, who regard it as an important agent for promoting definitions favorable to criminal behavior. As Akers says (1994:104):

It is in peer groups that the first availability and opportunity for delinquent acts are typically provided. Virtually every study that includes a peer association variable finds it to be significantly and usually most strongly related to delinquency, alcohol and drug use and abuse, adult crime, and other forms of deviant behavior.

As noted before, this position contrasts with that of control theory. In control theories, criminality leads persons to associate with others like them who also have a propensity to crime (*"birds of a feather flock together"*); in learning theories, it is the "flocking" — differential association — which causes the "feathering" — criminality (see Gottfredson and Hirschi, 1990; Akers, 1994). Social learning theory does not predict that differences appearing in early childhood will be as important as differential associations later in life.

Although learning theory identifies an important way in which criminal behavior can be learned, it does not completely account for crime. As Tittle (1995:3) points out, the theory does not address differences among individuals in their ability to learn, or differences in the degree of differential association required to learn, for example, definitions favorable to murder as opposed to alcohol use. Control theorists may note that the theory places too much emphasis on the group nature of criminal behavior, which is often *anti-social* in nature.

Another limitation of social learning theory is that it does not address the origin of definitions favorable to law violation. As Akers says (1985: 43):

> The theory does not say how or why the culture, structure, and social patterning of society sets up and implements certain sets and schedules of reactions to given behavior and characteristics.

Akers and other learning theorists do claim that theories which do attempt to link crime and social and cultural features of societies can be recast in terms compatible with learning theory (Akers, 1994; Pearson and Weiner, 1985).

Developmental Theories

Both control and social learning theories are general theories of crime. That is, they both attempt to explain all sorts of criminal and deviant behavior according to a limited set of processes. In contrast, developmental theories offer a more complex approach to explaining crime. Current versions of developmental theory are especially compatible with the social learning approach, but also use aspects of control theory.

Developmental theories are compatible with the notion of *criminal careers*. The term, "career," simply refers to the pattern of offending over the lifetime of the offender. Blumstein and his associates (Blumstein, Cohen, Roth, and Visher, 1986), the leading advocates of this perspective, suggest that there are important differences in the stages of offending, which they identify as onset, duration, and desistance from a career of offending. Thus the reasons why persons begin offending (onset), persist in offending (duration), and stop offending (desistance) may differ from each other and may differ for different types of offenders.

Building on this foundation, developmental theorists such as Moffitt (1993) and Patterson and Yoerger (1993) suggest that two major types of offenders can be identified. One group begins to exhibit antisocial behavior early in life and continues to do so throughout life. Patterson calls these

offenders *"early starters"* and Moffitt calls them "life-course-persistent" offenders. A second, larger group begins offending in adolescence and desists in the early years of adulthood. Patterson calls this group the *"late starters,"* and Moffitt calls them "adolescence-limited" offenders.

The early starting, persistent offenders are similar to the persons with low self-control described by Gottfredson and Hirschi (1990). Moffitt and Patterson both attribute early starting to poor socialization, which may be aggravated by neuropsychological difficulties. Ineffective socialization in early childhood produces a propensity toward criminal offending which is stable over the course of the offender's life.

In contrast, adolescence-limited, late starting offenders are similar to the learning theory image of the offender. According to Moffitt (1993), these offenders are well-socialized in childhood, but in early adolescence, they rebel against the constraints imposed on them by adults. This rebellion takes the form of associating with delinquent peers (the life-course-persistent offenders), which leads to learning and receiving reinforcement for delinquent behavior. Patterson and Yoerger (1993) give a similar account, but stress the importance of peers for both early and late starters.

Evaluation of Developmental Theories

Developmental theories have a great deal of appeal because they combine control and social learning explanations in a way that does not seem to require that one or the other be abandoned. The theories also provide an explanation for an important research finding: the vast majority of offenders do not persist in criminal behavior after early adulthood.

Explanations for this finding can also be constructed from other theories, especially Sampson and Laub's (1993) social control theory of the pathways and turning points in crime (Paternoster and Brame, 1997). But developmental theories, if they are empirically supported, hold the potential for allowing one to identify the two major groups of offenders and respond in differing ways to their behavior. For example, long-term incarceration would not be a cost-effective way of dealing with adolescence-limited offenders, although it might be appropriate for life-course-persistent offenders.

So far, attempts to test these theories have met with mixed results (Bartusch, Lynam, Moffitt, and Silva, 1997; Paternoster and Brame, 1997). One problem is correctly identifying the age at which persons first offend. Official records are not suited to this task, and self-reports of offending may differ systematically depending on the type of offender (that is, one type of offender may be more likely to lie about their criminal behavior than the other).

SOCIAL STRUCTURE AND CRIME

With the exception of social disorganization theory, the theories that we have examined so far deal with criminal behavior at the individual or situational level. There are other important theories which examine the ways in which the structure of society influences rates of criminal behavior.

Strain Theories

One of the major ways in which sociologists have tried to account for variations in crime rates is by examining the ways in which persons are encouraged to commit crimes by social forces. Strain theories attribute high crime rates to *criminogenic* (crime-causing) influences in society.

Currently, the leading version of strain theory is Messner and Rosenfeld's (1997) *institutional anomie theory*, which is based on an earlier theory of anomie proposed by Robert Merton (1938). "*Anomie*," refers to a state in which the norms of society lose their salience, and thus do not act to prevent persons from committing crime (Messner and Rosenfeld, 1997:44).

In a nutshell, *institutional anomie theory suggests that crime is caused by the "American Dream" of economic success*. American culture places a great deal of emphasis on the individual achievement of material wealth, and holds out this goal as desirable for every member of society. The emphasis on these goals has become so exaggerated in American society that they have weakened the *social institutions* which regulate conduct. For example, families and "family values" are considered less important than work — the person who works overtime is valued more than the person who requests family leave. Schools and colleges are shaped to meet the demands of the labor market rather than the goals of a liberal arts education. Social institutions such as schools become more "economic" in their operation, using grading methods and assembly-line production methods to turn out a standard product: the educated student.

Both the emphasis on material wealth and the weakening of major social institutions may contribute to crime (Messner and Rosenfeld, 1997):

> At the cultural level, the dominant ethos of the American Dream stimulates criminal motivations while at the same time promoting a weak normative environment (anomie). At the institutional level, the dominance of the economy in the institutional balance of power fosters weak social control.

Evaluation of Institutional Anomie Theory

Messner and Rosenfeld's theory is the latest in a long line of attempts to link inequities in the social and economic structure of society to criminal behavior. Similar ideas of crime causation are also presented by conflict theorists and radical theorists (Bohm, 1997). These theories help provide a context for individual level processes of social control and social learning.

As if often the case with social structural theories, Messner and Rosenfeld's contribution seems to be limited to accounting for crime in one society: that of the United States in the late twentieth century. What is needed are truly comparative theories of social structure and crime which relate differences in the features of society to differences in crime rates. That is an important part of the subject matter of comparative criminology and criminal justice.

CONCLUSION

This review of criminological theories is limited, by necessity, to only a few of the dozens of alternative formulations which are available. I have neglected any number of worthy and valuable theories in favor of describing a few examples in more detail.

I hope that this strategy has helped you to understand some major approaches to explaining crime, as well as the give and take of refining and testing the theories. Criminology is in an exciting period, characterized by its methodological sophistication, the increasing precision and specificity of theories, and, of course, a great deal of interest in applying successful theories to the prevention and control of crime.

Although the theories described in this chapter differ considerably in their specific policy implications, I am sure that most of the theorists would agree on one point: Americans need to take better care of their children if they wish to see a long-term reduction in crime. As we have seen, criminologists may differ about the specific aspects of socialization which produce crime, but it is socialization — the way in which children are taught the values and norms of society — which is the key to criminality.

✳ ✳ ✳ ✳ ✳

REFERENCES

Abadinsky, Howard
    1993   *Drug Abuse: An Introduction.* Second Edition. Chicago, IL: Nelson-Hall.
Adler, Freda, Gerhard O.W. Mueller, and William S. Laufer
    1995   *Criminology.* Second Edition. New York, NY: McGraw-Hill.
Akers, Ronald L.
    1985   *Deviant Behavior: A Social Learning Approach.* Third Edition. Belmont, CA: Wadsworth.
    1994   *Criminological Theories: Introduction and Evaluation.* Los Angeles, CA: Roxbury.
Babbie, Earl
    1996   *The Practice of Social Research.* Seventh Edition. Belmont, CA: Wadsworth.
Barlow, Hugh D.
    1978   *Introduction to Criminology.* Second Edition. Boston, MA: Little, Brown.
Bartusch, Dawn R. Jeglum, Donald R. Lynam, Terrie E. Moffitt, and Phil A. Silva
    1997   "Is age important? Testing a general versus a developmental theory of antisocial behavior." *Criminology,* 35: 13-48.

Beccaria, Cesare
    1764   *On Crimes and Punishments.* 1963 English Edition, H. Paolucci, Translator. Indianapolis, IN: Bobbs-Merrill.
Becker, Howard S.
    1963   *Outsiders: Studies in the Sociology of Deviance.* New York, NY: The Free Press.
Bentham, Jeremy
    1892   *An Introduction to the Principles of Morals and Legislation.* 1948 Edition. New York, NY: Hafner.
Blumstein, Alfred, and Jacqueline Cohen
    1980   "Sentencing convicted offenders: An analysis of the public's view." *Law and Society Review,* 14: 223-261.
Blumstein, Alfred, Jacqueline Cohen, Jeffery A. Roth, and Christy A. Visher (eds.)
    1986   *Criminal Careers and "Career Criminals."* Volume I. Washington, DC: National Academy Press.
Blumstein, Alfred, David P. Farrington, and S. Moitra
    1985   "Delinquency careers: innocents, desisters, and persisters." Pp. 137-168 in M. Tonry and N. Morris (eds.), *Crime and Justice,* Volume Six. Chicago: University of Chicago Press.
Bohm, Robert M.
    1997   *A Primer on Crime and Delinquency.* Belmont, CA: Wadsworth.
Bridges, George S., and Martha A. Myers (eds.)
    1994   *Inequality, Crime and Social Control.* Boulder, CO: Westview.
Burgess, Robert L., and Ronald L. Akers
    1966   "A differential association-reinforcement theory of criminal behavior." *Social Problems,* 14: 128-147.
Clarke, Ronald V. (ed.)
    1992   *Situational Crime Prevention: Successful Case Studies.* New York: Harrow and Heston.
Cohen, Albert K.
    1966   *Deviance and Control.* Englewood Cliffs, NJ: Prentice-Hall.
Cohen, Lawrence E., and Marcus Felson
    1979   "Social change and crime rate trends: A routine activity approach." *American Sociological Review,* 44: 588-608.
Cornish, Derek B., and Ronald V. Clarke (eds.)
    1986   *The Reasoning Criminal: Rational Choice Perspectives on Offending.* New York, NY: Springer-Verlag.
Curran, Daniel J., and Claire M. Renzetti
    1994   *Theories of Crime.* Boston, MA: Allyn and Bacon.
Datesman, Susan K., and Mikel Aickin
    1984   "Offense specialization and escalation among status offenders." *Journal of Criminal Law and Criminology,* 75: 1246-1275.
Earls, Felton J., and Christy A. Visher
    1996   *Project on Human Development in Chicago Neighborhoods: A Research Update.* Washington, DC: National Institute of Justice, U.S. Department of Justice.
Elliott, Delbert S., Suzanne S. Ageton, and Rachelle J. Canter
    1979   "An integrated theoretical perspective on delinquent behavior." *Journal of Research in Crime and Delinquency,* 16: 3-27.

71

Felson, Marcus

    1986   "Linking criminal choices, routine activities, informal control, and criminal outcomes." Pages 119-128 in D.B. Cornish and R.V. Clarke (eds), *The Reasoning Criminal: Rational Choice Perspectives on Offending.* New York, NY: Springer-Verlag.

    1994   Crime and Everyday Life: Insights and Implications for Society. Thousand Oaks, CA: Sage.

Fowles, D. C.

    1988   "Psychophysiology and psychopathology: A motivational approach." *Psychophysiology*, 25: 373-391 [cited in Raine, 1993].

Gibbs, Jack P.

    1966   "Conceptions of deviant behavior: The old and the new." *Pacific Sociological Review*, 9: 9-14.

Gottfredson, Michael, and Travis Hirschi

    1990   *A General Theory of Crime.* Palo Alto, CA: Stanford University Press.

Hagan, John

    1989   *Structural Criminology.* New Brunswick, NJ: Rutgers University Press.

Hagan, John, and Ruth D. Peterson

    1995   *Crime and Inequality.* Stanford, CA: Stanford University Press.

Hirschi, Travis

    1969   *Causes of Delinquency.* Berkeley, CA: University of California Press.

    1986   "On the compatibility of rational choice and social control theories of crime." Pages 105-118 in D.B. Cornish and R.V. Clarke (eds.), *The Reasoning Criminal: Rational Choice Perspectives on Offending.* New York, NY: Springer-Verlag.

Jeffery, C. Ray

    1978   "Criminology as an interdisciplinary social science." *Criminology*, 16: 161-162.

Karmen, Andrew

    1996   *Crime Victims: An Introduction to Victimology.* Third Edition. Belmont, CA: Wadsworth.

Kelly, Delos H. (ed.)

    1993   *Deviant Behavior: A Text-Reader in the Sociology of Deviance.* Fourth Edition. New York, NY: St. Martin's.

Kornhauser, Ruth Rosner

    1978   *Social Sources of Delinquency: An Appraisal of Analytic Models.* Chicago, IL: University of Chicago Press.

Lab, Steven P.

    1984   "Patterns in juvenile misbehavior." *Crime and Delinquency*, 30: 293-308.

Laub, John H.

    1996   "Crime in the making: Pathways and turning points through life." Pages 240-256 in P. Cordella and L. Siegel (eds.), *Readings in Contemporary Criminological Theory.* Boston, MA: Northeastern University Press.

Maxfield, Michael G., and Earl Babbie

    1995   *Research Methods for Criminal Justice and Criminology.* Belmont, CA: Wadsworth.

McKean, Jerome B.

    1996   "Self-control and social control: Applying general theory to variations in crime rates among geopolitical units." Paper presented at the annual meeting of the American Society of Criminology. Chicago, IL: 1996.

Merton, Robert K.

    1938   "Social structure and anomie." *American Sociological Review,* 3: 672-682.

Messner, Steven F., and Richard Rosenfeld
    1997   *Crime and the American Dream.* Second Edition. Belmont, CA: Wadsworth.

Miller, Stuart J., Simon Dinitz, and John P. Conrad
    1982   *Careers of the Violent: The Dangerous Offender and Criminal Justice.* Lexington, MA: D.C. Heath.

Moffitt, Terrie E.
    1993   "Adolescence-limited and life-course-persistent antisocial behavior: A developmental taxonomy." *Psychological Review*, 100: 674-701.

Nye, F. Ivan
    1958   *Family Relationships and Delinquent Behavior.* New York, NY: Wiley.

Osgood, D. Wayne, Janet K. Wilson, Patrick M. O'Malley, Jerald G. Bachman, and Lloyd D. Johnston
    1996   "Routine activities and individual deviant behavior." *American Sociological Review*, 61: 635-655.

Pallone, Nathaniel J., and James J. Hennessey
    1996   *Tinder-box Criminal Aggression.* New Brunswick, NJ: Transaction.

Paternoster, Raymond, and Robert Brame
    1997   "Multiple routes to delinquency? A test of developmental and general theories of crime." *Criminology*, 35: 49-84.

Patterson, Gerald R., and Karen Yoerger
    1993   "Developmental models for delinquent behavior." In S. Hodgins (ed.), *Mental Disorders and Crime.* Newbury Park, CA: Sage.

Pearson, Frank S., and Neil Alan Weiner
    1985   "Toward an integration of criminological theories." *Journal of Criminal Law and Criminology*, 76: 116-150.

Petersilia, Joan, Peter Greenwood, and Marvin Lavin
    1978   *Criminal Careers of Habitual Felons.* Santa Monica, CA: Rand Corporation.

Raine, Adrian
    1993   *The Psychopathology of Crime.* San Diego, CA: Academic Press.

Reiman, Jeffery
    1990   *The Rich Get Richer and the Poor Get Prison.* Third Edition. New York, NY: Wiley.

Reynolds, Paul D.
    1971   *A Primer on Theory Construction.* Indianapolis, IN: Bobbs-Merrill.

Roncek, Dennis
    1981   "Dangerous places: Crime and residential environment." *Social Forces*, 60: 74-96.

Sampson, Robert J.
    1987   "Urban black violence: The effect of male joblessness and family disruption." *American Journal of Sociology*, 93: 348-382.

Sampson, Robert J., and W. Byron Groves
    1989   "Community structure and crime: Testing social disorganization theory." *American Journal of Sociology*, 94: 774-802.

Sampson, Robert J., and John H. Laub
    1993   *Crime in the Making: Pathways and Turning Points Through Life.* Cambridge, MA: Harvard University Press.

Sampson, Robert J., and Janet L. Lauritsen
    1994   "Violent victimization and offending: Individual-, situational-, and community-level risk factors." Pages 1-114 in A.J. Reiss, Jr. and J.A. Roth (eds.), *Understanding and Preventing Violence, Volume 3: Social Influences.* Washington, DC: National Academy Press.

Sellin, Thorsten
    1938   *Culture Conflict and Crime.* New York, NY: Social Science Research Council.

Shannon, Lyle
    1988   *Criminal Career Continuity: Its Social Context.* New York, NY: Human Sciences Press.

Shaw, Clifford R., and Henry D. McKay
    1942   *Juvenile Delinquency and Urban Areas.* Chicago, IL: University of Chicago Press.
    1969   *Juvenile Delinquency and Urban Areas.* Revised Edition. Chicago, IL: University of Chicago Press.

Shelden, Randall G., John A. Horvath, and Sharon Tracy
    1989   "Do status offenders get worse? Some clarifications on the question of escalation." *Crime and Delinquency*, 35: 202-216.

Shover, Neal
    1985   *Aging Criminals.* Beverly Hills, CA: Sage.

Steffensmeier, Darrell
    1989   "On the causes of white-collar crime: An assessment of Hirschi and Gottfredson's claims." *Criminology*, 27: 345-358.

Sutherland, Edwin H.
    1947   *Principles of Criminology.* Fourth Edition. Philadelphia, PA: J.B. Lippincott.
    1937   *The Professional Thief.* Chicago, IL: University of Chicago Press.

Sutherland, Edwin H., Donald R. Cressey, and David F. Luckenbill
    1992   *Principles of Criminology.* Eleventh Edition. Dix Hills, NY: General Hall.

Tillman, Robert
    1987   "The size of the 'criminal population': The prevalence and incidence of adult arrest." *Criminology*, 25: 561-579.

Tittle, Charles R.
    1995   *Control Balance: Toward a General Theory of Deviance.* Boulder, CO: Westview.

Tracey, Paul E., Marvin Wolfgang, and Robert Figlio
    1990   *Delinquency in Two Birth Cohorts.* New York, NY: Plenum.

Vila, Bryan
    1994   "A general paradigm for understanding criminal behavior: extending evolutionary ecological theory." *Criminology*, 32: 311-359.

Warr, Mark
    1995   "Public perceptions of crime and punishment." Pages 15-32 in J.F. Sheley (ed.), *Criminology: A Contemporary Handbook.* Second Edition. Belmont, CA: Wadsworth.

Wolfgang, Marvin E., Robert M. Figlio, and Thorsten Sellin
    1972   *Delinquency in a Birth Cohort.* Chicago: University of Chicago Press.

Wolfgang, Marvin E., Robert M. Figlio, Paul E. Tracy, and Simon I. Singer
    1985   *The National Survey of Crime Severity.* Washington, DC: Bureau of Justice Statistics, U.S. Department of Justice.

Research Methods in Criminal Justice

By

Andra J. Katz and **Donald Blazicek**

This chapter is designed to acquaint students with relevant issues in research as they pertain to the field of criminal justice. Conducting research on the causes of crime and criminal justice has led to a number of controversial findings as well as support for some of those deemed intuitive in nature. The fact that the criminal justice system as a whole impacts every member of society whether directly or indirectly makes such research not only necessary, but welcome. Theories, popular opinion, and common sense beliefs have all been challenged regularly by findings from vigorous and insightful research conducted on a number of related issues. As has been illustrated with example after example, reliance solely on intuition and what is identified as being common sense is simply not adequate. Rather, both are quite vulnerable to personal biases and perceptions which, in turn, interfere with objectivity. Utilizing scientific investigation and inquiry helps to eliminate such biases and allows for a much more objective exploration of a particular topic. The scientific approach enables researchers of the hard sciences and behavioral sciences alike to proceed by way of an "objective, logical and systematic method of analysis of phenomena, devised to permit the accumulation of reliable knowledge" (Lastrucci, 1963:6).

Proceeding in a systematic fashion is standard regardless of the discipline. The traditional model of science incorporates the following basic operations: problem formation, operationalization, data collection, and data analysis. Decisions must be made regarding the problem or topic about which the research is going to be conducted. Merely identifying the problem is not enough. The individual conducting the research must define the problem or topic in a manageable form so as to make it satisfactory for purposes of research. Data collection is the next step in the process. It involves decisions relating to the observing, measuring, and recording of information. Data analysis, the final operation, involves the process of organizing and arranging the data to note its significance, to summarize its meaning, and to generalize about it.

The goal of research in criminal justice and criminology is to build and develop a body of knowledge about crime, criminals, and criminal justice systems and processes. This goal can be realized through the systematic collection of data which is integrated with theory. Furthermore, it is only through the application and employment of scientific procedures that we can objectively learn about these phenomena.

THE CLASSIFICATION OF CRIMINAL JUSTICE RESEARCH

Research in criminal justice may be characterized in numerous ways including: (a) the role of the research, (b) classification by the goal of the research — pure and applied, (c) classification by the purpose of the research — exploratory, descriptive, or explanatory, and (d) classification by the method of data collection or research design — observational, survey, or experimental research.

Role of the Research: Research enables us to explore and understand crime and criminal justice by utilizing a systematic approach. Adherence to the scientific method enables the researcher to follow an already established set of principles and steps while conducting the research. While there is no guarantee that following such steps will ensure a methodologically sound experiment, the scientific method provides a logical progression which may be viewed as a guidance tool. It is important to note that while the scientific method is not the only acceptable method utilized when conducting research, it clearly is the one most recognized and exemplifies the research process. Research challenges preconceived notions and has, in some cases, provided evidence which contradicts ideas and assertions relied upon heavily for personal decisions as well as decisions made by legislative bodies and criminal justice agencies. Research findings, on the other hand, may provide evidence which supports rather than refutes belief systems. Although research does not preclude the need for speculation and assumptions, it enables researchers, and society as a whole, to gain an understanding and insight into many of the everyday issues facing the criminal justice system.

Goal of the Research: In classifying research on the basis of its goal, we can distinguish between four types of research studies: (1) basic research, (2) applied research, (3) action research, and (4) instrumental research (Sommer and Sommer, 1991). Basic research, also known as pure research, may be defined as those research activities which seek knowledge merely for the sake of knowledge. Basic research involves finding answers to questions which are intellectually stimulating, but which have no immediate practical application. Applied research, on the other hand, involves the immediate use of research findings and conclusions to either solve a problem or to improve the effectiveness of a given program. According to Sommer and Sommer (1991), "(i)n practice, the division between applied and basic studies is far from clear. Most behavioral research arises from a combination of attempts to answer specific questions and the researcher's curiosity" (p. 6). Although distinguishing between the two is important, such a distinction is often blurred in practice. In an attempt to reconcile and acknowledge the practice whereby both basic and applied research are conducted simultaneously, Kurt Lewin (1946) pioneered what he termed action research (Sommer and Sommer, 1991). Action research, in essence, combines the testing of a theory, while at the same time, answering a practical question (Sommer and Sommer, 1991). Unlike the aforementioned types of research, instrumental research is that whose goal is to "demonstrate competence in research" rather than whether or not it is theory-oriented or application-oriented (Sommer and Sommer, 1991:7). For example, students taking a basic research methods course are usually required to complete some sort of research project. The focus is most often not on what the student is researching, but how it is being researched. It is the process that is the focus, not the subject matter or practicality of the data collection and/or findings.

Purpose of the Research: In categorizing research on the basis of purpose, we can distinguish between exploratory research, descriptive research, and explanatory research (Maxfield and Babbie, 1995). Exploratory research is most commonly utilized for one of the following reasons: (1) when some type of policy change is under consideration, (2) when the researcher wants to find out about something that little is known about, and (3) to help develop tests and methodologies for further research based on what is learned through the initial or preliminary studies. Exploratory studies, in this sense, may be considered as feasibility probes. They allow the researcher a great deal of flexibility and latitude in the conduct of the study so as to identify the hurdles or problem areas in a more careful subsequent study. According to Champion (1993), "the distinguishing feature of exploratory studies is that relatively little is known about the target of one's research" (p. 58). As a result, they provide a starting point from which other, more sophisticated, research follows.

Descriptive studies, in the literal sense, deal with describing phenomena and situations, and the distribution and occurrence of variables. Description tells us the "what," "where," and "when," of a particular phenomenon. In contrast to exploratory studies, with descriptive studies, researchers know in advance what they wish to describe, and their accumulated data reflect a focus of specific social and psychological dimensions of persons and their environments (Champion, 1993:60). In criminal justice, there are a plethora of examples. The National Crime Panel victimization surveys are an excellent example of descriptive criminal justice research projects. Under the auspices of the Law Enforcement Assistance Administration, the Bureau of Census conducted these surveys from 1972-1976. They were instituted to obtain a stable measure of crime that could show relationships between crime incidents and victim characteristics in different areas and across time (see Blumberg, 1979; Decker, et al., 1979; Pope, 1979; Nelson, 1979; Young, 1979 for application of these survey data to specific studies).

Explanatory studies represent the third general purpose of criminal justice and criminological research. By way of conducting such studies, the researcher is able to gain important insight into a particular phenomenon. While descriptive studies are concerned with observations and documenta-tion, explanatory studies go one step further and attempt to answer "why." For example, if we wanted to determine why the crime rate between two local neighborhoods is so dissimilar, we would attempt to identify and test variables that would provide an explanation for this observation. Simply noting the dissimilarity would be descriptive research, while seeking answers would be explanatory research.

In summary, while it is useful to categorize research on the basis of its purpose, it is important to recognize that most studies will have characteristics of each. Thus, for example, if one were to evaluate a new rape offender rehabilitation program, there would be exploratory aspects as one considers the various dimensions of the project. There would also be descriptive elements as one portrays the differences in rehabilitation rates. And, certainly there would be explanatory aspects, as one would want to know why certain offender types and which characteristics are most successful (see Groth, 1979 for an example of a study on the psychodynamics of rapists).

Method of Data Collection: When categorizing research on the basis of method of data collection, distinctions may be made between qualitative and quantitative research, as well as on the basis of the specific procedure employed (i.e., observational research, survey research, and experimental research).

Qualitative research refers to "any kind of research that produces findings not arrived at by means of statistical procedures or other means of quantification" (Strauss and Corbin, 1990:17). The data of qualitative research is most often expressed in words. For example, the participant observer takes field notes and keeps a running log of his/her observations. The researcher then begins to formulate questions and theorize about the meaning of these observations, as well as describes the analytic structure of them. The approach most commonly utilized in qualitative research is referred to as bottom-up or inductive reasoning. In other words, the researcher ideally approaches the situation, problem or circumstance he or she wishes to study with relatively limited preconceived notions. Rather than the researcher dictating the theory and then proceeding with the data collection, it is the information gleaned from the data by the researcher that guides his or her theory formation, analysis, and interpretation of the particular phenomenon under scrutiny.

Quantitative research, on the other hand, assigns numbers (i.e., the process of measurement) to the variables under investigation, and then statistically analyzes important relationships. Analyzing data in such a manner enables researchers to generalize, summarize, and potentially predict relationships between certain variables. Statistical analysis is not only predicated on the fact that the data must be converted to numbers, but that it must be analyzed in a manner consistent with the type of data collected. The approach most commonly taken by researchers conducting quantitative research is referred to as top-down or deductive reasoning and is considered by some to exemplify the traditional method of research. In sum, the researcher first develops a theory and supporting hypotheses based on speculation and/or assertions. He or she then collects and analyzes the data. The resulting interpretation is dependent upon its support or refutation of the initial theory on which the research was predicated.

Regardless of the fact that some view the two types of research as competing rather than supportive of one another, others realize the advantages each has to offer. As a result, many researchers utilize both types of research in the course of a research agenda or even within the same research project. Others, convinced that the other type has no merit, continue to conduct research in a relatively limited environment failing to realize the implications of their unwillingness to incorporate a technique that can prove to be quite insightful. In sum, a decision regarding which type or types of data collection to use should be predicated on the type of research conducted and the most beneficial technique(s) necessary to achieve the goal(s).

The specific research procedures of observation, surveys, and experiments will be discussed in detail below.

THE METHOD OF SCIENCE IN CRIMINAL JUSTICE

The term "scientific method" is employed to describe a process of investigation for the acquisition of knowledge. This process involves objectivity and utilizes empirical data in a systematic manner. Science as a way of knowing and acquiring knowledge, however, is only one such method. Other modes of inquiry and knowing include tradition, authority, experience, intuition, and faith (Babbie, 1979:7-9). These methods possess inherent deficiencies in that they are subjective, individualistic, and arbitrary. On the other hand, science and the use of the scientific method is progressive, public, cumulative, and self-correcting. Evidence reached through the use of the scientific method are open to public scrutiny and may be refuted. This refutation is acceptable because the counter-argument is gathered scientifically and not because the scientist says so, or because of emotional reasoning. Science is cumulative and progressive in the sense that we build upon our research findings to refine and clarify our understanding of the particular phenomena being investigated.

The method of science incorporates several factors or dimensions which distinguish it from other methods of knowing. Four such major characteristics include: objectivity, replicability, precision, and abstractness.

Objectivity: The idea of objectivity applies to both the individual scientist/researcher in terms of one's attitude and the state of mind in the conduct of research, and to science in terms of its factual basis. The researcher must adhere to the scientific ideals of being open-minded, unbiased, and "ethically neutral" when conducting research (see Parsons, 1968: 579-639 for a detailed discussion on the freedom of science from value judgments). Such conduct is truly a prerequisite to the criminal justice and criminological research profession, and it is indeed often difficult given the political nature of the phenomenon investigated. Honesty and integrity in the research process reflects adherence to such professional ethics (see Borate and Cecil, 1983 for further discussion on research ethics). The objectivity of science, as indicated above, lies in the employment of systematic data collection, the value free analysis of that data, and its factual basis.

Replicability: In order for science to be progressive and in order for findings to be verifiable, other researchers must be able to duplicate particular studies. Scientific facts are not unique and, in order for their veracity to be accepted, different observers or researchers must be able to repeat the study or experiment, and must also be able to obtain the same result. Failure to do either or both may prove highly suspect in some cases. As a cautionary note, reliance solely on the results of one study for policy implementation may prove devastating if it turns out that the particular study was flawed or skewed in some way. The ability to repeat or replicate studies increases our confidence in findings and contributes to the body of knowledge.

Precision: One of the requirements for replication is that of specification which implies precision. Thus, in conducting criminal justice research nothing should be casual. Researchers must be precise in conducting research, as well as in reporting their procedures and results. It does us little good, for example, to study police stress, unless we define exactly what we mean by "stress" and how we are going to measure it (see Webb and Smith, 1980 for a discussion on the conceptualization of police stress and its various dimensions). The need for precision is one reason that scientific is often quantitative. It should be noted, however, that precision, in and of itself, is not science, but rather only one characteristic of it.

Abstractness: Scientists, criminologists, and criminal justicians deal with concepts. A concept may be defined as "an abstraction from reality, a term that designates a class of phenomena or certain characteristics shared by a class of phenomena" (Ferman and Levin, 1975:11). Concept is a technical term for mental images which are representational of some phenomena. A concept is abstract if it is independent of any specific time or place. It is concrete if it is specific to a given setting or historical time. A concrete event is an instance of an abstract concept. Thus, for example, "crime" is an abstract concept. It has numerous dimensions, definitions, causes, and explanations. Crime has always occurred historically, and there is evidence of crime in all societies; thus it is not specific to any time or place. The specific crime or crime rate in a particular city is a concrete reality. Similarly, terms such as "crime prevention," "irresistible impulse," "insanity," "delinquency," "violence," "discretion," and other such criminal justice terms are concepts. That is, they are abstractions which have representational meaning in reality (see Maxfield and Babbie, 1995; Wallace, 1971, Chapter 3 for detailed discussions on conceptualization).

Theory and Research in Criminal Justice

One of the primary goals of social science is the building of theory, which can be defined as "an integrated body of assumptions, propositions, and definitions that are related in such a way as to explain and predict relationships between two or more variables" (Champion, 1993:19). The term "theory" may be thought of as a tool of science in the following ways: "(1) it defines the major orientation of a science by defining the kinds of data which are to be abstracted; (2) it offers a conceptual scheme by which the relevant phenomena are systematized, classified, and interrelated; (3) it summarizes facts into (a) empirical generalizations and (b) systems of generalizations; (4) it predicts facts; and (5) it points to gaps in our knowledge" (Goode and Hatt, 1952:8). As was described in an earlier section, theory and the relevant research can be either deductive or inductive in nature. Although in most social science research theory precedes data collection and analysis, the extrapolation of theory from the study of a specific problem or set of observations is perfectly acceptable, and, in some cases, preferred.

Theory and research should never be considered as mutually exclusive. Rather, they are highly interrelated and in constant interaction in the research process, and each serves to foster the other. Theory functions to organize, integrate, and incorporate known empirical findings into a locally consistent framework. It leads to the collection of relevant empirical relations, and to the systematic expansion of knowledge. Theory also functions as a proposition mill which spurs research. Research, on the other hand, initiates, reformulates, and clarifies theory. In general, research deals with facts, and theory deals with the relationship among facts (for in-depth discussions on the relationship between theory and research see Blalock, 1968; 1979; 1982; Coombs, 1953; Merton, 1967:139-171).

The relationship between theory and research is one of mutual contribution to the field of knowledge. As Selltiz, et al., (1962:498-499) state:

> Theory can point to areas in which research is likely to be fruitful, can summarize the data of a number of specific studies, and can provide a basis for explanation and prediction. Research findings, on the other hand, can test theories which have been worked out, can clarify theoretical concepts, and can suggest new theoretical formulations or extend old ones. Moreover, the process of reciprocal contributions is a continuing one; research stimulated by theoretical considerations may raise new theoretical issues, which, in turn lead to further research, and so on indefinitely.

The Two Realities

Social science research enables us to learn through what we personally observe and/or experience and also through well-designed experiments implemented by others. Experiential reality is that which we know due to our own personal experiences (Maxfield and Babbie, 1995). Clearly, the reality created by way of personal experience is often subjected to individual biases and perceptions. As a result, suffice it say that experiential reality may differ significantly from one individual to another. Agreement reality, on the other hand, is that which we believe to be real and accurate since

we have been told by others that this is so (Maxfield and Babbie, 1995). Reliance on what the ''experts'' have to say often takes precedence when we have little or no personal knowledge or experience with a given subject or topic. Our reality is made up of a combination of these two types of reality. The amount of each will vary on an individual level. Science embraces both realities in that one does not have to personally experience or test a given variable to believe a certain outcome. As long as a study is logical, methodologically sound, and has an outcome supportive of the theory, the reality that it generates is generally reliable and accurate.

The Research Process

Criminal justice research is an enterprise. Such an undertaking is a process involving a series of decisions or basic operations. More specifically, the research process includes: (1) formulating the research question, (2) formulating a testable hypothesis, (3) establishing a research design, (4) gathering data, and (5) analyzing the results (Defleur, et al., 1972:21-27). Similarly, Hagan (1982:13) summarizes the following general steps in the conduct of research: (1) problem formulation, (2) research design, (3) data collection methods, (4) analysis and presentation of findings, and (5) conclusions, interpretations, and limitations. Babbie (1979: 108) also suggests the following decision-making steps: (1) conceptualization, (2) choice of research method, (3) operationalization, (4) population and sampling, (5) observations, (6) data processing, and (7) analysis. Thus, even though there are variations, the same fundamental operations are present. However, to enhance the research process, it is necessary to conduct a literature review. Reading and learning about previous research that is relevant to the issue or problem at hand oftentimes proves insightful. Not only does one learn about what has been done prior to this point, but may utilize the research to help mold or modify one's own research project.

Problem Formulation: Formulation of a problem to be studied is the first step in the process. At this point, a decision regarding the actual topic or area that the researcher is going to investigate is made. It is necessary to specify the dimensions of that problem area, and to consider which factors among these dimensions are important. In addition to the selection of the specific problem to be studied, the researcher must make important decisions relating to conceptualization, operationalization, and measurement.

Once the specific topic or problem has been selected and identified, the researcher must engage in the process of conceptualization. That is, the researcher must determine: "(1) which concepts are most appropriate to your topic, (2) which variables follow from these concepts and how they are defined, (3) how your variables relate to one another, and (4) what the specific sources of your data will be" (Williamson, et al., 1982:41). Conceptualization may be viewed as "the process through which we specify precisely what we will mean when we use particular terms" (Maxfield and Babbie, 1995:95). It is necessary to establish precise meanings so as to avoid ambiguities. As an example, the term "crime" may invoke different images for different people. Some may envision "crime" as being violent and predatory, while others may view "crime" as being white collar in nature. To go one step further, one may go so far as to say that "crime" constitutes anything that is illegal. While the above definitions of "crime" are all accurate, it is clear that one's experience and/or exposure may affect his/her own perception.

As the process of research moves from one of conceptualization and defining, the measurement of variables becomes important. Measurement may be defined as "the assignment of symbols to observable phenomena. Of course, before any variable can be measured, it must be defined" (Philliber, et al., 1980:33). If, for example, we are going to study "self-concept" and "criminal behavior," we may define self-concept as a person's conception of his role in his interactions with others and the environment, and we may define criminal behavior as any overt violation of the criminal law. These definitions of the concepts are important, since they will allow the research findings to be related back to theory. Equally important, however, is that the concepts must be opera-

tionalized. That is to say, we must specify the operations to be used in measuring "self-concept" and "criminal behavior." Certainly, there are numerous ways in which we could measure these concepts, but our task is to precisely clarify how we measure them. This process is also strongly related to one of the characteristics of science mentioned above (replication). If other researchers cannot determine how we measure our concepts, they certainly could not repeat the study (see Maxfield and Babbie, 1995:9).

Other important decisions to be made during the problem formulation stage include: (1) the choice of the specific research method, (2) who the subjects are going to be and how they will be sampled (see Cochran, 1963; Slonim, 1960; Williamson, et al., 1982:103-122 for more information on sampling and sampling procedures), and (3) consideration of other obstacles or problems one might encounter in conducting the research. Once these considerations are concluded, the researcher is ready to collect information about the research topic.

Reviewing the Literature: Reviewing literature relevant to the problem or topic constitutes the next step. In doing so, one can best determine which approaches have been taken in the past by those conducting research on the same or similar topics. Information regarding the results and findings of past studies are advantageous as well. They provide the researcher with insight into the problem or topic at hand and may act as a mechanism for purposes of comparison and/or guidance. A variety of sources are available for review including, but not limited to, journals, books, and mediums of the mass media. Other useful information may be gleaned from anecdotal accounts from "experts" in the field of study.

Data Collection: Once the research design, and other related issues as indicated above are determined, the researcher is ready to empirically study the subjects or subject matter at hand. There are numerous procedures of data collection, with experimentation, survey, and observation being the most widely employed in criminal justice and criminology. Each of these will be discussed in more detail below. However, there are other issues related to the data collection phase of the research process.

The nature of the information sought by the researcher may, in itself, determine the most appropriate methodology. For example, if we were to conduct a study on prostitution and the attitudes held by prostitutes toward the police, a mailed survey technique would be inappropriate. Not only would we expect a low return/response rate, but we would have difficulty finding a suitable listing from which to draw a sample. On the other hand, if we wanted to find out the attitudes of college students toward prostitutes a survey and its appropriate sampling is more feasible as lists of students could be easily obtained. Also, although interviews could be conducted with incarcerated prostitutes, this might yield biased results. Thus, the investigator is directed into some other methodology, such as observation and field work or street interviews, which will produce data with greater integrity.

The methodology which is utilized in a given study may also be contingent on other factors which may, in fact, be out of the control of the researcher. Time constraints, lack of financial resources, lack of trained personnel, and the like may heavily influence the way in which the researcher is able to conduct the study. In turn, such constraints may affect the research overall, depending on their severity and relevance to the project. Limitations of the study, as they are often called, should be acknowledged by the researcher and taken seriously especially when such research may have far-reaching consequences.

Given the nature of the specific investigation, the data collection stage can be relatively mechanical or it can encompass many obstacles. This, of course, is related to how well the problem has been formulated. Data collection can range from merely awaiting returns from a mailed survey to spending innumerable hours interviewing and observing subjects. As a general rule, collecting data usually takes longer than anticipated.

After the problem has been formulated and specified, the researcher is anxious to go out and collect the facts. It is important to remember, as Simon (1969:77) so aptly states, that knowledge can be tricky to obtain, and common-sense knowledge gathering methods may not be sufficiently powerful. There are often many obstacles that prevent you from getting accurate knowledge easily. Simon (1969:77-173) details these obstacles, which can be summarized as follows:

1. Obstacles Relating to the Humanness of the Observer
   A. Observer Bias
   B. Observer Variability
   C. Cheating by Interviewers
   D. Variability Among Observers

2. Obstacles Relating to the Humanness of the Subjects
   A. Lack of Knowledge of the Subject Matter
   B. Forgetting and Memory Loss
   C. Cover-up by the Subject
   D. Trying to Please the Interviewer

3. Obstacles Relating to Obtaining Adequate Subject Matter
   A. Simple Bias
   B. Nonresponse and Low Return Rates
   C. Shortage of Subject Matter
   D. Unreliability of Data
   E. Inability to Experiment with the Subject Matter

In short, while the data collection phase is seemingly the most straightforward, it is nonetheless critically important that the researcher sustain his/her intimacy in the process so as to try to avoid any stumbling blocks. At the same time, one

should not become discouraged if things do not go just as you planned them. Whether your work is primarily deductive or inductive, there is still plenty of room for surprises, as well as the potential for spinning your wheels in frustration. Remember, however, that the same flexibility that allows for the possibility of error, and the occurrence of the unexpected, also allows for creativity. Your individual effort and inspiration can make a difference in the outcome of research (Williamson, et al., 1982:56).

Data Analysis: In the data analysis phase of the research process, the information obtained from the field or laboratory is coded/categorized, tabulated, and statistically analyzed. Coding involves the reduction of the information gathered in the field to a standardized form. It may involve: (a) the conversion of qualitative data into quantitative data (see Figure IA), (b) the sorting of qualitative data into various categories (see Figure IB), or (c) the reduction of quantitative data into a simpler form (see Figure IC). In any case, the data placed into categories must be mutually exclusive and exhaustive. That is, each datum must be placed in one and only one category, and we must account for all data.

Figure I. <u>Coding Examples of Questions in Criminal Justice Research</u>

A. *Qualitative to Quantitative Date*

In your opinion, what kind of a job do you feel the local police are doing to protect your neighborhood?

5	4	3	2	1
More than Adequate		Adequate		Less than Adequate

B. *The Sorting of Qualitative Data*

What was the most important reason why you did not report this crime incident to the police?

_____Nothing could be done — Lack of proof

_____Did not think it was important enough

_____Police wouldn't want to be bothered

_____Did not want to take the time — Too inconvenient

_____Private or personal matter — Did not want to report it

_____Did not want to get involved

_____Afraid of reprisal

_____Reported to someone else

_____Other — Please specify

C. *Reduction of Quantitative Date*

What was your gross family income for the past year:

_____(1) Below $7999   _____(5) $20,000 - $24,999

_____(2) $8,000 - $11,999   _____(6) $25,000 - $34,999

_____(3) $12,000 - $15,999   _____(7) $35,000 - $49,999

_____(4) $16,000 - $19,999   _____(8) $50,000 and over

Tabulation refers to the process of arranging data according to two or more categories simultaneously. A very common approach in criminal justice and criminological research is the cross-tabulation of two variables. An example of such a cross-tabulation on the relationship between degree of usage and the type of substance used by female robbers is shown in Figure II.

The statistical analysis of a body of data is essentially linked to answers to the following questions: (1) what relationships exist between and among the important variables in the investigation, (2) how confident are we in accepting or believing that these relationships are not the result of chance, and (3) how well can these results be generalized to the population from which the sample was drawn? There are numerous statistical tests appropriate to specific research designs which are applicable to answering these questions.

Figure II. **Percentage of Female Robbers Using Controlled Substance, Degree of Usage and Type of Substance used** (Source: Fortune, Vega, and Silverman, 1980:321)

Degree of Usage	Type of Substance					
	Alcohol	Hallucinogens	Stimulants	Depressants	Heroin	Cocaine
Heavy	39.4	36.4	21.2	15.2	24.2	18.2
Moderate	6.1	3.0	3.0	0.0	0.0	3.0
Light	30.3	3.0	9.1	0.0	0.0	9.1
None	24.2	57.6	66.7	84.8	75.8	69.7

For now, however, it is important to remember that many of the decisions surrounding the data analysis are really made earlier in the research process prior to the collection of the data, during the problem formulation stage. If the researcher is clear in setting up the problem to be investigated, and develops mock tables of how the data will look when it is tabulated, then the mechanics of the analysis are greatly simplified and straightforward.

This section has highlighted the specific components of the research process from formulating, conceptualizing, and specifying the research topic, to the data collection phase, and finally to the analysis of the data. This overview was intentionally brief. It was designed to provide the reader with the importance of the fact that research in criminal justice and criminology is a dynamic process which entails a constant interplay between theory and either qualitative or quantitative data collection. It involves a series of decision-making procedures, and the involvement of the investigator at each stage of the process.

METHODS OF DATA COLLECTION IN CRIMINAL JUSTICE RESEARCH

In the preceding sections emphasis has been placed on science, its characteristics and structure, as well as overviewing the research process. This section focuses on specific procedures for the collection of data in criminal justice research. There are a variety of research procedures, tactics, or strategies employed in criminal justice; however, certain approaches have become standards in the profession, as well as in the behavioral sciences in general. These strategies may be classified into the following: (1) survey research, (2) experimental research, and (3) observational research, each of which has important subdivisions.

Survey Research

There is no consensus on how to define a survey, but there is general agreement that the following factors are involved: (1) quantitative data, which implies standardized data from, and/or about subjects, (2) a substantial number of cases (no set number), but sufficient enough to allow statistical analysis, (3) the respondents are representative of some predefined universe or population (e.g. prison inmates), and (4) the data are obtained by interview or questionnaire.

Surveys may range from fact finding (e.g. the extent of computer crime) to field experiments (e.g. the testing of causal hypotheses). Surveys such as the Harris, Roper, and Gallop polls are strictly fact finding. These polls are mostly descriptive in nature since they make no attempt to scientifically provide reasons for the variations among categories.

The design of any survey is intricately linked to its analytic purpose as descriptive or explanatory. The basic design of a survey, however, involves the collection of standardized information from or about a sample representative of some universe. Within the basic design, there may be variations on the following dimensions: (1) the form of the instrument being structured or unstructured; (2) the method of administration, that is, a

mailed questionnaire, a personal interview, a telephone interview, a questionnaire administered to a group, or a questionnaire distributed individually and then returned (e.g. having prison inmates complete the survey in their cell and then returning it via prison mail); (3) the method of sampling among the various probability and non-probability sampling designs; and (4) the definition of the universe or population.

In summary, survey research is a procedure for systematically collecting information from and about individuals; their attitudes, beliefs, and experiences, and their behavior through the use of a questionnaire or interview. Survey research, like other strategies, has its limitations (see Williamson, et al., 1982:156-157), and is not an appropriate research strategy for every problem. Perhaps the greatest weakness of survey research is the total dependence on the respondent and their memory, their interest, their clarity of self-perception, their frankness, and their honesty in answering (Williamson, et al., 1982:158) as a means of data collection. Survey research also has its advantages over other types of research. In many cases, it is relatively inexpensive to conduct, and yields a great deal of information in a relatively short period of time, making it a rather desirable option for many researchers.

Experimental Research

The major purpose of experimental research is to test causal hypotheses. As such, it is perhaps the most rigorous approach or strategy in criminal justice research. It is important to mention, however, that the basic logic underlying experimental research is the same as other strategies in terms of the research process. Experimental research may vary from being eloquently simple to very elaborate in design. Experimental research is well suited for some jobs and poor for others. According to Maxfield and Babbie (1995:122):

> Experiments are especially well suited to research projects involving relatively well-defined concepts and propositions. A further requirement is being able to control the conditions under which the research is conducted. Experimentation, then, is

especially appropriate for hypothesis testing. It is better suited to explanation and evaluation than to descriptive purposes.

The basic logic of experimental research is relatively direct, and involves the following: (1) independent and dependent variables, (2) control and experimental groups, (3) random assignment of subjects to either the experimental or control group, and (4) control or manipulation of the independent variable. The researcher conducting the experiment is interested in seeing what, if any, effect the independent variable has on the dependent variable.

It is important to note that unlike the hard sciences where causality is relatively easily to establish, identifying a true causal relationship in the social sciences is a bit more tenuous and difficult than often assumed. As a result, in social science research, the phrase "causal inference" is deemed much more appropriate and is used only in those cases which meet the following criteria: (1) temporal precedence is established, in that the cause must precede the effect, (2) the independent variable, when manipulated, effects the dependent variable in some way, (3) the variables must go together, in that the relationship must make sense, (4) the variables must vary together, in that there must be some relationship (correlation) between the two (either positive or inverse), (5) the researcher must eliminate alternative explanations and/or extraneous variables which might otherwise contribute to the observed effect (Maxfield and Babbie, 1995).

In an experiment, subjects are randomly assigned to either a control group or an experimental group (or condition). Each group is given a pre-test on the dependent variable. The researcher then manipulates (or controls) the independent variable, and measures the difference in the dependent variable on a post-test. As an example, suppose we wanted to test the influence of a new prison intake program on the ability of incoming inmates to adjust to prison life. First, we would draw a sample of incoming inmates and give them a pre-test on "attitudes toward a prison life." Second, we would randomly assign them to either the experimental group (the prison intake program) or

the control group (do nothing different than before). Third, we would engage the intake program (i.e. control or manipulate the independent variable). Fourth, after a specified period of time we would retest the subjects on the dependent variable (attitudes toward prison life). Finally, we would assess any differences between the two groups. This design is schematically depicted in Figure III.

As stated, experimental designs can be fairly simple as illustrated in the preceding example, or they can be more elaborate. One example of this could be that rather than having only one level of the independent variable (i.e., either in the prison intake program or not) there would be various levels or degrees of intensity of the independent variable. Thus, if we were interested in the role that defendant characteristics have on juror decisions to assess punishment, we could establish several categories or levels of physical attractiveness of the defendant (i.e., the independent variable), and then observe any variations on juror or subject decisions on the severity of punishment. Similarly, if we were interested in the influence or degree to which different counseling or rehabilitation programs (i.e. the independent variable) had on inmate adjustment, we could design such an experiment as schematically represented in Figure IV.

The basic experimental design as illustrated in Figure III can be extended to incorporate a larger number of categories in the independent variable (Figure IV). It can also be extended to incorporate a larger number of independent variables. There are situations in criminal justice and criminology in which more than one variable may have an influence on a dependent variable. This type of experimental research is called a *factorial* design. In a factorial design, two or more independent variables are presented together. The design includes all possible combinations of the independent variables or factors (thus named the factorial design). The introduction of additional independent variables has several advantages. First, one can assess the joint effect of the independent variables on the dependent variable. Secondly, it better approximates the nature of the real world phenomena that the researcher is trying to explain (see

Figure III. Example of an Experimental Design for a Study on the Influence of a Prison Intake Program on Adjustment to Prison Life.

GROUP	EXPERIMENTAL	CONTROL
Pretest	*Attitudes toward prison life* O_1	*Attitudes toward prison life* O_2
Treatment	Complete prison intake program	Do nothing different than before
Posttest	*Attidues toward prison life* O_3	*Attitudes toward prison life* O_4
$(O_1 - O_3)$	OBSERVE DIFFERENCE	$(O_2 - O_4)$

Source: For further details on experimental design see Babbie, (1979:270), Ferman and Leven, (1975:38), and Hagan, (1982:19-41).

Kerlinger, 1979; Winer, 1971 for greater detail on experimental and factorial designs).

Experimental research as the most rigorous approach to data collection has the advantages of: (1) isolated crucial variables that the researcher can control or manipulate, (2) allowing replication which strengthens our confidence in the findings and, (3) allowing tests of causal hypotheses derived from theory. Experimental research also has several disadvantages, including: (1) its artificiality in that experimental conditions do not truly represent natural settings, (2) it is questionable if the findings can be generalized to the population and, (3) experiments generally do not provide descriptive data. Despite these limitations, however, experimental research is critical to criminal justice and its advancement as a scientific discipline.

Experimental research, as discussed above, deals only with the most ideal conditions and circumstances. In reality, it is important to note that other research designs, namely quasi-experimental and pre-experimental, are perfectly acceptable and used extensively by researchers in less than ideal circumstances. Clearly, choosing the most appropriate and suitable research design is a must.

Observational Research

The kind of data obtained from observational research is inherently different from the more quantitative obtained from survey and experimental methodologies. Information secured in observational research is conditioned upon two basic factors: (1) context and, (2) marginality. The context of observational research refers to the respondents basis for reacting or communicating to the researcher. Marginality refers to both the researcher's and the respondent's position in the group under study.

Figure IV. Example of an Experimental Design for a Study on the Influence of Different Prison Counseling Programs on Inmate Adjustment to Prison Life.

Group	Experimental Group I	Experimental Group II	Experimental Group III	Control Group
	Intensive Individual Counseling	*Group Counseling*	*Behavior Modification*	*Do Nothing Different*
Pretest	*Measure of Prison Adjustment*	*Measure of Prison Adjustment*	*Measure of Prison Adjustment*	*Measure of Prison Adjustment*
Treatment	Complete Program	Complete Program	Complete Program	
Posttest	*Measure of Prison Adjustment*	*Measure of Prison Adjustment*	*Measure of Prison Adjustment*	*Measure of Prison Adjustment*

OBSERVE DIFFERENCES AMONG GROUPS

Observational research may categorized as follows: (1) complete participant, (2) participant-as-observer, (3) observer-as-participant, and (4) complete observer (Gold, 1969:30-39). It is defined by the role the researcher plays throughout the duration of the study. Although in all cases observation is taking place, the role of the researcher varies along a continuum. In the role of a complete participant, the researcher is seen by his/her subjects purely as a participant, not as a researcher. In fact, the researcher never discloses to his/her subjects his/her true identity. While there are clearly some advantages to this type of research, it begs the question as to whether or not it is ethical. Additionally, questions regarding legal liability (i.e., in the case of posing as a drug dealer) and risks also arise.

The second category identified by Gold (1969) is referred to as participant-as-observer. In this case, the researcher participates, but reveals his/her role as a researcher. In this instance, there is no room for accusations of deception on the part of the researcher. However, there are disadvantages, the greatest of which is that the subjects, knowing that they are being studied, may shift their focus toward the researcher and the research at hand. As a result, the subjects may alter their behavior, either consciously or subconsciously, to fit what they believe the researcher is looking for (sometimes referred to as the Hawthorne Effect).

In the case where the researcher is an observer-as-participant, the researcher clearly identifies him/herself as a researcher, first and foremost. The participatory role is lessened, and the primary focus is on research. The researcher makes no false pretenses about being a participant. The researcher is in no way deceptive in terms of concealing his/her identity. However, the research may itself suffer. Questions regarding tainted research (i.e., the subjects severely modifying their behavior(s)) arise.

Lastly, Gold (1969) discusses the role of the researcher as a complete observer. In this instance, the research is unobtrusive. The researcher does not participate whatsoever, and does not even attempt to interact with the subjects under investigation. Once again, despite the advantages, there are also disadvantages. Ethical questions arise in cases where an individual's rights may be infringed upon since they do not know they are being watched. Another disadvantage is the fact that the researcher does not have the ability to gain insight from the perspectives of those being studied, something present in the other three roles.

Methodological issues arise with observational research. In fact, there are problems inherent to it. Some major difficulties include: (1) the fact that the observer modifies the context being observed simply by his/her presence in the situation, (2) by participating in the situation, the observer is influenced or changed by the context, (3) entry problems and, (4) sampling problems. Entry problems refer to issues concerning what role the observer should take, and how he will enter the group. Other entry problems include developing appropriate language or argot, dress, and demeanor. It is readily apparent that:

> Whenever research involves interaction between subjects and investigators, there is no such thing as total, bland unobtrusiveness. . . Participant observers should try to understand and take into account the identity that their subjects attribute to them. How do a researcher's race, sex, ethnicity, physical appearance, known affiliations, and the like affect respondents behavior? Does the researcher pose any kind of threat to the group or to any particular individuals or factions? . . . (Williamson, et al., 1982:199)

Sampling problems relate to two distinct issues in observational research. First, the researcher is faced with the problem of trying to generate an adequate and representative sample of subjects. The second issue deals with the behaviors being observed. That is, of the behaviors under study are those that are observed representative of those that occur? As indicated previously, the researcher modifies the context; thus, behaviors of the subjects may be altered from their natural occurrence. Also, unless the researcher witnesses all dimensions of the particular phenomena under study some misrepresentation may occur.

Despite these complications, such observational research is an important tool for criminal justice and criminological research. In some cases, it represents the only method for obtaining data and information, and this is particularly true when dealing with subject populations which are either deviant (i.e., criminals and other socially deviant groups) or suspicious or resistant to researchers (i.e., the police). In fact, Polsky (1967) details how he studied organized crime, drug dealers, pool hustlers, and confidence men through the use of participant observer research techniques. Similarly, Laud Humphreys (1970), through the use of observational research techniques, was able to study homosexuality in public places. Examples of observational research in criminal justice and criminology are numerous.

Observational research employs those research strategies which collect more qualitative data and information. This type of information is important in that it adds to our knowledge of the richness of behavior in natural settings. Additionally, as Hagan (1982:111) stresses, "(a)dvocates of participant observation. . . feel that we have been all too dependent on studies of imprisoned criminals in an unnatural environment, or of using unquestioningly official statistics, and that this has led to an inaccurate view of criminals and criminal behavior." Finally, as Chambliss (1975:39), in writing about the paucity of this type of research indicates:

> It is possible to find out what is going on "out there." We are not permanently stuck with government reports and college students' data on

organized crime and professional theft as well as other presumably difficult-to-study events. They are much more available for study than we think. All we really have to do is to get out of our offices and onto the streets. The data are there; the problem is that too often sociologists are not.

The preceding subsections have introduced the beginning student to three fundamental modes of data collection in criminal justice and criminological research. These are not the only strategies, but they are the most widely employed. It should be emphasized that each of these strategies has their own peculiar strengths and weaknesses. None is appropriate for all situations, but each contributes to the development of our knowledge about crime and criminal justice.

THE ANALYSIS OF DATA IN CRIMINAL JUSTICE RESEARCH

After gathering the data, regardless of the specific strategy employed, the researcher is confronted with the problem of making some sense about his/her findings. In one way, the statistical analysis is a fairly direct procedure, especially when this has been thought about early in the research process. It is merely a matter of compiling the data, plugging it into a statistical formula, and noting the result. On the other hand, the very mention of the word "statistics" is enough to send shivers up and down one's spine. The present section will not attempt a comprehensive review of statistical analysis in the behavior sciences, as this would be an impossible task given the space limitations. Rather, a brief overview of data analysis will be presented so as to acquaint the beginning student with the kinds of data and statistical analysis available for the criminal justice researcher.

The use of statistics has several major functions in research, including: (1) explaining how the sample data differ from the population to which it is generalized, (2) indicating how confident we are in accepting that the obtained results did not occur by chance alone, (3) explaining the relationships between and among the variables we are studying,

and (4) providing an accurate means for summarizing the data we have amassed. Statistics, as a branch of mathematics, deals with the "collection, classification, description, and interpretation of data obtained by the conduct of surveys and experiments. Its essential purpose is to describe and draw inferences about the numerical properties of populations" (Ferguson, 1966:4).

There are basically two kinds of statistics: (1) descriptive statistics, and (2) inferential statistics. We may also identify correlational analysis as a distinct statistical procedure.

Descriptive Statistics

Descriptive statistics, if taken literally, "describe" and summarize a collection of data. These types of statistical presentations may take numerous forms including: (1) frequency distributions, (2) graphs and pictorial presentations, (3) percentages and rates, (4) measures of central tendency or typicality (e.g. means or averages, modes, medians), and (5) measures of dispersion (e.g., range, standard deviation, and variance).

Each of these descriptive statistics has an important function depending on the purpose of the research, and the audience to which it is presented. Thus, for example, we often see the use of graphs, charts, or other pictorial versions summarizing the data. The Federal Bureau of Investigation *Uniform Crime Reports*, in addition to presenting tables and computing rates of crime, presents the so-called "crime clocks." In the crime clocks, the amount of crime is compared to a unit of time and then pictorially presented as shown in Figure V. This conversion and pictorial representation allow statements such as "there is one murder every 25 minutes," etc.

The Uniform Crime Reports also calculate rates of crime (i.e., the amount of crime as compared to a specific unit of population, usually 100,000). This conversion is important because it allows for the direct comparison of crime between cities of different sizes. So, for example, if there are 300 murders per year in City A and 150

Figure V. Federal Bureau of Investigation, Uniform Crime Reports, Crime Clock for 1995 (Based on Federal Bureau of Investigation, 1996)

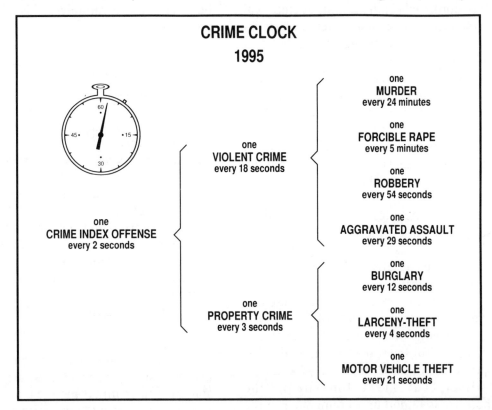

CRIME CLOCK
1995

one
CRIME INDEX OFFENSE
every 2 seconds

one
VIOLENT CRIME
every 18 seconds

one
PROPERTY CRIME
every 3 seconds

one
MURDER
every 24 minutes

one
FORCIBLE RAPE
every 5 minutes

one
ROBBERY
every 54 seconds

one
AGGRAVATED ASSAULT
every 29 seconds

one
BURGLARY
every 12 seconds

one
LARCENY-THEFT
every 4 seconds

one
MOTOR VEHICLE THEFT
every 21 seconds

The crime clock should be viewed with care. Being the most aggregate representation of UCR data, it is designed to convey the annual reported crime experience by showing the relative frequency of occurrence of the Index Offenses. This mode of display should not be taken to imply a regularity in the commission of the Part 1 Offenses; rather, it represents the annual ratio of crime to fixed time intervals.

murders per year in City B, we would be hard pressed to state that one would be twice as likely to be a victim of homicide in City A. We must consider the ratio of murders to the population, and then convert a comparable statistic (i.e., rate per 100,000 population). Suppose the population in City A is 2,000,000 and the population of City B is 500,000. If we convert to rates, the homicide rate in City A is 15 per 100,000 population, versus 30 per 100,000 in City B. Thus, we have a higher likelihood of being murdered in City B even though the actual number of homicides is smaller.

Descriptive statistics may be: (1) univariate (i.e., summarizing the distribution of a single variable), for example, a frequency distribution of the types of crimes committed in a specific geographic location within a given time frame, (2) bivariate (i.e., summarizing the distribution of two variables) for example, the cross-tabulation of two variables such as age of the offender and type of crime, or (3) multivariate (summarizing the distribution of more than two variables), for example, a table containing the age of the victim, the type of victimization, and the place of residence (city, suburb, or rural area).

Inferential Statistics

Inferential statistics go beyond the data at hand as is the case with descriptive statistics. Inferential statistics are composed of two ideas: (1) to generalize to the population from which the sample was drawn (estimation), and (2) the testing of empirical hypotheses (significance testing). Inferential statistics as a means of testing hypotheses incorporate a number of specific tests. Thus, there are procedures to test for: (1) differences between the means or measures of central tendency, (2) differences in measures of dispersion (i.e., the analysis of variance), as well as (3) testing to see if correlations or other measures of relationships between and among variables are significant (i.e., that the differences noted are not attributable to chance).

The use of statistical tests helps the criminal justice researcher to assess the validity of relationships obtained in data, as well as make interpretations about possible causality. There are, as mentioned above, many different tests of significance available to the researcher, and their usage depends on the kind and type of data obtained. It is clear that a knowledge of statistics and probability theory is essential for the researcher to make full and appropriate use of these statistical procedures, and as Philliber, et al., (1980:166) stress, "the logic of their use is important to remember in the beginning stages of data analysis." Thus, if in the conceptualization and operationalization phases of the research, the researcher meticulously formulates the problem, the type of statistical tests and descriptive statistics to employ will be obvious.

Correlational Analysis

The preceding sections addressed the use of statistics to describe and summarize data sets, and to conduct tests of statistical significance about empirical hypotheses. There are times in criminal justice and criminological research, however, when the investigator is interested in the degree of simultaneous or concomitant variation of two variables. For example, one might be interested in the degree of relationship between the severity of victimization impact and the victim's age. To do this, the researcher would need measures for both variables for each subject victim in the study. One measure would be the victim's age, the other some score of measure of severity of victimization

impact. From these paired data, it is possible to get a number that represents the degree of relationship between the two variables. This number is called a correlation.

Correlation refers to the degree of correspondence, co-relationship, or co-varying between two variables. It tells the strength of this relationship, as well as the direction of the relationship. Thus, for example, if as the victim's age increases and so does the severity of victimization impact we have a positive relationship or a positive correlation (i.e. both are increasing together). On the other hand, if age increases and severity of impact decreases, we have a negative correlation. Mathematically, the value of a correlation coefficient cannot be greater than one (1.00), and can range from -1.0 (a perfect negative correlation) to +1.0 (a perfect positive correlation). A correlation of zero indicates that there is no relationship between the variables under study, and the closer the correlation is to zero, the weaker the relationship.

In concluding this section on data analysis, we may best summarize and illustrate the relevance of statistics in criminal justice and criminology research as follows: (1) they permit the most exact kind of description, (2) they force us to be definite and exact in our procedures and in our thinking, (3) statistics enable us to summarize our results in a meaningful and convenient form, (4) they enable us to draw general conclusions, (5) they enable us to make predictions, and (6) they enable us to analyze causal factors.

EVALUATION RESEARCH AND POLICY DECISIONS

The previous sections of this chapter have concentrated on specific aspects of science and its characteristics, the research process, the collection of data, and data analysis. These considerations were mainly directed toward the idea of pure science, that is, seeking knowledge for the sake of knowledge. There are, however, program and policy needs which must be met through the application of these same procedures.

Crime and criminal justice have witnessed a resurgence of public concern in recent years. This increased attention has fostered and encouraged funding for solutions to the crime problem. This increase in sums of money being put into criminal justice programs has mandated the need for evaluation of such programming and policy. Evaluations are conducted at all levels of administration of the criminal justice system (i.e., federal, state, and local), as well as in all subsystems of law enforcement, courts and corrections.

Evaluation research serves a number of purposes, including: (1) to determine whether a program should be continued, modified, or abandoned altogether, (2) to determine whether local funding should be used to support a program after completion of its experimental stage, (3) to decide if the program should be promoted in other jurisdictions, and (4) to provide information which can lead to general principles and guidelines for administrators in setting their priorities for new program implementation (Maltz, 1972:1). Similarly, Weiss (1971) specifies four major types of utilization of evaluation research: (1) feedback for improving ongoing programs, (2) input at the end of a program cycle to decisions on whether to terminate, modify, or enlarge the program, (3) input at the highest policy making level to decisions on what to do with the overall program, and (4) ammunition for special-interest groups.

As with the pure science approach to research, evaluation research entails basically the same process in that decisions must be made in terms of: (1) formulating and conceptualizing the problem, (2) determining what should be measured and how it should be measured, (3) selection of the research design, (4) decisions concerning the sampling procedures to be employed, and (5) analyzing and interpreting the collected data (see Williamson, et al., 1982:332-344).

It must be remembered that although evaluation research has a pragmatic goal, it must maintain scientific objectivity in order to be useful. It does little good, and there is minimal program benefit, to collect data merely to support a particular program, administrative point of view, or political philosophy. The maintenance of objectivity is particularly acute since:

> The overall scientific quality of evaluation research remains low because of the many methodological problems that must be addressed and because of the relationship between researchers and program personnel, which is often less than fully cooperative. In order to improve the scientific quality of evaluation research, as well as its usefulness in solving human problems, researchers should exercise their responsibility to see that their work is fully and fairly reported by the sponsors and that improper use of research results be brought to light (Williamson, et al., 1982:344-345).

ETHICAL CONSIDERATIONS IN RESEARCH

A discussion of research methods is by no means complete without a discussion of the ethical principles that should guide researchers. Maxfield and Babbie (1995) identify the following, which are widely accepted by most professional organizations: "(1) no harm to participants, (2) voluntary participation, (3) anonymity and confidentiality, (4) deceiving subjects and, (5) analysis and reporting" (1995:153-158). The first ethical principle, referred to as "no harm to participants" by Maxfield and Babbie (1995), refers to the need for researchers to go to great lengths to ensure the safety (both physical and psychological) of the subjects. It is up to the researcher to decide whether or not to go forth with a given research process. Conducting a cost-benefit analysis to determine whether the gains elicited from the research outweigh any risks associated with it, is often relied upon by independent researchers operating under their own devices. On the other hand, those conducting research as affiliates of an educational institution or government agency are often monitored by a committee that oversees research projects which involve humans or animals. Prior to conducting studies, approval from a formal committee must be sought by the principle researcher. His/her research is subjected to scrutinization by the members of the committee who reach a consensus on whether the researcher should be allowed to go forth with such a project. Failure to do so may lead to serious consequences for the researcher.

Ensuring anonymity, when agreeing to do so, is another ethical principle identified by Maxfield and Babbie (1995). With reference to conducting research, anonymity, in the purest form of the word, essentially means that the researcher does not know who answered the questions and makes no effort to find out the identity of the respondent. An advantage of this is the fact that the researcher is much more apt to acquire a rich, insightful data set since the subjects have a tendency to feel that they having nothing to lose by disclosing information and are not usually in jeopardy of someone finding out. A clear disadvantage is the fact that there is no real way to follow up with a given respondent.

Along the same lines of anonymity is the principle of confidentiality (Maxfield and Babbie, 1995). Once again, if the researcher has made an agreement with the respondents, he/she is obligated to abide by such an agreement. However, unlike the case of anonymity, in a research project that guarantees confidentiality, the researcher is able to link the subject with the information gathered, yet does not disclose the subject's name or any other identifying information publicly. Knowledge of the identification of the subjects enables the researcher to do a follow-up study or report on specific individuals. The information revealed by the subjects may be somewhat limited in nature compared to projects ensuring anonymity.

The ethical principle that dictates that a researcher has an obligation to identify him/herself as a researcher and should reveal the purpose of the study is seemingly less definitive that the aforementioned principles (Maxfield and Babbie). As Maxfield and Babbie state:

> Even when it's possible and important to conceal your research identity, there is an important ethical dimension to be considered. Deceiving people is unethical, and within criminal justice research, deception needs to be justified by compelling scientific or administrative concerns. Even then, the justification will be arguable (1995:156).

The researcher must be careful how he/she treads in the area of deception. As Maxfield and Babbie point out, there are some instances where it may be justified, but such deception must not become commonplace or even an outwardly acceptable practice.

The last ethical principle discussed refers to the way in which a researcher analyzes and reports the data and subsequent findings (Maxfield and Babbie, 1995). According to this principle, the researcher has an obligation to be honest and open about the shortcomings and limitations of the research. The researcher is also obliged to report all the relevant findings even if they fail to support the theory. Manipulating, modifying, or "fudging" the data and findings in any way, shape, or form is in direct violation of this principle. Lastly, the researcher is expected to discuss, or at least mention, the existence of outliers or anomalies. Since it is understood by those in the research community that actually including them in the analysis may distort the data, interfering with the "true" findings, a brief discussion is often sufficient.

CHAPTER SUMMARY

This chapter has examined various dimensions of the use of research in criminal justice and criminology. It has concentrated on those general principles of the use of the scientific method, the research process, and the analysis of data. Emphasis was placed on the characteristics of science, particularly in terms of its objectivity as a method of knowledge acquisition. The research process was depicted as a dynamic process which incorporates a series of decisions in problem formulation — conceptualization, operationalization, and measurement — and the analysis and interpretation of collected data.

It is apparent that we are facing extraordinary crime problems in our society, as well as throughout the world. Criminal justice and criminological research alone will not solve these problems.

Unless we have objective, politically free, and an unbiased understanding of the numerous dimensions and the vast vicissitudes of crime, we will make no pragmatic progress towards its reduction or control. The blend between practice and knowledge is never-ending. As society, the structure of societal institutions, the stratification of populations, the international interrelationships of countries and peoples, and technological changes occur, crime will be omnipresent and ubiquitous. The task of criminal justice research is not to judge, but to explain; not to argue for some given or desired state of affairs, but to examine the workings of the criminal justice system and its various subsystems, as well as the consequences which derive from alternative ways of doing things. Any practical attempt to curtail and control criminal activities will certainly rest, as well as find its foundation, in systematic and theoretically grounded research. It is a challenge for the future.

✳ ✳ ✳ ✳ ✳

REFERENCES

Agar, M.H.
  1973   *Ripping and Running: A Formal Ethnography of Urban Heroine Addicts.* New York: Seminar Press.
Babbie, E.R.
  1979   *The Practice of Social Research.* Belmont, CA: Wadsworth Publishing Company.
Bachman, R., and R. Paternoster
  1997   *Statistical Methods for Criminology and Criminal Justice.* New York: McGraw-Hill Companies, Inc.
Becker, H.S.
  1963   *Outsiders: Studies in the Sociology of Deviance.* New York: The Free Press.
Blalock, H.M.
  1968   "The Measurement Problem: A Gap Between the Languages of Theory and Research," in H.M. Blalock and A.B. Blalock (eds.) *Methodology in Social Research.* New York: McGraw-Hill Book Company.
  1979(a) "Measurement and Conceptualization Problems: The Major Obstacle ot Integrating Theory and Research." *American Sociological Review,* 44: 881-894.
  1979(b) *Social Statistics.* New York: McGraw-Hill Book Company.
Blumberg, M.
  1979   "Injury to Victims of Personal Crimes: Nature and Extent," in William H. Parsonage (ed.) *Perspectives on Victimology.* Beverly Hills, CA: Sage Publications.
Boruch, R.F., and J.S. Cecil
  1983   *Solutions to Ethical and Legal Problems in Social Research.* New York: Academic Press.
Chambliss, W.
  1975   "On the Paucity of Original Research on Organized Crime: A Reply to Galliher and Cain." *American Sociologist,* 10: 36-39.
Champion, D.J.
  1993   *Research Methods for Criminal Justice and Criminology.* Upper Saddle River, NJ: Prentice-Hall Regents.

Cochran, W.G.
   1963   *Sampling Techniques*. New York: John Wiley and Sons, Inc.
Combs, C.H.
   1953   "Theory and Methods of Social Measurement," in Leon Festinger and Daniel Katz
            (eds.), *Research Methods in the Behavioral Sciences*. New York: Dryden Press.
Decker, D.L., R.M O'Brien, and D. Schichor
   1979   "Patterns of Juvenile Victimization and Urban Structure," in William H. Parsonage
            (ed.) *Perspectives on Victimology*. Beverly Hills, CA: Sage Publications.
DeFleur, M.L., W.V. D'Antonio, and L.B. DeFleur
   1972   *Sociology: Man in Society*. Glenview, IL: Scott Foresman and Company.
Eckhardt, K.W., and M.D. Erman
   1977   *Social Research Methods: Perspective, Theory, and Analysis*. New York: Random
            House.
Federal Bureau of Investigation
   1996   *Uniform Crime Reports — 1995*. Washington, DC: United States Department of Jus-
            tice.
Ferguson, G.A.
   1966   *Statistical Analysis in Psychology and Education*. New York: McGraw-Hill Book
            Company.
Ferman, G.S., and J. Levin
   1975   *Social Science Research*. New York: John Wiley and Sons.
Finsterbusch, K., and A.B. Motz
   1980   *Social Research for Policy Decisions*. Belmont, CA: Wadsworth Publishing Company.
Freeman, L.C.
   1965   *Elementary Applied Statistics*. New York: John Wiley and Sons.
Gold, R.L.
   1969   "Roles in Sociological Field Observation," in George J. McCall and J.L. Simmons
            (eds.) *Issues in Participant Observation*. Reading, MA: Addison-Wesley.
Goode, W.J., and P.K. Hatt
   1952   *Methods of Social Research*. New York: McGraw-Hill Book Company.
Groth, A.N.
   1979   *Men Who Rape: The Psychology of the Offender*. New York: Plenum Press.
Guilford, J.P.
   1950   *Fundamental Statistics in Psychology and Education*. New York: Mc-Graw Hill Book
            Company.
Hagan, F.E.
   1982   *Research Methods in Criminal Justice*. New York: MacMillan Publishing Company.
Hays, W.L., and R.L. Winkler
   1971   *Statistics: Probability, Inference, and Decision*. New York: Holt, Rinehart, and Win-
            ston, Inc.
Hirschi, T.
   1969   *Causes of Delinquency*. Berkeley, CA: University of California Press.
Hirschi, T., and H.C. Selvin
   1966   "False Criteria of Causality in Delinquency." *Social Problems*, 13: 254-268.
Homans, G.
   1950   *The Human Group*. New York: Harcourt, Brace, and World.
Humphreys, L.
   1970   *Tearoom Trade: Impersonal Sex in Public Places*. Chicago: Aldine.
Hyman, N.H.
   1963   "Reflections on the Relationship Between Theory and Research." *The Centennial
            Review*, 7: 431-453.
Johnson, E.S.
   1981   *Research Methods in Criminology and Criminal Justice*. Englewood Cliffs, NJ: Pre-
            ntice-Hall, Inc.

Kaplan, A.
    1964   *The Conduct of Inquiry: Methodology for Behavioral Science*. San Francisco, CA: Chandler Publishing Company.

Kerlinger, F.N.
    1979   *Behavioral Research: A Conceptual Approach*. New York: Holt, Rinehart, and Winston.

Klockars, C.P.
    1974   *The Professional Fence*. New York: The Free Press.

Lastrucci, C.L.
    1963   *The Scientific Approach: Basic Principles of the Scientific Approach*. Cambridge, MA: Schenkman Publishing Company.

Letkemann, P.
    1973   *Crime as Work*. Englewood Cliffs, NJ: Prentice-Hall, Inc.

Maltz, M.D.
    1972   *Evaluation of Crime Control Programs*. Washington, DC: United States Department of Justice.

Maxfield, M.G., and E. Babbie
    1995   *Research Methods for Criminal Justice and Criminology*. Belmont, NY: Wadsworth Publishing Company.

Merton, R.K.
    1967   *On Theoretical Sociology*. New York: Free Press.

Nelson, J.F.
    1979   "Implications for the Ecological Study of Crime: A Research Note," in William H. Parsonage (ed.), *Perspectives on Victimology*. Beverly Hills, CA: Sage Publications.

Nettler, G.
    1984   *Explaining Crime*. New York: McGraw-Hill Book Company.

Nunnaly, J.
    1967   *Psychometric Theory*. New York: McGraw-Hill Book Company.

Parsons, T.
    1938   "The Role of Theory in Social Research." *American Sociological Review*: 3.

Philliber, S.G., M.R. Schwab, and G.S. Sloss
    1980   *Social Research: Guides to a Decision-Making Process*. Itasca, IL: F.E. Peacock Publishers, Inc.

Polsky, N.
    1967   *Hustlers, Beats, and Others*. Chicago: Aldine.

Pope, C.E.
    1979   "Victimization Rates and Neighborhood Characteristics: Some Preliminary Findings," in William H. Parsonage (ed.), *Perspectives on Victimology*. Beverly Hills, CA: Sage Publications.

Reynolds, P.D.
    1971   *A Primer of Theory Construction*. Indianapolis, IN: Bobbs-Merrill Company, Inc.

Robinson, W.S.
    1951   "The Logical Structure of Induction." *American Sociological Review*, 16: 812-818.

Rowntree, D.
    1981   *Statistics Without Tears: A Primer for Non-Mathematicians*. New York: Charles Scribners' Sons.

Sanders, W.B.
    1977   *Detective Work: A Study of Criminal Investigations*. New York: Free Press.

Schafer, S.
    1969   *Theories in Criminology*. New York: Random House.

Schwartz, M.S., and C.G. Schwartz
    1969   "Problems in Participant Observation," in George S. McCall and J.L. Simmons (eds.), *Issues in Participant Observation*. Reading, MA: Addison-Wesley.

Selltiz, C., M. Jahoda, M. Deutsch, and S.W. Cook
    1962   *Research Methods in Social Relations*. New York: Holt, Rinehart and Winston.

Shavelson, R.J.
  1988   *Statistical Reasoning for the Behavioral Sciences*, second edition. Boston: Allyn and Bacon, Inc.
Siegel, S.
  1965   *Nonparametric Statistics for the Behavioral Sciences*. New York: McGraw-Hill Book Company.
Simon, J.L.
  1969   *Basic Research Methods in Social Sciences*. New York: Random House.
Slonim, M.J.
  1960   *Sampling*. New York: Simon and Schuster.
Sommer, B. and R. Sommer
  1991   *A Practical Guide to Behavioral Research: Tools and Techniques*, third edition. New York: Oxford University Press.
Strauss, A., and J. Corbin
  1990   *Basics of Qualitative Research: Grounded Theory Procedures and Techniques*. Newbury Park, CA: Sage Publications.
Turner, J.H.
  1991   *The Structure of Sociological Theory*, fifth edition. Belmont, CA: Wadsworth Publishing Company.
Vito, G.F., and R.M. Holmes
  1994   *Criminology: Theory, Research and Policy*. Belmont, CA: Wadsworth Publishing Company.
Vold, G.B.
  1978   *Theoretical Criminology*, second edition by Thomas J. Bernard. New York: Oxford University Press.
Wallace, W.L.
  1969   *Sociological Theory: An Introduction*. Chicago: Aldine.
  1971   *The Logic of Science in Sociology*. Chicago: Aldine-Atherton.
Webb, S.D., and D.L. Smith
  1980   "Police Stress: A Conceptual Overview." *Journal of Criminal Justice*, 8(4): 251-257.
Weiss, C. H.
  1971   "Utilization of Evaluation: Toward Comparative Study," 1971, in Francis G. Carr (ed.), *Reading in Evaluation Research*. New York: Russell Sage Foundation.
Williams, F.
  1992   *Reasoning with Statistics: How to Read Quantitative Research*, fourth edition. Fort Worth, TX: Harcourt Brace Jovanovich College Publishers.
Williamson, J.B., D.A. Karp, J.R. Dalphin, and P.S. Gray
  1982   *The Research Craft: An Introduction to Social Research Methods*. Boston: Little, Brown, and Company.
Winer, B.J.
  1971   *Statistical Principles in Experimental Design*. New York: McGraw-Hill Book Company.
Young, V.D.
  1979   "Victims of Female Offenders," in William H. Parsonage (ed.), *Perspectives on Victimology*. Beverly Hills, CA: Sage Publications.
Ziskin, J.
  1970   *Coping with Psychiatric and Psychological Testimony*. Beverly Hills, CA: Law and Psychology Press.

SECTION III

THE JUDICIAL SYSTEM

Chapter 5

The Law: At the Core of Government and American Justice

By

Richard G. Frey

There are many alternative ways of thinking about and defining law. This chapter offers answers to some of the specific questions one might ask such as: What is law? How does law come into existence and develop? How does government change the law? Where can answers to law questions be found? The beginning of full answers to such questions comes with accepting the fact no single philosophical approach or academic framework can explain law in all its facets. However, in order to provide a context with which to approach these questions, it is necessary to examine some of the history and philosophical roots that have shaped law in modern society.

WESTERN LEGAL TRADITIONS

In Western Civilization four great influences have shaped the development of law: Greek Philosophy, Roman Jurisprudence, Judeo-Christian Religion, and modern science. These influences, according to John Merryman (1969:1), have resulted in three major legal traditions which dominated the twentieth century world. These legal traditions are civil law, common law, and socialistic law. The oldest and most general tradition is civil law while common law is predominant in the "English" speaking countries. Socialistic law emerged after the Russian Revolution and spread as Soviet influence increased. None of these three traditions has given rise to operating systems wholly free from the influences of the others. Other traditions might be suggested, such as the Scandinavian, Moslem, and Hindu, but they would compose a miscellaneous fourth grouping with little in common with each other and so for simplicity will not be discussed.

A legal tradition is defined by Merryman (1969:2) as a set of deeply rooted, historically conditioned attitudes toward the nature of law, the role of law in society, the proper organization and operation of law, and the way law is (or should be) made, applied, studied, perfected, and taught. A legal system is an operating set of legal institutions, procedures, and rules, and it may be grouped by the underlying assumptions it shares with all legal systems following a particular tradition. The entire United States (with the exception of Louisiana, dominated by the civil law tradition) follows the common law tradition with politically separate legal systems in each of the various states and at the federal level.

101

In the course of the first twelve centuries A.D., Greek Classical Philosophy, Roman law and administrative practice, and Christian doctrine fused. The result was medieval theology, which flourished during the middle ages; this theology influenced all thought including law. Earlier, alongside Roman law, canon law was developing as the law of the Roman Catholic Church. Following the decline of the Holy Roman Empire, canon law fused with Roman law and became the basic law of Europe. This approach to law became known as the civil law tradition. It made the medieval ruler, the king, responsible to God and the church in a sacred society. This civil law tradition is based on written law called codes. In these codes behavioral situations are anticipated and right conduct is prescribed. The first of these civil law codes was the Justinian Code. The early codes were classical in orientation and made the individual responsible for exercising free will.

The common law tradition emerged in England just following the Norman conquest of the Anglo-Saxon King Harold in 1066 A.D. England of that time was covered by a network of local courts which administered most of the judicial business. In these assemblies of courts justice was administered for the ordinary citizen. Men of nobility under Anglo-Saxon law had resorted to the king and the members of the king's council called the *Witan* for their justice.

The Norman kings imposed their authority by building on the Anglo-Saxon judicial system. The common law tradition is based on decisions of judges; the body of law derives not from extensive codes but incrementally from precedents established on a case-by-case basis. The English common law tradition followed classical philosophy but gave secular authority greater responsibility. The revolt of the English nobility against the absolute power of the crown resulted in the Magna Charta in 1215, the establishment of parliament, and eventually the English "Bill of Rights" and the dominance of the protestant religion. The nobility attempted to establish a new tradition of justice free from the direct influence of sacred authority. This tradition was based on the concept

that free individuals could enter into a social contract form of government.

The Industrial Revolution in Europe brought changes in both the civil and common law traditions. The feudal system in which power was based upon the possession of land for agriculture was replaced by another in which money and the mercantile economy were the determining factors. The business class made increasing demands for freedom from authority. The American and French Revolutions in the latter eighteenth century led to the United States "Bill of Rights" and the French "Rights of Man" explicitly restricting government infringement on individual liberty.

The French Revolution emphasized the separation of government powers and a checks and balances system of justice. The power of the legislature was increased and judicial power was decreased. Prior to the Revolution the judiciary of France was seen as the tool of the monarchy in the enforcement of arbitrary law. The French Revolution reduced the power of the judges to that of clerks and gave the legislature the authority to decide issues of law. On the other hand, the American revolutionaries, though also supporting the checks and balances concept of government, saw the judge as an ally in gaining more freedom from the monarch. In the United States the Revolution increased the power of the judiciary and gave it almost absolute power to decide issues of law (Merryman, 1969).

After the American Revolution, the first formal written constitution was introduced, resulting from a Constitutional Convention composed of delegates selected from the various states. It set forth the structure of government, the duties and responsibilities of the various branches, a "Bill of Rights," and the process for amending the Constitution. The United States followed the English common law tradition with modifications. Each state within the federal system established a state constitution and enacted its own laws. This created a tension and struggle for dominance between centralized and decentralized authority. The Civil War, the 14th Amendment's guarantee of certain rights to all citizens, the 16th Amendment's legalization of the federal income tax, and demands emanating from the great depression of the 1930's helped tip the scales in favor of centralized federal authority.

Modern science has influenced the direction of law by modifying the free will and self-responsibility concepts of the civil and common law traditions. Under the classical philosophy all individuals were able to exercise self responsibility; no exceptions were made. The first exception to appear in law was for younger children who were not yet socialized in the expectations of the group and those older individuals classified as lunatics or insane by medical testimony. The modifications in the classical philosophy which accepted exceptions in exercising of free will were integrated into a reformulated "neo-classical" philosophy. As the knowledge of science increased, more exceptions were identified and introduced into law through the use of the hypothetical question. The scientists, doctors, or psychiatrists gave testimony on their professional opinion, and the court or jury determined whether an exception to the concept of free will would be made. The recognized exceptions appeared in code form and have become the basis for administrative commitments under specific circumstances; i.e., to specialized institutions, such as retardation colonies, mental hospitals, and hospitals for the criminally insane.

The rise of the under classes to power and the revolutions in the twentieth century, beginning with Russia, have introduced a third tradition of justice. This tradition is Socialist Law. Under this tradition, it is assumed that law corresponds to the needs and interests of the general public. The source of law is the will of the state, the sanctions lie with the coercive power of the state, and the nature of law is in a body of state rules. Communist assumptions and practices have become part of this tradition through Russian hegemony over much of Eastern Europe for more than half the twentieth century. Ironically, the goal of the Communists is the ultimate elimination of law in an Utopian society.

DEFINING LAW

Law as a concept has had many meanings during the course of history. Seen as a series of behavioral commands backed by government sanctions, it is a tool of social control. But it becomes ineffective without support from other important institutions of the culture.

Law can be written or unwritten. It can be based on a religious command, a command of a sovereign, a court decision, a legislative code, a constitution, or custom. The concept of law seems easy to define but difficult to understand. Law is like a puff of smoke in a tornado. Law can be just or unjust, fair or unfair. It can be discriminatory and favor one group or individual over another. It can bestow rights on a chosen few at the expense of the majority. For those who have power, law is what they say it is.

The subject matter of law is either public or private. Public law deals with the public generally and the state in its political or sovereign capacity. It can be divided into (a) constitutional law, (b) administrative law, (c) criminal law, (d) criminal procedures, and (e) the law of the state considered in its quasi private personality.

Private law covers law which is administered between individuals. It is concerned with the definition, regulation, and enforcement of rights in cases where both the person who has the right and the person who has the obligation are private individuals. Two major subdivisions of private law are (a) torts — breach of obligations imposed by society, including assault, libel and slander, fraud, and negligence, and (b) contracts — breach of obligations imposed by a private agreement, covering domestic relations, inheritance, sales of real and personal property, business organizations, agency, and negotiable instruments.

Law may also be divided into substantive law and adjective law categories. Substantive law is the law which creates rights and obligations.

Adjective law is the law of procedure which provides a method of enforcing and protecting the rights and obligations created by substantive law.

Philosophical Debates about Law

Philosophically, the debate on the issue, what is law, predates man's ability to write. The ancient concept of law centers around the belief that it comes from outside the group. God is usually the first of the outside law givers. He is believed to have communicated with a chosen person such as Hammurabi or Moses who, in turn, became God's spokesman within the group. The belief that law comes from outside the group is the basis for the natural law theories. These natural law theories which are based on the pre-existence of law give support to the possibility of a science of law. The task of the researcher becomes to discover the natural law that already exists. Discovery will reveal universal truths — or laws. These truths will then apply to all groups regardless of differences in culture.

The belief that law is man made rejects the theory of an outside law giver. Oliver Wendall Holmes, a Supreme Court Justice and American judicial realist, remarked that "law is what the courts do." Holmes saw justice rendered in the common law tradition where the judge has the power to make decisions of law. In the civil law tradition, where natural law theories predominate, judges must often defer to the legislature for clarification. This assumption that law is enacted or adopted by man himself and is the product of his own thinking is labeled legal positivism. Positivism, as a scientific movement, dates from Auguste Comte, the father of Sociology.

Lon Fuller (1940:4) identifies the major problem confronting those studying law to be choosing between the two competing directions of legal thought: legal positivism and natural law. These two polar positions, one assuming law is man made, the other giving credit to an outside source be it God, nature, or man's common denominator, have dominated jurisprudential speculation for

centuries. The two positions influence attitudes, definitions, and provide the frame of reference upon which a complete system of social control can be built. It is possible, however, to combine elements of both extreme positions and still have an effective system of law.

A definition common to both natural and positivist law would identify law as:

> "that which is laid down, ordained, or established. Law is a system of principles and rules of human conduct, being the aggregate of those commandments and principles which are either prescribed or recognized by the governing power in an organized jural society as its will in relation to the conduct of members of such society, and which it undertakes to maintain and sanction and to use as the criteria of the action of such members." (Black, 1933:1074)

Jural Postulates

Roscoe Pound, an early leader of the sociological approach to law, identified what he called jural postulates (or legal principles) that he felt provide the implicit guidelines for the operation of all legal systems regardless of their legal tradition. He wrote (1942: 113-115) that in civilized society people must be able to assume:

"1. ...that others will commit no intentional aggressions upon them.

2. ...that they may control for beneficial purposes what they have discovered and appropriated to their own use, what they have created by their own labor, and what they have acquired under the existing social and economic order.

3. ...that those with whom they deal in the general intercourse of society will act in good faith and hence

(a) will make good reasonable expectations which their promises or other conduct reasonably create;

(b) will carry out their undertakings according to the expectations which the moral sentiments of the community attaches thereto;

(c) will restore specifically or by equivalent what comes to them by mistake or unanticipated or not fully intended situation whereby they receive at another's expense what they could not reasonably have expected to receive under the circumstances.

4. ...that those who are engaged in some course of conduct will act with due care not to cast an unreasonable risk of injury upon others.

5. ...that those who maintain things likely to get out of hand or to escape and do damage will restrain them to keep them within their proper bounds." (1942:113-115)

Pound's framework saw law functioning to resolve societal conflicts and saw legal systems never free from the influences of the social pressures within society. Similarly, the legal results or adjudications produced by legal systems had consequences beyond their immediate audiences in the larger society.

The reduction of interpersonal conflict and the promotion of physical security are common justifications for law. Over 150 years ago Alexis de Tocqueville (1973 translation) in his commentary, *Democracy in America*, noted that scarcely "any political question arises in the United States that is not resolved, sooner or later, into a judicial question." Yet law has its limitations. Law cannot guarantee conformity by itself. It must have the support of the various institutions which are responsible for socializing or educating the individual. Some of these institutions are: the home, the church, the school, the work group, the government in general. Law cannot easily control behavior if the individual does not want to be controlled. Law supplies the authority which may justify coercive action directed at the correction or punishment of a person when other persuasive methods fail.

DEVELOPING THE AMERICAN MODEL OF CONSTITUTIONAL LAW

The period after the American Revolution was characterized by the development of key components of our federal legal system. The Constitution was established as a restraint on government and a symbol of the American commitment to the rule of law over personal privilege. At the same time the legal profession and the judiciary emerged as essential and powerful elements in the United States' legal model.

Establishment of the American Constitution

In a general sense a constitution is a set of fundamental rules governing the affairs of an organized group. A government, church organization, business arrangement, campus fraternity or sorority, or a social club may operate under the provisions set forth in a formal written document identified as a "constitution." Not all rules dealing with an organization will be found in its constitution. A government such as the United States has acts of Congress; state governments have statutes. A church, campus, business, or social organization will have by-laws.

The major objective of a constitution is to place limits on the governing authority. According to Fritz Kern (1956), the basis for limiting governing authority has its roots in the Middle Ages. During this period the medieval monarch was bound by the law because of three traditions. The first of these traditions, Germanic custom, grew from the practice of electing tribal leaders. Once elected, the leader had to satisfy the members of the tribe. Resistance was the basic method of controlling the leaders. If enough members of the tribe were resistant to the leader's authority, a new leader was elected to replace the ineffective one.

The second tradition came from the codification of the canon law. Church fathers interpreted

105

the moral imperatives of the law of nature. They determined that law was not left to the monarch's pleasure but that the law was absorbed into the monarch's will from the outside. All monarchs had to conform to the natural law and do what was "right" because it was God's command.

The third tradition originated with the Christian idea that every ruler is God's vicar and instrument of action. In this tradition the monarch was not above but below the law. The coronation ceremony became an ecclesiastical consecration of the new ruler. The King or Queen took an oath to God acknowledging subservience and gained in exchange a supernatural sanction for sovereign authority. These three traditions supported the idea that the supreme law stands over all, even over the monarch. The social control theorists linked the idea of a supreme law to the notion control of the governing authority eventually could be by the consent of the governed.

Constitutions have come into existence by several methods. Some have been the result of evolution such as the so-called unwritten constitution of the British. Others have resulted because of royal grant. If the monarch system of government was in control, the king or queen could compromise by consenting to demands and thereby reduce the possibility of rebellion. A good example of the royal grant concept is the Magna Charta.

Students familiar with United States history will recognize that a third method of developing a constitution is through the use of constitutional conventions. The United States Constitution was written by the Philadelphia Convention of 1787. Constitutional conventions usually produce a written constitution while the other two methods usually add to the collection of documents and practices referred to as an unwritten constitution.

All state constitutions in the United States show a similarity in written form and borrow from elements in the federal constitution just as it drew on parts of the English "Bill of Rights" and Magna Charta. Each state sets forth its government organization which usually follows the federal organization and separation of powers pattern. Each state constitution has a description for amending the original document. Finally, each state constitution has a "Bill of Rights" similar to that found in the United States Constitution. Yet, as Lawrence Friedman (1984:183) points out in his analysis, the state constitutions "are significant documents in their own right." They are the product of unique histories and often contain provisions without a federal counterpart. From the beginning of our country most of the law with which a citizen has had to be concerned was state law.

As mentioned previously, constitutions are either written or unwritten. The United States Constitution is a single document and frequently cited as an example of a written constitution. Great Britain operates under an unwritten constitution which is composed of a number of historical documents, all acts of Parliament, elements of the common law, and certain governmental customs which cover the subject of constitutional law.

When the subject of constitutional law is considered, even in the United States, one single document does not include the total field of legal research into its meaning. The United States Constitution, as adopted by unanimous consent at the Constitutional Convention on September 17, 1787, consists of seven articles. The first ten amendments were ratified by eleven of the original states by December 15, 1791, and made part of the Constitution. Since that date only seventeen additional amendments have been ratified by the states and made a part of the constitution.

In drawing up the constitution, the delegates to the Constitutional Convention had in mind certain principles that they deemed essential to a well ordered government. Those basic principles are:

1. The United States Constitution as the supreme written law.

2. Supreme power to reside in the people.

3. A federal government of delegated powers.

106

4. The separation of power into three branches: the legislative, the executive, and the judiciary.

5. The supremacy of the courts in interpreting the Constitution.

6. Certain natural rights to be guaranteed to all people.

The separation of power into three parts gives the legislature, the executive, and the judiciary each a law making, or law influencing power. The role of the judiciary deciding "case law" and the legislature enacting statutes fluctuated with regard to dominance in the early development of American law.

Three Stages of American Legal Development

American legal history has moved through three stages of development. The first stage of this development was from 1800 (the forming of the federal government under the Constitution) to the Civil War, 1861-1865. The second stage was from the Civil War and the Reconstruction to World War I. The last stage takes us from World War I to the present. Various authorities (Gilmore, 1977) have identified the stages as the Age of Discovery (before the Civil War), the Age of Faith (from the Civil War to World War I), and the Age of Anxiety (from World War I to the present).

Dominance of the judge is apparent during the frontier period prior to the Civil War — the judges created the legal system. The revolutionary trauma had instilled in many Americans a hatred of England and all its ways. This state of mind lasted through the events which culminated in the War of 1812 and remained for a generation after it might have otherwise disappeared. The prevalent Anglophobia led to statutes applicable in some jurisdictions which prohibited the use of English legal materials in court proceedings.

There were very few law books during this period. Perhaps Blackstone's *Commentaries on the*

Common Law or Kent's *Commentaries on American Law* had made their appearance to some, but most judges were not well versed on the "law." They used "good old common sense" in decisions, not unlike the judges of the old Anglo-Saxon communal courts and the royal judges established under the reign of the Norman King, Henry II. Very few court decisions were printed. There was no systematic method available for retrieving the case law then in existence. Judges were free to create a legal system and decide cases without restrictions. Lawyers had little or no formal education. Law education was on a personal basis. A good example was Abraham Lincoln who read a few books on law and then went into practice, first with an existing attorney. Lawyers had to rely on personal ability with little legal research. Jeremy Bentham in England and Justice William Story in the United States were reformers during this period advocating the codification of law.

By 1820 a substantial amount of American legal materials had accumulated. The decisions of American courts, state and federal, were being published. Books on American law were beginning to appear as well as American republication of English books and case collections (with added local annotations). There was an indigenous base of American law which had not existed a generation earlier. From the 1820's until the Civil War, American lawyers lived with the idea that the common law not only could be but probably would be codified. The general principles which were the basis of the hundreds and thousands of cases would be set out in a connected series of reasoned propositions. This readiness not to be tied to a single common law tradition or civil law (code law) tradition exemplified the extra-ordinary flexibility — the open-endedness — which became characteristic of American law during this period.

After 1800 the principal characteristics of American law had been its chaotic diversity, its sensitivity to changing conditions, its fluidity, and its pluralism. Until the Civil War the legislatures, state and federal, did very little; judges, by default, took over the task of answering the questions which someone had to answer. After the Civil War the legislatures became more active, and the first major administrative agencies were set up toward the end of the nineteenth century. It was also during the post-Civil War period that the legal truism emerged that "courts never legislate, that the judicial function is merely to declare the law that already exists." This truism became an article of faith for lawyers.

The pace of technological progress slowed during the Age of Faith period. Anyone born in 1800 who lived until 1860 experienced the shock of technological change. Anyone born in 1850 who lived until 1910 experienced relatively little change except for the addition of a few amenities like central heating and indoor plumbing. While many of the inventions which have unsettled our own lives occurred in this period, they did not have their impact until much later. Rapid technological change unsettles the law quite as much as it unsettles people. The slow pace of change during the half century after the Civil War contributed to the illusion that a stable body of law was not only a theoretical possibility but an accomplished fact.

The post-Civil War judicial product seemed to start from the assumption that the law is a closed, logical system. Judges, it was said, did not make law but merely declared law that in some Platonic sense already existed. The judicial function had nothing to do with the adaptation of rules to changing conditions; it was restricted to the discovery of what the true rules were and indeed always had been. Past error can be exposed, and in that way minor corrections can be made; but the truth, once arrived at, is unchangeable and eternal. Change can only be legislative, and even legislative change will be treated with a wary distrust. A statute in derogation of the common law would be strictly construed even if it could not be set aside on constitutional grounds as beyond the power of the legislature to enact.

The post-Civil War period saw the emergence of large-scale business enterprises, along with the vast fortunes which they generated. The historic bias in favor of the least possible government intervention and the belief that the best government is that which governs least had an obvious

appeal to the movers and shapers of our economy. The masters of the new wealth were left free in the name of competition to do their own thing in their own way based on the economic theory that the relentless pursuit of private gain was the best way of serving the public interest. Not surprisingly, an adversarial justice system developed along the same lines. Litigants with a personal stake in the outcome going all out to win their case would provide a court the arguments with which to reach the best result. The precedents provided by the rules pronounced in these individually self-interested decisions would further the public interest.

During this period of time legal education became formal and law schools appeared. Professional teachers of law wrote "case law books" to use as textbooks. The authors of these textbooks used them to teach the correct law and rejected the great majority of case law as useless and not worthy of further consideration in their opinion. The ever present symbiotic relationship in society between the academic establishment and the political/economic establishment was particularly strong at this time of institutional growth in both realms.

The Age of Anxiety, as Gilmore calls it, began with World War I and extends to the present day. World War I established the United States as a world power. During this period rural living and agriculture gave way to urbanization and industrial employment. Technology developed at a rapid pace with the automobile, airplane, radio/television, and computer becoming commonplace. There was even more emphasis on the competition to be bigger, to be best, to be first.

The great depression of the 1930's introduced "Big Government" as we know it with massive bureaucratic organizations administering executive policy. The legislature, the courts, and the executive were all required to make decisions in an unprecedented volume. Laws, case decisions, and administrative rules expanded at an ever increasing rate. The emphasis in law was to be current and up-to-date. Advance sheets, pocket parts, and other fast reference services became common place. The computer as a research tool for fast service became a reality. The paralegal was introduced into office practice to increase the efficiency of the lawyer. Continuing legal education was mandated in many states as a means of keeping licensed attorneys up-to-date. The life-long law license of past generations no longer exists in some states where it must be renewed on an annual basis.

Following World War I the study of law changed, too. As the social sciences focused on law, the behavioralist movement within the social sciences emphasized the difference between law on the books and in reported cases with the law as it operates in practice. The United States Constitution had expressed the assumption that law would operate above any individual aspiration in the "supremacy clause" of Article VI: "This Constitution, and the laws of the United States which shall be made in pursuance thereof...shall be the supreme law of the land..." Equal justice for all was the national promise as the "society of laws not men" concept rejected putting absolute powers in the hands of individual rulers. Numerous studies in the twentieth century, however, revealed law not to be neutral in its applications or consequences. United States law is not the product of nor does it serve the interests of an absolute ruler. But the reality of discretion exercised by individual personalities in the legal system prevents law from being in fact wholly rational and morally neutral. Academicians confirmed what many citizens already knew — the law is as much the product of the choices made by those charged with its enforcement as it is the product of formal courts and legislatures.

CHANGING LAW

Law is slow to change. When the purpose behind a particular law ceases to exist, the obsolete law can still survive. Departures from law force a constant re-evaluation of the system. It is the responsibility of the judiciary, the legislature, and the executive branches of government to facilitate change in the law in order to resolve conflict.

Charles A. Miller (1969) has identified certain values which influence the decision making process about law within a society regardless of what unit of government is making the decision. These values are: social philosophy, the role of government, the roles of the various branches of government, law and order, and stability and change.

Social Philosophy. Attitudes toward the organization and functioning of the economy, the rights of individuals, and their roles in society determine a society's social philosophy. The emphasis a society elects to place on the issue of public vs. private rights will have a direct bearing on law. If free enterprise, private property ownership, and private business expansions are emphasized, the rights of individuals may be given a low priority, and the roles they will be expected to perform will be in support of business expansion. The individual will be primarily a working person dependent on a job for survival. On the other hand, a society that places a higher value on personal freedom will sacrifice private business expansion. It may organize the economy with more public control of property and make the survival of the individual more a responsibility of government.

The Role of Government. The role government plays in a society depends on political control and the ideology of those in power. The types of acts passed by the legislature and then signed into law by the executive for subsequent enforcement are directly related to the political philosophy of those in power. Historically the two major political parties in the United States, the Republicans and the Democrats, have debated not only specific policies but also the role of government. The Republicans usually profess the laissez faire philosophy that "the government that governs least governs best." The Democrats have generally supported active government intervention to promote social goals and reduce the power of private property ownership.

The Roles of the Various Branches of Government. The roles of the various branches of government cannot be separated from political philosophy. Even in a society where the "checks and balances" concept of the separation of powers is followed, the government will be expected to accomplish important goals and objectives which require cooperation between the branches. The chief executive will suggest laws he deems necessary; the legislature will enact laws based upon those suggestions; and the courts will facilitate the accomplishment of the objectives set forth by those laws. In times of national crisis the chief executive has authority to assume extraordinary power. Even at other times the legislative branch will regularly delegate rule making and adjudicatory functions to administrative agencies in order to achieve governmental policy goals.

Law and Order. The political value of law and order affects the law. Government acts with greater unanimity during times of crisis. An especially brutal crime can revive interest in the death penalty. An assassination of a much loved political leader can stimulate demand for gun control. The shocking experience of seeing middle-class youth arrested and convicted in large numbers for drug violations can be the basis for repeal or modification of the laws dealing with the use of narcotics. During times of domestic tranquility, interest often shifts to the rights of the accused. Reforms in the correctional system are advanced during that period. A general interest in rehabilitation and treatment predominates; control of police enforcement activity may occupy the courts and legislators' attention. During periods of strife and increased crime, emphasis shifts to the victim. Demands for strict enforcement of the law and punishment to the criminal dominates. Legislation and court decisions will increase the latitude given police in combating crime and increase the sentences given offenders.

Stability and Change. The prevailing attitude toward stability and change has a direct effect on law. If change is desired, laws which will bring change will appear. The shift in the procedure followed in the United States in regard to eminent domain is an example. In the past the law made it a requirement of the government to show necessity for public use and to commence the legal action to take private property for only public use. Urban renewal legislation has shifted responsibility for starting court action to the property owner. A property is subject to eminent domain because urban planners have determined that it has depreciated in value and could be put to better uses. The government, by law, offers the owner a sum of money for his property. If the owner resists, he must start the court action.

Judicial Interpretation of the Law

The judges in a common law country such as the United States influence the laws by their power of interpretation even though the legislature may have the formal responsibility for passing laws. Not having this legislative law-making authority, a court must passively wait for issues to be brought to it by contesting litigants. Once before the court, however, a judge's ruling on a legal issue establishes the last word on it. The judge's decision establishes what is called "case law."

Judicial power in the United States was enhanced by the ruling of Chief Justice John Marshall in the famous case of *Marbury v. Madison* in 1803. This decision, holding that the Court had the power to declare an act of Congress unconstitutional, established a doctrine of judicial review and supremacy that made the United States Supreme Court unique in the world. The Court's power in the twentieth century has been further enhanced by the interpretation given the 14th Amendment. By this Amendment, passed after the Civil War, many provisions of the Bill of Rights have been held to be restraints not only on the national executive but on state governments as well.

The basic principles set forth in the United States Constitution are in words that are vague and convey several meanings. It is this vagueness and the intent of the original delegates to the Constitutional Convention which have resulted in many court decisions interpreting the Constitution. Articles and textbooks have been written attempting to clarify the meaning of the original document. The Court itself has been labeled "activist" when it appears to disregard old precedents or interpretations in light of changing conditions and "strict constructionist" when it appears resolute in leaving all changes to the legislative branch.

Legislative Policy Making

The United States Congress and the various states have the same general legislative procedures. The legislative body is bicameral (except for Nebraska with a unicameral system), divided into two houses, a senate and "lower" house. In the states both houses now are divided into districts based on near or equal populations, though the lower house has the larger number of districts. The representation in the United States Senate is based on two senators for every state.

The drafting of a bill is a highly technical job which requires thorough knowledge of the constitution, statutes, government, and the rules of the legislature. Often a bill passes through many drafts before it is introduced. Laws begin as bills and must pass both houses of the legislature and be approved by the executive. Bills can be introduced only by members of the legislature, but relatively few bills really originate with the members. Some of the most important bills are administration measures sponsored by the executive. Some are departmental bills originating with administrative agencies. Many other bills originate at other levels of government such as county boards or city councils. A great number come from organizations such as the League of Municipalities, the Isaak Walton League, a State Federation of Labor, State Conference of Social Work, and other interest groups or PACs (political action committees). Constituents, of course, are important sources for bills for a legislator.

Of central importance to the legislative process is its committee system. In the states any citizen can have a voice in the matters before the legislature by appearing at committee hearings or writing to various representatives to express their opinions. In committee, staff and elected officials can work less formally and less visibly to produce proposals responsive to a myriad of interests. Many legal proposals die in committee.

Each legislative body has a formal procedure for considering bills for passage. If a bill is successful and passes in the legislative body, it is sent to the chief executive for consideration. The chief executive, be he the president or governor of a state, may sign the bill into law or reject it by veto. A bill which has been vetoed is returned to the legislative body for further action. If sufficient legislators (usually two-thirds) feel the bill should be law, they can override the chief executive's veto; if not the bill dies. Some jurisdictions permit the chief executive to ignore the bill and permit it to become law without his signature. Statutes are usually effective only when signed and enrolled; they are referred to as written law or "black letter law."

Presidential Authority to Influence Law

An indirect but important effect the President of the United States has on law is through the power to appoint, with the advice and consent of the Senate, all federal judges, including members of the Supreme Court. When a vacancy occurs in the federal court system the President does not have to appoint an unbiased individual. Appointments to the United States Supreme Court usually have gone to people who substantially support the President's philosophy on certain issues. Once on the bench, the judge or justice is free from political control since the federal appointment is for life; removal can be only by impeachment.

Presidents can directly determine the meaning and effect of law through the exercise of many traditionally recognized constitutional powers. As the chief executive of one of the largest bureaucracies in the world, a president can influence the exercise of bureaucratic discretion by his appointment of agency heads and other staff. A president by law may issue proclamations and executive orders with the force of law; these are published in the *Federal Register* along with federal agency promulgations. Presidents negotiate treaties that constitutionally have the same effect as law. As commander-in-chief of the military and charged with maintaining domestic tranquility, many presidents have by-passed existing law in times of national emergency. Finally, as mentioned previously, much of the legislation considered by Congress will in fact have been proposed by the President or an executive agency.

The governors of the various states and the mayors of the cities possess in different forms many of the same prerogatives held by the President. For example the governor of a state can declare a state of emergency and order the state guard into an area to enforce order. A mayor of a city can invoke a curfew during a crisis. Both the governor and the mayor make suggestions to their legislative bodies and both are policy makers for their administrative organizations.

Law is seldom static and frequently changes. With every change some group or interest gains rights and privileges while others lose rights and may acquire added responsibilities. The law surrounds, guides, restricts, and, if necessary, punishes from birth to death.

The system which the United States has developed under the Constitution is a hybrid method of promulgating laws. Law-influencing power can be found in the three branches of government. The finished product, if law is ever a finished product, is the result of an evolutionary process. The courts use the Constitution to control the legislature and chief executive. The chief executive exercises discretion as to how, when, and where the laws are to be employed. The legislature can redraft, clarify, and change laws if the courts and chief executive range too far afield. Moreover, the impetus for some changes in law comes from a shift in public opinion, propaganda, or other external forces grounded in people not part of government.

FINDING LAW

Law can be found in a variety of repositories such as judicial decision, law texts, statute books, legal encyclopedias, administrative decisions, digests, treaties, legal periodicals, municipal rules, constitutions, and the minds of the people. However, legal research as we know it was made possible by the West Publishing Company's development of the National Reporter System in the late 1800's. For the first time all the decisions, not only of the federal appellate courts but of all the state courts, were accessible to lawyers throughout the country.

As the law business developed in the 1800's there was money to be made in writing law books, and a professional class of law-book writers emerged. One year a book on negotiable instruments might be published, a book on corporations the next year, and a book on insurance the year after that. Often the books were conceived as manuals for practicing lawyers and judges and consisted mostly of uncritical collections of case digests. Many of these publications became the stock and trade of the working bar. West Publishing Company and several major firms that followed built on the commercial success of these early efforts. They catered to the needs of the market and designed their books to be usable and often cross-referred them to other books so that practitioners would find it expedient to purchase all different kinds of books from the same company.

Successful legal research requires no magic, only common sense and a little background knowledge. In order to do successful legal research a student needs to know the basic types of legal reference books and how they are used or how they have been designed by the publisher to facilitate their use. Most legal research projects require three basic steps: locating a source that will provide the needed information, extracting the information in understandable form, and checking to insure the information is current. In discussing these steps below, we will survey the basic types of books one is likely to need or encounter as one seeks answers to legal questions.

STEP ONE: Using a Law Finder. Law finders are parts of books, devices, or full services that direct you to the place where your answer is found. The most used law finders are:

Classification Schemes — Most legal publications have a table of contents or other classification scheme identified for the book. This is usually found at the front of the publication and will give the searcher a quick reference to the page where the major data or subject matter of the publication can be found.

Indexes — In searching for the answer to any given problem, one usually starts with some index book. The most popularly used such books are the legal encyclopedias and indexes of digested cases, both of which are organized by subjects and within those subjects by extensive topic outlines. Legal encyclopedias and case digests exist for federal law as well as the law of many individual states.

Tables — When one knows the name of a relevant case, it can be used to locate other cases or the topic references to the same points of law discussed in that case. Tables of cases are organized by the name of the case (plaintiff v. defendant), but many book series also provide a reverse table (defendant v. plaintiff) for the instances the name may not have been remembered correctly or have been remembered by only one name. The name of the case may have been obtained from a textbook, encyclopedia, annotation, or other published source. Many law books have table of cases sections or volumes that will provide you the full citation of the case and the topic numbers assigned by various editors to the points of law abstracted from it. These topics and numbers are often used by publishers throughout their entire collection of books enabling researchers to locate other potentially relevant decisions under the same topic and number in another of a publisher's series, for example, going from a federal digest to a state digest.

Digests — The American Digest System comprises over 500 topics similar to those encountered in the encyclopedias. Each digest is subdivided into as many subtopics as are necessary to cover the points of law arising under that subject. Numbers are assigned to each specific subtopic. The topic name, together with the number, constitutes a reference to a particular point of law within the topic outline. Holdings and significant dicta from almost every decided appellate case are abstracted and published in digests under the appropriate topic and number. The ''Key-Number'' term along with a symbol in the form of a small key is the copyrighted device used this way in the American Digest System and most of West Publishing Company's other books.

Citators — When one wants to know a decided case's subsequent history and what other cases or collateral references have cited it, one turns to a ''citator.'' The authoritative citator system in America was developed by the Frank Shepard Company in publications popularly known as ''Shepard's Citations.'' Organized by legislative unit or court reporter, citators exist for the citations to statutes as well as cases. The use of this service permits a quick and accurate index for checking every case one might find in a code, digest, encyclopedia, textbook, or other legal work.

Cross References — Many publishers in addition to providing the natural cross reference possibilities created by their topic and numbering systems will provide explicit editorial information and directions to related information.

Words and Phrases — Since many legal problems turn on the meaning of a legally significant word or phrase, researchers frequently seek judicial decisions which have interpreted, construed, or defined such words or phrases. In addition to a multi-volume digest organized solely along these lines, many case digests and other references provide among their index volumes a words and phrases index. Similarly, some statutory collections have a table allowing one to find an enactment by its popular name.

STEP TWO: Going to the Law. The source which contains the statement of law for which you are searching may not always be the one you anticipated. The statement may be in a case, a statute, a regulation, or a ruling of an administrative agency. The statement may be a primary or secondary authority, but the point is that it states what the law is on your subject. Among the most commonly used sources are:

Statutes (Annotated and Unannotated) — Enactments of legislatures are compiled chronologically and published in bound form at the end of each session or term. However, an updated, ''official'' code containing all the existing statutes in force is published by or at the direction of each state and the federal government. ''Unofficial'' versions of these codes are published by private publishers with "annotations" which means they will have many helping features beyond the text of the statute itself — such as cross references, case notes, commentaries, or summaries. These unofficial versions are the most usable, but formal research and legal presentations may require citation to the official statutory source.

Case Reporters — Appellate court opinions are compiled chronologically and published for every state system and the federal appellate courts. Starting in 1879, the West Publishing Company began to publish the decisions of the various federal and state courts as they were rendered. These publications duplicated the official reports of the United States courts and those of the various states. West's National Reporter System, also, collects the case reports of the states in regional reporters (Northeastern, Atlantic, Southwestern, Southern, Northwestern, Southwestern, and Pacific). In recent years many government units have adopted the West publications as their official reporters. There are three long-published sources for United States Supreme Court cases: *The United States Reports* (the official reporter), *The Supreme Court Reporter* (the West publication), and *United States Reports, Lawyers' Edition* (originally published by the Lawyers' Co-op Publishing Company).

American Law Reports — Another type of case reporter developed by the Lawyers' Co-op Publishing Company takes a selective, subject approach. Drawing from litigation throughout the country, it contains only cases which are unique either from the facts involved or because of a controversial rule of law in issue. With each of the major cases reported the editors provide numerous annotations and a detailed treatise on the legal point involved. The *American Law Reports* and its companion publications are organized with a digest and subject numbering system similar in format to that used in the West books.

Encyclopedias — An encyclopedia of law is a publication which serves two purposes. First, it is a book in which legal topics are discussed in narratives that attempt to synthesize the relevant statutory and case law. Second, it is a book which in

footnotes or annotations cites the primary authority from which the conclusions in the narrative have been drawn. Because of its narrative format, encyclopedias are often easier to use for those new to legal research than the more unique publications. Two major national encyclopedias of law exist: *Corpus Juris Secundum* and *American Jurisprudence*. Some of the larger states, New York for example, have encyclopedias devoted solely to their law.

Restatements — A series of scholarly efforts in the field of legal commentary has found expression in various restatements of law published over the years by the American Law Institute, an organization founded in 1923. Works on such topics as criminal law, contracts, agency, conflict of laws, and torts have been cited by many courts. Rules of law are set out with extensive comments and illustrations drawn from discussions by the country's foremost scholars on the particular topic. Case citations are omitted, but in some cases committees from each state have published annotations for their respective states.

Articles and Textbooks — Most law schools publish law reviews composed of articles written by outstanding legal scholars that focus on current legal topics of interest to the legal community. Bar Associations also generally sponsor regular publication of a journal with articles and news of interest to its lawyer members. These periodicals are similar in format and diversity to scholarly journals in other professional and academic fields. Textbooks covering the range of subjects currently taught in law school may provide edited case reports, articles, explanations, and statutory material relevant to particular legal issues.

STEP THREE: Checking the Latest Law. As new statutes and cases are passed and decided, it becomes important in doing legal research to be sure the authoritative statement of law one has found is the latest word on the subject. When an item of legal information becomes available, it is the goal of publishers to convey it to the legal profession as soon as possible. To discharge this responsibility, publishers have devised various ways to keep their publications up-to-date and to assure researchers that they have the latest word. Typical supplements and services provided for this purpose are:

Advance Sheets and Slip Opinions — As courts and legislatures decide cases and enact legislation, each opinion and bill is printed. Variously called advance sheets, slip opinions, or slip laws, they may be ordered directly from a government printing office or provided to libraries or professionals as part of some existing publication or service. The slip laws of the United States Congress are accumulated chronologically into a permanent bound form at the end of each session as volumes of the *Statutes at Large.*

Pocket Parts and Bound Supplements — The two most common forms of updating are paper pamphlet supplementation such as that used with case reporters and pocket parts as used with legislative codes. Most law books, given the time necessary to produce them, are out-of-date in one respect or another at the time of publication, and it would be cost prohibitive to the publisher and customer to have to print new books just to include a few new cases, statutes, or editorial comments. Many books are kept current by periodically (usually yearly) printing the new material in an insert to be placed in a "kangaroo" pouch located on the inside of the back cover of the original publication. As these inserts increase in size they may be replaced by a paper bound supplement included next to the original volume. With case reporters, as a number of cases are decided they are published in paper bound pamphlets which are discarded when the permanent bound volumes are finally produced.

Loose Leaf Services — The loose leaf publications are a rapid form of updating used in several complex and rapidly changing areas of the law. Loose leaf pages inserted into ring or post binders can be updated at frequent intervals — monthly, biweekly, weekly, or even more often. The updating can be either cumulative, with pages added consecutively, or inter-paginated, with new pages replacing old ones at scattered points. Noted loose leaf services exist for taxation law, commercial law, administrative law, and constitutional law.

✳ ✳ ✳ ✳ ✳

REFERENCES

Black, Henry Campbell
    1933   *Black's Law Dictionary.* St. Paul, MN: West Publishing Company.
Friedman, Lawrence M.
    1984   *American Law.* New York, NY: W.W. Norton & Company, Inc.
Fuller, Lon L.
    1940   *The Law in Quest of Itself.* Boston, MA: Beacon Press.
Gilmore, Grant
    1977   *The Ages of American Law.* New Haven, CT: Yale University Press.
Holmes, Oliver Wendall
    1881   *The Common Law.* Boston, MA: Little Brown.
Kern, Fritz
    1956   *Kinship and Law in the Middle Ages.* New York, NY: Harper and Row Publishers.
Merryman, John H.
    1969   *The Civil Law Tradition.* Palo Alto, CA: Stanford University Press.

Miller, Charles A.
    1969   *The Supreme Court and the Uses of History*. New York, NY: Simon and Schuster,
             Clarion Books.
Pound, Roscoe
    1942   *Social Control Through Law*. New Haven, CT: Yale University Press.
de Tocqueville, Alexis
    1973   *Democracy in America, Volume I*. Translated by Henry Reeve, Francis Bowen, and
             Phillips Bradley, original copyright, 1945. New York, NY: Alfred A. Knopf, Inc.

Chapter

The Judiciary:
The Arbitration of Conflict

By

Rolando V. del Carmen and **Michael R. Smith**

This chapter addresses the formal and public resolution of conflict in current American society. For legal purposes, formal conflict may be classified into civil and criminal. Civil conflict exists primarily between private persons who fail to come to terms on an issue and therefore need the influence and power of the state to help resolve the dispute. Criminal conflict aligns the state on one side as the offended party seeking to assert authority over an erring individual who has run afoul of the law. The state seeks justice in the interest of society; law must prevail, otherwise society disintegrates. In reality, the victim of the crime loses and suffers much more than the state does in a criminal act, but the days of private retribution have given way to institutionalized justice; hence the state undertakes the role of an offended party seeking to redress the wrong.

The discussion in this chapter is limited to criminal cases. It looks at the criminal justice system, then characterizes the main participants in conflict arbitration, namely: judges, prosecutors, and defense lawyers. Central to the American system of justice is respect by public officials for the basic constitutional rights of the accused. The most significant rights are therefore discussed, followed by a description and evaluation of controversial practices in conflict arbitration. The discussion has a legal orientation because law, more than anything, provides direction and limits to the process of conflict resolution.

Every society has ways and methods of settling disputes. In less developed human settings, disputes are settled informally through the intervention of the family, the clan, or the tribe. In modern societies, conflict resolution is much more formalized — with codified rules passed by the legislature or drafted by the judiciary governing structures and procedures. In the United States, disputes are formally resolved by and in the courts, or in some cases, by alternative dispute resolution forums that operate on a more informal level.

The criminal justice system is composed of three subsystems: police, courts, and corrections. The police apprehend criminals and prevent crime; courts determine guilt or innocence; and the corrections subsystem isolates, exacts vengeance, deters, or rehabilitates. Although the three subsystems interact with each other as equals, the courts in reality predominate over police and corrections, primarily because they are the interpreters of constitutional provisions and laws under which all subsystems must function. They are therefore in a position to tell the two other subsystems what they can or cannot do. Consequently, the courts occupy the apex of the criminal justice system triangle. Their edicts and pronouncements filter down by means of court decisions handed down in actual conflict.

Courts perform various functions in American society. They resolve disagreements among members of the community in civil cases and enforce penal laws in criminal cases.[1] In the course of deciding cases, courts inevitably make social policies which affect individuals and determine the future of society. The higher the court, the greater its potential for policymaking. Most of the decisions of the United States Supreme Court in fact set national policies. Many current governmental policies emanate from judicial decisions, such as the policies on civil rights, education, abortion, rights of the accused, and treatment of prisoners. Judicial policymaking intrudes into legislative and executive domains, but it is accepted as the natural consequence of conflict adjudication in a society where the main policymaking branches are sometimes merely reactive and often unwieldy.

American courts also perform a slightly different form of conflict resolution — that of judicial review. This means that courts can declare any law passed by the legislature, or any act of an executive official unconstitutional and thus void and unenforceable.[2] Although the power of judicial review is not explicitly granted in the United States Constitution, its existence has been acknowledged for decades as part of the American scheme of government.[3] Despite the appearance of omnipotence resulting from the doctrine of judicial review, the judiciary is perhaps the most vulnerable branch of government. It is bereft of political power and completely dependent on the legislative and executive branches for financial resources. To ensure that the judiciary performs its functions without fear or favor, federal judges enjoy a high degree of independence. They hold tenure for life and their salaries cannot be diminished while in office. State court judges are much less protected, although they, too, enjoy a good measure of autonomy, power, and independence.

Criminal justice adjudication has aptly been categorized into *Crime Control and Due Process models*.[4] The Crime Control model produces a high rate of apprehension and conviction, oftentimes at the expense of individual rights. It is analogized to an assembly line conveyor belt, down which moves an endless stream of cases, never stopping, carrying the cases to workers who stand at fixed stations. Its emphasis is on speed and finality. In contrast, the Due Process model looks like an obstacle course. Each of its successive stages is designed to present formidable impediments to carrying the accused any further along in the process. Due Process is founded on an insistence on formal adjudicative, adversary fact-finding processes in which the case against the accused is publicly heard by an impartial tribunal and is evaluated only after the accused has had a full opportunity to discredit the case against him.[5]

Both models, though at odds with each other, are at work in the criminal justice system. While the American ideal proclaims adherence to the Due Process model, reality often falls far short of that goal and frequently lapses into a Crime Control mode. Limited resources and strong local sentiments oftentimes dictate the use of the more efficient Crime Control model, particularly when it best satisfies the public's perception of justice.

The United States adheres to the adversary system in the search for justice. This means that courts play a neutral role in the conflict among individuals and between individuals and the state. The system is based on the "fight theory" which postulates that parties-litigant in a lawsuit clash in courtroom combat — with the judge playing the role of an arbiter who makes sure that both protagonists play by the rules. Truth is supposed to emerge from the ashes and ruins of this courtroom struggle. The reality is often a mere shadow of the ideal; nonetheless, the process goes on and the myth continues.

In criminal cases, the state is represented by the prosecutor, while the accused's interests are championed by the defense lawyer. The judge or jury determines the facts from the welter of usually conflicting testimony; such determination having the ring of finality because appellate courts rarely disturb findings of fact by the lower court on appeal. Even in jury trials, the judge plays a crucial role in resolving the myriad of technical disputes that arise between the parties in the course of the proceedings.

THE PROCESS OF ADJUDICATION [6]

In general, the criminal process can be divided into three basic stages: procedure prior to trial, procedure during trial, and procedure after trial.

A. *Procedure Prior to Trial*

1. **Filing of a Complaint**: A *complaint* is a charge made before a proper officer alleging the commission of a criminal offense. It may be filed by the offended party or by a police officer who has obtained information about or witnessed the criminal act. The complaint serves as the basis for issuing an arrest warrant, Where the accused has been arrested without warrant, the complaint is prepared and filed, usually by the arresting officer, at the defendant's initial appearance before the magistrate.

2. **Arrest**: There are two kinds of arrest, namely: arrest with a warrant and arrest without a warrant. In arrest with a warrant, a complaint is filed and presented to the magistrate, who reads it and finds probable cause to justify the issuance of an arrest warrant. In contrast, arrest without a warrant usually occurs when a crime is committed in the presence of a police officer or if a state statute permits a warrantless arrest under the circumstances. In some instances, police may issue a citation or summons (a written notice to appear) rather than make a custodial arrest for less serious offenses. If the person fails or refuses to appear in court as scheduled, an arrest warrant is then issued.

3. **"Booking" at Police Station**: This usually involves filling out the appropriate paperwork and making an entry into a computer that details the identity of the person and the offense for which the person was arrested. If the offense is a serious one, the suspect may also be photographed or fingerprinted.

4. **Appearance Before Magistrate after Arrest**: In some states, this is known as an "initial appearance," "presentment," or

119

"arraignment on the warrant." In most states, statutes or court rules require that an arrested person be brought before a judge, magistrate, or commissioner "without unnecessary delay." The meaning of this phrase varies from state to state, depending upon the state law or court decisions; hence, it is possible to state a specific number of hours within which an arrested person must be brought before a magistrate. In *County of Riverside v. McLaughlin* (1991) the Supreme Court held that persons must generally be brought before a judicial official within 48 hours of arrest.

The magistrate first advises the arrested person of his or her rights, including the right to counsel if the person is charged with an offense for which incarceration is a possibility. If the case is not disposed of during this appearance, the arrested person is either sent back to jail, released on his own recognizance (ROR), or allowed to post bail in an amount determined by the magistrate.

5. **Preliminary Hearing**: Where the accused is charged with a felony, he is usually entitled to a preliminary hearing held before a judge or magistrate within a reasonably short time after arrest. Preliminary hearings closely resemble trials, except that their purpose is more limited and the hearing officer is generally not the same judge who will preside in the actual trial. Representation by counsel and cross-examination of witnesses are both allowed. After the preliminary hearing, the magistrate may do any of the following: "bind" the defendant over for trial, discharge the accused, or reduce the charge.

6. **Filing of Accusatory Pleading**: A criminal prosecution is commenced by the filing of an accusatory pleading in the court having jurisdiction of the offense. This may be done through an indictment or an information. An indictment is filed by the grand jury, while an information is filed by the prosecutor without referring the case to the grand jury. Some states require that serious cases be referred by the prosecutor to the grand jury (as a safeguard against possible arbitrary prosecution), while others permit the prosecutor to file an information with the court following the outcome of the preliminary hearing.

7. **Arraignment**: At a scheduled time and after prior notice, the accused is called to court, informed of the charges against him, and asked how he or she pleads. This is known as the arraignment. The accused's presence during arraignment is required. If the person has not been arrested, or if the person is on bail and does not appear, a bench warrant (warrant issued by the judge) will be issued to compel the accused to appear in court. In many states, an accused charged with a misdemeanor may appear through counsel at the arraignment and need not be physically present.

8. **Plea by Defendant**: There are generally three kinds of pleas in modern criminal practice: (a) guilty; (b) nolo contendere; and (c) not guilty. Where the defendant pleads "guilty," the record must affirmatively show that the plea was voluntary and that the accused had a full understanding of its consequences. Without these, the plea is invalid as a matter of constitutional law. A plea of guilty has the effect of giving up several important constitutional rights (such as the right to trial by jury and the right against self-incrimination). Hence, there is need to make sure the accused knew exactly what he or she was doing and was not coerced into making the plea. A nolo contenders plea literally means "no contest." The effect of this plea is the same as that of a guilty plea; however, the defendant may benefit in that the plea cannot be used as an admission of guilt in any subsequent civil proceeding arising out of the same offense. If the defendant pleads "not guilty" the case is will be set for trial at a later date. The delay is designed to give both the prosecution and defense time to prepare their cases.

B. Procedure During Trial

1. **Selection of Jurors**: A panel of jurors is assembled according to an established procedure — usually using voter's registration lists, municipal directories, telephone directories, or other available listings. The prospective jurors are then sent notification letters by the jury commissioner, with instructions to show up at a specified time and place for possible jury duty. Prospective jurors may be questioned to determine whether there are grounds for challenge. This is known as *voir dire*, meaning "to tell the truth." In federal courts, the trial judge usually asks the questions — although he may permit counsel to conduct the examination or submit questions for the judge to ask the jury. In state practice, the lawyers themselves often ask the questions. There are two types of challenges to prospective members, namely: (a) challenge for cause, and (b) peremptory challenge. Jurors can be dismissed for causes specified by law. These include actual bias, implied bias, or other factors which would prevent the juror from making a fair and impartial decision. Peremptory challenges are those for which no reason need be stated and are therefore entirely within the discretion of each party. The number of peremptory challenges allowed a party varies from one jurisdiction to another, and may also depend upon the seriousness of the offense. More serious offenses are allowed more peremptory challenges.

2. **Opening Statements**: After the jury is chosen, the prosecution and the defense present opening statements. In the opening statement, the prosecutor acquaints the jury with the nature of the charge against the accused and gives some description of the evidence that will be offered to sustain the charge. Opinions, conclusions, references to the accused character, argumentative statements, or references to matters on which no evidence will be offered are out of place, and the defense may object to the them.

Opinions differ over the tactical value of an opening statement by the defense. Some argue that the defense should not risk assuming the burden of proving something to the jury, which would be expected if an assertion of any kind is made. Others note that failure to make a statement may imply a weak or hopeless defense. In most cases, the defense elects to make an opening statement.

3. **Presentation of Government's Case**: After opening the case, the prosecutor offers evidence in support of the charge. While physical evidence may be introduced, most evidence tends to be in the form of witness testimony. Witnesses are examined in the following order:

   (a) Direct examination — by the prosecutor.

   (b) Cross-examination — by the defense lawyer.

   (c) Redirect-examination — by the prosecutor.

   (d) Recross-examination — by the defense lawyer.

   After presenting all of its evidence, the government rests its case.

4. **Presentation of Defendant's Case**: When the prosecution has rested, the defendant or his lawyer opens the defense and offers evidence in support thereof. Witnesses are examined in the order noted above, with the defense lawyer conducting the direct examination and the prosecutor cross-examining the witness. After presenting all the evidence, the defense rests its case.

5. **Motion Prior to Verdict**: Defendants may avail themselves of several different motions prior to jury deliberations and a verdict. The most common are:

   (a) *Motion for acquittal*: The defense normally moves for a judgment of acquittal at the close of the prosecution's case on

121

grounds of failure to establish a *prima facie* case. This motion alleges that the prosecution has failed to introduce evidence on a necessary element of the offense charged — such as intent in robbery, or death in homicide. If denied by the judge (as is usually the case), the defendant may renew the motion to acquit at the close of his case.

(b) *Motion for directed verdict of acquittal*: At the close of evidence in a jury trial, the defendant may ask the court for a directed verdict of acquittal — again on the ground that the evidence is legally insufficient to convict.

(c) *Motion for mistrial*: Improper conduct at trial constitutes a basis for mistrial. Examples of grounds for a mistrial include the introduction of inflammatory evidence and prejudicial remarks by the judge or prosecutor.

6. **Argument After Presentation of Evidence**: In most jurisdictions, the prosecution first presents its closing argument; the defense replies; and then the prosecution has a final argument to rebut the defense.

(a) *Prosecution argument*: The prosecution summarizes the evidence and presents theories on how the evidence should be considered to establish a defendant's guilt. The prosecutor's summation sometimes includes improper remarks to which the defense may object and (if serious enough) even secure a mistrial, new trial, or reversal on appeal.

(b) *Defense argument*: The closing argument by the defense is an important matter of tactic and strategy. Generally, the defense emphasizes the heavy burden of proof placed on the prosecution, particularly proof of defendant's guilt beyond a reasonable doubt. The defense then stresses that this burden has not been met and hence the defendant must be acquitted.

7. **Instructing the jury**: The trial judge must properly instruct the jury on all general principles of law relevant to the charge and on the issues raised by the evidence. In most criminal cases, the parties, especially defense counsel, will ask the court to give instructions to the jury proposed by the parties themselves. The judge will then decide which additional instructions to give; and advise counsel of his decision. Often an informal conference on instructions is held among the judge, prosecutor, and defense counsel.

8. **Jury Deliberations**: The foreman of the jury is usually elected immediately after the jury has been instructed by the judge and has retired from the courtroom to start its deliberations. The foreman presides over the deliberations and gives the verdict to the court once a decision is reached. Jury deliberations are conducted in secret and jurors are not subject to subsequent legal inquiry regardless of the result. There is conflict among various jurisdictions as to whether jurors — during the trial and/or during deliberations — should be kept together (sequestered) or allowed to return to their homes at night or during weekends. Most states permit the trial judge to sequester at his discretion.

9. **Conviction or Acquittal**: A verdict of guilty results in a conviction of the accused. After the jury has announced its verdict, the defendant has a right to have the jury polled. At this point, each jury member must express his or her vote in open court. Following a conviction, the court may order the defendant committed to custody or released on bail pending imposition of sentence.

C. Procedure After Trial

1. **Sentencing**: Sentencing follows a guilty verdict. Sentencing is defined as the formal pronouncement of judgment and punishment upon the defendant following conviction in a

122

criminal prosecution. The sentence is always imposed by the court; however, some states permit the jury to recommend or determine the punishment for certain offenses. The sentence generally must be imposed "without unreasonable delay." State rules frequently provide a time limit, while recognizing that some period between a verdict of conviction and the sentencing — usually 10 days to 3 weeks — is necessary for the probation officer to prepare a pre-sentence investigation report which judges use to help them determine a fair and appropriate sentence.

The sentence imposed by the court usually consists of one or a combination of the following punishments:

(a) Death

(b) Imprisonment in a jail or penitentiary

(c) Imposition of a fine and/or restitution

(d) Forfeiture of property

(e) Probation or community service

(f) Any other type of punishment deemed appropriate by the judge, as long as it is within the bounds of his or her authority.

Where the defendant has been convicted of two or more crimes, or is already serving a sentence on some other offenses, it is necessary to determine whether the sentence imposed will run concurrently (at the same time) or consecutively (one after the other, or "stacked"). In most states, this decision is entirely within the discretion of the judge who formally imposes the sentence.

The accused has a right to counsel during sentencing and if indigent, an attorney must be appointed for the accused by the state. Most courts also provide that the defendant is entitled to make a statement, known as the right of allocution, on his own behalf as to why the sentence should not be imposed. The accused has few other procedural rights during sentencing. Even the rules of evidence are relaxed so that the judge may rely on hearsay or unsworn reports and need not afford the defendant an opportunity to cross-examine.

2. **Appeal**: The right to appeal is not a constitutional right; however, all states, by statute, allow the accused to appeal a conviction. There are very few limitations on the right to appeal; hence, it can delay the final adjudication of a criminal case — to the detriment of the criminal justice process. In contrast, the prosecutor cannot appeal an acquittal because of the constitutional prohibition against double jeopardy. The appellate process can take years before a conviction is affirmed or overturned. If affirmed, the accused starts serving his sentence; if overturned, the accused can usually be tried again — at the discretion of the prosecutor.

3. **Post Conviction Remedies**: Even while serving sentence, there are remedies available which keep a convict's hope of freedom alive. The most popular is the writ of habeas corpus, a petition filed, usually in the court where the inmate was convicted, asking that the inmate be set free because he or she was deprived of constitutional rights during the trial. These petitions seldom succeed and even if they do succeed, the inmate can be prosecuted again in the place where the crime was committed.

ALTERNATIVE DISPUTE RESOLUTION

Beginning in the late 1960's and early 1970's, an alternative to the criminal court system began to emerge in American communities. In response to widespread dissatisfaction with court processing of minor criminal disputes, communities began developing alternative dispute center projects that diverted some criminal cases from the courts. These projects were designed to help alleviate overcrowding on court dockets, reduce delays, and to increase citizen satisfaction with case processing and outcomes. The early alternative dispute resolution projects were developed by local prosecutors and handled minor criminal matters. The first projects of this sort began in Philadelphia, Pennsylvania and Columbus, Ohio. The Columbus project is now 25 years old and handles over 10,000 cases per year.[7]

Gradually, alternative dispute resolution expanded to include other types of disputes. In an effort to extend the successes of the early dispute resolution projects begun by local prosecutors, the National Institute of Justice created three Neighborhood Justice Centers in 1977. These centers were established in Atlanta, Kansas City, and Los Angeles and were designed to resolve disputes between persons with ongoing relationships.[8] The types of disputes that these centers helped resolve are typical of what many alternative dispute resolution projects handle today. Thus, in addition to criminal matters, disputes typically heard by alternative dispute resolution centers include landlord/tenant disputes, domestic or family disputes, consumer complaints, employer/employee disputes, and neighborhood conflicts. By the late 1980's, it was estimated that between 180 and 400 alternative dispute resolution programs were in place in 40 different states.[9]

A. What is Alternative Dispute Resolution

Dispute resolution that takes place outside of a courtroom setting can generally be divided into three basic types. The first type of alternative dispute resolution is called *negotiation*. When negotiating a resolution to a dispute, the disputing parties meet directly and attempt to work out their differences. No outside third party takes part in the discussions, and the parties arrive at their own solutions. This type of alternative dispute processing is almost never used in a formal dispute resolution program, especially if the dispute involves a criminal matter.

The second method of dispute resolution is the one preferred by most dispute resolution professionals. This method is labeled *mediation*, and it involves a neutral third party who acts as a facilitator to help the disputants arrive at a mutually agreeable solution to their problem. The mediator does not take sides and does not impose his or her own solution on the disputants. Instead, the mediator helps the parties to compromise and to achieve their own settlement.

Arbitration is the final type of alternative dispute resolution process. With arbitration, a neutral third party is brought in to decide on a solution to the dispute. The parties present their sides of the dispute to the arbitrator who then decides on a settlement that the arbitrator believes is fair under the circumstances. The arbitrator's decision may be binding or nonbinding on the parties, depending on the particular dispute resolution program or on the parties agreement at the start of the arbitration.[10]

B. Alternative Dispute Resolution of Criminal Matters

In recent years the criminal justice system has shown an increased concern over the rights and needs of crime victims. As a result, more communities are developing *victim-offender reconciliation* programs. These programs take a variety of forms, but generally have one or more of the following goals in mind:

➤ To improve the conflict resolution capacity of the parties involved

➤ To help bring closure to the crime victim by allowing for the venting of feelings and the exchange of viewpoints

➤ To compensate victims for their losses

➤ To help reform offenders by allowing them to observe firsthand the harm caused by their conduct

➤ To achieve reconciliation between victim and offender

➤ To relieve overburdened courts of some of their cases

➢ To facilitate a speedier and less costly resolution to the case

➢ To improve case outcomes through fairer and more just solutions[11]

The types of cases that are usually processed through victim-offender reconciliation projects are minor in nature. Simple assaults, harassment, and property damage cases are typical of those resolved through these reconciliation projects. However, some jurisdictions have extended alternative dispute resolution to serious felonies such as robbery, aggravated assault, rape, manslaughter, and burglary.[12]

Most reconciliation projects receive their cases through referrals from criminal courts. Some centers, however, are set up and maintained independently of the criminal justice system and receive their cases from local residents who bring their disputes directly to the centers. In those instances where a case is referred to a victim-offender reconciliation project from a court, both the victim and the offender must agree to the alternative dispute resolution forum. Some projects divert cases from the courts before they are adjudicated. If the victim and offender are able to agree on an outcome, the offender will not be convicted and will not receive a criminal record so long as he or she completes the requirements set forth in the agreement with the victim. Other victim-offender reconciliation projects receive their cases after the criminal defendant has been convicted but before a sentence has been imposed. In these cases, the defendant's sentence may be reduced or suspended if he or she fulfills the terms of the agreement with the victim.

Almost all victim-offender reconciliation projects use mediation as their means for resolving cases. Mediators are usually laypersons who receive between 16 and 32 hours of formal training. Following their training, future mediators serve a period of apprenticeship under an experienced mediator.[13] One advantage of mediation over formal adjudication in criminal cases is that individually-tailored outcomes can be achieved. Offenders are frequently required to pay restitution to their victims under mediated agreements or are required to provide some other useful service to them. Sometimes all a victim wants from an offender is an apology, and alternative dispute resolution allows for this outcome.

C. The Future of Alternative Dispute Resolution

Research into the effects of alternative dispute resolution in criminal cases shows its impact to be mixed. A 1986 study by Schneider found that serious juvenile offenders who were randomly assigned to victim-offender mediation had lower recidivism rates than comparable offenders who received probation. Two earlier studies found no differences between mediation and traditional adjudication in reducing future hostilities between disputing parties.[14] On the other hand, victims who participate in mediation are usually satisfied with the outcome. According to Gehm and Umbreit (1986), 90 percent of victim-offender mediations resulted in a mutually acceptable outcome. In addition, some researchers have found high levels of victim satisfaction with the mediation process.[15]

If chronic courtroom overcrowding continues, then the need to divert criminal cases from the formal adjudication process will persist. Because of this, it seems likely that victim-offender reconciliation projects will continue to exist on a limited scale. Despite participants' satisfaction with mediation in criminal cases, however, it also seems likely that victim-offender reconciliation projects will remain limited in scope so long as public demand for harsher treatment of criminals continues.

COURT SYSTEM AND PROCESS

Article III, Section 1 of the United States Constitution provides that "the judicial power of the United States shall be vested in one Supreme Court and in such inferior courts as the Congress may from time to time ordain and establish." It further provides that judges shall hold their offices during good behavior and shall receive for their services a compensation which shall not be diminished during their stay in office. These provisions assure an independent judiciary, insulated from the pernicious effects of political pressure.

The United States has a "dual court system" meaning that it has one court system for federal cases and another for state cases. In reality, that term is misleading because what we in fact have are 51 different judicial systems, referring to the independent judiciaries of the 50 states and of the federal government. These systems are independent from each other and are not hierarchically related, except that constitutional decisions of the United States Supreme Court are binding on both state and federal courts at all levels.

A. The Federal Court System

1. **The United States Supreme Court**: This highest court is composed of one Chief Justice and eight associate justices. All are appointed for life by the President of the United States with the advise and consent of the Senate. The justices (as they are called on the Supreme Court level) may be removed only by impeachment. This is an extremely difficult process; no Supreme Court justice has ever been successfully impeached in the history of the United States. The Court is located in Washington, D.C.. and always decides cases *en banc* (meaning as one body), and never in smaller groups.

2. **The United States Courts of Appeals**: There are 13 Courts of Appeals distributed in various regions of the country. These courts are officially known as he Court of Appeals for the ___ Circuit. Judges of the Courts of Appeals are also appointed by the President with the advice and consent of the Senate. These courts may hear cases *en banc or* in divisions of three or five judges. Courts of Appeals judges enjoy tenure for life and may be removed only by impeachment.

3. **The United States District Courts**: There are more than 500 judges on the trial level, located in 94 judicial districts scattered throughout the United States and its territories. Each state has at least one judicial district, but each district may have as many as 40 judges, depending upon caseload. District court judges are appointed by the President of the United States for life, with the advice and consent of the Senate, and can be removed only by impeachment. Only six district court judges have lost their office by impeachment throughout the more than two centuries of United States history. Evidently, the impeachment process is not a threat to judicial independence.

Also under the federal system, but not considered a separate court, is the office of the U.S. Magistrate Judge. Magistrate judges are appointed by district court judges and must be lawyers. Their duties are limited, although they have been given more responsibilities in recent years. In addition to trying persons accused of minor offenses, magistrate judges perform various pretrial duties such as holding bail hearings, issuing warrants, reviewing civil rights petitions, and conducting pretrial hearings. Magistrate judges are adjuncts of district court judges and function primarily to ease the burden on regular court judges.

B. The State Court System

The structures of the various state court systems are idiosyncratic and differ from state to state; however, they have basic similarities which justify certain generalizations:

1. **State Supreme Court**: This highest state court makes final decisions in cases involving state laws and provisions of the state constitution. In some states, the highest state court is called the Supreme Court of Appeals, in others it is called the Court of Appeals, the Supreme Judicial Court, or simply the Supreme Court. Texas and

126

Oklahoma have separate supreme courts for civil and criminal cases; all other states have one highest court for civil and criminal cases.

2. **Intermediate Courts of Appeals**: Thirty-eight states have courts at this level. In some states, defendants must first appeal their cases to these intermediate courts before appealing to the state supreme court. In other states, defendants appeal directly to the state supreme court, which then assigns some cases to the intermediate court of appeals.

3. **Trial Courts**: State cases are originally tried in these courts. There are various names given to trial courts, the most popular of which are: district court, superior court and county court. Most states have an even lower level of original jurisdiction courts, to which have been applied a greater variety of names, such as: justice of the peace courts, municipal courts, and courts of common pleas. Courts at this level have limited and/or specialized jurisdiction and, in many cases, are not courts of record. Typically, the procedures in such courts are less formal than those observed in courts of general jurisdiction.

C. The Appeal Process

With rare exceptions, cases enter the federal and state judicial systems at the trial court level. At that level, a jury, or the judge in cases being heard without a jury, determines the facts of the case based on the evidence presented. By applying the applicable law to the facts to be settled, the judge or jury determines the outcome of the suit.

Every case has a winner and a loser. A party seeks review, and possible reversal, of an unfavorable judgment by appealing it up the judicial hierarchy. Courts of appeal do not hear further evidence; generally, they do not re-evaluate the evidence presented in the trial court. Their primary function is to determine errors of law and give a remedy for prejudicial errors.

A large majority of cases filed in any court system are with decided with finality at the trial court level because it is not appealed. In most cases, an appeal is therefore more of a potential rather than an actual part of the case. Of those cases appealed, most are found to have been rightly decided at the level below, or otherwise not subject to reversal.

The federal and state court systems merge at the Supreme Court of the United States. Because the supremacy clause of the Constitution makes the Constitution the "Supreme Law of the Land," and because the Supreme Court decides the meaning of the Constitution, that body can review state supreme court decisions insofar as they pass on claims or defenses founded on the Constitution or laws enacted under its authority. Conversely, the Supreme Court will not disturb a state decision that is based purely on state law and has no constitutional implications.

An important concept in the judicial process is *stare decisis* or the principle of judicial precedent. While the immediate function of every judicial decision is to settle the rights of the parties before the court, a secondary function is to forecast how subsequent, similar cases will be decided so other persons can conform their conduct to the demands of the law. This predictive aspect is the precedential value of a case, and often its persuasiveness varies with the level of the court that decided it. The Supreme Court of the United States hands down the decisions of greatest future significance; trial courts render decisions that have less value as precedent.

D. The Effect of Judicial Decisions

The jurisdiction of every American court is limited in some way. One type of limitation is territorial or geographic; meaning that each judicial decision is authoritative and has precedential value only within the geographic limits of the area in which the deciding court has authority. Hence:

➢   United States Supreme Court decisions

on questions of federal law and the Constitution are binding on all America courts because the whole country is under its jurisdiction.

➢ Federal court of appeals decisions on such issues are the last word within the circuit if there is no Supreme Court action. The First Circuit Court of Appeals, for example, settles federal issues for Maine, Massachusetts, New Hampshire, Rhode Island, and Puerto Rico, the areas to which its jurisdiction is limited.

➢ When a district court encompasses an entire state, as is the case in Maine, its assessment of federal law (again barring appellate action) produces a uniform rule within the state. In a state like Wisconsin, however, where there are multiple districts, there can be divergent rules.

The existence of a dual court system and the limited jurisdictional reach of the vast majority of courts make it inevitable that conflicting decisions on a point of law will be rendered by the courts. A core function of the appellate process is to provide a forum for resolving these conflicts. The existence of a conflict in court decisions could be a strong argument for an appellate review of an unfavorable decision.

Given the maze of courts, how is one to know whether a criminal act is to be tried in federal or state court? The basic rule is simple: if the penal provision used to prosecute is a federal law, then the case is tried in federal court; conversely, if the penal law invoked is a state law, then the case is tried in a state court. If a criminal act violates both federal and state laws (such as kidnapping, transportation of narcotics, counterfeiting, or robbery of a federally-insured bank), the crime can be tried in both federal and state courts, should the prosecutors in both jurisdictions be so inclined. Usually, however, state and federal prosecutors decide informally whether the defendant will be tried in state or federal court. In most cases, the second

jurisdiction will not prosecute the case again if the accused is found guilty and given the appropriate punishment in the first trial.

Jurisdiction and venue are two terms usually associated with courts but which are sometimes used interchangeably and are oftentimes confusing. They are, however, very different concepts. Jurisdiction refers to the power of a court to try and punish a person for an offense. Such power is derived from statutory or constitutional law. In contrast, venue means the place where the offense is to be tried. The rules for deciding the appropriate venue are specified by statute, which usually provides that the trial must be held in the place where the crime was committed. Jurisdiction is nontransferable (although some courts may have concurrent jurisdiction), but venue may be changed and the trial held in another place based on grounds specified by law. This is done to assure the accused a fair and impartial trial in cases where there has been massive pretrial publicity or a strong community prejudice against the accused which makes it difficult to select an impartial jury.

COURT PERSONNEL IN CONFLICT ARBITRATION

Three categories of court personnel are pivotal in formal conflict arbitration. These are: judges, prosecutors, and defense lawyers. They are the key participants in the adversary system; without them the system does not function.

A. Judges

Judges play the most dominant role as participants and supervisors in the litigation process. They occupy center stage and, in most cases, what they say or do determines the quality of justice litigants obtain. Judges perform a host of functions, among them:

1. Determine probable cause and issue search or arrest warrants

2. Set bail or determine when a suspect may be released on his own recognizance without bail

3. Decide if the terms of a plea bargain between the prosecutor and the defense lawyer are acceptable

4. Determine if an accused is indigent and, if so, assign the accused a defense lawyer at government expense

5. Preside at trials, decide what evidence to admit or exclude and which objections to sustain or overrule

6. Control the trial environment, particularly the behavior of the accused, lawyers, witnesses, and the mass media

7. Decide if a motion to dismiss is to be granted because the prosecutor failed to prove his case beyond reasonable doubt

8. Give instructions to the jury at the end of the trial

9. Impose the sentence in case of conviction

10. Decide if an accused is entitled to bail pending appeal, if convicted

Judges have traditionally wielded vast power in the conduct of litigation. Judicial authority is enforced through contempt citations which authorize a judge to place just about anybody in contempt of court and subject that person to confinement for interfering with court functions or disobeying court orders.

Like most other powerful professions, certain myths abound about the power and function of judges. One is that judges are well-trained for what they do. While some judges are in fact well-prepared to perform judicial functions, most judges do not have any specialized training other than experience gained in the practice of law. Most states, however, have workshops or seminars for newly elected judges. Many judges are former prosecu-

tors or were actively engaged in private law practice. This differs from the system in European countries where judges are trained to be career professionals without first becoming practicing lawyers. There is a college for new judges in Reno, Nevada, but attendance in the program is voluntary and training time is limited.

A second myth is that judges alone determine the punishment to be imposed on an on an offender. This may be technically true in most jurisdictions where the judge is required to impose sentence in his or her name in open court; however, there are many states where the judge is bound by the penalty the jury recommends. Moreover, judges are often limited in what they can do by penal code provisions which set minimum and maximum penalties, by the recommendation of a probation officer, by the recommendation of the prosecutor in plea bargained cases, and by the guidelines of the parole board which determine the actual time to be served by an inmate.

A third myth is that judges can effectively affect the crime rate by what they do or not do. The public is quick to attribute the upsurge in crime to judges who "coddle criminals" or to applaud "hanging judges" when the crime rate plummets. What may be closer to the truth is that what judges do have only a minimal effect, if any, on crime. Among the reasons are that only about 50% of crimes committed are ever reported to the police and out of this number only a few suspects are arrested, charged with an offense, and eventually sentenced. In most criminal cases, what the police do is far more significant than how a judge wields power or how tough or soft the judge may be on crime.

Finally, there is the myth that courts can effectively control the conduct of the police. Courts sometimes do tell the police what they can and cannot do.. This is done through court decisions defining which police behavior is constitutional or reprehensible as to violate individual rights. In many cases, however, the minutiae of police work is insulated from the effects of judicial prescription. For example, what the United States Supreme Court says ought to be done may not always be what a police agency does. As one writer observes: "Once uttered, these pronouncements will be interpreted by arrays of lower appellate courts, trial judges, magistrates, commissioners, and police officials."[16] The ideal may vastly differ from reality; yet the myth thrives because virtual omnipotence is ascribed by the public to the Supreme Court.

One way whereby courts control the conduct of the police is through the use of the exclusionary rule. This rule holds that evidence illegally seized by the police cannot be used as evidence during trial. In reality, the use by the courts of the exclusionary rule may be ineffective for various reasons. Only around 5% of cases are actually tried in court (hence there is no opportunity to invoke the rule), police officers oftentimes arrest suspects or confiscate evidence without expectations that the case would ever be brought to trial, and because in some cases the officer is not certain whether what he or she is doing is legal or not. The exclusionary rule has become the focus of much debate in legal circles and frequently has been re-examined and refined by the United States Supreme Court.

B. Prosecutors

Prosecutors in federal courts (known as United States attorneys) are presidential appointees, while those in state courts (called district or state attorneys) are elected. A prosecutor is the chief law enforcement officer of a geographical territory, hence a prosecutor's influence in criminal justice goes beyond prosecuting criminal cases. Among a prosecutor's functions are the following:[17]

1. Investigates possible violations of the law

2. Cooperates with the police in investigating a crime

3. Determines the charge to be filed

4. Reviews applications for arrest and search warrants

5. Subpoenas witnesses

6. Enters into plea bargaining agreements

7. Tries criminal cases

8. Represents the government in appealed cases

In most states, the district attorney is an independent public official who is accountable only to the electorate. The prosecutor does not have an immediate superior, neither are his or her decisions reviewed by anybody — except in states where felony charges must be presented to the grand jury for indictment. The use and abuse of discretion by district attorneys has been the subject of concern in criminal justice. The extent of discretion is exemplified by the fact that a district attorney may charge a suspect with a crime even if the evidence barely warrants prosecution. Conversely, in most states, there is nothing that compels a district attorney to prosecute despite ample evidence. The amount of discretion possessed by the district attorney is made more crucial by the absence of job visibility. In the words of a noted observer: "The fate of most of those accused of a crime is determined by prosecutors, but typically this takes place out of the public view."[18]

C. Defense Lawyers

Persons charged with an offense for which they are actually sent to jail or prison, even if it be for one day, are entitled to the services of a lawyer provided by the state if the accused is indigent.[19] The standard for indigence varies from one jurisdiction to another; hence it defies dollar amount precision. There is no uniform rule to determine indigence. Some standards used by judges to determine indigence are: unemployment, not having a car, not having posted bail, not having a house, etc. The judge enjoys wide discretion in making this determination and his or her decision is rarely reversed on appeal.

Defense lawyers for indigents are provided either through the appointment by the judge of private practitioners who earn a nominal fee from the state, or through the services of a public defender who is a full-time public employee. The choice of a legal service delivery system to indigents is likely to be dictated by economics. Smaller communities prefer private counsel because the caseload may not warrant a full-time public defender; on the other hand, bigger population centers find the public defender system cost-effective, efficient, and easier to manage. The effectiveness of either system for the accused is open to debate.

A question often asked of defense lawyers is: "Why should a lawyer defend a guilty defendant?" In reply, one writer says: [20]

1. Lawyers are advocates, and not judge or jury. If lawyers begin to judge their clients, the adversary system of justice will be destroyed.

2. The fact that a client appears to be guilty, indeed, has confessed to the commission of a crime, does not mean that he committed it. For every notorious crime, a number of people who could not possibly have committed the crime take credit for it.

3. The term "guilty" has neither a moral nor a factual connotation in the law. It is strictly a legal term which refers to a formal adjudication after a prescribed process has been followed.

4. Under our system, the prosecution has the burden of proving the defendant's guilt beyond a reasonable doubt. The fact that one human being, an attorney, may be persuaded of the guilt of his client does not mean that twelve other human beings, the jury, will be.

5. Criminal law is so complex that no defendant really knows whether he is guilty of any particular crime or not.

6. If lawyers refuse to represent defendants who they believe are guilty, the right of a defendant to be represented by counsel is eliminated and with it the entire traditional criminal trial.

Basic to understanding the role of a defense lawyer in the criminal justice process is the realization that in the American system of justice, the loyalty of a lawyer is to the client and not to society. In case of conflict, loyalty to the client prevails. A lawyer is obligated, by the oath of the profession, to do everything possible to defend a client, short only of doing anything that is illegal, unethical, or both. Society values the lawyer-client relation such that where what a client tells the lawyer in the course of a professional relationship cannot be divulged by the lawyer at any time, except upon consent of the client. The search for truth would be vastly simplified if a district attorney could place a lawyer on the witness stand and, under oath, ask what the lawyer's client told him or her in confidence. We do not do that because some relationships in American society are considered so important that they must be preserved even at the cost of truth. Unless the system mandates that the loyalty of a lawyer be to society instead of to the client (and in the process destroying the adversary system), the role of counsel in a criminal proceeding will most likely be viewed as betraying the public good for the benefit of the accused or for the glitter of gold.

BASIC RIGHTS OF THE ACCUSED [21]

The safeguards guaranteed in the Bill of Rights of the United States Constitution enjoy utmost protection during the trial stage of the criminal proceeding. Accordingly, those rights have been extensively developed, refined, and protected more than in any other stage of the criminal justice process. The primary safeguards for the accused in a criminal trial are:

➢ Right to Counsel

➢ Right to Trial by Jury

➢ Right to a Fair and Impartial Trial

➢ Right to Confrontation of Witnesses

➢ Privilege Against Self-incrimination

➢ Right to Protection Against Double Jeopardy

A. Right to Counsel

The Sixth Amendment to the U.S. Constitution provides that "in all criminal prosecutions, the accused shall enjoy the right ... to have the assistance of counsel for his defense." Consequently, a defendant has the right to be represented by counsel at "every critical stage" of the criminal proceeding. The Supreme Court has articulated the rationale for the right to counsel in criminal proceedings as follows:

Even the intelligent and educated layman has small and sometimes no skill in the science of the law. Left without aid of counsel, he may be put on trial without a proper charge, and convicted upon incompetent evidence, or evidence irrelevant to the issue or otherwise inadmissible. He requires the guiding hand of counsel at every step in the proceedings against him. Without it, though he be not guilty, he faces the danger of conviction because he does not know how to establish his innocence.[22]

Although the Sixth Amendment extends to "all criminal prosecutions," the Supreme Court has held that the right to counsel applies only (1) if the crime charges is a felony, or (2) if, upon conviction of the offense (whether felony or misdemeanor), actual imprisonment is imposed.[23] The United States Supreme Court has decided that the right to counsel under the Fifth or Sixth Amendments applies in the following instances: custodial interrogations, non-custodial interrogations after the accused has been formally charged, a lineup at the police station after the suspect has been charged, preliminary hearing, the trial itself, and the sentencing stage.

Conversely, the right to counsel does not apply in the following proceedings: grand jury hearings, purely investigative proceedings, police lineup prior to suspect being charged, prison disciplinary proceedings, probation and parole revocation, and military proceedings.

The defendant may challenge a conviction on the ground that his or her lawyer at the trial was so incompetent as to deprive the defendant of the effective assistance of counsel. This claim is frequently raised, but rarely succeeds. The Supreme Court has avoided setting minimum standards of competency for defense counsel in criminal proceedings. Rather, it has indicated that the question is primarily one within the "good sense and discretion of the trial courts."[24] The fact that counsel's advice turns out to be wrong does not mean that the accused was deprived of "effective" counsel. Rather, the question is whether the advice was "within the range of competency" expected of attorneys defending criminal charges.[25] An accused has a constitutional right to waive counsel and represent himself or herself in a criminal proceeding. But if an accused elects to do so, the accused cannot later claim denial of effective assistance of counsel.[26]

B. Right to Trial by Jury

Article III, Sec. 2, cl. 3 of the Constitution provides that "The trial of all Crimes, except in Cases of Impeachment, shall be by jury." The Sixth Amendment also provides that "In all criminal prosecutions, the accused shall enjoy the right to a speedy and public trial, by an impartial jury of the State and district wherein the crime shall have been committed."

In all federal criminal trials, a jury of 12 is required by statute. However, a jury of 12 is not required by the Sixth Amendment. The Supreme Court has upheld a Florida law providing for a 6-member jury in all criminal cases except those involving capital offenses.[27] In 6-member juries, the decision to convict must be unanimous. The Court has not indicated what minimum number of jurors could still properly constitute a jury in a criminal case.

In federal criminal cases, the Sixth Amendment requires a unanimous jury verdict. But a unanimous jury verdict, although mandated in most states, is not constitutionally required in state trials. The Supreme Court has upheld a 9 - 3 vote for conviction.[28] but has refused to say how far down it would go in declaring split decisions constitutional. In states that require jury verdicts to be unanimous, lack of unanimity results in a

132

"hung jury," which means that the defendant can be tried again for the same offense.

Since the Sixth Amendment guarantees a jury trial only where a serious offense is charged, a distinction must be made between serious and petty offenses. To determine this, the Court looks at the maximum sentence allowed by law for that offense instead of the actual sentence imposed. The Court has ruled that where the maximum punishment authorized by statute is imprisonment for more than six months, the offense is considered "serious" regardless of the penalty actually imposed, hence the accused is entitled to a jury trial.[29]

C. Right to a Fair and Impartial Trial

The Due Process Clauses of the Fifth and Fourteenth Amendments guarantee the accused a fair trial by an impartial jury. The publicity given to a notorious case may bias a jury or create a high risk that the jury will consider information other than that provided in court. A defendant claiming undue pretrial publicity or other circumstances that would endanger his right to a fair and impartial trial locally can move for a change of venue, meaning having the place of trial changed to another county where potential jurors might not have been exposed to massive pretrial publicity. This is allowable in both felony and misdemeanor cases. If there is danger that jurors will be exposed to prejudicial publicity during the trial, some states permit sequestration, at the judge's discretion, immediately following jury selection for the duration of the trial.

One of the most effective means of controlling prejudicial publicity is to impose a "gag rule" that prohibits the attorneys and other parties from releasing information or talking to the press. The "gag rule" is constitutional and used by many judges in highly-publicized cases. Generally, attempts to control the news media or the kind of news items they can print in connection with a criminal case are unsuccessful because of the First Amendment guarantee of free speech and a free press. Courts usually prohibit the taking of photo-graphs or the televising of courtroom proceedings. In some states, however, allowing the media to televise courtroom proceedings is discretionary with the trial judge. But if the judge allows televising court proceedings, care must be taken not to create a carnival atmosphere inside the courtroom. The Supreme Court has reversed a conviction because the trial was televised and the atmosphere was akin to that of a carnival. The Court found the televising process so distracting to the judge, jurors, witnesses and counsel that it denied the defendant a fair trial.[30] More recently, many lawyers and commentators have criticized the impact that television had on O.J. Simpson's trial for murder.

D. Right to Confrontation of Witnesses

The Sixth Amendment provides that "in all criminal prosecutions, the accused shall enjoy the right ... to be confronted with the witnesses against him." The right to confrontation is guaranteed in all criminal proceedings — including trials, preliminary hearings, and juvenile proceedings where the juvenile is suspected of having committed a crime. However, the right does not apply to purely investigative proceedings — such as grand jury proceedings, coroner's inquests, and legislative investigations.

The right to confrontation includes: (a) the right to cross-examine all opposing witnesses; (b) the right to be physically present during the trial; and (e) the right to know the identity of prosecution witnesses. Opportunity to cross-examine all opposing witnesses is an important right of the accused. It is the process whereby any falsehood or inaccuracy in the witness's testimony can be detected and exposed, and through which a skillful lawyer may elicit testimony which can be helpful to his client. The right to confrontation also means that the accused must have the opportunity to be physically present in the courtroom at the time any testimony against the accused is offered. The right to be present may, however, be waived if an accused is present at the start of the trial but is later voluntarily absents or if the accused's conduct in the courtroom is disruptive.[31] Any witness who testifies against the accused must reveal his or her true name and address. Such information may be crucial to the defense in investigating and cross-examining the witness for possible impeachment.

E. Privilege Against Self-Incrimination

The privilege against self-incrimination springs from the Fifth Amendment provision that "No person ... shall be compelled in any criminal case be a witness against himself." The privilege designed to restrain the state from using force, coercion, or other illegal methods to obtain any statement, admission, or confession. It is generally considered to guarantee two separate privileges. These are: (a) the privilege of the accused; and (b) the privilege of a witness.

1. **Privilege of the accused**: The accused in a criminal case has a privilege not to take the stand and therefore, not to testify. "He may stand mute, clothed in the presumption of innocence." No conclusion of guilt may be drawn from failure of the accused to testify during the trial; therefore, the prosecutor is not permitted to make any comment or argument to the jury suggesting that the defendant is guilty because he refused to testify. Should such comments be made, the conviction will be reversed. Once an accused takes the witness stand in his or her own defense, however, that person waives the privilege not to testify and must therefore answer all relevant inquiries about the charge for which the person is on trial.

2. **Privilege of a witness**: Any witness has a privilege to refuse to disclose any matter that may "tend to incriminate" the witness. A question tends to incriminate a witness if the answer would directly or indirectly implicate him or her in the commission of a crime. The privilege therefore does not extend to any form of civil liability. But if the answer would make the witness subject to both civil and criminal liability, the privi-

lege can be claimed. It cannot be claimed merely because the answer would hold the witness up to shame or disgrace (as long as no crime is involved). The decision whether or not an answer "tends to incriminate" the witness is made by the judge.

F. Right to Protection Against Double Jeopardy

The Fifth Amendment provides that "no person shall be ... subject, for the same offense, to be put twice in jeopardy of life and limb." A person who has committed a criminal act can be subjected to only one prosecution or punishment for the same offense. Accordingly, when a defendant has been prosecuted for a criminal offense and the prosecution has resulted in either a conviction or an acquittal — or the proceeding has reached a point at which dismissal would be equivalent to an acquittal — any further prosecution or punishment for the same offense is prohibited.

The general rule is that a defendant seeking a new trial or appealing a guilty verdict "waives" the protection against double jeopardy and therefore the defendant can be tried again for the same offense. For example, in the celebrated *Miranda* case, defendant Miranda appealed his original conviction for rape on the ground that his confession was obtained in violation of his right against self-incrimination. His conviction was reversed by the Supreme Court, but he was tried again for the same offense in Arizona and was reconvicted based on other evidence. There was no double jeopardy because his appeal of the first conviction "waived" his right against a retrial on the same offense.

If the same act is a crime under both federal and state law, there are two distinct crimes — because two "separate sovereignties" are involved. The acquittal or conviction of defendant on the federal crime in the federal courts generally does not bar prosecution for the state crime in state courts, and vice versa.

COURT PRACTICES IN CONFLICT ARBITRATION

A. Bail

Bail is the security required by the state and given by the accused to ensure his or her appearance before the proper court at the scheduled time and place. In theory, the only function of bail is to guarantee the appearance of the defendant at the time set for trial. In practice, however, bail has also been used to prevent the release of an accused who might otherwise pose a danger to society or whom the judges do not want to release. This practice is known as "preventive detention" and is used widely in many states.

Where the charge is merely a misdemeanor, most courts have bail schedules pursuant to which the arrested person may post bail with the police or clerk of court in an amount designated in the schedule without having to see the judge. In felony cases, the judge will fix the amount if there is sufficient evidence to justify charging the accused with a crime. Some offenses are not bailable, as when a person is charged with a crime punishable by death and the evidence of guilt is strong.

The amount of bail is usually determined in the light of facts then known to the judge. These include the nature and seriousness of the crime, previous criminal record of the accused, likelihood of flight from the state, and roots in the community. Bail determination is not subject to review by a higher court unless there is a gross violation of the constitutional guarantee against excessive bail.[32] Unfortunately, the term "excessive bail" is hard to define, making this constitutional right difficult for the accused to invoke. The release of an accused pending trial may be secured through four different types of bail, which are: [33]

1. **Fully secured bail**: The defendant posts the full amount of bail with the court.

2. **Privately secured bail**: A bondsman signs a promissory note to the court for the bail amount and charges the defendant a fee for the service (usually 10% of the bail amount). If the defendant fails to appear, the bondsman must pay the court the full amount. Frequently, the bondsman requires the defendant to post collateral in addition to the fee.

3. **Percentage bail**: The courts allow the defendant to deposit a percentage (usually 10%) of the full bail with the court. The full amount of the bail is required if the defendant fails to appear. The percentage bail is returned after disposition of the case although the court retains 1% for administrative costs.

4. **Unsecured bail**: The defendant pays no money to the court but is liable for the full amount of bail should he or she fail to appear.

Release through bail always involves money or property as collateral. There are other ways of releasing the accused without the use of money; the most common options used are: [34]

1. **Release on recognizance** (ROR): The court releases the defendant on a promise to appear in court as required.

2. **Conditional release**: The court releases the defendant subject to specific conditions set by the court, such as attendance at drug treatment therapy or staying away from the complaining witness.

3. **Third party custody**: The defendant is released to the custody of an individual or agency that promises to assure his or her appearance in court.

Bail practices have come under criticism because of their adverse impact on the poor. An excessively high bail discriminates against the poor and results in deprivation of liberty prior to trial. Studies show that an accused who is detained pending trial is less likely to present an adequate defense; hence more likely to be convicted, than one who is free on bail. Yet, at least in bailable offenses, the only reason a person languishes in jail pending trial is that he or she is too poor to afford bail. The practice of "preventive detention" has been criticized as haphazard and negates the presumption of innocence. Moreover, the use of private bail bondsmen to secure a defendant's release virtually gives bondsmen license to determine who should be let out (based on capacity to come up with the initial amount and post collateral) and thus the key to jail — for profit.

Since the early 1960's, several projects have been undertaken designed to cushion the impact of bail on the poor. Some states have eliminated bail bonding for profit. Kentucky dealt with both bondsmen and release programs in 1976 when it banned bondsmen and set up a statewide system of pretrial service agencies.[35] The use of court administered bail (whose effect is the elimination of bondsmen) has spread and more states are releasing defendants on recognizance procedures or are authorizing law enforcement officers to issue citations instead of arresting misdemeanants. Accordingly, the outcry against the inequities of bail has subsided although inequities continue to exist.

B. Plea Bargaining

Plea bargaining is the process of mutual concession whereby the state agrees to reduce the charge or penalty in exchange for a guilty plea from the accused. The practice has long been an integral part of the criminal justice process. Prior to the 1970's, plea bargaining was generally viewed a dubious practice unworthy of public acceptance. In 1971, however, the United States Supreme Court legitimized its existence by declaring that plea bargaining is an essential part of the criminal justice process.[36] This decision lifted the veil of secrecy that previously enshrouded the practice. Since then plea bargaining has been an accepted and indispensable part of court the adjudication process.

Plea bargains often result from inducements on both sides. Some inducements, however, may be so inherently unfair or coercive that a plea in reliance thereof is involuntary and therefore invalid. For example, a threat to prosecute the accused's wife as a co-defendant (despite lack of evidence), or to charge prior convictions (thereby increasing the possible sentence for the accused) would invalidate the plea because of improper pressure.[37] But a guilty plea that represents a voluntary and intelligent choice among alternatives available is not rendered invalid simply because it was made to avoid the possibility of the death penalty.[38] A guilty plea despite continued claims of innocence by the defendant does not invalidate the conviction as long as strong evidence on the record supports findings of guilt.[39] If a plea is based to any significant degree on a prosecutor's promise, that promise must be fulfilled. If not, the agreement or promise is either specifically enforced or the plea may be withdrawn.[40]

Critics maintain that somebody somehow gets the short end of justice in the plea bargaining process. They allege that plea bargaining is phony in that it rests on the assumption that acknowledgment of guilt is the first step toward rehabilitation; hence, the offender deserves leniency. What in fact happens is that culprits bargain because they get away with a lighter penalty, and not out of repentance. Society fails to get its share of justice because the criminal gets less than what defendant would have received had the law been formally enforced. On the other hand, criminals are dissatisfied with the plea bargaining because they are excluded from the negotiation stage and have little say as to the type and length of sentence they are to serve. The defense lawyer and the prosecutor "make a deal" and the defendant accepts it. The defendant can turn it down, but the risks of displeasing the defense lawyer and the prosecutor are high. In sum, critics maintain that plea bargaining is informal justice which fails to render justice to anybody.[41]

Those who defend plea bargaining maintain that the practice is necessary and functional for everybody in the criminal justice system. The prosecutor saves time and secures conviction where the evidence may otherwise be weak; the defense lawyer obtains a lower sentence for the client; the judge disposes of another case in a crowded docket; and the accused is spared the risk of getting a harsh penalty . The reality is that plea bargaining is a cost-effective and an expeditious way to dispense justice. Statistics show that courts are terribly congested, causing intolerable delays in the adjudication of criminal cases. With only about 5% of criminal cases going to trial, the delays would be even greater if plea bargaining did not exist. In the face of mounting congestion, criminal defendants can just about paralyze the criminal justice system by refusing to plea bargain and insisting instead on their constitutional rights to trial and to be proved guilty beyond reasonable doubt. Plea bargaining is certainly an easy way out of a caseload nightmare.

Some jurisdictions have in effect abolished plea bargaining. Prohibitions against plea bargains have been adopted in Alaska; New Orleans, Louisiana; El Paso, Texas; Blackhawk County, Iowa; Maricopa County, Arizona; Oakland County, Michigan; and Mulnomah County in Oregon. Many other jurisdictions have adapted plea bargaining guidelines for prosecutors.[42] A study of the Alaska plea bargaining ban shows that it resulted in longer sentences, as some had hoped for, but no backlogs in criminal cases, as some had feared. In fact, criminal cases were disposed of faster after the ban went into effect. Defendants continued to plead guilty in great number and the percentage of the accused choosing to exercise the right to trial increased only from 6.7% to 8.6%.[43] These encouraging figures, however, may not be of much consolation to other states because Alaska courts did not have the caseload of other states. Besides, other conditions existed in Alaska at the time of the ban which almost guaranteed positive results.[44]

The National Advisory Commission on Criminal Justice Standards and Goals recommended in 1973, that plea bargaining be abolished not later than 1978. On the other hand, the American Bar Association and the American Law Institute have both gone on record as in favor of retaining plea bargaining with some modifications. Obviously, the latter recommendation has prevailed.[45]

Despite shortcomings, plea bargaining will continue to be a part of the criminal justice process because it is economical, speedy, and convenient. In many states judges are required to bring the process out in the open by asking the prosecutor and the defense lawyer if a plea bargain had been arrived at in a guilty plea. If so, the judge asks for the sentence agreed upon by both parties. If acceptable, the judge affirms the agreement; if not, a "not guilty" plea is entered for the defendant and the case is scheduled for trial.[46] One writer has proposed that the plea bargaining discussion should include not just the defense lawyer and the prosecutor, but also the judge, the accused, and the victim.[47] The suggestion is interesting but has failed to gain acceptance.

C. The Jury System

The right to jury trial is a basic right in American society. Like any other constitutional or statutory right, the right to trial by jury may be waived by the accused and is implicitly waived in plea bargaining cases.

The right to trial by jury carries with it the assumption that the trial will be by a "jury of peers." The problem is that the term "jury of peers" is difficult to define and operationalize. Courts have generally interpreted the term to mean that what is needed is that jurors be selected from a larger pool that is a "representative cross-section of the community" wherein no segment of the community is purposely excluded from jury selection. Restricting jury service to special groups is forbidden; hence excluding women, minorities, or those who are against the death penalty (in capital punishment cases) is unconstitutional.

Although no one foresees the demise of the jury system in the United States, its use has generated a measure of dissatisfaction. Critics maintain that jury trials cause delay and court congestion, that jurors do not understand the complexities of the law and are incapable of grasping technical material, that juries are costly and do not assure better verdicts, that jury decisions are unpredictable because jurors can be emotional, that jurors unconsciously pay more attention to the demeanor of lawyers than to the facts of the case, and that a jury can be "loaded" for or against a defendant. The public is also critical of time waste. Studies show that most of the juror's time is spent waiting in the jury room and in jury selection rather than in determining guilt or innocence.[48]

The search for an improved jury system continues. The use of six-member juries in felony cases or of non-unanimous juries has won grudging acceptance by the courts and the public. Using computers for jury selection has cut down on time waste and has assured a wider pool of potential jurors drawn from a broader segment of the community. Limiting the number of excuses a potential juror can use has led to an equitable distribution of the burden of jury service. Courts in a number of states have adapted a practice where a juror is called for only one day to be available to sit in a single trial. Only if selected for a trial would a juror serve more than one day, until again randomly selected for jury service.[49] Courts in all 50 states have used a juror call-in system where jurors can dial a number to learn whether their attendance is needed on a particular day during their term of service.[50]

Despite shortcomings, jury defenders are legion. It is naive to assume that the system does not enjoy widespread citizen support or that its popularity has diminished. The Constitution, tradition, and the sense of "justice by peers" guarantee juries a hallowed spot in the American system of justice. The jury system is here to stay.

D. Sentencing

Sentencing represents the final stage of the trial process and is perhaps the most significant function performed by judges. It is a task most judges do not particularly enjoy and are least prepared to undertake.

The goals of sentencing reflect multiple and often conflicting concerns of society in dealing with law-breakers. The traditional objectives of sentencing are: rehabilitation, deterrence, incapaci-

tation, and retribution.[51] In many states, no sentencing goals or guidelines are available or articulated. The absence of a specific mandate allows judges to interject personal preferences, within minimum and maximum limits set by law, in meting out sentences. For example, one judge believes in rehabilitation, another spurns it, a third judge emphasizes incapacitation, while a fourth judge places high value on deterrence. The cacophony of philosophies is often further compounded by the absence of priorities judges are to follow.

Sentences may be classified into fixed, determinate, or indeterminate. Fixed sentences carry a specific time to be served, while determinate sentences usually provide for a minimum and a maximum. Fixed and determinate sentences are anchored on the retributive philosophy that the punishment should "fit the crime." In contrast, indeterminate sentences, in pure form, have no minimum or maximum (virtually a day to life). They rest on the positivist philosophy that the penalty should "fit the criminal" instead of the crime.

Indeterminate sentencing has attracted attention and concern in criminal justice. It is generally conceded that indeterminate sentencing results in sentencing disparity where persons convicted of similar offenses under analogous circumstances are give disparate sentences.[52] Sentencing disparity exists on several levels. It can exist between and among jurisdictions, among regions within a state, among judges in the same judicial district, and in sentences imposed by the same judge for similar offenses. Such disparity may be attributed to state and regional differences, community attitude towards certain crimes, a shift in a judge's sentencing philosophy, or to sheer judicial caprice.

National interest in sentencing disparity, with its corresponding dysfunctional effect on criminal justice, has set the stage for the adoption of sentencing guidelines by the federal government and by a number of states. Following the Sentencing Reform Act of 1984, Congress established a commission to develop a comprehensive set of sentencing guidelines to be used by federal courts.

Three years later the United States Sentencing Guidelines took effect.

The purposes of the guidelines are threefold. First, the guidelines were designed to promote honesty and fairness in sentencing. Theoretically, defendants will know exactly what sentence they will receive under the guidelines and how much time they will be required to serve. Secondly, the guidelines sought to reduce the widely disparate sentences that judges were imposing on similarly situated defendants. Finally, the guidelines were intended to promote proportionality in sentencing by ensuring that criminal sentences appropriately reflected the severity of the crimes for which they were imposed.[53]

A sentencing table is at the heart of the guidelines. The table contains 43 offense levels and six criminal history categories. Judges match the offense level with a particular defendant's criminal history score to obtain a relatively narrow range of months or years within which they can sentence defendants. Adjustments can be in certain cases to reflect a defendant's role in the crime or whether he or she obstructed justice. Adjustments are also allowed that reflect the status of the victim (for example, whether the victim was particularly vulnerable) and whether the defendant was convicted of multiple counts. If a judge wishes to depart either upward or downward from the sentence mandated by the guidelines, the judge must give reasons for doing so and must justify the departure in writing.

Ten years after the guidelines went into effect, reaction to them is mixed. Some federal judges believe that the guidelines represent an important step forward in making criminal sentences fairer and more predictable. Others claim that disparities in sentencing persist under the guidelines and that sentencing discretion has merely been transferred from judges to prosecutors who can now control sentences by the charging decisions that they make.[54] It is unquestionable that the guidelines have spawned a huge number of appeals as defendants look for loopholes in the increasingly complex set of sentencing rules. These challenges to the guidelines show no signs of abating, despite the Sentencing Commission's yearly efforts to amend them. Today, sentencing guidelines remain an important and controversial component of the federal adjudication process in criminal cases.

The controversy over disparate sentencing has ebbed during the past few years, but the effort to make sentencing more equitable has not receded. In the coming years more states are expected to limit vast discretion in judicial sentencing and make punishment more predictable, less capricious, and more rational.

SUMMARY

Courts perform various functions in American society. They resolve disagreements among members of the community in civil cases, enforce penal laws in criminal cases, and declare laws passed by the legislature unconstitutional if they fail to comport with the Constitution.

The United States adheres to the adversary model in the search for justice. This means that courts play a neutral role in the conflict among individuals and between individuals and the state. Truth is supposed to emerge from the ruins of courtroom combat. The reality is often far removed from this ideal; nevertheless, the myth thrives and the adversary system has become the accepted method by which justice is dispensed.

The process of adjudication is often long and complex. It starts with the filing of a complaint, followed by an arrest, a booking at the police station, and an appearance before the magistrate. If the case goes any further, a preliminary examination is held, followed by the filing of an accusatory pleading, an arrangement, and then the defendant's plea. The trial itself starts with the selection of jurors (in jury cases), followed by opening statements from the prosecution and the defense. The cases for the prosecution and the defense are presented, the final arguments heard, and then the judge instructs the jury. the judgment can be a conviction, an acquittal, or — if no agreement is reached — a hung jury. If a defendant is convicted, he or she is sentenced by the judge according to the forms of punishment prescribed by law. Although not a constitutional right, all defendants, by statute, are given the right to appeal a conviction. If the conviction is affirmed on appeal, the defendant starts serving the sentence imposed. While serving a sentence, a defendant may continue his fight for freedom by filing a writ of habeas corpus, alleging that his basic constitutional rights were violated during the trial. Writs of habeas corpus very seldom succeed, but hope springs eternal in the hearts of prisoners who have nothing to lose.

Over the past 25 years, a number of jurisdictions have adopted alternative dispute resolution projects that help resolve minor criminal matters informally. In most states, these alternative dispute resolutions centers receive their cases from court referrals. The purpose of these projects is to bring victims and offenders together in an effort to achieve fairness for victims. Studies have shown that satisfaction with these projects is usually high among victims who participate in them.

The United States has a dual court system, meaning that it has one court system for federal cases and another for state cases. In reality, what we have are 51 different judicial systems representing the independent judiciaries of the 50 states and of the federal government. The federal state court systems are separate from and independent of each other, except that both systems are bound by decisions of the United States Supreme Court. Criminal cases may be prosecuted in federal or state courts, depending upon the penal law invoked for the prosecution. If an act is punished by state and federal laws, prosecution can take place in both jurisdictions.

Three categories of court crucial in formalized conflict arbitration. These are the judges, prosecutors, and defense lawyers. Judges control the environment of the proceedings and impose sentences; prosecutors represent the interest of the state, and defense lawyers protect the rights of the accused. Prosecutors are obligated to render justice even if it means disclosing favorable evidence to the accused and losing the case. On the other hand, the loyalty of a defense lawyer is to the accused and not to society. The defense attorney is expected to zealously represent the interests of her client within the bounds of law and professional ethics.

The rights of the accused, primordial in our system of government, are given utmost protection during the trial. The right to counsel provides that an accused must be allowed his or her own lawyer and, if indigent, must be given one by the state. The right to trial by jury is guaranteed in every case where the offense carries a possible penalty of more than six months in jail or prison. The right to a fair and impartial trial prohibits exposing the accused to undue publicity which might prejudice his case and negate the presumption of innocence. The right to confrontation assures the accused of the opportunity to cross-examine the witnesses against him in an effort to expose false testimony. To minimize coercion and abuse, an accused enjoys protection from self-incrimination. This means that the accused does not have to take the witness stand and his or her failure to do so cannot be commented upon by the prosecutor. The right against double jeopardy states that no person shall be punished twice for the same offense; however, defendants who appeal their cases and are successful may be tried again because they are deemed to have waived this right.

Court practices are important in conflict arbitration. Foremost among these is the granting of bail, the practice whereby an accused is given his freedom pending trial in exchange for some type of security. Plea bargaining has been going on for centuries, but its use and legitimacy have been acknowledged by the United States Supreme Court only recently. The jury system has bad its share of critics, but the Constitution, tradition, and the sense of "justice by peers" assure juries a hallowed spot in the American system of conflict arbitration. Sentencing represents the final stage of the conflict resolution process and is perhaps the most important phase for the accused. It is the object of reform efforts because of the inequitable and dysfunctional effects of indeterminate sentencing.

Given what the public sees and reads daily, it does not take much wisdom to realize that the criminal justice system is beleaguered and its institutions and practices are undergoing critical scrutiny. While the system is admittedly far from perfect, it is perhaps the best that can be devised by a society that places a high value on freedom and basic liberties.It is a system that would rather set nine guilty people free than convict an innocent person. Criminal justice is basically a clash between the rights of offenders and the collective values of society as embodied in penal laws enacted by the legislature. The process has been going on for centuries, with imperfect results. There is no reason to believe that perfection will be achieved by this or any other society. Nonetheless, we continue to search and experiment in hopes that through self-analysis, we may bring about the kind of process and result that best resemble the kind of justice our democratic society seeks.

✳ ✳ ✳ ✳ ✳

ENDNOTES

[1] Spaeth, (1972).

[2] Abraham, (1980).

[3] Marbury v. Madison, (1803).

[4] Packer, (1968).

[5] Packer, (1968).

[6] del Carmen, (1995).

[7] McGillis, (1982).

[8] Roehl & Cook, (1982).

[9] Duffy, (1991).

[10] New Mexico Center for Dispute Resolution, (1992).

[11] Woolpert, (1991).

[12] Woolpert, (1991).

[13] Woolpert, (1991).

[14] Davis et. al., (1980); Felstiner & Williams, (1979-80).

[15] Launay & Murray, (1989); Marshall & Merry, (1988); Ruddick, (1989).

[16] Amsterdam, (1970, p. 285).

[17] Senna and Siegel, (1984).

[18] U.S. News & World Report, (1982).

[19] Argersinger v. Hamlin, (1972).

[20] Schwartz, (1961).

[21] del Carmen, (1995).

[22] Powell v. Alabama, (1932).

[23] Scott v. Illinois, (1979).

[24] McMann v. Richardson, (1970).

[25] del Carmen, (1995).

[26] Faretta v. California, (1975).

[27] Williams v. Florida, (1970).

[28] Apodaca v. Oregon, (1972).

[29] Baldwin v. New York, (1970).

[30] Sheppard v. Maxwell, (1966).

[31] Ilinois v. Allen, (1970).

[32] Stack v. Boyle, (1951).

[33] U.S. Department of Justice, (1983).

[34] U.S. Department of Justice, (1983).

[35] U.S. Department of Justice, (1983).

[36] Santobello v. New York, (1971).

[37] del Carmen, (1995).

[38] Brady v. U.S. (1970).

[39] North Carolina v. Alford, (1971).

[40] Santobello v. New York, (1971).

[41] Kaplan, (1979).

[42] U.S. Department of Justice, (1983).

[43] Time Magazine, (1978).

[44] Alaska courts had sufficient slack to absorb more trials. Efficiency techniques instituted 16 months before the 1975 ban continued to whittle down court delay. More careful screening-out of weak cases also helped.

[45] Reid, (1982).

[46] Article 26.13 *Texas Code of Criminal Procedure*.

[47] Morris, (1974).

[48] U.S. News & World Report, (1973).

[49] U.S. Department of Justice, (1983).

[50] U.S. Department of Justice, (1983).

[51] U.S. Department of Justice, (1983).

[52] Wilkins, (1978).

[53] United States Sentencing Commission, (1995).

[54] Flaherty & Biskupic, (1996).

REFERENCES

Abraham, Henry J.
   1980   *The Judiciary: The Supreme Court in the Governmental Process*. Boston: Allyn and Bacon, Inc. 5th edition, p. 175.
Amsterdam, Anthony G.
           "The Supreme Court and the Rights of Suspects in Criminal Cases," *45 N.Y.U.L. Rev*, pp. 285-94.
Apodaca v. Oregon, 406 U.S. 404 (1972).
Argersinger v. Hamlin, 407 U.S. 25 (1972).
Baldwin v. New York, 399 U.S. 66 (1970).
Brady v. U.S., 397 U.S. 472 (1970).
County of Riverside v. McLaughlin, 111 S. Ct. 1661 (1991).
Davis, R., M. Tichane, and D. Grayson
   1980   *Mediation and Arbitration as Alternatives to Criminal Prosecution in Felony Arrest Cases: An Evaluation of the Brooklyn Dispute Resolution Center (first year)*. New York: Vera Institute.

del Carmen, Rolando V.

    1982   *Potential Liabilities of Probation and Parole Officers*. Washington, DC: U.S. National Institute of Corrections.

    1995   *Criminal Procedure: Law and Practice* (3rd ed.). Belmont, CA: Wadsworth.

Duffy, Karen Grover

    1991   "Introduction to Community Mediation Programs: Past, Present, and Future." Pages 21-34 in Karen Grover Duffy, James W. Grosch, & Paul v. Olczak (eds.), *Community Mediation: A Handbook for Practitioners and Researchers*. New York: The Guilford Press.

Faretta v. California, 422 U.S. 806 (1975).

Felstiner, W.F., and L. Williams

    1979-80 *Community Mediation in Dorchester, Massachusetts*. Washington, DC: U.S. Government Printing Office.

Flaherty, Mary Pat, and Joan Biskupic

    1996   "Despite Overhaul, Federal Sentencing Still Misfires," *Washington Post*, October 6.

Illinois v. Allen, 397 U.S. 337 (1970).

Kaplan, John

    1979   *Criminal Justice: Teacher's Manual*. Mineola, NY: The Foundation Press, Inc.

Launay, G., and P. Murray

    1989   "Victim/Offender Groups." Pages 113-131 in M. Wright & B. Galaway (eds.), *Mediation and Criminal Justice*. London: Sage Publications.

Marbury v. Madison, 1 Cranch 137 (1803).

Marshall, T.F., and S. Merry

    1988   *Crime and Accountability: Home Office Research Study*. London: Her Majesty's Stationary Office.

McGillis, Daniel

    1982   "Minor Dispute Processing: A Review of Recent Developments." Pages 60-76 in Roman Tomasic & Malcolm Feeley (eds.), *Neighborhood Justice: An Assessment of an Emerging Idea*. New York: Longman.

McMann v. Richardson, 397 U.S. 759 (1970).

Morris, Norval

    1974   *The Future of Imprisonment*. Chicago: University of Chicago Press.

New Mexico Center for Dispute Resolution

    1992   *Mediation and Conflict Resolution for Gang-Involved Youth*. Washington, DC: U.S. Department of Health and Human Services.

North Carolina v. Alford, 400 U.S. 25 (1971).

Packer, Herbert L.

    1968   *The Limits of the Criminal Sanction*. Stanford, CA: Stanford University Press.

Powell v. Alabama, 287 U.S.45 (1932).

Reid, Sue Titus

    1976   *Crime and Criminology* (1st ed.). Hinsdale, IL: The Dryden Press.

    1982   *Crime and Criminology* (3rd ed.). New York: Holt, Rinehart and Winston.

Roehl, Janice A., and Roger A. Cook

    1982   "The Neighborhood Justice Centers Field Test." Pages 91-110 in Roman Tomasic & Malcolm Feeley (eds.), *Neighborhood Justice: An Assessment of an Emerging Idea*. New York: Longman.

Ruddick, R.

    1989   "A Court Referred Scheme." Pages 82-98 in M. Wright & B. Galaway (eds.), *Mediation and Criminal Justice*. London: Sage Publications.

Santobello v. New York, 404 U.S. 257 (1971).

Schwartz, Murray L.
    1961   *Cases and Materials on Professional Responsibility and the Administration of Criminal Justice*. New York: Council on Legal Education for Professional Responsibility.

Scott v. Illinois, 440 U.S. 367 (1979).

Senna, Joseph J., and Larry J. Siegel
    1984   *Introduction to Criminal Justice* (3rd ed.). St. Paul, MN: West Publishing Company.

Sheppard v. Maxwell, 384 U.S. 333 (1966).

Spaeth, Harold
    1972   *An Introduction to Supreme Court Decisions Making*. San Francisco: Chandler Publishing Company.

Stack v. Boyle, 342 U.S. 1 (1951).

Texas Code of Criminal Procedure, Article 26.13.

Time Magazine, 1978, August 24, p.44.

U.S. Department of Justice
    Report to the Nation on Crime and Justice. Washington, DC: Bureau of Justice Statistics.

United States Sentencing Commission
    1995   *United States Sentencing Guidelines Manual*. Washington, DC: U.S. Government Printing Office.

Wilkins, Leslie T., et al.
    1978   *Sentencing Guidelines: Structuring Judicial Discretion: Report on the Feasibility Study*. Washington, DC: National Institute of Law Enforcement and Criminal Justice.

Williams, v. Florida, 399 U.S. 78 (1970).

Woolpert, Stephen
    1991   "Victim-Offender Reconciliation Programs." Pages 275-297 in Karen Grover Duffy, James W. Grosch, & Paul v. Olczak (eds.), Community Mediation: A *Handbook for Practitioners and Researchers*. New York: The Guilford Press.

SECTION IV

LAW ENFORCEMENT

Chapter 7

History of Law Enforcement in the United States

By

Lyle Shook

To prognosticate the future of law enforcement, one must understand the system as it exists today; but, to do that, you must understand where the system came from. The history of any individual, organization, system, or nation is the foundation upon which it exists. Everything, including law enforcement, is a product of its past. Procedures, attitudes, law, appearance and methods used, all result from deeply ingrained traditions. Citizen attitudes, expectations of the enforcement officer, and the agency he or she represents, are the end result of history. Knowing history is therefore paramount to understanding the present.

American law enforcement history is, to a large extent, a sad story. A story full of low or no educational standards, inefficiency, poor administration, no or ineffective training, brutality and corruption. This history was, for the most part, undisturbed until as recently as the 1930's. This long period of neglect resulted in a public image of the "Keystone Cops." The impression was that the police were so inefficient, stupid, and corrupt that any effort they put forth was a comedy of errors. And often it was. The reputation of law enforcement in America was not something to be proud of. "Bad reputations die hard, and police-community relations are deeply affected by this legacy."[1] The American public, and to a large extent the police themselves, were not alert to, nor did they truly care about, conditions until the social and legal eruptions that occurred in the 1960's. To a considerable extent, the errors of the past are the roots to many of law enforcement's current problems.

ENGLAND

Almost all of the basic concepts of criminal justice in America come directly from English history. There is no way that one can understand our system of justice without looking at the history of English criminal justice. The first colonists were English. They brought with them what they knew and understood. The original thirteen colonies were legally bound to England. The political leadership of those colonies was appointed by the English Crown. For almost half of our history, we were part of the English Empire. England's history is extensive and only a few of her major events will be listed here, events that had a direct effect on American criminal justice. It should be noted by the reader that England reflected the history of many other countries going back through its ancient beginnings. Space does not allow an in-depth discussion in this chapter.

This review would be remiss without mention of the development of Christian thought and its overwhelming influence on England. Early English history was dominated by the Pope and the Roman Catholic Church. There was a time when the Church was the government. The church was the source of law. The church enforced its law and judged any and all violations of its law. This was a dark period of history, not only for England, but most of Northern Europe. The Christian codes of conduct were based on the Ten Commandments and church decree. Church law was harsh, especially for non-believers. Many heinous acts were part of this era. The student of American criminal justice history must become aware of the serious abuse of power during this early period when the church was everything to all people. The Christian codes of conduct had profound impact on American legal thinking and stands as evidence of the need for separation of church and state. Early Christian thinking contributed to laws about homicide, theft, perjury, drinking, gambling, sex, and almost every aspect of morality.

In Europe thousands upon thousands of people were put to death for the church violation of being a witch. Most were burned alive at the stake to "save their souls." A small amount of "witch killing" was conducted among the Puritans of Massachusetts. Virtually every law in America that deals with moral behavior is the direct result of church thinking and influence. Most such laws are violated by huge numbers of citizens, especially in the sexual arena.

In early times the King and Christianity were all powerful. The King appointed the Lord of the Manor. A Manor was an economic and political unit. It was the Lord's land and the serfs worked for the Lord. The Lord provided safety, collected taxes, led men to war, and handed out justice. Somewhere around 600 AD, bands of German and Danish people invaded England. They quickly intermixed with the local Anglos and became known as "Anglo-Saxons." Under the Anglo-Saxons, a system of policing known as "the

mutual pledge system" developed. It was apparently modeled after the Frank-Pledge system, which was developed in France around 700 AD.[2] This system of mutual pledge made every able-bodied citizen responsible for enforcing the law.

At this time of English history, most people lived in small groups or tribes. Where they lived was called a "tun" [town]. As tuns grew inadequate, the Angle-Saxons organized people into groups of ten families called "tithings." Each tithing elected a "tithingman" who had the responsibility to raise the "hue and cry" in case of crime or an emergency. When the hue and cry was put out, it became the responsibility of every able-bodied man to respond, chase the criminal and bring him back for justice. The tithingman punished the offender. This system is the forerunner of the authority of citizen arrest.[3]

The next step was to organize ten tithings into a group call a "hundred," which was led by an elected "reeve." In time a group of hundreds became a "shire." A "shire-reeve" was appointed by the King or a nobleman. The shire-reeve enforced the law and collected taxes. A shire is very similar to an American County. In America, the shire-reeve became known as the Sheriff. The shire-reeve was a powerful, political official. The shire-reeve was given the power of "posse-comitatus," which allowed him to order every able-bodied man to assist him in the hunt for criminals. This is the same power an American Sheriff has today to organize a "posse." Rounding up a posse is seldom used in modern times, but the concept played an important role in our early history. If properly used, posse-comitatus could play an important role in the future, especially in rural areas. Each hundred also elected an officer called a constable. This officer was responsible for weapons and the horses of the entire community. Evidence indicates that the constable was the first police officer in England.[4]

In 1066, England was conquered by William, Duke of Normandy. In history, we know him as William the Conqueror. He brought with him a very different concept for law enforcement. The

148

Normans imposed a strong centralized form of government and enforcement of the King's law. This was the beginning of modern organized policing. The new King appointed his own Sheriffs and retained control over each. The concept of responsibility for law enforcement shifted from local communities to the central government; however, this concept was not popular with the people.[5]

In 1116, Henry I issued an act called the "legis Henrici," which divided England into 30 judicial districts, and identified certain offenses (arson, robbery, murder, counterfeiting, and crimes of violence) as violations of the "Kings peace."[6] Legis Henrici established levels of crime by declaring some as misdemeanors and others as felonies. With this act, we see the idea develop that when a crime is committed, the government is injured and the government should judge the issue. If there is to be a fine, the money goes to the government. Other moneys could be paid to the victim in the form of restitution. The thirteen colonies used both Anglo-Saxon and Norman concepts. Evidence of both are still in use in America today. Restitution goes to the victim and fines go to the government. From this period of history, we see the development of fear of too much power in the hands of central government and the need to keep that power in check, a concept that established America's decentralized system of government and police power. Fragmented law enforcement and government authority, in America, was by choice.

In 1213, a group of barons and church leaders met near London to call for a halt to the King's (John) injustices. They drew up a list of rights they wanted King John to grant them. After the King refused to grant these rights on two separate occasions, the barons raised an army and forced him to meet their demands. On June 15, 1215, King John signed the Magna Carta.[7] King John had been a brutal ruler and the Magna Carta, by force of arms, placed restrictions on his power and the power of his police. Magna Carta is extremely important to American history because parts of our Constitution and especially the Bill of Rights are patterned after this document.

As crime in England continued to rise, King Edward I issued the Statute of Winchester in 1285, and established the "Watch and Ward" form of government, which demanded that all able-bodied men in a given town serve on the night watch. All citizens were required to pursue the criminal when the watch sent out the "hue and cry." In the early days of America, when the Sheriff rode into town and formed a posse, he in effect was putting out the hue and cry. The hue and cry made all citizens responsible for crime. This statute also required all males to have weapons in their home for use in protecting the public peace. These two concepts, have to a large extent, been lost in modern America.

A "marching watch" evolved out of the night watch. This appears to be the forerunner of the foot patrol, which is still used in many locations in America. In addition, the *police des mouers* appear. Their duties were intended to regulate and control prostitution and keep it in certain parts of the city, the start of the "red light district." In America, this approach to prostitution has been tried in many cities, only to be met with failure. The *police des mouers* appears to have been the first vice squad. Edward the First also gave us the first use of a curfew.

The "statutes of treason" appeared in 1352, under King Edward III. This law made it illegal to give aid and comfort to enemies of England and to counterfeit English money. Laws in the United States dealing with treason and counterfeiting were patterned after these early English statutes.[8]

The office of "Justice of the Peace" was created by Edward the Third in or near the year 1361. This office took over many of the duties of the Sheriff and was given the additional power to try and punish. The office of Justice of the Peace had a role in U.S. history, but in the last two or three decades, this office has lost considerable ground and in many states has been eliminated.

We can even find the origin of the use of paid informants in early England. In 1434, Henry VI created the position of "State Informer."[9] These individuals were paid to identify citizens who opposed the King or his policies, which was considered subversion.

Soon after Columbus accidentally found the West Indies, major population shifts started to take place in England. England was beginning to be a major factor in world trade. English wool was highly prized and landowners began to raise more and more sheep. This left less land for farming and farmers were forced to move to cities to find work. This population explosion led to overcrowding, poverty, slums, and crime. Children were starving and families had to get food or money any way they could. They stole goods, and many young girls resorted to prostitution in order to survive.[10] Crime quickly got out of control and riots were common. As a last resort, the army was ordered in and often was very repressive in its efforts to restore order. Harsh repression increased people's fear of centralized power and enforcement by a military police state.

In 1653, Oliver Cromwell assumed power. Crime continued to increase at every level and England came under military rule. Cromwell divided England into twelve districts and placed a general who exercised discretionary police powers in charge of each district. Cromwell's system was very effective in maintaining law and order, but it totally suppressed any form of democracy, and the English people did not like being ruled by a dictator.[11] Political pressure resulted in England's elected Parliament gaining more power. Parliament passed legislation that restricted the King's power even more. When Charles the Second was asked to be King by Parliament in 1660, it was established that the King could not overrule laws passed by Parliament. England took its first giant step in establishing a democratic government. In 1679, Parliament passed the "Habeas Corpus" Act. This law forced the police to produce a prisoner in court and explain to the judge and state the charges upon which the prisoner was being held. If the judge felt the reason was not good enough, the prisoner was released. Habeas Corpus became, and still is, a major factor in American criminal justice.[12]

Crime continued to be an ever increasing problem in England. In 1692, a system of rewards was established to help identify and arrest criminals. Large numbers of people were very poor. In an attempt to gain money, false reporting quickly became a major problem. In 1737, came the beginning of tax supported police. At this time, King George II allowed city councils to levy taxes to pay the night watchmen.[13]

In 1784, Henry Fielding was appointed magistrate of the Middlesex and Westminster districts in London. Fielding was a lawyer and popular writer. Fielding studied the out-of-control crime problem and concluded that a full-time police force was the answer. Parliament gave its support and Fielding and his brother, John, (who was blind), developed a full time force that operated from a station on Bow Street. Although not well-liked in the beginning, the force had a foot patrol, horse patrol, and a detective unit. They were semi-uniformed and became known as the Bow Street Runners. The people soon recognized that the "Runners" were a better choice than the Army. The Bow Street Runners covered only a small area of London, but they laid the foundation for an organized and well-trained police force.[14]

In 1796, another Middlesex Magistrate, by the name of Patrick Colquhoum, wrote a paper titled "A Treatise on the Police of the Metropolis," which drew considerable attention. He stated that London needed a centralized and well-trained police force.[15] Colquhoum, with the assistance of Sir John Harriot, formed the Marine Police Establishment with the intent to protect the docks in the Port of London. This force was so successful that in 1800, Parliament passed the Thames River Police Act which gave the force permanent status, and it was called the Thames River Police.[16]

The most important single act in the history of English-American police history occurred in 1829, with the passage of the London Metropolitan Police Act. Sir Robert Peel was Home Secretary and introduced a bill in Parliament entitled "An Act for Improving the Police In and Near the Metropolis," otherwise known as the Metropolitan Police Act.[17] Part of the act eliminated a number of laws and reformed the criminal code in general.

Effort was made to make the remaining laws simple and understandable. This "Peelian Reform" also established a police force for the city of London. Candidates were to be paid and recruited from the ranks of non-commissioned army officers. This new police force was to be operated based on a strict set of principles, some of the most notable being:

1. The police must be stable, efficient, and organized along military lines.

2. The police must be under governmental control.

3. The absence of crime will best prove the efficiency of the police.

4. The distribution of crime news is essential.

5. The deployment of police strength both by time and area is essential.

6. No quality is more indispensable to a policeman than a perfect command of temper; a quiet, determined manner has more effect than violent action.

7. Good appearance commands respect.

8. The securing and training of proper persons is at the root of efficiency.

9. Public security demands that every police officer be given a number.

10. Police headquarters should be centrally located and easily accessible to the people.

11. Policemen should be hired on a probationary basis.

12. Police records are necessary to the correct distribution of police strength.[18]

The reform brought about by Peel and his supporters was radical but progressive. Today, we would refer to the change as a "quantum leap." Although desperately needed, Peel's ideas were not popular with the people of London in the beginning. There was great fear that he was starting his own army and that he had intent to become a dictator. Peel took great care to keep the police out of politics and politics out of the police. Within a short period of time, attitudes dramatically changed and the people of London grew to respect and trust their police. Within a period of ten years, the people were referring to their police as "Bobbies" in honor of Sir Robert Peel. It needs to be noted that in 1883, the London Metropolitan Police appointed two women. In 1914, they appointed female officers to work in uniform on the street. By 1918, this practice was common. This act of equality was not matched in American until the early 1970's.[19]

Like all great men, Peel stood on the shoulders of many who went before him. But, Peel is commonly given credit for being the "father of modern policing." There is no doubt that he deserves credit for many of the foundation blocks of modern American police principles and practice. Many of Peel's principles have been widely accepted in the United States, but there are noticeable differences. The British established a high degree of police centralization and standardization of law enforcement. America designed a highly decentralized system with very little standardization. England kept politics out of law enforcement, America did not. The British police were very proactive in community relations and crime prevention. American police separated themselves from the public, and became re-active. As a result, these differences undoubtedly contributed to unequal law enforcement, vast differences in the quality and training of officers, political influence within police departments, corruption, and brutality.

AMERICAN LAW ENFORCEMENT DEVELOPMENT

The Colonial Period

Many of the early settlers who came to America were, by English standards, religious misfits or criminals. The development of the English empire was an opportunity for England to rid itself of undesirables and at the same time populate its expanding territories. Many were seeking freedom from direct English rule and taxes, and freedom of religion. But for many, the new world was an escape from jail or worse. To a large extent the new settlers were intolerant people. They were intolerant to English rule and other religious interpretations. They immediately set about taking the land and anything of value from the native Indians. When the Indians figured out what was happening and began to resist, the good people simply killed them. There are no records as to how many Indians were robbed, raped, and murdered. Today, some people wonder why America is so violent. American violence started almost as soon as the white man set foot on our Eastern shore and continues today. When our forefathers said, "The only good Indian is a dead one," that was exactly what they meant. We have always been quick to shoot and ask questions later.

Alone in this vast new country, surrounded by "savages" and "heathens," the settlers realized that there had to be some form of society and rules to follow. The only system they were aware of was England's. There was little need of criminal justice in their small groups and when judgment had to be made, their church set the standard. As the population increased, and more formal government systems were needed, they turned to the English Watch, Constable, and Sheriff.

The early settlers had to have some organization to their society. The systems that developed varied according to the local religion, size of the population, and the natural resources available. These influences are still factors today. The southern colonies found vast areas of good land and hot weather which was ideal for agriculture. Large plantations developed and were supported by slave labor. The county was the primary unit of government and the Sheriff was the chief law enforcement officer. The Sheriff became a very powerful official. Considerable law enforcement effort went into slave-patrol. For example, Charleston, South Carolina, had a slave-patrol of about 100 officers as early as 1837.[20] Other Southern communities maintained similar systems to police the slaves. The violence associated with slavery is well documented and adds to the nation's history of violence. Slaves were property and, of course, had no rights.

People who settled in the north did not find good climate or agricultural land, and tended to live in towns and cities. They turned to trade, fishing and industry. They were very independent people and had experienced tight English control, which they did not like. Therefore, they also avoided centralized government and its enforcement of the law. In 1631, Boston formed the first night watch. It was organized in a military fashion with one officer in charge and six men.[21] In 1636, Boston's night watch was supplemented by "volunteer" citizens who were expected to serve on the night watch.[22] Needless to say, some of the so-called volunteers were not eager to serve and would even pay someone to serve for them, regardless of the substitute's ability. In some cases, courts would even sentence misdemeanants to serve on the night watch.[23]

New Haven, Connecticut, appointed two constables in 1673. Overall, these early colonial police were inefficient and all but worthless. New York City developed a "rattle watch" (a night watch) in 1685. They carried large rattles made of wood to announce their presence and communicate with each other.[24] In 1700, Philadelphia also developed a night watch force.[25] Finally, in 1712, the people of Boston voted to hire, and pay, full-time night watchmen.[26] The pay amounted to about fifty cents per night. Cincinnati and New Orleans developed their night watch forces in 1803, and 1804, respectively.[27]

Night policing continued until 1833, when Philadelphia created a 23-man daytime force and expanded their night watch to 120 men. The mayor appointed one captain to command both the day and night forces.[28]

After the Broad Street riot in Boston in 1837, a man by the name of Francis Tukey was appointed Marshal. Tukey created a very effective police force in Boston, and became one of America's first notable police officials. He divided Boston into districts and created precinct stations.[29]

Day and night forces existed separately until 1844, when New York started adopting some of Robert Peel's recommendations and consolidated its day and night forces. A police superintendent was appointed by the mayor and confirmed by the city council. He organized day and night duty shifts.[30] Because of this action, New York City seems to have legitimate claim to being the first around-the-clock police force in America. In 1850, Boston consolidated its day and night watches. Consolidation was accomplished in Chicago in 1851, in Baltimore and Newark in 1847, and in Providence in 1864.[31]

American cities borrowed heavily from the London Police, but they borrowed selectively. The London Police were highly centralized. Our police were very decentralized. London was highly professional and well-trained but we were not. The British had removed their police from politics. American police were extremely political. The London Police were highly professional with considerable attention being given to good administration, community relations and crime prevention. Police in most American cities were almost totally unprofessional, corrupt, untrained, and showed little concern for citizens. Every aspect of policing was influenced or controlled by local politics. There were no personnel standards other than your political party, religion and ethnic background. To be an officer, you had to have an "in with the political machine in power." There was no job security, and if your political party lost the election, you lost your job. The appointment of Barney McGinniskin, the first Irish-American police officer in Boston, created a major political crisis in 1851. Soon, however, the Irish gained control of most American police departments.[32]

What American people needed in protection from crime, enforcement, service, and prevention was all but non-existent. Political influence was the direct cause of police inefficiency and corruption. Much of the early corruption was by non-enforcement. The police received pay-offs for "looking the other way" on vice such as prostitution, gambling, and illegal liquor. Officers often paid for promotions with money they obtained from graft. The concept of America being a great melting pot led to open conflict between various religious and ethnic groups. Control of alcohol consumption was the major issue in local politics.

Sobriety and temperance was a badge of respectability for many people of Protestant and Anglo-Saxon background. They sought to impose their morality on other groups, especially the Irish and Germans, by controlling or outlawing drinking.[33] The attempts of one group to force their morality on others, especially religious groups, remains a major problem for the police even today.

It is no secret that in modern America, the police chose the laws they wished to enforce and used considerable discretion with the laws they didn't agree with. Early police were treated with disrespect, contempt, and often laughed at. The Keystone Cops were the joke of the day. Unfortunately, old habits and attitudes are hard to break. Many police officers were honest and hard working men, who did their best with what little they had to work with.

The American Civil War

The Peel-based New York City model of policing was adopted by several American cities by the start of the Civil War in 1861. While the basic principles of the New York model were largely acceptable, the new police system confronted three issues:

1. A controversy over the adoption of uniforms,

2. A concern about arming the police, and

3. The issue of appropriate force in making arrests.[34]

The purpose of the uniform was to make the police readily visible to victims, to deter potential offenders, and to compel officers to perform their duty and avoid hiding. In 1853, New York City became the first city to require officers to wear uniforms. The Commissioner refused to hire any officers who refused to wear the uniform. There were many arguments however, against wearing uniforms. Some felt that the uniform would simply make officers more visible to thieves, that it was un-American, or that it undermined officers' masculinity.[35] After the Civil War there was a

153

surplus of blue uniforms and blue became the accepted color for police uniforms in most communities.

Firearms and shooting people have always been part of American history. As our society developed, so did the use of firearms. Before the Civil War a few police officers were shot in the line of duty, but not many. In most communities the police could carry a gun by choice. Many chose not to be armed. After the Civil War there was widespread use of hand guns as a weapon of self defense for law enforcement officers. The war made large numbers of weapons available and produced a population that knew how to use them. After the war, many had experience at killing. The arming of the police was a response to an armed citizenry.

In America it can be argued that all history leads up to the Civil War or away from it. Rebellion is generally not looked upon as a local law enforcement issue, but it was an issue of law, order, and justice at the highest level of our Constitution. The Civil War was the most violent period of our entire existence as a nation. The assassination of President Lincoln was one of our worst criminal acts. The violence that tore our nation apart contributed heavily to our reputation as a violent people. The police responded to violence with violence.

Post Civil War

After the Civil war, thousands of displaced Americans drifted West to find a new start. They ventured into a frontier without government, a land without law and order. The only law was the fastest gun. With no choice, people formed vigilante groups and took the law into their own hands. Vigilante law was swift, but not always sure. As vast areas of land opened up and became territories of the United States, the role of the US Marshall was important. But, with thousands of square miles to protect, his job was nearly impossible. In many cases the only protection came from the US Army. The slaughter of American Indians went on unabated. The "savage" had no rights. Entire

tribes were wiped out — men, women, and children. Their society, language, religion, and even their food supply was deliberately destroyed. Settlers and cowboys needed their land. The systematic destruction of the American Indians is one of the ugliest chapters in American history. Justice did not exist for the red man. "Thou Shalt Not Kill" was not part of frontier thinking.

Frontier towns began to spring up, especially as the railroads moved west. Cattle drives brought vast herds of beef for the rapidly growing cities "back east." These cowtowns were often lawless. Citizens elected sheriffs and hired constables and town marshals, like Wyatt Earp, Wild Bill Hickok, Bill Tilghman, and others. These "lawmen" were nothing more than a fast gun. There was little time to worry about constitutional rights — it was law and order at any cost. That cost was often a dead body lying in the street. In this part of the country and period of time, law enforcement bore little resemblance to criminal justice today.

Allan Pinkerton

Allan Pinkerton is normally associated with private security, but he played an important role in the development of the American police. He was born in Scotland, married, and joined the radical Chartist group. With the authorities after him, he fled to the United States as a fugitive. He and his wife settled in Chicago and he worked as a cooper (making barrels out of wood). One day, by accident, he stumbled upon a gang of counterfeiters and helped the Cook County Sheriff arrest them. He later sold his business and was appointed deputy sheriff in Cook County, Illinois. In 1843, he was appointed the first detective in the city of Chicago. There is evidence that Allan Pinkerton was the first professional detective in America. In 1850, Pinkerton took on the Rock Island and Illinois Central Railroads as private clients and soon thereafter formed the Pinkerton National Detective Agency. Pinkerton became the first law enforcement officer to protect railroads. He is the beginning of the "railroad police."[36] Pinkerton also hired Kate Warne, who was the first female detective in America.[37]

154

As the railroads spread west, the agency became the only organized source of law enforcement available and served in many ways like a national police agency, even though they were privately owned. Public law enforcement was so corrupt and incompetent that the well trained, professionally dressed, and honest Pinkerton agents were refreshing. There seemed to be no limits to the spread of Pinkerton's business. Pinkerton agents worked under a strict code of ethics, they developed the art of "shadowing," (surveillance) and "assuming the role" (going undercover). Pinkerton established the art of handwriting examination. He pushed for the creation of centralized criminal identification records and worked hard for international police cooperation. He is given credit for building the foundation for the modern international organization known as Interpol.

When the South opened fire on federal property at Fort Sumpter in Charleston Harbor, North Carolina, and the Civil War started, Pinkerton offered his services to the North. He was immediately given the task of protecting newly elected President Lincoln. He detected an assassination plot while Mr. Lincoln was on the way to be sworn in as President. The assassination plot failed. President Lincoln called on Pinkerton to "ascertain the social, political, and patriotic relations of numerous suspected people in and about Washington."[38] This was the start of his extensive intelligence work for the North during the rest of the war. Pinkerton's espionage and military intelligence contributed heavily to the war's outcome. Pinkerton often went on spy missions himself, and was in fact caught several times, but talked his way out of trouble every time.

The Start of State Police

As early as 1835, Texas organized a state military unit to patrol the Mexican border and deal with Indians, outlaws, and cattle rustlers. They were known as the Texas Rangers, but they did not have state-wide general police powers.

In 1865, Massachusetts appointed several "state" constables.[39] Their main mission was the reduction of vice throughout the state. These officers were given general police power state-wide, and therefore, claim to be the first true state police. Because of the unpopularity of the agency, they were abolished in 1875.[40] In 1901, the Arizona Rangers were formed, followed by the New Mexico Mounted Police in 1905. Both were border patrol and similar to the Texas Rangers.[41] About 1905, (this date is in question) The Pennsylvania State Police was established.

Today, state police agencies are strong in the Northeastern states, but tend to play a secondary roll in the rest of the nation. In most Southern, Mid-Western and Western states, State police efforts focus on "State Troopers," who patrol major highways and Interstates, a state investigative agency, crime lab, and a police training academy. There is still considerable fear in placing too much police power in a centralized government. Most people feel that they can maintain better control over a local police department which has an elected mayor and city council, or a locally elected sheriff, than they can a large bureaucracy at the state level. At the local level, the average person feels he has a chance. At the state level, chances are greatly diminished, and at the national level, the average person feels he has little to no chance.

Federal Law Enforcement

Federal law enforcement starts with our second government. Immediately after the American Revolution our first government was known as the Articles of Confederation. For all practical purposes, we were thirteen separate states bound together in a very loose confederation. Our young nation went too far in decentralization of power. The United States was in jeopardy and about to go under when our leaders called a Constitutional Convention and adopted our Constitution in 1789. This action created a new and stronger government for America. The Constitution divided power between state governments and a centralized federal government. The Constitution created a Supreme Court. Nothing is said in the Constitution

155

about a federal enforcement system. The original document said nothing about individual rights of the citizens. By agreement, a "Bill of Rights" was added in 1791. The founders of our government had considerable fear of centralized police power and government in general. The Constitution of the United States is full of "checks and balances" in a deliberate attempt to control government power. The Bill of Rights was added to the Constitution to protect every citizen from its own Federal government, because it was the Federal Government that our Founding Fathers feared. The Bill of Rights had almost no impact on state criminal procedure. Each state had its own Constitution where its local criminal procedure was spelled out.

Immediately after the Civil War, in 1866, the Fourteenth Amendment was added to the Constitution. This Amendment stated that "no state shall deprive any person of life, liberty or property without due process of law, nor deny . . . the equal protection of the laws."[42] Much of the intent of this amendment was to provide protection for the new black citizens, especially from criminal justice in Southern States. Many states conducted business as usual and it took a long list of decisions by the United States Supreme Court to force compliance by the individual states. But gradually, The Fourteenth Amendment brought sweeping changes in state criminal procedure. Three cases in the 1960s, were especially important. The cases of Mapp v. Ohio, Escobedo v. Illinois, and Miranda v. Arizona made it very clear that Constitutional rights applied to all citizens at all levels of government. At the time there was a hue and cry from local law enforcement that they had been handcuffed in their fight against criminals. This of course did not happen. With the guidelines from the court in effect, the police had a clear set of procedures to follow. In effect, local and state law enforcement were told that they must also obey the law of the land. As a direct result of these three cases, law enforcement standards and training have vastly improved, although there are hold-outs who still feel that present criminal procedure provides too much protection for the individual being accused of a crime. But we must be very careful to ensure that every person has equal protection under the law from all governments,

whether they be local, state, or federal. All modern law enforcement officers must be ethically, morally, and legally required to obey the law the same as government requires the citizen to obey the law. These three landmark cases gave definition to criminal procedure and were a major step forward.

In the division of powers between the states and federal government, the federal government was given control over a standardized system of money and counterfeiting, the postal system and interstate commerce. In time, agencies were established to allow the federal government to enforce its mandate.

In 1789, the Revenue Cutter Service was created to fight smuggling. The issue was the government collecting taxes. Also in that year the office of U.S. Attorney was created. Its responsibility was to investigate crimes committed against the U.S. government. The U.S. Post Office created an investigation unit in 1829, to combat mail fraud. In 1865, the Secret Service was authorized to deal with counterfeiting. There was a rapid expansion of federal enforcement in the five years after the Civil War. The Internal Revenue Service, Customs Service and the Department of Justice were all created and put into effect. It should be noted that up to the end of the Civil War in 1865, almost all federal investigations and enforcement was contracted out to private security.

President Theodore Roosevelt ordered the Attorney General to create an investigative bureau for the Department of Justice in 1908. By 1909, the new agency was in operation and was known as the Bureau of Investigation. The White Slave Traffic Act, also known as the Mann Act, was new and responsibility for its enforcement was given to the Bureau. This act forbids interstate transportation of women for prostitution. Sex for hire was in great demand. Gangs of men tricked, coerced and kidnaped females, broke their resistance, transported them across state lines, and forced them into prostitution. Those that could not be broken, were killed. One of the famous cases involved heavyweight boxing champion, Jack Johnson, who ended up in jail as a result of a trip with his fiancee, a former prostitute.

When the Bureau of Investigation was established, there was immediate fear of too much power in the hands of an ever growing Federal government. "... once initial suspicions were allayed that it would turn into some big, secretive, czarist police force, it did precisely that. The bureau quickly built its empire of white men in white shirts, chasing anarchists and Bolsheviks in the 20's, gangsters and bootleggers in the 30's, fascists in the 40's, communists in the 50's and civil-rights leaders and antiwar protesters in the 60's."[43]

Until the early 1900's, the role of federal enforcement was limited. But, when World War I started in Europe, two big criminal justice issues impacted on our Federal Government. First, in 1914, the nation became involved with drugs when Congress passed the Harrison Act. Under this act, the Department of Treasury was made responsible for regulation of importation, manufacturing, and distribution of narcotics. With our entry into World War I, national security took center stage and the Espionage Act was passed in 1917, followed by the Sedition Act of 1918. Federal law enforcement power rapidly increased during this dramatic time.

In 1917, the Communists had been successful in the Russian Revolution and our first "Red Scare" broke out in America. The Justice Department placed J. Edgar Hoover in charge of its Intelligence Division. Under Hoover's leadership, the Intelligence Division "prepared dossiers on 450,000 people, 60,000 of whom he designated as important radicals."[44] Hoover made mass arrests of suspected communists. Centralized federal power, as feared by so many, was turned loose. This "Red Scare," the first of many, subsided in the early 1920's. But, it did not die, and is still with us today. Unfortunately, law enforcement is the tool of government. Government helps to create the problem by passing unwanted or unnecessary laws, and uses enforcement to force people to do its bidding. As a result, enforcement often winds up taking the responsibility for violations of peoples rights.

The Roaring 20's

America's fight against gangsterism was getting more intense. As the nation entered the 1920's, a large group of morally motivated people thought they could correct many of Americas social and criminal problems if they could require people to stop drinking liquor. With the Volstead Act, the Constitution of the United States was amended and the manufacture, sale, and distribution of booze was prohibited. On January 16, 1920, America went "dry." World War I had just ended and the public's mood seemed to be, "Live today for tomorrow we may die." Thousands had fought and died for freedom, not moralistic control. The thought was noble, but two errors in judgment were made. First, Americans did not like to be told they could not drink, and second, the majority wanted to drink. Prohibition drove liquor underground and created a huge and highly profitable illegal market for gangsters who were willing to supply the outlawed products that so many people wanted. The 1920's became known as the "Roaring Twenties." The moralists unwittingly set off one of the most criminal periods in our history. It became fashionable and exceedingly profitable to disobey the law. The fact that these "products" were illegal contributed to their desirability, and guaranteed uncounted millions of dollars of profit. The gangsters were more than willing to make murder a necessary tool of their "business." The Thompson .45 caliber submachine gun became so popular with gangsters, it became known as a "Chicago typewriter."

The law made illegal booze so profitable that gangsters soon fought over control of larger and larger territories. It can be demonstrated that prohibition created hoodlums like Al Capone and hundreds like him. Capone often described himself as a business man supplying products "respectable" Americans wanted. Capone combined the three areas of illegal booze, gambling, and prostitution, putting them under one roof, and paid off hundreds of law enforcement officers to "look the other way." Police corruption was at an all-time high.

The moralists may have been well-intended,

but like so many times before and after, they created worse problems by attempting to control the desire of their fellow man. Instead of moral reward, tranquility, and the improvement of society, they eroded American morality and contributed to the new menace of armed gangsterism. We have done the very same thing with our modern "war on drugs."

J. Edgar Hoover

The Bureau of Investigation had a bad reputation for corruption. In 1924, a major restructuring took place and a young lawyer working in the Bureau, J. Edgar Hoover, was named to the directorship of the Bureau of Investigation. From that point on, high standards of employment, promotion based on merit, and high ethical expectation became the standard. In time, these standards resulted in a highly respected agency. Hoover hired the best of the best. All were college graduates and most new agents were lawyers. He weeded out agents of questionable background and fired large numbers of "honorary" agents who had been given badges for political reasons. He quickly established a criminal laboratory based on the highest standards of evidence analysis. He established a National Police Academy. All new FBI agents were trained there along with selected law enforcement officers from all over the United States. Academy training was, and still is, the best available. Loyalty to the FBI and to Mr. Hoover quickly expanded to all parts of the country. As the FBI became stronger and stronger, Hoover asked for, and was granted, permission for agents to be armed. The power of the FBI over interstate and other crimes was expanded. Hoover and his internal leadership became masters of the media. During the 1920's, many notorious criminals were created by the media and with encouragement from the FBI. They in turn were arrested or killed by special agents, always with great publicity for the Bureau.

As the nation reeled under the increase in crime, important new laws involving such matters as extortion, kidnapping, stolen property, bank robbery, etc., were added to FBI responsibility.

When the stock market crashed in 1929, money was hard to come by. Armed gangsterism turned to bank robbery. The media was eager for the next FBI Wanted Poster. The mass media hung on every episode of gangsterism and the well-published and relentless pursuit by the FBI. Bank robbers became famous as they out-ran and out-gunned local police. Kidnapping was another popular way to turn quick cash. Headlines blared with names like "Machine Gun Kelly," "Bonnie and Clyde," "Baby Face Nelson," and the most notorious of all, John Dillinger.

Dillinger was a bank robber and killer, who roamed the Midwest and Chicago. In July of 1934, working on a tip, the FBI tracked him to Chicago, where he was betrayed by a female "friend." The FBI set a trap, and as he walked out of a theater he was confronted. As he tried to draw his gun he ran down an alley and was gunned down. In death, Dillinger was seen by the public as a modern day "Robin Hood," and with considerable help from the press was elevated into a folk-hero. But the FBI got their man.[45]

As the FBI brought down mobster after mobster there was considerable fear that the Federal Government was moving closer and closer to a national police force. By the mid 1930's, horror stories were already pouring out of Nazi Germany about the Gestapo. Many Americans began to see J. Edgar Hoover and the FBI as one and the same. Hoover was a respected but feared man. After his death, the Freedom of Information Act opened many thousands of pages of "secret files" that clearly demonstrated that Hoover and the FBI were very political, and worked to help certain candidates. Hoover's claim that the FBI was politically impartial was a total sham. Using illegal electronic and photographic surveillance, Hoover and his FBI had built dossiers on just about every important person in the nation, including critical files on Adlai Stevenson for Eisenhower, and on Senator McGovern for Nixon. Many feel that the FBI was closer to a Gestapo-type operation than the public ever realized. One thing is certain; Hoover had extraordinary power, and it seemed that no one could touch him, not even Presidents.

The capture of one big-time mobster led to the FBI's first popular nickname. Resulting from an Oklahoma City, Oklahoma, kidnapping and ransom case, the FBI's suspect was George "Machine Gun" Kelly. They tracked him to a hideaway and caught him without his machine gun in hand. Totally surrounded by agents with guns pointed at him, he pleaded for his life by saying, "Don't shoot, G-men! Don't shoot, G-men!" The American press picked it up and for a long time, FBI agents were commonly known as G-Men. Many popular movies were made about the exploits of G-Men and later hundreds of television programs portrayed then as super cops. Thousands of headlines and magazine articles made the FBI the number one law enforcement agency and Mr. Hoover was crowned the number one G-man. There was no question in anyone's mind that the FBI was at war with crime, and that Mr. Hoover was the FBI.

As World War II approached, the FBI developed files on Americans suspected of being sympathizers with Germany, Japan, and Italy. When the United States became involved in the war on December 7, 1941, thousands of these sympathizers were immediately rounded up. With the war came additional laws and expansion of the FBI and its power.

In 1950, Hoover and his bureau hit on a publicity gold mine when they came out with the "Ten Most Wanted" criminals in the U.S. Never one to miss a story, Hoover named the first ten, not in one release, but listed them one at a time and got ten stories for the FBI and, of course, for Mr. Hoover. It was on May 14, 1950, when "Tough Tommy" Holden was given the number one spot on the top ten. Thomas J. Holden was a train robber, prison escapee and had murdered his wife and her two brothers in Chicago. The American public was eager to help and the sudden nationwide notoriety resulted in his arrest on June 23, 1951.

Hoover and his FBI, from the beginning, recognized the power of information and the use of the public press. Through the years, the FBI expanded its information gathering ability and today has extensive information on a large number of American citizens.

The Push for Professionalism

There were many outside the FBI who worked tirelessly for law enforcement professionalism. By the early 1900's, a much broader reform movement known as progressivism was sweeping the United States. Police reform was but one aspect of progressivism.

Richard Sylvester, Superintendent of the District of Columbia Police, became the head of the International Association of Chiefs of Police in 1901. The IACP grew out of the National Chief of Police Union that began in 1893. Sylvester quickly transformed the IACP into the voice of law enforcement professionalism and the leading source for new ideas in police work, especially administration.[46]

Even more famous than Sylvester was August Vollmer, who became Chief of Police in Berkeley, California. His greatest contribution was his desire to have college-educated officers with a degree in Criminology. Vollmer created the first formal training school for police officers in 1908. He was instrumental in organizing the first police-science courses at the University of California in 1916. In that same year he assisted in the establishment of the first college-level training program for police at San Jose State College, in San Jose, California. After his officers gained a degree and police experience, he urged them to become Chiefs of Police in other California cities and duplicate his example. August Vollmer gave lectures and seminars throughout the country and acted as a consultant to many police departments. A few cities like Berkeley, Cincinnati, and Milwaukee enjoyed high standards of professionalism. Others could not change and failed. Vollmer spent a year as chief of police in Los Angeles, but gave up in despair and went back to Berkeley. Chicago was, and has been, impervious to reform. The reformers put all their effort into police administration, which proved to be an error. This tended to make police organizations into highly centralized and isolated bureaucracies. You can not wage war on crime and only involve the chiefs.

After World War I, technology began to have an impact on law enforcement. First was the patrol car. It's not certain which city had the first, but the time was just before the war started for America. The police had to use cars just to keep up with the criminals. Many great things can be said in favor of police cars, but they took the patrol off the street and isolated the police from the citizen. Police-community relations suffered and isolation of the police remains a problem even today.

The telephone had been patented in 1877. This breakthrough put the public in immediate touch with the police. Any citizen could quickly call the police for help or to provide information about a crime.

A third technological breakthrough was the two-way radio. At first, radio was one-way, but by the late 1930's, two-way radio communication was reasonably common in police work. For the first time, police headquarters and the officer on the street could maintain around-the-clock communication. Now, the chief knew his officer was on duty and could be quickly sent to the source of trouble. But, that also meant that everyone could "call the cops." The police workload increased dramatically as public expectations expanded. The public quickly learned two things about the police: No matter what the problem was, the police were available and the police had authority. This was not always true, but the public thought so, and expected action. The demands for service calls exploded. The police soon received more service calls than criminal calls.

An understudy of August Vollmer became chief of police in Wichita, Kansas in 1928. O.W. Wilson made contributions to police administration and developed new methods for efficient police patrol. He pushed the concept of one-officer patrol cars and demonstrated that they were just as safe as a two-man car, but, with two cars you could cover twice the territory. Wilson went on to become the Dean of the School of Criminology at Berkeley. In 1960, he was appointed superintend-

ent of the Chicago Police Department. In Chicago, he made improvements, especially in administration, but he failed to get the department under control and end corruption. He was a principal author of the International City Management Association text, *Municipal Police Administration*. In 1950, he authored a leading textbook on Police Administration, and became the leading authority on police administration in the U.S.

Wickersham Commission

At the urging of many, especially August Vollmer, President Herbert Hoover in 1929 appointed the National Commission of Law Observance and Enforcement, to study the American criminal justice system. The chairperson was George Wickersham, and the study became known as the Wickersham Commission Report. Two of the fourteen reports dealt with the police. Report number 11 was the most sensational and was titled "Lawlessness in Law Enforcement." It thoroughly examined and exposed the problem of police brutality. The report concluded that "The third degree . . . the infliction of pain, physical or mental, to extract confessions or statements . . . is extensively practiced." It found that the police commonly used beatings, threats, protracted questioning, and illegal detention.[47] There had been much concern about police brutality and the Wickersham Commission confirmed it. America and police leaders were deeply embarrassed. There was much discussion, but in the end, very little changed.

World War II

World War II found almost every country in the world either directly involved in the conflict or touched by it in some way. Large numbers of men and women were in the service, especially young men who are most likely to commit a crime. Crime dropped but so did the number of police officers. Thousands of police were either drafted or enlisted. Although there was lots of black market crime, violence, to a large extent, was vented on our enemies. The war brought an "understanding" between our government and organized crime. For example, for certain privileges, the criminal element agreed to protect our shipping docks from violence, sabotage, and espionage. America had no problem on our docks during the entire war, thanks to the mob.

One of the really ugly chapters in American history and in criminal justice occurred in 1942, with the forced internment of 110,000 American citizens of Japanese descent. After the attack on Pearl Harbor, the West Coast of America was in panic, and thought that they would be invaded at any moment. The U.S. Army, with the help of the FBI and local police, rounded up men, women, children, and even babies, of Japanese background and placed them in concentration camps located out in the desert and other inhospitable places. The criminal justice system did nothing to protect their constitutional rights. In fact, these American Citizens, known as Nisei, suddenly had no rights whatsoever. The real issue was racial. In Hawaii, where invasion was a real possibility, only a handful of Japanese-American citizens were arrested and detained. Most of the west-coast Japanese lost everything to the whites who were eager to buy their land and property very cheaply. The Republican Governor of California was Earl Warren, who made no effort to protect the rights of so many of California's citizens. Warren later became Chief Justice of the United States Supreme Court.

Post World War II

After World War II, the nation was busy re-adjusting to a peacetime economy. Marriages and the number of babies dramatically increased. This "baby boom" would later have a direct affect on street crime. Thousands of former GIs went to college on the new GI Bill. Many of these new college graduates found their way into police work. Many had military police or investigation experience. For the first time in the nation's history, there were highly trained, educated, and experienced men coming into law enforcement. Some of these men began to demand higher police standards, training, and professionalism.

The late 1950's, and early 1960's, brought the rapid spread of television. Suddenly, every night, citizens could see what was happening all over America. Police events were given lots of coverage, and the American public, for the first time, were in a position to judge what the police were doing or not doing. With knowledge came questions. Because of the excitement in police work and the interest in criminal activity, "cop shows" became very popular with the American TV and motion picture public.

In Los Angeles, William H. Parker had been appointed Chief of Police. Parker brought many new ideas and methods in his attempt to bring police corruption under control. He also introduced "aggressive patrol," to wage war against street crime. This form of professionalism backfired because it resulted in greater separation of the police and the public and proved to be very insensitive to blacks and Hispanics. The police seemed to forget that when you push people too far, they push back.

The Tumultuous 60's

Five major events occurred in the decade of the 1960's, that turned the criminal justice world upside down. Early, we see large-scale racial riots across America and the Assassination of President John F. Kennedy. By the mid 60's, a series of landmark Supreme Court cases rocked law enforcement. Fourth was the American involvement in Vietnam. Finally, there was considerable interest and usage of illegal drugs.

By the early 1960's, black people were fed-up with discrimination by government and harsh enforcement by its various police agencies. The spark was a young black woman by the name of Rosa Parks, in Montgomery, Alabama, who took a seat in the front of the bus, which was considered the white section, because there were no seats in the back, which was the black section. She was arrested by the police and the Montgomery Bus Boycott was on. The issue was brought into everyone's living room that night by TV. Soon they saw a church bombing in Birmingham, Alabama. They saw the bodies of the little girls who were killed, and they watched the street riots that resulted. TV showed police officers beating blacks with nightsticks, and police dogs biting and ripping the clothing off blacks who protested. Fire hoses were turned on and blacks were knocked off their feet by the pressure. In Selma, Alabama, at the Edmund Pettis Bridge, TV showed America a large number of blacks getting ready to peacefully march to Montgomery to protest their treatment, when suddenly and without provocation, State Troopers and local police charged the crowd, nightsticks swinging, tear gas bursting, people falling and bleeding, and being dragged from harm's way.

TV showed blacks being arrested in Montgomery, Alabama and other cities for trying to eat in all-white restaurants. TV showed the nation a young Montgomery preacher by the name of Martin Luther King, being arrested and put in jail. There were black and white water fountains and toilets, etc. In Mississippi and other Southern states, white "Freedom Riders" were being murdered. Federal troops were sent to Little Rock, Arkansas, so that black children could go to public school. The Governor of Alabama, George Wallace, "stood in the doorway" of the University of Alabama to prevent the entrance of black students and the Federal government had to federalize the national guard to force integration. All across America, riots, arson, and looting broke out in the black sections of many major cities. Most of the riots were precipitated by an incident involving the police.

The most dramatic of these riots were in Watts (a district in Los Angeles), Detroit, and New York City. Police agencies seemed to be helpless. Night after night, America was burning, and the police were swinging their nightsticks, using dogs and throwing tear gas, and the people sang, "We shall overcome." But it was all happening in our front room. It was no longer somewhere far away. America was mesmerized by the events. Most Americans were shocked, fearful for the nation, and could not believe it could happen here — in America. Large numbers of people began to ask if this was what America was about. The police lost

respect, they were no longer the "Keystone Cops." They were mean, vicious bullies, who enforced the status quo, with little or no regard for people's constitutional rights. It was obvious that equal rights did not exist. The police were there to protect the rich, but not the poor.

In the middle of all of this turmoil, President John F. Kennedy was assassinated in Dallas, Texas. Kennedy was young, full of energy, and very popular with the American public. We saw him playing with his small children, and his attractive wife Jackie. Much of the nation was in love with "Camelot." Then we saw them riding down the street in Dallas. Right there in our front room, we saw him gunned down. We observed his head explode, and TV replayed it time after time. We saw the blood on Jackie's dress. In shock, the nation almost came to a standstill. Even crime on the street dramatically dropped. All of this could not be happening in America. Where were the police? The FBI? The Secret Service? There was talk of CIA involvement, or was it an organized crime hit? America saw everything, and asked hard questions, but received few answers that they could believe. Even today, there is considerable question as to what really happened in Dallas. Many felt the police, and especially the government, lied to us to cover its error and incompetence. Did the government lie to us? If so, why?

The "Hippie" generation brought "flower children" who dared confront authority on many issues, especially on the draft and the ever increasing involvement in some far-off jungle called Vietnam. As the years passed, the body count got higher and higher. The passive resistance of the early 1960's, became more vocal and less passive. Government responded with tough enforcement and the hippies put flowers in their gun barrels. Many hippies were well-educated people, who challenged police with questions the police could not answer. Police were called "pigs." Drugs became popular and were used openly in public. Great music concerts drew thousands to places like Woodstock. Rock music, drugs, and sex were seen by the public on TV, in their front room, on the news, almost every night. The police seemed to do nothing about this defiance of the law. As major issues and our society changed, government, the law, and the police did not.

Public expectations about the role, performance, and efficiency of the police had changed rapidly. To a large extent, the police had not been prepared, nor were they ready for the Supreme Court to drop the "due process revolution" on them. In three landmark decisions, the Court, over a period of five years, insisted that all state and local law enforcement officers follow the rules as established by the Bill of Rights. These rules are collectively known as "Due Process." In Mapp v. Ohio (1961), Escobedo v. Illinois (1964), and Miranda v. Arizona, (1966), the high court established specific guidelines that the police had to follow when officially dealing with citizens. In essence, the Court said the Government makes the law and the citizen is expected to obey the law, but, the police also have rules and they are expected to follow those rules also. Today, the public is aware of due process, and expect that it will be followed. Back in the 1960's, these decisions fell on law enforcement with great impact.

Due process had been established for, and was followed by, all federal law enforcement agencies and about half of the various states. But, after Mapp, Escobedo and Miranda, there no longer was a choice. Local police now had to follow the rules. Police agencies thought they had been handcuffed. There was a feeling that they would never be able to convict another criminal. In police eyes, these were very controversial decisions.

In the 1960's, American police were placed under the microscope of public scrutiny and the public did not like what it saw. We observed discrimination, a disregard for civil liberty, and little consideration given for constitutional rights. Police officers were ill-prepared for the changes taking place. Officers were under-educated, many had little or no training, efficiency was low, salaries were poor, equipment was second rate, and administration often weak. Crime was on the rise and became a major political issue. "Law and Order" became the "hot button" of the day. The more the police were scrutinized, the more they were criticized.

In response, the International Association of Chiefs of Police and the International Association of Police Professors (now known as the Academy of Criminal Justice Sciences), put out the call for the academic community to offer degrees in Police Science. Starter money began to appear. With money on the street, academic institutions quickly became interested. The University of Iowa, for example, in 1967, received a grant to help start six two-year programs in the state Community College System. That grant called for a Director who had a college degree in something, (Criminal Justice degrees were almost non-existent at the time), who was a certified teacher, (which was required to teach in a Community College) and someone who had both law enforcement and teaching experience. A survey of all police officers in the state of Iowa, found only four officers with a degree in anything. None were certified teachers. The Iowa experience would have been typical for the time. The author of this chapter was the only person in the state who could meet all the requirements, and became the director for that grant.

The six community colleges came on-line, but no law enforcement instructors could be found. As a solution to the problem, the law enforcement students were brought to the university for the summer, where the enforcement classes were taught by experienced people with degrees, but the university did not require certification.

In 1965, conditions had deteriorated to the point that President Johnson called for a President's Commission to study the entire criminal justice system. Their report was called The Challenge of Crime in a Free Society, and was issued in 1967. Many recommendations were made. One, for example, was to educate every officer to the level of a Bachelors Degree by 1984. The Federal government made billions of dollars available to pay for education and hundreds of other things. Cities saw the opportunity to build new jails, buy squad cars and all kinds of equipment. States built more prisons and bought everything in sight. "Snake oil" dealers were everywhere. Police officers found that with the GI Bill and Law Enforcement Assistance money, they could make more money going to college than they could working two or three part-time jobs. Colleges noted that the government was throwing money in every direction and overnight came up with degree programs. In a period of ten years, the nation went from a mere handful of degree programs in criminal justice to somewhere over 1,700. There is an old police saying that states, "When there is lots of money on the streets, there will also be prostitutes." Frankly, this was a period of prostitution for law enforcement, colleges, and universities across America. Quality was not a major concern, and law enforcement education developed a poor reputation. But, the money was flowing and the hookers were there to take it. In time, people began to realize that you can not solve social problems by throwing money at them. As the money dried up, fewer officers enrolled, classes were dropped, and entire programs vanished.

Although there was tremendous waste, some good did result from The Law Enforcement Assistance Act (LEAA). Some research challenged old methods of doing things. New police stations, jails, and prisons were built. New equipment and badly needed squad cars were added. More officers were hired. Communications centers were added and radios became standard items. Police training and educational standards improved. Many states used LEAA money to establish police academies and set minimum standards for all officers. Until the mid 60's, and early 70's, most police officers were still hired, given a badge and a gun, and told to go get the bad guys. Thousands of officers went to college. Officers with an education did better on their promotional tests and soon we began to see college-educated Chiefs of Police in many communities. By the mid-1980's, and about five billion dollars later, the Law Enforcement Assistance program was shut down. The number of officers working on degrees dropped, as did the number of degree programs. Criminal justice research, without money to fund it, substantially decreased. All-in-all, President Johnson's "war on crime" had not lived up to expectations.

The President's Commission on Law Enforcement and the Administration of Justice had made many recommendations. In 1967, the Johnson Administration was able to get The Safe Streets and Crime Control Act passed and implemented. As a direct result of the turbulence of the 1960's, and pressure demanding police change from many other social forces, the 1970's and 80's saw many changes in American criminal justice. Federal laws demanding equal opportunity for women and minorities resulted in major hiring changes. Laws and court orders demanding that minorities and females be promoted to all ranks, opened command positions to officers who ten years prior, did not have a chance to achieve.

Law Enforcement Today

Modern law enforcement is a far cry from what it was just a few years ago. The level of professionalism has steadily improved. Large numbers of police administrators are college educated. Many have Masters Degrees and a few have a Doctorate. Many street level officers have degrees or are working on one. Many police agencies provide incentive pay to officers working on degrees. Many agencies require continuing education for officers. Police schools and seminars are available on a wide variety of law enforcement topics. The FBI Academy continues to offer state-of-the-art training for local and state officers. State academies are also providing advanced training along with upgraded basic training. Unfortunately, some departments continue to lag behind in training and education.

Today, we observe a few females and many blacks as police chiefs. This is especially true in large cities. Almost all local, county, and state law enforcement agencies are integrated, although there are still some problems, especially in rural areas.

Many new concepts of police work are now in use, again, mostly in larger departments. Today, departments are doing crime analysis, intelligence gathering, team policing, preventive patrol, profiling, new methods of management, and community oriented policing, to mention a few. Equipment has been upgraded. Police cars have computers and mounted TV cameras. Most officers are wearing bullet- and stab-resistant vests, and are armed with magazine-loaded pistols rather than the lower-firepower revolver. By satellite monitoring, it is now possible to track the exact (within a few feet) location of a squad car. Headquarters can even tell the direction and how fast the squad car is moving. The touch of one panic button and a signal can tell immediately when an officer is in danger, and exactly where the car is.

Police work today involves a wide variety of methods of transportation and communications. There is a movement to get patrol officers back into various forms of foot patrol. Automobiles are used extensively along with four-wheel drive vehicles for rugged areas. Four-wheelers and snowmobiles are in common use. Fixed-wing aircraft and helicopters are found in state and big-city patrol. A variety of marine police use airboats and fast patrol boats. Large departments even have robots that enter dangerous places, such as for bomb disposal, plus bomb transport trucks. Horses are used in many large cities, especially for crowd control and park patrol. Horses are used in the far West for off-road areas. Motorcycles are used for patrol and so are bicycles.

In recent years we have observed a steady increase in the use of trained dogs for patrol, explosives, arson accelerants, drugs, tracking missing persons, and finding people and bodies buried in buildings after earthquakes, explosions, etc.

As society changes the police have been forced to change also. Today we face domestic terrorism from religious and political groups. It is only a matter of time until someone or some group will use nuclear threat or attack against the civilian population. There is also the new threat of chemical and biological attack. These domestic threats will happen, but no one is prepared for them. Hate crime is on the increase. There are over five hundred groups that are busy hating someone or something. Social and moral issues such as abortion, obscenity, child pornography, and all the vices still present age old problems, but are becoming more sophisticated all the time. Just a few years ago, who would have though that today we would have police officers in so many public

schools or that we would have cyber-police working the Internet and World Wide Web?

In so many areas, the criminal has learned to use advanced technology. In doing so, they often have left the police in the dust. There is no question that police officers of the future will have to be much better educated, just to try and keep up. To do so, the police will have to be more and more specialized.

The FBI crime laboratory and academy, and most notably, the Behavioral Science Unit within the academy, have made many breakthroughs in mass-murder and serial-crime investigation. The FBI crime lab has developed single fingerprint classification, new methods of finding fingerprints, and DNA identification. DNA databanks are now being built and are offering positive identification that was not possible just two or three years ago. It is likely that DNA investigation is the biggest breakthrough for investigators since the Henry system of fingerprint classification.

Until recently, the FBI and its various functions have been almost without criticism. "For the better part of a generation, both political parties have thrown money and laurels at the FBI for one reason: to stop crime."[48] But by the mid 1990's, many FBI errors have raised a series of questions and criticism of its handling of several major cases. The April 28th, 1997 issue of *Time* magazine has as its cover story a major article titled, "What's wrong at the FBI?" There has been "virtually no congressional oversight (of the FBI) . . . any lawmaker who raised concerns risked being flayed as soft on crime. But without accountability, several things happen, all of them bad. Money gets wasted, officials get sloppy, innocent people go to jail, and cases that should be won are lost."[49] The issue that triggered such sharp criticism was an Inspector General's report that questions the crime lab's credibility and accuses the lab of slanting evidence to help prosecutors get convictions. Major cases such as the World Trade Center Bombing, The Unabomber, The O.J. Simpson murder case and others are mentioned. The Bureau has received sharp criticism for cases that went wrong at Ruby Ridge and

Waco. Evidence at the Oklahoma City bombing was tainted. The very sloppy handling of the Richard Jewell situation resulting from the Atlanta bombing at Olympic Park was a classic case of convicting a person through the media before going to trial. The FBI was the source of the information leaks. The FBI also failed to warn Jewell that he was a suspect. All of that and now there is word that the Inspector General is ready to blast the FBI for "dragging its feet in pursuing CIA traitor Aldrich Ames, (CIA agent) who worked for the Russians in Washington (...under the FBI's and CIA's nose) for nine years before he was finally captured."[50] It only takes a few mistakes to tarnish an otherwise outstanding record.

When we look at the history of American law enforcement and consider where we are at present, it is apparent that the future will be exciting, and hopefully progressive.

SUMMARY

To understand American police history, the reader must look back through world history for the roots of major thought concepts that we currently use. Specifically, we have to look at the history of England. Because the original thirteen colonies were English, our ancestors brought with them English thinking traditions and law.

English history is long and many events contributed to the development of their police. The most important was the founding of the Metropolitan London Police Department in 1829. So many of the original concepts pioneered by Sir Robert Peel are still the cornerstones of American police today. Unfortunately, we were not able to keep politics out of law enforcement and our fear of centralized police power caused us to fragment our police to an extreme extent. That fear is still with us and at times we observe merit for such fear.

From the very beginning of our history, we proved to be a violent and often intolerant people. The treatment of native Americans is a long story of murder, theft of their property, rape, and almost total destruction of their religions and life style. Almost all of our history reflects violence. Therefore, violence in America today should not come as a surprise to anyone. We are a violent people.

America used the concept of the English Sheriff for our rural enforcement of the law, and the constable and watch systems for our cities. Early on, all were inefficient and ineffective. New York City, in 1844, was the first twenty-four hour, modern police force in America, and was designed based on the London Police.

The Civil War period resulted in the creation or expansion of Federal enforcement and brought weapons and uniforms to local police. In the developing West, law-and-order often was found in "the fastest gun." In many locations, organized law enforcement did not exist. Where police were found, they were often corrupt and inefficient. In large cities, especially in the East, the Irish immigrants took over police departments and used the police force as a way to become Americanized. Many law enforcement issues were sub-contracted out to private-security companies, such as the Pinkerton Agency.

In the 1920's, crime was out of control. The moralist movement had set the stage for organized crime and illegal liquor; prostitution and gambling ruled, under the leadership of gangsters like Al Capone. Many police were paid off by gangsters and the honest police did not have the ability nor education to deal with the mob. But out of the confusion and lawlessness, there developed the need for police professionalism. Police reformers like August Vollmer and others begin to have an impact. Most of this professional movement was aimed at administration.

The 1930's was a period of world-wide depression and the beginnings of World War II. Police professionalism portrayed the ideal officer as a crime fighter. Bank robbery increased and the media made heroes out of our gangsters who shot it out with local police, then made daring getaways. J. Edgar Hoover and his FBI carefully built the "G-Man" reputation and expanded the agency. They became masters at the improvement of their image as they arrested bank robber after bank robber. Local police inefficiency created a need for expansion of state police and investigative agencies.

The first half of the 1940's was devoted to World War II. Policing was given a low priority. Most officers and criminals were either in the service or making good money in the war effort. Our docks were protected by a deal with organized crime. There was no work interruption nor did we have any sabotage. Because of panic, 110,000 Japanese-American citizens were put in American concentration camps and given no constitutional rights or protection. In the second half of the 40's, America readjusted to peace. The baby boom was on and crime increased. Thousands of GIs went off to college. The GI Bill allowed the average American access to higher education for the first time. Some of these graduates found their way into police work, a field not accustomed to educated people.

A major "Red Scare" opened the 1950's. California led the way in police professionalism and television and Hollywood made the public aware of the need for police improvement and professionalism. The Federal government continued to expand its influence in the enforcement of law.

The lid blew off in the 1960's. Law enforcement and much of society was in social, sexual, and racial turmoil. Crime figures shot up as "baby boomers" hit the high-crime age. Black citizens were saying "enough is enough." They demanded equal treatment, demonstrated for their rights, and America was burning. Civil disobedience often could not be controlled by local and state law enforcement and Federal troops had to be called in. Many times a local police "incident" was the trigger for mass rioting and burning. The very popular president of the United States, Jack Kennedy was assassinated and soon thereafter the

Attorney General and brother of the late president, Robert Kennedy, was also assassinated. To add to the confusion, the Supreme Court issued three landmark cases: Mapp v. Ohio, Escobedo v. Illinois, and Miranda v. Arizona — all demanding that local enforcement follow procedural rules as established by the Constitution and Bill of Rights. The Court, for the first time, told the police that they would have to follow the rules also. Vietnam was a serious political issue and was being challenged by a new "hippie" culture that fought with non-violence and flowers. They also greatly expanded the use of illegal drugs. To a large extent, the police were totally unprepared and often responded with the only thing available — force. All of America began to ask serious questions about the police. President Johnson created the President's Commission on Law Enforcement and the Administration of Justice. The commission report called for a better-educated police force that was highly trained to do their difficult job. President Johnson initiated the "war on crime" concept and got the Safe Streets and Crime Control Act passed. Federal involvement in criminal justice, even at the local level was greatly expanded.

The 1970's, brought equal opportunity and the entry of females and blacks into the ranks of law enforcement. Police training academies were created and mandatory training for entry-level police was required. Because of Federal money, research involving police matters was greatly expanded. More police officers were added and thousands of police used LEAA money to go to college to quickly earn created degrees in police science.

The 1980's saw an increase in crime as the nation experienced a "ripple effect" of the post World War II baby boom. More young people in the high crime age equaled more crime. The Federal government used this opportunity to pass new laws giving the federal government more power in the enforcement of law. The "war on drugs" filled our prisons and consumed a large share of police efforts. Females and minorities expanded their numbers in police forces and many officers continued to seek college degrees. Minimum standards for police work were expanded and professional organizations encouraged research in Criminal Justice.

Today, the drive for professionalism has not been reduced. Money from LEAA has disappeared, but research continues to find new methods of doing things. Society has changed and new challenges confront law enforcement — from hate groups, religious and political terrorism, to the computer net and the world wide web, and many other concerns. Experts in criminal justice have begun to recognize that it is impossible to win the war on drugs, and that the system may be a contributing factor to the problem, just as we experienced in prohibition back in the 1920's. Substandard levels of education, poor community relations, corruption, and brutality still are problems in some locations. Efforts to reduce the police mission, and to privatize some police responsibilities are under consideration. Everyone seems to agree that there will always need to be law enforcement officers and that they will have to be better educated to meet the challenges of the future.

✳ ✳ ✳ ✳ ✳

ENDNOTES

[1] Samuel Walker, *The Police In America*, (New York: McGraw-Hill Book Co., 1983), p. 2.

[2] A.C. Germann, Frank D. Day, and P.J. Gaillati, *Introduction to Law Enforcement and Criminal Justice*, (Springfield, IL: Charles C. Thomas, Publisher, 1976), p. 3.

[3] Henry Worbleski, and Karan M. Hess, *Introduction to Law Enforcement and Criminal Justice* 5th. Ed. (Minneapolis / St. Paul: West Publishing Co. 1997), p. 6.

[4] Michael J. Palmiotto, *Policing*, (Durham: Carolina Academic Press, 1997), p. 10.

[5] Wrobleski, op. cit. pp. 7-8.

[6] Ibid., p. 8.

[7] Ibid., p. 8.

[8] Ronald L.Tannehill, "The History of American Law Enforcement." *Introduction to Criminal Justice: Theory and Application*, (Lake Geneva, WI: Paladin House, 1985), p. 156.

[9] Germann, op. cit. p. 57.

[10] Vern L. Folley, *American Law Enforcement: Police, Courts, and Corrections*, 3rd. ed. (Boston: Allyn and Bacon, Inc., 1980), p. 58.

[11] Patrick Pringle, *Hue and Cry: The Story of Henry and John Fielding and Their Bow Street Runners*, (New York: William Morrow and Co., 1969), pp. 12-16.

[12] Wrobleski, op. cit., p.10.

[13] Germann, op. cit., p.58.

[14] Frank Schmalleger, *Criminal Justice Today*, 4th ed. (Upper Saddle River, NC: Prentice-Hall., 1997), pp. 161-162.

[15] J. L. Lyman, "The Metropolitan Police Act of 1829: An Analysis of Certain Events Influencing the Passage and Character of the Metropolitan Police Ace in England," in *Issues in Law Enforcement*, George Killinger and Paul Cromwell, Jr., eds. (Boston: Holbrook Press, Inc. 1975), pp. 18-19.

[16] Germann, op. cit., p. 59.

[17] Lyman, op. cit., p. 31.

[18] Germann, op. cit., pp. 61-62.

[19] Schmalleger, op. cit., p. 162.

[20] Walker, op, cit. p. 6.

[21] Folley, op. cit., p. 70.

[22] Roger Lane, *Policing the City, Boston 1822-1835*, (Cambridge: Harvard University Press, 1967), p. 10.

[23] Germann, op. cit., p. 67.

[24] Irving Crump and John W. Newton, *Our Police*, (New York: Dodd, Mead and Co. 1935), p.32.

[25] Folley, op. cit., p. 70.

[26] William J. Bopp and Donald O. Schultz, *A Short History of American Law Enforcement*, (Springfield: Charles C. Thomas Publisher, 1972), pp. 15-18.

[27] Folley, op. cit., p. 70.

[28] Raymond B. Fosdick, *American Police Systems*, (New York: The Century Co., 1921), pp. 63-65.

[29] Foley, op. cit., p. 71.

[30] Fosdick, op. cit., p. 63.

[31] Ibid., p. 67.

[32] Walker, op. cit., p. 15.

[33] Ibid., p. 9.

[34] Palmiotto, op. cit., p. 15.

[35] Ibid., p. 15.

[36] Karen M. Hess and Henry M. Warbliski, *Introduction to Private Security*, (Minneapolis/St. Paul: West Publishing Co., 1996), pp. 17-19.

[37] Ibid., p. 18.

[38] Ibid., p. 18.

[39] Raymond B. Fosdick, *Police Systems in the United States*, (Montclair, NJ: Patterson-Smith, 1969), p. 147.

[40] Palmiotto, op. cit., p. 20.

[41] Fosdic, op. cit., p. 148.

[42] Warbleski, op. cit., pp. 218-219.

[43] Nancy Gibbs, *Under the Microscope*, (New York: Time Magazine, Inc., 1997), pp. 28-35.

[44] Palmiotto, op. cit., p. 21.

[45] Mark Sabljak and Martin H. Greenberg, *Most Wanted*, (New York: Bonanza Books, 1990), pp. 9-13.

[46] Walker, op. cit., p. 10.

[47] Ibid, pp. 14-15.

[48] Gibbs, op. cit., p. 28.

[49] Ibid, pp. 28-29.

[50] Ibid, p. 31.

Chapter **8**

Contemporary Policing in America

By

James A. Fagin

The existence of the police in a democratic society is a phenomenon of considerable interest. In a society that talks about the importance of the values of personal freedom and individual rights, the police officer is a constant reminder that these values have not been achieved. In a country which upholds the constitutional right to the "pursuit of life, liberty and happiness," the police are a constant reminder that it is still necessary to place limitations and restraints upon people's actions and interactions and that formal means of regulating and controlling individual behavior are still necessary.

Previous chapters have outlined the evolution of legal institutions and formal authority in the Untied States such as courts and laws. However, important as these institutions are it seems that many people perceive that it is the "police" who have primary responsibility to maintain public order and regulate human behavior. The police are one of the most visible formal control agencies in society. It has been remarked that the police are like Volkswagen "beetles" — they are out-of-date, but they appear to be everywhere. While they may be everywhere, many people do not seem to know who the police are, what they do, or how they are organized. Public opinion toward the police varies dramatically. There are two phrases frequently spoken by the average citizen concerning the police which seem to reflect the range of the public's attitude toward the police: (1) "where are the police when you need them?" and (2) "why aren't you out fighting crime instead of giving me a ticket?" Much of what people know about the police comes from images portrayed by the entertainment media.

This chapter will discuss contemporary American police agencies and the role they perform in the administration of justice. It will answer the questions: (1) what do the police do?, (2) who are the police?, and (3) how are they organized? Other chapters discuss the history of policing and the role of the private police so this chapter will focus upon public funded municipal, county, state, and federal law enforcement agencies. The chapter omits a discussion of law enforcement activities performed by military agencies and it should be mentioned that there is no discussion of the Central Intelligence Agency (CIA). Contrary to the myth portrayed in the entertainment media, the CIA is not a police or law enforcement agency and is not authorized to perform any law enforcement activities in the United States or its territories, nor is the CIA authorized to assist any police agency. (Also, its agents do not have licenses to kill.)

WHAT DO THE POLICE DO?

Much of what the police do defines the relationship between the ordinary citizen and the higher abstractions of law, order, authority, and justice. Hahn has argued that in the absence of the police "to supervise the division between personal actions and political authority, the task of relating governmental regulations to individual behavior would be nearly impossible." The police seem to be involved in almost every aspect of regulating human behavior and maintaining public order (Hahn, 1970:1). The role of the police has become so prominent that to many citizens the police officer is the "government," whether the citizen is seeking help and information or is in conflict with the law.

The core mission of the police is to control crime (Moore, et al., 1988, p. 1). History acknowledges their role as crime fighters, the public holds them accountable when the crime rate rises, the media most frequently shows the police in this role (although admittedly an exaggerated and unrealistic depiction), and police officers often aspire to be crime fighters. Some evidence seems to indicate that they must be doing a pretty good job as crime fighters as they apparently are catching more and more criminals. According to the U.S. Department of Justice Bureau of Justice Statistics (1996), in 1994 the number of adults under some form of correctional supervision was 5.1 million or about 2.7% of the U.S. adult resident population. This percentages is up from the 1.1% reported in 1980. Despite the increase in the number of "caught" criminals, the crime rates seems to continue to rise and the public's fear of crime appears to be unabated. If the police are crime fighters, and if as Sir Robert Peel remarked that the absence of crime is the best test of police efficiency, then it appears that many citizens may not give the police a passing grade in evaluating their crime fighting performance. We will revisit this question after discussing "who are the police" and "how are they organized."

WHO ARE THE POLICE?

It is not proper to speak of "the police" when referring to the various law enforcement agencies in the United States. The police in the United States do not consist of a single national organization as in some countries. Despite the fact that the public often fails to distinguish among or appreciate the difference, there are nearly 17,000 publicly funded semiautonomous police agencies employing nearly 750,000 full-time employees (Justice Expenditure and Employment 1990, 1992). Nearly every incorporated municipality has its own autonomous police department and in addition there are county, state, and federal police agencies. Of the nearly 17,000 publicly funded separate police agencies approximately 72 percent (12,288 agencies) are local police, 18 percent (3,093 agencies) are sheriff departments, 9 percent (1531 agencies) are special police, i.e., park police, game wardens, etc., and less than 1 percent (49 agencies) are state police. In contrast to the nearly 17,000 state and local law enforcement agencies there are only about 50 federal law enforcement agencies. Of the nearly 750,000 full-time employees in law enforcement agencies only 65,490 or about 9 percent are employed by federal agencies.

The powers, functions, and goals of each law enforcement agency differ. For example, some agencies have very broad police powers, whereas other police agencies have very specifically limited powers and authority. The various law enforcement agencies are organized by (1) political boundaries, i.e., federal, state, county, and municipal; (2) by geography, i.e., the various states, counties, cities, and regional areas of the United States, and (3) function(s) they perform, i.e., Customs, Postal Inspectors, park police, etc. The creation of agencies to perform various law enforcement duties has historically been an on-going creation process. At various times in history difference law enforcement agencies have been formed to serve a perceived need. Some of these agencies have continued to exist into contemporary times, some have evolved into new agencies, and some have simply passed into history. One should remember that at the birth of the United States in the late 18th century there were only three law enforcement agencies. Two of these were federal agencies: the Office of the U.S. Marshal and the Office of the Postal Investigation Service, and one was a county agency: the Office of Sheriff. There were no state police agencies, no municipal police agencies, no highway patrols, and no FBI. In a little over 200 years the number of law enforcement agencies has grown to nearly 17,000!

Federal Law Enforcement Agencies

There are only about fifty federal police agencies. In general these agencies perform specialized law enforcement activities and enforce federal laws. The size of these federal agencies range from less than 20 to 20,0000. Each federal law enforcement agency is autonomous from the control of the other agencies. The police powers given to the agency and its personnel depend upon the responsibilities of the agency. Even though they are federal law enforcement agencies, some personnel have very limited arrest powers and serve a very limited geographical area, and other agencies and their personnel have police powers throughout the United States. Each federal law enforcement agency is under the control of one of the branches of government. The larger and more well-known agencies are controlled by the Executive Office (President) and the Treasury Department.

A few of the more prominent federal law enforcement agencies will be briefly discussed. Many of the smaller, lesser known law enforcement agencies provide very specific and limited police services which are generally well defined by their title. For example, the small police agencies of the Smithsonian Institution Police, the Zoological Park Police, and the Library of Congress Police are limited in their authority and responsibility to provide limited police and security services to the respective governmental agency they serve. For the most part these agencies go unnoticed by the public unless some specific event brings them to public attention such as the death of Vincent Foster, President Clinton's friend and White House employee. The investigation of his death in a Washington, DC park was handled by the Park Police rather than the Federal Bureau of Investigation. The discussion as to whether the Park Police should handle the investigation or whether it should be turned over to the Federal Bureau of Investigation focused national attention on an otherwise obscure law enforcement agency. These small federal law enforcement agencies provide essential services but will not be discussed in this chapter.

U.S. Marshal Service

One of the oldest federal law enforcement agencies in the United States is the U.S. Marshal Service, an English law enforcement office established in the United States by the Judiciary Act of 1789. The Federal Marshal Service has had a colorful past as it was the primary law in western territories in the late 19th century. Legendary figures of the "wild west" such as Wild Bill Hickok, Buffalo Bill Cody, Bat Masterson, and the outlaw Bob Dalton served as deputy U.S. Marshals. The federal marshals of the "wild west" left a rich legacy of myth and fact. Presently the ninety-four United States marshals and their deputies are chiefly occupied by such responsibilities as the execution of federal arrest warrants, the movement and custody of federal prisoners, the capture of inmates from federal penitentiaries, the security of federal court facilities and personnel, and the protection of federal witnesses whose lives may be in danger because of their testimony.

One of the significant and far reaching influences upon contemporary law enforcement brought about by the actions of the Western federal marshals of the late 19th century was the Posse Comitatus Act of 1878. During the late 1800s the federal marshals were responsible for maintaining law and order in the territories but they often lacked the necessary manpower and resources to carry out such responsibilities. For example, during the era of "Bleeding Kansas" the federal marshals were granted the power of *posse comitatus*. This authority granted them the power to deputize or command the assistance of private citizens and/or the military to assist the marshal in performing his law enforcement duties. (All of the U.S. Marshals and their deputies during this period were male.) Because of the expense involved in using private citizens the federal marshal frequently used military troops. Thus, from 1854 to 1878 it was quite common for the federal marshal to command the assistance of military troops to assist him to perform civilian law enforcement duties. Due primarily to abuse, the power of *posse comitatus* was revoked in 1878. In contemporary times when it was suggested that military personnel and equipment be used to help in the interdiction of drug traffickers, early efforts were thawed by the prohibitions of the Posse Comitatus Act. Congress found it necessary to rethink the issue of the use of military personnel and resources for civil law enforcement purposes. As a result of this reconsideration by Congress, military personnel and equipment are used to perform important surveillance and interdiction roles in the fight against illegal drugs.

The Federal Bureau of Investigation (FBI)

Although not the oldest of federal agencies, The Federal Bureau of Investigation (FBI) is perhaps the most well-known federal law enforcement agency. The FBI is considered by many to be an outstanding example of law enforcement professionalism. The forerunner of the FBI, the Bureau of Investigation, was created in 1908 by President Roosevelt by executive order following legislative defeat of a proposal to create the Bureau. The primary purpose of the Bureau of Investigation was to provide detective services to the Executive branch of the government. These services had previously been contracted out to private firms or "borrowed" from the Secret Service. The Bureau of investigation had few responsibilities until the 1930s. The FBI became a prominent federal law enforcement agency during the 1930s under the leadership of J. Edgar Hoover. During this time, the fame of the FBI was spread by media coverage of its "daring" crime fighting exploits as agents of the FBI killed John Dillinger, Pretty Boy Floyd, Baby Face Nelson, Ma Barker, Alvin "Creepy" Karpis, and other gangsters.

Since 1930 the responsibilities of the FBI have steadily grown. In 1930 the FBI was designated the national clearing house for the newly legislated Uniform Crime Reports and in 1935 the FBI established the National Police Academy. These have remained major law enforcement services performed by the FBI. The powers of the FBI were expanded again when in 1939 the FBI was charged by presidential directive with responsibility for domestic intelligence matters relating to espionage, sabotage, and subversive activities. The investigative and enforcement authority of the FBI, like all federal police agencies, is strictly limited to federal laws and specifically delegated federal authority. However, through legislation such as the Mann Act (1910), the Lindbergh Law (1932), The Fugitive Felon Act (1934), and the National Firearms Act (1934), the FBI has been able to assume additional criminal responsibility for "local" crimes which would otherwise not be a violation of federal law. Contemporary efforts to combat street crime has resulted in legislation further expanding the power of the FBI to include carjacking, drug-related crime, gang-related crime, and organized crime.

The FBI is not a "national police" and cannot by law act as such. The FBI does not have direct or indirect power to supervise, discipline, or control other federal, state, county, or municipal law enforcement agencies. The FBI must depend upon the voluntary cooperation of other agencies. As the powers of the FBI expand some have suggested it may be appropriate for the FBI to assume such national police powers. However, the general citizenry appears to be hesitant to encourage the idea of a national police. As the powers of the FBI extend into the investigation of "street crime" the problems of conflicting authority, jurisdiction, and responsibility between the FBI and other law enforcement becomes a more frequent problem. The strife generated by this interagency conflict is sometimes depicted in movies as the FBI and local police go head-to-head over "who is in charge." While these media depictions may be based in truth they are often exaggerated to enhance the plot of the movie.

In addition to their criminal investigation and

domestic intelligence responsibilities, the FBI also maintains and operates a sophisticated crime lab and makes the technical expertise of the crime lab available to other police agencies upon request. The FBI crime laboratory provides invaluable expertise to police departments. Perhaps the best known service provided is the assistance the FBI provides in fingerprint identification. Unlike its British counterpart Scotland Yard which selectively collects fingerprints, the FBI has attempted to amass a universal personal identification system. As early as 1935 J. Edgar Hoover proposed to the public that every person in the Untied States, including children, should have his or her fingerprints on file with the FBI Civil Index Division. The idea of an universal fingerprint system has never been accepted but the FBI has collected numerous sets of fingerprints. The FBI also maintains the National Crime Information Center (NCIC) which is the nation's largest data bank of computerized criminal information on wanted felons and certain stolen items such as automobiles, boats, guns, and securities. Nearly every police agency participates in NCIC and it has been an invaluable tool in law enforcement in this highly mobile contemporary society. Recent allegations of unprofessional practices by the FBI crime lab in high profile cases has subjected the FBI Crime Lab to public and Congressional examination. However, the reputation of the FBI Crime lab is still one of the most respected in the world.

Drug Enforcement Agency

When J. Edger Hoover was offered the responsibility of investigating drug crimes he declined. As a result Congress created a number of agencies to deal with the enforcement of drug laws. The Drug Enforcement Agency has emerged as the primary federal law enforcement agency responsible for enforcing federal drug laws. While there have been some recent discussions suggesting that the FBI and DEA should be merged because of overlapping responsibilities, no serious proposals have emerged. The forerunner of the DEA was the Bureau of Narcotics and Dangerous Drugs. In the early days the agents of this agency were not armed and their powers were primarily limited to

inventory accountability of narcotics and dangerous drugs. As this model of enforcement proved inadequate, Congress revised the agency giving it broad powers to combat drug crime and making its agents one of the most heavily armed of the federal law enforcement agencies.

The Department of the Treasury

The Department of the Treasury has several law enforcement agencies under its direction. The largest of these is the United States Customs Service which guards the nation's borders against the smuggling of contraband into the United States. The Internal Revenue Service Intelligence Division is the second largest law enforcement agency in the Department of the Treasury. The primary function of the IRS Intelligence Division is the investigation of tax fraud and tax evasion. Its agents investigate what is best described as "white collar" crime and organized crime. The detective work of the IRS Intelligence agent requires expertise in accounting, computers, and other special investigative skills not typical of law enforcement detectives.

Also under the department of the Treasury is the Bureau of Alcohol, Tobacco, and Firearms (BATF) and the Secret Service. These agencies perform limited law enforcement duties enforcing specifically defined federal laws and having limited responsibilities. BATF as its name suggests investigates violations of federal laws regarding alcohol, tobacco, and firearms. Popularized in the media for their campaign against the legendary and infamous "rum runners" and "moonshiners," recent social and economic changes have significantly curtailed the illegal production and sale of alcohol and BATF is now much more active in the investigation of firearms violations and illegal explosives. Unfortunately, the involvement of the BATF in the Waco, Texas standoff between the members of a religious cult and the government, resulting in the death of most of the members of the cult group, has for many marred the image of the BATF.

The Secret Service was founded in 1865 and was first charged only with investigating the widespread counterfeiting and currency violations which followed the Civil War. Motivated by the assassination of President William McKinley at Buffalo, New York in 1901, the duties of the Secret Service were expanded by Congress to include the protection of the President and certain members of his family. This protection responsibility has been expanded and presently the Secret Service is responsible for the protection of the Vice President and designated members of his family, former Presidents, widows of former Presidents, major presidential and Vice-Presidential candidates, and visiting heads of foreign states or foreign governments. The Secret Service also provides protection of certain national treasures such as the Declaration of Independence and the Constitution of the United States. The Secret Service has retained its responsibility for counterfeiting and currency violations but these responsibilities are often surpassed in importance by its Presidential protection duties. Fortunately, the latest currency designs are making counterfeiting more difficult; thus, there is little danger that the Nation will suffer from some serious attack on the integrity of its currency due to the Secret Service neglecting its performance of this duty.

United States Postal Investigation Service

The United States Postal Investigation Service is a highly specialized agency that is responsible for the security of the United States mail, mail carriers and personnel, and the investigation of mail fraud. Like the Marshal's Service the U.S. Postal Investigation Service dates from the founding of the nation (U.S. Post Office Department, n.d.). Its agents are called "postal inspectors." The Postal Investigation Service has always had a low-key profile despite the fact that it is one of the largest staffed federal law enforcement agencies and has an impressive record of effectiveness. This is because its responsibilities are strictly limited to crimes affecting the delivery of the mail. Thus, striking a mail carrier or stealing a letter from a mail box are federal crimes which are investigated by the U.S. Postal Investigation Service, not the local police.

The Office of Sheriff

The office of sheriff is the oldest local law enforcement agency in the United States. The office of sheriff dates back to the mutual pledge system of 10th century England. Under the mutual pledge system the responsibility of apprehending law breakers was the collective duty of the private citizens. To aid in performing this task the citizens were organized into groups known as a tithing, a group of ten free males (usually related to each other). A person appointed by a local nobleman was responsible for ten tithings known as "the hundred."

This person was called the "constable" and his primary duty was the responsibility for the weapons and equipment of the hundred. The constable was supervised by a "shire-reeve" who was appointed by the Crown. The shire-reeve supervised a number of constables within a geographical area known as a "shire" which is equivalent to a county in the U.S. The shire-reeve answered to the local nobleman and was responsible for effective law enforcement by the different hundreds. The office of shire-reeve developed from a supervisory post to the office of sheriff which had the responsibility of actual pursuit and apprehension of lawbreakers. Many Americans' image of the English office of Sheriff is rooted in the "corrupt" sheriff of Nottingham of Robin Hood legends.

When the English immigrated to the American colonies in the 17th and 18th century they also brought with them their law enforcement structure. The Sheriff was the primary law enforcement officer for the colonists. During the colonial era the Crown-appointed governors of the colonies were responsible for appointing sheriffs. After the American Revolutionary war the citizens of the new government retrained the office of sheriff as their primary law enforcement organization. Municipal policing was not to develop until the 19th century. However, there must have been great mistrust of the sheriff by the new citizens as rather than have the office continued as an appointed position, it was subjected to the democratic process and the sheriff was elected to office by popular vote (Richardson, 1976:16-17). The sheriff is the only head of a major law enforcement agency in the United States who obtains office by election.

Most sheriffs in the United States are still elected to office by popular vote. Until fairly recently, the elected terms of many sheriffs still reflect early mistrust and suspicion of authority. It was almost universal for the sheriff to be elected to office for a term of two years (Walker, 1970:6). Furthermore, many sheriffs were limited in the number of terms they could serve and some sheriffs were prohibited from serving consecutive terms. While the election of the sheriff by popular vote subjected the office to democratic control, it also had several disadvantages. In the selection of a sheriff by popular vote frequently the credentials of the candidate may be obscured by political issues. The office of sheriff becomes a political office rather than a law enforcement position and the elected sheriff may be totally incompetent to perform the law enforcement duties of the office as there are no professional or job-related prerequisites. The short tenure of many sheriffs meant that they were constantly involved in a re-election campaign which detracts from the time they have to devote to administering the office. Furthermore, because of the constant exposure to public opinion some sheriffs tended to attempt to temper law enforcement with politics. Recognition of these problems has resulted in many states revising the terms of office for the sheriff. While it remains an elected office and few or no professional prerequisites are required to run for sheriff, many states now provide for four-year terms and have removed prohibitions against the sheriff serving consecutive terms.

Sheriff departments usually have three areas of responsibility: (1) rural law enforcement, (2) work related to the administration and security of the county jail, and (3) work related to the courts. The sheriff has the title of chief law enforcement executive in many counties. While this title designates that the sheriff is responsible for law enforcement throughout the county, in practice the sheriff usually only provides law enforcement and police services to the unincorporated populations of the county. In counties that have jails the sheriff may be responsible for the administration of the jail and the custody of its prisoners. However, as the population of county jails has grown (some county jails have 1,000 or more inmates) some counties have removed the responsibility of the jail from the sheriff and have developed county departments of corrections which run the jail. Some counties do not have a jail. Several counties may share a common corrections facility run by an agency independent of the sheriff's office. In Hawaii, for example, the state administers all correctional institutions and there are no county jails in the state. The final area of responsibility of the sheriff is the serving of civil papers of the court, such as summons, eviction notices, divorce papers, etc., and providing security for the county court.

Sheriff departments are frequently redundant in that they provide law enforcement services already provided by urban police departments. In some counties the city limits and the county limits are so similar that the rural area of the county, traditionally that area to which the sheriff has provided law enforcement services, is very small or even non-existent. Thus, it is not surprising that many sheriff departments are small. According to the U.S. Department of Justice (Reaves, 1992) two-thirds of the 3,100 sheriff's departments have less than 25 sworn officers. Only 12 sheriff departments have more than 1,000 sworn officers. Many sheriff departments have only a single officer — the sheriff. For this reason some counties have combined the municipal police and the law enforcement responsibilities of the sheriff to create a metropolitan police. This combined law enforcement agency usually is administered by both the county and the city and provides for consolidation of police service to create a single agency responsible for all law enforcement service throughout the county. This does not abolish the office of the sheriff or the municipal police department but only provides for cooperative and unified policing. The primary advantage is a significant financial savings realized from the elimination of the dualism of the two agencies. The state of Hawaii is the only state which has radically redefined the office of the Sheriff. The sheriff is a state administrator who is appointed to office and has very limited law enforcement responsibilities and is not responsible for jail administration or prisoner custody as there are no county jails.

The State Police

State police agencies were formed as early as 1835 when the Provisional Government of Texas formed the famous Texas Rangers. However, there was no significant movement by the states to develop the concept of a state police until the early 1900s. In the early 20th century several states developed state police agencies. For example, Pennsylvania established the Pennsylvania State Constabulary in 1905, New York established a state police in 1917, and Michigan, Colorado, and West Virginia commissioned state police agencies in 1919. One of the primary factors motivating the development of state police agencies was the widespread corruption, incompetence, and political control of local police departments (Walker, 1970). Most state police agencies of the era were small, poorly financed agencies with limited criminal investigation responsibilities and they did not assume significant criminal justice responsibilities or make a significant impact upon the improvement of effectiveness and efficiency of criminal justice.

It was the widespread use and popularity of the automobile that was to define the primary role of the state police. The majority of the state police agencies spend most of their time on traffic services. It is evident that the primary responsibility of the state police is general patrol of the interstate highways, freeways, and state routes. Basically their primary function is traffic safety and speed control and many of the state police agencies reflect the predominance of this activity in their title as numerous agencies are called "highway patrol," e.g., California Highway patrol, Nevada Highway Patrol, Kansas Highway patrol, etc.

Other than general patrol, some state police also have responsibility for rendering technical assistance and support, specialized police, criminal investigation, and unincorporated area patrol. Most states maintain state crime laboratories which provide technical assistance and expertise to local police departments in scientific crime investigation. The National Advisory Commission on Criminal Justice Standards and Goals (1973:299) has recognized the importance of this vital assistance to local police departments and has encouraged state police agencies to improve these support services. In addition to criminalistic, scientific, and technical support, several state police agencies provide radio communications support for local police and maintain state-wide communications/information systems for the distribution of criminal justice information.

Some state police agencies are also responsible for specialized patrol such as the patrol of state parks, enforcement of the hunting and fishing laws, and the state capital grounds. In some states these functions are performed by separate and autonomous police agencies such as park police.

Finally, state police in some states have criminal investigation responsibilities and provide law enforcement services to unincorporated areas. Because of their limited manpower and resources, state police are usually selective in the type of criminal activity they investigate. Generally, state police tend to investigate "state-wide" crime such as organized crime and drug trafficking and do not investigate "street crime" and other local crime which is more appropriately handled by municipal police departments. A few state police agencies have the responsibility for investigating complaints about local police departments or politicians. For example, complaints of police brutality or the misappropriation of funds by politicians may be investigated by the state police based upon the assumption that they can conduct unbiased and impartial investigations.

The Urban Police

Although the concept of the municipal police department with paid, full-time personnel did not emerge until the mid-nineteenth century, they have become the predominant law enforcement agency in the United States. When most people mention "the police" they are referring to the local municipal police department. According to Reaves (1996), eighty percent of U.S. residents are served by public police. In the typical city there are about 21 police officers for every 1,000 citizens. Most of these officers are non-minority males. Only 11.3 percent are black, 6.2 percent are Hispanic, and 8.8 percent are females. The typical officer has about 900 hours of pre-service training. The largest municipal police department is the New York Police department with over 35,000 sworn officers. The typical starting pay for municipal officers in 1993 was $21,300. The pay for chiefs ranged from $22,900 to $91,700 and the average pay for chiefs was $34,600 (Reaves, 1996).

HOW ARE THE POLICE ORGANIZED?

Chief Administrative Officers

Federal law enforcement agencies are created by Congressional legislation or Executive Order. The typical title for the administrative head of most federal law enforcement agencies is "Director" and the position is obtained by Presidential appointment. State police are created by state legislation and likewise its chief administrative officer is called "Director." The position is usually obtained by appointment by the governor. Municipal police departments are headed by a "chief" and the position is usually obtained by appointment. Chiefs are usually appointed by the mayor, city manager, or a special committee representing the mayor or city manager charged with selecting the chief, e.g., the "police commission." Nearly all sheriffs obtain their position by wining a county-wide general election.

Municipal Police Departments and Sheriff Departments

Municipal Police

A common job title for line-level personnel in municipal police departments is "police officer."

The municipal police department is organized in a hierarchy of authority which resembles the military and is often called a "semi-military" organizational structure. The typical ranks in order are: patrol officer, sergeant, lieutenant, captain, major, and deputy chief. There is no use by police of the military rank of "private" and many smaller departments do not use the rank of corporal. Patrol officers are frequently classified as "I," "II," and "III," or some other similar scheme in lieu of the rank of corporal.

"Detective" is normally a job description rather than a rank. In many departments a minimum rank of sergeant is required to be a detective. Thus, a person could be a sergeant-detective or a lieutenant-detective. A sergeant-detective normally has the same hierarchical rank as sergeant. Detective denotes the investigative responsibilities of the person as opposed to patrol or administrative responsibilities.

Municipal police departments are "closed hierarchies." For nearly all municipal police departments the only way to enter the organization is at the lowest rank — recruit. All promotions to higher ranks are filled from the personnel in the lower ranks. Only patrol officers presently employed by the agency can apply for the position of sergeant. Only sergeants presently employed by the agency can apply for the position of lieutenant, etc. Since detectives usually must be sergeants, no one can obtain employment with the department as a detective without first serving several years as a patrol officer.

Municipal police departments are organized to provide round-the-clock service to all areas of the city. The resulting administrative structure is several "shifts" of service units and as many divisions as necessary to provide service to all geographical areas in the city.

The first American urban police departments were modeled after the London Metropolitan Police founded by Sir Robert Peel. However, there are significant differences in the formal administrative structure of the American police organizations and the British model (Miller, 1974-1975).

First, the London Metropolitan Police was a highly centralized agency. The Head of the agency was the Home Minister who answered directly to the Crown. The early American urban police were extensively involved in partisan politics and police officers were not considered so much as public servants as they were considered agents for a given political faction. Police work during the 19th century was considered a form of casual labor, not a lifelong career (Walker, 1970). O.W. Wilson (1957:12) has remarked concerning the origin and development of urban American police departments that their "past hangs as a millstone about the neck of the professional minded police."

Secondly, The Home Office of the London Metropolitan Police was essentially an extension of the British national government. Americans were skeptical of a strong, centralized police and strongly opposed any development of national police. The result was that the American urban police were fragmented, autonomous police agencies ruled by local governments.

Finally, British police commissioners were recruited from the ranks of the upper class and were usually individuals trained for professional civil service careers whereas American police executives frequently were incompetent and chosen because of partisan politics. Increased professionalism by the American police has made significant changes in reducing the role of partisan politics and improving the quality of police personnel and police executives.

The American Police Officer as a Generalist

The results of this ill-defined growth in American policing and political control of the police departments has been that the urban police have assumed numerous and often seemingly unrelated and even contradictory responsibilities. The role of the American urban police officer has not developed as the role of a specialist or a technician but as a generalist, and the urban police officer must be proficient at a variety of tasks rather than skilled in a limited field (Garmire, 1972:2; National Advisory Commission on Criminal Justice Standards and Goals, 1973).

Upon first examining the activities of the urban police officer it appears that there is no order to the seemingly endless variety of tasks that they perform. The police direct traffic, catch stray animals, catch criminals, escort officials and citizens, deliver babies, patrol businesses and residential premises, take crime reports, administer first aid, assist in natural disasters, mediate domestic disputes, and perform many other functions. The President's Commission on Law Enforcement and Administration of Justice, after a comprehensive analysis of the activities of the American police officer, concluded that their role could best be comprehended as divided into two major types of activities or roles which the Commission labeled as "law enforcement" and "community service" (President's Commission on Law Enforcement and Administration of Justice, 1967:91-99).

Similar investigations by the National Commission on the Causes and Prevention of Violence and the National Advisory Commission on Criminal Justice Standards and Goals also concluded that these two major roles constituted the totality of police activities in the community (Campbell, 1973; President's Commission on criminal Justice Standards and Goals, 1973). The law enforcement role is that role in which the police enforce the criminal laws and perform activities related to the enforcement of criminal laws, such as the prevention of criminal activity and participation in court proceedings. The community service role is that role in which the police provide essentially a social service to the community, performing a noncriminal service capacity such as control of traffic, providing assistance, and resolution of day-to-day conflicts among friends, family, or neighbors.

While the actual composition of these two major roles varies, depending upon such factors as the size of the department, emphasis, and need, the National Advisory Commission on Criminal Justice Standards and Goals (1973) identified several activates which they considered basic to each role. The fundamental elements of the law enforcement role were: prevention of criminal activity, apprehension of criminal offenders, participation in court proceedings, and protection of constitutional rights. The fundamental elements of the community service role were: providing assistance for those who cannot care for themselves or who are in anger of physical harm, control of traffic, resolution of day-to-day conflicts among friends, family, neighbors, etc., and the promotion and preservation of civil order.

Based upon the identification of these two basic roles, many authorities have called for the development of separate police roles. No major police department has so divided the duties of its police officers.

The Sheriff's Department

The Sheriff's Department is usually organized in a manner very similar to the municipal police department. One difference is that line-level personnel in the Sheriff's Department are called "deputy sheriffs," and the second-in-command in the Sheriff's Department is called the "Undersheriff."

Another difference is that because the Sheriff usually has responsibilities related to the jail, the courts, and law enforcement, deputy sheriffs perform duties not performed by municipal police officers. Some sheriff departments have dual-entry career tracks and a recruit applies either for a job related to law enforcement and court service or jail-related duties. In these departments there are usually different requirements for the two positions and the pay for jail-related duty jobs is usually lower. (The starting salary for deputy sheriffs in 1990 was $16,000 to $26,000.) Other departments require all recruits to first perform jail-related duties and then some personnel are selected at a later time to perform law enforcement and court-service duties. It is not uncommon in a Sheriff's Department to find that assignment to jail-related duties is used as a form of punishment for "road" officers who violate departmental rules.

Federal Law Enforcement

Rather than the primary organizational goal being to deliver round-the-clock patrol and law enforcement services, most of the larger federal law enforcement agencies are organized more like businesses. Line-level personnel are not called patrol officers or deputy sheriffs. A more common title for federal law enforcement personnel is "agent" or "special agent." Supervisors may be called "Agent in Charge" or "Regional Director" rather than traditional military ranks. Few federal law enforcement agencies use the traditional military rank titles associated with municipal police departments. Federal agencies are usually organized around delivery of services to a geographical area in the United States. This area could include part of a state, an entire state, or several states.

The Hiring Process

While there is no universally agreed-upon procedure for the hiring of municipal, county, state, and federal law enforcement personnel, the procedures used by many agencies are very similar. The benchmark scores for passing may differ and the prerequisites for applying for the job may be higher or lower but generally there is more commonality than differences in the hiring process.

The U.S. Department of Justice Office of the Attorney General (1992:41) has recommend that law enforcement departments invest in quality law enforcement personnel. The process of hiring new recruits is a rigorous process designed to eliminate "bad candidates." One of the reasons that the agencies invest so much in the selection of recruits is the fact previously mentioned that all future administrative ranks will be filled from within the department. Thus, not only is the department hiring candidates with the skills, knowledge, and abilities to perform as police officers, some candidates must possess skills, knowledge, and abilities that would allow them to advance to the position of sergeant, lieutenant, captain, major, or even chief as all these positions are filled by people who were once recruits.

Job Requirements

The hiring process usually begins with an announcement of the job opening. Ever since 1972

181

law enforcement agencies have had to conform to the equal employment provisions of the Civil Rights Act. Prior to 1972 law enforcement agencies were exempt from this Act and nearly all police officers were non-minority males. Since 1972 the hiring practices must provide equal opportunity for all candidates. All prerequisites for the position must be job related. The minimum age for municipal police officers and sheriff deputies is 21. This minimum age requirement is related to state and federal laws regulating the carrying of concealed handguns. The typical job announcement requires the candidate to be in good physical health, have good moral character, be licensed to operate a motor vehicle, and a resident of the state or municipality. While experts advocate the advantages of a college-educated police department (Meese, 1993:3) the minimum educational requirements vary by department. Nearly all federal law enforcement agencies require a bachelor's degree. Few, if any, require that the degree be related to law enforcement. Less than one percent of municipal police departments require a bachelor's degree. The most common requirement for local police departments is a high school diploma.

Good physical health is usually determined by an examination by a medical doctor and the ability to pass a test of physical strength and endurance. The presence of any back problems, or any disease which would effect job performance, may disqualify the candidate. The physical ability test must test only for job related abilities. The most common abilities tested for are upper-body strength, cardiovascular fitness, eye-sight, and hearing. Upper-body strength is usually tested for by the ability to perform a minimum number of exercises such as push-ups or pull-ups in a specified time. Standards for eye-sight have relaxed considerably over the past decades. Whereas 30 years ago most law enforcement agencies required 20/20 vision without correction, many agencies will now allow for the wearing of eyeglasses or contact lenses to correct vision. Most agencies will reject applicants who are color blind.

Good moral character usually means no felony arrests, no misdemeanor arrests for violent crimes such as assault, and no arrests for domestic violence. Federal legislation effective in 1997 prohibits firearm ownership or possession by anyone convicted of domestic violence. This new legislation has caused all law enforcement agencies to redefine their qualifications for employment. A conviction for domestic violence, even a misdemeanor conviction, most likely will disqualify the candidate. In about half of the states and most federal law enforcement agencies, homosexual activity may disqualify the candidate for employment.

A difficult question concerning good moral character is the question of drug use. In nearly all departments any drug use of any kind in the last year will disqualify the candidate. Use of a narcotic drug at any time will usually disqualify the candidate. Use of a drug such as LSD at any time during one's life including "years ago in high school" will usually disqualify the candidate. If the candidate has ever sold drugs, even if it was "a long time ago," they will be disqualified for employment. For those agencies who specialize in enforcement of drug laws such as the DEA, the tolerance for any illegal drug use by the candidate may be zero.

The Examination and Interview Process

The following steps highlight the procedures in the hiring process which are common to many law enforcement agencies. After submitting his or her application the candidate must pass a written examination which may test for reading comprehension, problem-solving abilities, grammar, and basic math skills. General intelligence tests are prohibited by civil rights case law. It has not been possible to demonstrate that general intelligence tests discriminate based upon job related criteria. While there is a minimum passing score the process is competitive so the higher the candidates score, the better.

If the candidates passes the written examination there will be an oral interview. The purpose of the oral interview is to determine the suitability of the candidate for police work. Most police departments call their interviews "stress interviews," which means that the purpose is to conduct the interview in an environment which places some stress upon the candidate. The candidate will be asked questions which have no "right" answer. A candidate may be asked if he would give his mother a traffic ticket. If he says "yes," he will be questioned about the honesty of his answer. If he says "no," he will be questioned about his favoritism and failure to perform his sworn duties. It appears that the oral examination committee places a great deal of importance upon the truthfulness of the candidate based upon the assumption that if the candidate would tell a small lie now, given the right conditions as a police officer he may yield to the temptation to lie or be dishonest in performing his duties.

The Psychological and Polygraph Examination

If the candidate continues in the process there will be a psychological evaluation by a trained professional. This evaluation normally consists of taking several "standard" personality assessment instruments such as the MMPI (Minnesota Multiple Personality Inventory) or Briggs-Meyers Instrument.

The final hurdles are a background check and perhaps a polygraph examination. The purpose of the background check is to verify information provided in the employment application and to investigate for illegal drug use, excessive use of alcohol, poor management of finances, evidence of racial, gender, religious prejudice, domestic violence, or character disorder. Usually the candidate provides a list of references, past addresses and past employers. The extent of the background investigation will depend upon the size of the agency and the "security clearance" which may be required for employment. Some federal positions may require a background investigation going back 15 years or more in the candidate's life.

Many agencies advise the candidate that he may have to take a polygraph examination but not all of those agencies actually administer a polygraph examination. Despite public distrust of the reliability and validity of the polygraph examina-

tion, they are routinely used by law enforcement agencies. Research indicates that the polygraph examination is 80 to 95 percent reliable. The primary purpose of the polygraph examination is to attempt to tell if the candidate indicates deception in certain areas which are difficult to verify. Frequent areas upon which the polygraph examination tests focus are illegal drug use, concealed debt, excessive alcohol consumption, sexual orientation, and sexual activity with minors.

It is not uncommon for a polygraph examination to take two to four hours. The reason for this is because the polygraph examination consist of several stages. The candidate may be asked to complete a fairly lengthy questionnaire covering a great number of illegal behaviors which the candidate may have done sometime in his life. After the questionnaire is completed the polygraph examiner will interview the candidate concerning any admitted illegal activity and further questioning the candidate if no illegal activity is admitted. After the interview the candidate will be advised of the questions to be asked on the polygraph examination. Usually there are about a dozen questions on the polygraph examination. The examiner will normally ask the same set of questions several times. The actual polygraph examination may last 20 to 30 minutes. During that time the candidate may experience some physical discomfort because the examination requires the use of a blood pressure cuff to record relative blood pressure during the examination. Many people find that the blood pressure cuff creates physical discomfort.

The Academy, Field Officer Training Program, and Probationary Period

Even if the candidate is successful in passing all these steps, he is still a long way from becoming a police officer. Next the candidate will be invited to attend a rigorous academy — stressing both academic learning and physical training. The average academy is approximately 900 hours in length or about six months. The candidate will be paid during this time as a recruit. If the candidate passes the academy, he or she will be "sworn-in" and placed in the field officer training program.

For a period of time the candidate will receive additional on-the-job training by an experienced police officer. During this period of time and usually up until the new police officer has completed one year of employment, the employee can be dismissed without the need of the department to show cause. During this probationary period of employment it is necessary for the new officer to demonstrate exemplary behavior. Once this probationary period passes the employee is granted the benefits of civil service protection and can only be dismissed from his job if the employer can show cause.

Municipal police officers and deputy sheriffs will serve their entire career in the city or county in which they were hired. Federal law enforcement officers most likely will serve in several geographical locations during their career. Their assignment to a geographical area will be based upon the needs of the agency. Most new agents in the FBI and DEA serve their first few years in major cities.

SUMMARY

The American police are historically rooted in English tradition; however, contemporary policing reflects the unique development of American politics and history. Contemporary policing in America is performed by numerous fragmented and autonomous police agencies. There are basically four types of police agencies: (1) federal police agencies, (2) state police agencies, (3) sheriff departments, and (4) urban police agencies.

The urban police agency, commonly known as the "police," has the greatest impact upon the average citizen as more citizens come into contact with the municipal police than any other police agent. The state police primarily perform general patrol and traffic safety of the highways, provide crime laboratory assistance to local police departments, and perform special investigations. The federal law enforcement agencies are the fewest in number and have specialized responsibilities and powers. Neither the FBI nor any other federal law enforcement agency is a national police agency having command and control over state and local police agencies.

The sheriff is the oldest local law enforcement agency in the United States and still reflects much of the early mistrust of authority, as most sheriffs are elected to office. In addition to rural law enforcement services the Sheriff usually also performs jail-related responsibilities and serves the county court. The law enforcement duties of the sheriff are often redundant and some counties have taken steps to eliminate this redundancy.

✳ ✳ ✳ ✳ ✳

REFERENCES

Campbell, James S., *et al.*
    1970   *Report on the Task Force on Law and Law Enforcement to the National Commission on the Causes and Prevention of Violence.* New York: Bantam Books.
Garmire, Bernard L.
    1972   "The Police Role in an Urban Society,". in Robert F. Steadman (ed.), *The Police and the Community.* Baltimore: The Johns Hopkins University Press.

Hahn, H.
    1970   *The Police in Urban Society*. Beverly Hills, CA: Waveland.

Kelling, George
    1988   *What Works — Research and the Police*. Washington, DC: National Institute of Justice.

Meese, Edwin III
    1993   *Community Police and the Police Officer*. Washington, DC: National Institute of Justice.

Miller, Wilbur R.
    1974-5   "Police authority in London and New York City, 1830 - 1870." *Journal of Social History*, VIII No. 2.

Moore, Mark H., and Mark A.R. Kleman
    1989   *The Police and Drugs*. Washington, DC: National Institute of Justice.

Moore, Mark H., Robert C. Trojanowicz, and George L. Kelling
    1988   *Crime and Policing*. Washington, DC: National Institute of Justice.

National Advisory Commission on Criminal Justice Standards and Goals
    1973   *Police*. Washington, DC: U.S. Government Printing Office.

President's Commission on Criminal Justice Standards and Goals
    1973   *A National Strategy to Reduce Crime*. Washington, DC: U.S. Government Printing Office.

President's Commission on Law Enforcement and Administration of Justice
    1967   *Task Force Report: The Police*. Washington, DC: U.S. Government Printing Office.

Reaves, Brian a.
    1992   *Sheriff's Department, 1990*. Washington, DC: U.S. Department of Justice.
    1996   *Local Police, 1993*. Washington, DC: U.S.. Department of Justice.

Richardson, James F.
    1976   *Urban Police in the Untied States*. Port Washington, NY: Kennikat Press.

United States Department of Justice
    1992   *Justice Expenditure and Employment*. Washington, D.C.: U.S. Government Printing Office.

United States Department of Justice Bureau of Justice Statistics
    1996   *Correctional Populations int he Untied States, 1994*. Washington, D.C.: U.S. Government Printing Office.

United States Department of Justice Office of the Attorney General
    1972   *Combating Violent Crime*. Washington, D.C.: U.S. Government Printing Office.

United States Post Office Department
    1972   *Survey, History of the Postal Inspection Service, Part I*. Washington, D.C.: U.S. Government Printing Office.

Walker, Samuel
    1970   *A Criminal History of Police Reform*. Lexington, MA: Lexington Books.

Wilson, O.W.
    1957   *Parker on Police*. Springfield, IL: Charles C. Thomas.

Chapter 9

Criminal Investigation and Criminalistics

By

Wayne W. Dunning

Criminal investigation and criminalistics are best considered as two separate fields, generally involving different specialists. The investigator works primarily in the field and deals mostly with people, while the criminalist works primarily in the laboratory and deals mostly with things. Some areas, such as evidence, certainly overlap, and meaningful communication between the two fields of specialty is vital. The investigator who does not understand what the criminalist can accomplish, or who cannot properly interpret the results from the laboratory, is working under a definite handicap. Likewise, the criminalist should be aware of the various ways in which he might be able to assist an investigation, and should be able to communicate his findings in an understandable and useful manner. Some illustrations are given later.

INVESTIGATION

Perhaps the best definition of criminal investigation is that given by Weston and Wells.[1] It consists of four factors, all of which should be constantly borne in mind by anyone involved in investigative work. It is a **(1) lawful search (2) for people and things (3) useful in reconstructing the circumstances of an illegal act or omission (4) and the mental state accompanying it.** In simpler but less descriptive terms, it is a search for the truth, insofar as it can be determined in an after-the-fact inquiry. Many factors, including personal prejudices, may influence an investigator in the course of his duties, but none should ever diminish his dedication to searching for the truth.

An investigator should be a keen observer of people and events, and should be able to record his observations accurately and report them correctly. He should have extensive knowledge of the laws and procedures governing police work and investigative processes, and he should be well versed in the rules of evidence. Since so much of the investigative process requires dealing with people, many of whom are not very anxious to be dealt with, the investigator should be something of a practicing psychologist and should hopefully be able to establish a sincere rapport with the people he contacts. Although already mentioned, the requirements for accurate and truthful recording and reporting cannot be overemphasized. However, note that the reporting is for official records and court purposes; interviewing and especially interrogation may well require some "stretching of the truth."

The investigation starts when a crime is dis-

187

covered or reported. In order to cover as many factors as possible, we will consider a crime — such as a homicide — that has been recently committed, in which there is a fairly well-defined crime scene. The crime scene is a critical area; the first officer on the scene has a number of duties which must be discharged almost simultaneously, and the actions taken at this stage can have a profound effect on the course of the investigation — either good or bad. The actions or mistakes of the first officer can literally "make or break" the case.

In those few instances where the perpetrator is (or appears to be) present, apprehension is the first duty. Although arrest is preferred, safety for officers and bystanders is the overriding consideration. The second duty is to render whatever medical aid may be required. The victim of a homicide is, of course, in no need of medical attention, and unless there are unusual circumstances the body should not be disturbed or moved until some time later — at least not before photographs have been taken and measurements made. A police officer can not legally make the distinction between an injured victim (live) and a body (dead), although in practice this determination must usually be made by the first officer. Without going into medical details, the difference is generally pretty easy to detect. (In any case, no one is perfect. It is well established that "bodies" are sometimes returned by morticians to the hospitals from which they had come, but are usually sent back to the morticians in a day or two.)

Next, the officer must protect and preserve the scene. In general, it needs to be protected from family, friends, neighbors, curious onlookers, and news reporters. Among these people will be those who wish to clean up the scene before other officers arrive, those who like to collect souvenirs, and those who like to have the opportunity to handle any physical evidence that may be present. For the most part, protection of the scene from these people is not too difficult. Unfortunately, there is another type of crime scene disturber that is extremely difficult to handle — the police officer of some rank who feels that he rightfully belongs

there even though he may be unqualified to properly process a crime scene. In some jurisdictions, this type of scene disturber can include prosecuting attorneys, coroners, city commissioners, and the mayor. There is probably not a whole lot the officer or investigator can do in such situations except to try to make the best of it. Fortunately, in recent years there has been heightened awareness of this problem, and an increasing number of police agencies are now able to properly contain a crime scene.

Once the scene is secure, the search for evidence can begin. Testimonial evidence is obtained from witnesses, survivors, or any other person at the scene who has knowledge of the crime. Physical evidence is obtained from the scene, hopefully by persons especially trained in its recognition, documentation, collection, preservation, etc. The evidence is then taken or shipped to the laboratory, where the criminalist will begin his work.

If, as is the usual case, the crime has not been solved at this point, there are three general avenues that may lead to its solution. Ordinarily they must be taken together; very rarely will only one of them suffice.

The laboratory can give extremely valuable assistance to the investigation, but *by itself* it is relatively helpless. It relies on material brought to it by others, and the results of the laboratory tests and analyses must be properly interpreted and coordinated by the investigators.

The second avenue relies on the imagination of the investigator, and may include hunches, intuition, and experience gained in similar cases. While some of these factors may not be reducible to an absolute scientific basis, they do frequently serve to direct an investigation into a profitable area. The workings of the human mind have not yet been brought to a computer-circuit status, and an investigator should not ignore any such inspiration.

The third avenue is the routine sequence of frequently dull "detective work" that should be followed for every crime. This routine work is necessary to ensure that no profitable area of inquiry or source of information is overlooked. Also, if the usual routine is not followed in any given crime, the defense may be able to raise considerable doubt in the jurors' minds about the validity of the entire investigation. There should be no loose ends unattended; any time there is a loose end, there will be somebody waiting to grab it and unravel the investigator's work.

Sources of Information

This third avenue is primarily one of information gathering. At first glance that might seem to be a relatively simple task, but there are many different information sources and some of them take a great deal of time, effort, and expertise to properly exploit.

The investigator may have his psychological abilities put to the test in the process of interviewing witnesses. If the person being interviewed is relatively normal and not hostile, the process can be fairly straightforward. However, the person is frequently hostile — perhaps to all police activities and inquiries or perhaps just in this particular case; he could be a friend or relative of the participant(s), or even be the guilty party himself. There might be fear of retribution, concerns about losing time from the job, anxieties about court appearances, and the unfortunately common attitude of "just not wanting to get involved." Many people have had some kind of unpleasant experience with the criminal justice system and therefore have what appear to them to be good reasons for being uncooperative. The investigator must handle these problems on an individual basis in an attempt to gain cooperation and elicit information. And throughout, it must be remembered that the job of the investigator is to *get* information, not to divulge it. It is not a social event, or a time for sharing. Also, the information sought is that which the person actually has, and not what the investigator would like to hear in order to confirm his theory of the case.

Questions should be directing, but not leading. They should ask for a detailed response, not merely a yes or no. "Who did you see running from the scene?" would be a proper question. "Was it Sam Dude you saw running from the scene?" would not.

Surveillance of some sort may be necessary. It may be a simple visual surveillance on foot, from a vehicle, or from a convenient building. A binocular or telescope may be used to assist, and a camera may be used to record. For agencies with sufficient resources, a wide variety of exotic electronic devices is available to assist and enhance visual and audio surveillance. The general rule is that anything the investigator can see from a place where he is legally entitled to be is fair game, but there are occasional exceptions. If the surveillance is to involve electronic bugging, wiretapping, etc., then there are strict legal requirements that must be met. Otherwise, the information gathered may be legally useless, and the investigator could find himself subject to criminal or civil prosecution.

Many types of records may have to be checked. These may include official records, such as police, court, tax, driver's license, auto registration, etc., and a wide variety of business or unofficial records such as utilities and credit bureaus. This may be a time-consuming, unexciting endeavor, but it can yield valuable information.

The Criminal Investigation Division in Great Britain relies very heavily on informants, and makes no secret of that fact. A 1976 report of the Rand Corporation said in effect that in the United States the image of the detective running a network of informants helping him to solve cases is a myth. It may well be that U.S. detectives do not rely so heavily on informants as their English counterparts, but the simple fact still seems to be that informants are a vital source of information, and that perhaps the Rand Corporation's informants were not very reliable. Informants may be willing to give information freely, or willing to trade it for favors or money, or they may be basically unwilling and therefore require some type of "arm-twisting" on the part of the investigator.

Regardless of the class of informants being dealt with, information obtained from them must be carefully checked; informants have been known to sometimes provide totally erroneous information. However, information from an informant who has proven to be reliable will generally be sufficient to serve as the basis for obtaining a search warrant.

Search and seizure are governed by the U.S. and State Constitutions, federal and state laws, and case law. Changes in requirements and procedures are frequent and drastic enough that only basic guidelines can be given here. The investigator should attempt to stay abreast of all of these changes — or be willing to ask for help — so that any evidence obtained will not be ruled inadmissible. (In some jurisdictions, a prosecutor may accompany the officers on a search in an effort to ensure that all legal requirements are met.) While every case can present its own problems and unusual circumstances, the best advice is that if it is possible and feasible to obtain a warrant before any search is made, it should be done. (There are special situations such as search incident to a lawful arrest, but we are primarily concerned here with the extensive search for physical evidence.)

All of the basic guidelines have been violated at one time or another, and sometimes the result is a hearing before the U.S. Supreme Court. Essentially, the investigator should consider the following:

(1) The warrant specifies the place to be searched. The address on the warrant should be correct, and the correct address should be searched. Going to the wrong place does not win public admiration, especially if a forced entry is made. (2) A copy of the warrant should be given to, or left for, the occupant. (3) The warrant specifies the item or items to be seized. Technically, the investigator can search or inspect only those areas where the designated item(s) could physically be. If a console television set is the object of the search, the investigator has no authority to look in desk drawers. (4) Other items which may be evidence, and are found in places where the investigator is entitled to search, may not be seized

unless they can be classified as contraband. If they are not contraband, there is then probable cause to obtain another warrant specifically listing such items. (5) A receipt for all items taken must be left with or for the occupant. (6) Although the law does not specify the exact means by which the search is to be made, damage and disarray should be kept to a minimum. There have been some terrible abuses and destructive searches, especially by some federal agents, and that problem does not seem to be improving.

If a likely suspect is found, one of the last stages of the investigation is the interrogation (sometimes called "custodial interviewing") of the suspect. The goal is to gain as much additional information as possible about the crime and the reasons for it — and perhaps to even obtain a confession. In an ideal situation, both the interrogation and the confession would be unnecessary. Hopefully, by the time the interrogation is conducted, sufficient information has been gathered that the case may be considered complete. In any event, the interrogator should know as much as possible about the case before he proceeds with the questioning.

Interrogation is another area that is subject to provisions of the Constitution, legislation, and case law. And again, revisions are frequent. Effective interrogation can be, and of course should be, carried out within these guidelines. Even if a confession is lawfully obtained, it should not be forgotten that it is merely hearsay (see page 193) at this stage. Only if repeated in open court does it become direct evidence (see page 192).

Throughout the information gathering process, the investigator should constantly be updating and revising, as necessary, his theory of the case — the who, what, where, when, why, and how. One of the greatest traps into which an investigator can fall is an unwillingness to revise his theory — he reaches a point where he believes he knows who committed the crime, and then all further efforts are directed toward proving that suspect guilty, rather than continuing to search for the truth.

CRIMINALISTICS

Criminalistics, broadly defined as "scientific crime detection" and frequently called "forensic science," is that part of the criminal justice system which utilizes the natural sciences (chemistry, biology, physics, mathematics, medicine, etc.) to detect and solve crimes, and otherwise aid the justice system. While all of the natural sciences are broad and complex fields, that of medicine is particularly so. Therefore, the forensic medicine branch of criminalistics is usually limited to doctors of medicine who have specialized in pathology. The remaining sciences may be handled by persons with broad scientific training and experience, although the help of specialists is sometimes necessary.

In some criminal cases, especially the current and frequent drug-law violations, criminalistics plays a crucial role — the entire case may depend upon the accurate identification of the alleged drug. In other cases, the success of the criminal is dependent upon how well he can conceal evidence (or avoid leaving it at all), and how capable the investigators and criminalists are in finding and properly utilizing that evidence. Criminals are not necessarily inferior persons, although many are frequently unlucky; some are very scientifically oriented. To a certain extent then, we find competition between the technology of crime and that of crime detection. Police technology must advance just to remain even with crime technology. If the conviction rate is to increase, police technology must advance at an even faster rate. Criminalistics is one of the big factors in this technology and should receive more attention if the police are to be more effective. Otherwise, we may never be able to repeal that unfortunate aphorism that "Crime Does Indeed Pay."

Most work with the natural sciences requires, in addition to trained personnel, proper physical facilities, the sum of which is generally called a laboratory. Most smaller police departments, and even quite a few larger ones, have neither a laboratory nor personnel trained in the natural sciences. These departments must then rely on other laboratories, including state and federal, or do without the help that the criminalist can provide. Unfortunately, there are quite a few departments that choose the latter option.

Questions about the necessary education or training of criminalists are difficult to answer precisely, since criminalistics covers so many areas. While most universities offer courses in the natural sciences, few offer criminalistics courses. Consequently, there are relatively few criminalistics graduates, and most forensic laboratories employ chemists or biologists and give them further training to meet their own specific needs. The big factor that the chemist or biologist lacks, is the understanding of how things chemical or biological relate to crime and its solution, and the inter-relation between the laboratory and the legal system.

Sometimes the scientist will go into police work for a time, or the police officer may take courses in the sciences. Both of these approaches can work very well, although in the author's experience both are rare. Courses in criminalistics, if available, will combine both the scientific and police viewpoints while adding areas not covered in the usual science courses, such as firearms identification, document examination, bloodstain analysis, etc. The average police officer, though he may not intend to ever become a criminalist, can gain valuable knowledge from such courses about the nature of evidence, its proper handling, its overall value, etc.

The popularity of television shows and motion pictures which portray police work and criminal investigation has resulted in a great deal of misunderstanding, by the general public, about the abilities of the crime scene technicians and criminalists and the means by which they accomplish their objectives. Although there have been a few realistic programs, it is probably safe to say that if a person were to watch all of these presentations and average them all together, he would obtain a very distorted picture of all categories of police work and investigation.[2] These widely held misconceptions cause frequent misunderstandings between police and citizen; the citizen expects the police to conform to their "TV image" and is disappointed, puzzled, or angered when they do not. In particular, the citizen may expect or demand certain services or results from the criminalist because they "know" these things can be done.[3] While it is true that shortages of trained personnel, money, and equipment prevent full utilization of criminalistics in practically all crimes, some citizens nevertheless have expectations which exceed the capabilities of even the most advanced facilities and skilled personnel.

Evidence

If a case ultimately goes to court,[4] two opposing sides will attempt to establish the guilt, or lack of guilt, of the defendant. The prosecution will attempt to "prove beyond a reasonable doubt" that the defendant committed all the elements of the crime charged. The defense will normally use any and all legal means available to counter the prosecution. The establishment of "proof," or lack of it, is of critical importance to the trial — especially to the defendant — and is the essential purpose *of* the trial. The proof with which the opposing sides are concerned is the result of the evidence.

Evidence is the means by which the "triers of fact" (the jury, or the judge in a non-jury trial) arrive at their conclusion concerning the truth or falsity (the "proof") of the charges and allegations involved. If there is no hung jury or other mistrial, then a "finding of fact" (guilty, not guilty, not guilty by reason of insanity or self-defense, etc.) is the final result of the presentation of the evidence. The "fact" so found may have no relation to what actually happened in true physical fact, but is a legal determination by which the parties involved are bound. The evidence consists of the testimony of witnesses, and physical objects along with the testimony of those presenting such objects. Attorneys and judges present no evidence.

Before evidence can be classified as to type, one must consider what the "point at issue" is. In other words, with what crime is the defendant charged, and what finding of fact is the jury trying to determine.

Direct evidence is evidence which, *if true*, can by itself prove or disprove the point at issue. In practical terms, this usually means eye-witness testimony concerning the crime charged. If Mary is charged with killing John by shooting him, there is no direct evidence that can be presented unless someone saw her do it (or unless Mary confesses in court). The prosecutor should by no means rely on direct evidence alone if any other is available. The eye-witness may well be mistaken, for any number of reasons, or lying. In the above example, the eye-witness testimony of the gun dealer who sold the weapon in question to Mary is not direct evidence; in this case Mary is not charged with buying a gun. If she were charged with the illegal purchase of a gun, then the dealer's testimony would be direct evidence.

Physical evidence is "indirect" or "circumstantial" evidence; that is, it cannot by itself establish the truth or falsity of the allegations — it can only suggest, or point to, or be a link in the chain which ultimately leads to the result. One sometimes hears it said that "you cannot get a conviction on circumstantial evidence alone." This is not true; in many cases the only evidence available is circumstantial. Subsequently, if there is a sufficient amount, properly linked together, then the jury can arrive at a finding of fact of "guilty."

In the above example of Mary and John, let us suppose that a person nearby heard a shot, heard Mary laugh, ran into the room and saw Mary standing over John's bleeding body and holding a smoking pistol in her hand. That is all circumstantial evidence.

The forensic pathologist must determine that John is indeed dead, the approximate time of death, and that he died from a gunshot. The criminalist must determine (if possible) that the fatal bullet was fired from the gun in Mary's hand. If

Mary's palm prints or fingerprints are on the gun (and that is by no means certain) they should be recovered and identified. Mary's hands should be processed for traces of primer residue; if any are present, they indicate recent firing of a gun. However, all of this is only circumstantial evidence. None of these factors by themselves can prove or disprove the point at issue.

Physical evidence is often considered the most reliable type, the thought being that "objects cannot lie." That is true, but merely because objects cannot talk. They also cannot tell the truth; someone must speak for them. For our purposes, this speaker is the criminalist. He may on occasion be mistaken, though the dedicated professional will make every effort to keep this to the absolute minimum. Regrettably, it must be recognized that some criminalists have been known to commit perjury; there is no justification for that behavior, and it is to be thoroughly condemned.[5]

Strictly speaking, items become evidence only when they are admitted into court. However, the convention is to classify items which the criminalist believes *may* eventually be evidence *as* evidence, and that convention will be followed in this chapter.

There is one type of evidence that is of little concern to the criminalist but of great importance to the investigator — it is known as hearsay evidence. A simple three-part definition of hearsay is: (1) statement(s), usually written or oral, (2) made outside of *this* court, and (3) offered to prove or disprove the matter asserted (which is not the point at issue). The basic rule is that hearsay is not admissible, unless it meets certain specific qualifications, because having been made outside of this court it is not subject to cross-examination. Since so much of the information found by investigators is hearsay, knowledge of what may be an admissible exception is important.

For any evidence to be admissible in court, it must meet four requirements. First, it must have been obtained legally. (Prior to 1961, evidence obtained illegally by federal agents could be used in state trials.[6]) Second, it must be relevant; it

must have some value in proving or disproving the point at issue. Third, it must be material; it must be important. Fourth, it must be competent. For physical evidence, competency is established by laying a broad foundation which includes a number of factors. One of these is the "chain of custody" or "chain of possession." This is the written record of every person who has handled the evidence from the time it was first picked up until its appearance in court. This record must be complete, and should be as short as possible — no one who doesn't need to handle the evidence should ever do so. Another factor is the proper identification or marking of the evidence; can it be definitely established that this is the same item, and not some similar but different item? Can it be verified that this is indeed the photograph of a particular scene, and not merely one of some similar scene? Except for disturbances made necessary by some examination, is the evidence in essentially the same condition as when originally found? If these (and other) questions cannot be honestly answered "yes," then the court may declare the evidence to be incompetent, and therefore not admissible. A great deal of time, effort, and expense may then be for naught, because of what appears to be a minor error in procedure. However, there are no minor errors in the handling of evidence — there are only errors, and every reasonable effort should be made to avoid them.

Physical Evidence at the Scene

Physical evidence frequently begins its value at the scene of the crime. While all steps in the handling and processing of evidence may be considered critical, the steps taken at the crime scene are especially so. In the laboratory, tests or procedures which fail may usually be repeated, or another method may be used. However, at the crime scene if evidence is overlooked or mishandled there will usually not be an opportunity to find it later, or to correct mistakes in its treatment. In most cases the control of the scene is returned to the owner or occupant after the scene investigator has made his investigation and collected the available evidence. Generally one cannot go back the next day or the next week and expect to find the scene undisturbed. Therefore, it is especially important that everything be done correctly at the scene the first time through because that is usually the only chance that will be available.

Before any item or substance can become evidence, it must be found and recognized as having some potential evidential value. Almost anyone can, with the proper care, engage in the search for evidence. The burden upon the searcher is eased considerably if he knows what he is looking for. For example, if there has been a shooting and the bullets found in the victim do not account for all that were fired, then a thorough search is made of the structure, furniture, etc., for any missing bullets. If the searcher is not sure what he is looking for, then he will have to call upon the criminalist to evaluate possible evidence that his search may uncover.

If the scene is of reasonable size, the search is best done by people experienced in the recognition of evidence. Material which may have great potential value at one scene may be of no interest at a different scene, even though the crimes may be very much the same. For example, consider a residential burglary where the point of entry is a window. If the window has been pried open, chipping off paint in the process, or if the paint is flaking, there is the possibility of transfer of some paint chips to the burglar's clothes. In a case like this, paint chip samples should be taken for later comparison. However, if the paint has not been chipped, or is not flaking, then there would be little point in taking samples. Because no two scenes will be exactly alike, it would be very difficult to give a general set of instruction for the inexperienced searcher to follow.

Before the evidence is handled, its nature and position must be recorded in the investigator's notebook. At this time a rough sketch may be made of the scene, showing its dimensions, pertinent features, and the location of items being collected. If the items are unusual and/or especially significant, they should be photographed in place. Notes must be kept of the location, description, time, and direction from which the photograph was taken. If the photographic system utilized allows

the identification of individual pictures, the identification number should also be noted. All of these factors assist in establishing the competency of the photographs. While all necessary photographs should certainly be taken, not all pictures are worth a thousand words. If the investigator or criminalist does not feel that a picture can readily aid the investigation or court presentation, it would be a waste of time and effort to take it; in such cases, a simple written description will suffice. Many agencies also make videotape recordings of major crime scenes.

In any case, regardless of who finds real or possible evidence, only one person — the leader of the search or the person in charge of collecting evidence at the scene — should handle it from that point on, until it is delivered to the examining facility. The general rule covering this situation can be stated simply: "If you pick it up, it's yours." This does not mean to imply a matter of finders-keepers, but that the first person to touch or pick up evidence is responsible for it until such time as it must pass out of his possession — when it is turned in to the laboratory, for instance. On television, one will sometimes see the first officer on the scene pick the gun up, handle and examine it, pass it to the second officer who does likewise and who then passes it to the third who puts it in his pocket. This represents an extremely poor technique, and it would be very unlikely that evidence so treated could be considered competent — the chain of custody could certainly not withstand cross-examination.

Once the evidence has been picked up or collected, it must be properly marked, tagged, or otherwise identified so that there will be no doubt in court that it is the item it is represented to be. Because of the tremendous variety in types of physical evidence that may be found, it is difficult to give general rules about the means that should be used to identify them. One reasonable rule is that any item which is likely to be presented in court, and which can be permanently marked without damaging its intrinsic or evidential value, should be so marked. This can avoid any possible suggestion that a tag or label may have been switched. While such an action on the part of the investigators would be despicable, defense attorneys are known to pluck at any possible straw which may aid their case.

Many items will require packaging and/or preservation. Once again, the nature of the evidence will have a major influence on the techniques to be employed. For example, a sample of liquid blood should be placed in an airtight, impervious container (such as glass) no larger than necessary, tightly stoppered or sealed, and refrigerated. (Some authorities suggest the addition of a small amount of preservative; others prefer to add nothing, thereby avoiding any suggestion of contamination.) On the other hand, items which are bloodstained must be treated in a somewhat different fashion; they must not be placed in an airtight container. After the bloodstains are thoroughly dry, the item is packaged in paper or some other semi-porous medium. If material containing wet bloodstains is tightly packaged, the blood will undergo serious and foul-smelling decomposition.

Likewise, the nature of the package or container used is governed by the nature of the intended contents. A common clean Styrofoam cup may make an excellent temporary container for a water-based liquid, but it would be a total disaster as a container for gasoline; gasoline dissolves Styrofoam rather rapidly.

Paper and plastic envelopes, glass and plastic bottles and vials, cardboard pill boxes, and small metal ointment tins are used for packaging a very wide variety of evidence. Some items, such as recovered bullets which should be protected from all unnecessary physical contact, should first be wrapped in clean cotton or tissue.

In most cases the package, in addition to providing protection to the item, must serve as the means of identifying the contents. Therefore, it needs to be properly and sufficiently marked so that there can be no later question of exactly what it contains.

The next step in the life history of evidence is usually transportation. (However, it should be noted that many items are actually transported to a local facility before they are marked and packaged. This would especially be the case if, for example, an electric engraver were to be used for the marking.) If there is a local laboratory with facilities for examining this particular evidence, transportation should be a very simple matter. However, even under these circumstances, serious errors have been occasionally committed. It is not unknown for the evidence to be handed at this point to a lower-ranking officer with instruction to "turn this in to the lab." While that may ease the burden of the higher-ranking officer, it does no good whatsoever to the chain of custody.[7]

If the evidence cannot be transported by the collecting officer to the examining laboratory, then it must be shipped. This requires proper packaging for protection, registration to protect the chain of possession, information on the case and the examinations desired. The information should be enclosed in an envelope in such a manner that the sealed evidence need not be disturbed in opening the envelope. This enables the person who will be doing the actual examination to be the one who opens the evidence package, and prevents secretaries and clerks from being possibly included in the chain of possession. The actual packing procedure will vary depending on the size and nature of the evidence.

Examination

In the majority of cases, the officer collecting the evidence will not be the person who does the actual examination. It is important for the collecting officer, or someone else in authority in the case, to establish intelligent communication with the examiner, especially in the area of what tests are requested and what information is desired from the evidence. Requesting the laboratory to "tell me all you can about this" will generally result in relegation of the evidence to the inactive file. The laboratory usually has more work that it can handle, and any unnecessary tests should be avoided. For example, in the case of a bottle of liquid suspected of containing some alcohol, is it merely necessary to determine if alcohol is present? Or is it also necessary to determine the exact alcohol content? It if is not alcoholic, is it necessary to determine what liquid it is? Ideally, investigators will communicate with the laboratory about the problems and questions in the case, and the criminalist may then be able to suggest laboratory examinations that may help.

After the examinations have been made and the reports prepared, the investigator (and the attorneys for both sides) should be certain that they understand exactly what the laboratory *is*, and sometimes more importantly is *not*, telling them. On occasion, the laboratory may even suggest problems that may be faced in court concerning the case.

Generally, the person examining the evidence will be the last person in the chain of possession before the evidence goes to court. As a member of this chain, he must pay all necessary attention to keeping the chain intact — to make any necessary records of the opening, handling, examining, resealing, etc., of the evidence. He must also take particular care to preserve the integrity of the evidence. This means that it is undamaged, uncontaminated, and affected as little as possible by the tests that will be performed upon it. In some cases it is not possible to prevent destruction or significant change to the evidence. Some samples are too small; some tests are naturally destructive. However, insofar as it is reasonably feasible, the integrity should be maintained. If any unnecessary damage or loss has occurred, this can be another fertile field for defense attack.

Known samples of evidence, and control standards, constitute a vital area of criminalistics that is often overlooked by the neophyte. Most laboratory examinations ultimately compare the crime scene evidence to a known or control sample. A list of all examples would be far too long, but a few typical ones will be given.

Latent fingerprints must be compared against known prints of suspects. A possibly forged signature must be compared to a legitimate one. A piece of carpet thought to contain traces of an accelerant in arson cases must be compared to a piece thought to be free of such traces. Bullets suspected of having been fired from a particular weapon must be compared to a bullet known to have been fired from it. Paint chips in the suspect's clothes must be compared to chips known to have come from the scene. Similar examples could be given for dust and dirt traces, glass, fibers, hair, and a great many other items.

Control standards do not come from the crime scene or from people involved with it, but from suppliers and manufacturers of standardized materials. These are used to calibrate instruments and to test and verify various laboratory procedures. Before results from a breath analyzer can be accepted in court, it must be verified that the instrument was working properly; this requires a control standard of certified purity. Instruments and procedures to test or analyze drugs must be calibrated and checked with certified samples. While the known samples of evidence change from case to case, control standards generally remain the same.

Testimony

After the examinations and tests have been completed and the reports written and filed, the criminalist may then (usually after some considerable delay) look forward to an appearance in court. Hopefully he has had this possibility in mind throughout his work, and has conducted that work in such a manner that his court appearance will not be a waste of time, nor an embarrassment to himself or the side presenting the evidence.

Regardless of the nature of the tests or instruments employed in the examinations, the results to be expressed in court are only opinions. We would hope that any qualified person doing any particular test would come to the same result or conclusion — nevertheless, the results of laboratory tests and examinations are still only the opinions of the examiner. While any witness is entitled to testify in certain legally specified areas on matters of opinion, only an expert may testify on other matters of opinion or on matters of conclusion. Furthermore, the expert may express these opinions or conclusions *only* in the fields in which he is considered qualified by the court.

Who is a qualified expert? Basically, whomever the court chooses to so declare! Judges do not all come from the same mold, and a person who may be accepted by one judge as an expert in a particular field may not be so accepted by a different judge. It is an individual decision by an individual judge. Generally the factors considered include education, training, apprenticeship, and experience. A judge will usually give due consideration to the fact that a person has been qualified in the field in question in another court, but he need not consider this as binding. Once a person has been qualified in a particular field in a given court, he will usually be accepted by that court in later cases without the necessity of requalification.

Once qualified and in position to give testimony, the expert faces certain dangers from attorneys on both sides. Probably the most severe of these are the attempts to lead him into testifying outside his field of expertise. The attorney calling the expert may get carried away and attempt to get more opinions or conclusions than he should in an effort to bolster his case. The opposing attorney may deliberately try to lead the expert into an area outside his field and then pounce upon him, thereby discrediting some or all of the expert's testimony.

In general, an investigator should have a somewhat easier time testifying than does a criminalist. Although occasionally the investigator may be qualified as an expert in some phase of police work, the questioning will ordinarily be straightforward and not require (or allow) opinions or conclusions.

Once testimony has been given, it is up to the triers of fact to make their decision. The results may not agree with what the person testifying thinks is proper or just, but if he has done his job competently and honestly he should not allow himself to be upset.

EXAMPLES OF EVIDENCE

The totality of types of evidence with which the criminalist may be confronted is far greater than can possibly be considered here. Some examples are presented, along with typical misconceptions concerning them, and some of the information obtainable from them.

Imprints and Impressions

Most commonly, these are made by fingers or hands but may also be produced by feet and other items. The general public now accepts the basic premises about fingerprints without it being necessary to lay a complete foundation for each court appearance — that the individual ridge patterns of the friction skin (fingers, palms, soles of feet) are essentially invariable throughout a person's lifetime, and that no two people have yet been found whose prints are not readily distinguishable.

There are three types of fingerprint information that may be found at crime scenes. First, and by far the most common, are the latent prints. These are generally considered to be invisible, but on many surfaces they can be readily seen if the lighting is proper. (On such surfaces the criminalist will usually make a visible light search before proceeding with the processing.) These prints have been made by the deposition of body oils, salts, and sweat when the hand or foot contacted an appropriately receptive surface. Whether visible or not, they require some form of processing before they can be utilized for identification purposes. The particular method of processing will depend on the surface on which the prints are located, and the established procedures of the department. Typically, prints on smooth, non-porous surfaces will be dusted. In this process, a fine, fluffy powder will be brushed over the surface with a very soft brush. Or, a magnetic powder may be applied with a device looking much like a pen or pencil, containing a retractable magnet. If all goes well, the powder will adhere to the oil traces making up the latent print, and not to the rest of the surface. If a powder of color contrasting to the surface has been used, the developed print can be photographed. Or a strip of a special cellophane-type tape or adhesive-coated rubber may be carefully pressed down on the print, smoothly lifted, and then protected by applying smooth plastic to the lifted print. The rubber lifter has the distinct disadvantage in that the lifted print is on an opaque surface, and is a mirror image of the original print, or of the known sample.

Prints on surfaces such as paper, into which the oil is absorbed relatively quickly, cannot be dusted but may be chemically processed by several methods. One excellent method is to spray the surface with a solution of ninhydrin. This chemical forms a colored compound with the amino acids present in the body oils which have made the print. Prints have been successfully developed by this method many years after they were left on the paper.

Surfaces which are naturally greasy, such as kitchen ranges and automobiles, can be dusted but specially compounded powders are necessary so that one does not end up with a solid layer of powder, rather than just a developed print. Latent prints have even been lifted or processed from skin using special techniques.

Some other chemical methods, similar in principle to the ninhydrin process, may be used to develop a print which can then be photographed. However, these methods also have certain drawbacks, such as staining or corroding certain surfaces. The criminalist should bear these factors in mind and attempt to choose a method appropriate to the occasion.

Unfortunately, to the disappointment and consternation of many victims of crime, there are many surfaces which are too rough and/or too porous to accept good latent prints, such as real wood surfaces. While powder applied to metal surfaces is fairly readily removed, surfaces such as wood or plastic with a porous or grainy structure may be almost impossible to thoroughly clean after the dusting operation. For this reason, some thought needs to be given, before dusting, to the probability of the surface containing a usable print and to the likelihood of permanent damage to a valuable item.

Several new techniques have been developed to allow the recovery of latent prints from a wider variety of surfaces. The proper laser or other high-energy light will cause fluorescence of the riboflavin molecules in perspiration and this fluorescence can be photographed. This technique is non-destructive.

An accidental discovery led to the development of a fuming process using a modern adhesive containing a cyanoacrylate ester (the so-called SuperGlue method). Items exposed to the fumes of this ester will develop white patterns on fingerprint residues and these patterns may be photographed or even dusted to enhance them. This technique can give good results on a variety of surfaces, including leather, vinyl, and cloth. Although a relatively simple process, it is a fuming process and therefore not applicable to all objects.

The second type of fingerprint found at crime scenes is the patent (pā-tent) or visible, and is left by hands or fingers containing such materials as blood, ink, or paint. In most cases these can simply be photographed without any further treatment.

The third type is the impression, found in things such as putty, uncured paint, and other soft materials. The nature of the processing will depend upon the exact nature of the impression. In some cases the entire impression can be removed and taken to the laboratory. In others it may be photographed with oblique lighting; sometimes powders can be carefully applied to increase the contrast. Sometimes a cast will be taken of a finger impression, using a material such as silicone rubber.

At a typical crime scene, the criminalist should feel quite satisfied if a good partial print of a single finger of the perpetrator is recovered. That amount of information is ordinarily sufficient for positive identification by comparison to known prints. Formerly there was the very significant problem of obtaining the known prints — if one did not have a relatively few suspects already in mind there was no practical way of searching the massive fingerprint databases for the needed information. (The FBI has over 213,000,000 fingerprint records, most of which are criminal.) A complete set of properly classified fingerprints from any person will allow a search of the databases for matching prints, but a partial print from an unknown finger presented an almost unsolvable problem with respect to searches. Fortunately, technology is coming to the rescue.

New techniques allow fingerprint cards to be optically scanned, the fingerprint data to be digitally classified and stored, and the databases to be searched electronically to identify possible candidates; a skilled examiner can then check those relatively few cards manually against the crime scene prints. The FBI is developing IAFIS, the Integrated Automated Fingerprint Identification System. IAFIS will support a law enforcement agency's ability to digitally record individuals' fingerprints and other related information, and electronically exchange this information with the FBI. It is expected that IAFIS will respond to urgent fingerprint identification requests in as little as two hours. In the past, it could take many days, if not weeks. This new technology is not inexpensive, but in recent years many law enforcement agencies have found it to be a good investment. In addition to being a valuable tool for the solution of new crimes, many old cases have finally been solved.

Feet, clothing, tires, teeth, and tools can also leave imprints or impressions. Evidence left by bare feet is just as distinctive as that left by fingers, and would be treated in the same fashion (except that there are no significant databases of footprints). Clothing can leave distinct impressions on furniture with soft finishes, on incompletely cured painted surfaces, and on hard painted surfaces if sufficient force is used. Hit-and-run vehicles frequently have cloth impressions in their paint from the victim's clothes. If the vehicle is found this can be significant evidence.

Tire prints are occasionally found on hard, smooth surfaced areas, but the usual situation is an impression in moist soil. If the impression appears to be sharp and distinctive, it is photographed and then a cast is made, generally with plaster but sometimes with a silicone rubber. A good tire cast can identify the brand of tire, and sometimes the make and model of car if the tire is the same one that came on the vehicle when new. As the tire wears, the distinctive wear patterns, cracks, and marks can be used to identify that particular tire and distinguish it from others of the same model.

Shoe prints and impressions are closely related to those made by tires. Dirty shoes may leave prints which can be photographed or lifted, and impressions in soil are preserved by making casts. The distinctive markings and wear patterns of heels, and occasionally soles, can lead to individualization.

Teeth marks may be found in food, such as cheese, and casts can be made of them. Teeth marks in flesh do not lend themselves to casting, due to the resiliency of body tissues. However, photographs of the marks may be useful since teeth vary in size, shape, and alignment.

Tool marks are left by jimmies, crow bars, wire cutters, bolt cutters, knives, axes, screwdrivers, etc. The neophyte investigator is sometimes tempted to try a suspect tool in the tool mark to see if it is a good fit. That might sound like a reasonable idea to some people, but it makes as much sense as trying to ram a bullet back down the barrel of the gun from which it may have been fired. Placing any tool in contact with any tool mark can destroy the evidential value of the mark.

If it is at all possible, the tool mark itself should be taken to the laboratory. If this is not feasible, a silicone rubber cast can be made. If a cast is used, it can be compared to the suspect tool under the comparison microscope (see "firearms"). If an original tool mark is available, it can be compared with marks made with the suspect tool on copper or lead sheets. A variety of marks may need to be made due to the various angles at which the tool can be held. A similar procedure is used with wire or bolt cutters — cutting a copper or lead wire and comparing its marks with the original evidence. A series of cuts may have to be made due to the length of the cutting portion of the tool as compared to the width of the wire.

Weapons

Here we consider some weapons other than firearms, which will be covered separately. For countless years man has used a wide variety of weapons with which to do away his fellow man. Knives, swords, spears, axes, picks, and broken bottles have been used to stab, cut, and slash. Hammers, bricks, and bats have been used to smash and crush. Ropes, ties, belts, wires, and hands have been used to strangle. Pillows, plastic bags, illuminating gas, carbon monoxide, and water have been used to suffocate. Automobiles, airplanes, fire, explosives, drugs, and poisons have all been used to inflict injury or death. Basically, just about anything that can cause damage to the human body has been used as a weapon at one time or another.

In cases of assault, the victim may have good knowledge of the weapon used against him. In the event that drugs or poisons are not self-administered, it will be somewhat less obvious; this is more a problem for toxicologists than criminalists, as the usual forensic laboratory will not be equipped for toxicological work.

If the assault results in death, the criminalist can certainly assist in the autopsy (if local policies permit), but the bulk of the work should be done by a forensically trained pathologist. Unfortunately, such personnel are not available in many localities and the autopsies are performed by physicians. A physician's training may make him adept in the healing arts, but does not prepare him to make the adequate and accurate determinations of cause of death in many situations.

Among the things to be determined at the autopsy are the nature of the weapon, and the manner in which it was used. Careful examination of stab wounds can establish whether a single or double-edged blade was used, and whether it was sharp-pointed or blunt-ended. It is often possible to

establish whether the attacker was left- or right-handed, and from what position the attack was made. Also, it may be established that the wounds were self-inflicted. Suicide is occasionally committed by the use of a knife. In a Wichita, KS case, a very intoxicated woman committed suicide by stabbing herself in the heart; she was very determined, and finally successful.[8]

Instruments used to smash may be identified by the size or shape of the impressions they make, particularly since they are usually used against the skull. A suggestion of the type of weapon used for strangulation may be gained from a study of the marks left and the tissue damage caused. There have been cases where a very obese person has been thought to have died from natural causes, only to have the mortician discover a tight ligature around the neck beneath the third chin.

Pedestrians killed by automobiles usually died from obvious causes. However, the operator of a car or airplane involved in a fatality may have died from other causes. Heart attacks, strokes, epileptic seizures, and fatal concentrations of carbon monoxide in the blood are among causes leading directly to death or to the crash causing death. In all cases it is important that the medical facts in the matter be established.

Fire is frequently used as a weapon, both directly to cause injury or death and indirectly in an attempt to cover up or disguise another crime or method of homicide. However, even if the body is quite severely burned, it is ordinarily a relatively simple matter to determine whether or not the victim was alive during the fire. If the victim was alive, there will be carbon monoxide in the blood; also there will be distinct charring and smoke deposition in the throat and lungs, whereas a dead body will be essentially unaffected in these areas by the fire. That the person was dead when the fire started does not itself indicate foul play. People have suffered heart attacks while smoking, and then set fire to their surroundings. Once again, it is important to establish the exact cause of death if at all possible.

It is also important to establish the cause of the

fire. A natural or accidental cause is to be assumed until proven otherwise, but a high threshold of suspicion should be maintained during the determination of cause.

There are many motives for arson, including pyromania, revenge, assault, insurance fraud, and trying to cover up other crimes, e.g., burglary or homicide. Except for such goals as insurance fraud, it is not too important for the arsonist to try to disguise the fact that the fire was not accidental. Even in fraud cases it may not be too important, as long as it does not appear that the beneficiary was responsible.

Typically, arson will involve the use of flammable liquids as accelerants. Gasoline, kerosene, and turpentine are typical accelerants. If a prompt and thorough investigation is carried out, there is an excellent chance of recovering identifiable traces of these substances. Fire generally burns upwards, and if the structure has not collapsed or been totally destroyed, the origin of the fire is most likely at the lowest portion which has been burned, or appears to have burned the longest. Samples of flooring, carpeting, wallboard, etc., should immediately be taken from the scene and placed in containers which are then tightly sealed. Likewise, known samples of these materials should be taken from areas thought to not be near the origin; these will be used for comparison purposes. It is not sufficient in court to be able to say that the carpet near the origin contained traces of gasoline, unless one can also testify that the carpet at the other end of the room contained no such traces. Otherwise it might be claimed by the defense that the entire carpet had just been cleaned with gasoline — something that at least a few people would be foolish enough to do.

Solid accelerants are used by some arsonists. Although in many respects they are not as effective in fire starting as the liquids, it is often far easier to arrange for a simple, inexpensive, delayed ignition system. They will generally leave very significant traces of residue. They have been frequently employed in foreign countries in terrorist campaigns, as they are readily carried and placed without suspicion. They then burst into flame some minutes or hours later, depending upon their exact construction.

Especially in arson investigation, in addition to looking for things which should not be there, the criminalist should be on the lookout for anything which should be there but isn't. For instance, if a merchant or homeowner is claiming that certain items were destroyed in the fire and should be reimbursed by insurance, it should be ascertained that any appropriate ash or residue from such items is indeed present. Merchants have been known to conveniently forget that they moved their stock to another location just before the fire "accidentally occurred."

Firearms

Contrary to the opinion of some people that firearms are used in all cases of personal assault, in Wichita, KS in 1975 seven successive homicides were committed without involving guns — two by axe, two by knife, two by sword, and one by strangulation and beating. Guns are, however, very frequently used in crimes, and there are a number of questions the criminalist may need to attempt to answer concerning them: Has this suspect recently fired a gun? In what order were the shots fired? From what range was the victim shot, and from what direction did the shot come? Is this the particular gun from which this particular bullet was fired? It may not always be possible to answer all of these questions, or perhaps any of them, but once again the best possible job should be done. Since the possible matching of a bullet and gun is the first test that usually comes to mind in a crime involving firearms, we will start with that aspect.

The proper name for this particular task is "firearms identification." It is usually referred to as "ballistics," even though that word properly describes the motion of projectiles, both within and outside of the gun, and really has nothing to do with identification. Another common misconception is that any fired bullet can be positively matched to the gun from which it was fired; that is by no means always the case. First, let's consider why positive matching can sometimes be done,

201

and how, and then under what conditions it is not possible.

The manufacture of rifled arms, whether revolver, pistol, or rifle, involves certain procedures that leave both *class characteristics* (which are usually constant in a given make and model) and *individual characteristics* (which differ between even apparently identical guns) within any particular barrel. Since some of these class characteristics — all, in exceptional cases — can be determined from recovered bullets, it is possible to suggest what make or model of gun may have fired the bullet. Many manufacturers may use the same class characteristics in their barrels, and they may change these characteristics from time to time, so one cannot usually be absolutely certain about the type of gun used from just an examination of the bullet.

Although a number of different manufacturing methods are in current use, each individual barrel will still have its own individual characteristics in addition to its class characteristics. Even with modern precision manufacturing methods, so far there is no evidence that any two barrels contain the same individual characteristics.

If one is to be able to state that a particular gun fired a particular bullet, then a match of individual characteristics in addition to class characteristics must be made. This requires the firing of a bullet — preferably the same type as that of the crime scene or clue sample — through the suspect weapon, and recovery of the bullet in as perfect a condition as possible. Water or snow is best, but cotton waste is frequently used because of its convenience. The two bullets, clue and known, are mounted for study under a comparison microscope. This is a device consisting of two identical microscopes attached together with an optical bridge. This arrangement allows the criminalist to study the two bullets while they appear to be a single bullet — the front half of one joined to the rear half of the other (although some instruments also allow a superimposed view). In modern instruments, the field of view can be swept from side to side, and if the bullets match it will appear that a line is moving across the length of a single bullet.

In the entertainment shows, something less than a minute is spent with the comparison microscope before the results are announced. In reality it is not nearly that easy. It may be necessary to compare all combinations of grooves on the two bullets. The clue bullet may be deformed, making certain comparisons difficult and others impossible. In addition to the marks that do match there will be a number which do not, even though the bullets may have been fired successively from the same gun. In this respect, bullet comparison differs from fingerprint comparison. With fingerprints if two particular marks or points definitely do not match, the prints are different, regardless of the number of similarities. With bullets, it is the number that match compared to those that don't, and the criminalist's judgment based on his training and experience that make the final determination: yes, no, or maybe. Why maybe? In some cases, the match is not good enough for a yes, but is still too good to say no.

There are other problems which may arise. Unlike fingerprints, which do not change over a lifetime, barrel markings may indeed change. Wear, rust, and neglect may affect the individual marking of a barrel over a period of time. There have been cases where two bullets fired successively from the same gun could *not* be matched — in one, the barrel was too worn and rusted, and its characteristics were changing from shot to shot.[9]

Guns may also be identified from fired cartridge casings. These are generally left behind at the crime scene when semi-automatic or self-loading firearms have been used, and sometimes also from other types of guns. The cartridge cases, of relatively soft metal and subject to high pressures and forceful treatment, will be impressed with a number of class and individual characteristics. The primer especially, being of even softer material and subject to higher pressures, will pick up distinct marks and impressions from the firing pin and the breech of the gun. The firing pin and breech will have their own machining marks. Most self-loading guns contain both an extractor and an ejector. The size and relative positions of the marks left by these parts are class characteristics, and they will also have their own particular machine marks. Therefore, any cartridge cases found at a crime scene should be considered valuable evidence.

Despite the differences between fingerprints and firearms identification, there are enough similarities to warrant establishing a computer database of crime-related bullets and cartridge cases, especially since criminals are becoming more mobile. As of early 1997, such work is underway, and some interstate links have been established.

Good examples of successes and difficulties are found in several Wichita cases. In one instance, the two fatal bullets were too badly battered to enable any comparisons to be done; the fatal weapon was identified from firing pin impressions on the ejected cases found near the victim. In the second case, the victim was shot eleven times in the head, six times from a gun of one caliber, and five times from one of another caliber. Two suspects were finally picked up. Only one of the eleven bullets was in good enough condition to allow positive identification, and even that one required extensive study. Those were plain lead bullets. Many modern bullets are designed to expand or fragment upon hitting the target. This can add to the difficulty of identification.

A final note: The criminalist must avoid routinely concluding that a particular bullet or cartridge was necessarily fired in a weapon intended for it. The criminal may sometimes make considerable improvisation in matching (or not matching) weapon and ammunition.

Has the suspect recently fired a gun? In years past, the so-called "paraffin"[10] or dermal nitrate test was employed to verify the presence of nitrates (a product of all propellant powder burning) upon the skin. Unfortunately, there are many other sources of nitrates, some more common than gunpowder, which may find their way to a person's hands. This test has therefore rightly fallen into disrepute. Swabs from the front and back of both the suspect's hands can be tested by several different sensitive techniques for the presence of metals found in primer compounds; these metals may find their way back to the hand or hands of a shooter. Antimony, barium, and lead are common primer constituents, although their relative amounts vary, and not all primers contain all three metals. Some contain lead only, and some newer compositions have no lead in an effort to cut down on possible lead poisoning in indoor ranges. The suspect must be examined as soon as possible, as the residues do wash off.

In what order were the shots fired? One might think this would be an impossible question to answer, but in some crimes such a determination can indeed be made. A revolver is a frequently used crime weapon, and in many cases the criminal has an assortment of ammunition for it, of different brands and bullet types gathered from a variety of surfaces. If the revolver is recovered before being emptied of cartridge cases or reloaded, the position of the fired cases in the cylinder can sometimes tell in which order they were fired. If the fired bullets can be recovered, it is often possible to identify them by brand or type; they can then be matched to the fired cases and the order of discharge determined. In one case, the suspect claimed that he fired in self-defense, killing the victim only after a warning shot had been fired. Because of the differing brands of ammunition in the gun, it was clearly established that the warning shot had been fired after the fatal shot.

From what range and direction was the victim shot? The range may be a critical matter in possible suicides, alleged self-defense, etc. From contact to a range of 3 to 6 feet, depending upon the firearm and ammunition, a fairly accurate determination can be made if the same gun and ammunition are available for test purposes. Even if they are not, reasonable estimates can be made by the criminalist. Firearms discharges produce quantities of nitrite salts, and at close range these are deposited upon the clothing or skin of the victim. In addition to these deposits (which are invisible until chemically processed) there will often be unburned powder grains, and visible burning and destruction caused by the muzzle blast. The nitrites can be made visible by a relatively simple chemical process, and the patterns of nitrites, powder, and burning on cloth samples fired at from known ranges can be compared to the crime sample.

If the weapon in question is a shotgun, the

distribution of the pellets (pattern size) and location and penetration of the wadding or shot-cup are important factors in determining the distance from which the gun was fired.

Determining the bullet's path may involve some difficulties, since bullets can glance or ricochet off many surfaces, change directions, and travel considerable distances. The author has personally witnessed a shooter being struck by his own bullet after it had glanced off of two oak surfaces; fortunately, it had little energy left and the injury was very minor. The pathologist can trace the path of a bullet in the body, and that may not be a straight line either. The angle of entrance into the body, the position the victim was in at the time, any ricochets or penetrations of walls or windows, and the location of any expended cartridge cases are all items of information that may allow the criminalist to make an accurate determination of projectile path.

Blood and Other Body Fluids

The history of the advances in scientific crime detection and determination may perhaps be best illustrated by the history of blood, as it relates to crime. From the identification of human blood by Uhlenhuth and the basic blood typing by Landsteiner in 1901, through the discoveries of many further blood sub-groups, secretors, etc., to the present time when blood samples can *almost* be individualized, the advances in forensic serology have been among the most exciting and far-reaching of any in the field of criminalistics.

At many crime scenes, the apparent presence and distribution of blood is obvious, but never forget that the laboratory must verify that the substance is indeed blood, and of the proper species. To the specialist, the size, shape, and distribution of blood spatters and stains can suggest the means by which the blood was deposited in those locations. One of the most famous examinations of this type was conducted by Dr. Paul Kirk in the Sam Sheppard murder case in 1954.[11, 12]

Bloodstains on certain surfaces, or stains which have dried, may have a deceptive appearance. Depending upon the age of the stain, conditions to which it may have been subjected, the state of decay and the nature of the underlying surface, the color may vary from gray, through blue and green, red and brown, to almost black. It very frequently just doesn't look like what a beginner would expect; sometimes it can even fool the expert. For these reasons, field tests have been developed for blood. These tests are easy, fast, inexpensive, and can quickly determine whether any given stain is "most likely blood," or is "almost certainly not blood." One of the easiest of these tests employs the Hematest tablets (™ Ames Laboratories). This tablet, looking very much like an aspirin tablet, is placed on the suspect stain and a few drops of distilled water are run down the side of the tablet, moistening the junction of the tablet and the stain. If the stain is blood (not merely human, but any vertebrate animal blood) the moistened tablet will turn blue within two minutes. Stains upon vertical surfaces, or upon expensive fabrics, can be lifted sufficiently with filter paper moistened with saline solution, and the test run upon the filter paper. If the test is negative, and there is no reason to believe the stain has been subjected to unusually harsh treatment, then it can be safely assumed that the stain is not blood. If the reaction is positive the stain should be taken to the laboratory for further tests. (There are a few substances besides blood that will cause a positive reaction.)

Sometimes a search must be made for possible bloodstains. Ultraviolet light, which will cause many other substances to fluoresce, does not do so with blood, and bloodstains are therefore black under UV. Occasionally, the *luminol* test for blood may be employed. Luminol is a chemical which, when sprayed on bloodstains, causes the stains to luminesce or glow; the luminescence must be viewed in the dark.

Blood found at the scene, or upon clothing, etc., must be properly handled to preserve its evidential value and to prevent the courtroom from being cleared when it is introduced as evidence. As mentioned before, blood stains that are tightly packaged when moist will undergo decomposition, resulting in the destruction of the blood as possible evidence, and the production of putrefaction products of almost indescribably foul odor.

If the stains have passed the field tests the laboratory can determine if they are indeed blood and of what species, if not human. The extent to which further tests will be performed will depend very much on the nature of the case. It could be as simple as a basic blood typing, which gives minimal information but can exclude a particular suspect, or as complex as an RFLP DNA procedure which could narrow the list of possible matches down to one in several billion. All of the tests rely on factors sometimes known as *genetic markers*, so termed because their nature is determined by the usual rules of heredity, and because they give information about the genetic makeup of the person who has them. Although there are many different categories of these markers, we will consider only the two suggested above: the basic blood-group systems, and the relatively new DNA procedures.

The blood group markers were the first discovered, are relatively stable, are found in the normal secretions of most people, and are of fundamental importance in such medical matters as blood transfusions. These particular markers are found on the surface of the red blood cells, and are generally called *antigens*. A characteristic of all antigens is that there can exist a complementary substance known as an *antibody*, and an antigen and its specific antibody will neutralize or destroy each other upon contact in a reaction known as *agglutination*. This general property is the basis of the body's immune system, since foreign antigens introduced into the body will cause production of the complimentary antibody, which will then destroy any further invasions of that particular antigen.

Thus, to prepare a material that will agglutinate human blood for instance, human blood is injected into some other animal, such as a rabbit or sheep. This causes the animal's system to produce antibodies to the antigens found in human blood, and some of those antigens are common to all human blood. The animal is then "processed" and the serum from its blood is now anti-human serum. When such serum reacts with any human blood or blood antigen-containing cells, the agglutination reaction will take place and is fairly easily observed. Other anti-species sera can be prepared by a similar process, and used to determine from what species the blood or other tissue came.

If the blood is determined to be of human origin, it can be classified in the basic ABO system. There are two antigens to consider in ABO grouping: the A and the B. The presence of either, both, or neither of these determines the person's basic blood type. That is, type O blood (in a sense, type zero, as there is no O antigen) has neither, type A has the A antigen only, B has B only, and AB has both antigens. As previously mentioned, mixing the A antigen with anti-A antibody results in agglutination, whereas A and anti-B would cause no reaction. One of the most interesting things about these two antigens is that all normal humans form, during their first year of life, the antibodies to whichever of these antigens they do *not* have in their blood. Thus a person with type O blood has both anti-A and anti-B antibodies in his blood, type B has and anti-A, and type AB has neither. It is the presence of these antibodies in the blood of most people that is responsible for the rules governing allowable blood transfusions. A person with type O blood cannot be given any other type, because his system already contains the antibodies to counteract any type A, B, or AB blood. This limitation may soon be overcome by a new method of processing donated blood that will actually remove the A and B antigens, thereby converting all blood-bank blood into type O.[13]

Because of the above, anti-A and anti-B sera are readily obtained from persons with type B or A blood respectively, and the use of animals is not necessary. If liquid blood is to be typed, it is teased into the appropriate anti-sera on a microscope slide, and watched to see if agglutination, or clumping, takes place. Sera prepared from an unknown sample of blood can also be tested with known red cells to determine what antibodies are present in the unknown blood; this may be done as a verification. Grouping of dried blood follows the same principles, but is somewhat more difficult in practice, and will not be described here.

There are a number of other grouping chemicals in blood, but these tend to be less stable and more difficult to type, especially in dried samples. The A and B antigens are sturdy, and can be determined in blood stains that are many years old; such grouping has even been done on Egyptian mummies.

Somewhere between one-half and three-quarters of the population are secretors; that is, their normal body secretions (sweat, saliva, etc.) contain various quantities of their A/B antigens. Therefore, if the criminal has left any of these secretions behind, it may be possible to determine the blood type. If neither antigen is found, was the person a type O secretor, or a non-secretor? For many years it was not possible to answer that question, but eventually it was discovered that one other antigen is found in the secretions of secretors; this is the H antigen, and a test with anti-H will allow the above distinction to be made.

One of the most significant developments in recent years is popularly known as *DNA Fingerprinting*.[14] The "fingerprinting" has nothing to do with the friction ridges of the skin, but refers to the potential identification abilities of the new techniques. The analysis is actually done on blood, hair, saliva, semen, etc.; indeed, cells from almost any part of the body. As noted by David Bigbee, "The most dramatic advancement in the field of forensic science since the discovery of fingerprints is recombinant DNA technology.... [It] may well be the most powerful tool the law enforcement community has ever seen for the administration of justice."[15]

DNA is the abbreviation for deoxyribonucleic acid, an organic substance found in the nucleus of living cells that provides the genetic code determining a persons' individual characteristics. DNA is the genetic "blue-print" of most living organisms, including humans. In every cell of the same human that contains DNA (virtually all cells, with the exception of red blood cells as they have no nucleus), the "blue-print" is identical, whether it is a white blood cell, a piece of skin, spermatozoa, or a hair root cell.

Pictorially, the DNA molecule resembles a twisted ladder, or double helix. The "steps" within the ladder consist of four chemical subunits or bases, which always pair in a specific way, called complementary base pairing. Thus if the sequence of one strand is known, the sequence of the other strand can be determined; this is the basis of all DNA tests. There are over 3 billion base pairs in human DNA, and the probability of finding another person (other than an identical twin, triplet, etc.) whose DNA would be identical is approximately 1 in 10^{32}. Expressed another way this means that, except for a possible identical twin, no person having the same DNA is now alive, or indeed has ever lived.[16]

In forensic DNA testing, typing, or analysis, polymorphic genes (different forms in different people) are analyzed and detected in both the crime sample and the known sample. As in traditional serology, if the characteristics of the samples are dissimilar then they exclude one another. If the characteristics of the samples are the same, then they *cannot be excluded* from each other. A particular DNA profile may be found to be consistent with one in a million, tens of millions, or more individuals, and thus has very high identification potential.

Two important advantages of forensic DNA testing over conventional forensic serology are the discriminating power of DNA tests and the nature of the crime scene samples that can be studied. DNA testing can generally be performed on more types of evidence, including hair, bone, and tissue, and moreover can generally be performed on smaller samples. DNA can even differentiate sources of mixed stains, which are common in cases of sexual assault. When amplification-based DNA techniques are employed, it is not uncommon for DNA analysts to obtain meaningful results even when other means of testing are unsuccessful.

For forensic DNA purposes, there are two procedures in current use: RFLP and PCR. Restriction Fragment Length Polymorphism (RFLP) as of this writing is used more often in forensic casework than Polymerase Chain Reaction (PCR). Forensic DNA technology is evolving very rapidly, and methods are in development that will incorporate certain parts of the two technologies.

RFLP requires a somewhat larger sample than PCR and is time-consuming, taking several weeks to complete the assay. It is a very labor-intensive technique requiring much hands-on laboratory work. The benefit of RFLP testing is that it is able to individualize a sample to a very small segment of the population — sometimes as small as one person in several billion.

PCR, on the other hand, is relatively easy to use and works on very small samples. Results can be obtained much more quickly than with RFLP techniques. PCR population results are much more closely related to traditional forensic serology test results and may be on the order of one person in thousands, compared with the very small numbers generated by RFLP.

The potential of forensic DNA testing to resolve investigative and legal issues of identity in violent criminal cases has given rise to a significant FBI commitment of resources. These FBI resources have been organized into an aggressive national forensic DNA identification program. The FBI's DNA program consists of four major components: applied research and development, case work, technology transfer, and a national data-base of DNA identification records (CODIS).

CODIS is a fully integrated local/state/national law enforcement network of DNA records. It consist of four primary indexes or databases: anonymous population records, forensic or crime scene records, convicted offender records[17], and missing persons records. By comparing DNA profiles recovered from crime scenes, the CODIS programs can help to link serial cases, identify repeat offenders, provide probable cause for unknown suspects identified by DNA, and assist in identification of missing or unidentified persons across the nation.

A classic tenet of the American criminal justice system is that "it is better that a dozen guilty men go free rather than one innocent man being convicted." Unfortunately, innocent people *do* get convicted by our imperfect system. One of the great accomplishments of DNA identification has been the clearing and freeing of innocent people who have been wrongly convicted and incarcerated.

Glass

Glass is actually a very viscous liquid, manufactured in varying compositions and colors. Although technically a liquid since it has no crystalline structure and no definite melting point, it is generally quite hard and brittle and therefore easily broken, and thus frequently an item of evidential value in crimes.

The side from which a pane of glass was broken, the side from which shots were fired through it, and the order in which the shots were fired, are factors which are generally easy to determine. If the glass is broken by a large, slow moving object such as a fist or brick, the break occurs in two stages with the stresses being applied on opposite sides of the glass as the break progresses. The different stresses cause the formation of two different types of cracks. If the broken glass can be pieced together sufficiently to tell which type of crack one is examining, the stress marks along the broken edge will tell the criminalist from which side the force was exerted. While the majority of the broken glass will fall on the side opposite the force, not all of it will do so. Also, people have been known to break windows from one side, and transfer the glass to the other in an effort to fool investigators.

Although it is generally fairly easy to tell from which side a piece of glass was broken, how does one tell which side of the glass was inside or outside? If the glass is perfectly clean, then one has a problem unless the pieces can be fitted together, or sufficient glass remains in the frame.

In most cases one side is significantly dirtier, or is coated with a different type of dirt, and as long as some glass remains in the frame, or in an adjacent pane, it is easy to tell which side is which.

High speed objects, such as bullets, have a different effect on glass. They will generally punch out a cone of glass, larger on the exit side, and cracks may form (or, they may not) around the hole. If there is more than one hole, and cracks have formed, those from any given hole will not cross any cracks already there. The order of formation of the holes may therefore be fairly readily determined.

Objects need not penetrate the glass in order to make a hole and form a cone. BB guns, rocks thrown up by cars, etc., will frequently make such holes and cones even though there is no penetration. People may be mistakenly lead to believe they have been shot at.

Burglars who break glass may frequently take small particles of glass with them, embedded in their clothes. Victims of hit and run mishaps may have broken headlight glass in or on their bodies. The question then arises, did this particular piece, sliver or chip of glass come from this particular window, lens, bottle, etc. As with many other substances, glass has both class and individual characteristics. Class characteristics include chemical composition, density (mass per unit volume), refractive index (the degree to which the glass bends light), fluorescence under ultra-violet light, and precise color. All of these are fairly easily determined in the laboratory. Unfortunately, a large quantity of glass is manufactured and the majority of modern glass of a particular type is rather uniform in these characteristics. Also, unfortunately, the only individual characteristic of glass that can definitely distinguish one item from another is the pattern of marks along the broken edge. If a piece of glass can be "jig-saw" fitted to another, with perfect matching of the edges, then it can be said that they were originally one piece. Otherwise, the best that can be said is that they could have been one piece originally, if all the class characteristics are the same.

Other items

The above list of evidential items is certainly not intended to be all-inclusive of those dealt with by the criminalist. Many others of equal importance could have been described. The ones given here are typical, and hopefully the student will have gained some appreciation for the problems faced by the criminalist, and the results that may be gained by proper study of the evidence.[18]

ENDNOTES

[1] Weston and Wells, 1990.

[2] In particular, it is *much* slower than TV and the movies suggest.

[3] Peterson, 1974.

[4] In most jurisdictions, most felony cases are resolved by means of plea-bargaining, rather than by trial.

[5] What may be the world's most famous forensic laboratory has come under fire recently. The Justice Department's inspector general has issued a draft report charging that "procedures in the FBI laboratory are lax and handling of evidence is sloppy." ("FBI lab flaws could create havoc in courts," *The Wichita Eagle*, Sunday Feb. 9, 1997, page 1A.) Feature articles on the problems of the

FBI have appeared in national magazines; e.g., "What's Wrong at the FBI?" in *TIME*, April 28, 1997, and "Good Cop, Bad Cop" in *The New American*, May 26, 1997. Some experts of the author's acquaintance have had severe reservations about FBI laboratory work and testimony for many years.

[6] Mapp vs Ohio, 367 US 643, 6 LEd(2d) 1081, 81 SCt 1684 (1961).

[7] On more than one occasion while the author was working as a crime-scene investigator, he was involved in such a situation. The item would be taken to the laboratory, and on the evidence ticket would be written: "Officer so-and-so ordered me to turn in this item. Here it is."

[8] In April, 1997, in Wichita, KS, a 46 year-old woman committed suicide using a butcher knife. She was small in stature, 5'2", and weighed approximately 105 pounds. She was known to be suffering from bipolar disorder. The body was found five days after the suicide occurred. From details of the body and the scene, the suicide is thought to have followed this chronology: she began the process in the living room, and stabbed herself in the fight side, about 6 inches below the armpit. She then moved to the bathroom, and used the knife to make numerous cuts on both wrists, some of which were deep enough to contact bone, but none of which severed any artery. She then moved to the bedroom. The wounds thought to occur next were deep stab wounds to the groin and abdomen. These resulted in extensive bleeding. There was a deep wound which pierced the heart, and a slash to the throat which severed an artery, either of which could have proved fatal. Altogether, there were 32 knife-inflicted wounds on the body.

[9] Burd and Gilmore, 1967.

[10] The name derives from the material used to remove the chemical residue from the skin. It is said that the more uncooperative the suspect, the hotter the melted paraffin tended to be. Paraffin could be employed as a lifting material in the modern tests, but the use of cotton swabs is much more efficient.

[11] Thorwald, 1967.

[12] At the time of this writing (February, 1997), DNA analysis has found the blood and semen of a third person on crime scene items. A key genetic marker matches that of another suspect, but the match is not sufficient for positive identification of the suspect.

[13] *ABC World News Tonight* with Peter Jennings, February 19, 1997.

[14] On January 9, 1992, the U.S. Court of Appeals ruled that DNA evidence was admissible in criminal trials. This avoids the necessity of detailed explanations and qualification of the procedure in every case.

[15] Bigbee, *et al.*, 1989.

[16] Approximately 10% of the DNA in a human cell consists of genes — segments of DNA that contain instructions for the manufacture of proteins by the cell. Other segments of DNA exert a regulatory function, determining whether certain genes will be switched on. However, much of human DNA has no known function. Although this DNA is properly called noncoding DNA (in contrast to the coding DNA of the genes), some researchers have coined the name "junk DNA." Ironically, it is this noncoding DNA that is used in forensic DNA analyses. The reason that noncoding DNA is valuable for such analyses is that its sequences are more variable than those of functional DNA. Because changes in functional DNA would probably have devastating effects on a cell or organism, cells have built-in mechanisms to prevent mutational changes in their DNA. Mutational changes in genes are thus rare, but mutational changes occur in noncoding DNA much more rapidly. This has the effect of making noncoding DNA more variable across the human population than genetic DNA. See Fowler, et al.

[17] By 1996, forty states had passed statutes requiring convicted offenders to provide samples for DNA analysis.

[18] The alert student will note that no mention of the infamous O. J. Simpson criminal case has been made in this chapter. The author considers that particular case to be a bad example of almost everything. The civil case was somewhat less so.

REFERENCES

Bennet, Wayne W., and Kären M. Hess
 1991   *Criminal Investigation* (3rd Ed.). St. Paul, MN: West Publishing Co.
Bigbee, David, Richard L. Tanton, and Paul B. Ferrara
 1989   "Implementation of DNA analysis in American Crime Laboratories," *The Police Chief*, October, pp. 86-89.
Burd, David, and Allan Gilmore
 1967   "Unusual Bullet Fingerprints," *The American Rifleman*, March, p. 24.
Fisher, Barry A. J.
 1992   *Techniques of Crime Scene Investigation* (5th Ed.). New York: Elsevier Science Publishing Co.
Fowler, J. C. S., L. A. Burgoyne, A. C. Scott, and H. W. J. Harding
 1988   "Repetitive Deoxyribonucleic Acid (DNA) and Human Genome Variation — A Concise Review Relevant to Forensic Biology," *Journal of Forensic Sciences*, Vol. 33, No. 5, pp. 1111-1126.
O'Hara, Charles E., and Gregory L. O'Hara
 1994   *Fundamentals of Criminal Investigation* (6th Ed.). Springfield, IL: Charles C. Thomas, Publisher.
Peterson, Joseph
 1974   *The Utilization of Criminalistics Services by the Police*. U.S. Dept. of Justice, March, 1974, pp. 24-34.
Saferstein, Richard (Editor)
 1982-88 *Forensic Science Handbook*, (2 Volumes). Englewood Cliffs, NJ: Prentice-Hall, Inc.
Thorwald, Jurgen
 1967   *Crime & Science*. New York: Harcourt, Brace & World, Inc. pp. 149-155.
Weston, Paul B., and Kenneth M. Wells
 1990   *Criminal Investigation*, Basic Perspectives. (5th Ed.) Englewood Cliffs, NJ: Prentice-Hall, Inc.

SECTION V

CORRECTIONS

Chapter 10

The History of Punishment and Correction

By

Ronald G. Iacovetta

Vengeance, retribution, deterrence, and reform have been the Historic purposes of Corrections. These purposes have been represented in various configurations in different societies, and within societies at different points in time, and they have been typically achieved by the infliction of some measure of pain and punishment.[1] While it is clear that the infliction of physical pain as a means of punishment is no longer condoned in the American correctional system, punishment, nevertheless, continues to be basic to its operation. Economic sanctions, restrictions on personal freedom (probation and parole) or incarceration in a formal institution (detention facilities, training schools, jails, and prisons) are the primary means of punishment.

Punishment in the interest of revenge and retribution (a repayment to society for injuries incurred) is considered vital to some. However, punishment in the interest of deterrence is more widely endorsed in the modern era. Punishment or restraint in the interest of reform has also been a popular view. Sanctions are imposed in order to facilitate the treatment of the offender. The restrictions and limitations on individual freedom are not designed to cause suffering but to insure the application of treatment in the interest the offender. The treatment (or therapeutic) approach has played a significant role in the development of modern corrections and will continue to have its advocates even in the recent move to more hard line conservative approaches to dealing with the offender population.[2]

The objectives of deterrence and reform have often been considered complimentary. Nonetheless, the predominant view is that they are often contradictory objectives. Punishment in the interest of deterrence takes quite a different directions than does punishment in the interest of reform. In fact, the basic conflict in correctional philosophy in the modern era is between the "hard liners" (or conservative ideologists) and the "treatment and reform" advocates (liberal ideologists). The "hard line" conservative ideologists do not perceive punishment as the ultimate goal but rather, an appropriate means to the goal of deterrence. Deterrence will be achieved by swiftly carrying out the threat of punishment so that it will not be perceived as an idle threat. Swift sure punishments will not only deter the offender from further offenses but will deter the potential offender. Treatment advocates take a contrary position contending that the goal should be rehabilitation and that treatment is the means to that goal. Furthermore, treatment advocates argue that in order for rehabilitation to occur a nonpunitive therapeutic environment is essential. This, obviously, is a matter of degree, since restriction, regulation, and control exist even in the most ideal therapeutic setting.

Deterrence and reform represent quite different approaches, although they are not polar opposites. Each advocates a different combination of treatment and punishment. Hard liners are primarily concerned with minimizing the appeal of criminal activity by making the offender and potential offenders fearful of the consequences. Treatment advocates are concerned primarily with changing the offender so that he/she may become a law abiding member of the community. Each position claims to protect the public. Treatment personnel argue, however, that institutional confinement under negative adverse conditions is not a deterrent to future criminal acts nor conducive to reform of the offender. In fact, one argument presented by the liberal ideologists is that incarceration serves only to maximize the potential for future criminality. Whether general deterrence of others (as opposed to specific deterrence of the individual offender) is achieved is a more difficult question. One must assume, however, that if those individuals who have been subjected to incarceration under the most adverse and trying conditions have not been deterred, its presence is not likely to have a discernible impact upon those who have not experienced it. "Hard liners" may argue, however, that there is no assurance of going to an institution upon conviction and this lack of certainty precludes effective specific or general deterrence.

PUNISHMENT vs TREATMENT APPROACH

The correctional system in America and around the world reflects disjointed and conflicting objectives. Some of these objectives are punishment directed and some are treatment directed. The result of this confusion is the existence, side by side, of correctional programs that were intended primarily for deterrence and retribution, and others designed to reform and rehabilitate offenders. Punishment and treatment objectives seldom complement each other. More often than not the focus upon these two components results in an ineffective and inefficient system having little impact on criminal activity. History illustrates and documents these bi-polar objectives. This chapter will trace the historical development of corrections and the impact of changing philosophies and influences. In so doing we are able to better understand, and place in perspective, modern correctional practices and philosophies.

In early societies lacking an economic base to provide for the costs of incarceration there are no workable alternatives to banishment or corporal and capital punishment. Punishment may satisfy important psychological and political needs of society.[3] Penalties may reflect and illustrate changing views about the nature of man and our ability to control and regulate human behavior. The penalty proscribed, and the manner of its execution, may have important philosophical and psychological implications.

More economically and technologically advanced societies developed the ability to process and detain large numbers of prisoners. Banishment and corporal and capital punishments become less palatable. Prisoners also become a valuable commodity that can be employed to increase production and profit. For example, John Langbein notes that beginning in the 16th and continuing into the 17th century there was a clear economic need to utilize prisoners to perform dangerous mining operations or to power oar-driven ships.[4] Given these economic needs prisoners who normally would have been executed provided a valued work force. However, technological advances transformed ships to steam and produced more effective mining implements and tools creating a commensurate reduction in the need for a prisoner "slave labor" force. These changes came after the internalization of a strong belief that incarceration and labor as punishment was appropriate and should be maintained. Old ships no longer used and abandoned mine shafts were sometimes transformed into depressing and omnipresent prisons in response to this belief.

English penalties were severe and hanging represented the most common sanction imposed for nearly every offense.[5] Early Colonial America mirrored this tendency to impose harsh penalties where branding, flogging, maiming, and death were commonplace and confinement as a form of punishment rarely existed.[6] Eventually these practices were questioned by reform groups and by citizens.[7]

The punitive approach saw its development in primitive societies where punishment of tribal members was required to avenge behavior that was defined as a violation of their customs and codes. The reaction to violations varied depending upon the nature of the offense, with strong punitive reaction representing one of many alternatives. For centuries, many primitive societies viewed crime as a manifestation of evil spirits or forces, often referred to as Demonology. These societies believed that a cure could only be achieved through prayer, ritual, torture, or total destruction of the body to remove and cast out the evil spirit.

Although illegal acts were not always precisely defined in early primitive societies they were generally recognized and understood. Reaction to violations varied with punitive responses representing only one alternative. With the onset of feudalism, elementary court systems were developed and wrongs were seen as crimes against the group as well as against the individual victim. As a consequence the society felt obligated to react to lawbreaking and the normal reaction was a puni-

tive reaction, and severe corporal punishments were often administered. Nevertheless, the philosophy that punishment had a well defined intrinsic value was not established. This reality is illustrated in W.L. Lee's description of the objective of punishment during the beginning of the feudal period in England:

> "A detected criminal was either fined, mutilated, or killed, but punishment, as we now understand the term, was seldom inflicted; that is to say, the dominant idea was neither to reform the culprit nor to deter others from following in his footsteps. If a man was killed it was either to satisfy the bloodfeud or to remove him out of the way as a wild beast would be destroyed; if a man was mutilated by having his fore-finger cut off or branded with a red-hot iron on the brow, it was done not so much to give him pain as to make him less expert in his trade of thieving and to put upon him an indelible mark by which all men should know that he was no longer a man to be trusted; if a fine was levied, it was more with a view to the satisfaction of the recipients of the money or cattle or what not, than with the intention of causing discomfort or loss to the offender."[8]

The notion that inflicting pain on the offender had some intrinsic value was not widely recognized until the beginning of the 18th century. Even so, controversy and debate centered around the merit, effectiveness and wisdom of the punitive approach and spawned the development of several distinct schools of criminological thought. These schools became known as the classical school, the neo-classical school, and the positive school.

The classical school was grounded in the doctrine of psychological hedonism, a doctrine that held that individuals weigh the pleasures and pains of individual actions and regulate behavior by selecting the action that will bring the greatest pleasure and the least pain. Each person was assumed to have a free will, and acted primarily on the basis of the anticipated hedonistic calculations of pleasure and pain. The classical school, in principle, advocated that a calculated amount of pain be applied to each criminal act. The precise amount of pain needed to be specified so that the offender, or prospective offender, would be able to calculate the amount of pleasure versus pain that would be realized. Ideally the amount of resulting pain should be greater than the pleasure anticipated by committing the act. The position advocated that the amount of punishment must be equal for all, regardless of social position or financial status, age, mental capabilities, or other conditions. Jeremy Bentham, a noted criminal law authority in the 18th century, attempted to develop precise mathematical laws for assigning punishments based on certain categories of offenses.[9]

The neo-classical school held that the classical doctrine was basically sound but needed to be modified in some ways. For example, children and lunatics were not believed capable of calculating pains and pleasures, and it was therefore believed they should not be treated as criminals or punished in the same fashion. In addition, the neo-classical approach advocated that consideration be given to mitigating circumstances, such as crimes that may have been committed for self preservation. The neo-classical view became the predominant philosophy of western nations in the 19th century. The major characteristic of this approach was that reaction to crime should not be purely punitive. Rather, some lawbreakers should be viewed as accountable and deserving of punishment and others may not be accountable or deserving of such measures but, rather, should be dealt with by other non-punitive approaches. Nevertheless, the predominant concept of the neo-classical school was the notion of individual responsibility and the application of punitive sanctions when failure of this responsibility led to criminal acts.

In direct conflict with the classical and neo-classical schools of thought was the "Positive" (or Italian School) which was based on the philosophical principle that lawbreakers are not responsible for their acts and should not be punished. Crime is a natural phenomenon created by genetics or other forces and can not be deterred by punishment. Some lawbreakers may be candidates for rehabilitation, while others must be incarcerated or put to death for society's protection (not for the sake of punishment). In the positivist view individual responsibility played an insignificant role and a system which assessed guilt and punishment for a lack of responsibility was viewed as inappro-priate and ineffective. Some of the modern approaches to treating, rehabilitating, and reintegrating offenders into the community are grounded in some of the views exhibited in the positive school.

The last three decades witnessed a general decrease in the employment of the punitive approach in dealing with offenders. Treatment approaches prevailed in the 1970's and 80's. Beginning in the Early 1990's we began to witness a gradual shift back to a more punitive approach. Nevertheless, in the current era both approaches are employed and are often in conflict with each other. The sharp movement back to a more "hard line" conservative neo-classical approach in the 1990's is buffered by those who continue to advocate treatment and reform. With the treatment approach the social situation and personality of the lawbreaker is studied. Individual needs and reasons for the criminal behavior of the individual are assessed and a treatment plan is developed. These practices include a variety of services and treatment modalities involving vocational training, education, housing, medical services, job finding, individual and group counseling and the like. Should the offender be perceived as a threat to society, or resort to further criminal activity, the alternative is often segregation and removal from the broader society (jail, imprisonment, or capital punishment) in order to protect society from further harm.

ORIGINS OF PUNISHMENT AND TREATMENT

Correctional philosophies and approaches have undergone a good deal of transformation throughout the ages reflecting changing political and religious beliefs, customs, and economic conditions.[10] Nevertheless, the modern era, and the philosophical dilemmas we face, mirror those evident in bygone ages. Elements of revenge and retribution still exist. Historical developments and changing philosophies have clearly promoted a more civilized and reflective approach to the offender population. Nonetheless, age-old controversies still exist in modern approaches to dealing with the offender population. We will review the historical record and its impact and influence. The contemporary correctional system can best be understood in the context of these historical developments.

In every society there are certain forms of behavior that have been prohibited, controlled, or otherwise constrained by decrees of law or the custom of a people. Some of the more universal prohibitions include homicide, rape, kidnapping, assault, and theft. While societal response to these offenses have changed over the centuries and vary in degree from country to country they represent relatively universal prohibitions with punishments that are often severe. The objectives of punishment have ranged from retribution and revenge to deterrence and reformation. History reveals that each have been placed at the forefront over time and cycles of emphasis have occurred.

In early times the remedy most commonly employed was some form of retaliation. The "eye for an eye, tooth for tooth" doctrines depicted in the book of Exodus as well as in earlier Sumerian codes (and the code of Hammurabi) had great influence. The Code of Hammurabi (around 1875 BC) specifically urged the "eye for an eye" approach in dealing with the offender population. These early codes established the belief that punishment was required in order to satisfy the need for vengeance by, or on behalf of, the victim. In the name of the state various forms of punishment were used to exact measures of pain and vengeance. Branding, mutilation, burning, execution, torture, public humiliation (stocks and pillory) fines, and imprisonment were all utilized to achieve this goal. Punishment under this philosophy was for retribution purposes. With the development of court systems in feudal history, the state assumed the authority and responsibility for dispensation of penalties for commission of illegal acts.

In more recent times a rationale for using punishment was deterrence. The belief was that punishment may provide an effective means of providing both specific deterrence (deter the offender form committing further illegal acts) and general deterrence (deter those who have not committed illegal acts from doing so). This view is based on the hedonistic assumption that people control their behavior by a process of calculation and assessing probable pleasures and pains in committing a criminal act. Should the pain caused by the penalty be greater than the calculated pleasure derived by committing the act there will be restraint. Nevertheless, it is quite evident that there are other conditions and variables that enter into whether a crime will be committed than that considered by the hedonistic philosophy. For example, value internalization, peer influences, emotions and passions (as in crimes of passion) and acts or behaviors of others that may invite or create opportunity for crime (leaving house unlocked, possessions easily assessable). Hedonistic philosophy also assumes an individual will have the capability to calculate the risk and probability of being caught and arrested for committing an illegal act.

The final rationale, endorsed in earlier and modern times, is that punishment is an effective tool in reforming and changing the offender. The argument is that punishment creates an aversion to the possibility of further punishment and fosters a recognition that crime does not pay. As a means of breaking criminal patterns it is argued that imprisonment may destroy undesirable habits by preventing the opportunity for their expression. Behavior modification may result by a judicious application of punishment. Research indicates that new desirable behavior patterns are best learned through positive reinforcement (rewarding approaches) rather than threatening punitive approaches.

The argument is that punishment may often create more hostility and deviant reaction rather than positive change. Nonetheless, advocates of punishment as a tool for reform continue to exist and advocate the need to promote individual responsibility. Punishment may help foster this development. Others argue that punishment, all too often, results in a temporary suppression of undesirable behavior and when given the opportunity the individual returns to the prior patterns of criminal activity.[11] For example, during 17th century England branding of offenders for theft and other crimes did not reform them. Instead it increased the probability of future crimes since criminals were publicly labeled, making it extremely difficult for them to earn a living without returning to criminal activity.[12]

History reveals that the mid 1700's were a time of unprecedented transformation and changing views of the temperament and nature of man. The 17th century cast away much of the superstition of the middle ages and developed a period that become known as "The Enlightenment" — a period that exhibited concern for the rights of humanity and the ability of human beings to change in the face of cultural, social, and religious influences. Prior to the "enlightenment" there was little concern for humanity and the concept of "corrections" had very little following. In fact, it can be argued that prior to this period the ideas of reform or rehabilitation hardly existed. While there is no doubt that society may have believed that painful methods of dealing with the offender may have had some deterrent value, "correction of the offender" was not the primary purpose of the early approaches.

An Italian, Cesarre Beccaria, is responsible for the transition from a focus on vengeance and punishment to prevention and reform in his essay "On Crimes and Punishments," which depicted the following principles and beliefs:

1. The basis of all social action must be the greatest good for the greatest number of people.

2. Crime is an injury to society, not only to the individual.

3. Prevention of crime is more important than punishment. Punishment is justified only when it deters crime.

4. Imprisonment should be more widely used, but when used, it should be humane.

5. Secret accusations and torture should be abolished, and there should be speedy trials.[13]

Beccaria believed that the idea of a social contract supported by colonists created undue emphasis upon punishment and incapacitation (including the application of the death penalty) and that man should not give the state the power to take life as part of the social contract. Beccaria argued for sanity in application of penalties and spoke out against torture and capital punishment. Punishment was viewed a means to deter crime and imprisonment should be used judiciously to that end.

There is no question that Beccaria had a significant impact on the French Code of Criminal Procedure and on the United States Constitution. Beccaria's convictions had significant influence on the development of democratic governments and the implementation of correctional practices designed to serve the needs of the masses and not the favored and powerful in society.

While the historical record is clear that brutal and inhumane methods of dealing with the offender population continued after Beccaria, his philosophy and writings reflected the beginning of a series of more reflective social responses to criminal behavior, including deterrence and rehabilitation as well as retribution and incapacitation. In fact, it may be argued that the construction of correctional facilities became necessary when societies decided that they could no longer summarily banish or execute a large number of offenders. Therefore, the emergence and development of correctional philosophy can best be understood through an assessment of the historical development of institutions in Europe, and of the events that took place in the American colonies in the 1800's and 1900's.

EARLY HISTORY OF IMPRISONMENT

The extensive use of imprisonment as a punishment did not occur until the 13th century in England, followed thereafter by other European countries. Edward I, in the latter half of the thirteenth century, utilized incarceration on a large

218

scale to compel offenders to pay fines. Association between prisoners was permitted in many facilities along with some allowable gambling and feasting. Jailers were also sometimes involved in graft by keeping the food or money of prisoners. Most of these early prisons were situated in the dungeons of castles where conditions were extremely poor.[14]

Many church authorities during the fifth century also occasionally imprisoned those who committed offenses against the church. The Church believed such segregation had reformative value through contemplation. The Roman Catholic Church used imprisonment during the inquisition era as a punishment for heresy. From about 1500 to 1700 imprisonment of offenders in galleys was commonplace in many European countries. For example, during the 17th century France directed the courts to regularly use this penalty for all able-bodied male offenders in order to provide crews for the galleys of ships. This practice was discontinued after large sailing vessels replaced the galley ships.

In 1552 London authorities placed beggars and prostitutes in a palace situated at St. Bridgets's Well. This facility represented a forerunner to the modern prison. The purpose was to securely detain offenders, institute forced labor, and engage in corporal punishments such as flogging and other punishments. In 1576 the English parliament enacted legislation providing for imprisonment in "Houses of Correction." These Houses were designed to compel "sturdy Beggars" to work. The belief was that hard labor would reform criminals and the institutions would make a profit. Vagabonds and Idle persons were committed along with "lewd" women with illegitimate children and men who had deserted their families. Over a period of time legislation was passed which broadened the offenses for which persons could be incarcerated.

By 1609 the English government had approved construction of houses of correction in every county in England. These houses of corrections were named Bridewells in honor of the first facility at St. Bridget's Well. These first penal institutions incarcerated only misdeameanants, since most convicted felons were put to death.[15] Beginning in the 17th century, houses of corrections and workhouses were established and used extensively in Europe and in the United States. Workhouses were originally designed to house the victims of the poor relief system or debtors where they were given work and industrial training. However, the distinction between houses of corrections and workhouses gradually became muted since debtors and misdemeanant offenders were commonly placed together in the same facilities.

By the 18th century there was evident an increasing need for prisons due directly to a decrease in the reliance upon executions. Executions were gradually declining in popularity. During the first half of the 17th century executions at Tyborn averaged 300 per year. For the period from 1665 to 1700 the number dropped to ninety and executions continued to drop during the five decades from 1750-1790, averaging somewhat less than forty annually during the period. Goals, or jails, as local houses of correction were labeled, were often places of hardship, debauchery, and cruelty during the 17th century. Segregation did not exist and debtors were indoctrinated with practices of thievery and immorality. Poor conditions often led to disease and death before trial. The problem finally gained the attention of the ruling classes since many knights and court workers were infected. In 1750 the Mayor of London, some aldermen, two city judges, an undersheriff, several lawyers, and some spectators succumbed to typhus.

John Howard, an English businessman, became concerned about the conditions in the English prisons. Howard was elected High Sheriff of Bedfordshire after retiring from business and set about the task of instituting change. He had personally witnessed the horrible conditions in English prisons and prisons across Europe in 1775. As a result of this assessment he published in 1777 his classic in penology, "The State of the Prisons."[16] This work provided vivid and shocking descriptions of the institutions he had visited, including overcrowding, disease and unsanitary conditions, leading to disease and death. His Critique also extended to the lack of discipline, segregation, or meaningful employment of inmates. Prisoners were often locked in a single room without restrictions and inmates made their own rules, with the weak being exploited by the strong, and prostitution abounded.

Based upon what he had found Howard proposed widespread reform. He was impressed with the Vilan's Maison de Force and the Hospice of San Michel at Rome. The Hospice (1704) was built along monastic lines by Pope Clement XI for the treatment of wayward youth. Young offenders worked together in a central hall. However, incorrigible youth were segregated day and night in small cells.[17] Howard liked the arrangement and recommended separation of classes of inmates, housing criminals in individual cells and utilizing criminals in productive work.[18] Although Howard's suggestions were incorporated in the Penitentiary Act of 1779, establishing penitentiary houses throughout the realm, none were actually built until after his death in 1790. Nonetheless, some of Howard's principles were influential in the United States. In England, a model prison incorporating his philosophy was built at Pentonville in 1842. Within a period of six years fifty-four other penitentiary houses were constructed in England. Howard's belief in the value of segregation was established in English prisons.

During the Early 1700's to 1850 there were many prison reform efforts. These included the establishment of several prison reform societies in the America. Studies revealed that hardened criminals were corrupting young offenders. Prison conditions were criticized, including the use of liquor, sexual orgies, swearing, gambling and personal lewdness of jail keepers. Changes were advocated and partially adopted, to include separating male prisoners from female prisoners, separating adults from children, holding religious services, separate confinement in cells, prohibition of liquor, and establishment of provisions of good behavior for inmates who had behaved well in prison. By the beginning of the 19th century imprisonment had become the primary method of punishing those convicted of serious crimes. Furthermore, the increased use of incarceration also reflected the growing opposition to corporal and capital punishments.

Corrections in America

Meaningful correctional reform began in the United States. The United States correctional system had its origin in Pennsylvania under the direction and influence of William Penn.[19] By the end of the 17th century William Penn was instrumental in revising Pennsylvania's criminal code to forbid torture and other forms of physical maiming. These practices were to be replaced by the punishment of incarceration, fines, forfeiture, hard labor, and mild whipping. All material possessions owned by the felons were to be utilized to make restitution to victims with a cap limited to twice the value of the damages incurred. When no property or possessions were owned felons were required to labor in the prisons until compensation could be accomplished. Penn required that new facilities be built to replace the many forms of public punishments (pillories, gallows, stocks, and branding irons and the like) with a sanitary lockup correctional facility. Every county was required build these facilities, resembling today's jails. These requirements were in effect until Penn's death in 1718, at which time the criminal code was abandoned, and punishment reverted, in large part, to many of the earlier harsh public practices.

In spite of the reversion to many of the earlier practices following Penn's death, facilities for detention were developed in the American colonies. Originally the function of these facilities was to hold those awaiting trial. Later they were used as a means of punishment after conviction and they became similar in function and purpose to houses of correction. Like those in European countries, conditions inside these facilities were very poor, with vice and drunkenness commonplace and inmates dependent upon charity for their existence. In the early facilities time was spent in idle association with others with no separation of the young and old, or separation of the sexes. The development of houses of correction had little commonality to what had transpired in Europe since it occurred on such a broad scale. These developments were based on values and philosophical orientations unique to Colonial America. The emphasis upon the value and importance of liberty helped support the belief that the perfect punishment was deprivation of liberty, or death.

220

The early colonists adapted the use of small goals and workhouses. However, the formal establishment of a prison did not occur until the 18th century. The first prison in the United States was opened in 1773 in Connecticut. This prison was constructed in a converted mine shaft near Simsbury where prisoners were confined in chains attached to their necks and iron bars fastened to their feet. They slept on platforms covered in straw. This prison was in operation until 1835. At the same time similar facilities were developed in Virginia and Maine where prisoners were secured in underground cells or pits. The cells were accessible only by ladder through a trap door at the top and were dank, dark, and cold.[20] In 1775 Massachusetts converted a military post on an island in Boston Harbor into a prison for offenders sentenced to solitary confinement. State Prisons increasingly served only the purpose of providing secure detention for offenders serving long terms and, through regimented labor, offset most of the costs of incarceration.

In 1776 Pennsylvania once again adapted William Penn's code, and in 1787 a group of Quakers developed a modern correctional system that was based on a philosophy that man had the ability to repent for wrong committed and to reform. The first modern penitentiary based on this premise was completed in 1787 in Pennsylvania. The Quakers has been concerned with the care of prisoners for some time. This concern resulted in the formation of the Philadelphia Society for Alleviating the Miseries of Public Prison and this became the driving force for reform in the prisons.

Dr. Benjamin Franklin and Dr. Benjamin Rush were among those initially involved in this organization. The Quakers argued that State prisons should be "penitentiary" in concept. This approach was similar to the approach used in Medieval prisons run by the church, and was premised on the belief that the purpose of prisons should not be for vengeance and retribution, but to produce penitence and reform. The local jails were the only models of corrections that Penn had established. These facilities suffered from many limitations given their design and purpose. They served only to detain offenders awaiting other punishment, or to confine those who were working to pay back the cost of their crimes. The jails thrust men, women, and children together indiscriminately in large rooms where debauchery and insanitary conditions prevailed. The Quakers insisted that these conditions be corrected and changes initiated that would facilitate penitence and reform.

Through the efforts of Dr. Rush and Dr. Franklin of the Pennsylvania Society, the Walnut Street Jail in Philadelphia was changed from a temporary lock-up facility to a penitentiary. On April 5, 1790, a law was passed by the Pennsylvania Legislature establishing the first prison administration. Management was under the direction of a board of paid inspectors. Through legislative approval the beginning of the "Pennsylvania System" was born — a system that was premised upon the principle of "solitary confinement to hard labor in total abstinence."[21]

In this newly created facility most prisoners were place in solitary confinement and remained there in isolation from other prisoners and with no provisions for work.[22] The section of the facility containing the solitary or separate cells was referred to as the "penitentiary house," reflecting a custom in existence in England. The new Pennsylvania system claimed early success in reducing the crime rate between 1789-1793.[23] The prison was looked upon as a model of reform. Nevertheless the Walnut Street jail had its problems. Overcrowding became a problem and undermined the objectives of solitary confinement for serious offenders. Soon it became necessary to place more than one inmate in each cell and a compromise of the original objectives occurred. Nevertheless, the model formed the basis for the development of other institutions incorporating the basic concepts originally implemented at the Walnut Street Jail.

The Pennsylvania System

In the model Pennsylvania system, inmates were locked in individual cells with only a bible. They were instructed to do penance and reform their evil ways. The Quakers believed that solitary confinement and reflection would result in reformation of the offender. Work was made subordinate to reflection. Prisoners were not allowed to communicate with each other, although they were encouraged to speak with the prison staff, clergymen, or members of the Philadelphia Prison Society.[24] The principle of solitary confinement was applied in two different styles. Inmates convicted of serious offenses were confined without labor in sixteen solitary cells and were fed a diet of maize and molasses. Less difficult inmates were locked together in eight larger rooms where they worked at crafts such as tailoring, shoe making, carpentry weaving, and nail making. Women worked at weaving, washing, and mending, with wages being applied to the cost of confinement. Except for female prisoners, silence was strictly enforced in the shops and at meals. However some quiet conversations were permitted in the night quarters before retiring.[25]

The early Pennsylvania system was successful for several years as indicated in a report of the Board of Inspectors in 1791. The Board stated that "From the experiments already made we have reason to congratulate our fellow citizens on the happy reformation of the penal system. The Prison is no longer a scene of debauchery, idleness, profanity: an epitome of human wretchedness; a seminary of crimes destructive to society; but a school of reformation and a place of public labour."[26] Following this early success the system become overcrowded and industrial activity and personal attention was eliminated. Nevertheless, the major principles of the "Pennsylvania System" were more fully realized in the development of the Western and Eastern State Penitentiaries that followed.

In 1818 Pennsylvania developed a prison that housed inmates in individual cells for the entire period of incarceration, and classifications were eliminated. The individual cells were to be isolated mini-prisons where prisoners could not contaminate each other. The new facility was the Western Penitentiary. This facility was built in a semi-circle with cells located along its circumference. Inmates were allowed out of their individual cells for only an hour a day under strict supervision. In 1820 a second essentially similar facility, called the East-

ern Penitentiary, was built in Philadelphia. Supporters believed that the penitentiary, by removing offenders from society and providing for a period of complete isolation, would promote reflection and atonement for crimes committed. Advocates also believe that isolation and in-cell labor would make normal work so enticing and desirable that the inmate would welcome a productive, law abiding existence upon release.

The Auburn System

In 1774, Quaker philanthropist Thomas Eddy of New York inspected the Philadelphia Penitentiary on Walnut Street. In 1775, at the insistence of Eddy, a commission was appointed to inspect the prison. Governor John Jay, following a report by the commission, promptly endorsed a bill (which became law on March 26, 1796) authorizing construction of additional prisons. Newgate Prison, with Eddy as Warden, was built on the bank of the Hudson river in New York City. This prison had 54 rooms, 12 by 18 feet, designed to accommodate 8 persons each.[27] The prison was regulated by a board or inspectors which included Judges of the Supreme Court, the State Attorney General and City Mayor. These inspectors were authorized by the Governor to set regulations for the management of the prison and could visit and inspect at any time. The first residents arrived at Newgate in 1797 although workshops and other construction was not completed for another two years. The prison provided opportunity to work at shoe making, blacksmithing, iron working, and nail making.[28] Within a span of 10 years, in spite of the innovative focus on penitence and reform rather than punishment, Newgate Prison had become fraught with overcrowding, boredom, and idleness, forcing the governor to pardon many convicted felons.

A second commission was established in 1816 to build a prison at Auburn, New York. Inmates were transferred from Newgate to aid in construction of the facility. The core building and one wing of the prison was completed by 1818. While the plan, as originally constituted, incorporated the idea of solitary confinement, the idea of separate cells was not observed. In order to cut costs in construction, the cells, three and a half feet by seven feet, were designed for two prisoners each. The Auburn system was known as the "Tier System" since the cells were built vertically, encompassing five floors of the structure. The system also became known as the "congregate system" given that inmates worked and ate together. In addition, 28 larger cells were constructed designed to hold from ten to twenty inmates each. In 1819 construction on a wing of solitary cells to house incorrigible inmates began. Although discipline at Auburn resembled Newgate in many ways, inmates were employed during the day and kept in groups at night. As with Newgate, overcrowded conditions and other problems began to take their toll and reforms became necessary.

Following the death of Auburn's Warden in 1821, Captain Elam Lynds was charged with the responsibility to run the prison. Captain Lynds instituted a procedure of segregating inmates at night while continuing to work together during the day. In order to reduce the problem of overcrowding, Lynds imposed a "rule of silence," lockstep marching and serving food to inmates in their cells rather than in a common dining area.[29] A New York senate committees, impressed with the new system following a visit to the institution, convinced the legislature to adopt the policy of solitary confinement in prisons in the state.[30]

The program developed by Lynds was completed with the development of a system of classification for segregation of inmates. Inmates were divided into three categories to include (1) the most dangerous who where placed in solitary confinement twenty four hours a day, (2) the less incorrigible who were alternated between solitary confinement and labor or recreation, and (3) the inmates who were most susceptible to rehabilitation were allowed to work during the day and placed in seclusion at night. The three class system was inaugurated Christmas day and eighty-three of the most hardened prisoners were committed to total solitary confinement. The program became known as the Auburn System. In the span of a year five prisoners had died and others begged to be

allowed to work.[31] In 1824 a legislative committee recommended the abolishment of total segregation and was successful in getting approval from the New York State Legislature. Continuous solitary confinement was replaced by having prisoners work in silent association during the day and being confined alone at night. Since the system was first developed at Auburn, it became known as "the Auburn Plan."

During the four decades that followed, the merits of the Auburn vs. the Pennsylvania model was discussed and debated with passion. European countries generally believed the Pennsylvania plan was superior, and many began modeling their prisons after it. In the American states there was a preference for the Auburn plan given the reduced cost of operation and the belief that work in and outside the prison was "good for the soul" as well as for the institution.

Auburn vs. Pennsylvania

In 1826, the first report of the Prison Discipline Society of Boston was issued. This report noted that 3,500 persons were confined in state prisons in the United States, with the predominant number being in the states of New York, Pennsylvania, and Massachusetts. The prevailing philosophy of the time was that the prisons could reform criminals, and the debate revolved around whether the Pennsylvania or Auburn System was more effective. Both systems were striving to achieve the goal. The ideological conflict that developed between these two approaches to inmate reform was based upon differences in philosophy and practice. Although the two systems were similar in many respects, the predominant differences centered around their basic design, philosophy, and daily handling of the prison population. The Auburn system was run on the congregate or "silent" system and the Pennsylvania system was operated on the "segregate" system.

The Prison Discipline Society of Boston expressed support for the Auburn system and the Philadelphia Society For Alleviating the Miseries of Public Prisons endorsed the Pennsylvania system. Supporters of the Auburn System contended that the congregate system had the following advantages: (1) It was cheaper to develop; (2) provided better opportunities for vocational training; and (3) provided more revenue for the state since inmates could work and help pay their keep. The proponents of the Pennsylvania system argued that the system of isolation and silence (1) made it easier to control prisoners; (2) reduced contamination through contact with other prisoners; (3) allowed for greater consideration of individual needs; (4) afforded greater opportunity for reflection, meditation and repentance by the offender; and (5) insured more complete anonymity for the prisoner upon discharge.[32]

Proponents of the Pennsylvania system also noted that the system reduced the need for a large custodial staff or disciplinary procedures for violation of rules that are necessary in a congregate system. They argued that the system was more efficient and humane and offered the best opportunity for reform of prisoners. They contended that the congregate system created temptations to talk and promoted criminal associations. Advocates of the Auburn System argued that this system was much cheaper to operate and charged that the Pennsylvania system of solitary confinement was cruel and inhuman and had negative physical and mental consequences for the prisoner population that far outweighed any negative effects of inmate interaction.

During this period in America, a strong appreciation of the value of work and occupation was being cultivated. Individual occupations, such a farming, were beginning to be supplanted by factory and industrial work of all kinds. The Pennsylvania system more closely reflected the society's view of the value of work as a solitary activity, while the Auburn system emphasizing congregate activity more closely reflected the changing work emphasis on factory assembly lines and mass production, where people worked in close association and cooperation with each other. Puritan religious beliefs and colonial cultural values clearly emphasized the value of work.

The Auburn system borrowed many elements from the Pennsylvania system. The allowable degree of interaction between inmates in the Auburn system represented a compromise between the almost complete congregate system typified by county jails and the presumed benefits of separate confinement and isolation as endorsed by the Pennsylvania system. More importantly, men worked in association during the day in the Auburn system to achieve maximum production, but were separated completely at night to facilitate the benefits of isolation. Communication inside the prison was forbidden. Both systems required strict obedience. Enforced perpetual silence in Auburn and lockstep marching was strictly enforced, and severe penalty resulted for failure to obey commands. Warden Lynds correctional philosophy included the belief that reformation could not take place until the spirit of the offender was broken.[33]

In addition, the Auburn System was premised upon the notion of crime prevention through fear of punishment and isolated confinement for the most incorrigible inmates. A combination of solitude and silence, along with harsh discipline, was considered necessary to restrain the will of offenders and transform them into law abiding citizens. This concept is considered in a book "Discipline and Punishment," by the French sociologist, Michael Foucault. Foucault poses the argument that as social systems become more advanced they develop a need for more complex mechanisms to restrain and punish the more unruly members of society, and transform them into receptive law abiding citizens. In earlier times, punishment was directed toward the physical being in the way of torture and mutilation, as a necessary means of retribution and revenge, with no concern for reform or deterrence.

The objective in the 19th century was to discipline as a means to promote psychological reform and changes in behavior. According to Foucault, punishment which once targeted the body was now designed to have an affect on the heart.[34] This philosophy is still evident in modern correctional practices. A violation of discipline in the Auburn system resulted in immediate administration of a whip to the back of the inmate. This method was said to be extremely effective and disciplinary problems were uncommon. Sing Sing Prison was built in 1825 with 100 inmates from the Auburn system and none attempted escape even though they were not locked behind walls or barbed wire.[35]

Prisoners at the Pennsylvania Penitentiary at Cherry Hill were separated from each other and the community at large. They were housed in separate quarters which connected to an individual exercise yard. What work they performed was restricted to cottage industry tasks within the cell itself. Penitence was expected in Pennsylvania as inmates were given bibles, moral instruction, and spent the entire time in their cells except for an hour of exercise each day. Other people were neither seen nor heard, and visits and correspondence was forbidden. Food was given to inmates in their cells through a small opening in an iron door.[36] The emphasis was on atonement and penitence. The Quakers believed that reform could be accomplished only through a process of divine forgiveness through a period of penitence. The system was expensive since all services, work material, and food had to be brought to the cell and removed. Physical and mental problems developed as a result of long periods of confinement without other activity or diversion.

In the congregate system at Auburn, prisoners worked outside their cells during the day and were only locked down in separate cells at night. The primary benefits included greater productivity and reduced operating costs, along with fewer health problems and mental disturbances. Manpower requirements were considerably lower, and the work prisoners did during the day benefited the prison and provided revenue for the state. Primarily for reasons of cost effectiveness, and the contribution of inmates by way of a regimented work schedule, the Auburn system prevailed and became the model for the penitentiary system to evolve in the United States.

In the early 18th century a few states attempted to develop institutions based on the Pennsylvania system but abandoned these efforts in favor of the Auburn system. The Auburn system formed the basis of institutions to follow. By the late 19th century this system was adapted in all states except Pennsylvania. These institutions included the employment of congregate working conditions, firm discipline, regimentation, and the use of solitary confinement for problem inmates. In these facilities inmates activities were on a rigid schedule (sleep, work, and meals) and regulated in military style.

While Auburn system was considered to be an improvement over the prior open practices of torture and corporal punishment, it did not completely eliminate these elements. In fact, in many institutions conditions were very depressed and prisoners were often subjected to whipping and other forms of physical punishment. Historian Samuel Walker has noted that prison brutality continued to exist in these facilities, representing an irony given the fact that the facilities had been developed as an alternative to corporal and capital punishments. The new system often became even more brutal in dealing with prisoners, even though they were where they were not subject to public view.[37]

PRISON INDUSTRY OF THE 19th CENTURY

The prisons in the latter part of the 19th century were similar in function and operation to those of today. Except for Pennsylvania they were operated according to the Auburn congregate system. As today, the prisons of the time experienced problems of overcrowding and it became necessary to place more than one prisoner in each cell. The needs of the prison and the desire to cut the cost of its operation led to the development of prison industries. The prisons were organized to facilitate the involvement of inmates in the prison industries. The focus of operation varied in different prisons with some prisons employing the "Contract System" of prison labor. In this system the labor of inmates was contracted (or sold) to private business.

Supervision of inmates was sometimes done by the contractor within the prison, but labor was also performed outside the prison walls. A "Convict Lease System" was also conducted in some prisons. In this system, prisoners were leased to individual businesses for a specific annual fee and were under their supervision and control. A third system which became progressively important over time was the "State Account System" in which prisoners were employed inside the prison to produce products (soaps, paints, cleaning products, license plates) to be used by the state.[38] During the Civil War, prison labor was used to produce shoes, furniture, and clothing among other items.

The prison industry concept often led to abuse of inmates and corruption and profiteering by prison administrators and business associates that were using these services. Beginning in the 1980's, the widespread use of prison labor to produce items to be sold on the open market came under the attack of trade unions. The argument that prison labor represented unfair competition, and served to reduce the profitability of private companies marketing similar products, resulted in restrictions on interstate commerce in prison-made goods.

The Reformatory

Beginning in the second half of the 19th century, advocates of reform argued that all prisoners did not need the regimentation and supervision that existed in the penitentiaries. In particular they argued that a prison to serve young, first offenders was necessary in order to promote reformation. This reformatory concept was recommended and endorsed by the American Prison Congress in 1870 at a meeting in Cincinnati. The system developed was based on a model developed in Australia and Ireland, known as the "Irish System," which was originally developed by Captain Maconochie. This system advocated the use of the indeterminate sentence in a system where prisoners could secure their freedom by earning points for good conduct.[39] The system emphasized productive labor, reformation, education, and parole.

The development of the first reformatory based on this model was opened in 1876 in Elmira, New York, and was aptly named the "Elmira Reformatory." The construction of this first reformatory was the accomplishment of a reformer, Zebulon R. Brockway, who also became the first warden of the facility. Brockway was familiar with the Irish System in operation by Sir Walter Crofton, Director of the Irish Convict Prisons during the period of 1854 to 1862. The Irish facility was an alternative prison where inmates worked together in outdoor labor or public works. The Irish facility was a compromise between solitary confinement and conditional release.

Brockway was convinced, given experiments at the Detroit House of Corrections with education programs, that training and education offered more promise for felons below the age of 30 than did punishment and isolation. In Elmira, Brockway instituted a variety of classes and workshops designed to promote academic and vocational education. He offered vocational classes in plumbing, tailoring, telegraphy, and printing in addition to classes to promote social education. Teachers from nearby high schools taught classes. Organized Sports were also implemented as a part of the program. As a result of the success of the program, Brockway authored an indeterminate sentencing act that was passed by the New York legislature in 1877. Brockway noted that this act "...put upon the managers the function of determining the duration of imprisonments on the basis of public safety, and left open to the managers the selection and use of measures to fit the prisoners for safe discharge."[40]

Prisoners at Elmira were placed in three grades which set the base for earning of good behavior. Prisoners entered the facility in "second grade" but could earn movement to "first grade" within six months subject go good conduct. "Third grade" was given to inmates exhibiting poor conduct and required a month of good conduct to move back to second grade. Maintaining "first grade" status for 6 months entitled the prisoner parole.[41] Clearly, this reformatory model incorporated the American belief in the importance of education and hard work.

Following the development of Elmira, Michigan opened a reformatory at Iona in 1878. Ten more reformatories were opened by 1901. The reformatory model was also developed for women beginning in 1873 when Indiana opened a facility exclusively for women. Three other states, Massachusetts in 1877, New York in 1901, and New Jersey in 1913, and the District of Columbia followed Indiana's lead. Until this time women were detained in special sections of traditional prisons. Since the 1930's dozens of women's institutions have been constructed. These facilities were smaller than male institutions, generally following a campus design containing small dormitories and cottages.[42]

The reformatory concept has been the predominant mode for women's prisons, and programs to train, educate, and socialize women have been incorporated in these facilities., However, programs in women's facilities have been more limited than in male institutions, and the emphasis has been more on "womans work" (sewing, weaving, ironing, cooking) than on education and training that would lead to real-world jobs. Much of the problem had to do with the cultural view that the appropriate place for women was in the kitchen and at home and not in the workplace.[43] This emphasis has now changed in most facilities, given a change in societal values regarding the role of women.

The Elmira Model has been transformed into many facilities today. Many reformatories have become practically identical to prisons in terms of function and structure. While originally designed to house the young and less recalcitrant offenders, many institutions now house all categories of offenders, with little differentiation from their sister "penitentiaries." This has come with a change in the nature of the prison population and the increasing problem of overcrowding. As a result, older and more serious offenders are often now housed with younger reformatory inmates. The size of reformatories often exceed 1,000 inmates, minimizing the ability to maintain a meaningful classification system. As a result, the differences between the inmate population in reformatories and prisons are much less distinct that they were in the past.

American prisons are still distasteful, depressing, and dangerous places. Nevertheless, the modern prison has eliminated the horrors and abuse that occurred in prisons in earlier times. In addition, training and rehabilitative programs have been implemented in these facilities and inmate rights have been affirmed by the courts, essentially eliminating long-term solitary confinement and corporal punishment. Today's prisons promote contact with the outside world via prison visitations, television, and reading material. Nevertheless, the conflict between punitive and treatment approaches are still quite evident in the operation of the correctional system. While the 70's and early 80's witnessed an increased emphasis upon treatment and reform in programs in and out of prison, the late 80's and 90's have witnessed a swing of the pendulum back to a more conservative "hard line" approach calling upon tougher penalties for offenders. The result has been a dramatic increase in the size of the prison population. Getting tougher on crime in general, and drug related offenses in particular, has resulted in a doubling of the prison population in the last ten years.

OTHER PRISON TYPES

Other facilities have been developed to deal with the offender population. Maximum security institutions were designed to deal with the more difficult and dangerous criminals. While many penitentiaries of the past were essentially maximum security facilities, they did not distinguish their purpose in terms of the nature of the population. Approximately one-third of all prisons in the United States are maximum security facilities built before the beginning of the 20th century. They represent the old bastille facilities where inmates are housed in cells and work within the confines of the walls.[44] These facilities were generally patterned after the Auburn System. A typical facility was Central Prison in Raleigh, North Carolina. This facility was built after the Civil War and was used up until 1976. The prison was constructed of granite walls 20 feet high with a base that extend-

227

ed underground fifteen feet deep. These walls were sixteen feet wide at the bottom and four feet wide at the top with guard towers.

An exception to the Auburn Model was Statesville in Illinois. This facility was copied after Milbank Penitentiary in England and was based on the ideas of Jeremy Bentham. Construction began in 1812 and was completed nine years later at a cost of $2,500,000. The prison was extremely large and had many guard towers. The Panopticon, as Bentham's original plan was named, was in the form of a huge spoked wheel encompassing three miles of corridors and hundreds of cells. Milbank Penitentiary was based on this master plan and emphasized a circular cell house which was surrounded by corridors connecting to the dining area, the administration building, and other areas of the prison. This structure allowed for surveillance of inmates with a minimum of security personnel. Inmates were confined in individual cells, reflecting the Quaker philosophy of reformation by way of solitary confinement.

The Maximum security prison built on Alcatraz Island in California was an even more specialized facility designed originally to house the most notorious gangsters of the thirties and forties. Alcatraz closed in 1963 but represented the ultimate symbol of an efficient maximum security facility. The prison was essentially escape-proof as a result of the high wall and the ocean water barrier (which completely surrounded the island). Many famous criminals spent time at Alcatraz. Institutions for the criminally insane were also developed. These facilities were ''Maximum Security'' but resembled a hospital more than a prison. Guard towers were maintained but wire mesh replaced stone walls and psychiatric aides took the place of guards. Shortly after congress passed legislation creating the Federal Prison system in 1930, a medical center at Springfield, Missouri was built to serve the criminally insane.

Asylums existed for the mentally disturbed prior to the facility at Springfield. However, it represented a milestone in an attempt to diagnose and treat the criminally insane utilizing current psychiatric theories of human behavior. Neither the Pennsylvania model, emphasizing meditation and exposure to religious teachings, or the Auburn emphasis upon the curative value of work, was viable for offenders who were mentally disturbed. A new approach had to be developed to deal with this population. These people were no longer thought to be under the influence of demons. The psychiatric community believed that these conditions were a result of explainable social phenomenon or trauma and could be treated medically or through counseling.

In addition to the development of the maximum security prisons and psychiatric prisons, it became necessary to develop a facility that would serve needs once reserved for the reformatories. The solution was ''minimum security'' facilities designed with open dormitories without high walls, fences, or guard towers. These facilities allowed more freedom of movement and reduced restrictions on association with other inmates. The minimum security prison is small, generally housing fewer than 500 inmates, and is reserved for those offenders considered a minimal risk to the community. A greater emphasis is placed upon rehabilitation and reform rather than the punishment and control evident in maximum security facilities.

Medium security facilities were also constructed serving purposes falling somewhere between those of the maximum security institution and the minimum security institution. These different facilities represent gradations in the level of security and emphasis upon treatment. Historically, treatment and reform objectives have been more of a priority in minimum security facilities and less so in maximum security institutions. Female institutions are more often medium or minimum security facilities in design, function, and correctional philosophy. An example of a female ''minimum'' security facility was a facility built in Seagonville, Texas in 1940 for female offenders. Since 1945 it has been used for male offenders and has represented a model in the use of a minimum security facility for ''security risk'' male inmates. However, despite the campus plan and minimum security the escape rate has been very low.[45]

Prison Camps

The Prison Farm concept developed in the 19th century with southern states developing the largest number. Mississippi commenced the development of the state farm system in 1890 following the state prohibition against leasing of convicts. The Mississippi state farm system was designed for the specific purpose of providing work for prisoners. Initially two farms were opened. One was to serve the needs of those considered a minimum security risk. In Mississippi in 1921, 28,750 acres of land provided work for state convicts. Other states had also acquired land for this purpose. Texas has over 73,000 acres, Florida 17,000, Louisiana 15,600, Pennsylvania 5,000, South Carolina 4,168 and Wisconsin 2,000 acres.[46]

Work camps also became quite popular in the early part of the 20th century. During the depression, states modeled prison work projects after the Civilian Conservation Corps and Works Progress Administration. During World War II the use of prison work camps expanded. Prisoners were used in an attempt to reduce the prison populations and to reduce cost of prison operation. Prisoners in the work camps were often housed in cages that could be moved from work site to work site. Ten to twelve men were assigned to each cage and remained there when not working. During work the prisoners were shackled together with chains attached to the ankles creating the name "chain gang" for this prisoner work group. A second type of work camp was a permanent location where prisoners were housed in very large congregate living quarters, where 50 or more inmates in a unit were not uncommon. In this system the work site, such as a state park or farm, was in close proximity to the camp.[47] Prisoners would be walked to the work site or be transported by truck.

The use of work camps has been more predominate in southern states. Georgia had work camps in 125 of its 159 counties in the 1930's. Roads were constructed and maintained for the counties. Each camp set its own rules and standards which resulted in a good deal of variability between camps. The state instituted a prison commission which was charged with inspection of the camps but fulfilled this duty infrequently.[48] In 1940 in Alabama thirty percent of the prison population was handled in work camps. In 1953 camp inhabitants in Alabama were still primarily black with 55% of all black inmates in the Alabama prison system living in road camps. In comparison only 7% of all white inmates lived in such camps.[49] In California by 1952 there were 21 work camps employed for fire fighting, fire prevention, and restoration.[50]

Prison work camps have formed the basis for movies like "Cool Hand Luke" and the book "I Am a Fugitive from a Georgia Chain Gang." This work depicted the abuses at prison farms and work camps (to include flogging, various forms of torture, use of sweat boxes). More recently the corruption and inmate abuse in the Arkansas Prison System has been depicted by Tom Murton in a book "The Dilemma of Prison Reform" and in a movie based on this book entitled "Brubaker," starring Robert Redford. Tom Murton served as superintendent of the Cummins Prison Farm and uncovered evidence of widespread graft, corruption, prisoner abuse, and cruelty which included the use of chains, straps, hoses, and the "Tucker Telephone" to torture and maim prisoners. The Tucker telephone was a mini generator with electrodes that were attached to the testicles of prisoners as a form of punishment and as a means of extracting information desired by the superintendent or guards. The story of the Arkansas prison system and its abuses received nationwide attention in 1968 when Murton uncovered the skeletons of three prisoners that appeared to have been murdered and dismembered. The book "Accomplices to the Crime" tells this story in vivid detail.[51]

Subsequent investigation and court cases revealed that corruption and inmate abuse had became common in prison farms and camps in several states. In the 1960's and 70's the operation of prison camps in Arkansas and other states came under close scrutiny and investigation as a result of widespread abuse and corruption. Court cases resulted in mandated changes in many of these states.[52]

Military Prisons

Military Prisons were constituted in the United States by Congress on March 3, 1873. Originally, the first military prison was to be located at Rock Island, Illinois. The Secretary of War at the time wanted the site to be developed into an ammunition ordinance facility and the plans were changed. The Act of Congress was amended a year later and the first military prison was constructed at Ft. Leavenworth, Kansas. The facility referred to as "The Disciplinary Barracks" was designed to hold only members of the U.S. Army who been convicted of violations of the military code. Between 1895 and 1906 the facility was under the direction and supervision of the Department of Justice. Some prisoners were housed in guard houses at local Army Posts instead of at Leavenworth. As the number of military prisoners grew it became impractical for the justice department to supervise the facility and the control of facility was returned to the Army in 1906. Within a span of thee years a second military prison was needed and the decision was to place the facility on Alcatraz Island located in San Francisco Bay. 774 prisoners were housed at Fort Leavenworth and 336 were housed at Alcatraz by June 30, 1909.

In 1908, a naval prison was constructed at the Portsmouth Naval Base in New Hampshire. The Air Force was not a separate branch of military service until following World War II and the development of facilities for Air Force Personnel did not develop until that time. In 1952 the 320th Retraining Command commenced operation of a military prison at Amarillo Air Force Base in Texas, and in 1967 moved the facility to Lowry Air Force base in Denver. This facility was designed more as a reformatory with a chain link fence topped by rows of barbed wire.[53]

Federal Prisons

Before 1895 Federal prisoners were detained in state prisons. Congress passed a law in 1889 authorizing the construction of three Federal facilities. However, appropriations were not forthcoming to implement the law. Finally, on July 1, 1895, the justice department began operating the military prison at Ft. Leavenworth, Kansas. Construction began construction on a penitentiary at the same location two years later to house 12,000 non-military inmates. The second Federal prison went into operation in 1902 in Atlanta, Georgia. Atlanta, Leavenworth, and a small jail that later became McNeil Penitentiary, represented the total Federal system until 1925. In 1925 congress approved development of a reformatory for men at Alderson, West Virginia, and a facility for women at Chillicothe, Ohio.[54]

Following the depression of 1930, congress enacted into law the Federal Bureau of Prisons and formally approved construction of an additional four facilities. These included a medical center at Springfield, Missouri. As a result of this initiative, the federal prison system assumed a leadership role for correctional operations around the country and opened up many jobs at a time when unemployment was high. Within a little over four decades the system expanded dramatically. By 1965, thirty-seven institutions made up the Federal Correctional System. These included six penitentiaries, five reformatories, five prison camps, four pre-release centers and eight medium or minimum security facilities.[55]

SUMMARY

History has revealed a colorful and distasteful history. Corrections has moved from a punitive, retributive system evidenced in the 17th and 18th centuries to a more reflective and multifaceted system emphasizing both punishment and reform. The focus on rehabilitation and reform during the early history of America (as evidence by the philosophy of the Pennsylvania system), to a more punitive approach in the development of prisons that followed more closely the Auburn Model, provides a perspective on where we are today. Clearly, the torture, mutilation, and corporal punishments carried out in 18th century Europe and in part in our Colonial heritage has given way to a more humane process in dealing with the criminal population.

A pendulum that swung back toward a greater emphasis on rehabilitation and reform in the 70's and early 80's has now moved back to a more hard line, "lock 'em up and throw away the key," approach. The recent "get tough on crime" posture is a reflection of the current political and social climate in response to the widespread concern of the citizenry about drugs, the increases in gang violence and drive-by shootings, and the rise in serial killings. These events have resulted in a heightened sense of insecurity and vulnerability. The efficacy and constitutionality of the application of the death penalty has continued to be affirmed by the Supreme Court and the citizenry remain in favor of its application. This, notwithstanding that England and other Western European Nations have abolished the death penalty.

What is in store for the future? History suggests that the pendulum will continue to move in different directions. Indications are that the current tough "hard line" approach toward dealing with the criminal population may give way, once again, to a more treatment or therapeutic approach. This may come as a necessity given the overcrowding our prisons have experienced as a result of the tougher penalties imposed for different categories of crime, especially drug-related criminal activity. As a result the prison population has more than doubled in the last ten years and the system is stretched to the limit in many states.

History has revealed that grand experiments and new philosophies do not create dramatic successes in dealing with the criminal element. However, the experiments and failures of the past do provide a foundation for the future. The past provides a blueprint for what has failed and what may still have promise in the future. At the very least, history serves to make us more aware of the blunders (as well as successes) of the past. History also has a way of repeating itself. However, with the historical record as a guide, we are provided with the insight and understanding to prevent the errors of the past and refine ways of dealing with the offender population. Although enlightened reform has eliminated many of the horrors of the past, there remain remnants in the current correctional system. Imprisonment and restraint have not been supplanted by utopian, crime correcting, alternatives. The reality of incarceration as a punitive measure in response to crime is still evident. The architectural design of many prisons still emphasizes control and limited freedom of movement. Most of these facilities were built before the turn of the century.

Progressive developments have taken place. In 1870 the National Prison Association adapted a set of principles that encouraged and promoted reform. This Association, and the resolutions set forth in 1870, began a renewed emphasis on reforms and transformation of the American Prison System. The Elmira Reformatory, notwithstanding its problems in fulfilling its mandate, became a symbol for the reform movement. Meaningful institutional reform did not occur until the 1940's. In 1944, the State of California began the process of upgrading their correctional system incorporating reception and guidance centers, a rehabilitation center for drug offenders, and the opening of satellite facilities to deal with different elements of the offender population. Texas began the process of reform in 1947 following exposure of the squalid conditions and corruption in the operation of prison farms. Reforms were also initiated in other states, including Louisiana, Alabama, and North Carolina in the 1950's. Other states like Wisconsin, South Carolina, and Iowa followed these leads in revamping and upgrading their systems.

Abuses and corruption characterized by the prison farm systems, and depressing conditions within many of our major penitentiaries, continued into the 70's and 80's with some states coming under court order to institute changes. Riots, prison takeovers, and a death toll of prisoners and security personnel have occurred. Major prison outbreaks occurred in the 70's with the most notable being the death of inmates and guards in the Attica Riot in Attica, New York, and the torture and killing of inmates in the takeover at the New Mexico State Penitentiary. In spite of reform efforts and legal intervention, the correctional system continues to have problems characteristic of the past. Newer facilities are operated according to a more progressive philosophy. Others, especially facilities built before the turn of the century, continue to harbor conditions which reflect the earlier era. Overcrowding and staff limitations have created explosive conditions and abuses. A wider use of alternatives to incarceration may be required to remedy these conditions. Closure of prisons built before the turn of the century, and replacement with modern facilities, is also imperative to minimize abuse and promote a safer, more positive environment.

✳ ✳ ✳ ✳ ✳

ENDNOTES

[1] Barnes, Harry E. (1972) *The Story of Punishment*. Montclair NJ: Patterson Smith. pp. 38-55.

[2] Allen, Francis A. (1959) "Criminal Justice, Legal Values and the Rehabilitative Ideal," *Journal of Criminal Law, Criminology and Police Science*, 50. September-October. pp 226-232.

[3] Newman, Graeme. (1978) *The Punishment Response*. Philadelphia, PA: J.B. Lippincott. p. 8.

[4] Langbein, John. (1976) "The Historical Origins of the Sanction of Imprisonment for Serious Crime," *Journal of Legal Studies*, 5:35.

[5] Clear, Todd. (1978) *A Model for Supervising the Offender in The Community*. Washington, DC: National Institute of Corrections.

[6] Graeme, Newman. (1983) *Just and Painful*. New York: MacMillan.

[7] Rothman, David. (1971) *The Discovery of the Asylum*. Boston: Little Brown

[8] Lee, W. L. M. (1901) *History of Police in England*. London: Methuen. p. 10

[9] Sutherland, Edward H., and Donald R. Cressey. (1970) *Criminology, 8th edition*. Philadelphia: J.P. Lippincottt. p. 302

[10] Germane sources include Alper, Benedict, *Prisons Inside Out*. (Cambridge, MA, 1974); Gustave De Beumont and Alexis de Tocqueville, *On The Penitentiary System in the United States and Its Application in France*. (Carbondale, IL: Southern Illinois University Press, 1964); Orlando Lewis, *The Development of American Prisons and Prison Customs, 1776-1845*. (Montclair, NJ: Patterson Smith, 1967); Samuel Walker, *Popular Justice*. (New York: Oxford University Press, 1980); Graeme Newman, *The Punishment Response*. (Philadelphia: Lippincott, 1978); David Rothman, *Conscience and Convenience*. (Boston: Little Brown, 1980).

[11] Jones, Edward, and Harold Gerhard. (1967) *Fundamentals of Social Psychology*. New York: John Wiley.

[12] Sutherland and Cressey, op. cit., p. 309.

[13] Beccaria, Cesare. (1963) *On Crimes and Punishments*. Translated by H. Paolucci. Indianapolis, IN: Bobbs-Merill.

[14] Zastrow, Charles. (1976) "A History of Corrections" in *Fundamentals of Criminal Justice*. Geneva, IL: Paladin House. p. 197.

[15] Ives, George. (1914) *A History of Penal Methods*. London: Stanley Paul and Co. p. 15.

[16] Howard, John. (1929) *The State of The Prisons*. New York: E.P. Dutton and Company.

[17] Barnes, Harry Elmer, and Negley K. Teeters. (1959) *New Horizons in Criminology*. Englewood Cliffs, NJ: Prentice-Hall, Inc. pp. 333-335.

[18] Howard, J. op. cit., pp. 94-96, 114-118.

[19] Walker, Samuel. op. cit., p. 34.

[20] Ives, op. cit., pp. 188-190, 174-175.

[21] Teeters, Negley K. (1937) *They Were in Prison*. Philadelphia: John C. Winston. p.30.

[22] Lewis, Orlando. (1922) *The Development of American Prisons and Prison Customs, 1776-1845.* Albany, NY: Prison Association of New York. p. 17.

[23] Ibid. p. 29.

[24] Haskell, Martin R., and Lewis Yablonski. (1974) *Criminology, Crime and Criminality.* Chicago: Rand McNally College Publishing Company. p. 524.

[25] Lewis, op. cit., pp. 26-27, 30-31.

[26] Teeters, Negley K. (1955) *The Cradle of the Penitentiary.* Philadelphia: Pennsylvania Prison society. p. 54.

[27] Lewis, op. cit., p. 29.

[28] Foucault, Michael. (1978) *Discipline and Punishment.* New York: Vintage Books.

[29] McKelvey, Blake. (1936) *American Prisons.* Chicago: University of Chicago Press. p. 8.

[30] Lewis, O. op. cit., pp. 43-44.

[31] Cromwell, Paul F. Jr. (1973) "Auburn: The Worlds Second Great Prison System," in *Penology,* Edited by George Killinger and Paul Cromwell Jr. St. Paul, MN: West publishing Company 1973. p.69.

[32] Caldwell, Robert G. (1965) *Criminology.* New York: The Ronald Press Company. p. 509.

[33] Martin, John Bartlow. (1951) *Break Down The Walls.* New York: Balantine Books, Inc. p. 115.

[34] Foucault, op. cit., p. 16.

[35] Orland, Leonard. (1973) *Justice, Punishment and Treatment.* New York: Free Press. p. 143.

[36] Ives, op. cit., p. 134.

[37] Walker, op. cit., p. 34.

[38] Ibid., p. 70.

[39] Carpenter, Mary. (1872) *Reformatory Prison Discipline as Developed by the Right Honorable Sir Walter Crofton in the Irish Convict Prisons.* London: Longman and Co. Chapter 1.

[40] Brockway, Zebulon Reed. (1912) *Fifty Years of Prison Service.* Montclair, NJ: Patterson Smith. pp. 224-298, p. 171.

[41] Barnes and Teeters, op. cit., 1959 edition, p. 426.

[42] Goldfarb, Ronald L., and Linda R. Singer. (1973) *After Conviction.* New York: Simon and Schuster. p. 49.

[43] Iacovetta, Ronald G. (1975) "Corrections and the Female Offender," in *Resolution of Correctional Problems and Issues* (Volume 1, no. 4, Summer) South Carolina Department of Corrections.

[44] Caldwell, op. cit., p. 529.

[45] Ibid., pp. 498, 523.

[46] Robinson, Lewis N. (1921) *Penology in the United States.* Philadelphia: The John C. Winston Company. p. 89.

[47] McKelvey, Blake. (1936) *American Prisons.* Chicago: University of Chicago Press. p. 188, pp. 222-223.

[48] *Eighteenth Annual Statistical Report of the Department of Welfare (1952) Bulletin No. 102. Penal.* Harrisburg: Commonwealth of Pennsylvania. Section B.

[49] *Annual Report, 1952-1953.* (1953). Montgomery Alabama. Board of Corrections, State of Alabama.

[50] *Prisoners in State and Federal Prisons and Reformatories, 1943.* (1946) Washington DC: Bureau of the Census. pp. 30-31.

[51] Murton, Tom, and Joe Hyams. (1969) *Accomplices to the Crime.* New York: Grove Press. pp 3, 7, and 13. For a detailed consideration of the abuses of the Arkansas Prison System see also Murton, Tom (1976) *The Dilemma of Prison Reform.* New York: Holt, Rinehart and Winston. pp. 146-162.

[52] Murton, T. (1976) ibid. p. 29-51, 131-162.

[53] Brodsky, Stanley, and Norman E. Egglestron. (1970) "Military Correctional Institutions," *The Military Prison.* Carbondale Illinois: Southern Illinois University Press. pp. 18-21.

[54] *Prisoners in State and Federal Prisons and Reformatories,* op. cit.

[55] *Directory: Juvenile and Adult Correctional Departments, Institutions, and Paroling Authorities.* (1977) College Park, MD: American Correctional Association.

234

Contemporary Corrections: Issues and Trends

By

Robert Scott

Plato believed that a stay in confinement should make an offender emerge a better man, or failing that, less of a wretch. The truth of Plato's statement may appear to be questionable on its face, based upon the realities of the 1990's. Correctional facilities, Plato would be surprised to learn, are but a single tool in the arsenal of correctional services, used for the "handling" of those who do ill against society and its members. Laurin Wollan (1994:2) noted that polls indicate that the public is now concerned about crime as much as it is about the economy. Accordingly, the world of correctional services has grown to become the fifth leading industry in the United States from the standpoint of annual expenditures (Scott, ACJS, 1996).

Paul H. Robinson (1995), law professor at the Northwestern School of Law, questioned why people obey the law. Robinson believed that the law had to have a certain moral credibility in order for it to seem just and worthy of adherence. Allen and Simonsen's (1992) portrayal of conflicting correctional ideologies as a swinging pendulum, moving back and forth over time between the two often polar extremes of the punishment and treatment philosophies, poses many of the same intellectual dilemmas as Robinson's query regarding law abidance. Why be good, when to be good, and how to be good, coupled with the questions why to punish, when to punish, and how to punish are questions whose answers change, for a variety of reasons, over time and place.

When Michael Fay was sentenced to caning for the crime of vandalizing automobiles in Singapore in 1994, the American populous was divided as to whether this punishment was horribly barbaric, or an appropriate response for a crime so senseless and mindless in nature. Many Americans, as we approach the 21st century, are divided with respect to the appropriate nature of punishment in general. Is punishment, dispensed by correctional services, meant to rehabilitate, seek societal retribution, to incapacitate wrongdoers, or to deter others from doing ill, based upon the example we make out of convicted transgressors?

GOALS OF CORRECTIONS

Thomas Mathiesen (1990), the Scandinavian criminologist, questioned the "defensibility" of contemporary corrections. In order to determine, or even debate the defensibility, desirability, or necessity of the battery of initiatives which make up contemporary correctional services, it is important to define the goals and objectives of the system and its various parts.

Correctional services maintain an oft changing balance between rehabilitation, deterrence, incapacitation, and retribution. Since Robert Martinson's classic pieces in the mid 1970's, delivery of correctional services, at least at the institutional level, has appeared to be much more concerned with incapacitation of the offender and extracting societies "pound of flesh" (retribution), and much less about rehabilitating and treating the offender. The conservative wave has been felt at both the federal and state levels. In fact, some have argued in response to Martinson's work, the Bureau of Prisons officially shifted the mission of the federal prison system from rehabilitation to incapacitation and retribution.

The debate over correctional ideology is clearly delineated in the federal legislation presently being sponsored by Rep. Bill McCollum (R-Florida). Congressman McCollum is seeking to tie federal moneys that are earmarked for the states, to their compliance with an initiative which would make juveniles much more accountable for their actions. The bill would, in fact, allow juveniles as young as thirteen to be tried as adults in the federal system for certain violent crimes. The debate arises when Congressman McCollum claims that such initiatives are an appropriate response to competent individuals and their law breaking. These laws are essentially "tough love." Conversely, Congressman Patrick Kennedy (D-Rhode Island) argues that these initiatives will simply push already troubled children over the edge into a full-fledged criminal lifestyle, and that Congressman McCollum and his ideological allies have completely disregarded the value of prevention programs (Charles Grodin, CNBC, 15 May 1997). Either way, ideological rightness and wrongness

cannot be determined at this stage of our understanding of the criminal mind-set. When speaking of such issues, we are dealing with shades of gray, and not absolutes.

The Contemporary Correctional System

The correctional system in America today is a multi-faceted entity. It no longer simply involves institutions. Probation, parole, community service, work release, halfway houses, electronic monitoring, boot camps, substance abuse and mental health treatment programs, as well as a multi-layered institutional structure, including municipal, county, state, federal, and military structures, add to many more initiatives to make up the world of contemporary corrections.

OVERVIEW OF INSTITUTIONAL STRUCTURES

...in several countries, the institutional growth pattern is so marked that one wonders whether we are entering a new stage in the use of prisons... (Mathiesen, 1990)

Federal Prison System

The federal prison system, known as the Bureau of Prisons (BOP), was created by Congress in 1930, under the auspices of the Department of Justice (DOJ). At present, the Bureau of Prisons consists of some 80 units, with several under construction. These 80 units house over 90,000 persons guilty of federal crimes (Butterfield, 1995, p. 201).

Facilities within the federal system consist of correctional institutions, detention centers, medical centers, prison camps, metropolitan corrections centers, and penitentiaries. These units are arranged in a hierarchy known as the level system.

Bureau of Prison facilities are classified from level 1 through level 6. Level 1 facilities are typically the work camps, facilities without detention wire or intensive supervision. Offenders in low level facilities, such as the level 2 facility at Yankton, South Dakota, are typically non-violent and not considered to be escape risks. Interestingly, the facility at Yankton, until the late 1980's, was Yankton College. Relatively few alterations to the facility itself were made during the transformation from educational institution to federal prison.

The seeming informality and relatively unrestrictive environment of the low-level facility is in stark contrast to the higher-level units in the system. Level 5 facilities are known as U.S. Penitentiaries, and are high security, freedom restricted units. Examples of level 5 units are USP-Atlanta, USP-Lompoc, CA, USP-Lewisburg, PA, USP-Terre Haute, IN and USP-Leavenworth, KS.

The most restrictive and high security units in the federal system are the level 6 units. The nations level 6 unit is also known as the "SUPERMAX" facility. Alcatraz Island was the first such facility, meant to house the most dangerous federal offenders and the highest escape risks. Alcatraz was replaced by Marion, Illinois, which has served as the nation's SUPERMAX for the past three decades. At present, Florence, Colorado is in the process of being transformed into Marion's replacement for the 21st century.

Types of crimes which offenders may be sentenced to the federal system for include a battery of drug offenses, offenses involving interstate commerce and criminal activity, kidnapping, bank robbery, tax offenses, federal firearms offenses, certain white collar crimes (embezzlement etc.), immigration law violators, as well as counterfeiting and forgery, plus many more.

A significant date with respect to the Bureau of Prisons is 1987. In 1987, Federal Sentencing Guidelines were initiated, establishing a sentencing key for offenses to ensure consistency in sentencing, as well as the requirement that federal inmates serve a minimum of 85% of their sentence. The immediate difference which can be seen between a federal and a state sentence can be viewed in the relative length of incarceration for the same offense. A non-violent drug conviction, and subsequent 20 year sentence in the federal system, requires the serving of a minimum of 85% of the sentence, or 17 years. Conversely, the same 20 year sentence in the state level Texas Department of Criminal Justice-Institutional Division, is likely to involve only 2-4 years of time served.

The typical federal inmate is 25-34 years old (36%) or 35-44 years old (32.9%), which is older than state prison demographics. The median age of a federal inmate is 36, compared to 30 in the state systems. With respect to other demographics, the typical federal inmate is married (37.9%), has a high school diploma (48.5%) or some college (28.1%), with a median education level of 12 years, was legitimately employed (74.4%) at the time of their arrest, and was making a relatively high (compared to state inmates) $25,000 or more (27.3%) per year (Clear and Cole, 1997, p. 250).

State Prison System

All fifty states operate a state level corrections division. All told, state level correctional departments employ over 300,000 persons in a variety of capacities. Approximately 1,100 facilities house nearly 1,100,000 inmates (Welch, 1996, p. 138).

State Departments of Corrections (DOC) are typically divided along security designations, into minimum, medium and maximum security units. Minimum security units are roughly equivalent to level 1 and 2 federal facilities. Medium security units are closer in form to maximum security units than minimum security, in that medium and maximum security designations involve greatly heightened security over that of the minimum facility.

States such as New York, Texas and California have a wide variety of units encompassing all levels of security and beyond. Smaller states have somewhat fewer facilities, but often are innovative in the provision of correctional services. The Alabama Department of Corrections, for example, consists of several prisons: a disciplinary rehabilitation unit, an honor farm for very-low-security inmates, a state cattle ranch for similarly classified inmates, a prison for women, a youth camp for male felons under the age of 25, and a battery of community based facilities (Welch, 1996, p. 362).

Departments of Corrections in the 1990's often put an enormous financial strain on state budgets. Consider a typical Midwestern state, Kansas for example. The Kansas Department of Corrections consists of nearly 7,700 bed spaces, with a relatively reasonable annual cost of about $17,000 per bed. Conversely, the New York Department of Correctional Services houses some 60,000 prisoners at a cost of nearly $40,000 per bed space (Risley, 1997). Some quick math indicates the enormity of the funding dilemma of correctional institutions, particularly in states that do not possess the large tax bases of the New Yorks, Texas and Californias of this country.

The typical offender in a state prison system is aged 18-34 (67%), never married (55.3%) or divorced (18.3%), possessing only a median tenth-grade education, and earning between $0 and $9,999 (51.9%).(17) State prison inmates, relative to their federal counterparts in the 1990's, are a much more marginal group of individuals (Clear and Cole, 1997, p. 250).

Jails and Other Detention Facilities

Jails are a distinct and unique part of the institutional network that helps make up the correctional service industry in the United States. Welch (1996) notes that the 3,300 jails that operate in this country (2,700 county control; 600 municipal control) house both pretrial and sentenced prisoners. As of mid-1995, 52% of those persons being held in such facilities were not convicted offenders (Bureau of Justice Statistics, 1995, pp. 2-3). Most recent statistics indicate that there are approximately 13,000,000 jail admissions made each year in this country, with approximately 490,000 persons being held at any one time (Bureau of Justice Statistics, 1993, p. 1).

The transitory nature of these facilities seems to preclude them from any form of effective treatment and rehabilitation. The rapid turnover of inmates makes these units much more likely to perform a simple "holding" function. Nancy Schafer (1986) points out that the local control that these units enjoy makes them much more responsive to local mores and beliefs than the generic nature of state and federal facilities (p. 497). Todd Clear (1997) showed that, although the vast majority of local jails do, in fact, service the relatively small populations which they are located in, several of the jail facilities in larger cities are amongst the largest institutions at any level in this country. Los Angeles County Jail, for example, houses 20,113 inmates, the New York City Jail system houses 18,171 prisoners, and Harris County Jail (Houston) houses 10,716 (p. 149).

An interesting phenomenon of jail facilities which is continuing to evolve into the 1990's is that of the rented bed space. Jails, both large and small, have been getting into the business of generating revenues by renting out bed space in local facilities to overcrowded jurisdictions, both local and state. In Texas, where the Texas Department of Criminal Justice-Institutional Division is hopelessly overcrowded, the Harris County Jail houses thousands of state prisoners on a yearly basis (Houston Chronicle, 16 March 1990, A12). This revenue-generating strategy is not restricted to large jurisdictions. Russell County, Kansas, for example, is situated in the west-central portion of the state. Although the county jail only holds 24 prisoners, the local demand for bed space never exceeds just a fraction of the total. The sheriff, Tim Holmes, houses 12-16 prisoners from Johnson County, Kansas (Kansas City), an overcrowded jail, for a fee of $42 per space per day. At this rate, the rural Russell County Jail makes a tidy profit, and Johnson County saves a tidy amount over their own local cost of housing their prisoners (Holmes, 1997). This trend looks to extend into the 21st century as the forces of supply and demand affect the local detention frontier.

Clear and Cole (1997) show that, on average, the typical prisoner confined to a jail facility in this country is white (54.5%), male (90%), not yet

238

convicted of a crime (52%), poor, and possessing low levels of educational attainment. Jail inmates have been called the great unwashed amongst American prisoners.

Community Corrections

Community corrections may be viewed as a macro title for many micro programs. Unlike their correctional counterpart, the prison and jail network in America, community corrections involves punishment, supervision, and treatment free from the institutional environment. A sampling of programs contained under the big umbrella of community corrections includes, but is not limited to: probation, parole, diversion, community service, work release, intensive supervision probation, and electronic monitoring.

Probation

Probation in the 1990's has evolved into a critical component of correctional services in America. Partially because of a search for alternatives to incarceration for low level offenders, and partially because prison overcrowding has forced certain jurisdictions to consider this as an option, there are approximately 2,900,000 adults on probation in this country today (Bureau of Justice Statistics, 1991, p. 1). A Rand study indicated that 70% of convicted offenders are now sentenced to a term of probation: an established period of time imposed by the court whereby the offender must meet terms and standards of conduct, as well as meeting and reporting regularly to an assigned probation officer (Samaha, 1997, p. 489).

The foundation of probation as we know it today, has its genesis in the case of *Roberts v. United States* (1943).[1] Roberts found probation to be acceptable when it involved an individualized program, free from institutional walls, with positive role models (probation officers) guiding their lives and actions, so that young offenders and persons not yet hardened by a criminal lifestyle may be reformed. Inflated probation officer case loads and other factors may have eroded some of

the specific intent described in Roberts, but the essential mission remains the same.

Parole

The term parole is often confused by the general public with probation. In fact, they are two distinct and wholly different programs with different missions. Parolees are released from prison, subject to certain conditions. The offender agrees to abide by certain pre-established rules for living, which includes remaining law-abiding. The length of parole is usually restricted to the uncompleted portion of an offenders prison sentence. The term parole, of French descent, means, appropriately, "word of honor" (Welch, 1996, p. 393).

Recent statistics from the Bureau of Justice Statistics indicate that there are approximately 500,000 persons on parole in this country (Bureau of Justice Statistics, 1991, p. 1). The use of parole has become an interesting paradox over the past decade. In some states, such as Texas, where prison overcrowding has forced the state to adapt a strategy of early releases, the use of parole is both integral and heightened. Conversely, both the Bureau of Prisons and the Virginia Department of Corrections have abolished the concept of parole entirely. Other states, such as Florida, are embracing a concept known as "truth in sentencing." Given this attempt to make the prison term that one is sentenced to more representative of the actual time served, Florida now requires its prisoners to serve 75% of their sentence, following in the footsteps of the Bureau of Prisons 1987 initiative requiring 85% time served by federal inmates.

It is unclear what the ultimate judgment will be with respect to the future of the use of parole as a tool of correctional services departments. The relatively poor (45%) success rate for parolees, meaning not being returned to prison for a new offense, or a parole violation, questions its effectiveness as a treatment tool; but, in the day and age of prison overcrowding, the importance of parole as an administrator's option cannot be diminished (Bureau of Justice Statistics, 1991).

Diversion

Diversion is becoming an increasingly popular option for the relatively minor or youthful offender. In the simplest of terms, diversion involves a process whereby the offender has his or her incarceration and/or prosecution delayed until a program of diversion is completed. A diversion program can involve a period of time during which the offender must remain crime free, diversion condition violation free, and may be forced to complete a form of community service program.

Diversion programs are meant, in their most basic form, to filter out non-violent drug offenders, first time offending juveniles and young adults, and other relatively minor or low priority offenses and/or offenders (Allen and Simonsen, 1992). The thinking with respect to diversion programs is that it is more desirable for the "system" to manage the low-level and youthful offender in the community, than in the institutional setting.

Community Service

Community service in the 1990's continues to be an effective and less costly method of dealing with non-institutionalized offenders. Beyond many of the same issues which have made other forms of community based corrections popular, community service, as a functional concept, was aided by the enactment of the Federal Comprehensive Crime Control Act of 1984. The Act, which took effect November 1, 1987, stated:

> ...if sentenced to probation, the defendant must also be ordered to pay a fine, make restitution, and/or work in community service...

Some advocates of community service argue that the use of community service may give the offender a sense of bonding with the community, rather than further alienating him or her from it. Similarly, Sam Souryal, a prominent theorist regarding the principles of corrections system ethics, believes that community service, whether effective or not, is certainly more humanitarian an approach than other available options (Souryal, 1997, p. 343).

It is difficult to compute statistics relative to the number of persons presently serving a term of community service since, unlike terms of incarceration in state or federal prisons, community sentence orders often sentence the person to as little as 10 hours. The transitory nature of community service, for lack of a better term, makes tracking virtually an impossibility. The figure, though, totals at least three million at any one time (Bureau of Justice Statistics, 1991, p. 1).

A unique attraction of community service is that it generates utility, and input, rather than being strictly expenditure based on the part of the correctional service agency. Hours spent picking up trash, aiding social service agencies in support positions, or involvement in public works projects all save the jurisdiction affected money that would otherwise have to be spent paying people to perform certain of these job functions. The utilitarian direction which community service has taken in the 1990's, interestingly, seems to mimic much of the intent of the ancient Greek and Roman societies, when utilitarian "pay-back" to the offended community was viewed as noble repayment of a debt.

Work Release

The original use of work release in the United States, as a form of punishment, can be traced to the Huber Law of the State of Wisconsin in 1913. However, the concept can be traced to ancient Rome. In Rome, prisoners aided in massive public work projects (Welch, 1996, p. 404). The Romans viewed the prisoner labor as a repayment of debt to the offended society. In contemporary America, however, the rationale is more offender-based. The intent is to allow certain low risk, non-violent offenders to maintain employment in the community during the day and return to their institutional setting at night.

The profits of the inmate's labor can be distributed in a number of fashions: it may be used as victim restitution, fine payment, to keep an inmate's family off of the welfare rolls while the bread earner would otherwise be incarcerated full-time, or it may be used to build a nest egg for the day when the offender is free from his or her institutional stay. Also important is the fact that offenders, earning income, pay taxes under this program, whereas they do not while behind prison walls.

In the 1990's however, in light of certain high profile cases of offenders on work release or a furlough program committing heinous acts (such as Willie Horton in Massachusetts), the screening processes for offenders to be admitted to such an alternative have been heightened considerably.

Electronic Monitoring

Annesley Schmidt (1991) posed the question of what can realistically be expected from electronic monitoring (EM). Souryal (1997) points out that electronic monitoring is not necessarily a punishment as much as it is an enforcement mechanism. Persons will be fitted with an ankle bracelet, or some other form of transmitter which can tell a central location if the offender has wandered outside of a predetermined radius (often 150 to 200 feet). If the offender does wander, authorities can be immediately notified, and the offender apprehended (Souryal, 1997, p. 347).

Much like many of the other community corrections options being utilized by states in the 1990's, electronic monitoring has critics as well as supporters. Morris and Tonry have noted that there have been arguments of class bias raised against this method. While certain states have liberalized definitions of a "home," most consider a home to be a dwelling. Souryal (1997:347) points out that many offenders do not own or rent a house or apartment in a fashion stable enough for most community correction divisions' liking. Also important is the contention of Souryal that this is not punishment, in the sense that most of the general public views punishment. With the issuance of a timetable of acceptable daily routines, the offender may work, go to school, shop, play, have visitors and the like, while under "control" of the state.

Electronic monitoring is, however, also a huge money-saving instrument. While the cost of maintaining an offender in a prison setting in the 1990's can range from about $17,000 per year up to about $40,000, the value of a system which can monitor the low level offender for about $3,500-$4,000 per year has obvious appeal (Leiker, 1997).

There is some debate however, about what constitutes a low-risk, or no-risk offender. Is the felony three-time drunk driver low risk? Is the non-violent, first-time drug dealer low risk? How about the child molester? The point is this: given the relative amount of freedom and access to all the creature comforts of the "free man," does electronic monitoring sufficiently deter and incapacitate the offender from recidivating.

ISSUES AND PROBLEMS IN COMMUNITY CORRECTIONS

Issue #1: Overcrowding

Overcrowding of inmates at both the state and federal levels have become chronic dilemmas for a great number of jurisdictions. Most recent statistics indicate that state prisons, taken as an aggregate, are presently filled to 118% of capacity. The situation in the federal system is actually worse, currently filled to 136% of capacity (Bureau of Justice Statistics, 1994, p. 6). In fact, Bureau of Justice Statistics information indicates that only 13 states are operating at or below 99% capacity. All other states, the District of Columbia, and the federal system are operating at or over 100% capacity (Bureau of Justice Statistics, 1994, p. 6).

The point has been made that the net effect of this overcrowding is that an exacerbation effect is taking place with respect for prison life, effecting both inmates and staff alike (Clements, 1979, p. 217). In fact, prisons in many of the jurisdictions with chronic overcrowding problems, have become the first resort option, rather than a last step. The warehousing approach to crime control in states such as New York, California, and Texas has aided the magnitude of each states overcrowding problems.

Further, Welch (1996) described several factors which have most strongly contributed to the problem of prison overcrowding: (1) the war on drugs, (2) demographic changes and the shifting age curve, (3) mandatory sentencing laws, (4) larger sentences, and (5) tougher parole boards (p. 178). The war on drugs, and the accompanying sentencing keys which have been its legacy, have, in particular, facilitated a situation whereby inmates are serving longer sentences, and requiring the incarceration for individuals who otherwise would not have even been sentenced to prison. This condition has effected the Bureau of Prisons most profoundly, where nearly 2 in 3 federal prisoners is now incarcerated for a drug, or drug related offense.

A similar situation exists in the nations 3,300 county and municipal jails. Bureau of Justice statistics indicate that, through the mid and late 1980's jail populations have increased by 77% (Bureau of Justice Statistics, 1991). Further, Mauer (1992) found in his study of New York City jails that their populations increased by 300% between the critical years of 1980 and 1992 (Bureau of Justice Statistics, 1991). Substantiating Clements (1979) findings discussed earlier that overcrowding exacerbates the already bad situation, Welch (1996) found that in the early 1990's there was an average of 3,000 assaults on staff and inmates per year in the Rikers Island facility alone (p. 177).

Agnes Baro (1988) from Grand Valley State University in Michigan indicated that state legislatures and federal courts were most responsible for taking autonomous control of state prison systems out of the hands of corrections administrators. Irrespective of whether this point is contributory to prison overcrowding or not, the strength of "right the ship" has been compromised. This being the case, states such as Kansas and Texas, one close to "overcrowding status" and the other having faced this problem since 1979 respectively,

are contemplating options such as privatization of prison services, blanket releases of low-level offenders, as well as unique diversionary programs.

Table A provides a typical example of a federal court order, in this case meant to ease overcrowding at Harris County (Houston, Texas) Jail (Houston Chronicle, 16 March, 1990, A12).

Issue #2: Problems Faced by the Correctional Officer

Ben Crouch and James Marquart (1996) have completed some of the most interesting and intriguing work, relative to the dilemmas and shortcomings faced by correctional officers in the contemporary prison system. Work conducted by both Crouch and Marquart, as well as Lombardo some years earlier, indicate that danger on the job is viewed as one of the most significant drawbacks to work in the American correctional network. Erosion of the power of the guard to discipline and control the institutional environment, by the courts, administrators, and politicians, has contributed greatly to this feeling of insecurity. Toch and Klofas (1982) found that this sense of abandonment by powers that be, has led to a dangerous trend towards avoidance of authority altogether on the part of the correctional officer.

Cheek and Miller (1993), followed by Crouch and Marquart, describe the physical and mental effects of the institution on the correctional officer. The term "working personality," also coined in describing law enforcement officers, refers to the change in one's personality brought on, either voluntarily or involuntarily, by the workplace. Problems arise when officers take this "working personality" home with them. Problems with respect to alcoholism, abusive speech and actions, health problems and the like are all common reactants to this line of work (Allen and Simonsen, 1992).

Racial and gender interaction amongst guards involves the breakdown of the archaic, yet com-

Table 1.   Jail Crowding

Highlights of a Federal Court Order Designed

to Ease Overcrowding at Harris County Jail

➤ Effective immediately, jail population limited to 6,700 prisoners. There were 6,663 Thursday afternoon including 2,400 state inmates.

➤ State inmate level must be cut by 300 by May 31. Total jail population must drop to 6,400.

➤ State inmate level must be cut by another 300 by Aug. 31. Total jail population must drop to 6,100.

➤ Over the next six months, the state must increase normal transfer of prisoners from the jail, averaging 182 per week, to an average of 353 per week. The state can imprison, parole or grant early releases.

➤ The county must limit new inmates by increased use of alternatives, such as early release and electronic home monitoring.

➤ If limits don't work, inmates get early release in this order:
First, those held for trial on low-level misdemeanors. Examples: speeding, running a red light, writing a bad check.
Next, low-risk prisoners held for trial on lowest-level felonies. Examples: official misconduct, auto theft or carrying a firearm in a business licensed to sell alcoholic beverages.
Next, those with low-level misdemeanors who have completed sentences but still owe fines or court costs. Examples: speeding, running a red light or writing a bad check.
Finally, those with more-severe misdemeanors who have completed sentences but still owe fines or court costs. Examples: driving while intoxicated, burglary of a coin-operated machine, trespassing.

fortable ''old boys network.'' It is not surprising that we show resistance to the unfamiliar. The advent of female and black prison guards has caused certain adaptation problems in certain segments of the correctional institution network.

Finally, Crouch found that institutional problems such as theft, drug dealing, homosexuality, extreme use of force and assisted escapes were not only tolerated by correctional officers, but in many instances the guard was a major contributor to the respective issue.

Issue #3: Computer Technology

The past decade has seen a renaissance in the use of technology in order to aid and assist corrections system workers in the nature, scope, and efficiency of their position. From innovation as simple as a small sheriff's department like Russell County, Kansas, with a population of barely over 7,000, with a department consisting of 4 deputies now using laptop computers and advanced software to take and write reports in the field in place of the more traditional written report, to tremendously advanced computer systems linking the nation's police and correctional forces into a single crime control network, technology and criminal justice agencies are forging an evolving and growing partnership.

In southern California, response to an inability of local corrections officials and law enforcement agencies to "talk" to each other's computer systems inspired the CHEERS system. The Night-stalker, Richard Ramirez, was the subject of a nationwide manhunt by local, state and federal agencies. The interesting factor, which underscored the necessity for CHEERS was that Richard Ramirez was not hiding in Canada, Mexico, or the hills of Kentucky. He was locked up in a southern California jail, being held under an assumed name on a drunk driving charge. The officers in that same department were part of an investigation for a man who was locked up in their own jail (Lemov, 1997, p. 58).

Robert Davis (1995) outlined a unique victim sensitive system installed by the City of Louisville, Kentucky, and copied in several other jurisdictions. The VINE system (Victim Information Notification Everyday) is a victim notification system which allows people to check inmate numbers and locations automatically. Persons can also determine offender release dates, as well as register to receive a phone call upon an inmate's release. A safety mechanism of the system is that the inmate cannot find out who has accessed information regarding their situation.

The VINE system cost the City of Louisville $55,000 to install the system, and costs approximately $57,000 per year to run (p. 59). The expenditure is viewed as a small price to pay for the added protection afforded the community, as well as the public relations value derived from the systems presence.

Passaic County, New Jersey has developed a system modeled on the Kentucky experience. Passaic County, however, has created a procedure whereby they fund the systems presence with confiscated and seized moneys. The criminals themselves are then, in an essence, paying for the system and its operation (p. 59).

Issue #4: Institutional Privatization

As the cost of business with respect to prison operation continues to spiral upwards out of control, more and more states are turning to privatization as an alternative. Texas is a prime example of a privatization experiment deemed successful, which is being expanded on a year-to-year basis.

The biggest of the private prison companies, CCA (Corrections Corporation of America), as an example, presently dominates the $250,000,000 industry. Although private prisons make up less than 2% of total state and federal prison bed spaces, and are at present in use in only 13 states, the future appears bright, particularly for CCA (Ramirez, 1994).

CCA claims that they "can do it better and cheaper" than the state. Their contract with the State of Texas requires that they provide total prison operations at a rate at least 10% less than the cost of a Texas Department of Criminal Justice-Institutional Division facility. In Texas, that means operating bed spaces at a rate of $40 per day per space. CCA accomplishes this mandate successfully (Ramirez, 1994).

CCA claims that attention to detail allows them to do the job that they do. Details like programs, treatment options, open lines of communication between inmates and administrators and the like, which William C. LaRowe, Director of the Texas Center for Correctional Services, a self-described cynic of private prisons, says have changed his mind about CCA and other players like Wackenhut. LaRowe noted that the level of programs and quality of those programs are as good or better than those provided in state-run institutions (Ramirez, 1994). Private prison officials claim that this is not by accident. Unhappy inmates break things, stab people and generally cost the system money — costs that, for a private operation, come right out of the profits. The rationale, therefore, is to keep them busy and keep them happy.

So how does CCA do it? How do they do it better, but also do it cheaper? The answer is quite simple. Wages are generally on a par with counterpart state run prisons. CCA does not, however, offer a pension plan which Ramirez claims saves the employer approximately 15% of total personnel costs. Additionally, CCA, a publicly traded company, offers its employees a stock purchase plan. This encourages employees to essentially "give back, or reinvest" a portion of their salary into the organization. In the end, the steady flow of reinvested capital allows CCA to expand or sign new contracts at a moment's notice, and their 15% personnel savings and streamlined management allows them to provide total prison management for the 10% premium guaranteed in the Texas contract.

Although private prisons, as mentioned, are still in control of a relatively small number of total institutional bed space, the future appears bright. President Clinton's Crime Bill spoke directly to the issue of private prisons, and the response was favorable. Additionally, CCA stock has more than doubled in value in a single 12 month period, and the company expects 85% annual growth, in a business community where 3-5% is considered healthy (Ramirez, 1994).

Issue #5: AIDS in an Institutional Environment

In a legal age when informed consent is essentially a pillar of certainty, the testing of inmates for HIV and AIDS has become an administrator's hot potato. Courts have upheld the rights of prison administrators to test inmates within a number of functional guidelines (see Harris v. Thigpen).[2] Perhaps the most significant case to date was that of Harris v. Thigpen (1990). *Harris v. Thigpen* contested mass screening, segregation of HIV positive inmates from the general population, and contested that the medical care given HIV and AIDS infected inmates by the Alabama Department of Corrections was inadequate. This case provided a conditional victory for the state, and created a blueprint for several issues related to AIDS for other states to follow.

According to most recent statistics, the Bureau of Justice Statistics reports that there are 21,538 HIV positive inmates in state and federal prisons (approximately 2.4% of the total population), and another 6,711 locked up in jails and detention centers (approximately 1.8% of the total population) (Brien and Harlow, 1995, p. 3). Brien and Harlow (1995) found the state with (by almost a 2:1 margin) the highest rate of HIV positive inmates in its Department of Corrections was New York at 12.4%, six times the national average. Connecticut (6.6%), Massachusetts (3.9%), Maryland (3.8%), and New Jersey (3.7%) round out the top five. It is interesting that all of the top five states are from the northeast. This fact is, however, hardly indicative of more than the fact that only 15 states test all prison inmates, of which most are northeastern states (p. 3). States without mandatory, universal, and frequent testing are able to artificially underreport the number of cases in their respective systems.

Hammett and Moini (1990) do point out that the cost of mass screening is often prohibitive. Thus cost considerations may render truly efficient detection and "count gathering" measures hopelessly unattainable.

Fiegley v. Fulcomer, 1989 a pre-cursor to the *Harris v. Thigpen* decision, confirmed that the Constitution allows correctional administrators to decide whether to segregate or not based upon a local, institution based decision.[3]

William C. Collins (1990), from the American Correctional Association, notes that, with respect to medical treatment, provision of AZT can cost up to $50,000 per year per case. This situation helps contribute to the fact that states are spending larger and larger proportions of their correctional budget on medical care. Georgia for example, spends nearly 25% of its annual budget on the medical care of inmates. Care of HIV/AIDS infected inmates encompasses much of this expenditure. *Harris v. Thigpen* provided states some relief when it was decided that provision of expensive and often experimental treatments by state prison systems are not necessarily mandated.

One issue in which corrections administrators

have been granted little exception and/or freedom is that of disclosure. Collins (1990) noted that, although staff and administrators often feel that they have the right to know which inmates they work around are HIV/AIDS infected, such disclosures are generally considered unnecessary since with universal precautions, the risk of infection by staff is no greater than work environments outside of the correctional setting (p. 130).

Issue #6: Sexual Predator Laws

Frightened communities are rising up against sex offenders, but that vigilantism will not always work. One thing which the scare of sex offenders and cries for justice have managed to do is to refocus attention on the treatment of sex offenders in prison and beyond. The six years served by Jesse Timmendequas for a brutal sexual attack on a child in the state of New Jersey, and the blatant, unremorseful attitude of Richard Allan Davis in California (Megan Kanka and Polly Klaas cases respectively) have been particularly antagonistic to the sensibilities of the American public.

In 1996, the Supreme Court entertained arguments by Carla Stovall, Attorney General of the state of Kansas, with respect to an intriguing response to dangerous sexual predators: sexual predator units. In Kansas, a 31-bed wing located at the Larned Correctional Mental Health Facility was set aside in the mid 1990's for dangerous sexual predators who had completed their sentence in the Department of Corrections. These offenders would then be civilly committed to the mental health block of the Larned facility. The facility presently is holding only eight such offenders as a result of the Court blocking future transfers until the Supreme Court determines if this process constitutes double jeopardy, or violates equal protection of due process rights. As of May 1997, the case has yet to have been ruled upon, and several states other than Kansas are awaiting the results (e.g., Washington and Minnesota).

Parts of this macro level case have in fact already been scrutinized. A Washington case from the early 1990's challenged that state's transfer policy as violative of the principals of double jeopardy — punishing a person twice for the same offense. The State weathered that challenge on the basis that the mental health commitment following the prison stay was not punishment, but treatment. The second stay (mental health) was not a criminal proceeding, therefore it could not be considered double jeopardy (In re Young, 122 Wash.2d1.)

The validity of sexual predator laws, as they exist in Kansas, Washington, Minnesota, and other states, is clarified by Justice Dwyer of Seattle, Washington. Justice Dwyer indicated that the standard which this, and similar cases may revolve around is whether the mental health commitment can be considered legitimate treatment, or is it simply a prison-like warehousing in a mental health setting (Young v. Weston, CN480C).

Issue #7: Regimented Inmate Discipline

The state of Oklahoma has enacted a program, which since its 1986 passage, has allowed young adult offenders to delay their sentencing pending the completion of a boot camp-like experience (Scott and Allen, in Press, p. 1). Participants in the Oklahoma program must be 18-21 year old male offenders (a female program is being developed) facing a felony charge, but not having a long history of felony convictions.

The purpose of this program, according to Scott and Allen, is the deterrent effect gained through military boot-camp-style discipline building. The resultant discipline building reinforces a positive self image, and hopefully shocks the young offender into conformity (Scott and Allen, in Press, p. 3).

The program itself consists of a 120 day regimen of scheduled, military style physical training, education and self-development sessions. The goal was that the "training" would not necessarily be generic, but somewhat individualized. Participants receive any number of the following treatment options during the 120 day period: substance abuse education (SAD), stress management and relaxation training (SMART), adult basic education (ABE), general education development (GED), and VO-TECH skill training (Scott and Allen, 1996, p. 4).

Joan Petersilia, in a 1993 report to the Bureau of Justice Statistics, noted the need to measure the effectiveness of the battery of initiatives that make up the world of community corrections. Petersilia's concerns for true measures of success, rather than anecdotal accounts, is appropriate, yet not feasible at this point with the RID program, as well as many of the boot camp initiatives in other states. The relative youth of the programs, difficulty in determining "successful" and "unsuccessful" program participants, as well as the relatively small numbers of available subjects, all contribute to a difficulty in developing meaningful outcome measures for these initiatives.

One, admittedly unscientific but certainly professional, opinion on the results of the RID program in Oklahoma, comes from David Alexander, a senior probation and parole officer in the Oklahoma Department of Corrections. Mr. Alexander notes "tremendous improvement" in most of the 20-25 Bryan County youth who have gone through the program successfully. Improvement, according to Alexander, came in the form of attitude and self-confidence. Interestingly, Alexander noted that offenders typically agree the experience was worthwhile, but feared returning. This fact in itself may be reason enough to consider the program, and others like it, a limited success.

Issue #8: Substance Abuse Counseling and Treatment

The use of substance abuse counseling and treatment as an integrated tangent of contemporary corrections has grown in favor in the early to mid 1990's (Scott and O'Connor, 1997). Models for usage vary greatly between using drug treatment as a small portion of a total institutional experience (Foote et al., 1994), to a model which views drug treatment as an outright alternative to the institutional setting (Van Stelle et al., 1994).

As a form of compromise, Barthwell (1995) described a twelve step model, similar to Alcoholics Anonymous and Gamblers Anonymous programs, which has found its way into the correctional setting. The Kansas Department of Corrections is an example of a state which provides facilities for comprehensive drug treatment, through the Larned Correctional Mental Health Facility. The unit, open since 1992, caters to KDOC inmates who display mental health and/or dependency problems while in the custody of the corrections department (KDOC, 1994, p. 1). The unit is an example of the specialized types of services that are increasingly being delivered by correctional services in the 1990 s.

TO THE FUTURE: PEEKING OVER THE RIM

Several other issues facing corrections administrators in the 1990's are worthy of note. Each of these issues is a growing trend, a unique program, or significant concern. Each of these issues promises, like those mentioned previously, to be significant well into the next century:

1. THREE STRIKES LAWS: In place in many states, this trend towards punishing three time felony offenders with a life, or automatic sentence is a popular and growing option for state legislatures. Georgia, in fact, has moved to a two strike law, and Michigan has passed a one strike drug trafficking law (Harmelin Law).

2. CIVIL LIABILITY CONCERNS: Section 1983 lawsuits filed against corrections personnel and administrators will continue to be a concern into the next century. Although the relative success rate of such lawsuits is small from the plaintiff's standpoint, loses for the corrections industry are typically expensive and often require a change in departmental policy, which is often time consuming and costly.

3. DEATH PENALTY: May 1997 brought two cases which illuminate just how this society is "pushing the envelope" with respect to the death penalty. Texas executed Terry Covington, a man who, by all standards and admissions, was retarded (USA Today, 7 May, 1997, p. A3). In North Carolina, a jury tried to sentence Thomas Richard Jones to the death penalty for what was, essentially, two counts of vehicular homicide (drunk driver). Only the court ruling that drunk driving precluded the killings being planned and premeditated saved Mr. Jones (USA Today, 7 May, 1997, p. A3).

4. CHAIN GANGS: A return to the use of the chain gang has been a popular trend in the mid-1990's in the American south. Alabama is the state which has drawn the most national publicity from their return to this long abandoned punishment, although many other states, including Georgia, Mississippi, and Arizona have toyed with the idea in various forms and fashion.

5. TENT CITY: The sheriff's department of Maricopa County, Arizona (Phoenix), headed by a no-nonsense ex-DEA agent, began the trend in the 1990's of alleviating their counties overcrowding problem — not by farming inmates out to other facilities, but by erecting military surplus tents, and housing county inmates there. The cost is predictably cheap, and has drawn national attention to Maricopa County. The state level Kansas Department of Corrections actually solicited information regarding this method, while considering options to deal with its own overcrowding problem (Risley, 1997).

CONCLUDING THOUGHT

It is clear that as we approach the new millennium, the world of correctional services is becoming a more and more dynamic entity. Prisons are no longer simply the old stone gulags they once appeared to be. Rather, prisons are coming to resemble very specialized role players in the entirety of a correctional division of a corrections department. Community corrections continues to expand the use of traditional options, while constantly striving to create new ones. Expansion appears to be the one constant for the future of correctional services in America.

✻ ✻ ✻ ✻ ✻

ENDNOTES

[1] For a discussion of this and related cases, see Charles Lindner (1993), "Probation's First 100 Years: Growth Through Failure, *Journal of Probation and Parole*, Spring.
[2] See Michael Welch, (1996), *Corrections: A Critical Approach.* New York: McGraw-Hill, pp. 430-436.
[3] Ibid.

REFERENCES

Allen, H., C. Simonsen
    1992   *Corrections in America: An Introduction*, 6th Ed. New York: Macmillan.
Baro, A.
    1988   "The loss of local control over prison administration." *Justice Quarterly*, 5, 79-93.

Barthwell, A.
  1995   "A continuum of care for substance abusers in the criminal justice system." *Journal of Psychoactive Drugs*, 27, 1, 39-47.
Brien, P., and C. Harlow
  1995   "HIV in prisons and jails, 1993." *Bureau of Justice Statistics Bulletin*, August, pp. 1-3.
Bureau of Justice Statistics
  1989   *Prison Rule Violators*. Washington, DC: U.S. Department of Justice.
Bureau of Justice Statistics
  1991   *Probation and Parole, 1990*. Washington, DC: U.S. Department of Justice.
Bureau of Justice Statistics
  1992   *National Update*. Washington, DC: U.S. Department of Justice.
Bureau of Justice Statistics
  1992   *Prisons and Prisoners in the United States*. Washington, DC: U.S. Department of Justice.
Bureau of Justice Statistics
  1993   *Jail Inmates, 1992*. Washington, DC: U.S. Department of Justice.
Bureau of Justice Statistics
  1994   *Prisoners in 1993*. Washington, DC: U.S. Department of Justice.
Bureau of Justice Statistics
  1995   *Bulletin*. Washington, DC: U.S. Department of Justice.
Butterfield, F.
  1995   "More in U.S. are in prisons." *New York Times*, August 10, p. 14.
Cheek, F., and M. Miller
  1983   "The experience of stress for correction officers." *Journal of Criminal Justice*, 11(2), 105-112.
Clear, T., and G. Cole
  1997   *American Corrections*, 4th Ed. Belmont: Wadsworth.
Clements, C.
  1979   "Overcroded prisons: A review of psychological and environmental effects." *Law and Human Behavior*, 3(3), 217-225.
Collins, W.
  1990   *Correctional Law for the Correctional Officer*. Washington, DC: St. Mary's.
Crouch, B., and J. Marquart
  1996   "On becoming a prison guard." In M. Welch, *Corrections: A Critical Approach*. New York: McGraw-Hill.
Davis, R.
  1995   "Computer technology comes to aid of crime victims." *USA Today*, September 15, p. A9.
Foote, J., M. Seligman, S. Magura, and L. Handelsman
  1994   "An enhanced positive reinfiorcement model for the severly impaired cocaine abuser." *Journal of Substance Abuse Treatment*, 11(6), 525-539.
Hammett, T., and S. Moini
  1990   *Update on Aids in Prison and Jail*. Washington, DC: National Institute of Justice.
Holmes, T.
  1997   (Interview with Sheriff Tim Holmes of Russell County, Kansas), January.
Kansas Department of Corrections
  1994   *Larned Correctional Mental Health Facility Fact Sheet*. Topeka, KS: KDOC.
Martinson, R.
  1974   "What works? Questions and answers about prison reform." *Public Interest*, 35, 22-54.
Mathiesen, T.
  1990   *Prison on Trial*. London: Sage.

Mauer, M.
1992   "Lock 'Em Up is Not Key to Crime Control." *New York Newsday*, Feb. 11
Murphy, J.
1995   *Punishment and Rehabilitation*, 3rd Ed. Belmont: Wadsworth.
Petersilia, J.
1993   "Measuring the performance of community corrections." *Performance Measures for the Criminal Justice System, Bureau of Justice Statistics — Princeton University Study Group on Criminal Justice Performance Measures*, 61-84.
Plato
1995   "Punishment as healing for the soul." In J. Murphy (Ed.), *Punishment and Rehabilitation*. Belmont: Wadsworth. Pp. 8-13. [A reproduction of a dialogue entitled *Gorgias*, between Socrates and Polus, debating the merits of Plato's thought. The dialogue is undated, except for a reference to the fourth century B.C.]
Ramirez, A.
1994   "Privatizing America's prisons, slowly." *New York Times*, August 14.
Risley, H.
1997   (Discussion with Henry Risley, Deputy Secretary of the Kansas Department of Corrections). February.
Robinson, P.
1995   "Moral credibility and crime: Why people obey the law." *Current*, 6, 10-15.
Samaha, J.
1997   *Criminal Justice*, 4ed. St. Paul: West.
Schmidt, A.
1991   "Electronic monitors: Realistically, what can be expected?" *Federal Probation*, 6, 2, 47-53.
Schafer, N.
1986   "Jails and judicial review." In S. Stojkovic, J. Klofas, and D. Kalinich (Eds.), *The Administration and Management of Criminal Justice Organizations*. Prospect Heights: Waveland. Pp. 497-511.
Scott, R.
1996   "Treatment in Transition." In Debra Stanley (Chair), *Psychiatric Care and Corrections*. Meeting of the Academy of Criminal Justice Sciences, at Louisville, Kentucy, March.
Scott, R., and T. O'Connor
in press "A four year follow up to the development of a psychiatric in patient transitional correctional facility." *Journal of Contemporary Criminal Justice*.
Scott, R., and L. Allen
in press "Regimented inmate discipline: An analysis." *Inside Corrections*.
Souryal, S.
1997   "Romancing the stone or stoning the romance." In P. Cromwell and R. Dunham (Eds.), *Crime and Justice in America: Present Realities and Future Prospects*. Upper Saddle River, NJ: Prentice-Hall. Pp. 342-353.
Toch, H., and J. Klofas
1982   "Alienation and desire for job enrichment among correction officers." *Federal Probation*, 46, 35-44.
Welch, M.
1996   *Corrections: A Critical Approach*. New York: McGraw-Hill.
Wollan, L.
1994   "Punishment and prevention." *The World & I*, 4, 36-43.
Van Stelle, K., E. Mauser, and P. Moberg
1994   "Recidivism to the criminal justice system of substance abusing offenders diverted into treatment. *Crime and Delinquency*, 40(2), 175-196.

Chapter *12*

Delinquency and the Juvenile Justice System

By

Galan M. Janeksela

Delinquency can be defined in various ways depending upon one's orientation. From a psychologist's viewpoint, delinquency may be determined by motivation (i.e., intentional non-compliance with the dictates of constituted authority; Rogers 1972). Sociologically, delinquency may be defined as that behavior which is considered unacceptable by community norms. Legalistically, delinquency includes those offenses "committed by minors which may or may not be punishable if they are committed by adults" (Scarpitti 1974). Minors can be arrested for violations which apply to adults in the same jurisdiction; i.e., criminal law violations. In addition to the legal codes for adults, juveniles are subject to the jurisdiction of a set of laws which are age specific and are known as juvenile status offenses (e.g., habitual vagrancy, truancy, sexual promiscuity, incorrigibility, and behavior endangering the morals, health, or general welfare of the child). Juvenile status offenses provide the court with the opportunity to intervene in many non-criminal matters. Some states have an omnibus clause in the juvenile code which allow the court to intervene when the court deems it appropriate (usually based on the best interests of the child). The children who are apprehended under the juvenile status codes or the omnibus clause are, for the most part, viewed as delinquents by the community.

OFFICIAL AND UNOFFICIAL DELINQUENTS

An official delinquent is someone who has committed a delinquent act and was apprehended. Official delinquents are more likely to commit delinquency acts with greater frequency than unofficial delinquents. Also, frequent offenders are more likely to have a court record; i.e., the chances of being apprehended and formally processed through the juvenile justice system increase as one's law violating behavior increases in frequency and seriousness. Many other variables influence this process (e.g., police discretion, juvenile intake decisions, chance factors). However, it should be emphasized that those who are apprehended by the police are a minority, and those who end up in an institution represent a small percentage of those who appear in juvenile court.

An unofficial delinquent is someone who has committed a delinquent act without being arrested.

Self-report studies are useful because a large percentage of delinquent acts and the identities of children who committed them are unrecorded in the official records of the police and the courts. The frequency and nature of delinquency committed by adolescents, but for which no one is arrested, are important but unknown dimensions of delinquent behavior. The chances of being apprehended are not very good. In several studies, researchers have found that over 90 percent of those admitting that they had committed an offense were not apprehended.

THE NATURE OF DELINQUENT BEHAVIOR

Numerous self-report studies have found that over 85 percent of juveniles admit committing an act for which they could have been brought to court. However, many of the committed acts are relatively trivial (e.g., fighting, truancy, running away). When asked only about criminal acts committed, the percentage drops significantly. However, many juveniles commit both criminal offenses and juvenile status offenses during the same period of time; i.e., the juvenile does not choose to be a "status offender" or a "criminal offender" — he may be involved in both types of offenses during the same time period.

What are the characteristics of the typical delinquent? The literature suggests that the typical delinquent has the following characteristics: male, from a large city, a broken home, and suffers from social, cultural, and economic deprivation. Generally, the family is poverty stricken, has low social status, and lives in an unstable home. The juvenile has a history of truancy, poor adjustment, and non-achievement. The Office of Juvenile Justice and Delinquency Prevention (1996) has specified a number of research findings regarding juvenile crime which will help the student to better understand the nature of juvenile crime. These findings are as follows:

• Most juveniles have committed at least one delinquent act.

• Black juveniles are twice as likely as white juvenile to come in contact with law enforcement.

• Most juveniles who come in contact with the juvenile justice system do so only once.

• Juvenile offending is characterized by some specialization amidst a large amount of versatility.

• Serious offending increases as the delinquent ages and as the criminal career lengthens.

• A small number of juvenile offenders account for the majority of the juvenile crime (Wolfgang et al. found that six percent of the juvenile offenders committed over fifty percent of the crime).

• The probability of adult arrests increases with the number of juvenile arrests.

• Serious adult offenders are likely to have more serious juvenile careers than are non-serious adult offenders.

• Juvenile offending is less predictive of adult offending as an adult ages.

• There is a strong relationship between illegal gun ownership, delinquency and drug abuse.

• Gun possession is common for serious juvenile offenders and some inner-city high schools students.

• More than 4 in 10 serious juvenile offenders in 1993 reported illicit drug use.

• The majority of homicide victims ages 10 to 17 are killed by a friend or other acquaintance, and the majority of these victims were shot to death.

• Personal crimes involving a juvenile victim occurred most often in school or on school property.

• 15% of students reported that gangs existed in their schools.

• The recent growth in homicides involving juvenile offenders has surpassed the growth in homicides involving adult offenders.

• A growing number of juveniles kill in groups of two or more.

The most recent data on juvenile crimes, based on an analysis of unpublished arrest data, found the following: The arrest rates of juveniles for murder between 1984 and 1993 increased by 170 percent; the arrest rate of juveniles for murder between 1994-1995 decreased by 17 percent. The juvenile arrest rates for robbery declined during most of the years in the 1980's, but between 1988 and 1994 it increased by about 70 percent. Juvenile arrest rates for aggravated assault increased by more than 120 percent between 1983 and 1994, and then dropped by 5 percent in 1995. The juvenile arrest rates for weapons law violations followed a pattern similar to the pattern of murder rates described above. Juvenile arrest rates for drug abuse violations was relatively stable from 1980 through 1993, but then jumped by 50 percent by 1995. Between 1980 and 1995 juvenile arrest rates for property crimes remained relatively constant (within the category of property crimes, the specific types of property crimes had different trend patterns: Snyder 1997).

Note that the above findings are just a sample of the research relevant to juvenile crime. The challenge of the theoretician is to develop a theory that would explain all juvenile crime. Ideally, social scientists would like to explain all delinquent behavior with a given set of variables. However, there is little consensus on a definition of delinquency, and the research evidence in the area of delinquency is contradictory and inconclusive (Hirschi and Selvin 1973:15). Furthermore, delinquent behavior is so complex that no single theory has been developed which will explain all delinquency. Each theory of delinquency deals with some variables that have an effect on delinquent behavior. Therefore, a combination of concepts from different theoretical orientations may be needed to explain delinquency. It may be useful to consider how much effect each of several theories has on delinquency (Reynolds 1971:137). An additional consideration is that the word "cause" implies that certain factors precede delinquency and that these factors were the sole determinants of delinquency. In reality, it is often difficult to establish which occurs first — the delinquent behavior or the factors which are supposed to be the "causes" of delinquency. In addition, one can not unequivocally state that these factors are the sole causes of delinquency. There are many variables which may influence the development of a delinquent child, and these variables could be different for each category of delinquent behavior. There are factors which social scientists know about and there are other factors which social scientists may not know about. In short, a skeptic can always identify other variables which the social scientist did not include in his theory of delinquency.

QUESTIONS FOR STUDENT REFLECTION:

Could you have been brought to court for your behavior as a juvenile? What is your theory of delinquency? How does your theory of delinquency compare to the above description of the typical delinquent? Are there other variables which you think are important? Prioritize the five variables that you think are the most important determinants of delinquency?

Specific information about delinquency theory is provided in the next two sections: "Demographic Factors in the Etiology of Delinquency" and "Theories of Delinquency."

DEMOGRAPHIC FACTORS IN THE ETIOLOGY OF DELINQUENCY

Sex

"Crime and delinquency rates for males are greatly in excess of rates for females: in all nations, all communities within a nation, all age groups, all periods of history for which organized statistics are available, and for all types of crime except for a few which are peculiar to women, such as prostitution, infanticide, and abortion" (Cohen and Short 1971:108). Sex status is of greater significance in differentiating criminals from non-criminals than any other trait (Sutherland and Cressey 1970:126). This accounts for the formulation of lower-class-male-oriented theories of delinquent behavior (Miller 1958:5-19; Cohen 1955; Cloward and Ohlin 1960).

The over-representation of males in the official crime rate may reflect the more docile and dependent role played by females in society (Bloch and Flynn 1956:37; Sutherland and Cressey 1960:115). In addition, females are more supervised and sheltered from deviant influences (Clark and Haurek 1966:496-508; Marwell 1966:35-7). "From infancy, girls are taught that they must be nice, while boys are taught that they must be rough and tough; a boy who approaches the behavior of a girl is regarded as a sissy" (Sutherland and Cressey 1970:130). In addition, males have different life goals, different means, different socialization, and different attitudes than females (Coleman 1962).

One study found that there is a greater proportion of males involved in delinquency (in comparison to females), especially for those who admitted committing offenses four or more times (Clark and Haurek 1966:496-508). During the recent past, female crime has been on the increase. Snyder (1997) states that between 1991 and 1995, increases in arrests rates for juvenile females were higher than for juvenile males in most offense categories. This may be due to the increasing autonomy for females which has resulted from the changing role of females within society. In general, social norms governing female behavior have become less restrictive and many women are expressing themselves in legitimate and illegitimate achievements.

Age

Different age groups have different arrest rates. Differential involvement of juveniles in delinquent behavior by age can be explained by the dissimilarity of roles prescribed for persons who occupy different age statuses. "An elementa-

ry knowledge of American cultural definitions of adult and child roles obviously leads to anticipated differential rates of behavior for age groupings" (Clark and Haurek 1966:501).

Adolescent age groups are more likely to display differential rates of behavior because it is a period of transition from childhood to adulthood. During this time the adolescent is most deviant (Neumeyer 1961; Sutherland Cressey 1960:108). The idea that older adolescents are more involved in criminal behavior is verified by official statistics which show that older juveniles (15-18 age group) have higher arrest rates than any other age group. In 1995, violent crime arrests peaked at age 18 and property crime arrests peaked at age 16 (Snyder 1997). However, the statistics also show that kids are becoming involved at younger and younger ages.

It can be argued that juvenile crime statistics may reflect the following factors: a growing discontent among youth; feelings of hopelessness; powerlessness; frustration about the lack of opportunity to achieve; and, estrangement from society. This discontent may be rooted in the nature of contemporary society, societal focus on material things, the decline of family control over juveniles, and increased social mobility resulting in the impersonal nature of social relationships. Other factors contributing to the discontent include increased juvenile autonomy resulting from the decline of the familial institution, and the increased access to money and automobiles

Race

In a longitudinal study of 9,945 boys in Philadelphia, the researchers found that race and socioeconomic standing were most strongly related to delinquency (Wolfgang, Figlio and Sellin 1972). A study by Monahan found that age for age, black rates exceeded white rates in 1923, 1941, 1949, and 1957 (Monahan 1960:387-97). Merton (1938: 146) states that rates of deviant behavior within a society vary by social class and by racial and ethnic groups.

Blacks comprised one-tenth of the population in 1967; however, blacks constituted nearly one-third of all persons arrested in that year (Wolfgang and Cohen 1970:31). In 1995, blacks are over-represented in the arrest statistics, and several studies have found that the "actual crime rate" of blacks is higher than for whites. In 1995, 80 percent of the juveniles in the U.S. were white (Hispanic ethnicity was included within the white category), and 15 percent were black. However, approximately half of the violent crimes committed by juveniles were committed by whites, and half by blacks (Snyder 1997). Different authors have accounted for this phenomenon in different ways. The social position of blacks may account for the over-representation of blacks in the crime statistics. The culture of the black community may be in conflict with the culture of the white community. Discrimination by the criminal justice system may also account for the over-representation of blacks in the official statistics. A study by Wolfgang et al. (1972) found that after the police take an adolescent into custody, he is most likely to be processed if he is non-white and poor. In another study, it was found that black youths were more often approached by the police because blacks were stereotyped as potential troublemakers. "In conjunction with police crime statistics, the criterion of demeanor led police to concentrate their surveillance activities in areas frequented or inhabited by Negroes. The consequences of this is reflected in police statistics showing a disproportionally high percentage of Negroes among juvenile offenders, thereby providing 'objective' justification for concentrating police attention on Negro youths" (Piliavin and Briar 1964:33).

Socioeconomic Standing

Theories of lower-class delinquency rest heavily on evidence from official sources (Gold 1966). The problem is that official records do not accurately reflect the distribution of delinquency by social class, race, age, sex, and other variables (Gould 1966; Williams and Gold 1972). Official records may exaggerate the differences in delinquency among different social classes (Gold 1966).

Self-report studies which draw their data from subjects in the public school system have shown that delinquency cuts across all social levels (Short and Nye 1958; Dentler and Monroe 1961). Gold (1966) found that the official ratio of lower-class delinquents to higher-class delinquents was reduced when a self-report instrument was used. The visibility and economic harm of lower-class crime may solicit more comprehensive surveillance by law enforcement. The negative consequence of this processing is a push toward serious delinquency. Therefore, one would expect lower classes to be involved in more serious delinquency than other social classes. There is evidence to support this notion.

A self-report study found that lower-class boys were more frequently delinquent and committed more serious offenses (Gold 1966). For those committing the most serious offenses, lower-class boys reported almost four times as many offenses as did middle- and upper-class boys.

THEORIES OF DELINQUENCY

Ecological Theory

According to Shaw and McKay, the most significant factor is the part of the city in which one is living. This is confirmed by an extensive study of four different nationalities (Germans, Irish, Poles, and Italians). For each of these four nationalities, Shaw and McKay found that delinquency rates were highest in the center of the city and lowest on the outskirts. Similarly, in a study of black delinquency, McKay found that delinquency rates for blacks decreased as one moved from the center of the city outward.

In areas of similar economic status, the differences between whites and blacks is markedly reduced. This implies that the difference in delinquency rates for whites versus blacks may be due to the greater concentration of blacks in the slum areas. The major conclusions from Shaw's research were as follows: There were marked variations by residential area in the rates of truancy, delinquency, and adult crime. These rates tended to vary inversely according to the distance from the center of the city. Those nearest the center had the highest rates while those furthest from the center had the lowest rates. Also, the highest rates were found in areas characterized by physical deterioration and high population density (President's Commission on Law Enforcement and the Administration of Justice, 1967A:57).

Family Environment Theory

The family environment orientation focuses on the social structure of the family, the nature of family relationships, and the implications for criminal and delinquent behavior. "The family institution provides the child with his first experiences in social living, and these experiences have an effect on most of his later development" (Trojanowicz 1973:62). The family environment can have a significant impact on how the child behaves in other social institutions and on whether or not he becomes defined as normal or delinquent.

Difficulties which can lead to delinquent behavior may arise from faults in the roles played by members of the family, from the nature of the interrelationships between family members, and from the social structure of the family.

Psychologists believe that early emotional deprivation is directly associated with later psychological disturbances and emotional problems. The family should provide the child with love, security, and a protective shelter from outside pressures (Aichhorn 1969).

Early familial experiences lay the framework for the child's future behavior and the development of the child's attitudes, values, and life-style. If the family does not help the child to adjust to his social environment, the child does not receive the most important means of psychological support; i.e., the most effective agent for socialization is without effect.

Parent hostility, affection, and inconsistent punishment patterns can all contribute to delinquent behavior (Berman 1964). Those families which have one or more delinquent youngsters are often characterized by some type of pathology (Aichorn 1969). The following characteristics are some possible pathologies which may exist in such a family: open hostility, shallow relationships between family members, a lack of concern by parents for their children, absence of a role model with whom the youngster can identify (Berman 1964). When parents fail to transmit positive community norms and values and when they fail as positive identification models, the children may come in conflict with community institutions.

While psychology emphasizes the process of personal or internal control that is represented by the conscience, sociology emphasizes the institutions that directly influence the external social control processes. The psychological and sociological approaches are complimentary, and both can enhance the understanding of delinquency (Trojanowicz 1973). Delinquent behavior can be viewed as the result of that situation where both personal and social controls have failed.

> Delinquency results when there is a relative absence of internalized norms and rules governing behavior in conformity with the norms of the social system to which legal penalties are attached, a breakdown in previously established controls, and/or a relative absence of a conflict in social rules or institutions of which the person is a member. Hence, delinquency may be seen as a function or consequence of the relationship established among the personal and social controls (Reiss 1951:196).

When community institutions of social control are ineffective, delinquency and crime are more prevalent. When internal personal control is ineffective, delinquency and crime are more prevalent. When a lack of internal control is combined with a lack of social control, it is likely that crime or delinquent behavior will result. The family can influence the development of the internal control structure, and it can have an effect on the external control social process by its methods of direct control and discipline.

256

Community institutions of control may intervene when the family has been unsuccessful in controlling the individual's behavior. If the parents are not adequate role models, if the parents do not facilitate the development of a child's conscience, and/or if their methods of discipline are not effective, then community social control mechanisms will address the problem behavior.

Lower-Class Culture Theory

"Unpleasant family experiences are more likely to produce delinquency in circumstances where there is an alternative cultural pattern that is favorable to the violation of law" (Stanfield 1966: 414). Miller's lower-class culture theory is based on the following premise: The probability of encountering a cultural pattern outside the family that supports behavior that violates the law is high for those boys from low socioeconomic status families. These boys are more likely to come in contact with a delinquency supporting culture. Delinquency results from learning a pattern of culture that supports the violation of law. The lower-class culture can be viewed as a milieu which generates for delinquency (Miller 1958).

The male adolescent peer group provides the training milieu in which lower-class males seek a sense of maleness, status, and belonging. Lower-class membership automatically puts youth in a situation that contains a variety of direct influences toward conduct which is defined as deviant by society (Miller 1958). The motivation underlying legal violations is the desire to conform to the value standards as defined by the lower-class community. The lower-class culture has a specific set of focal concerns which may differ from the American middle-class standards (Miller 1958). Therefore, deviance may result from conforming to different standards than those which are upheld by the those who define deviance (e.g., legislature, city govern-ment).

Each socio-economic class has unique values and norms, which has the potential for conflict between social classes. The class in power defines deviations from its norms and values as unacceptable and the other classes are the "bearers" of these definitions. The "bearers" may not accept the norms and values of the power group as guides to their behavior. Therefore, the extent of crime in the various social classes may be a function of how each social class defines crime. For example, Gold (1967) found that higher classes defined trivial behavior (such as name scratching on desks) as being a crime while lower classes did not. The extent of self-reported crime may be influenced by different opinions of what constitutes criminal or delinquent behavior.

Differential Association Theory

Sutherland's theory of differential association focuses on the learning of attitudes and behavior from those who are already delinquent or criminal. "...[T]his theory is probably one of the most systematic and complete theories of delinquency causation that has yet been constructed" (Trojanowicz 1973:38). According to differential association theory, criminal behavior is learned in interaction with other persons in the process of communication. The principal part of this learning occurs within intimate personal groups. The learning of criminal behavior includes the techniques for committing the crime and the specific direction of motives, drives, rationalizations, and attitudes that are consistent with criminal behavior. The specific directions are learned from definitions of legal codes as favorable and unfavorable.

The process of learning criminal behavior by association of criminal and anti-criminal patterns involves all of the mechanisms that are involved in any other learning. The child is exposed to both criminal and non-criminal patterns of behavior. Delinquent behavior is predictable if there is an excess of definitions which are favorable to the violation of laws versus those definitions which are unfavorable to the violation of laws. If a juvenile associates mostly with delinquent youths, chances are greater that he will become involved in delinquent behavior. Conversely, if a juvenile associates mostly with non-delinquent youths, chances are greater that he will not become involved in delinquent behavior. The quality and quantity of an individual's associations are defined by the frequency, duration, priority, and intensity of such relationships. Involvement in delinquent behavior is more likely if an individual has many contacts with criminals over a long period of time, and if those contacts are important to him as well as intense (Sutherland and Cressey 1970).

Differential Opportunity Theory

Cloward and Ohlin's theory of differential opportunity focuses on the strains which affect lower-class individuals and the alternative means of adapting to these strains. The United States culture stresses equality for all participants. However, our society does not allow all groups to have equal access to institutionalized means to achieve goals, and strains may result. Within every society there are: cultural goals which are learned during socialization; the norms for achieving the goals; and, the institutionalized means that are available for goal achievement. Social structure consists of the patterned sets of human relationships which determine the actual distribution of the opportunities for achieving cultural goals (Merton 1938).

The work ethic states that everyone can achieve their goals if they are diligent. However, the promise of equal opportunities is denied in reality. Subjective reaction to this situation can take a variety of forms, one of which is alienation. Alienation is a process of withdrawal of allegiance to the legitimacy of established social norms. A common source of alienation from established social norms is failure, or the anticipation of failure, in achieving success-goals by socially approved means. Lower-class males often find themselves at a competitive disadvantage in gaining access to legitimate routes to success-goals (Cloward and Ohlin 1960). The competitive disadvantages relate to the different cultural experiences which lead to achievement of conventional goals. Lower-class cultural experiences may place limits on a juvenile's life chances in a social structure which stresses middle-class goals. The result may be an intense sense of frustration that may alienate some youth from conventional rules and expectations.

Faced with a situation of unfulfilled aspirations and blocked opportunity, many lower-class youth turn to illegitimate means which might offer a possible route to middle-class goals (Cloward and Ohlin 1960). Lower-class youth can be viewed as victims of a contradiction between the goals toward which they have been taught to strive, and the socially structured means of striving for these goals. In this situation, there is a definite pressure toward deviant behavior (Merton 1957). The means of achieving success goals are not as readily available to lower-class youth; therefore, deviant adaptions are more likely in the lower classes (Marsh 1961).

Labeling Theory

Labeling theory focuses on the impact of social control mechanisms on the individual. Although social control is necessary, inappropriate or insensitive control mechanisms may intensify those behaviors which the mechanisms are designed to control. Regardless of the outcome of a formal contact with the system, other people may define the individual as a permanent deviant. Formal sanctioning can alienate the juvenile from the system by exposing him to alienated people, exposing him to impersonal criminal justice processes, and allowing him to learn neutralization techniques, skills, attitudes, and values from hardened criminals. Therefore, official contact with social control agencies for minor deviations may be harmful to the individual's self-concept, his reputation, and his attitudes toward the system and its controlling agents.

Gibbons (1973) has stated that "one of the major factors that may drive juveniles toward delinquency as a systematic role is the extent to which community organizations have defined the individual as a delinquent and a bad boy." Lemert (1971) has suggested that agency contacts may be of major significance in this process, and the police department is the agency which is most likely to have contact with juveniles. Formal sanctioning can be viewed as a stigmatization and criminalization process in that the individual is identified to society and to himself as being deviant. If an individual is frequently involved in delinquent behavior, then it is more likely that he will be observed and/or apprehended; and, as apprehension increases, the probability of formal sanctioning increases. The process is circular. The formally sanctioned individual is subjected to negative contact with the juvenile justice system, and he is identified to himself and the community as a deviant. The affects on self-concept can decrease an individual's motivation to achieve prescribed cultural goals, and stigmatization by the community can decrease the individual's opportunity to function as a normal member of society.

QUESTIONS FOR STUDENT REFLECTION

The above theories have a long standing presence in the field of criminology. However, no one theory has "proven" to explain all delinquency. Therefore, the criminologist must decide which theory is most credible, or which combination of theories explains the greatest percentage of delinquent behavior. In your view, which theory is most credible? Which types of juvenile criminal behavior does this theory "best" explain?

EARLY HISTORY OF JUVENILE JUSTICE

In the early development of law, the treatment of juvenile delinquents depended solely on their age. Children under seven were viewed as incapable of forming the intent necessary to commit a crime. Children between seven and fourteen years of age were only presumptively incapable of forming the requisite intent. Those over fourteen were treated as adults.

The English concept of *parens patriae* provided the basis of the American system of juvenile

justice; i.e., when the parents fail, the king is the father who "determines the family rules, budget limitations, family activities, and the disciplinary action for violation of family rules" (Coffey 1974:35).

The development of the juvenile court had its origin in the parental responsibility that the king, as representative of the state, took in matters of juvenile misconduct. In the middle of the nineteenth century, courts began to consider a child's relationships with his family and society. Thus, the courts shifted from merely punishing a child to trying to help and protect him from the destructive influences in his life. If the parents of a child defaulted in performing their responsibilities of the child, the state intervened on the basis of *parens patriae*. The proceedings involved were civil (rather than criminal); the state was providing the protection to which the child was entitled. The earliest effort to administratively assist the king in his role as parent of the country was the Court of Chancery (also known as the Equity Court) which handled a variety of problems including dependent children. Although the Chancery Court did not completely separate adults from juveniles, it did forward the concept of individualized justice which served as the basis for a distinction between adults and juveniles.

The transfer of the English Chancery Court to American juvenile justice was quite swift. In 1861, the criminal court processes of Chicago began separating children from adults. In Massachusetts, a 1869 law established a position for a person to represent children under sixteen in criminal court. In 1870, 1872, and 1877, Massachusetts passed other laws which established special trials for children's cases. Also, in 1870, the State of New York passed a law prohibiting the confinement of children with adult offenders. In 1893, the State of Indiana established the principle of "petitioning the court on behalf of the child." This law allowed the court an alternative to the criminal court complaint for children who were neglected or delinquent. Furthermore, this law called for placement with the Board of Children's Guardians (rather than prison) if the child was found to be neglected or delinquent. It is very likely that this law was based on the above described New York law of 1870 which called for separation of adult and juvenile offenders. Prior to 1899, juveniles who violated the law were treated as adults who violated the law. Juveniles who were arrested were allowed to post bail. If they could not post bail, they were jailed. Juvenile offenders were indicted, tried, and disposed of in a manner similar to adult offenders (Coffey 1974:35-36).

THE JUVENILE COURT MOVEMENT IN THE UNITED STATES

In the 1800's, the Child Savers, a reform group in Illinois, played an aggressive role in the development of laws which control the behavior of juveniles.

The Child Savers were stimulated by the problems associated with rapid industrialization and urbanization, the influence of environmental factors on behavior, claimed by social sciences that they could treat the problems which lead to deviance, and the inhumane conditions under which children were incarcerated. The philosophy behind the reform movement was that the child who broke the law should be handled by the state in a way that a wise parent would deal with his wayward child (Platt 1969).

Platt argued that the child savers should not be considered libertarians or humanists for the following reasons: their reforms did not herald a new system of justice, but rather expedited traditional policies which had been informally developing during the nineteenth century; they implicitly assumed the "natural" dependence of adolescents and created a special court to impose sanctions on premature independence and behavior unbecoming to youth; their attitudes toward "delinquent" youth were largely paternalistic and romantic, but their commands were backed up by force (they trusted in the benevolence of government and similarly assumed a harmony of interest between "delinquents" and agencies of social control); and, they promoted correctional programs requiring longer terms of imprisonment, long hours of labor and militaristic discipline, and the inculcation of middle-class values and lower-class skills (Johnson 1975). The juvenile court was created in the name of social duty, and it was not based on a sound philosophical scheme. There was a lack of a set:

...of systematized generalities that any philosophy must entail. If any juvenile court philosophy is to develop, therefore, it must be in jurisprudential terms — as a matter of the meaning of justice in the context of childhood. Inquiry must be made, for example, if the interrelationships between formality and compassion, between the judicial concepts of responsibility and equality. Since the juvenile court process is so heavily infused with concepts from the social sciences, the role of science in legal affairs is an essential conceptual component of a new philosophy (Fox 1971:63-64).

In 1899, Illinois established the first statewide juvenile court system. This legislation entitled "An Act to Regulate the Treatment and Control of Dependent, Neglected and Delinquent Children" was passed into law due, in part, to the efforts of the Child Savers. The act placed all children who came in contact with the courts under one jurisdiction; i.e., the court had control over dependent, neglected, and delinquent children. Under this act, the first Juvenile Court of Illinois was established in Cook County, which includes Chicago. Children under the age of sixteen, who were alleged to be delinquent, fell under the jurisdiction of the juvenile court.

Juvenile courts were created by legislatures as courts of limited jurisdiction. The goals of the juvenile courts were as follows: Correction and protection of the delinquent child...

...in order to make good citizens of potentially bad ones. In the case of the dependent or neglected child, the purpose is to provide protective services including placement of the child in an approved family or other surrounding where the child receives as nearly as possible the care his natural parents should have given him. It was envisioned that the juvenile court setting would be informal, that the proceedings were to be non-criminal in nature and that a wise and humane judge would act as a substitute parent prescribing and applying individual treatment which best would meet the needs of both the child and society (Stevenson 1973).

The juvenile court was to have the following attributes: a judge designated to handle juvenile cases; the record keeping function would be separate from adult records; the records would be confidential; the juvenile court would have a less formalized procedure than the adult court; and, the juvenile courtroom would be separate from the courtroom where adults were tried. In the eyes of the juvenile court, the delinquent child had ceased to be viewed as a criminal. He/she was redefined as a child in need of care, protection, and discipline directed toward rehabilitation. The procedures did not involve the machinery of due process to the extent found in criminal courts, and the powers of the court included punishment for violation of specific laws, and the responsibility for determining if a child is immoral, wayward, in need of supervision, incorrigible, or in an unfit home. "The problem for determination by the judge is not, has this boy or girl committed a specific wrong, but what is he, how has he become what he is, and what had best be done in his interest and in the interest of the state to save him from a downward career" (Mack 1909). The most significant distinction between adult crime and juvenile delinquency was the initial philosophical distinction between responsibility and accountability. This distinction is illustrated in the following example.

Imagine a state in which the deliberate setting of a fire in a residence is a felony — an arson seen as a serious crime punishable by many years in a state prison. Further, imagine that the state laws correspond to the federal law granting the eighteen-year-old the right to vote; that is, the state law defines as an "adult" one who is at least eighteen years old. Imagine that juveniles are defined as any person seventeen years or younger — meaning that in no case can a person under 18 be an adult criminal (Coffey 1974:2).

Given these factors, consider the following two cases of felonious arson: An eighteen-year-old is arrested, tried, and convicted for burning down a neighbor's house; a seventeen-year-old is arrested, brought before the juvenile court, and declared a ward of the court for burning down a neighbor's house (Coffey 1974:2-3). Throughout most of the history of the juvenile court in the U.S., these cases would be handled as follows: In the adult system, the adult would be held accountable and responsible; in the juvenile system, the juvenile would be held accountable, but not responsible. During the past two decades, the juvenile system has moved in the direction of the crime-control model which results in holding juveniles both responsible and accountable for their behavior.

The original Illinois statute gave the new Cook County Juvenile Court jurisdiction over all dependent, neglected, and delinquent children between 12 and 16 years of age. With the realization that many of the children it wished to help were not involved in crime, but instead were incorrigible. Six amendments, which passed in 1901, expanded the definition of delinquency to include status offenses, such as frequenting gambling establishments, incorrigibility, growing up in idleness, running away from home, loitering, and using profanity. These status offenses exposed minors to the same actions by the juvenile court as children engaging in criminal behavior.

The goal and hallmark of the juvenile court was to promote the rehabilitation of juvenile offenders and help them become useful, respectable citizens. Toward this end, a separate judge was appointed with the exclusive responsibility of handling children's cases, and the court was authorized to hire probation officers to carry out its child-saving efforts.

Hearing facilities were to be separately located from the adult courthouse, and the physical surroundings were less severe and imposing. By sitting at a desk or table instead of behind an elevated bench, the juvenile court judge could convey a paternal and sympathetic image of concern that was firm and authoritative at same time. The Illinois state-wide juvenile court system contained most of the features which characterized the ideology and administration of juvenile justice until the mid 1960's. In the 1960's the landscape of juvenile justice began to change.

261

LANDMARK U.S. SUPREME COURT DECISIONS IN JUVENILE JUSTICE

Several decisions by the United States Supreme Court have defined the requirements of due process for juveniles: Gallegos v. Colorado; Kent v. United States; In Re Gault; In Re Winship; Breed v. Jones; and McKiever v. Pennsylvania. The case of Gallegos v. Colorado, 370 U.S. 491 (1962), involving a criminal prosecution of a minor, demonstrated that the juvenile offender would have to be dealt with in a special way. The Supreme Court of Colorado affirmed the conviction of a fourteen year old accused of murder resulting from a robbery. The juvenile was arrested shortly after the crime and confessed. After being kept by the police for five days, a formal statement was taken from him in which he freely admitted that he was not physically coerced, intensively questioned, or psychologically threatened. The United States Supreme Court, in reversing this conviction, stated the following:

The prosecution says the boy was advised of his right to counsel, but that he did not ask either for a lawyer or his parents. But a fourteen year old boy, no matter how sophisticated, is unlikely to have any conception of what will confront him when he is made accessible only to the police. That is to say, we deal with a person who is not equal in knowledge or understanding of the consequences of the questions and answers being recorded and who is unable to know how to protect his own interest or how to get the benefits of his Constitutional rights. The prosecution says that the youth and immaturity of the petitioner and the five-day detention are irrelevant, because the basic ingredients of the confession came tumbling out as soon as he was arrested. But if we took that position it would with all deference be in callous disregard of the boy's Constitutional rights. He cannot be compared with an adult in full possession of his senses and knowledgeable of the consequences of his admissions. He would have no way of knowing what the consequences of his confession were without advice as to his rights — from someone concerned with securing him those rights — and without the aid of more mature judgment as to the steps he should take in the predicament in which he found himself. A lawyer or an adult relative or friend would have given the petitioner the protection which his own immaturity could not. Adult advice would have put him on a less unequal footing with his interrogators. Without some adult protection against this inequality, a fourteen year old boy would not be able to know, let alone assert, such Constitutional rights as he had. To allow this conviction to stand, would in effect, be to treat him as if he had no Constitutional rights.

Kent v. United States, 383 U.S. 541 (1966), involved the transfer of a case from juvenile court to criminal court so that the youngster could be prosecuted as an adult. The U.S. Supreme Court decided that "the basic requirements of due process and fairness" must be met in all important actions determining vitally important statutory rights of the juvenile. The Court concluded that as a condition to a valid waiver order, the juvenile was entitled to the following: a hearing; representation by legal counsel; access by his counsel to the social records and probation or similar reports which are presumably considered by the court; and, access by his counsel to a statement of the reasons for the juvenile court's decision. This statement of reasons allows the judge's decision to be reviewed. Prior to transferring cases, a hearing must be held and counsel for the juvenile must have an opportunity to examine and present witnesses. Furthermore, the judge must state his reasons for transferring the case to adult court.

The court listed eight factors to consider in making the decision to transfer the case to adult court, as follows: seriousness of the offense; was it an aggressive act; was it an act against person or property; sophistication and maturity of offender; history of the offender; likelihood of reasonable rehabilitation; desirability of one trial for joint offenders when some are adults and some are juveniles; and, weight and stature of cases in terms of prosecutorial worth.

In the Kent case Justice Fortas stated, "There is evidence...that there may be grounds for concern that the child receives the worst of both worlds: That he gets neither the protections accorded to adults nor the solicitous care and regenerative treatment postulated for children."

RELATED ISSUES:

Several issues are raised by the Kent decision: How does one know if the juvenile is amenable if he has not been through the juvenile system? Will the juvenile be amenable within the time period that he is under the juvenile systems jurisdiction? Who will determine the jurisdiction? How does the Kent decision relate to the concept of concurrent jurisdiction over a juvenile? For example, in Nebraska, 16-18 year-old's are under concurrent jurisdiction of the juvenile and adult courts.

The case of In re Gault, 387 U.S. 1 (1967), focused on the clarification of the constitutional rights of juveniles. The events of the case are delineated in this paragraph. On June 8, 1964, Gerald Gault and another youth were taken into custody by the sheriff of Gila County, Arizona. Gerald Gault, who was on juvenile court probation at the time, was immediately placed in a detention home; at the time of the arrest, Gault's parents were both at work, and they were not notified of their son's custody or detention. Mrs. Cook, a neighbor of the boys, reported to the police that she had received an obscene telephone call.

On June 9, 1964, an adjudication hearing was held in the Chambers of Juvenile Court Judge McGhee. The complainant, Mrs. Cook, was not present; no one presented sworn testimony; no transcript, recording, or formal record of what transpired was prepared; no memorandum or record of the proceedings was prepared. Neither Gault nor his parents were informed that he had a right to remain silent and a right to counsel. At the hearing, the probation officer filed a petition in juvenile court; the petition contained no specific charges. The petition stated that "said minor is under the age of 18 years and in need of protection of this Honorable Court [and that] said minor is a delinquent minor" The petition was never served on the Gaults; they saw the petition for the first time two months later. The hearing was continued on June 15, 1964.

Mrs. Gault had requested that the complainant be present at the hearing "so she could see which boy done the talking, the dirty talking over the phone." The juvenile court judge replied that Mrs. Cook "didn't have to be present," and she was not present for the hearing. The judge had not communicated with Mrs. Cook at any time up to that point, and the probation officer had only spoken to the complainant once by phone. A referral report prepared by the probation officer and filed with the court stated that the charge against Gerald Gault was "lewd phone calls." Although the report was formally filed with the court, this information was not disclosed to Gault or his parents.

At the June 15 hearing, the judge committed 15-year-old Gerald Gault to the State Industrial School "for the period of his minority [until 21], unless sooner discharged by due process of law." The judge's order stated that "after a full hearing and due deliberation, the Court finds that said minor is a delinquent child."

The Supreme Court held that the child and his parents or guardian had: a right to be notified in writing of the specific charge or factual allegations sufficiently in advance to the hearing to permit preparation, a right to counsel, a right to confrontation and cross-examination of witnesses, and a privilege against self-incrimination. In the course of his opinion, Justice Fortas quoted Justice Frankfurter as follows: "The history of American freedom is, in no small measure, the history of procedure." Justice Fortas went on to state the following:

But, in addition, the procedural rules which have been fashioned from the generality of due process are our best instruments for the distillation and evaluation of essential facts from the conflicting welter of data that life and our adversary methods present. It is these instruments of due process which enhance the possibility that truth will emerge from a confrontation of opposing versions and conflicting data. Procedure is to law what scientific method is to science.

As a result of the Gault decision, the juvenile can no longer be deprived of his basic rights by adherence to a *parens patriae* philosophy.

RELATED ISSUE:

In some states, juveniles who commit status offenses do not have the right against self-incrimination. Delinquents have this right as a result of the Gault decision. However, status offenders do have a number of other rights which delinquents have: the right to adequate notice of the specific charges, the right to a hearing, and the right to have hearsay testimony excluded from evidence.

In Re Winship (1970) held that a finding of delinquency by the court must be based on proof beyond a reasonable doubt that the juvenile committed the act for which he is accused. This decision places emphasis on the attainment of evidence for the prosecution of juveniles, thereby pushing the juvenile system in the direction of the criminal system where the emphasis is on the determination of guilt or innocence. The implications for the police are evident; e.g., investigate thoroughly, do not base a case on an invalid confession, and do not violate the juvenile's rights.

In 1975 the U.S. Supreme Court, in Breed v. Jones, held that juveniles are entitled to the protection of the Fifth Amendment double jeopardy prohibition. The above five decisions have provided the foundation for a new due process era in juvenile justice. One decision that indicated that there is still a distinction between adults and juveniles was the McKiever vs. Pennsylvania case in which the Supreme Court ruled that juveniles did not have a constitutional right to a trial by jury; however, the court did not prohibit the states from establishing jury trials for juveniles.

THE 1974 JUVENILE JUSTICE AND DELINQUENCY PREVENTION ACT

Relevant to its constitutional role to "establish justice and ensure domestic tranquility," Congress passed the Juvenile Justice and Delinquency Prevention (JJDP) Act in 1974 with strong support from both political parties. This Act created the Office of Juvenile Justice and Delinquency Prevention, and it included a method for assuring state and local participation in designing programs for preventing and controlling delinquent behavior. Tragic stories, combined with compelling statistics on confinement of status offenders, provided the impetus for Congress to enact the Act, as amended, requiring the deinstitutionalization of status offenders and separation of juvenile and adult offenders in institutional settings.

Bobby Nestor was sent to Camp Hill Correctional Facility, an adult prison, to "learn a lesson." Following four and one-half months of incarceration, he hung himself after being sexually assaulted by adult inmates. Bobby Nestor was sent to Camp Hill for incorrigibility (Office of Juvenile Justice and Delinquency Prevention, 1995).

The Act has been repeatedly re-authorized with consistent bipartisan political support. The Act codifies the congressional evolving view of the key issues in juvenile justice, and it reflects congressional awareness of the differences between managing juvenile and adult offenders. The act expresses congressional belief in the key role of prevention and early intervention in controlling juvenile crime and violence. The Act also addresses the need for national standards for the administration of juvenile justice; participating states currently undertake to meet five standards as follows:

The first three standards are based on research which documented the negative impact of exposing non-violent juveniles to more serious delinquents or adult offenders; the fourth standard identified the non-secure custody guidelines to be used when juveniles are in the custody of the system; the fifth standard addresses the apparent over-representation of minority youth in the juvenile justice system. The standards are as follows:

1. Deinstitutionalization of Status Offenders. The deinstitutionalization of status offenders (DSO) requirement provides, as a general rule, that no status offender or non-offender may be held in secure detention or confinement. The Formula Grants Program regulation issued by OJJDP (Office of Juvenile Justice and Delinquency Prevention), creates a temporary-hold exception for accused status offenders and non-offenders in juvenile detention centers. Status offenders or non-offenders may be held for up to 24 hours, excluding weekends and holidays, for purposes of identification, investigation, release to parents, or transfer to a non-secure program or to court. The 24-hour exception applies only to accused status offenders and non-offenders. It begins when the juvenile enters a secure custody status in a detention facility. A second 24-hour "grace period" may follow an initial court appearance. Another statutory exception, for "valid court orders," provides that a status offender accused of violating such an order may be held in a juvenile detention facility longer than 24 hours. In order for a state to invoke this exception, the juvenile must have received all constitutional due-process protections at the initial adjudication and must be afforded a detention hearing within 24 hours. In addition, prior to a dispositional commitment to secure placement, a public agency (other than a court or law enforcement agency) must have reviewed the juvenile's behavior and possible alternatives to secure placement, and submitted a written report to court.

2. Separation. The separation requirement provides that juveniles shall not be detained or confined in a secure institution in which they have contact with incarcerated adults, including inmate trustees. This requires complete separation such that there is no sight and sound contact with adult offenders in the facility. Separation must be provided in all secure areas of the facility.

3. Jail and Lockup Removal. The jail and lockup requirement states that all juveniles who may be subject to the original jurisdiction of the juvenile court (based on age and offense limitations established by state law) cannot be held in jails and law enforcement lockups in which adults may be detained or confined. The OJJDP Formula Grants Program regulation provides a six-hour hold exception for accused delinquent offenders, for the limited purposes of identification, processing, interrogation, transfer to a juvenile facility or court, or to detain pending release to parents. The exception does not apply to status offenders, non-offenders, or adjudicated delinquents. Sight and sound separation from incarcerated adults during the six hours is required. The statute and regulation provide a "rural exception" for jails and lockups located outside a Standard Metropolitan Statistical Area (SMSA). Facilities outside an SMSA may hold an accused delinquent for up to 24 hours, excluding weekends and holidays, while awaiting an initial court appearance, if state law requires such a detention hearing within 24 hours, and provided no existing alternative facility is available. If weather or road conditions do not allow for reasonably safe travel, the facility may detain the juvenile until conditions allow for safe travel, up to an additional 24-hour period. If conditions of distance or lack of highway, road or other ground transportation do not allow for a court appearance within 24 hours, a brief (not to exceed 48 hours) delay is authorized. Again, separation from adult offenders must be maintained at all times. A final regulatory exception concerns juveniles under the jurisdiction of a criminal court for a felony offense. It applies only after such jurisdiction has been invoked through the official filing of criminal felony charges in a direct file situation, or after a juvenile has been officially waived to criminal court through a judicial waiver process.

4. Non-Secure Custody Criteria. To accommodate the needs of law enforcement, OJJDP policy guidance allows juveniles, including criminal-type offenders, status offenders, and non-offenders to be held non-securely in an adult jail or lockup facility. The OJJDP policy establishes "non-secure custody criteria" to guide law enforcement officers in providing non-secure custody for juveniles in their custody. The criteria include the following: holding the juvenile in an unlocked multi-purpose area not normally used as a secure area, or if it is a secure area, used only for processing purposes; the juvenile is not physically secured to a stationary object; the use of the area is limited to providing non-secure custody only long enough and for the purposes of identification, processing, release to parents, or arranging transfer to an appropriate juvenile facility or court; the area is not designed or intended for residential purposes; and, continuous visual supervision is provided by a law enforcement officer or facility staff during the period of non-secure custody.

5. Disproportionate Minority Confinement. The disproportionate minority confinement requires states to address efforts to reduce the number of minority youth in secure facilities where the proportion of minority youth in confinement exceeds the proportion such groups represent in the general population (OJJDP 1996).

The JJDP Act anticipated a future which had a reduced role for the Federal government in developing programs to meet the needs of local communities, and recognized the importance of state initiatives for solving local and state problems. Congress constructed the block grant program to be administered by State Advisory Groups (SAGs) which were gubernatorially appointed boards representing professionals and volunteers interested in or working in the juvenile justice field. The more than 1000 local volunteer leaders that constitute the State Advisory Groups represent a broad spectrum of political and philosophical views, thus creating a cross-section of the views of the general public. The State Advisory Groups provided for a local investment in the fight against youth crime and violence, and insured local input in identifying the needs of communities and in developing strategies to meet the specific needs of each community and each state. The State Advisory Groups coordinate JJDP Act funds with other existing state and Federal funds so as to maximize resources and prevent duplication of effort.

OVERVIEW OF THE CONTEMPORARY JUVENILE JUSTICE PROCESS

The juvenile offender may be apprehended by: a community agency; his parents; a school authori-

ty; a truant officer; a concerned citizen with knowledge of a child's misbehavior or parental neglect; or a probation officer. However, in most cases the juvenile will be apprehended by the police. Once a juvenile is apprehended, the juvenile justice process is under way. However, the juvenile justice process need not involve legal proceedings as will be demonstrated later in this chapter.

The operations of the juvenile justice system vary from state to state and from city to city because each state has the authority to legislate its own juvenile law, and each city has a different level of development regarding juvenile justice alternatives. Some cities will have more alternatives at each stage of the system and others will have fewer alternatives. The community determines who will be processed through the official justice system, and the juvenile must eventually return to the community.

Police Procedures

The apprehended juvenile may be reprimanded and released or the police officer may serve as a conflict resolver between the complaining party and the juvenile and/or his parents. If the conflict is resolved, disposition of the complaint is informal, but the police will usually make a written report of the incident. Informal disposition is usually an alternative when less serious offenses are involved; i.e., informal disposition is usually not an alternative when a serious offense is involved. Goldman (1963) states that there are several factors which impact an officer's disposition of an apprehended juvenile:

• The policeman's attitudes toward the juvenile court.

• The impact of special individual experiences in court, or with different racial groups, or with parents of offenders, or with specific offenses, or an individual policeman.

• Apprehension about criticism by the court.

• Publicity given to certain offenses either in

the neighborhood or elsewhere may cause the police to feel that these are too "hot" to handle unofficially and must be referred to the court.

- The necessity of maintaining respect for police authority in the community.

- Various practical problems of policing.

- Pressure by political groups or other special interest groups.

- The policeman's attitude toward specific offenses.

- The police officer's impression of the family situation, the degree of family interest in and control of the offender, and the reaction of the parents to the problem of the child's offense.

- The attitude and personality of the child.

- The black child offender is considered less tractable and needing more authoritarian supervision than a white child.

- The degree of criminal sophistication shown in the offense.

- Juvenile offenders apprehended in a group will generally be treated on an all-or-none basis.

Many police departments have Police-Juvenile Units. If the juvenile is apprehended and brought to the Police-Juvenile Unit of the Police Department, the Police-Juvenile Unit may attempt to resolve the conflict between the complaining party and the juvenile and/or his parents; however, resolution is more likely in the field by the apprehending officer. If a department does not have a Police-Juvenile Unit, the officer who apprehends the juvenile is responsible for the subsequent law enforcement functions related to the juvenile, or a detective is assigned the case. Upon review of the case, the police will do one of the following: the juvenile will be released to his parents with an official reprimand; the juvenile will be released with an official report; the juvenile will be released to some other juvenile agency; or, the juvenile will be referred to juvenile court.

Intake

The initial stage of the juvenile court process is the intake department which is also known as intake service. The intake department functions in the screening of juveniles. At this time, some juveniles are referred to social agencies for treatment, and some juveniles are unconditionally released. In addition, some juveniles are released on certain conditions. For example, some courts have a diversion program whereby first offenders can be released if the child and his family agree to certain conditions to be fulfilled during a defined period of time. These conditions might include informal supervision restitution, family counseling, improvement of school attendance, improved school performance, marriage counseling, periodic visits to the intake service, and other ancillary services available to the juvenile court. In some cases, juveniles are diverted without special provisions of supervision. The concept of diversion will be further discussed later in this chapter. If an intake officer and/or a judge decide further legal proceedings are necessary, the district or county attorney is notified, and a charge sheet is drawn up. If there is a time lapse between the court hearing and the adjudication hearing, the juvenile can be released to his parents during the interim, or the juvenile may be held in a detention facility.

Detention

Before a juvenile is placed in a detention facility, an intake officer obtains information regarding the incident, the juvenile, and his family. If the intake officer refers the juvenile to a detention facility, a written report must be submitted to the juvenile court. In many states, the juvenile can be held in detention for up to forty-eight hours without a court order. When the need for a detention hearing is determined, the court is required to do the following: set the time and place for the hearing immediately; appoint a guardian *ad litem* for the child if he is not represented by counsel; and, provide a written notice to a juvenile's parents (guardian) 24 hours prior to the detention hearing. In most courts, the intake officer makes a recommendation to the judge who determines if there is probable cause to believe that the juvenile committed the alleged act. At the detention hearing, the presiding judge will decide whether or not the juvenile will be held while awaiting the plea hearing and the adjudicatory hearing.

THE JUDICIAL PROCESS

The initial procedural steps in the juvenile court are as follows: (1) complaints go to the clerk of the court; (2) a probation officer is assigned; (3) the probation officer interviews the child; (4) the probation officer inquires into circumstances of the alleged problem; (5) arraignment; (6) probation officer presents complaint; (7) public defender is appointed. Many states have four separate hearings for juveniles as follows: detention, plea, adjudicatory, and disposition. A recommendation from the police department or a Complainant's Petition is required before a juvenile appears in Juvenile Court. When a petition is filed with the Juvenile Court, a probation officer is assigned, but he does not become involved with the juvenile unless he is detained prior to adjudication. The plea hearing is that hearing where the juvenile admits or denies involvement in the alleged misbehavior. The adjudicatory hearing is to determine whether or not the juvenile committed the alleged delinquent act. The disposition hearing is the hearing to determine a disposition which is in the best interest of the child and the community. However, in some states, the judge conducts the plea hearing and the adjudicatory hearing at the same time, or the adjudicatory hearing and the disposition hearing at the same time.

If the juvenile "pleads" guilty or *nolo contendere* (no contest) at the plea hearing, the adjudicatory hearing must be scheduled within a specified time period (e.g., within two weeks of the plea hearing). At the adjudicatory hearing, the juvenile is represented by a *"guardian ad litem"* (a court appointed representative) or a privately retained attorney. In most states, there is no jury. As a result of the adjudicatory hearing, the case may be dismissed on a legal technicality or on the merits

of the evidence. In some cases, the judge releases the juvenile with a warning to both the juvenile and his parents. Or, the judge may conclude that the juvenile did not commit the alleged act. If the court finds that the juvenile is guilty of the alleged act (beyond a reasonable doubt), the judge will then schedule a disposition hearing.

Transfers to Criminal Court is Not a New Phenomenon

In rare cases, the juvenile may be transferred to adult court. Prior to transfer of jurisdiction, a waiver hearing must be held; criteria for transfer are specified in the Kent decision (see above). If the juvenile is tried in an adult court and is found guilty, he may be sentenced to an adult prison. However, some countries and some states in the United states allow the convicted juvenile to serve their time in an institution that is age specific.

A juvenile's delinquency case can be transferred to criminal court to be tried as an adult in one of three ways: judicial waiver (usually, the prosecutor makes a request to waive the case to adult court); prosecutorial discretion (the law provides for concurrent jurisdiction of certain cases and the prosecutor has the discretion to select either the juvenile court or the adult court for prosecution of the case); and, statutory exclusion (state law excludes certain juvenile crimes from juvenile court jurisdiction). In a given state, one, two, or all three transfer mechanisms may exist.

Several states have permitted juvenile offenders to be transferred to criminal court since before the 1920's — Arkansas, California, Colorado, Florida, Georgia, Kentucky, North Carolina, Ohio, Oregon, and Tennessee; some states have permitted transfers since at least the 1940's — Delaware, Indiana, Maryland, Michigan, Nevada, New Hampshire, New Mexico, Rhode Island, South Carolina, and Utah.

Historically, the decision to transfer a youth to criminal court was made by a juvenile court judge. This decision was based on the individual circumstances in each case, and on the need of the juvenile. Since the 1970's, however, state legislatures have increasingly transferred juveniles to criminal court based on age and offense seriousness — the case-specific assessment offered by the juvenile court process. In half the states, laws have been enacted that exclude some offenses from juvenile court and a number of states have also expanded the range of excluded offenses. One quarter of the states have given prosecutors the discretion to charge certain offenses either in juvenile or criminal court.

Juvenile Court Disposition

If the judge conducts the adjudicatory process and the disposition process in the same hearing, he will have information about the alleged offense and the social history of the child and his family prior to the hearing. Prior to disposition, the juvenile court judge reviews the social history (also referred to as the pre-disposition investigation) of the juvenile. The social history is prepared by a probation officer, and it includes information regarding prior offenses, current offenses, family relationships, school, prior contact with the police, and the probation officer's recommendations. At the dispositional hearing, the judge will make a decision in the best interests of the child and the community.

When a juvenile goes to juvenile court, there are only specific decisions that can be made: no action — child remains at home; supervision by probation officers — child remains at home; supervision by probation officers — child removed from home and placed with a relative or a foster or group home; remain in the community — commitment to residential treatment facility; and commitment to a juvenile correctional institution.

The primary considerations a judge employs in deciding what action is to be taken are as follows: Can the parents deal with the child and his problems? Is the child uncooperative or resistant at home, school, or work? What is the juvenile's juvenile court record? If he has been on probation, what was his behavior and attitude, and what does the probation officer recommend? Other factors which affect the disposition include the seriousness of the act, prior court and police contacts, the attitude of the child and his parents, and the age of the child. These factors are as ambiguous as laws which state that the disposition should be in the best interest of the child and the community. Some of the other structural variables of the juvenile justice system which affect disposition are as follows: availability of probation officers; financial resources; age; race; the offenses (severity and number of prior offenses); and, court variables (the presiding judge, and whether counsel represented child). Written guidelines for juvenile court dispositions are now being used in a number of states so as to avoid inequities in the process.

JUVENILE CORRECTIONS

The traditional alternatives available to the judge at the disposition hearing include the following: probation; a state juvenile institution; foster care; a private agency; or, a community based facility. In some states, parents may request that their child be placed in a private institution; however, this is financially unfeasible for most families. The relative frequency of dispositions made by the juvenile court are as follows: probation, institution, case dismissed, and placement in special programs. When placed on probation, the child is under the supervision of a probation officer, and the probation officer facilitates the juvenile's functioning in the community. If the child's home is unsuitable, he may be placed in a foster home or in a group home while on probation. If the juvenile has committed a serious offense or is a recidivist, he may be committed to a juvenile institution. When the juvenile is released from the institution, he is usually placed under the supervision of a parole officer for a given period of time. In most cases, the juvenile will eventually return to the community.

The juvenile justice system needs a graduated system of dispositions, including pre-judicial alternatives. Technically, the pre-judicial alternatives are not dispositions. However, if the non-judicial disposition focuses on treatment, then it logically can be considered as one alternative that the judge has in disposing of a case in a manner which reflects the *parens patriae* philosophy of the court. Diversion is a concept which is pre-judicial, but it can also be considered a correctional alternative for dealing with juvenile offenders.

Diversion

Diversion removes the person from the system. Therefore, any strategy (whether formal or informal) which removes the child from the subsequent processes of the juvenile justice system can be referred to as diversion. Diversion usually is used in reference to some specific formal program designed to divert the child from the system. For example, many courts have a diversion program whereby first offenders can be released if the child and his family agree to comply with certain conditions to be fulfilled during a defined period of time, usually a six month period. These conditions may include informal supervision, restitution, family counseling, improvement of school attendance, improved school performance, marriage counseling, periodical visits to the intake service, and involvement in ancillary services available to the juvenile court. In some cases, juveniles are diverted without special provision of supervision. Many juvenile courts do not have access to a diversion program.

In recent years, there has been a trend toward diversion of youth from the juvenile justice system. There are several reasons for this trend: the juvenile justice system has proved ineffective in controlling or preventing delinquency; in theory, the juvenile justice system focuses upon rehabilitation, but, in practice, traditional juvenile justice processes have been punitive; and, increasing awareness that treating juvenile offenders before they become adults is in the best interest of society.

Most diversion programs have similar procedures. Usually, status offenders and/or first offenders and their families are interviewed after a petition is filed. The goal of the interview is to obtain a consent agreement (from all people involved) to suspend formal proceedings for an agreed period of time. During this period, the child and the child's parents agree to certain provisions (e.g., informal supervision, restitution, family counseling, improvement of school attendance and performance). In some cases, suspending formal action without special provisions of supervision is all that is required. The petition is dismissed if the child takes responsibility as defined in the diversion agreement.

Youth Services Bureau

The administration of diversion programs is based on the knowledge of alternatives to the juvenile justice system. Therefore, the crucial factor in the development of a successful diversion effort is the determination of referral alternatives within the community and evaluating the effectiveness of these various alternatives. Traditionally, the problem has been that public and private social service agencies allow children and their families to fall between them because no one agency is responsible for anyone (Mangel 1971). The Youth Services Bureau concept is designed to facilitate coordination of these agencies; its goal is the maximum elevation of community resources, continuity of treatment, and feedback of information. A Youth Services Bureau is designed to supply a broad range of services for "trouble-making" youth who have been referred to the bureau by police, probation departments, schools and community agencies, or by parents. The Youth Services Bureau administers a variety of services for youth (e.g., individual counseling, foster home placements, work assignments, special education), and the bureau provides opportunities for involvement in social, cultural, and recreational activities. It can help to link youth to services that exist within the community, and it can also help to link or coordinate community resources with legislative action and develop resources to get at the problem of reducing delinquency. This approach provides an effective mechanism for dealing with non-serious "delinquents," and it reduces the number of cases handled within the juvenile justice system, thereby allowing it to function more effectively and more efficiently.

The idea of the Youth Services Bureau is to divert minor offenders from the justice system and keep them out of it before they are branded delinquents by the courts. This enables probation to focus its effort on the more serious offenders, while the Youth Services Bureau helps to identify and find solutions to delinquency breeding problems (Norman 1973). The main concern of such a coordination agency should be changing juveniles' attitudes toward society and changing the community's attitudes toward the juvenile. Youth Service Bureaus have brought social workers, teachers, administrators, and parents together to determine the causes of truancy and other behavioral problems in the schools, and to discuss what can be done about those causes. Such an approach stops the practice of each group blaming the others and referring the child to the juvenile court which is further removed from the cause of the problem.

Examples of programs which may be a part of the Youth Services Bureau are as follows: a program focused on changing public attitudes toward young offenders and increasing employment opportunities for those youth who are returning to the community; a truancy diversion program in which cases are no longer accepted by the court, but are handled in the schools with the help of the Youth Services Bureau; and a youth volunteer program where volunteers aid the juvenile justice process by referring youngsters on the verge of trouble to community resources (Norman 1973).

OTHER CORRECTIONAL ALTERNATIVES

Diversion and the Youth Services Bureau concepts can be viewed as alternative efforts to rehabilitate/treat the juvenile. A graduated system of dispositions should include the placement of a juvenile in the least restrictive alternative which can insure public safety and which simultaneously provides a reasonable certainty that the juvenile can be more effectively treated within the selected correctional alternative. All correctional options should focus on treatment. This necessitates that non-judicial institutions for guidance, treatment, and other services, are used to carry out the diagnosis and treatment function.

There is a need for quality in-depth assessment of youths. In most juvenile justice systems, this does not occur. A recent trend in juvenile justice is to establish a Juvenile Assessment Center (JAC) to administer quality assessments to youth. The juvenile's particular deficits and needs can then be a part of the juvenile justice decision-making process. For example, the JAC can refer youths who are identified as having a potential alcohol/other drug abuse or mental health problem for additional assessment, and if needed, the juvenile will be placed in a facility for treatment services.

Many non-legal agencies are regularly utilized by the justice system in the disposition of cases at the adult level and at the juvenile level. The agencies that are needed for the treatment process are usually classified under one of the following concepts: social service, drugs and alcohol, mental health, retardation, and developmental disabilities. Services/programs from these agencies are routinely incorporated into the selected correctional disposition alternative (e.g., judges often utilize drug and alcohol treatment programs as part of a sentencing disposition). The same type of treatment needs to be available to people placed on diversion or on probation or in another correctional alternative, including institutions. Those who are in institutions will need to have treatment while in the institution and a re-integration plan (including treatment during their gradual release).

The following treatment-related goals should be a part of the correctional process for juveniles: placement of juvenile offenders according to needs/risk assessment; coordinate referrals to community services as appropriate; provide access to drug and alcohol programs while on diversion and after the diversion is completed; provide continuing support for juveniles returning to "high risk environments;" and, provide access to temporary residential shelter care programs as needed.

Juveniles are amenable to treatment, if the treatment is relevant to their needs (Adams 1967: 48-57). The task is to develop treatment programs which are sensitive to: juvenile needs; the differences in offenses committed; and the negative consequences of traditional formal sanctioning ceremonies. The emphasis should be on early problem discovery, low-profile processing, and treatment approaches which recognize the needs of each individual. The relative cost of such changes in the present system is not nearly as great as the economic and social harm that will be forthcoming by those processes under the current system.

"We know how to identify many kids who are likely to get into trouble by the time they reach the third grade. We are beginning to understand that many children who misbehave flagrantly, perhaps as many as half of them, have basic medical problems that if treated would allow them to control weird impulses that lead to assault, even murder" (Mangel 1971:3). There are experiments in juvenile rehabilitation that indicate promising ways to reduce recidivism and the cost of the juvenile justice system. Some of the other treatment alternatives are delineated below.

Treatment in the Home

According to legal statute, the home is regarded as the best place for the child to receive care and treatment (Stevenson 1973:13). However, it can be argued that many of the behavioral problems of juveniles are caused by or intensified by the nature of the home environment. Logically, the solution lies in changing the home environment. However, access to the home is often difficult to achieve, and when achieved, parental attitudes may prevent significant changes. The goal is to solicit parental cooperation in a problem-solving effort.

If it is necessary to remove the child from the home, two factors are of utmost importance: the child's cooperation and acceptance of a new home; and continued parental involvement if this is the desire of the child and his parents. Such parental involvement must be under the control of a social agency, and, it must not disturb the authority of the foster home in which the child is placed. The foster home care should be defined as a temporary measure and goals related to the home environment should be delineated. It should be emphasized that another approach is to sever parental and juvenile ties until the home environment has been straightened out. However, the juvenile should not be removed from the home unless there is no other alternative.

Familial problems, including juvenile misconduct, can be more effectively dealt with in a voluntary cooperative setting. The filing of a formal petition of delinquency is so threatening that it may serve to deter successful treatment. Furthermore, filing of a formal petition is a symbol, which if identified by the community, will have negative consequences for the employment opportunities and the social functioning of the individual. To accomplish anything, the probation officer must have the trust and confidence of the child and of the parents. Even when the parents' or child's attitude is extremely hostile, it is desirable to construct a situation where both the parents and the child are willing to accept intervention of an outside agency.

Treatment in the Educational System

There is ample evidence which suggests that schools do attempt to deal with deviant behavior of youth. Unfortunately, in many cases the emphasis is not on diagnosis and treatment but rather on control and punishment. "There is also substantial evidence that schools contribute to a student's academic failure and this in turn adds to his problems, reinforces his negative evaluation of himself and either creates resentment towards society or reinforces a resentment which was already there" (Stevenson 1973:13). The typical delinquent youth is behind in school. Many delinquent youths are several years behind the normal grade level in mathematics, reading, and language arts. The delinquent youths are often perceived as a "behavior problem" and as a failure by their teachers and family. Also, delinquent youths are characteristically truant from school, and they are multiple offenders (National Institute of Law Enforcement and Criminal Justice 1974).

New Jersey has supported a policy of defining youth problems as educational rather than delinquent. In 1931, Mayor Hague of Jersey City laid the foundation for this policy by stating that children in trouble should not be subject to arrest, and if at all possible, they should not be sent to the Juvenile Court.

In St. Louis, the Providence Educational Center was established to deal with young delinquent youths, 12 through 16 years old, who had been charged with stranger-to-stranger crimes and who had histories of poor school performance and social failure. This program assumes that the long-term rehabilitation of delinquents who are exhibiting poor school performance and social failure is contingent on the development of human reactions and communication skills which are needed for successful experiences in school, in the family, in social living, and on the job.

The Center's goals are: to provide delinquent youths with effective alternative ways of relating and functioning in the community; to improve their self-image, school performance, and social skills; and, to provide the child with support and guidance in the reintegration process (National Institute of Law Enforcement and Criminal Justice 1974). Teams of professionally trained counselors, educators, and social workers develop, implement, and individualize a program for each child, to improve his educational and social adjustment skills. The program has demonstrated notable effectiveness in treating adjudicated delinquents with a history of truancy, poor school performance, and behavioral problems. The Center has decreased the incidence of further offenses among the youngsters it served, has increased their ability to function in the public schools and on the job, and has strengthened their family relationships. The recidivism rate of this program is only twenty-eight percent, and because this program is non-residential, it is able to provide services to delinquent youths at a lower cost per juvenile.

Treatment in the Community

There are a multitude of treatment strategies for incarcerated juveniles, too numerous to discuss here. One relatively successful treatment effort is the "family treatment program." This program involves groups of boys or girls living together in family units. The juveniles talk about their feelings and thoughts and the purpose is to change attitudes and behavior (United States Dept. of Health, Education, and Welfare 1971). The probation officer acts as the group leader and the catalytic agent for producing change and discussion. Some of the goals are to bring about awareness, self-respect, identity, respect of peers, and interpersonal maturity.

The parents also meet in group sessions so that they can realize that they are not alone in coping with the problems of raising an adolescent. The youngsters are allowed to go home on weekends so parents and child can implement their new skills. This allows them to operate in the environment of which they are an integral part, and it allows them to discuss some of the problems they are having in that environment upon return to their group. Additionally, after release these people can receive out-patient counseling for a period of up to six weeks (Trojanowicz 1973).

Treatment in Secure Facilities

Juveniles often have treatments/services available to them while they are in a detention facility. A detention facility is a youth jail. It usually involves a short stay for the juvenile while he is awaiting subsequent hearings or awaiting space in a correctional alternative. The juvenile can also be sentenced to the detention facility if the time is less than one year. However, this approach is rarely used because the detention facility does not have the resources for treatment that a correctional center would have.

A juvenile correctional facility (e.g., youth center, industrial school) is usually a secure facility. However, it is not impossible for a juvenile to escape. In fact, compared to a maximum- or medium-security adult facility, the juvenile correctional facility is not very "escape-proof." Within correctional facilities, there are treatment programs and services to meet the needs of the juveniles, as follows: medical, dental, educational programs, behavioral programs, drug and alcohol programs, skill development programs, group therapy, and special-needs programs (illiteracy, mental retardation, developmental disabilities, learning disabilities). However, in a state-by-state comparison, one will find that there are marked differences in the availability and quality of treatment programs and services. There is even a difference within states (e.g., rural vs. urban counties, wealthy vs. poor counties).

✳ ✳ ✳ ✳ ✳

REFERENCES

Adams, Stuart
    1967   "Some Findings from Correctional Caseload Research," *Federal Probation*, 31, (December) pp. 48-57.
Aichorn, August
    1969   *Delinquency and Child Guidance*. New York: International University Press.
Albanese, Jay
    1985   *Dealing with Delinquency: An Investigation of Juvenile Justice*. Lanham, MD: University Press of America.
Albanese, Jay S.
    1993   *Dealing with Delinquency: The Future of Juvenile Justice*. Chicago: Nelson-Hall Publishers.
Bartollas, Clemens, and Stuart J. Miler
    1994   *Juvenile Justice in America*. Englewood Cliffs, NJ: Regents/ Prentice-Hall.
Berman, Sidney
    1964   "Antisocial Character Disorder," In *Readings in Juvenile Delinquency*. Ruth S. Cavan, ed., Philadelphia: J.B. Lippincott Company, p. 142.
Bernard, Thomas J.
    1992   *The Cycle of Juvenile Justice*. New York: Oxford University Press.
Bloch, Herbert A., Frank T. Flynn
    1956   *Delinquency: The Juvenile Offender in America Today*. New York: Random House, p. 37
Breed v. Jones, 421 U.S. 519, at 531, 95 S.Ct. 1779 at 1786.
Clark, John, and Edward Haurek
    1966   "Age and Sex Roles of Adolescents and Their Involvement in Misconduct: A Reappraisal," *Sociology and Social Research*, Vol. 50 (4), pp. 496-508.
Cloward, Richard A., and Lloyd E. Ohlin
    1960   *Delinquency and Opportunity*. New York: The Free Press of Glencoe.
Coffey, Alan R.
    1974   *Juvenile Justice as a System: Law Enforcement to Rehabilitation*. Englewood Cliffs, NJ: Prentice-Hall.

Cohen, Albert K., James F. Short, Jr.
    1971   "Crime and Juvenile Delinquency," In *Contemporary Social Problems*. Robert K.
            Merton and Robert Nesbit, eds. New York: Harcourt Brace Jovanovich, Inc., p. 108.
Cohen, Albert K.
    1955   *Delinquent Boys*. New York: The Free Press of Glencoe.
Coleman, James
    1962   *The Adolescent Society*. New York: The Free Press of Glencoe.
Cottle, T.
    1977   *Children in Jail: Seven Lessons in America Justice*. Boston: Beacon Press.
Dentler, R.A., and L.J. Monroe
    1961   "Social Correlates of Early Adolescent Theft," *American Sociological Review*, Vol.
            · 26, p.733-44.
Erickson, Maynard L., and LeMar T. Empey
    1963   "Court Records, Undetected Delinquency and Decision-Making," *Journal of Criminal
            Law, Criminology, and Police Science*. Vol. 54 (4), pp. 456-69.
Fox, Sanford J.
    1971   *The Law of Juvenile Courts in a Nutshell*. St. Paul, MN: West Publishing Company.
Gallegos v. Colorado (1962) 370 U.S. 49, 82 S.Ct. 1209.
Gibbons, Don C.
    1973   *An Introduction to Criminology*. Englewood Cliffs, NJ: Prentice-Hall, Inc., p. 114.
Gold, Martin
    1967   "On Social Status and Social Delinquency," *Social Problems*, Vol. 15 (Summer),
            pp. 114-16.
Gold, Martin
    1966   "Undetected Delinquent Behavior," *Journal of Research in Crime and Delinquency*,
            Vol. 3(1), pp. 27-46.
Goldman, Nathan
    1963   "The Differential Selection of Juvenile Offenders for Court Appearance," National
            Council on Crime and Delinquency.
Gould, Laurence J.
    1966   *The Alienation Syndrome: Psycho-Social Correlates and Behavioral Consequences*,
            Storrs, CT: University of Connecticut. Unpublished Ph.D. Dissertation.
Hahn, Paul H.
    1971   *The Juvenile Offender and The Law*. Cincinnati: The W.H. Anderson Company.
Hirschi, Travis, and Hanan C. Selvin
    1973   *Principles of Survey Analysis*. New York: The Free Press, p. 15.
In re Gault. (1967) 387 U.S. 1, 40 Ohio Op (2d) 378, 18 Led (2d) 527, 87 Sct 1428.
In re Winship. (1970) 90 Sct 1068, 51, Ohio Op (2d) 323, 25, Led (2d) 368, 397 U.S. 358.
Janeksela, Galan M.
    1978   "Systems Analysis in Juvenile Justice," *Juvenile and Family Court Journal*, August,
            p. 14.
Janeksela, Galan M.
    1979   "Juvenile Delinquency and the Juvenile Justice System." Chapter 14 (pages 331-354)
            in *Introduction to Criminal Justice: Theory and Application*, edited by Dae H. Chang,
            Dubuque, IA: Kendall/Hunt Publishing Company.
Johnson, Thomas A.
    1975   *Introduction to the Juvenile Justice System*. St. Paul: West Publishing Company, p. 20.
Kent v. United States. (1966) 833 U.S. 541, 555-556, 40 Ohio Op (2d) (270).
Lemert, Edwin M.
    1971   *Instead of Court*. Washington, DC: U.S. Government Printing Office.
Mack, Julian
    1909   "The Juvenile Court," *Harvard Law Review*, Vol. 119.

Mangel, Charles
> 1971   *How to Make a Criminal Out of a Child*. Hackensack, NJ: National Council on Crime and Delinquency.

Mannheim, Ernest
> 1965   "Reactions to Alienation," *Kansas Journal of Sociology*, Vol. 1(3), pp. 108-111.

Marsh, Robert W.
> 1961   *The Mandarin's: The Circulation of Elites in China 1600-1900*. New York: The Free Press of Glencoe.

Marwell, Gerald
> 1966   "Adolescent Powerlessness in Delinquent Behavior," *Social Problems*, Vol. 14 (1), pp. 35-7.

McKiever v. Pennsylvania. (1971) 403 U.S. 528, 91 S.Ct. 1976.

Merton, Robert
> 1938   "Social Structure and Anomie," *American Sociological Review*, Vol. 3 (October), pp. 672-82.

Merton, Robert
> 1957   *Social Theory and Social Structure*. New York: The Free Press of Glencoe.

Miller, Walter B.
> 1958   "Lower Class Culture as a Generating Milieu of Gang Delinquency," *Journal of Social Issues,* Vol. 14 (3), pp. 5-19.

Monohan, Thomas
> 1960   "Broken Homes by Age of Delinquent Children," *Journal of Social Psychology,* Vol. 51, May, 1960, pp. 387-97.

National Institute of Law Enforcement and Criminal Justice
> 1974   *An Exemplary Project: Providence Education Center*. National Institute of Law Enforcement and Criminal Justice.

Neumeyer, Martin
> 1960   *Juvenile Delinquency in Modern Society*. New York: D. Van Nostrand Company, Inc.

Norman, Sherwood
> 1973   "Kids, Crime and Communities," National Council on Crime and Delinquency. The Journal. Washington, DC: The American Chamber of Commerce Executives.

Oaks, Dalin H., and Warren Lehman
> 1968   *A Criminal Justice System and the Indigent*. Chicago: The University of Chicago Press.

Office of Juvenile Justice and Delinquency Prevention
> 1995   *Office of Juvenile Justice and Delinquency Prevention's Fact Sheet #22*. Washington, DC: U.S. Department of Justice.

Office of Juvenile Justice and Delinquency Prevention. (Located on the INTERNET)
> 1996   *An Effective Approach to Juvenile Crime and Violence: The Juvenile Justice and Delinquency Prevention Act, State Advisory Groups and the Federal Office of Juvenile Justice and Delinquency Prevention*. Washington, DC: U.S. Department of Justice.

Piliavin, I., and S. Briar
> 1964   "Police Encounter with Juveniles," *American Journal of Sociology*, Vol. 70 (2).

Platt, Anthony
> 1969   "The Rise of the Child Saving Movement: A Study in Social Policy and Correctional Reform," *Annals of American Academy of Political and Social Sciences,* 381 (January).

President's Commission on Law Enforcement and the Administration of Justice
> 1967   *The Challenge of Crime in a Free Society,* Washington, DC: U.S. Government Printing Office.

President's Commission on Law Enforcement and the Administration of Justice
> 1967   *Juvenile Delinquency and Youth Crime*. Washington, DC: U.S. Government Printing Office.

Reiss, Albert J.
> 1951   *The Police and the Public*. New Haven, CT: Yale University Press.

Reiss, Albert J., and Albert L. Rhodes
    1961   "The Distribution of Juvenile Delinquency in Social Class Structure," *American Sociological Review*, Vol. 26 (5), pp. 720-32.
Reynolds, Paul Davidson
    1971   *The Primer in Theory Construction*. New York: The Bobbs-Merrill Company, p. 137.
Rogers, Dorothy
    1972   *Adolescence: A Psychological Perspective*. Belmont, CA: Brooks-Cole.
Rosen, Bernard C.
    1956   "The Achievement Syndrome: A Psycho-cultural Dimension of Social Stratification," *American Sociological Review*, Vol. 21, pp. 203-24.
Scarpitti, Frank R.
    1974   *Social Problems*. Chicago: Holt, Rinehart and Winston, Inc.
Schwartz, I.
    1989   *(In)justice for Juveniles: Rethinking the Best Interest of the Child*. Lexington, MA: Lexington Books.
Short, James F., and Ivan F. Nye
    1958   "Extent of Unrecorded Delinquency: Tentative Conclusions," *Journal of Criminal Law, Criminology and Police Science*, Vol. 49 (4), pp. 296-302.
Snyder, Howard
    1997   "Juvenile Arrests 1995," *Juvenile Justice Bulletin* (February), Washington, DC: Office of Juvenile Justice and Delinquency Prevention.
Snyder, Howard, and Melissa Sickmund
    1995   *Juvenile Offenders and Victims: A National Report*. Washington, DC: Office of Juvenile Justice and Delinquency Prevention.
Stanfield, Robert
    1966   "The Interaction of Family Variables Gang Variables in the Etiology of Delinquency," *Social Problems*, Vol. 13 (4).
Stevenson, Margaret
    1973   "The Juvenile Justice System in Iowa," unpublished manuscript No. 733. Iowa City: League of Women' Voters.
Sutherland, E.H., and D.R. Cressey
    1970   *Criminology*. New York: J.B. Lippincott Company.
Torbet, Patricia, Richard Gable, Hunter Hurst, Imogene Montgomery, Linda Szymanski, and Douglas Thomas
    1996   *State Responses to Serious and Violent Juvenile Crime*. Washington, DC: Office of Juvenile Justice and Delinquency Prevention.
Trojanowicz, Robert C.
    1973   *Juvenile Delinquency: Concepts and Controls*. Englewood Cliffs, NJ: Prentice-Hall, Incorporated.
United States Department of Health, Education, and Welfare
    1971   "National Strategy to Prevent Delinquency," Washington, DC: Social and Rehabilitation Service, Youth Development and Delinquency Prevention Administration, U.S. Government Printing Office.
Williams, Jay R., and Martin Gold
    1972   "From Delinquent Behavior to Official Delinquency," *Social Problems*, Vol. 20 (2).
Wolfgang, Marvin, and Bernard Cohen
    1970   *Crime and Race Conceptions and Misconceptions*. New York: Institute of Human Relations Press.
Wolfgang, Marvin E., Robert M. Figlio, and Thorsten Sellin
    1972   *Delinquency in a Birth Cohort*. Chicago: The University of Chicago Press.

SECTION VI

THE APPLICATION
of
CRIMINAL JUSTICE THEORY
IN SOCIETY

Chapter 13

ON GUARD:
The Private Security Industry in America

By

Ken Peak and **Ken Braunstein**

> *"It's no use filling your pockets with money if you have got a hole in the corner."*
>
> --- George Eliot

Saul Astor said, "We are a nation of thieves." And, it might be added, one of murderers, rapists, robbers, and other types of offenders. There are about 42.5 million offenses committed each year in America, 11.5 million of which are against persons (Maguire and Pastore, 1996). According to the National Institute of Justice, personal crime is estimated to cost $105 billion annually, and if one includes the costs of pain, suffering, and the reduced quality of life that are associated with criminal behavior, the cost soars to $450 billion (National Institute of Justice, 1996). We are indeed a nation at risk.

Given this situation, it is not surprising that Americans have turned to other sources of protection than that which can be provided by the public police. Indeed, as the 1990s began there were more than 1.5 million persons employed in private security agencies, and Americans were paying more than $52 billion per year for their services (Cunningham et al., 1991); this compared with about 550,000 full-time local police officers and expenditures of about $20 billion for local police protection (Maguire and Flanagan, 1991). Both employment and expenditures for private security are expected to greatly increase well into the 21st century.

Additionally, contemporary trends in crime, such as terroristic acts against people and places around the globe, have forced us to become even more security minded. Even our own White House, which has been attacked frequently by people in airplanes and others shooting guns, is now vulnerable. With security concerns now present with a broad range of places and people, including computers and lotteries, celebrities and college campuses, casinos and nuclear plants, shopping centers, mass transit systems, hospitals, railroads, and a host of others, a higher level of protection is demanded beyond that which can be provided by public policing agencies.

More and more, these vulnerable entities within our society demand protection and security from "the other police" — people in the private sector. Private police now outnumber the local police by more than three to one. The private security sector relieves much of the pressure for the regular police and serves a productive function (Peak, 1985). Furthermore, there is an increasing realization that not all functions require full police powers and armed police.

This chapter examines America's burgeoning security industry, including discussions of its historical development, modern-day nature and functions, personnel education and training, the question of whether or not private police should be armed, public/private police cooperation and interface, the problem of liability, and the future of private security and its technology, to include Web sites where students and practitioners alike can obtain further information.

HISTORICAL DEVELOPMENT OF PRIVATE POLICING

In Tribes and Early Communities

Since prehistoric times, people have sought security — safety, protection, and comfort in their persons and property — from enemies and beasts of prey. With their simple weapons and through the use of caves and lakes or elevated cliff dwellings, they hoped to fend off attackers. The home site was designated for safety and security. Human-made barriers were placed between the individual and his or her environment. The most elaborate security system in ancient times was the Great Wall of China, stretching 1500 miles in length and requiring 15 years and a half million workers for its construction.

Private individuals also sought safety and protection by banding together to form communities, which provided greater safety through numbers. As tribes became nations, rulers of small domains became kings and emperors. The equivalent of police forces were often established from the ranks of the military. For example, the Roman Emperor Augustus created the Praetorian Guard, a form of bodyguard police, as well as the Vigiles, who were police-firemen. Ancient Egypt had its feared Mamelukes; the early sultans were guarded by their Janissaries.

During the Middle Ages, about 476 A.D. to 1453 A.D., the "mutual pledge" system was initiated by the Anglo-Saxons in England. Under this system, groups of 10 families, called tithings, banded together for security and to provide collective responsibility for order maintenance. Castle moats and spectacular bridges also became commonplace during this period as a means of controlling ingress and egress for security purposes.

The Statute of Winchester

A milestone in the evolution of private security and policing came in 1285 when King Edward issued the Statute of Winchester. Under this broad statute were originated the idea of a curfew, the night watch, and the office of bailiff. It has been said that the Statute was the only significant public measure enacted to regulate the policing of England between the Norman Conquest of 1066 and the Metropolitan Police Act of 1829 (Critchley, 1967). The Statute established three practical means of reaching its stated objective, which was to "abate the power of felons": (1) the watch and ward; (2) the hue and cry; and (3) the assize of arms.

The **watch and ward** provided night watchmen in England's larger communities. The night watchmen, given full powers of arrest, augmented the day (ward) duties of the constable. All the men in the towns were pressed into service on a rotating basis and were punished if they failed to serve. The merchants of England, however, were not pleased with this mode of protection; the watch and ward was eventually termed colloquially as the "snooze and snore" watch, for its obvious shortcomings. When some men rebelled against the compulsory nightwatch service and paid apathetic replacements to serve in their stead, merchants were forced to hire private police to guard their businesses or investigate crimes committed thereon (Peak, 1985).

The **hue and cry** was the Statute's method of restraining those persons who would resist the watchmen. When resistance occurred, the watchmen cried out so that all within hearing distance were obliged to join in the pursuit of the offender. Finally, the Statue required compliance with the **assize of arms**, whereby every male between the ages of 15 and 60 was compelled to keep a weapon in his home as a "harness to keep the peace" (Peak, 1985).

Although largely ineffective the watch and ward was the primary means of security and law enforcement until the Industrial Revolution (Hess and Wrobleski, 1982). When extensive social and economic problems struck England during the Industrial Revolution, private citizens collectively hired special police for protection. Radzinowicz (1956:202) also noted that "No one had even questioned the principle that if a man were able and willing to pay, he could ensure greater security for himself or his property by organizing a private police force of his own."

Nineteenth Century Private Security

It is clear that England's attempts at part-time public policing prior to the nineteenth century were largely ineffective and unprofessional; furthermore, these attempts were made at the expense of men who were disinterested and/or ill-equipped to be defenders of the laws. However, the *private* police, hired by groups of private citizens in the early 1800s in England and the United States, contributed greatly to keeping the peace. Private,

armed watchmen could be found protecting shipping docks, industrial firms, and railroad companies. These security officers, like the new, full-time members of London's Metropolitan Police agency founded by Sir Robert Peel in 1829, concentrated on the *prevention* of crimes. Even after the "Bobbies" were legislated into being by Parliament, the private security officers were remembered as having been a valuable adjunct to public law enforcement (Peak, 1985).

During the mid-1800s the Western frontier of America was awash with train robbers, pickpockets, bootleggers and common outlaws; indeed, United States Congressmen carried guns as they debated on Capitol Hill in the days of the Wild West, for protection against these unsavory characters. Because of these criminals, railroad companies were allowed to establish their own in-house, proprietary security forces. This was also the beginning of the "contract security" system for private concerns (Peak, 1985), explained more fully below.

In 1851, Allan Pinkerton, a pioneer in the private security industry, founded the Pinkerton National Detective Agency. The agency, specializing in railroad security. Pinkerton established the first private security contract operation in the United States. His company's motto was "We Never Sleep," and his logo, an open eye, was probably the genesis of the term "private eye." Pinkerton authored 18 books on private security matters, many of which described him and his operatives' colorful investigative exploits. He also established a code of ethics for his agents which reflects the extent of labor unrest of the day:

The Agency will not represent a defendant in a criminal case except with the knowledge and consent of the prosecution; they will not shadow jurors or investigate public officials in the performance of their duties, or trade union officers or members of their lawful union activities; they will not accept employment from one political party against another; they will not report union meetings unless the meetings are open to the public without restriction; they will not work for vice crusaders; they will not accept contingent fees, gratuities, or rewards. The Agency will never investigate the morals of women unless in connection with another crime, nor will it handle divorce cases (Horan, 1967:30).

One of the staples of the security industry, the alarm operation, had its inception in the mid-nineteenth century; also, in 1858, Edwin Holmes began the first central office burglar alarm operation, which evolved in Holmes Protection, Inc. (National Advisory Commission, 1976).

Other pioneers in the security industry were Henry Wells and William Fargo, who in 1852 formed their contract (fee-for-service) security company, Wells Fargo, that provided private detective and shotgun riders on stagecoaches west of the Missouri River.

Early Twentieth Century Advances

In 1909, William J. Burns, a former Secret Service investigator and head of the Bureau of Investigation (forerunner of the Federal Bureau of Investigation) founded the William J. Burns International Detective Agency; Pinkerton and Burns had the only national investigative agencies until the formation of the FBI in 1924. In 1917, after two of Washington Perry Brink's payroll delivery guards were murdered in holdups, the Brink's "armored car" was unveiled; today Brink's handles about half of the cash that is transported by private couriers in the nation. Later, in 1954, George R. Wackenhut and three other former FBI agents formed the Wackenhut Corporation (Peak 1985).

While security concerns had existed during World War I, largely because of the fear of sabotage and espionage, World War II was a significant catalyst in the growth of contract private security. Munitions plants and all manner of classified documents and defense secrets needed protection from sabotage and espionage. As a result, the war industry employed more than 200,000 plant watchmen during World War II. After the War, the use of private security services expanded to encompass all segments of the private sector (National Advisory Commission, 1976).

MODERN DAY PRIVATE SECURITY

Definition, Nature, and Function

Today, Pinkerton, Wells, Fargo, and the other pioneers of the security industry might well be amazed with the growth in employees and expenditures of the private security industry, discussed in the introduction. The private policing field has become larger in both personnel and resources than the federal, state, and local forces combined (Cole, 1995). Clearly, this industry has survived the growing pains that are usually attendant to any new or innovative concept, attempting to proactively prevent losses from occurring due to both internal and external causes.

A succinct definition of private security was given by a Task Force of the National Advisory Commission on Criminal Justice Standards and Goals in 1976 (p. 30):

> Private security includes those self-employed individuals and privately funded business entities providing security-related service to a specific clientele for a fee, for the individual or entity that retains or employs them, or for themselves, in order to protect their persons, private property, or interests from varied hazards.

Some contemporary writers object to the "profit" aspect of the above definition, on the grounds that airports, hospitals, school, and many other types of institutions now employ private security personnel without the profit orientation (Green, 1981). Another, perhaps better, contemporary definition of private security is "those individuals, organizations, and services other than public law enforcement and regulatory agencies that are engaged primarily in the prevention and investigation of crime, loss, or harm to specific individuals, organizations, or facilities" (Green, 1981:25). Both of these definitions, however, exclude the fastest growing segment of private security — the manufacture, distribution, and installation of security equipment and technology. This segment will be discussed more fully below.

The most common security services being provided today are contract guards, alarm services, private investigators, locksmith services, armored car services, and security consultants (Cunningham et al., 1990). An important consideration for any business or property owner (or "end-user") is deciding whether loss prevention can be most effectively achieved by having one's own security personnel or by hiring an outside agency to supply such personnel. In-house security services, directly hired and controlled by the company or organization, are called *proprietary* services; conversely, *contract services* are outside firms or individuals who provide security services for a fee. Today the proprietary sector continues to be one of the major employers of security personnel, representing more than 25 percent of all private security employees (Cunningham et al., 1990).

Many companies prefer to have their own security personnel because they are likely to be more loyal, more motivated due to promotion possibilities, more knowledgeable of the specific operation and personnel of the organization, more courteous to patrons, and more amenable to training and supervision. However, some disadvantages of proprietary security services include cost, lack of flexibility, and administrative burdens (Hess and Wrobleski, 1992). Such services are provided not only to stop lawbreakers and uphold order, as with the public police, but also to regulate behavior according to policies unique to private property. For example, if a person were to walk barefoot in Disney World, a behavior that is prohibited by the property's owner, a security officer would probably escort that person off of the premises (Shearing and Stenning, 1987).

An example of the rapidly expanding area of contemporary private security — casino security — is presented in Table 1.

Power and Authority

The activities of private security personnel vary widely; some employees merely act as watchmen and call the public police at the first sign of trouble; others are deputized by public authority to carry out patrol and investigative duties similar to those of public officers; still others rely upon their presence and ability to make a "citizen's arrest" to deter lawbreakers. More ambiguous is the issue of a private guard's search of the person or property of a suspect.

Although some of the duties of the security officer are similar to those of the public police officer, their overall powers are entirely different. First, as security officers are not law enforcement officers, recent court decisions have stated that the security officer is not bound by the Miranda warnings of rights. Furthermore, security officers generally possess only the same authority to effect an arrest as does the common citizen (the exact extent of citizen's arrest power varies, depending upon the type of crime, jurisdiction, and the status of the citizen). In most states, warrantless arrests by private citizens are allowed when a felony has been committed and reasonable grounds exist for believing that the person arrested committed it. Most states also allow citizen's arrest for misdemeanors committed in the arrester's presence (Fennelly, 1989).

This power of citizen's arrest is very significant in the private sector, because it allows security officers to protect their employer's property; however, given the serious nature of placing someone under full physical custody arrest, there is very little room for errors of judgment. The public police officer is protected from civil liability for false arrest if probable cause existed to believe a crime was committed; however, the security officer (citizen) can be liable if a crime was not committed. And with respect to searches of offenders after their arrest, unless the security officer fears that a weapon may be hidden on the arrestee, in general it is best for the security officer to await the arrival of the public police to conduct a search, unless permission is given for such a search (Fennelly, 1989).

285

Table 1. CASINO SECURITY

A decade ago only Nevada and New Jersey had legal casino gambling, commonly called gaming. Today, only Hawaii and Utah have no kind of legal gaming. From full casinos, Indian casinos and river boat casinos, to card rooms, bingo parlors, racetracks, betting parlors, legal bookmaking and lotteries, an old vice has blossomed into a new socially acceptable recreational pastime.

Gaming often includes 24 hour access, convenient and often free availability of alcohol and food, and a continuous flow of gaming's product—money, most often in the form of tokens, chips or cash. Gamblers win or lose in public view, and may become victims of serious crimes like theft, assault, robbery or murder. Providing a safe environment for gaming is the responsibility of the establishment. This includes not only the casino, or other gaming establishment, but also hotels, restaurants, shops and parking lots or garages that are part of the facility. Sometimes adjacent and even nearby facilities must be kept safe by casino security forces. Since the growth of gaming has been extremely rapid, there has been a very limited supply of well trained and experienced casino security officers and supervisors.

Casinos usually have two very different kinds of security. The first is what most of us would think of when we envision security officers, uniformed personnel on patrol. The other type is surveillance, which is often totally separate from security and is responsible for the protection and integrity of the game. It protects guests from illegal practices (cheating) by the house, as well as protecting the house from cheating by its guests. Surveillance personnel often have experience and skills as dealers or other gaming practitioners. They are trained in the use of closed circuit television (cctv) and recording devices to detect suspected irregularities in the game. Much of the activity of surveillance units is mandated and controlled by state statutes.

Casino security usually involves three different yet interrelated functions: the protection of guests and employees, protection of the physical plant (including non-public areas, often called gray areas), and protecting and servicing gaming activities. The first area, protection of guests and employees, requires a physical presence. It is from this area that almost all inadequate security lawsuits come. During a recent three-year period in Nevada, more than 70 percent of all lawsuits filed against casinos were security related (Combs, 1990).

The second area, protection of the physical plant, is little different from other large facilities where large numbers of people gather. However, in casinos, very large sums of cash, often many millions of dollars, are present; also, some gaming properties are so large that they serve as destination resorts or independent communities. The ten largest hotels in the world are all in Las Vegas, Nevada, and the largest of all, the 6,000 room Sands Hotel/Casino, is currently under construction.

The third area, protecting and servicing gaming, is unique to the industry. It includes such tasks as performing drops or fills which relate to the pick up, replacement and delivery of chips, tokens or money. Much of this responsibility is also mandated by state statutes. The courts have often held that too much emphasis has been placed on this area, and too little on the protection of guests and employees (see, for example, *Early v. NLV Casino Corp.*, 1984, and *Craigo v. Circus Circus*, 1987).

Typical areas of concern and responsibility in casino security include adequate hiring, training, written policies and procedures, supervision, and documentation. Although these responsibilities are not notably different from non-gaming security departments, the financial consequences of failure to adequately perform in casino security seem to be disproportionately high. Many lawsuits result in settlements or plaintiffs' awards in the millions of dollars, as in the much publicized United States Navy Tailhook case, where a federal jury in Las Vegas held a Hilton Hotel liable for $6.7 million (see *Coughlin v. The Tailhook Assn., Inc.*, 1993).

Although the recent elections of 1996 have slowed the rapid growth of gaming nationwide, its popularity is proven. Gaming is an integral part of American society. Gaming security has improved, and will continue to improve in the future. Professionalism of gaming security will provide employment opportunities for many years to come.

PERSONNEL EDUCATION AND TRAINING

A Tradition of Problems

A long-standing controversy concerns the amount of formal education and training that is possessed, and is appropriately needed, for private security personnel. For example, the five-volume 1971 RAND Corporation study of the security industry (Kakalik and Wildhorn, 1971:133-137) described the "typical" security guard in less than glowing terms:

> "...an aging white male who is poorly educated and poorly paid...between 40 (and) 50; he has little education beyond the ninth grade; he has had a few years of experience in private security; he earns a marginal wage...some have retired from a low-level civil service or military career..."

A federal task force also noted the variety of types, duties, and educational needs of these personnel saying "Of those individuals involved in private security, some are uniformed, some are not; some carry guns, some are unarmed; some guard nuclear energy installations, some guard golf courses; some are trained, some are not; some have college degrees, some are virtually uneducated" (Shearing and Stenning, 1987:III).

Studies have also shown that security personnel are often recruited from among persons with minimal education and training; because the pay is low, the work often attracts only people who cannot find other jobs or who seek only temporary work. Thus, most of the work is done by the young and the retired (Cole, 1995). A RAND Corporation study also found that fewer than half of all private security guards have a high school education, and their average age was 52. Ninety-seven percent of the respondents failed to pass a "simple examination designed to test their knowledge of legal practice in typical job-related situations" (Kakalik and Wildhorn, 1972).

Postsecondary Security Education

Historically, security education has been offered mostly by state universities as an adjunct to their criminal justice programs. The practical effect of this arrangement is that security education is perceived by many people to be a "subset" of the sponsoring department, and that students must often satisfy department requirements that are irrelevant to their vocational interests but are necessary for graduation. The impact on the market, they argue, is even more frustrating, as employers are left with the impression that universities do not understand the nature of security education. It is felt that the biggest challenge for security education in the future will be the collaborative process involving industry, senior leaders in the field, and academics from a variety of institutions. The appropriate courses to be included in a model security program must be identified, then course content must be detailed. It is generally felt that this will not be an easy task to accomplish (*Security Management*, 1994).

During the late 1970s and early 1980s, security education programs were developed primarily by those departments offering police science and criminal justice (CJ) programs. Various studies, including a Task Force on Private Security (National Advisory Commission on Criminal Justice Standards and Goals, 1976) had recommended the development of such programs, with a curriculum that was 10 percent sociology, 10 percent law enforcement/cj, 20 percent security, 20 percent business, and 40 percent general education. Unfortunately, most educational programs of this period were not in line with this recommendation; in fact one observer noted that the programs of the 1970s were preoccupied with "locks, safes, vaults, alarms, and access control" (Parsons, quoted in Chuvala and Fischer, 1994:78). In addition to being narrow in scope, authorities perceived that these programs had several other problems: security education was dominated by police practitioners, little or no concern was shown for theory in program designs, and little research was conducted on the effectiveness of programs (Parsons, quoted in Chuvala and Fischer, 1994). Most of these programs were said to be "tacked on" to CJ programs.

By 1983, 26 programs offered baccalaureate or higher level degrees in security; however, in 1985 it was reported that more than 60 programs of security education in colleges offering associate's degrees and higher had been discontinued. Many observers felt that there was an academic conflict in basic theory between those persons interested in theory, or criminology; those interested in public enforcement, or criminal justice and law enforcement; and those interested in a profit-oriented approach, or private security (Chuvala and Fischer, 1994). By 1989, the first issue of *Security Journal* could report that the education and experience characteristics for one proprietary security organization had approached those of the public police. The private security organization also employed more female officers, and the staff had a greater diversity of ethnic backgrounds than found in the local police departments (Walsh, 1989).

It now appears that many such academic programs have bridged this gap between theory and practice. Even though many security programs have been dropped at colleges and universities, many of those that remain are felt to be quite strong, well-thought out interdisciplinary programs. A survey by Chuvala and Fischer (1994) found 59 programs offering baccalaureate degrees or above. The majority of these programs were still called CJ degrees with a security emphasis or option. On average, only one or two full-time faculty members instruct in these programs, with one or two part-time faculty members assisting. The backgrounds of these faculty are quite diverse, with about a third having police backgrounds, and 70 percent having no security background. Most (70 percent) of the students in security education programs are male, and 80 percent are pre-service.

A Curriculum of Relevancy

As this chapter will demonstrate, the role of the security manager has changed. The security manager of today is likely to be an individual with more than 25 years of experience, a graduate degree, and certification as a protection professional (Chuvala and Fischer, 1994) or security

---

Table 2.   WHAT'S A "CPP" and "CST"?

The CPP designation, for Certified Protection Professional, was created by the American Society of Industrial Security (ASIS) in 1977. The designation recognizes persons having the specialized knowledge necessary to perform as quality security managers in the private sector. All candidates wishing to take the CPP examination must meet rigorous educational and experiential qualifications. The 4.5-hour test is composed of nine subject areas and is given in a multiple-choice format on a wide range of security and loss prevention topics, including the law, physical security, personnel security, investigation, loss prevention, and substance abuse. One recent survey revealed that CPPs earn about $10,000 per year more than non-CPPs in similar positions (*Security Management*, 1996).

The CST Evaluation Program, for Certified Security Trainer, was founded under the auspices of The Academy of Security Educators and Trainers in 1980, and is located in Berryville, Virginia. Recognizing that several recent court decisions emphasized deficiencies in security training, this program seeks to provide a foundation for the future growth of personnel involved in security training. The program's tuition is $1400, and attendees must complete a three-phase process to earn the CST designation: submit a complete resume for credential review and background check, attend a 5-day annual assessment and evaluation program, and, during this program, complete a series of written and oral examinations, personal interviews, training exercises, and three actual training presentations for the certification board (Academy of Security Educators and Trainers, 1997).

trainer (see discussions of the "CPP" and "CST" certifications in Table 2). These managers need to possess business, computer, and legal knowledge in addition to human resource skills. Current educational programs are attempting to meet these multidisciplinary needs, but many authors are arguing that more must be done to provide security managers with a career pathway. Experts recommend that classes be offered at all levels of education, and as a separate discipline at universities and colleges. Classes should be offered in commerce crime, information systems security, and security management in government and industry, which covers terrorism, kidnapping, and hostage taking issues. The focus should be on prevention, not apprehension.

Courses are also recommended in such specialty areas as museum, church, and library security; students can also study insurance and organizational management through the business school, management of information systems through the computer science department, and fire safety through the campus academic or safety department. Some current security management faculty already emphasize the business aspects of the field, assigning students case studies in which they have to identify the security needs of the organization and determine how each need affects the company's profits (Ortmeier, 1996).

A recent survey of 200 security service providers by Ortmeier (1996) attempted to identify the training and education needs of modern security personnel. Eighty-five percent of the respondents felt that an officer academy for basic training was needed; self-defense; first aid; tear gas, baton, and firearms training; patrol procedures; and traffic regulation were identified as training needs in this academy. They also felt that the legal aspects of security, public relations, and report writing should be emphasized.

Ninety-five percent of the respondents also favored an associate's degree in security at community colleges, for entry-level management. Here, emphasis should be placed on accounting, general business practices, public and human rela-

tions, law, written communications, investigations, computer literacy, specialized security applications, speech, and social science.

Ninety-two percent favored a bachelor's degree in security at colleges and universities, for mid-level management. Competencies to be developed in these students included business law and ethics, budgeting, contracting, personnel management and labor relations, planning, organizational theory, communications and behavior, public relations, policy formulation, statistics, systems engineering, technical writing, and threat assessment and analysis.

Perhaps the above overview of desired courses of study at the basic academy, two-year, and four-year levels best demonstrates how security management has evolved, and the kinds of challenges that face this industry in the twenty-first century.

Indeed, a master's program in security administration already exists and is thriving. Webster University, of St. Louis, Missouri, began operating in the late 1980s in cooperation with the ASIS Foundation; since then, it has prospered. In September 1996, Jacksonville, Florida, became the ninth city to offer the Webster master's degree program (in addition to Albuquerque; Bolling Air Force Base, Washington, D.C.; Chicago; Pope Air Force Base, North Carolina; San Diego; St. Louis; Merritt Island, Florida; and Denver). And as of September 1996, Webster's security management program had produced nearly 200 graduates and had approximately 200 graduate students enrolled nationwide (Thompson, 1996).

Training Needs

Security training has been an issue in court cases involving claims of negligent security. An example of such a case was *Early v. N.L.V. Casino Corp.* (1984), where a woman was severely beaten in a Las Vegas casino restroom, suffering psychological trauma as a result. She sued the casino for negligence. The trial court dismissed the case, but the state Supreme Court reversed, finding that the casino could be held liable for Early's injuries. On appeal, the court called into question the casino security's training program. For example, evidence indicated that the security department did not hold regular, formal training sessions or meetings. No security manual existed, and the only instruction security officers received pertained to carrying money boxes from the casino counting room. This case illustrates the importance of security training, not only with regard to day-to-day performance but also with respect to a company's ability to defend itself against charges of negligent security in the event of a lawsuit.

At a minimum, the security manager must ensure that training complies with all local, state, and federal laws. Such managers should consult legal counsel to identify any statutory provisions and case law that may apply to training programs, particularly those concerning the use of force. Notably, local peer review may be more important than comparisons with distant or national industry training guidelines, as community standards can often override industry standards in the courtroom (Nichter, 1996). Training records, program or course outlines, attendance sheets, examinations, procedural manuals, and policy statements are all subject to subpoena and should be maintained in up-to-date fashion.

All too often the new security officer is taught only the security "primer": the chain of command, how to use a radio, and uniform wear standards. Some organizations "train" their employees by merely having them accompany other security offices around the company's facility (Chuda, 1995). The most effective security training program is a combination of classroom lecture and hands-on training, using computers, lectures, and videotapes. Furthermore, as court cases have pointed out, the course material must be related to the security officer's job. Trainers, of course, must be qualified and have a firm understanding of their subject matter. Trainers and security managers can also review any relevant professional standards that are promulgated by professional organizations, such as ASIS, the American Society of Safety Engineers, Risk and Insurance Management

Society, the International Foundation for Protection Officers, and the Academy of Security Educators and Trainers.

Building Legislative Support

One example of state interest in, and control over, minimum training standards and licensing procedures for the security industry is that of Oregon. In 1995, Oregon's governor signed into law S.B. 60, becoming effective on January 1, 1997.

The main goal of the legislation was to standardize regulation statewide. Prior to the legislation there were no state training or certification requirements. Some municipalities regulated security, but the regulations were not standardized. Private security industry representatives had made several attempts at legislation over the past 20 years, but prior to S.B. 60 they could not garner the necessary support for passage. Much groundwork obviously had to be laid before this legislation would be signed into law.

Private security executives in Oregon felt strongly that their industry would benefit from regulatory support. Therefore, this legislation was drafted and supported by a group of such practitioners, with critical collaboration from law enforcement, private industry, and state agencies. Then a statewide, annual training session was conducted, discussing public/private relationships, media relations, the status of the pending legislation, and other topics. Building bridges with public police executives, legislators, and other key persons was very important in gaining support for S.B. 60. One of the most critical partnerships was that established between contract and proprietary security personnel. These two groups formed a private security council that promoted professionalism of the industry, pushed for legislation that would require licensing of private security companies and certification of security officers, and form active partnerships with public police agencies (Langford, 1996).

ARMING SECURITY PERSONNEL

An Enduring Controversy

A study conducted more than a quarter century ago (Kakalik and Wildhorn, 1971) found that half of both contract and proprietary guards carried firearms at least a quarter of the time. A 1980 study by the federal National Institute of Justice (NIJ) found that only 10 percent of the guards were armed, and the rise in insurance premiums and liability litigation suggests that by the year 2000 perhaps only 5 percent will be armed (Cunningham et al., 1991). However, there are other observers who believe that, where comparisons over several years are able to be made, the percentage of armed guards appears to be growing (Harowitz, 1995). A survey by *Security Journal* found that the percentage of armed guards averages 10 to 20 percent in the states.

A long-running debate concerning private security personnel is whether or not these individuals should even be armed at all. The question that is often raised is whether those officers who carry weapons use them wisely. Information needed to address this question is difficult to acquire. Ten states require that weapons discharge reports be filed with the regulatory agency, but only three states compile and analyze statistics from these reports (Harowitz, 1995).

One of the most common arguments against arming private security personnel is that only public police officers should be armed. In the view of security practitioner Henry DeGeneste (1995:49), "guns up the ante. Split-second decisions with lethal weapons can result in death or serious injury; a visible weapon may cause a criminal to assume a more violent attitude that could in turn trigger more violent action." He argued that another concern is the mindset of the security officer. Such officers, DeGeneste maintained,

"...are rarely prepared, either mentally or physically, to carry guns or make informed deci-

sions about the use of deadly force. (They) generally do not have the training and preparation for armed public contact assignments. Approximately 40 percent of armed contract security personnel report being 'self taught' in the use of firearms. Is this level of training enough for an armed officer? Absolutely not. Most security officers lack the tactical savvy to make decisions regarding the use of deadly force, even under optimal conditions. Add the stress, fear, and confusion that accompany an armed confrontation, and the prospect of armed security officers is problematic at best."

That reasoning, according to another security practitioner, Bill Clark (1995), fails on two counts: because of the widespread availability of weapons among criminals, and because many private security officers are now asked to handle the equivalent of public police duties. Clark argues that the decision to arm private security officers should be based on whether it is necessary and prudent for the site in question. Clark felt that the most legitimate concern of those who oppose arming private security forces is the liability issue. Armed security personnel can increase a company's exposure to liability, and therefore must take appropriate steps to cover the liability. If a security situation does not expose the security officer to dangerous criminal situations, then the officer need not be armed. And if these personnel are neither sufficiently trained nor disciplined to avoid reckless use of their weapons, they should not be armed (Clark, 1995).

This is probably a debate that is not going to be settled in the foreseeable future. However, both sides agree that there are some roles in which security officers must be armed, such as protecting high risk or high value assets like nuclear plants, and certain shipments in transit such as armored cars. Yet, this concern remains and it is justified; as the renowned Hallcrest II report (Cunningham et al., 1990) reminded us, "One inescapable fact...is that firearms tend to be used when they are carried" (p. 143).

When the critical decision is made by an employer to arm security personnel, then the type and level of firearms training that is provided those security personnel is justifiably called into closer scrutiny. Much ado has been made about security officers carrying weapons who have received little or no prior training or have undergone no checks on their criminal history records, but are carrying a weapon. While an eight-hour block of pre-service instruction is recommended for all security personnel, it is further recommended that armed security officers attend another 24-hour block on general matters and a 23-hour block on firearms instruction. And, because private security personnel may encounter violent or dangerous situations, it is recommended that proper legal training be provided as well (National Advisory Commission, 1973).

The National Advisory Commission's Task Force on private security recommended that these personnel receive 24 hours of firearms training, including three hours' instruction on legal and policy restraints, before assignment. Fewer than 10 states have such stringent requirements. However, 23 states mandate some firearms training for armed guards; only 14 require training for unarmed guards. Surveys and interviews indicate that the typical uniformed guard receives an estimated 4 to 6 hours of training before assignment (Cunningham et al., 1991). Today, training requirements for armed security officers are far from consistent. Where required at all, firearms training varies widely, from four hours in Arkansas and South Carolina to 47 hours in New York (Harowitz, 1995).

THE PUBLIC-PRIVATE POLICE INTERFACE

A Radical Revolution

The relationship between private security and the public police has experienced what has been termed a "radical evolution" (Patterson, 1995:33), from being a very poor working relationship to one that has now improved considerably.

Research sponsored by NIJ in the early 1980s revealed few collaborative efforts until that time between police and private security, with the exception of crime prevention programs. Public police officials described their relationship with private security managers as fair to good at best. Historically, this lack of communication and poor working relationship resulted in botched investigations, destruction of evidence, and overzealousness by the private police.

Another wedge between these two entities, from the standpoint of public officials, has to do with public police "moonlighting" in private police jobs. Indeed, private firms now hire an estimated 150,000 regular police officers to provide security in their off-duty hours (U.S. Department of Justice, National Institute of Justice, 1988). With the growth of police brotherhoods and unions in the 1930s, the local police began to have more time to perform second jobs.

There are major concerns about police officers performing secondary employment. They can become overextended in their off-duty labors to the point that they can become exhausted and therefore unfit for police duty. Their off-duty job may threaten the dignity and status of the policing profession, or may physically disable the officers. There may be conflicts of interest between the officers' regular job and the moonlighting jobs, such as working for a tow companies or bail-bonding firms. As a result of these concerns, many police agencies have written extensive policies to control their officers' secondary employment. To this point, the federal courts have been sympathetic with the need for police administrators to restrict outside employment.

In the mid-1980s, the International Association of Chiefs of Police, the National Sheriffs' Association, and the American Society for Industrial Security (ASIS) established the Joint Council of Law Enforcement and Private Security Associations. A number of local and regional groups also set up cooperative programs involving the police and private security. The public-private police interface now involves a number of positive cooperative efforts with such tasks as the transportation of hazardous materials, protecting dignitaries, and control of crowds. Furthermore, there has been an expanded role of private security in recent natural disasters, where there is a need to provide emergency response, protect property and persons, and prevent looting.

With private security forces far outnumbering police personnel and recent budget cuts causing reductions in National Guard personnel, these forces are expected to be used more and more to respond to natural disasters and emergency situations. Cooperative public police and private security initiatives are also evidenced in large public special events. Municipal police also encourage a stronger role by private security in burglar alarm monitoring and response, and in patrolling churches, residences, and business districts. And, where carjackings, drive-by shootings, rape, and robbery raise employee safety concerns, employers are hiring drive-by security services to patrol parking lots. Private security employees are also conducting government security-clearance background investigations, required for certain positions with the federal government (Patterson, 1995).

THE PROBLEM OF LIABILITY

Civil liability has become an increasing concern in the private security industry. Civil actions may be brought against any private security personnel who commit an unlawful action against another person. Often, the officer's employer is sued as well as the officer (Hess and Wrobleski, 1992). For example, in *Granite Construction Co. v. Rhyne* (1991), a California court held that the term "person" includes incorporations and that therefore a corporation could be prosecuted for manslaughter.

The legal landscape, as one attorney described it, is "studded with liability land mines for security officers and their employers" (Houska, 1995:70). To prevent costly jury verdicts, today's security manager must be aware of the basic laws governing the actions of security officers as well as steps a security company can take to minimize its civil liability.

The common scenario develops when a person is attacked while on property that is either patrolled by a private security company, has a security officer stationed on the premises, or has no security present. As with most crime, the act is usually unexpected and completed in a matter of seconds. Then, when the assailant is not caught or has no assets to compensate the injured victim, the victim turns to the landowner and security company for recovery (Feliton and Owen, 1994). Thus, reasonable precautions must be taken to try to prevent innocent people from being victimized. Where the line between reasonableness and unlimited liability should be drawn, and who should be liable when the line is crossed, are questions that are taken to the courts. It is also important to note that a landowner cannot "contract away culpability" merely by hiring a private security firm or officers to work on the premises; after problems arise the courts may still look to see if reasonable precautions were taken to avoid negligence.

Some cases have dealt specifically with the private security officer's obligation and legal duty; generally, however, the courts indicate that the security officer's liability is intertwined with the landowner's. Also, it is typical that the liability of a security officer is based on some form of negligence or failure to provide adequate security. By examining the individual elements of negligence — duty, breach, and causation — the extent of a security officer's liability can be determined.

Another question that often arises with respect to security officer performance is foreseeability. Although, as noted above, their liability is said to be intertwined with the landowner's, a criminal act may not be considered foreseeable to the landowner unless there have been prior similar criminal acts. A "totality of the circumstances" test may be used to determine foreseeability when there have not been prior, similar criminal acts (see *Isaacs v. Huntington Memorial Hospital*, 1985). Once the landowner is put on notice, he or she can fulfill his or her duty by hiring private security officers to patrol the property. It is also important for the landowner to document these actions taken; if he or she cannot document that they did take some affirmative action, then generally they are considered to *not* have properly done so. Then, since the officer acts as the landowner's agent and is hired after the landowner has notice of criminal activity, the notice is imputed to the guard force. Any crime occurring on the premises under those circumstances could be considered foreseeable (Feliton and Owen, 1994).

However, several cases have held that unanticipated criminal acts are superseding factors that exonerate an otherwise negligent landowner or security officer. An example is the case of *Toscano-Lopez v. McDonald's* (1987), where a heavily armed individual entered the McDonald's restaurant in San Ysidro, California, and opened fire on the patrons. Twenty-one people were killed before the gunman was shot and killed by the police. At trial, it was found that, since the restaurant was located in a high-crime area, McDonald's had breached its duty by failing to provide adequate security precautions — at least to the extent of having an unarmed security officer on the premises. Still, McDonald's was absolved from liability because of the random nature of the offense.

Various steps can be taken to help protect security companies from liability, including adequate training of personnel. The security officer should also become thoroughly familiar with the neighborhood in which he or she is working, including the manner and type of criminal activity that may be expected (Feliton and Owen, 1994).

THE FUTURE OF PRIVATE SECURITY AND TECHNOLOGY

A Changing Philosophy

The corporate vision and operational objectives have changed — and will continue to change — as managers adopt business philosophies such as Total Quality Management (TQM). One result is that companies will demand more from security contractors. Contract guard service companies must be prepared to operate in this new, tougher business environment. The movement toward quality is accelerating like never before, due to the ever-increasing availability and acceptance of new, improved, and cheaper technology. Such technology is transforming training methods, communications, and operations (Sundberg, 1994).

How do these advances affect the security industry? First, many corporations with routine guard requirements have already gone beyond the learning stages of TQM, enacting programs to provide increased customer value-added service at ever lower costs. This new corporate customer is looking at the guard company vendors for similar attitudes; the guard service contractor must learn to fit into this environment. Furthermore, the basics of guard duty are rooted in risk management. The guard industry must continue in the future to strive to close the gap between its performance in delivering the appropriate level of risk management services and the customer's perception of the service provided. Technology also provides a guard service company with the opportunity to upgrade its performance significantly by tracking client company asset changes, and automatically making the corresponding changes in guard services (Sundberg, 1994).

But some practitioners, like Richard Juliano, do not agree with the view that security managers must change the way they do business. They disagree that the security professional "must be someone with a master's degree in business administration and operate from a corporate perspective" (Juliano, 1996:222). He argues that these executives need not go so far as to fall in line with the corporate management image and treat employees as a customer base that must be kept happy.

Security need not be user-friendly. And the many popular management theories that advocate these approaches run the risk of taking the security department's focus away from its real mission of protection. Security executives around the country are using techniques such as total quality management (TQM) effectively. However, the fact remains — and rightly so — that the average security department is run more as a quasi-police operation than as a corporate accounting department.

294

Juliano also finds "disturbing" the view often expressed in the security literature that trained police personnel cannot easily understand security's main function of prevention and deterrence, thereby precluding present or former police officers from becoming truly useful as security officers.

Law enforcement officers already have a level of training that makes them highly suitable and adaptable to the concepts of private security. Indeed, there are more similarities than differences between the skills and goals of law enforcement personnel and security professionals. These [police] individuals also bring unique life experience with them from policing to security, which gives them a strength of character that helps them function well in stressful situations.

Trends That Will Drive Industry Growth

While in-house corporate security practitioners continue to face budget pressures, the private security industry is doing well and should continue to expand. Worth nearly $2 billion, the commercial and industrial security equipment market in the United States is forecast to expand its revenue base at a compound annual growth rate of 13.8 percent. By 2001, this market could be worth as much as $4 billion. Technological approaches to security problems will continue to expand, with greater emphasis on total systems solutions (Bowman, 1996).

A recent questionnaire of 100 companies listed in the *Security Industry Buyers Guide*, conducted by Erik Bowman, discovered that three trends are driving growth in private security: the public's concerns about crime, the United States government's reluctance to increase expenditures on public safety measures, and technological advances in security products. Bowman believes that, in the early 21st century, one of the most striking changes will continue to be the consolidation of operations and technologies. Systems integration is the wave of the future for security, such as combining access control, closed circuit television (CCTV), and intrusion detection into a single computer-controlled unit. Rather than new pro-

ducts being created, future growth is likely to come in the form of combinations of technologies that already exist. End-users will continue to search for turn-key solutions that provide them with the means of coordinating the many responsibilities faced by security from access control to facility management (Bowman, 1996).

The physical security industry can be divided into three broad segments: perimeter security, interior security, and access control. Taken together, electronic access control and interior physical security comprise over 97 percent of the technology market. Next we examine what the future appears to hold for these three segments.

There are four categories of perimeter security: microwave sensors, video motion detection systems (VMDs), barrier sensors, and buried sensors. The emergence of VMDs has sparked most of the growth in the perimeter security market. Perimeter security has an annual market of about $20 million today; it is expected to grow to about $39 million by 2001. Within the barrier sensor segment of the market, fiber optic cable sensors have the most potential for growth.

The largest physical security equipment market segment is "electronic access control," which represents about 58 percent of the entire industry and has annual market revenues of about $1 billion. Security professionals can expect to see falling prices for electronic access control systems. The biometrics market is expected to experience significant growth, at a rate of about 35 percent per year. Biometrics is a statistical study of biological data and uses unique individual physiological characteristics to positively identify people (Thompson, 1985). This is done by recording, recognizing, and comparing the stored patterns of retinal configurations of the eye, fingerprints, or the geometry of one's palm or hand (Fennelly, 1989). However, there is concern over performance and user acceptance of biometric devices. But there are eye recognition devices that may replace the current hand geometry or fingerprint technologies.

Equipment in the "interior physical security"

category is used to detect and monitor intruders inside buildings. It includes microwave sensors, magnetic contacts, glass break sensors, passive infrared sensors, and CCTV. Motion detectors allow end-users to give authorized personnel a way to open doors automatically. Annual sales of equipment in this market are worth more than $700 million, and are expected to exceed $1.9 billion by 2001. Recently CCTV has experienced price declines and technological advances. CCTV systems vary greatly in design. The advent of a new chip, replacing the image tube, has reduced camera size and cost, extended camera life, and increased durability and reliability. Technology is also providing cameras that can operate well even in low-light security and surveillance applications (Bowman, 1996).

An interesting use of CCTV that is likely to see future expansion is in monitoring open, public places — an undertaking that until recently was viewed as too Orwellian and an infringement on civil rights. An estimated 120 communities throughout Britain are now using CCTV technology for public area surveillance of parking lots, shopping centers, and sporting events (following several riots at football stadiums). Citizens now report feeling safer and being more willing to shop, eat, and be entertained in public. Several communities with CCTV monitoring report that this is a costly but successful concept; decreases in serious crimes and acts of vandalism are commonplace. Some American cities are using CCTV as well. For example, Baltimore recently launched a pilot program to install 16 cameras in one crime-infested neighborhood, and city councils in Cincinnati and Memphis have already had success with surveillance cameras (Poole and Williams, 1996).

The use of robots is also anticipated to experience enormous expansion in the future. Robots are about one-third the price of humans and, in their security application, will be equipped with sensors which, in effect, makes them nonstationary, or mobile, detectors (Cathey, 1983).

The future of security education programs is far from certain. Such programs continue to fade away. There appears to be little financial or philosophical support for these programs at many postsecondary educational institutions, making planning for program changes difficult if not impossible. Financial uncertainty, the needs of the security community, and control by other departments all appear to be key issues. One of the problems inherent in security education programs, as revealed in a national survey by Chuvala and Fischer (1994), is that many of the people instructing in these programs have little or no experience in the field of security or loss prevention. Another possible need is for such programs to use advisory boards. The programs that are most successful have used such boards; input from experts and practitioners is very helpful.

On The Web

Another area that security executives of the future must master to remain competitive is cyberspace. There is a wealth of security resources available on the Internet. While the idea of connecting to the Internet is intimidating to some people, it is no longer as complicated as it once was. What is complicated and frustrating is finding the information you want rapidly and efficiently. The solution is knowing how to navigate through the vast resources of the Internet to get to the right information with minimal effort.

What are some of the security-related "places" people are able to access once connected to the Internet? The list grows daily as more and more organizations and individuals claim their cyberspace, but following is a short list of sites that can be accessed through the addresses listed:

➢ National Industrial Security Board (http://nisb.jcte.jcs.mil/). This is the site of the Defense Investigative Service bulletin board, providing guidance in support of the National Industrial Security Program.

➢ Security Management (http://www.securitymanagement.com). You can download a monthly publication, *Legal Reporter*, free of charge.

296

- National Criminal Justice Reference Service (gopher://ncjrs.aspensys.com:71/). Through this service one can access copies of research papers, criminal justice data, or connect to any of the many international agencies on the "Police Resource List."

- Criminal Law Links (http://dpa.state.ky.us/~rwheeler/). This site leads to state and federal law resources.

- FBI Homepage (http://www.fbi.gov) Through this site, you can access FBI bulletins and related agency information.

- Drug Enforcement Administration (http://www.usdoj.gov/deahome.htm). This page gives DEA press releases and employment opportunities.

- Vera Institute (http://broadway.vera.org/pub/ocjsites.html). This site is hosted by a research organization that has complied a list of other criminal justice resources.

- U.S. Department of Justice (http:www.usdoj.gov/) This site offers information on issues such as the Americans with Disabilities Act (ADA), as well as data on major crimes.

- CopNET (http://police.sas.ab.ca/) This is an index of national, state, and local law enforcement and other public agencies' homepages.

- Terrorism. Numerous sites around the Web contain information on terroristic threats. Among them are The Counter Terrorism Page (http://www.interlog.com/~vabiro/) and Terroristic Profiles (http://www.tezcat.com/~top/terrorist/)

Those who are new to the Web need to remember that our world is in constant flux; if the address of a particular organization does not work, it may have changed. Try doing a key word search with the organization's name using one of the directories (like Yahoo) if that occurs (Lander and Roughton, 1996).

SUMMARY

This chapter has examined the rapidly growing private security industry, to include its history and contemporary methods, issues, and challenges. It is clear that many challenges still lie before this industry's administrators — particularly in an era when lawsuits can and do arise from security personnel negligence and abuse.

However, in the defense of the administrators in this industry, state statutes have not often required that they do much more than what they have been doing, especially in the areas of training and general accountability. Consequently, improper treatment of members of the public and a lack of knowledge of basic elements of security work (for example, how to properly arrest and restrain someone) is not uncommon. Hopefully this increasingly troublesome problem will be addressed soon through appropriate legislation. Meanwhile, this industry will continue to burgeon and provide much of the protection of society as it moves into the 21st century.

✳ ✳ ✳ ✳ ✳

REFERENCES

Academy of Security Educators and Trainers
   ·1997   "The Certified Security Trainer (C.S.T.) Evaluation Program," program information brochure, p. 2.

Astor, S.
   1978   "A Nation of Thieves," *Security World* 15 (September): 18.

Bowman, Erik J.
   1996   "Security Tools Up for the Future," *Security Management* 40 (January), p. 30.

Cathey, William Cole
   1983   "The Robots Are Coming!" *Security Management* 27 (September), p. 112.

Chuda, Thomas T.
   1995   "Taking Training Beyond the Basics," *Security Management* 39 (February), pp. 57-59.

Chuvala III, John, and Robert James Fischer
   1994   "Where Have All the Programs Gone?" *Security Management* 38 (August), pp. 76-81.

Clark, Bill
   1995   "A Call to Arms," *Security Management* 39 (October), p. 49.

Cole, George.
   1995   *The American System of Criminal Justice*, 7th ed. Belmont, CA: Wadsworth Publishing Company.

Combs, E. Leslie
        Personal communication, January 25, 1990.

Critchley, T. A.
   1967   *A History of Police in England and Wales*, 2d ed. Montclair, NJ: Patterson Smith Publishing Corp.

Cunningham, William C., John J. Strauchs, and Clifford Van Meter
   1990   *The Hallcrest Report II: Private Security Trends, 1970 to 2000.* McLean, VA: Butterworth-Heinemann.
   1991   "Private Security: Patterns and Trends." U.S. Department of Justice, National Institute of Justice, Research in Brief, August 1991, p. 2.

DeGeneste, Henry I.
   1995   "A Disarming Question," *Security Management* 39 (October), pp. 49-51.

Feliton, Jr., John R., and David B. Owen
   1994   "Guarding Against Liability," *Security Management* 38 (September), pp. 125-132.

Fennelly Lawrence J. (ed.)
   1989   *Handbook of Loss Prevention and Crime Prevention*, 2d ed. Boston, MA: Butterworths.

Green, Gion
   1981   *Introduction to Security* (3d ed.), Stoneham, MA: Butterworth.

Harowitz, Sherry
   1995   "A Shot in the Dark," *Security Management* 39 (October), p. 47.

Hess, Karen M., and Henry M. Wrobleski
   1992   *Introduction to Private Security*, 3d ed., St. Paul, MN: West Publishing Company.

Horan, James
   1967   *The Pinkertons.* New York: G. P. Putnam's Sons.

Houska, Maureen M.
   1995   "Guarding Against Liability," *Security Management* 39 (April), pp. 70-71.

Juliano, Richard
   1996   "Has Security Lost Its Perspective?" *Security Management* 40 (September), p. 222.

Kakalik, James, and Sorrell Wildhorn
    1971   *Private Police in the United States*, five vols., Washington, DC: National Institute of
            Justice. See specifically Volume 2, *The Private Police Industry: Its Nature and Extent*.
Lander, Ronald, and James E. Roughton
    1996   "The Security Professional in Cyberspace," *Security Management* 40 (January), pp.
            40-41.
Langford, Jo Ann
    1996   "Building Support for Security Legislation," *Security Management* 40 (September),
            pp. 176-177.
Maguire, Kathleen, and Ann L. Pastore
    1996   *Sourcebook of Criminal Justice Statistics — 1995*. Washington, DC: U.S. Department
            of Justice, Bureau of Justice Statistics.
Maguire, Kathleen, and Timothy J. Flanagan
    1991   *Sourcebook of Criminal Justice Statistics — 1990*. Washington, DC: U.S. Department
            of Justice, Bureau of Justice Statistics, pp. 2, 18.
National Advisory Commission on Criminal Justice Standards and Goals
    1973   *Private Security* volume (Washington, DC: U.S. Government Printing Office.
National Institute of Justice
    1996   "Victim Costs and Consequences: A New Look," NIJ Research Report, January 1996,
            p. 3.
Nichter, D. Anthony
    1996   "Training on Trial," *Security Management* 40 (September), pp. 75-78.
Ortmeier, P.J.
    1996   "Adding Class to Security," *Security Management* 40 (July), p. 99.
Patterson, Julien
    1995   "Forging Creative Alliances," *Security Management* 39 (January), p. 33.
Peak, Ken
    1985   "On Guard: The Private Security Industry in America." In eds. Dae H. Chang and
            James A. Fagin, *Introduction to Criminal Justice: Theory and Application* (2d ed.)
            (Geneva, IL: Paladin House, 1985), pp. 273-287.
Poole, Robert, and Derek Williams
    1996   "Success in the Surveillance Society," *Security Management* 40 (May), pp. 29-33.
Radzinowicz, Leon
    1948   *A History of English Common Law*. New York: Macmillan Company.
Reiss, Jr., Albert J.
    1988   *Private Employment of Public Police*, National Institute of Justice, Research in Brief,
            February.
Security Management
    1994   "Security Education and the Marketplace," Vol. 38 (June), pp. 85-86.
Security Management
    1996   "CPP Candidates Multiply," Vol. 40 (October), p. 89.
Shearing, Clifford D., and Philip C. Stenning (eds.)
    1987   "Say 'Cheese!': The Disney Order That Is Not So Mickey Mouse," in *Private Polic-
            ing* (Newbury Park, CA: Sage), p. 13.
Sundberg, Edward A.
    1994   "Is the Security Guard Industry Ready for Its Future?" *Security Management* 38
            (August), p. 134.
Thompson, Amy
    1996   "Jacksonville Offers Webster Master's Degree," *Security Management* 40 (Septem-
            ber), pp. 180-181.
Thompson, Michael
    1984   "The Newest Wave: Biometric Security," *Security World*, February, p. 55.

United States Department of Justice, National Institute of Justice
1988   *Private Employment of Public Police.* Washington, DC: U.S. Government Printing Office.

Walsh, W.
1989   "Private/Public Police Stereotypes: A Different Perspective," *Security Journal* , pp. 21-27.

CASES CITED

Coughlin v. The Tailhook Association, Inc., 818 F.Supp. 1366 (D.Nev., 1993).

Craigo v. Circus Circus, 106 Nev. 1, 786 P.2d 22 (1990).

Granite Construction Co. v. Rhyne, 107 Nev. 651, 817 P.2d 711 (1991).

Early v. NLV Casino Corp., 100 Nev. 200, 678 P.2d 683 (1984).

Isaacs v. Huntington Memorial Hospital, 204 Cal.Rptr. 765 (Cal. App.2 Dist. 1984).

Toscano-Lopez v. McDonald's, 238 Cal. Rptr. 436 (1987).

Chapter 14

Minorities and the American Criminal Justice System[1]

By

Ineke Haen Marshall and **Chris E. Marshall**

"...and justice for all." These are the final words of the American Pledge of Allegiance. These words embody the highest of ideals at the heart of the American experiment of democracy. It calls upon us to treat all American citizens — black or white, male or female, rich or poor — equally. Our 200-year history shows that this goal remains one of the most elusive and difficult to achieve. It is also clear that until such time as we are able to reach this goal, we will not in good conscience be able to call our American experiment of democracy a success. One part of our government which is constantly wrestling with achieving this ideal is the American criminal justice system. This system, charged with the administration of the criminal laws of our country, is perhaps the most visible of all the parts of government. The success of the American criminal justice system in meeting the goal of *justice for all* is an important measure of how well we as a nation are doing.

The American population is very diverse. It is divided along many, many dimensions including those of ethnicity, religion, national origin, gender, wealth, and age. Underlying these different dimensions is that most important division of them all: access to power — economic, political, cultural or social. By far the most powerful group in the United States is that made up of white males of Northern European or English descent. Those further down the ladder of power are blacks, Hispanics, Native Americans, and those of East European or Asian heritage — groups we usually refer to as "minorities." A minority group is any group with a (perceived) shared racial, ethnic, or cultural heritage, whose members are subject to stereotyping and discriminatory treatment, and whose members are relatively powerless vis-a-vis the majority in a society. This definition connects different population groups based on ethnicity or race, nationality or country of birth.[2] Many critics contend that where there exist such great disparities of power, "justice for all" will remain only a high-sounding ideal and that our American great experiment is doomed to fail.

We examine the effects of minority group status (primarily race and ethnicity) on the functioning of the American criminal justice system. We ask ourselves the question: Is the American criminal justice system successful in its attempt to approximate the ideal of justice for all? Do blacks, Hispanics, and recent Asian immigrants receive the same kind of treatment as their white counterparts by the police, the courts, and in prisons? And what about those people living in the U.S. who are

301

not American citizens? What are their experiences with the American justice system? As you will soon see, this topic is quite complex. The issues of "power" and "justice" have been analyzed by countless scholars for many years. Questions concerning "ethnicity" and "race" also have been the topic of much debate and research.[3] Any one of these concepts is difficult on its own. There are no simple or quick answers. In this chapter, we can only discuss the main issues and key controversies; for a more indepth understanding of the topic, we refer you to the extensive body of writings in this area. We have listed some of the leading texts at the end of this essay.

Most of our discussion in this chapter centers around "race"[4] or "ethnicity," but we will also include studies and arguments with primary emphasis on citizenship or immigrant status ("foreigners"). The red threads throughout the chapter are the themes of justice, power, and inequality. As we will illustrate throughout the following pages, power differences and inequality are reflected *both* in the type and extent of criminal involvement of minorities *and* in the manner in which the police, prosecutors, juries, judges, and correctional personnel deals with minorities.

CLASSIFYING AND SORTING OUR POPULATION

To most of us, it is common-sense that the government has the responsibility and need to gather information — including racial/ethnic information — about the people living within its borders. The list of race/ethnicity choices on the U.S. Census questionnaire seems innocuous enough — just something that "has to be done." However, it is important for us to consider another possibility.[5] The racial and ethnic classifications employed by government agencies, such as the Census Bureau, are not necessarily neutral statistical devices. Instead, they determine the types of comparisons which _can_ be made in government reports summarizing American racial/ethnic conditions; they reinforce racial, ethnic and national distinctions; they shape our citizens' self-identification.

These classification schemes can also have a significant impact upon research and policy in the areas of race/ethnicity. This is most convincingly illustrated by the manner in which the American government statistically divides the population into only four "racial" groups: American Indians/Native Americans, African-Americans/blacks, Asian-Americans, and Caucasians/whites. [It is likely that the U.S. Census will include the category of "mixed" race in the year 2,000.] Each of these four "racial" categories consists of a large number of subgroups of often widely divergent national, ethnic, or racial characteristics.[6] Figure 1 shows the racial/ethnic breakdown of the 248,79,873 people formally living in the U.S. In addition to "race," the United States Bureau of the Census uses "ethnic" background (defined as Spanish-speaking or not).[7] A person classified as "Hispanic," may be either White, Black, Asian, or Native American. As will be explained at different points in this chapter, this scheme fails to capture essential distinctions and commonalities among and between minority groups. Furthermore, the researcher who has to rely on formal statistics (i.e., police, court, prison data) has no choice but to work within the limits imposed by these artificial distinctions between population groups.[8]

AFRICAN-AMERICANS AND CRIME

The white perception of blacks in America has long included an aspect of criminality (Myers,

Figure 1. U.S. Population in 1990.

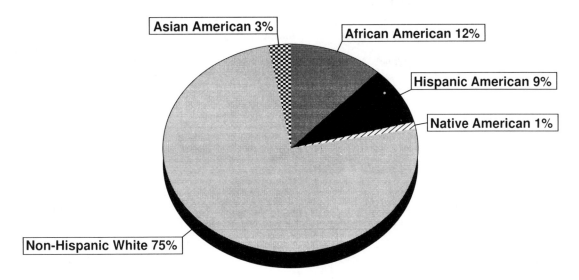

Source: U.S. Bureau of the Census, *Current Population Reports*, Series P25-1092 (Washington, DC: Government Printing Office, 1992); *Statistical Abstract of the United States 1994* (Washington, DC: Government Printing Office, 1994) *[adapted from Parillo (1996, p. 78)]*.

1995:146). In American society, public concern with crime has been (and continues to be) primarily focused on "blacks."[9] Not only the public and politicians have long equated "crime" with "black crime": American scholars, too, have a significant history of discussions about the crime rates of blacks versus whites (See, for example, Hawkins, 1995A; Tonry, 1995).[10]

Official Statistics on Black Crime: Data from the Government Agencies

The dramatic rates of involvement in the criminal justice system of black males (and increasingly females) in present-day America are having a substantial impact on black Americans (Mauer, 1995), as well as on society in general. "On an average day in America, one out of three African-American men aged 20-29 was either in prison or jail, on probation or parole" (The Sentencing Project, 1995, cited in Donziger, 1996:105). This statement underscores the urgency

of the problem of race and justice in America. The United States is "on the verge of a social catastrophe because of the sheer number of African-Americans behind bars — numbers that continue to rise with breathtaking speed and frightening implications" (Donziger, 1996:99).[11] Historically, African-Americans have always been overrepresented in our jails and prisons, but the differences have widened tremendously over recent decades.[12]

At every stage of the criminal justice system from arrest through incarceration, blacks are present in numbers greatly out of proportion to their presence in the population. In 1994, for example, blacks made up about 12% of the U.S. population but 44.7% of those arrested for violent index crime (murder, forcible rape, robbery, and aggravated assault)[13] (see Table 1). More than one-half of the arrests for homicide (56.4%) and robbery (60.8%) in 1994 involved a black suspect; about one-third of the arrests for index property crimes (burglary, larceny-theft, car theft and arson) was cleared by the arrest of an African-American. The 1994 data (not presented in Table 1) show a

Table 1. Total arrests, distribution by race, United States, 1994.

Offense Charged	Total arrests					Percent distribution[1]				
	Total	White	Black	American Indian or Alaskan Native	Asian or Pacific Islander	Total	White	Black	American Indian or Alaskan Native	Asian or Pacific Islander
Total	11,846,833	7,894,414	3,705,713	126,503	120,203	100.0	66.6	31.3	1.1	1.0
Murder/nonnegligent manslaughter	18,475	7,705	10,420	126	224	100.0	41.7	56.4	0.7	1.2
Forcible rape	29,759	16,683	12,419	327	330	100.0	56.1	41.7	1.1	1.1
Robbery	146,793	55,055	89,232	737	1,769	100.0	37.5	60.8	0.5	1.2
Aggravated assault	449,179	264,466	176,062	4,063	4,588	100.0	58.9	39.2	0.9	1.0
Burglary	319,466	215,363	97,867	2,844	3,392	100.0	67.4	30.6	0.9	1.1
Larceny-theft	1,235,016	796,212	407,231	12,803	18,770	100.0	64.5	33.0	1.0	1.5
Motor vehicle theft	166,119	95,216	66,544	1,562	2,797	100.0	57.3	40.1	0.9	1.7
Arson	16,727	12,555	3,853	168	151	100.0	75.1	23.0	1.0	0.9
Violent crime[2]	644,206	343,909	288,133	5,253	6,911	100.0	53.4	44.7	0.8	1.1
Property crime[3]	1,737,328	1,119,346	575,495	17,377	25,110	100.0	64.4	33.1	1.0	1.4
Crime Index total[4]	2,381,534	1,463,255	863,628	22,630	32,021	100.0	61.4	36.3	1.0	1.3

[1] Because of rounding, the percentages may not add to total.
[2] Violent crimes are offenses of murder, forcible rape, robbery, and aggravated assault.
[3] Property crimes are offenses of burglary, larceny-theft, motor vehicle theft, and arson.
[4] Includes arson.

somewhat lower degree of overrepresentation of blacks for vandalism, sex offenses (other than rape and prostitution), driving under the influence, liquor law violations, drunkenness, curfew, and loitering law violations, and runaways: approximately one of every five arrests for these offenses involved a black suspect. For all 29 offense types included in the FBI's *Uniform Crime Report* data, 31.3% of the arrests nationwide was cleared by the arrest of an African-American.

Aggregate national data such as those presented in Table 1 only provide a very crude index of the involvement of blacks in the criminal justice system. There are, of course, major geographic variations; there is a greater overrepresentation in cities (in 1994, 48.5% of arrests for violent index crimes in cities was African-American) than in suburban areas (32%), or in rural counties (24.5%).[14]

Impact of the "War on Drugs"

In spite of public beliefs to the contrary, rising violent crime rates among blacks are not responsible for the alarming growth in the locking up of America's blacks (Chambliss, 1995); the proportion of African-American arrests for violent crime has not changed significantly for 20 years (Mauer, 1995; Tonry, 1995, 1996). For instance, the percentage of violent crime arrests of blacks in 1979 (44.1%) was virtually the same as in 1992 (Tonry, 1995:49). Between 1979 and 1992, arrest rates ("Index Crimes") for youth under 18 decreased slightly for whites and for blacks; arrest rates for adults (18 and over) increased slightly for both whites and blacks (Bureau of Justice Statistics [BJS], 1994A:378). Today, young blacks are twice as likely as young whites to be arrested for one of the index crimes; this risk is about five times higher for a black person (18 or older) than for a white person (18 or older). This was true in 1979, and it still holds true today.

Drug law enforcement as part of the War on Drugs is primarily responsible for the increase in incarceration of African-Americans (and Hispanics). The drug-related arrest rates for blacks have increased much faster than those for whites (see Figure 6 in Tonry, 1996:51). Ninety percent of current prison admissions for drug offenses are African-American or Hispanic. Since 1980, non-white drug arrest rates have risen steadily and then skyrocketed until by 1988 they were five times higher than white rates (Tonry, 1996:49).

Are blacks that much more involved in drug use and dealing than whites, then? While African-Americans are estimated to constitute about 13% of drug users,[15] they make up 35% of arrests for drug possession, 55% of convictions, and 74% of prison sentences (for drug possession) (Mauer, 1995). It appears, then, that blacks are arrested and confined in numbers grossly out of line with their use and sale of drugs (Tonry, 1995, 1996). There is a growing consensus among American scholars that the skyrocketing of drug-related arrests of African-Americans is a result from the over-surveillance of innercity black areas in the name of the War on Drugs (Tonry, 1995, 1996; Mauer, 1995).[16]

Self-Report and Victimization Surveys: Alternatives to Police Data

Is the persistent and high black overrepresentation in arrests the result of racial bias and discrimination, or does it simply reflect a higher level of involvement in crime? When self-report studies (mostly among youth) of offending were first done some forty years ago, black/white differences in self-reported offending were found to virtually disappear, or to diminish greatly (compared to police arrest statistics), a finding which supported the discrimination thesis. This is no longer the case. Most researchers now believe that differences between race and crime estimates from the FBI's Uniform Crime Reports — police data —

and from self-report surveys exist largely because self-reports overemphasize *less serious forms of crime* and juvenile delinquency (Elliott and Ageton, 1980 in LaFree and Russell, 1993:278). Black/white differences in offender reports are trivial for non-serious offenses such as drunkenness, truancy, and drug violations, but race differences are "unmistakable" for the more serious forms of delinquency (Harris & Meidlinger, 1995:125).

Confidence in the validity of UCR arrest data regarding race has also grown because of the results of the ongoing survey of victimization, the National Criminal Victimization Survey (NCVS). For instance, comparisons of crime rates by race for the UCR and NCVS show "remarkable correspondence" between the percentage of robbery offenders identified as black by victims and the percentage of blacks among UCR arrests for robbery; a similar finding was made with regard to burglary (LaFree and Russell, 1993:278). NCVS data also suggest that racial differences in victim reporting to the police are minor, thus eliminating another potential source of racial bias in police statistics.[17]

The NCVS shows that African-Americans report a higher level of personal victimization than whites. In 1993, the violent crime annual victimization rate for persons age 12 or older was 66.1 per 1,000 blacks and 49.7 per 1,000 whites. Blacks experienced higher annual victimization rates than whites for rape, robbery, and aggravated assault, but there were virtually no differences with whites in simple assault (see Table 3.5 in BJS 1994A:232).

Crimes against black Americans cause greater injury than similar crimes committed against persons of other races; they are also more likely to involve guns (BJS, 1994B). In large cities, blacks had higher annual robbery and household burglary rates than whites regardless of the age or family income of the victim or the household head. In the suburbs and nonmetropolitan areas, blacks had higher rates than whites for these crimes, but there were fewer differences when age, family income, and home ownership were taken into account (BJS, 1994B).

Violence, Guns, Drugs, and Gangs in America's Ghettos

It is true that, compared to some hundred, fifty, or even twenty years ago, black Americans have made considerable progress toward economic, educational, and political equality with their white American counterparts. But blacks in the United States continue to experience a much lower quality of life in terms of income, jobs, education, health, housing, and personal safety than do white Americans (Hacker, 1992). Furthermore, the National Minority Advisory Council on Criminal Justice (1980, cited in Young and Sulton, 1994:4) concludes that the relative involvement of African-Americans in crime is not disproportionate at all, considering their ranking on the "misery index."

Recent decades have witnessed the increasing polarization of America's black population: a growing, well-to-do black middle class, increasingly separated from an expanding number of poor "underclass" blacks whose homes tend to be clustered in slum neighborhoods of the larger American cities. There are, of course, poor white Americans, also: 16% of white children in 1990 lived below the poverty line, compared with about 45% of black youngsters (Hacker, 1992:99). However, most of America's poor whites live in rural areas or in the suburbs; there are few white ghettos. Urban black families are much more visibly segregated: 70% of these households are concentrated in what commonly is referred to as ghettos. And, it is in America's slum areas where crime — violent crime, in particular — has grown to be a tremendous problem. How do the recent disturbing developments in the American crime story fit with the picture painted by national crime statistics?

The good news is that the most recent crime statistics for the nation are generally encouraging. Victimization data and police data show a trend pattern of overall declining victimization of the population since 1975.[18] The bad news is that these global crime statistics oversimplify reality. The "average American" so often referred to in these contexts is merely a statistical construct; developments in crime are not the same for the young and the old; for blacks and whites; for males and females; or, for city-dwellers and rural citizens. For example, victimization among whites is decreasing, but for certain segments of the black population crime — especially violent crime — is currently touching more, rather than fewer, lives.

Violence, and homicide in particular, has historically affected the African-American population disproportionally (Reiss and Roth, 1993). Nonwhites have always been more likely to be murdered than whites in the U.S. Today, the chance of being a homicide victim is about seven times higher for blacks than whites. Gun-related lethal violence has started to grow disproportionately among the very young blacks.[19] Much of the youth violence is associated with the sale of drugs (crack and power cocaine, and heroin) (Sanders, 1994; see also Schatzberg and Kelly, 1996, and Block and Block, 1993). Drug profits are a powerful incentive to teenagers living in these areas, and drug gangs are "springing up on street corners in ghettos" (Schatzberg & Kelly, 1996:169).

Intra-Racial Nature of Black Crime

One of the few undisputed facts about street crime is that crime is largely intraracial: black offenders tend to choose black victims, and whites victimize whites. Both NCVS data and studies based on police statistics confirm this.[20] Furthermore, contrary to current political rhetoric and public opinion, victim reports consistently show that the bulk of all street crime including assaults, rapes, thefts, and burglary is committed by whites against whites. The only exception to this pattern is robbery where the majority of the victims of black robbers is white.[21]

Anti-Black Bias in the Criminal Justice System

The volume of research on racial discrimination by the American public, police, prosecutors, judges, juries, parole boards, and parole officers is massive, and it has become increasingly sophisticated. A simple summary always runs the risk of

306

oversimplification. The blatantly racist discrimination against blacks considered normal a century ago, or even thirty years ago, is today much more subtle and, therefore, difficult to prove (see Zatz, 1987). Partly as a result of legislative pressures and partly because of more general social changes, the grossest racial inequities in the criminal justice system have been reduced or eliminated. This has led a few researchers to conclude that the problem of racial discrimination by police and criminal justice is exaggerated and as good as gone (Wilbanks, 1987). However, there are very few scholars who would even seriously consider the claim that racism has been completely *eliminated* from the American criminal justice system.

As we saw before, African-Americans are disproportionally involved in street crimes; however, does this overinvolvement account completely for their huge overrepresentation in America's jails and prisons? We think not. Michael Tonry (1995:50), one of the leading scholars in the field of racial discrimination and criminal justice, concludes that "the apparent influence of the offender's race on official decisions concerning individual defendants is slight."[22] Yet, most anybody has to acknowledge that there remain undeniably troubling and well-documented pockets of racial discrimination in the American system of justice. Whenever a study finds evidence of differential treatment based on race, this treatment is invariably to the disadvantage of blacks, very seldom to the disadvantage of whites (see, for example, Chiricos and Crawford, 1995). There is also a lack of evidence for leniency toward blacks (Kleck, 1981, cited in Chiricos and Walters, 1995:300).[23] Institutional racism remains a reality in the American criminal justice system (Mann, 1993, 1995). A convincing example is current drug law policy and enforcement (discussed a few pages ago), where the existence of racial bias has been well-documented (e.g. Chambliss, 1995).

The allegation of pervasive and systematic discriminatory treatment based on race remains a controversial issue. Donziger, for example, argues that there are

"...so many more African-Americans than whites in our prisons that the difference cannot be explained by higher crime among African-Americans — racial discrimination is also at work and it penalizes African Americans at almost every juncture in the criminal justice system" (1996:99).

Evidence about police behavior and the death penalty further documents that racial discrimination in the criminal justice system is not something of America's past.

Black Experience with the Police

The much-publicized Rodney King incident, where Los Angeles Police Department and California State Troopers brutally beat a black suspect, exemplifies the tense relationship existing between the police and blacks in the United States. Police use of excessive force — including deadly force — against racial minorities has become the cause célèbre of the 1990s. The federal government has initiated a nationwide data collection effort of police abuse cases; research funds have been made available; and there is a growing interest in improving the handling of citizen complaints (Walker and Wright, 1995). Early studies concluded that police officers were more likely to shoot and use excessive force when dealing with blacks; more recent research, though, shows that the racial disparity in people shot and killed by police has declined (Walker *et al.*, 1996:93-95).

"Many minority communities in America feel both overpoliced and underprotected" (Donziger, 1996:160). Black Americans more than whites feel verbally and physically harassed by the police; police protection in black neighborhoods is viewed as worse than that in white neighborhoods. Response to 911 calls is often slow in black neighborhoods. Violence associated with gangs and the drug trade make assignment to the impoverished black inner city neighborhood one of the least desirable job assignments for police officers, thus placing the youngest and least experienced officers in charge of the most violent and volatile precincts. Police gang and drug operations such as

Chicago's *Operation Clean Sweep* in predominantly black housing projects often involve blatant disregard for the rights and dignity of the project residents, the vast majority of whom are quite innocent of any wrong-doing. Further, these operations frequently result in very few arrests or convictions.[24]

Although it is painful to admit, it is fair to say that black American citizens who encounter police as either victims or suspects will have a lesser chance of receiving civil and fair treatment than whites in similar situations. In support of this claim, a recent report by the Criminal Justice Institute at Harvard Law School, based on hearings in six cities on the issue of police brutality against minorities, found that for minorities ANY encounter with police "carries the risk of abuse, mistreatment or even death" (cited in Donziger, 1996:169).

Death Penalty[25]

Death penalty research has consistently and thoroughly documented that this ultimate punishment is definitely not color blind (Baldus *et al.*, 1983). Instead, a rather uniform pattern of discrimination based on race of the victim has been found: offenders killing whites are more likely to be given the death penalty than those killing blacks (Gross, 1985, cited in Smith, 1995). The "race-of-the-victim" effect is made more disturbing due to the relative *infrequency* of death sentences for blacks who kill other blacks. One interpretation of this is that the death penalty system is more lenient towards black murderers, since the large majority of black murderers kill black victims. More convincing is the counterargument that the lives of black victims simply have less value in the criminal justice system than do those of whites. Complicating interpretation of this body of research is the mixed evidence on discrimination by race of offender. In *McCleskey v. Kemp* (1987), the U.S. Supreme Court rejected the body of scientific research showing patterns of racial discrimination as insufficient to challenge the constitutionality of the death penalty. In practical terms this means that in the U.S., a white person convicted of killing a black person continues to have much smaller chance of receiving the death penalty than a black person who has killed a white person.

Blacks as Workers in the Criminal Justice System

In the United States, efforts to recruit more racial minorities (i.e., African-Americans, Hispanics, Asian-Americans, and Native Americans) by the police, courts, and corrections have taken place for several reasons: it is required by law; and it is believed to reduce racism and to improve the relationship between the criminal justice system and racial minorities, who are, after all, the system's single, largest "client." Federal affirmative action programs have helped to increase the presence of racial minorities in the criminal justice system (Hacker, 1992). Most large American cities now have a sizable proportion of black officers (in 1992, Washington D.C, had 67.8% black officers in the police force, Detroit had 53.3%, and Atlanta had 54.6%), and in most of the 50 largest cities, the situation has improved between 1983 and 1992 (see Table 1.36 in Walker & Turner, cited in BJS, 1994A:49). However, only a handful of these cities (e.g., Los Angeles and Washington, D.C) had a representation of black officers equal to their proportion in the general population. Several large cities now have a black mayor, or a black police chief.

Similar trends, although less pronounced, are seen in the other branches of the criminal justice system. America now has more black prosecutors, judges, and correctional officers then ever before in history; however, they are still seriously underrepresented. In 1992, 20% of all correctional personnel was black (Walker *et al.*, 1996:211). Using the proportion of arrestees for index crimes (one-third), or the proportion of blacks in the prison population (almost 50%), even these considerable gains are not satisfactory.[26]

308

HISPANICS

U.S. census forms include one question about "race," and another question about "ethnicity" ("Hispanic" or not)[27] [Hispanics may be of any race.] The category of "Hispanic" (or Latino) includes a wide variety of Spanish-speaking groups: those of Mexican heritage, those from Puerto Rico or Cuba, those from Central or South America; a mixture of long-term habitants of the U.S. and newcomers, Latino immigrants and refugees, and their descendants (Parrillo, 1996:131). In 1990, about nine percent of the U.S. population was Hispanic (see Figure 1).

Paralleling the experiences of black Americans, Hispanics are relatively powerless; also, they have been (or are) seen as "different," threatening, problematic, or deviant; they have been subject to discriminatory laws and regulations, prejudice and negative stereotyping; they have been the focus of public fear and violence; and they have been targets of political campaigns. Generally, Hispanics are more likely to be unemployed, poorer, less healthy, and less educated than the non-Hispanic population (Hacker, 1992). But there are huge differences between the different Hispanic groups: some are more wealthy and better educated than the rest of the "average American" (e.g., some Cubans who came to the U.S. to escape from Castro in the 1960s); while others rank at the bottom of the scale (e.g., many from Puerto Rico and Mexico).

In a recent volume on criminal justice and Latino communities, Lopez (1995) laments the lack of research and attention paid to issues related to criminal justice and the Latino community. The absence of official data (Hispanics are often categorized as "white") is one explanation for the relative absence of research on Hispanics; another reason is the assumption that Hispanic crime is a "mirror image of that of blacks, who have been studied extensively" (Flowers, 1988:96). Further, some critics claim that criminological research has stereotyped and created negative images of Lati-

nos, which have influenced the objectivity of the research (Lopez, 1995:ix). Most available research concerns Mexican-Americans, the numerically largest Hispanic group; this is also the group that has attracted most of the public fear and allegations of crime by illegals.[28]

Official Statistics on Hispanic Crime

For a short time (1980-1986), the FBI collected arrest information on Hispanics. The 1986 arrest statistics indicated that the Hispanic arrest rate was about double that expected based on the size of the Hispanic population; alcohol- and drug-related arrests were prevalent (Flowers, 1988). Current national aggregate arrest data on Hispanics are no longer available.

Prison statistics, on the other hand, do distinguish "Hispanic" and "non-Hispanic" inmates, but there are substantial variations in classification procedures, as well as a large percentage of "unknowns" which make these statistics of questionable utility. According to the 1993 *Census of Jails*, Hispanics made up 12.8% of the nation's inmate population (more than their 9% presence in the general population), and 27% of the federal prisoners; Hispanic inmates were incarcerated disproportionally for drug-related offenses. Hispanics constituted the fastest growing minority group in prison from 1980 to 1993. During that period, the proportion of inmates of Hispanic origin nearly doubled and the rate of imprisonment for Hispanics more than tripled (Donziger, 1996:103-104).[29]

Other Data on Hispanic Crime

Victim surveys show that Hispanic households have higher victimization rates for burglary, car theft, and household larceny than non-Hispanic households. Hispanics also run a slightly higher risk of personal victimization, in particular for robbery. As in the case of black citizens, a large proportion of criminal victimization is intra-ethnic (i.e. Hispanics victimizing other Hispanics).

Hispanics figure prominently in the youth gang literature; life in the urban 'barrios' has historically been associated with gangs, and since the 1980s guns, drugs, and violence have become a more central feature of these gangs (Sanders, 1994; Klein, Maxson and Miller, 1995). The notions of machismo and the subculture of violence are among the more popular explanations of gang membership (see Erlanger, 1995 for a critical note).

Anti-Hispanic Bias in the Criminal Justice System

Some of the overrepresentation of Hispanics in police and prison cells may reflect the impact of discriminatory treatment by the criminal justice system. Studies have documented: (1) harsher treatment of Chicanos (compared to Anglos) at each stage of the criminal process in Monterey County, California (Garza, 1995); (2) Hispanics (compared to the general population) in Texas feel less safe, do not trust the police, and do not feel they have adequate police protection (Carter, 1995A, 1995B); (3) defendants of Mexican origin (and blacks) are considerably more likely to receive a severe sentence than comparable Anglo defendants (Holmes and Daudistel, 1995); (4) there has been a marked increase in racial violence against Latinos (Hernandez, 1995); and (5) Hispanic criminal defendants received less favorable pretrial release outcomes, were more likely to be convicted in jury trials and received more severe sentences than whites in Tucson, Arizona and El Paso, Texas (LaFree, 1995). Language barriers handicap many Latino criminal defendants (Lopez, 1995), contributing to misunderstandings and reinforcing of prejudice among police (Mann, 1993:103).

ASIAN-AMERICANS

The generic term "Asian" includes not only Japanese and Chinese and Koreans, but also Indonesians and Indians along with Burmese and Thais, Filipinos, and Pakistanis (Hacker, 1992:5), a strange amalgam of racial, national, and cultural identities, together constituting three percent of the American population. Some Asian-Americans are doing extremely well, both socially and economically, while many others such as those of Chinese and Filipino origins seem barely able to survive economically. There is ample documentation that this small, yet fast-growing Asian-American population has been the subject of legal discrimination, police harassment, and hate crimes, both in the past and present (Hacker, 1992; Mann, 1993; Flowers, 1988, Jacobs and Henry, 1996).

Not a "Model Minority"

Asian-Americans have a lower arrest rate than their presence in the population (see Table 1) — lower than whites, blacks, and American Indians. Asian-Americans also have a very low rate of incarceration. Only sixteen Asian-Americans were on death row in 1993 (.6%), less than their proportion in the general population (3%). May we conclude then, that Asian-Americans are a "model minority," and that the relative absence of research on Asian-American criminal involvement and contacts with criminal justice agencies is therefore justified? Probably not.

First, there exist important variations in criminality when comparisons are made among the diverse Asian-American groups. Japanese Americans have consistently had lower crime rates than Chinese Americans — explained, among other things, by strong family ties (Mann, 1993:94). Even though Chinese crime rates within Chinese communities were low prior to 1965, crime and violence among Chinese have increased since that time (Chin, 1995:46). This increase is because of two influences: (1) the influx of young immigrants from Hong Kong who have formed youth gangs [see later discussion] and (2) the "extremely high unemployment rates, depressing poverty, and disheartening living and social circumstances" of the people living in Chinatowns (Takagi and Platt, 1978, cited in Mann, 1993:97).

310

A second reason to challenge the notion of Asian-Americans as "model citizens" is the fact that arrest statistics probably do not fully capture the involvement of Asian groups in organized crime. Both Chinese and Japanese organized criminals have been active in drug trafficking, gambling, and prostitution in the U.S. from the early beginnings of immigration [see later discussion of gangs]. Also, national data are providing a distorted picture because Asian-Americans are concentrated in a few states (California, Washington, New York, Nevada). Indeed, state-level statistics provide a less favorable picture. To illustrate, the California Youth Authority reports that Asian and Pacific Islanders constitute six percent of incarcerated youth, but nine percent of new admissions — mostly immigrants from Southeast Asia, China, and the Philippines (Donziger, 1996:104).

NATIVE AMERICANS

This is the smallest "racial" group identified by the U.S. Census data; According to the 1990 census there are about 1,800,000 Native Americans — American Indians, Eskimos and Aleuts — less than one percent of the U.S. population. The identification of who is and who is not Native American is a serious problem in investigating this minority. Another factor which makes research difficult is the problem of multiple jurisdictions: tribal members are subject to tribal, to state, and to federal government jurisdiction depending upon the type of crime, whether it happened on or off the reservation, and whether Indians or non-Indians were involved (Zatz et al., 1991:101). Most Native Americans, the original inhabitants of this rich country, ironically have no share in the American Dream. Moreover, they have the lowest life expectancy, very high rates of illiteracy, unemployment, infant mortality, and alcoholism. They are a very small and powerless group; maybe not surprisingly, there still is very little sound research on this population group.

Crime, Criminal Justice, and Native Americans

Native Americans are with 1.1% of the total arrests slightly overrepresented (.7% of the population) (See Table 1). Again, these aggregate official police statistics tell only a small part of the story. The arrest figures for homicide (.7%) in particular are grossly misleading since they do not include crimes committed on reservations, where about half of the Indian population lives. The homicide rate for American Indians is much higher on-reservation than off-reservation. For instance, Bachman reports that the national homicide rate for American Indians is 9.6 per 100,000 population, but the rate may be over 100 per 100,000 population in some reservation counties (1992, cited by Snyder-Joy, 1995:318). Alcohol use plays a large role. This is seen in the overrepresentation of Native Americans in the arrest statistics in a limited narrow range of mostly alcohol-related (drunkenness, liquor law violations, driving under the influence, disorderly conduct) offenses.

American Indians are overrepresented in federal prisons (BJS, 1995); this may be explained by the fact that there is federal jurisdiction over particular offenses committed by Indians. About six of every ten juveniles in federal custody are Native American (Donziger, 1996:104). States with a heavy concentration of Native Americans — including New Mexico, Oklahoma, South Dakota, Montana, and Arizona — have an overrepresentation of Native Americans in state prisons. In 1993, twenty-two Native Americans were on death row (less than one percent of the total).

Very little self-report research has been done on this population; however, Mann concludes that these studies show few differences between Indians and whites in frequency of crime, and that numerous and repetitive arrests among a minority of Indians greatly inflate the rates of arrest and incarceration for all (1993:100). Overall, few studies have examined the involvement of Native Americans in the criminal justice system (Zatz et al., 1991:100-101; Snyder-Joy, 1995:316-317). It has been suggested that discrimination and over-surveillance in Indian communities may explain the higher arrest rates, as well as the higher incarceration rates of American Indians (Mann, 1993:98). Native Americans are more likely to receive a prison sentence than are non-Indians, and they serve a longer portion of their sentence before parole release (Snyder-Joy, 1995:317). Other theories of criminality among American Indians make use of the concepts of social disorganization, culture conflict, and economic deprivation (Mann, 1993).

CRIME AND THE THREAT FROM WITHOUT: RECENT IMMIGRANTS AND CRIMINAL ALIENS

America is a nation of immigrants and it may be natural that the activities and, indeed, the crimes of foreign-born people and newly-arrived immigrants become an issue (Hawkins, 1995A). Over the last few years, there is a renewed public and political interest in the link between immigrants and criminality. In the scholarly community, concepts such as "country of origin," "nationality," and "citizenship" are drawing interest once again.

The popular belief that alien criminality is becoming a more serious problem finds support in both court and prison data. For example, the number of non-citizens who were prosecuted in U.S. District Courts from 1984 to 1994 increased an average of ten percent annually compared to a two percent annual increase in overall federal caseload (BJS, 1996:5). The growth in the number of noncitizens prosecuted between 1986 and 1989 was generally attributable to an increase in the number of noncitizens charged with drug and immigration offenses (BJS, 1996:5-6). Drug and immigration offenses account for the majority of the offenses for which noncitizens are prosecuted in federal courts (Table 5, BJS, 1996).[30]

There is little doubt: Foreigners (noncitizens) are becoming increasingly visible in the American criminal justice system. For many of these nonciti-

zens, the only illegal act is their failure to possess a legal residence permit; they are law-abiding people who have come to the U.S. in search of a better life. Some may drift into an illegal way of life when the American Dream turns out to be an illusion (see next section). For yet another category of (legal and illegal) aliens, however, criminal motives are the sole reason for crossing American borders. It is this latter group which exemplifies a qualitatively new type of "foreigner" crime (i.e., terrorism, drug trafficking, trafficking in humans, and in human organs).

Migrants, Ethnic Organized Crime and Ethnic Gangs

Scholarly and public interest in differences between white ethnic groups started to wane some fifty years ago, with one important exception: white ethnic groups remained persistently tied to organized crime (Hawkins, 1994).[31] Indeed, organized crime has long been thought of as an underworld enterprise comprised almost exclusively of traditional white ethnic groups such as Italians, Irish, and Jews. Organized crime has provided a "vehicle for upward mobility for lower-income ethnic minorities in their odyssey towards the fulfillment of the American Dream" (O'Kane, 1992:139).

Recent evidence suggests that new ethnic groups are "waiting their turn" on the ethnic queue: blacks (American and Caribbean), Hispanics (Cuban, Mexican, Puerto Rican, Colombian, Venezuelan), and Asians (Chinese, Japanese, Vietnamese, Filipino, and Korean), Soviet Jews, Nigerians, Ghanians (O'Kane, 1992:89). Many of the ethnic criminal organizations exist in their native countries and simply expand into the U.S. Some of these groups consist primarily or solely of American-born, others are mostly made up of foreigners or recent immigrants.

"Domestic" American developments in organized crime reflect global political changes and population movements. For instance, after the collapse of the Soviet Union, police departments throughout the U.S. have come in contact with

Russian organized emigre crime networks (Finckenauer, Waring & Barthe, 1996). A different example concerns Asian-based organized criminal influence in the U.S. Although by no means a new phenomenon, organized criminal activities by Asian immigrants is rapidly becoming a more visible problem, particularly in cities such as Los Angeles and New York with a large Asian population. The increasing number of Chinese immigrating to the United States has affected the stability of the Chinese-American communities (Chin, 1995:46). These communities, unable to absorb the large influx of immigrants, have witnessed the growth of gangs: Chinese gangs have developed in San Francisco, Los Angeles, Boston, Vancouver, and New York City. Chinese gang involvement in heroin trafficking, money laundering, and other racketeering activities has led to the prediction that "Chinese criminal organizations will emerge as the number one organized crime problem in the 1990s" (Chin, 1995:46).[32]

With the influx of new immigrants the youth gang picture is no longer dominated by the "domestic" urban (black and Hispanic) gangs. Today, America's urban landscape provides an increasingly complex mixture of gangs. For instance, in Chicago, there are black and Hispanic gangs, but also Chinese, Cambodian, Vietnamese, Filipino, and Greek gangs; in Los Angeles, Pacific Islander gangs (Samoans, Tongans, Guamanians, and Hawaiians) have emerged, as well as Filipino, Salvadoran, Mexican, Korean and Vietnamese gangs (OSS, 1995:44). More often than not, members of these gangs are legal or undocumented aliens; also, these gangs are frequently involved in a variety of crimes.

EQUAL JUSTICE FOR ALL?

This chapter has barely scratched the surface of the complex issues related to minority status, criminality and criminal justice in the U.S. We have not discussed the many criminological theories related to criminality and minorities; we barely touched on issues related to organized

crime or the globalization of criminality, and its impact on racial and ethnic minorities in this country. However, as we have shown, the basic facts — regardless of some of the controversies surrounding their interpretation — do speak loud and clear. That is, delinquency, crime, and contacts with the criminal justice system are "massive risk factors" in the lives of poorly educated and economically disadvantaged minorities in the U.S. (Hagan and Peterson, 1995:17). As we have hinted at throughout the chapter, there typically have been two competing explanations of this undisputable fact. The first is that race-linked structural economic inequality and discrimination, segregation, and concentrated poverty produce high levels of delinquent and criminal behavior among young minorities. The second explanation posits that young black (and other minority) males are victims of prejudice and discrimination in the form of more frequent arrest, prosecution, and punishment for delinquent and criminal behavior (Hagan and Peterson, 1995:17). Today, most criminologists — regardless of their political or ideological stance — are convinced that *both* of these explanations describe reality; and, as Hagan and Peterson (1995:17) argue, these realities together produce an additional important problem: a legacy of suspicion and distrust of the justice system in America, in particular among minorities.

In the INTRODUCTION, we said that the success of the American criminal justice system in meeting the goal of *justice for all* is an important measure of how well we as a nation are doing. As long as American society remains divided into winners and losers, as long as large sections of the American population remain systematically excluded from a realistic pursuit of the American Dream, as long as race, ethnicity, or national origin remain intimately tied to one's chances of a reasonable "pursuit of happiness" and fair treatment by the justice system, there is no chance that "justice for all" will be achieved. Although instances of blatant discrimination based on race, ethnicity, or citizenship are becoming less common, we are still a long way from concluding that the American criminal justice system is successful in its attempt to approximate the ideal of justice for all. Blacks and whites, Hispanics,

American Indians, and recent immigrants do *not* receive the same kind of treatment by the police, the courts, and in prisons. It is very simple, really. There can be no legal formal justice in a society that lacks substantive justice (cf. Savelsberg 1995).

Minority groups in the U.S. grow at a faster pace than the dominant white groups. Migration — both legal and illegal — is bound to continue. By the middle of the next century, according to U.S. Census projections, the U.S. population will be evenly divided between non-Hispanic, white, and other minorities.[33] Presently, there is an on-going and strong backlash against immigration and immigrants. A bill severely limiting the rights of illegal and legal noncitizens has been signed by the President. The INS is receiving an expanded budget to deal with illegal aliens. Children of illegal immigrants no longer have the right to receive public education (including school lunches). Another bill, seriously undermining current welfare guarantees, has also been signed into law. The cutting of welfare benefits has a potentially disastrous effect on the quality of life of some recent immigrants, who are often poorly skilled and poorly educated. The new federal welfare bill also will have a disproportionate effect upon the economic and physical well-being of many African-Americans, Hispanics, Native Americans, and some Asian groups, groups which tend to rely more on public assistance than white Americans. In the short run, then, the prospects for a society with "justice for all" are pretty grim. The disproportionate criminal involvement and criminalization of minorities will continue as long as pervasive power differences and other forms of inequality remain part and parcel of American society. Until such day that the power balance will shift and the white (Northern and Western) European descendants will no longer be the majority group in the U.S. Perhaps at that time, this nation will have grown mature enough to realize that the key to preserving the American democratic experiment is by inclusion rather than exclusion of people who are not "like us."

* * * * *

ENDNOTES

[1] This chapter draws from I. Haen Marshall, "Minorities, Crime, and Criminal Justice in the United States." In I. Haen Marshall (ed.), *Minorities, Migrants, and Crime. Diversity and Similarity Across Europe and the United States.* Thousand Oaks, CA: Sage (1997).

[2] American society's complex patchwork of minority groups, based on race, ethnicity, national origin, is constantly changing; some "minorities" have been part of American society for a long time, others are foreign-born, recent legal immigrants or undocumented aliens; some come from Europe, others from Asia, South America or Africa; they are political refugees, migrant workers, members of international organized crime groups, or highly educated professionals. Some are considered and consider themselves "white;" others, "people of color." In the United States the measuring rod for normal behavior and appearance continues to be the "Americanized" white (northern and western) European; this reduces, by definition, all other ethnic, national and racial groups to minorities.

[3] The American community of scholars has contributed a massive amount of work on the topics of race, ethnicity, and crime. This body of information leads to many, sometimes conflicting, conclusions regarding the current state of affairs.

[4] "Race" is placed between quotation marks to signify the socially constructed nature of this concept. In the remainder of the chapter, these quotation marks have been omitted.

[5] This following point is not meant to imply some lurking "conspiracy" by the government but rather to suggest some possible and subtle consequences of government practice.

[6] The gross oversimplification of the popular racial and ethnic classification is discussed by Parrillo (See, for example, 1996:127).

[7] Approximately 9% of the population in the 1990 Census was classified as Hispanic (i.e., from Mexico, Cuba, Puerto Rica, Middle- and Southern America); the remaining 91% as non-Hispanic.

[8] Most of research on American minorities is restricted to making rather crude "black/white" comparisons, with only occasional "Asian-Americans," "Native Americans," or "Hispanic/NonHispanic" contrasts. Driven by this classification, most reviews of the field (e.g., Flowers, 1988; Mann, 1993) classify research and theory into these four "minority" groups ("Blacks," Hispanics, Asian-Americans, Native Americans).

[9] This overly-broad and inexact category — blacks — includes American-born persons of African ancestry; recent African immigrants mainly from Ethiopia, Nigeria, and Ghana; and those of a Carribean background such as Haitians and Jamaicans (Parrillo, 1996:127). African-Americans are currently America's largest minority group comprising about twelve percent of the US population; they continue to seriously lag behind white Americans in terms of education, income, quality of housing, life expectancy and health, and political power (Hacker, 1992; Parrillo, 1996).

[10] Research and writing on the involvement of blacks with the criminal justice system has exploded over the last twenty years, reflecting the impact of urban race riots, the continuing evidence of racial disproportionality in rates of crimes and punishment (Hawkins, 1995A:28; see also LaFree and Russell, 1993), practical concerns about the costs of prison construction, growing intolerance of unequal justice, and last but not least, the fast-growing supply of academic researchers in criminology, criminal justice, and sociology departments all over the United States who have made crime their business. Research funding is more generous, publication outlets more ample, and the obstacles to access to information less formidable when studying America's blacks (or Hispanics or Native Americans) than when investigating the deviance of powerful corporations, government agencies, or politicians.

[11] The United States locks up African-American men at a rate six times that of white men: 1,860 per 100,000 vs. 289 per 100,000, respectively (Table 2.1 in Tonry, 1995:62). More than a half million blacks were incarcerated in US prisons and jails in 1990; blacks make up nearly 50% of those in prison on an average day (Tonry, 1995:49).

[12] Donziger explains that in 1930, 75% of all prison admissions were white and 22% African-American, but that ratio has roughly reversed in 1992, when 29% of prison admissions were white, while 51% were African-American and 20% were Hispanic (1996:103).

[13] This disproportionality becomes even more marked when one considers that the majority of arrests for serious crime involves males, and that black MALES make up only about six percent of the general population.

[14] Over one-half of the African-American population lives in the large cities of the North and the Midwest.

[15] These estimates are based on national drug use surveys; they probably underestimate the extent of serious drug abuse among marginal populations. Recent trends indicate a decline in casual use, a growing abstinence among middle-class users, and the spread of addiction among the poor and unemployed, pointing to an increasing importance of race and class in shaping patterns of drug abuse (Schatzberg & Kelley, 1996:165).

[16] Another factor which may explain the high number of drug-related black offenders in prison is that federal sentencing guidelines require much more severe penalties for crack than for powder cocaine. Crack is most typically used by African-Americans, while powder cocaine is more common among whites.

[17] Needless to say, not all criminologists agree with this assessment. Many criminologists argue that official crime statistics should not be used to conclude that blacks are more criminal than whites (Young and Sulton, 1994:4); in this view, offical statistics should never be used as a valid measure of criminal involvement.

[18] The NCVS violent crime rate in 1992 was lower than in the early 1980s. Police data show that the violent crime rate in 1994 (716 per 100,000) was 2% below the 1990 rate (732); the property crime rate for 1994 (4,658) was 8% lower than the 1990 rate (5,088); this reflects a reversal of the trend during the 1980s of increasing violent (and stable property) crimes for the "average" American (BJS, 1994C).

[19] With exploding drug-trafficking business in the mid-1980s, a "dramatic change in violent crime committed by young people" took place, particularly among black innercity youth (Blumstein, 1995:3).

The 1992 UCR data show that black males age 12 to 24 represented 17.2% of single-victim homicides (they make up 1.3% of the population); this translates to a homicide rate of 114.9 per 100,000 black males in this age range, more than eleven times higher than the U.S. average rate (BJS, 1994B).

NCVS data on assault, rape, and robbery parallel the trends seen in recent homicide statistics. A BJS (1994B) publication presents the following highlights. Between 1973 and 1992, the rate of violent victimizations of young black males increased about 25%. In 1992, black males age 12 to 24 experienced violent crime at a rate significantly higher than the rates for other age or racial groups. Males age 16 to 19 were especially at risk; their violent victimization rate was almost double the rate for white males and 3 times that for white females in the same age range. Excluding murder, the most serious violent crimes (rapes, robberies, and aggravated assaults) comprised 60% of all violent victimizations of black males age 12 to 24 in 1987 and 65% in 1992. The proportion of these crimes against white males in the same age range remained stable at about 45%. The average rate of handgun victimizations per 1,000 black males age 16 to 19 was 39.7 from 1987 through 1992, 4 times the rate for white males. Persons under age 21 committed two-thirds of the victimizations of black males between 12 and 21.

[20] In 1994, approximately 40% of homicides having a single victim and a single offender involved a white offender and a white victim; 46% involved a black offender and a black victim (see Table 2.8 in UCR, 1995:17). Among the victims of rape, robbery, and assault age 12 to 24, 82% of the victimizations of black males (and 71% of the victimizations of white males) involved an offender or offenders of the same race (BJS, 1994B).

[21] Besides robbery, there is another, very important exception to the intra-racial character of America's street crime: these are the so-called "hate crimes." These acts are apparently motivated by simple racism and xenophobia and are most commonly committed by whites against blacks or other minorities. Regrettably, many believe that these crimes motivated by racial hate may be on the rise (Garofalo, 1991:164).

But for a convincing counterargument, see Jacobs and Henry (1996) strong challenge of the "uncritical acceptance of a hate crime epidemic" (1996:391).

[22] The analysis of "empirical race bias" as discussed here is limited to decision-making points in the criminal justice system (cf. Harris and Meidlinger, 1995). However, racial bias enters discussions on "race and crime" much earlier. At the point of analyzing police statistics and victimization studies most researchers, for example, limit their focus to street crime, a focus which will exaggerate the involvement of blacks in criminality in general. High-profit, low-risk crime remains the privilege of the well-to-do, primarily white middle class. This "a priori race bias" also is seen in legislative decisions, law enforcement priorities, and media coverage of "criminality" (Harris and Meidlinger, 1995). Consider the altogether unlikely possibility that scholarly and popular focus were to radically shift to white collar crime — "crime in the suites." Plainly, the underrepresentation of blacks as offenders would be one of the most striking early observations, wouldn't it?

[23] The O. J. Simpson case is one of the most well-known examples where a defendant's race was used to his advantage. Whether the favorable outcome for the defendant was a reflection of his class or race remains open to discussion.

[24] Several cities now are using "community policing models" in an effort to improve police relations with minority communities. The hope underlying this approach to policing is to help improve the quality of life of poor blacks, reduce crime, increase confidence in the police, and lessen fear of crime. The verdict is still out at the the real success of these programs although there is considerable enthusiasm surrounding them, especially among politicians and some police administrators.

[25] After a five year moratorium ending in 1977, capital punishment is now used with growing frequency in the United States.

[26] As history has shown with the Attica uprising, American prisons can be hotbeds of racial tension. Often, urban black offenders are incarcerated in prisons away from the city, in a rural setting, guarded by rural, working-class whites. Unfortunately, the recent increase in black correctional personnel may come to an abrupt halt with the dismantling of federal affirmative action programs and the backlash of the "white angry male" against preferential hiring and promotion practices. The increasingly tough stance on prisons (i.e., federal funds for inmate education have been eliminated, together with exercise equipment and other "frills") may escalate the smoldering racial unrest in America's prisons.

[27] In California, about one-half of the "Hispanics" did not self-identify with any race; the other half picked either black or white, and in a few cases, Native American or Asian. (Hacker, 1992:6).

[28] Another example are the 1980 Mariel Cuban 'Banditos' who were viewed as a "danger to law enforcement and society in general" (Mann, 1993:101).

[29] In 1990, ten percent of all Latino males were either on probation, on parole, or in prison (Poupart, 1995:179). In 1993, 206 Hispanics were on death row.

[30] In 1994, these two offenses — drug and immigration offenses — accounted for over 78% of the prosecutions of noncitizens in Federal court (up from 69% in 1984). While in 1984, 35% of noncitizens prosecuted in Federal court were charged with a drug offense; by 1994, the proportion charged with a drug offense had increased to 45% (BJS, 1996:1).

[31] Woodiwiss (1988, quoted by Bailey, 1991:12) describes the "nativist xenophobia" in the years after World War II, the fear of "alien conspiracies" by Sicilians and Italians, the belief that something called the "Mafia" was responsible for America's organized crime problem.

[32] Most gang members are young immigrants; few are American-born. Asian gangs include not only Chinese "organized criminal groups involved in street crime" (OSS, 1995:14) such as the Wah Ching gang, comprised of Cantonese Chinese with youthful, illegal immigrants as members (OSS, 1995:43), but also "Viet-Chings" (Vietnamese of Chinese ethnicity), Koreans and Filipinos. There is further some speculation that there is a serious escalation of Japan-based Yakuza activity in the U.S.: Yakuza members are thought to be involved with factions of La Costa Nostra on the east coast (OSS, 1995:44). In a recent article, Reuter suggests that the Italian Mafia is no longer a serious threat to the US; instead, new ethnic gangs mostly from East Asia, have "become wealthy through their control of large scale illicit drug distribution systems" (Reuter, 1996:33).

[33] By 2010, Hispanics will be the U.S. largest minority group, outnumering blacks; the Asian group is also expected to grow at a very fast rate.

317

REFERENCES

Bailey, F. Y.
   1991   "Law, Justice, and 'Americans': An Historical Overview." Pages 10-21 in M. J.
           Lynch and E. Britt Paterson (eds.), *Race and Criminal Justice*. Albany, NY: Harrow
           and Heston, Publishers.

Baldus, D. C., C. Pulaski, and C. Woodworth
   1983   "Comparative Review of Death Sentences: an Empirical Study of the Georgia Experi-
           ence." *Journal of Criminal Law and Criminology*, 74:661-753.

Block, C., and R. Block
   1993   *Street Gang Crime in Chicago*. National Institute of Justice: Research in Brief. Office
           of Justice Programs, U.S. Department of Justice. U.S. Government Printing Office

Blumstein, A.
   1995   "Juvenile Homicides." *National Institute of Justice Journal* (August).

Bureau of Justice Statistics
   1994A   *Sourcebook of Criminal Justice Statistics, 1994*. U.S. Government Printing Office.

Bureau of Justice Statistics
   1994B   *Highlights from 20 Years of Surveying Crime Victims*. Washington, DC: U.S. Depart-
           ment of Justice.

Bureau of Justice Statistics
   1994C   *Young Black Male Victims*. Washington, DC: U.S. Department of Justice.

Bureau of Justice Statistics
   1995A   *Criminal Victimization in the United States, 1993*. Washington, DC: Department of
           Justice

Bureau of Justice Statistics
   1996   *Noncitizens in the Federal Criminal Justice System, 1984-94*. Washington, DC: De-
           partment of Justice.

Carter, D. L.
   1995A   "Hispanic Interaction with the Criminal Justice System in Texas: Experiences, At-
           titudes and Perceptions." Pages 57-72 in A.S. Lopez (ed.), *Latinos in the United
           States. Volume 3. Criminal Justice and Latino Communities*. New York and London:
           Garland Publishing, Inc.

Carter, D. L.
   1995B   "Hispanic Perception Of Police Performance: an Empirical Assessment." Pages 73-86
           in A. S. Lopez. (ed.), *Latinos in the United States. Volume 3. Criminal Justice and
           Latino Communities*. New York and London: Garland Publishing, Inc.

Chambliss, W. J.
   1995   "Crime Control and Ethnic Minorities: Legitimizing Racial Oppression by Creating
           Moral Panics." Pages 235-258 in D. F. Hawkins (ed.), *Ethnicity, Race, and Crime:
           Perspectives Across Time and Place*. Albany, NY: State University of New York
           Press.

Chin, K.
   1995   "Chinese Gangs and Extortion." Pages 46-52 in M .W. Klein, C. L. Maxson, and J.
           Miller (eds.), *The Modern Gang Reader*. Los Angeles, CA: Roxbury Publishing Co.

318

Chiricos, T. G, and C. Crawford
    1995   "Race and Imprisonment: a Contextual Assessment of the Evidence." Pages 281-309
            in D. F. Hawkins (ed.), *Ethnicity, Race, and Crime: Perspectives Across Time and
            Place*. Albany, NY: State University of New York Press.
Donziger, S. R. (ed.)
    1996   *The Real War on Crime. The Report of the National Criminal Justice Commission*.
            New York: Harper Collins Publishers.
Erlanger, H. S.
    1995   "Estrangement, Machismo and Gang Violence." Pages 207-220 in A. S. Lopez (ed.),
            Latinos in the United States. Volume 3. Criminal Justice and Latino Communities. New
            York and London: Garland Publishing, Inc.
Finckenauer, J. O., E. J. Waring, and E. Barthe
    1996   "Law Enforcement Perceptions of Soviet Emigre Crime Networks in the United
            States." *Trends in Organized Crime*, 1(3):37-40.
Flowers, R. B.
    1988   *Minorities and Criminality*. New York: Praeger.
Garofalo, J.
    1991   "Racially Motivated Crimes in New York City." Pages 161-173 in M. J. Lynch and E.
            B. Paterson (eds.), *Race and Criminal Justice*. Albany, NY: Harrow and Heston, Pub-
            lishers.
Garza, H.
    1995   "Administration of Justice: Chicanos in Monterey County." Pages 47-56 in A. S.
            Lopez (ed.), *Latinos in The United States. Volume 3. Criminal Justice and Latino
            Communities*. New York and London: Garland Publishing, Inc.
Hacker, A.
    1992   *Two Nations: Black and White, Separate, Hostile, Unequal*. New York: Ballantine.
Hagan, J., and R. T. Peterson
    1995   "Criminal Inequality in America. Patterns and Consequences." Pages 14-36 in J.
            Hagan and R. D. Peterson (eds.), *Crime and Inequality*. Stanford, CA: Stanford Uni-
            versity Press.
Harris, A. R., and L. R. Meidlinger
    1995   "Criminal Behavior: Race and Class." Pages 115-144 in J. F. Sheley (ed.), *Criminolo-
            gy* (2nd Edition). Belmont, CA: Wadsworth Publishing Company.
Hawkins, D. F.
    1995   "Ethnicity, Race, and Crime: A Review of Selected Studies." Pages 11-45 in D. F.
            Hawkins (ed.), *Ethnicity, Race, and Crime: Perspectives Across Time and Place*.
            Albany, NY: State University of New York Press.
Hawkins, D. F.
    1994   "Ethnicity: The Forgotten Dimension of American Social Control." Pages 99-116 in
            G. S. Bridges and M. A. Myers (eds.), *Inequality, Crime, and Social Control*. Boulder,
            San Francisco, Oxford: Westview Press.
Hernandez, T. K.
    1995   "Bias Crimes: Unconscious Racism in the Prosecution of 'Racially Motivated
            Violence'." Pages 139-158 in A. S. Lopez (ed.), *Latinos in the United States. Volume
            3. Criminal Justice and Latino Communities*. New York and London: Garland Publish-
            ing, Inc.
Holmes, M. D., and H. C. Daudistel
    1995   "Ethnicity and Justice in the Southwest: The Sentencing of Anglo, Black, and Mexican
            Origin Defendants." Pages 125-138 in A. S. Lopez (ed.), *Latinos in the United States.
            Volume 3. Criminal Justice and Latino Communities*. New York and London: Garland
            Publishing, Inc.

Jacobs, J.B., and J. S. Henry

1996   "The Social Construction of a Hate Crime Epidemic." *The Journal of Criminal Law & Criminology*, 86:366-391.

Klein, M. W., C. L. Maxson, and J. Miller

1995   *The Modern Gang Reader*. Los Angeles, CA: Roxbury.

LaFree, G. D.

1995   "Official Reactions to Hispanic Defendants in the Southwest." Pages 159-184 in A. S. Lopez (ed.), *Latinos in the United States. Volume 3. Criminal Justice and Latino Communities*. New York and London: Garland Publishing, Inc.

LaFree, G., and K. K. Russell

1993   "The Argument for Studying Race and Crime." *Journal of Criminal Justice Education*, 4(2):273-289.

Lopez, A. S. (ed.)

1995   *Latinos in the United States. Volume 3. Criminal Justice and Latino Communities*. New York and London: Garland Publishing, Inc.

Mann, C. R.

1993   *Unequal Justice. A Question of Color*. Bloomington and Indianapolis: Indiana University Press.

Mann, C. R.

1995   "The Contribution of Institutionalized Racism to Minority Crime." Pages 259-280 in D. F. Hawkins (ed.), *Ethnicity, Race, and Crime: Perspectives Across Time and Place*. Albany, NY: State University of New York Press.

Mauer, M.

1995   "Disparate Justice Imperils a Community." *Legal Times* (October 16, 1995).

Myers, M. A.

1995   "The New South's 'New' Black Criminal: Rape and Punishment in Georgia, 1870-1940." Pages 145-168 in D. F. Hawkins (ed.), *Ethnicity, Race, and Crime: Perspectives Across Time and Place*. Albany, NY: State University of New York Press.

O'Kane, J. M.

1992   *The Crooked Ladder. Gangsters, Ethnicity, and the American Dream*. New Brunswick: Transaction.

Operation Safe Streets [OSS]

1995   "Street Gang Detail L.A. Style: A Street Gang Manual of the Los Angeles Country Sheriff's Department." In Klein, M. W., C. L. Maxson, and J. Miller, *The Modern Gang Reader*. Los Angeles, CA: Roxbury.

Parrillo, V.

1996   *Diversity in America*. Thousand Oaks, CA: Pine Forge Press.

Poupart, L. M.

1995   "Juvenile Justice Processing of American Indian Youth: Disparity in One Rural Country." Pages 179-200 in K. L. Leonard, C. E. Feyerherm, and W. H. Feyerherm (eds.), *Minorities in Juvenile Justice*. Thousand Oaks, CA: Sage Publications.

Reiss, A. J., Jr., and J. A. Roth (eds.)

1993   *Understanding and Preventing Violence*. Washington, DC: National Academy Press.

Reuter, T.

1996   "The Decline of the American Mafia." *Trends in Organized Crime*, 1(3):27-34.

Sanders, W. B.

1994   *Gangbangs and Drive-Bys: Grounded Culture and Juvenile Gang Violence*. Hawthorne, New York: Aldine de Gruyter.

Savelsberg, J.
    1995   "Crime, inequality, and Justice in Eastern Europe: Anomie, Domination, and Revolutionary Change." Pages 206-224 in J. Hagan and R. D. Peterson (eds.), *Crime and Inequality*. Stanford, CA: Stanford University Press.

Schatzberg, R., and R. J. Kelly
    1996   *African-American Organized Crime*. New York and London: Garland Publishing.

Smith, M. D.
    1995   "The Death Penalty in America." Pages 557-572 in J. F. Sheley (ed.), *Criminology* (2nd Edition). Belmont, CA: Wadsworth Publishing Company.

Snyder-Joy, Z.
    1995   "Self-Determination and American Indian Justice: Tribal Versus Federal Jurisdiction on Indian Lands." Pages 310-322 in D. F. Hawkins (ed.), *Ethnicity, Race, and Crime: Perspectives Across Time and Place*. Albany, NY: State University of New York Press.

Tanton, J., and W. Lutton
    1993   "Immigration and Criminality in the U.S.A." *The Journal of Social, Political and Economic Studies*, 18(2):217-234.

Tonry, M.
    1995   *Malign Neglect: Race, Crime and Punishment in America*. New York and Oxford: Oxford University Press.

Tonry, M.
    1996   "The Effects of American Drug Policy on Black Americans, 1980-1996." *European Journal on Criminal Policy and Research*, 4(2):36-62.

Walker, S. and B. Wright
    1995   *Citizen Review of the Police, 1994: A National Survey*. Washington, DC: Police Executive Research Forum.

Walker, S., C. Spohn, and M. DeLone
    1996   *The Color of Justice. Race, Ethnicity, and Crime in America*. Belmont, CA: Wadsworth.

Wilbanks, W.
    1987   *The Myth of a Racist Criminal Justice System*. Monterey: Brooks/Cole.

Young, V., and A. T. Sulton
    1994   "Excluded: The Current Status of African-American Scholars in the Field of Criminology and Criminal Justice." Pages 1-17 in A. T. Sulton (ed.), *African-American Perspectives on Crime Causation, Criminal Justice Administration and Crime Prevention*. Newton, MA: Butterworth-Heinemann.

Zatz, M. S., C. C. Lujan, and Z. K. Snyder-Joy
1991 "American Indians and Criminal Justice: Some Conceptual and Methodological Considerations." Pages 100-112 in M. J. Lynch and E. B. Patterson (eds.), Race and Criminal Justice. New York: Harrow and Heston.

Zatz, M. S.
1987 "The Changing Forms of Racial/Ethnic Biases in Sentencing." Journal of Research in Crime and Deliquency 24:69-92.

15

Crime Prevention and the Victim

By

Michael J. Palmiotto and **Michael Joseph Palmiotto**

The concern about personal safety and the securing of personal property can be traced to our tribal ancestors. The informal process of tribal members handling disorder and violence against members of the tribe or clan, eventually evolved over the centuries into a formal process now known as law enforcement. Informal customs and rules eventually became formalized as laws. The concept of crime and the elements of distinctive crimes such as murder, assault, and rape evolved over the centuries. A crime cannot be considered an illegal act unless some legal body makes it so. The concept that the citizen and the community were responsible for maintaining order and preventing crimes against persons and property has survived to the present day and plays an important part in keeping crime under control. With the advent of a formalized policing structure, it became one of the goals of the police organization to be involved in crime prevention.

The idea of *crime prevention* as an important function of policing can be traced to Sir Robert Peel. He established crime prevention as one of London s Metropolitan Police goals. For the last several decades the police have recognized crime prevention as one of their functions. They have established crime prevention units or departments to assist home owners, apartment dwellers, and business owners to avoid being a victim of a crime. The police recognize that to prevent crime they need to gain the cooperation of the citizenry. Also, citizens must understand that they must take preventive measures against becoming crime victims.

In the twentieth century the American legal system has formalized its crimes. The legislative branch of our federal and state governments have passed laws outlawing specific behavior as criminals. Crime can be defined as "a positive or negative act in violation of the penal law; an offense against the state."[1] Criminal acts are further divided into crimes against people and crimes against property. Crimes against people include: homicide, assaults, robberies and rape. Crimes against property include: burglary, theft, and auto theft.

Since the 1964 presidential election when crime was made an issue for the first time in a national election crime has been one of the top concerns of the American people. Politicians are consistently debating the crime problem during elections. The news media — print and electronic — keep crime news in the forefront of the public mind. Their motto seems to be "if it bleeds then it leads." The constant bombardment of crime news, along with our politicians attempting to **"out tough"** one another have created a "fear of crime" among many Americans.

For many Americans crime is a fact of life. Crime has either increased, or at the least, is considered to be at unacceptable levels by a good portion of the general public. At least since the 1960s, crime has been considered a serious problem and Americans want something to be done about it. Public opinion often rates crime as the number one social issue facing America.

Opinion polls have rated crime as a major concern among Americans living in our cities. For example, residents of the City of Wichita declared crime their number one concern. A poll by *The Wichita Eagle* in August 1994 revealed that the fear of crime was considered the region's number one problem.[2] The *Eagle* indicated that those polled were concerned about their safety and the violence projected by the news and entertainment media. Approximately 92 percent of those polled considered violent crime to be either an extremely important or a very important issue. Eighty-four percent responded that safety was an extremely important or a very important concern.

Typically, people estimate their risk to crime on limited information. They rely on secondhand information, media accounts, and their personal perceptions of crime. Based on misinformation about crime, various segments of our population believe they have a greater chance of being a victim of a crime than what statistics bear out. One factor that could contribute to American's fear of being a victim of a crime is their belief that crime has not been decreasing but increasing. With the perception of crime escalating many people feel their chances of becoming a crime victim are increasing.

One scholar who believes that crime has been increasing is Kenneth Ferraro. Ferraro claims that crime rates have continued to increase since the 1970s. He claims that crime soared from the mid-1960s to the mid-1970s. He further maintains that after the mid-1970s, there have been increases in rates for certain types of crimes, but, since the mid-1980s the index crimes have continued to increase.[3] It appears many average citizens are in agreement with Ferraro, believing that crime is on the increase. Because of the perception that crime has been on the increase police agencies and citizens are pooling their resources to prevent crime. However, the United States Justice Department reported that the year 1996 saw an overall decrease of crime in America by three percent. New York City even saw its murders go below 1,000. This was the first time in decades that the cities murder rate was below 1,000. Although there are numerous reasons given for the decrease in the crime rate ranging from community policing to enforcing nuisance offenses, such as panhandling, as well as a decrease in teenagers committing crimes, there exists no scientific data to substantiate the reasons given. It is rather difficult to determine why crime either increases or decreases. The trend of lower crime rates in America are not expected to last due to the fact that crime rates run in cycles.

Generally, there are three elements present when a crime has been committed. First, the individual wants to commit the crime. Second, the opportunity to commit the crime is present and third, the individual has the ability to commit the crime. The purpose of crime prevention is to eliminate either one or all three elements that make it possible for an individual to commit a criminal act.

THE DIMENSIONS OF CRIME PREVENTION

There are a wide variety of view points as to who has the responsibility for crime prevention. One approach would be that the individual himself has the sole responsibility of avoiding becoming a victim of a crime, thereby shouldering the responsibility for crime prevention. The second approach would be that the neighborhood or community has the responsibility of crime prevention. Another approach suggested that the police have the primary responsibility of preventing crime. Upon close examination it appears that the individual, the community and the police all have a responsibility for preventing crime. For crime prevention to work it involves the participation of all formal and informal structures and the willingness of individuals to be aware of dangers that place them in harms way.

Crime prevention involves education, training, public relations and the development of strategies to prevent criminal activities. In the last several decades there has been a number of crime prevention studies, programs, and strategies advocated in order to prevent the individual, neighborhoods, and governmental and private organizations from being crime victims. There are several definitions of crime prevention but we will only provide the definition of the organization that has been devoted to crime prevention since 1971. The **National Crime Prevention Institute** describes "crime prevention as any kind of effort aimed at controlling criminal behavior." The **Institute** further divides crime prevention into: "Direct controls of crime includes only those which reduce environmental opportunities for crime, and Indirect controls include all other measures, such as job training, remedial education, police surveillance, police apprehension, court action, imprisonment, probation and parole."[4]

The National Crime Prevention Institute delineates ten operational goals of crime prevention. They are:

1. Potential crime victims or those responsible for them must be helped to take action which reduces their vulnerability to crimes and which reduces their likelihood of injury or loss should a crime occur.

2. At the same time, it must be recognized that potential victims (and those responsible for them) are limited in the action they can take by the limits of their control over the environments.

3. The environment to be controlled is that of the potential victim, not of the potential criminal.

4. Direct control over the victims's environment can nevertheless affect criminal motivation, in that reduced criminal opportunity means less temptation to commit offenses, and learn criminal behavior and consequently, fewer offenders. In this sense, crime prevention is a practical rather than a moralistic approach to reducing criminal motivation. The intent is to discourage the offender.

5. The traditional approaches used by the criminal justice system (such as punishment and rehabilitation capabilities of courts and prisons and the investigative and apprehension functions of police) can increase the risk perceived by the criminal, and thus have a significant (but secondary) role in criminal opportunity.

6. Law enforcement agencies have a primary role in crime prevention to the extent that

they are effective in providing opportunity-reduction education, information and guidance to the public and to various organizations, institutions and agencies in the community.

7. Many skills and interest groups need to operate in an active and coordinated fashion if crime prevention is to be effective in a community-wide sense.

8. Crime prevention can be both a cause and an effect to efforts to revitalize urban and rural communities.

9. The knowledge of crime prevention is interdisciplinary and is in a continual process of discovery, as well as discarding misinformation. There must be a continual sifting and integration of discoveries as well as a constant sharing of new knowledge among practitioners.

10. Crime prevention strategies and techniques must remain flexible and specific. What will work for one crime in one place may not work for the same crime in another place. Crime prevention is a "thinking person's" practice, and countermeasures must be taken after a thorough analysis of the problem, not before.[5]

The goal of crime prevention is to prevent people from being crime victims and the protection of property. The concept of crime prevention holds that measures can be taken where people can prevent being a victim. A crime prevention program has several distinct characteristics:

1. It will be set in motion *before* the crime is committed, not after.

2. It will focus on *direct* controls over behavior, and not on indirect controls.

3. It will focus on the *environment* in which crimes are committed, and on the organism with his environment, and not on the individual behavior.

4. It will be an *interdisciplinary* effort, based on all disciplines dealing with human behavior.

5. It will be *less costly* and *more effective* than punishment or treatment. This means that crime prevention is a more just and moral system than the system currently under use.[6]

Both the government and the private sector have been involved in crime prevention efforts to decrease the chance of individuals and business from being crime victims. Crime prevention programs can involve attempts to reduce crime, the fear of crime, and the elimination of annoying offenses such as drunkenness and urinating in public places. The various crime prevention studies, programs, and strategies will be discussed briefly.

Police Role in Crime Prevention

The police mission, as outlined by Sir Robert Peel, holds that the police have the responsibility of preventing and controlling crime. No other component of the criminal justice system has the vantage point the police possess in working with the community. The police are the first to know if a crime has been committed. They have to investigate crimes, solve crimes, arrest criminal offenders, and recover stolen property. By the nature of their positions, the police know how offenders commit crime. They are aware of the criminals method of operation. When a criminals method of committing a crime becomes known, the next obvious step implies taking measures to prevent the crime from occurring.

Many police departments have crime prevention units or at the minimum have an officer who does security checks for residents and businesses. The police attempt to obtain the cooperation of neighborhood and business associations in order to convince them to put in place crime prevention strategies. The primary role of the police in crime prevention is educating and providing consulting services to the neighborhood and community. There are a wide variety of specialized crime prevention programs. These include programs dealing with preventing rape, mugging, shoplifting and juvenile delinquency. This chapter cannot go into detail to cover all the specialized programs pertaining to crime prevention. Students are recommended to take a crime prevention course if one is available at their college or university.

Although the police have been involved in a wide variety of crime prevention programs, not all can be discussed in this chapter. However, the **Neighborhood Watch** because of its impact on crime prevention should be mentioned. The Neighborhood Watch has received a great deal of national media attention and students of criminal justice should have an understanding of how it operates. Neighborhood Watch programs are instituted to reduce crime as well as the fear of crime. The concept requires that citizens of a neighborhood play an important role in controlling crime in their neighborhood. Residents of a specific neighborhood, can be either homeowners or apartment dwellers, who ban together to establish a sense of security and safety. The Neighborhood Watch Association meets regularly in order to provide information about residential and personal security. The Association works with all its members to create a genuine neighborhood and to exchange information on crime prevention techniques. The police crime prevention specialist should only function as an advisory to the Neighborhood Watch Association. If the crime prevention specialist runs the meeting this makes residents feel that they should not be actively involved. The success of Neighborhood Watch depends on neighborhood residents being actively involved to make their own neighborhood secure and safe.

Not only should the crime prevention specialist be actively involved in crime prevention; the patrol officer should be vigorous in looking for ways to improve the security and safety of residents and businesses on his beat. The patrol officer should seek out conditions that could potentially lead to a criminal offense. He should be looking for poor or inadequate locks and recommend that the owner replace them. Owners who leave their establishments open or unlocked need to be informed of the danger of this action. The patrol officer has the responsibility to check the physical security of his beat which should reduce the opportunity to commit an offense. The officer should check the exterior security of buildings on his beat. When doing this, the officer should check on the following: fire escapes, doors, locks, windows, ladders, boxes, and equipment left out.[7] The officer should also perform an inside security check and if he lacks the knowledge then he should contact the crime prevention specialist who can perform a detailed survey of the premises.

Community Crime Prevention

The community has a role to play in crime prevention. The police now recognize that they cannot solve crime when left to their own means. They need the assistance of the community. More importantly, they can not prevent crime on their own; they need the cooperation of the community to put in place successful crime prevention strategies. Effective crime prevention can only be obtained with community involvement. Only when there exists citizen participation in crime prevention can we expect that crime will be reduced. Even when crime has been decreased crime prevention participation by citizens needs to be a continuous process so crime will not take an upward turn. One of the major problems of citizen's involvement in crime prevention is their long term staying power. Most citizens can muster enough energy for the short term but long term involvement is needed to keep crime under control. Paul Whisenand in his classic text on crime prevention indicates that its essential for community organizations to identify problems, and that priorities should be established. Whisenand had the following to say about community crime prevention programs:

> First, the course of action selected should fall within the scope of interest of the organization's members. Second, the problem selected for attack must be tractable within the organization's geographical base and its available manpower, funding, and other resources. A third concern in determining priorities is to be sure that the action program selected does not create more problems than it solves.[8]

The term community has multiple definitions depending upon an individuals perception. It means the entire city, for example the community of Wichita, or it could be viewed as a section of the city, for instance the north side or the east side. Crime prevention strategies or plans function more efficiently when specific geographical areas are focused upon. An entire city or community usually do not have similar crime problems. This often can be due to the socio-economical composition of the city. Poorer neighborhoods will not have similar crimes that occur in middle-class and upper class neighborhoods. Lower socio-economical areas may have drive-by shootings and drugs being sold on street corners while the upper middle-class neighborhood have as their biggest crime problem burglaries. Police departments are well aware of where violent crime usually occurs. They are also aware of those geographical areas where specific crimes such as robberies, burglaries, auto theft and drug dealing take place. In order to keep crime under control the police not only need the cooperation of citizens who live in the locality where crime occurs, but need to concentrate on these geographical neighborhoods. A neighborhood implies a smaller geographical unit. The following quotation provides a good explanation on what comprises a neighborhood.

> First, and most basically, a neighborhood is a small physical area embedded within a larger area in which people inhabit dwellings. Thus, it is a geographic and social subset of a larger unit. Second, there is a collective life that emerges from the social networks that have arisen among the residents and the sets of institutional arrangements that overlap these networks. That is, the neighborhood is inhabited by people who perceive themselves to have a common interest in that area and to whom a common life is available. Finally, the neighborhood has some tradition of identity and continuity over time.[9]

To obtain the involvement of residents of a specific neighborhood may require a great deal of effort. It has been estimated that approximately 10 percent to 20 percent of neighborhood residents will, at any one time, be involved in crime prevention activities. The goal of neighborhood crime prevention programs is to reduce the opportunity for crime in order to reduce crime. There are a wide variety of programs that can be implemented that can include improved housing, education, and employment opportunities to name only a few.

According to the *National Crime Prevention Council* a neighborhoods crime problems begin with decay which further deepens the spiral of destruction. To improve the neighborhood crime prevention and improvement are tied together. There exists numerous methods to make neighborhoods safer and at the same time improve their quality of life. Not only do neighborhoods need to reduce crime, they also have to correct the underlying causes of their crime problem.[10] The success of a crime prevention program can be measured in several ways. They are:

> ➤ **Is crime reduced?** Are there fewer robberies, assaults, vandalism, burglaries, than last month? Than this time last year?

> ➤ **Is fear of crime reduced?** Do residents see crime as being reduced? Do they act in ways which show they are less afraid to move about their neighborhoods?

> ➤ **Are attitudes changed?** Do citizens have more confidence in their community and its institutions? Are they more convinced that their actions can improve the community? Are they more involved in civic activity?

> ➤ **Are the needs of the community and its residents met?** Are teenagers finding positive recreation, employment, leadership opportunities? Do children have access to crime prevention and child protection instruction, reliable adults with whom to speak if scared or threatened? Can people and businesses function free from intimidation? Are senior citizens comfortable walking and driving in their community? Are all citizens provided with the chance to lend their skills to community betterment?[11]

Because of the difficulty in obtaining citizen involvement in crime prevention programs the federal, state and local authorities have periodically been involved in media campaigns.

Media Campaigns

Since 1980, the Bureau of Justice Assistance within the U.S. Department of Justice has supported the **National Citizens' Crime Prevention** media campaign. The purpose of the media campaign has been to make the public aware of crime prevention strategies and programs that allow citizens to protect themselves and their property. The goals of the media campaign are to achieve the following:

a. change unwarranted feelings and attitudes about crime, drug use, and the criminal justice system;

b. generate an individual and community sense of responsibility for crime and drug prevention;

c. initiate individual and community action toward preventing crime and illicit drug use;

d. mobilize additional resources for crime and drug prevention efforts;

e. enhance existing crime and drug prevention programs and projects conducted by national, state and local agencies and organizations;

f. develop organizational capacities to implement crime and drug prevention programs.[12]

The success or failure of mass media campaigns rests with the willingness of mass media programmers to disseminate crime prevention announcements and for local police officials to support crime prevention efforts. Findings indicate that both police officials and media programmers support crime prevention media campaigns.[13]

At the local level **crime newsletters** can provide specific crime information targeted for certain neighborhoods. A newsletter can supply detailed news about crime problems and offer preventive measures to avoid becoming a victim. The crime newsletter can include the class of crime committed, where the offense was committed, and description of the offenders if available. Another media method used for both the print and electronics media is **Crime Stoppers**. The media informs the general public of a specific crime. Persons having knowledge of the crime are encouraged to telephone Crime Stoppers providing information on the individual or individuals who may have committed the offense. The caller can remain anonymous and can receive an reward if an offender is arrested. The monetary amount of the reward will be based upon the seriousness of the crime. The more serious the crime the greater the reward.

In the 1990s television shows re-creating a crime have been successful in apprehending fugitives. We are familiar with many of these television shows, including "America's Most Wanted" and "Unsolved Mysteries." At the local level the Sheriff of Sedgwick County/Wichita Kansas announces on cable television his "Ten Most Wanted" list. A pictured of the wanted person along with a physical description is provided to the viewing audience. The Wichita Police Department on cable television announces the names of individuals having warrants for their arrest. The local cable network of Sedgwick County/Wichita also places on television the names and ages of those offenders convicted of drunk driving.

As we can see, the news media can play an influential role in crime prevention strategies. However, the media cannot be expected to provide all the information needed by citizens to prevent becoming a crime victim. The individual citizen has to assume responsibility for obtaining knowledge about his own security and safety.

In addition to media support and individual responsibility, there are a variety of sophisticated strategies that can be implemented at the local level. One of these strategies is the utilization of **defensible space**.

Defensible Space

The term *defensible space* can be traced to a conference held in 1964 at Washington University in St. Louis, Missouri. Two sociologist and two architects, along with police officers from the St. Louis Police Academy, discussed physical features that produced security for public housing.[14] "Defensible space is a surrogate term for the range of mechanisms — real and symbolic barriers, strongly defined areas of influence, and improved opportunities for surveillance."[15] Oscar Newman who coined the phase defensible space expounded the goals of defensible space. He stated:

> Defensible space is a model for residential environments which inhibits crime by creating the physical expression of a social fabric that defends itself. All the different elements which combine to make a defensible space have a common goal — an environment in which latent territoriality and a sense of community in the inhabitants can be translated into responsibility for ensuring a safe, productive, and well maintained living space.[16]

The defensible space concept provides residents of public housing an milieu of security from crime. To feel secure in their public housing environment defensible space includes areas other than their individual apartments. Areas including defensible space include lobbies, hallways, playgrounds, and adjacent streets. According to Oscar Newman, a founder of defensible space, four elements of physical design, can contribute to a secure residential environment. The four elements are:

1. The territorial definition of space in developments reflecting the areas of influence of the inhabitants. This works by subdividing the residential environment into zones toward which adjacent residents easily adopt proprietary attitudes.

2. The positioning of apartment windows to allow residents to naturally survey the exterior and interior public areas of their living environment.

3. The adoption of building forms and idioms which avoid the stigma of peculiarity that allows others to perceive the vulnerability and isolation of the inhabitants.

4. The enhancement of safety by locating residential developments in functionally sympathetic urban areas immediately adjacent to activities that do not provide continued threat.[17]

The preceding four elements of defensible space — territoriality, natural surveillance, positive picture of locality, and environment are all perceived to influence disorder and crime in the area. Defensible space concepts holds that the inhabitants of public housing can control disorder and crime in their public housing complex. The theory claims that residents can assert territoriality for their public housing complex while natural surveillance allows the inhabitants to observe legitimate residents along with potential offenders. The last two elements of the concept — positive picture of locality and environment should project a feeling of safety from disorder and crime for residents of public housing. To a great extent, public housing in the late 1980s and 1990s, with grants from the Department of Housing and Urban Affairs, put into operations all or segments of the four elements of defensible space. Residents of public housing complexes in a joint effort with their local police department reclaimed their living environment from drug dealers, drug users and other criminal offenders. The criminal element was chased away with police cooperation. The residents reclaimed their territoriality, their housing complex. Natural surveillance helped them to identify the legitimate residents from law violators. Playgrounds were reclaimed so that children could again play on them. This led to a positive feeling about the locality where they resided. The environment was cleaned up with graffiti removed from walls and grass planted where none existed.

Crime Prevention Through Environmental Design

Environmental techniques to the prevention of crime were initially made popular by Oscar

Newman in his study of **defensible space**. These methods have been used for residential areas, commercial businesses, schools, and parking garages. J. Ray Jefferies, the theorist who developed the concept of crime prevention through environmental design (CPTED), believed that crime prevention involved the physical design of buildings along with citizen involvement and the effective use of police agencies. According to Jefferies, the physical environment in terms of buildings, each floor of a building, and each room in a building should be examined. Jefferies correctly claims that usually a small area of the city is responsible for the majority of crime. However, he maintains that analysis of crime ignore house-by-house or block-by-block variations in crime rates. He advocates that for the purpose of crime prevention, crime data be utilized to determine in what areas of a community crime generally occurs.[18]

The thrust of the CPTED model implies that the physical environment can be orchestrated to prevent potential offenders from committing incidents of crime along with improving the quality of life. Those individuals prone to criminal activity can have this inclination removed by a physical environment that places stumbling blocks in the way of the potential offender. CPTED involves creating a physical environment that people can be free from the fear of crime and have a feeling of safety. The CPTED model includes information from the architectural field but also includes information from the sociological, psychological, and law enforcement fields. It's a cooperative effort to reduce crime and to meet the needs of individuals and the community. Planning is extremely important to the CPTED model and strategies are needed if CPTED is to be put into operation.

Timothy D. Crowe indicates that there are three overlapping strategies in CPTED: "natural access control, natural surveillance, and territorial reinforcement."[19] The purpose of access control is to reduce the opportunity to commit a crime. Methods used to control access to an area can include gates, guards, locks, and shrubbery. The aim of this strategy should be to create an allusion that the risk for attempting a criminal act is greater than the opportunity. The purpose of surveillance is to observe outsiders or intruders into the neighborhood. When strangers are under surveillance, the risk of committing an offense increases. Strategies of surveillance include police and security guard patrols, lighting and windows. The third strategy, territoriality; implies that physical design contributes to a perception of territoriality. A sense of ownership or influence can be created by the physical environment. Potential offenders can recognize the residents ownership or influence over a geographical area. Also, natural access control and surveillance contribute to a feeling of territoriality.[20]

CPTED, to be successful must be practical and be understood. Residents, store owners, school officials, and parking garage owners must visualize the benefits of CPTED before they will implement the model. Crowe advocated a Three-D approach to space assessment to be used as a guide for the nonprofessional. The Three-D concept is based on the three function or dimensions of human space:

1. All human space has some designated purpose.

2. All human space has social, cultural, legal, or physical definitions that prescribe the desired and acceptable behaviors.

3. All human space is designed to support and control the desired behaviors.[21]

According to Crowe, by using the Three-Ds as a guide, space may be evaluated by asking the following questions.

Designation

* What is the designated purpose of this space?
* What was it originally intended to be used for?
* How well does the space support its current use? Its intended use?
* Is there conflict?

331

Definition

* How is the space defined?
* Is it clear who owns it?
* Where are its borders?
* Are there social or cultural definitions that affect how that space is used?
* Are the legal or administrative rules clearly set out and reinforced in policy?
* Are there signs?
* Is there conflict or confusion between the designated purpose and definition?

Design

* How well the physical design support the intended function?
* How well does the physical design support the definition of the desired or accepted behaviors?
* Does the physical design conflict with or impede the productive use of the space or the proper functioning of the intended activity?
* Is there confusion or conflict in the manner in which the physical design is intended to control behavior?[22]

The three strategies of access control, surveillance, and territoriality are intrinsic in the Three-Ds as proposed by Crowe. The Three-Ds should assist in putting the CPTED model into operation. CPTED can be successful when carefully planned and thought-out.

The concept of "defensible space" developed by Oscar Newman and the concept of "crime prevention through environmental design (CPTED)" developed by Jefferies preceded *situational crime prevention*.

Situational Crime Prevention

Situational crime prevention refers to *reducing opportunities for crime*. It can be defined as "(1) directed at highly specific forms of crime (2) that involve the management, design, or manipulation of the immediate environment in a systematic and permanent way as possible (3) so as to increase the effort and risks of crime and reduce the rewards as

perceived by a wide range of offenders."[23] Techniques used in situational prevention can include a wide variety of crime prevention categories. They can include: burglary alarms, fenced yards, graffiti cleaning, street lighting, baggage screening, CCTV systems, identification cards, and credit card photographs to name only a few techniques.

Under this concept the criminal act is examined. Situational crime prevention holds that specific crime situations have unusual features that can be appraised and examined for solutions. The focus of situational crime prevention is on specific problems and searches for solutions to those problems.[24] Situational crime prevention considers crime analysis to be the first step. The following questions are asked, "What are the detailed characteristics of the problem? When and where is the problem occurring? Who might be committing the offenses or causing the difficulty and why? What elements in the socio-physical background environment could be contributing, in an immediate way, to the observed crime pattern?"[25] Situation crime prevention uses twelve techniques to prevent crime. A brief review of them follows:

1. **Target hardening**. The most obvious way of reducing criminal opportunity is to obstruct the vandal or the thief by physical barriers. This "target hardening" involves the use, for example, of locks, safes, screens or reinforced materials.

2. **Access Control**. Access control is now widely practiced by large employers in offices and factories, particularly in the cities.

3. **Deflecting Offenders**. This technique involves channeling inappropriate behavior to more acceptable directions. For example, place public urinals in areas which has a persistent problem of people urinating in public parks/streets.

4. **Controlling facilitators**. The low rates of homicide in Britain, where handguns are much less readily available than in the United States, provide one reason for believ-

ing that effective gun controls can reduce levels of violent crime.

5. **Entry/exit screening**. Entry screening differs from access control in that the purpose is less to exclude people than to increase the risk of detecting those who are not in conformity with entry requirements. Exit screens serve primarily to deter theft by detecting objects that should not be removed from the protected area, such as items not paid for at a shop.

6. **Formal surveillance**. Personnel such as police, security guards and store detectives, whose main function is to furnish a deterrent threat to potential offenders, are the principal providers of formal surveillance. Their surveillance role may be enhanced by electronic hardware, for example by burglar alarms, radar speed traps, and closed circuit television (CCTV).

7. **Surveillance by employees**. In addition to their primary role, some employees, particularly those dealing with the public, also perform a surveillance role. They include shop assistants, hotel doormen, park keepers, parking lot attendants and train conductors.

8. **Natural surveillance**. Households may trim bushes at the front of their homes and banks may light the interior of the premises at night, in attempts to capitalize upon the "natural" surveillance provided by people going about their everyday business.

9. **Target removal**. This can include the removal change makers that are the frequent target for thefts, cash limits at convenience stores, and exact change on public transportation.

10. **Identifying property**. Cattle branding is a crude, but effective way to identify property. Modern organizations pursue essentially the same logic when they mark their property. Property marking was extended to house-

holder's valuables through "operation identification."

11. **Removing inducements**. In certain parts of New York City it is unwise to wear gold chains in the streets or to leave cars parked, such as the Chevrolet Camaro, which are highly attractive to joyriders. Some inducements are less obvious. For example, extensive experimental research has suggested that the mere presence of a weapon, such as a gun, can induce aggressive responses in some people.

12. **Rule setting**. In order to protect themselves from crime, all organizations find it necessary to regulate the conduct of their employees.[26]

A negative aspect of situation crime prevention is the concern about *displacement*. Displacement simply means that crime has been displaced to an adjacent geographical area. When opportunities to commit crime are blocked in one area this creates an opportunity to commit crime in another area. However, there are contradicting studies pertaining to displacement as it relates to situational crime prevention.

Crime Prevention and Community Policing

Crime prevention and community policing are interrelated. A number of police agencies have integrated their crime prevention efforts into community policing. Crime prevention contributes information to the community on techniques and strategies to reduce and prevent crime. Both physical and social aspects of the neighborhood are addressed by crime prevention. Crime prevention deals with problem-solving and can and should be incorporated into the community policing operations. The Chicago Police Department made it one of their principles for change to community policing:

Crime control and prevention must be recognized as dual parts of the fundamental mission of policing. Solving crime is and will continue to be an essential element of police work. But preventing crime is the most effective way to create safer environments in our neighborhoods.[27]

The state of Oregon's Board of Public Safety and Training being committed to the belief that crime prevention is an essential element of community policing provides an eighty (80) hour course in crime prevention especially designed for community policing officers. The course was developed because state administrators realized that crime prevention officers have been doing the work described by the community policing concept. This includes problem-solving, empowerment of the citizen and a police partnership with the community. Under the Oregon program, crime prevention officers function as mentors, resources, catalysts, and troubleshooters for community policing officers who are responsible for the day-to-day community policing activities. The crime prevention officers instruct community organizations in conflict resolution, volunteer management, and program development.[28] There are five basic arguments for linking crime prevention and community policing. They are:

> Crime prevention and community policing share a common purpose — making the public safer and making communities healthier.

> Crime prevention offers information and skills that are essential to community policing.

> Crime prevention and community policing have great potential for enriching each other.

> Crime prevention responsibilities may be repositioned within the department as it moves to community policing, but successful departments have found a need for a clear focus of responsibility for crime prevention and a driving necessity for the capacity to apply and teach crime prevention knowledge and skills.

> Thoughtful, planned action that carefully

nurtures a core of crime prevention expertise while making the skills and knowledge available to all officers, especially those working at the street level, can substantially benefit the transition to community policing as well as its practice.[29]

The linkage of crime prevention and community policing can only strengthen the security and safety of neighborhoods and the community as a whole. The goal should be to integrate crime prevention into community policing operations. Crime prevention programs have discovered that neighborhood associations and individuals can play a successful part in their own security and safety. Programs such as block watch, neighborhood watch, business and security surveys, and security training have all proven useful in involving the citizen in crime prevention. These programs often involved the citizen in problem-solving and the initiation of a police-citizen partnership. It also left the citizen with a sense of empowerment over their own safety. Crime prevention closely parallels the philosophy of community policing. Community policing delineates problem-solving, empowerment, a community-police partnership to prevent crime and more importantly, give the community a sense of security and safety. Crime prevention and community policing have six major premises in common. They are:

> Each deals with the health of the community.

> Each seeks to address underlying causes and problems.

> Each deals with the combination of physical and social issues that are at the heart of many community problems.

> Each requires active involvement by community residents.

> Each requires partnerships beyond law enforcement to be effective.

> Each is an approach or philosophy, rather than a program.[30]

Differences do exist between crime prevention and community policing. As a philosophy community policing administers public safety while crime prevention has to be considered a central goal of policing. Crime prevention provides information and instruction to the community on how to prevent specific types of crime, how to motivate residents in prevention endeavors, and how to create an hostile environment to crime. Community policing is incorporating crime prevention into its operations.[31] Both rural and urban police departments are incorporating crime prevention strategies into their community police operations. One rural police department that used its Neighborhood Watch program to introduce community policing at the block level was Caldwell, Idaho, a city with a population of 22,000. The Neighborhood Watch was expected to identify three problems and come up with possible solutions. Neighborhood Watch Captains were kept informed of criminal activities and civic events. Many of the skills of crime prevention strategies have become the basis for community policing. Another example of integrating crime prevention into community policing is Knoxville, Tennessee. Knoxville with a population of 180,000 people incorporated crime prevention into the beat officer's work. The police department established a 100 member community advisory board to include representatives from neighborhood associations, Neighborhood Watch groups, business associations, and civic leaders. The community policing advisory committee was involved in developing the city's crime prevention plan. Specific goals of the crime prevention plan was to focus on resources and results. The obvious goal of the community policing philosophy of Knoxville was to police the community with residents assistance and for residents to play a role in crime prevention by policing themselves.[32]

Crime prevention for the last several decades has sold to our individual citizens, neighborhoods, communities, businesses and governmental agencies that it offers a viable means to reduce crime, the fear of crime and to provide a sense of security and safety to those areas implementing programs. However, crime prevention strategies do not address those concerns of individuals who by

chance, either by being in the wrong place at the wrong time or by be targeted, are victims of criminal offenders. The President's Commission on Law Enforcement and Administration of Justice in their 1967 report *The Challenge of Crime in a Free Society* reported that the victims were the neglected subjects in the study of crime. The report not only recommended that studies be done to determine the role of victims in a crime, but also recommended that they be compensated for their injuries.[33] The next section examines the changes that has occurred pertaining to how the criminal justice system views victims since the printing of The President's Commission findings in the late 1960s.

VICTIMS

As a result of the growing crime rate and increased violence in our society, the victims movement has become more vocal with their demands for justice. This outcry has triggered both federal and state governments to respond by proposing and passing legislation enhancing the rights, assistance, and protection for victims. The criminal justice system is responsible for delivering more services to victims which in turn, forces many agencies to reshape their policies, and provide additional training.

Throughout the 1950s and 1960s the criminal justice system placed emphasis on offender rehabilitation, and neglecting the needs of crime victims and leaving them with a sense of vulnerability. The Kennedy and Johnson administrations believed crime would decrease dramatically if the socioeconomic problems in the nation, like poverty and unemployment were solved.[34] With to much emphasis placed on offender rehabilitation it was acknowledged in the 1970s that criminal cases were being dismissed or lost as a result of witnesses failing to appear in court.[35] Victims play a vital role assisting police officer and prosecutors in bringing criminals to justice. Criminal justice practitioners realized that victims/witness cooperation was needed to prosecute cases. This recognition led to a federal funded program called the Law Enforcement Assistance Administration (LEAA), established in 1974. LEAA initiated the first ten prosecutor-based victim/witness assistance programs in various counties throughout the country. The program encouraged cooperation with victims and witnesses by providing them with information concerning their role as a witness and the court process.[36] Due to the lack of funding, the program eventually became defunct.

Most of the victim assistance legislative activity has been influenced by individuals who have been affected by crime, seeking laws that recognize and compensate crime victims. To assure that this activity is generated, interest groups have been formed which focus on victims rights. Some of these groups include the ACLU, NOVA (National Organization for Victim Assistance), MADD (Mothers Against Drunk Driving), and women's groups. Their work is not confined to the national level, it includes state and local programs as well.[37]

Shortly after taking office in 1981, President Reagan responded to the victims assistance movement, proclaiming an annual National Victims of Crime Week recognizing the problems that surround victims.[38] The victims movement has raised enough support to create legislation.

The 1980s was significant in that it led to a dramatic increase in victims rights and victim/witness service programs. The turning point occurred in 1982 when the President's Task Force on victims of crime was formed. Their final report included over 60 recommendations directing criminal justice personnel at the federal, state, and local levels to establish more services for victims.[39] This report also led to the creation of the federal office for victims of crime within the Department of Justice in 1983.[40] Legislation efforts began to form more intensely on retribution for victims, as opposed to treatment and rehabilitation for the offender.

The first piece legislation passed was the *Victim Witness Protection Act of 1982* which provided more protection for victims of crime. The

Act allows the use of victim impact statements at sentencing in criminal cases.[41] This enables crime victims to express to the court how the crime has impacted their lives and families. Victims acquire a better understanding of the overall situation and feel that justice is being served when they participate in sentencing offenders. Allowing victims to be involved in the sentencing of offenders assists them psychologically in the healing process. Probation departments include victim impact statements in their presentence reports which reflect the effects of the crime on victims, as well as the appropriateness and amount of restitution. This can often influence the final sentence imposed by the court. The Act also allows greater protection for victims and witnesses from intimidation, allows more flexibility for judges to order restitution to victims for medical expenses, and made it illegal for felons to profit from their stories until victims receive full restitution.[42] Federal law enforcement agencies were directed to develop guidelines insuring that they treated victims and witnesses of crime fairly. For example, the U.S. Capital Police responded by developing a manual implementing guidelines for the fair treatment of federal crime victims and witnesses.[43]

Victim witness assistance coordinators are appointed from within the agency and respond to the crime scene to assist victims and witnesses. Officers must be able to communicate with the public more effectively, giving the victims a more positive experience with the criminal justice system. Information is also provided for the victims concerning their case or services that are available to assist them with recovery.

Another important piece of legislation, the *Victims Crime Act of 1984*, established a Crime Victims Fund. This federal fund allowed victim compensation and victim assistance programs in the states to supplement their funding. Money is allocated from fines and forfeitures that have been previously collected from offenders convicted in the federal system. "Included in this fund are names collected from federal funds, new penalty assessment fees for federal felons, forfeiture bad bonds, and criminals literary profits."[44] State and local governments can provide adequate services to victims using the funds they receives for the Victims of Crime Act.

Legislation in the 1980s will always be a significant part of history for the victims rights movement, however, pressure is still being applied to create new laws. In recent years, the Clinton administration signed new legislation strengthening the rights and improving services for victims. In 1994, the Crime Control Act was passed which reinforces the use of victim impact statements and proposed that states have similar laws. It also amended the 1984 Victims of Crime Act giving states more flexibility in use for allocated funds to improve their training programs. Services for sexual assault and domestic violence victims have also been upgraded, including mandatory restitution for women who are victims of violent sexual crimes.[45]

The Victim Restitution Act was passed in 1995 making it easier for victims to collect restitution. The victim can be reimbursed for medical expenses, in addition to income being lost, or any other expense that are a result of the crime. The court also has the leverage of choosing the method of payment, whether it be in a lump sum, or established a monthly payment schedule.[46] Many times, the restitution will be ordered as a condition of probation, parole, or supervised release.

Today victim/witness assistance programs have been developed in many counties and cities throughout the country. Many criminal justice agencies realize that victims must often cope with physical pain, psychological trauma, or financial loss. It is necessary that they show compassion and deliver services accordingly, otherwise the victim will experience the feeling of being "revictimized."[47]

As stated above, many agencies have become more efficient in providing an array of services to victims. Many victim assistance programs are located in prosecutor s offices, designated to assist victims and witnesses throughout the criminal proceedings. This is important were most individuals are unfamiliar with the court process and often become confused and disgruntled. Informa-

tion is provided for them in response to questions concerning the court proceedings such as bail status, various motions, and continuances.[48] Referrals are also given to certain victims who need basic necessities like shelter, food, and clothing. Others may require long term services such as counseling, and legal or medical assistance. There are some crimes such as domestic violence, sexual assault, and child abuse where the psychological pain is so great, moral support is needed while in the courtroom. Victim assistance personnel may often accompany the victims for that purpose. Another reason is to interpret the legal jargon that often takes place during the proceedings. Providing transportation to court or intervening with the employers of victims are other services that may be offered.

In order to comply with federal and state legislation, criminal justice agencies are providing training for their personnel to improve services to crime victims. The Justice Departments Office for Victims of Crime, for example, provides training and technical assistance to federal, state, and local victim assistance programs addressing various issues. Some of the tapes include trauma of victimization, crisis response team training, advocacy for victims in the criminal justice system, legal rights of victims, crime victim compensation programs, program standards for victim services, stress management for care givers, and many others.

Police departments have also felt pressure from the community to provide additional training to enhance public relations.[49] Since police officers are often the first to have contact with the victim, their demeanor can impact significantly the attitude the citizenry has toward the criminal justice system. If procedures are improved and better training is provided, the police will be able to interact more effectively with the community. This will increase the likelihood of attaining more information about the crime.[50]

Services for victims and witnesses have improved dramatically over the past 20-30 years as legislation mandated funding for programs, better training for criminal justice personnel, and expanding victim rights. Although the movement is heading in the right direction, there is still more that can and should be done. Crime hits hardest among the poor and undereducated and often times they are not aware of the services available to assist them. Information needs to be filtered into the community so they can be better educated as to their rights as victims. Additional training should be offered on victims legal rights and working with special victim populations which include the elderly, juveniles, the mentally ill, and members of various ethnic groups. As the victims movement continues its efforts toward expanding the rights of victims, the criminal justice system will offer more services and programs. Hopefully this will aid healing for the psychological trauma resulting from a crime.

SUMMARY

The idea of crime prevention as an important function of policing can be traced to Sir Robert Peel. He established crime prevention as one of the London Metropolitan Police goals. The concept that crime prevention is one of policings responsibilities has been transferred to the goals of American policing.

Crime prevention involves education, training, public relations and the strategies to prevent criminal activities. In the last several decades there have been a number of crime prevention studies, programs, and strategies advocated in order to prevent people from being crime victims and the protection of property. The concept of crime prevention holds that measures can be taken where people can prevent being a victim.

The police mission holds that the police have the responsibility for preventing and controlling crime. Many police departments have crime prevention units or at the minimum have an officer who does security checks for residents and businesses. Not only do the police have a major role to play in crime prevention, the community has one also.

Since 1980, the Bureau of Justice Administration has supported the National Citizens Crime media campaign. The purpose of the campaign has been to make the public aware of crime prevention strategies and programs that allow citizens to protect themselves and their property.

As a result of the growing crime rate and increased violence in our society, the victims movement has become vocal with their demands for justice. This outcry has triggered both federal and state governments to respond by proposing and passing legislation enhancing the rights, assistance, and protection for victims. The criminal justice system is responsible for delivering more services to victims which is forcing many agencies to reshape their policies, and provide additional training.

✳ ✳ ✳ ✳ ✳

ENDNOTES

[1] Henry Campbell Black, *Black's Law Dictionary*, Fourth Edition, St. Paul, MN: West, 1968, p. 444.
[2] Tom Webb, "No. 1 Fear? Crime," *The Wichita Eagle*, September 4, 1994, p. 1A.

[3] Keneth F. Ferraro, *Fear of Crime: Interpreting Victimization Risk*, Albany, NY: State University of New York, 1995, p. 44.

[4] National Crime Prevention Institute, *Understanding Crime Prevention*, Boston: Butterworths, 1986, p. 2.

[5] Ibid. pp. 20-21.

[6] C. Ray Jefferies, *Crime Prevention Through Environmental Design*, Beverly Hills, CA: Sage Publications, 1977, p. 37.

[7] Tim Perry, *Basic Patrol Procedures*, Salem, WI: Sheffield Publishing Company, 1994, p. 38.

[8] Paul M. Whisenand, *Crime Prevention*, Boston: Holbrook Press, 1977, pp. 290-291.

[9] Robert J. Bursik, Jr. and Harold G. Grasmick, *Neighborhood and Crime*, New York: Lexington Books, 1993, p. 6.

[10] National Crime Prevention Council, "The Success of Community Crime Prevention," *Topics in Crime Prevention*, in *Canadian Journal of Criminology*, Volume 31, No. 4, October, 1989, p. 488.

[11] Ibid. p. 488.

[12] Garrett J. O'Keefe, Dennis P. Rosenbaum, Paul J. Lavrakas, Kathleen Reid, and Renee A. Botta, *Taking A Bite Out of Crime: The Impact of the National Citizens' Crime Prevention Media Campaign*, Thousands Oaks, CA: Sage Publications, 1996, p. 21.

[13] Ibid. p. 58.

[14] Oscar Newman, *Architectural Design for Crime Prevention*, Washington, DC: U.S. Department of Justice, 1973, p. 1.

[15] Oscar Newman, *Defensible Space: Crime Prevention Through Urban Design*, New York: Collier Books, 1973, p. 3.

[16] Ibid. p. 3.

[17] Ibid. p. 8-9.

[18] National Crime Prevention Institute, *Understanding Crime Prevention*, Boston: Butterworth, 1986, p. 120.

[19] Timothy D. Crowe, *Crime Prevention Through Environmental Design: Applications of Architectral Design and Space Management Concepts*, Boston: Butterworth-Heinemann, 1991, p. 30.

[20] Ibid. pp. 30-32.

[21] Ibid. p. 33.

[22] Ibid. pp. 33-34.

[23] Ronald V. Clark, Editor, *Situational Crime Prevention: Successful Case Studies*, New York: Harrow and Heston, 1992, p. 4.

[24] Patrick L. Brantingham and Paul J. Brantingham, "Situational Crime Prevention in Practice," *Canadian Journal of Criminology*, Volume 32, No. 1, January, 1990, p. 25.

[25] Ibid. p. 26.

[26] Ronald V. Clarke, *Situational Crime Prevention in Practice*, New York: Harrow and Heston, 1992, pp. 12-20.

[27] Chicago Police Department, *Together We Can*, Chicago: Chicago Police Department, 1992, p. 6.

[28] Criminal Justice Management and Training Digest, "Crime Prevention and Community Policing: A Vital Partnership, Part II," Washington, DC: *Washington Crime News Service*, Volume 2, No. 3, February 7, 1996, p. 3.

[29] Criminal Justice Management and Training Digest, "Crime Prevention and Community Policing: A Vital Partnership Part I," Washington, DC: *Washington Crime News Service*, Volume 2, No. 1, January 24, 1996, p. 1.

[30] Ibid. p. 3.

[31] Ibid. p. 4.

[32] Criminal Justice Management and Training Digest, "Crime Prevention and Community Policing: A Vital Partnership Part III," Washington, DC: *Washington Crime News Service*, Volume 2, No. 4, February 21, 1996, pp. 4-8.

[33] The President's Commission on Law Enforcement and Administration of Justice, *The Challenge of Crime in a Free Society*, Washington, DC: Government Printing Office, 1967, pp. 38-41.

[34] Marion, Nancy E., "The Federal Response to Crime Victims, 1960-1992," *Journal of Interpersonal Violence*, Volume 10, No. 4, December 1995, p. 421.

[35] Roberts, Albert R., "Delivery of Services to Crime Victims: A National Survey" *American Journal of Orthopsychiatry*, Volume 61, January 1991, p. 129.

[36] Roberts, Albert R., "Victim/Witness Programs, Questions and Answers," *FBI Law Enforcement Bulletin*, Volume 61, December 1992, p. 13.

[37] Marion, Nancy E., p. 428.

[38] Davis, Robert C., "Crime Victims: Learning how to Help Them," *National Institute of Justice*, No. 203, May/June 1987, p. 1.

[39] Sloan, John J., Brent L. Smith and Richard M. Ward, "Public Support for the Victims' Rights Movement: Results of a Statewide Survey," *Crime and Delinquency*, Volume 36, No. 4, October 1990, p. 490.

[40] Lutheran, Joseph R., "Victim-Witness Assistance," *FBI Law Enforcement Bulletin*, Volume 60, March 1991, p. 5.

[41] Davis, Robert, p. 2.

[42] Marion, Nancy E., p.422.

[43] Lutheran, Joseph R., "Victim-Witness Assistance," *FBI Law Enforcement Bulletin*, Volume 60, March 1991, pp. 1-5.

[44] Roberts, Albert R., p. 130.

[45] Franklin, Sloan R., "New Legislation Makes Victims' Rights a Priority," *Corrections Today*, Volume 57, July 1995, p. 153.

[46] Ibid. p. 153.

[47] Sloan, John, J. et al., p. 489.

[48] Roberts, R., p. 132.

[49] Hendricks, James E. and Gary L. Webb, "Confronting Citizen Fear of Crime: Police Victim Assistance Training," *The Police Chief*, Volume 59, November 1992, pp. 30-31.

[50] Ibid. p. 31.

REFERENCES

Black, Henry Campbell
    1968   *Black's Law Dictionary*, Fourth Edition. St. Paul, MN: West Publishing.
Brantingham, Patrick L., and Paul J. Brantingham
    1990   "Situational Crime Prevention in Practice", *Canadian Journal of Criminology*, Volume 32, No.1, January.
Bursik, Robert J., and Harold G. Grasmick
    1993   *Neighorbood and Crime*. New York: Lexington Books.
Clarke, Ronald V.
    1992   *Situational Crime Prevention in Practice*. New York: Harrow and Heston.
Chicago Police Department
    1992   *Together We Can*. Chicago: Chicago Police Department.
Criminal Justice Management and Training Digest
    1996a   "Crime Prevention and Community Policing: A Vital Partnership, Part I," *Washington Crime News Service*, Volume 2, No.1, January 24.

1996b   "Crime Prevention and Community Policing: A Vital Partnership, Part II," *Washington Crime News Service*, Volume 2, No.1, February 7.

1996c   "Crime Prevention and Community Policing: A Vital Partnership Part III," *Washington Crime News Service*, Volume 2, No.4, February 21.

Crowe, Timothy D.
1991   *Crime Prevention Through Environmental Design: Applications of Architectural Design and Space Management Concepts.* Boston: Butterworth-Heinemann.

Davis, Roert C.
1987   "Crime Victims: Learning How to Help Them," *National Institute of Justice*, No. 8, May/June.

Ferrari, Kenneth F.
1995   *Fear of Crime: Interpreting Victimization Risk.* Albany, NY: State University of New York

Franklin, Sloan R.
1995   "New Legislation Makes Victims Rights a Priority," *Corrections Today*, Volume 57, July.

Hendricks, James E., and Gary L. Webb
1992   "Confronting Citizen Fear of Crime: Police Victim Assistance Training," *The Police Chief*, Volume 59, No. 11.

Lutheran, Joseph R.
1991   "Victim-Witness Assistance," *FBI Law Enforcement Bulletin*, Volume 60, No.3.

Jefferies, C. Ray.
1977   *Crime Prevention Through Environmental Design.* Beverly Hills, CA: Sage Publications.

Marion, Nancy E.
1995   "The Federal Response to Crime Victims, 1960-1992," *Journal of Interpersonal Violence*, Volume 10, No. 4.

National Crime Prevention Council
1989   "The Success of Community Crime Prevention," *Topics in Crime Prevention*, in *Canadian Journal of Crime Prevention*, Volume 31, No.4.

National Crime Prevention Institute
1986   *Understanding Crime Prevention.* Boston: Butterworth.

O'Keefe, Garret J., Dennis P. Rosenbaum, Paul J. Lavakas, Kathaleen Reid, and Renee A. Botta
1996   *Taking A Bite Out of Crime: The Impact of the Nationa Citizens' Crime Prevention Media Campaign.* Thousands Oaks, CA: Sage Publications.

Perry, Tim
1994   *Basic Patrol Procedures.* Salem, WI: Sheffield Publishing Company.

Roberts, Albert R.
1991   "Delivery of Services to Crime Victims," *American Journal of Orthopsychiatry*, Volume 61, No.1.

Roberts, Albert R.
1992   "Victims/Witness Programs, Questions and Answers," *FBI Law Enforcement Bulletin*, Volume 61, No.12.

Sloan, John J., Brent L. Smith, and Richard M. Ward
1990   "Public Support for the Victims' Rights Movement: Results of a Statewided Survey," *Crime and Delinquency*, Volume 36, No.4.

The President's Commission on Law Enforcement and Administration of Justice
1967   *The Challenge of Crime in a Free Society.* Washington, DC: Government Printing Office.

Webb, Tom
1994   "No. 1 Fear? Crime" *The Wichita Eagle*, September 4.

Whisenand, Paul M.
1977   *Crime Prevention.* Boston: Holbrook Press.

Criminal Justice in Other Countries

By

Philip L. Reichel

A man's feet must be planted in his country, but his eyes should survey the world.

--- George Santayana

Throughout this book you read about criminal justice as it operates in the United States. It is also desirable to understand how other countries conduct their criminal justice procedures. One reason why a more global appreciation of justice issues is important is the increased understanding that knowledge gives us about our own system. Learning more about something familiar by contrasting it with something strange seems an odd way to proceed. However, it is a strategy we all use on occasion. While learning a foreign language, it is not uncommon for students to increase their knowledge of word meaning and sentence structure in their native tongue. People familiar with American football may be surprised at how their understanding of that sport increases when they start reading about and watching Australian football and Canadian football. This increased understanding of the familiar is the result of our mind trying to make sense out of the different. In other words, understanding the familiar is increased through appreciation of the different. A goal of this chapter is to increase your understanding of the American criminal justice system by offering examples of how other countries respond to their law violators.

In addition to understanding better our own justice agencies and procedures, an international perspective has the advantage of preparing us for increased crime and justice activities at the international level. Crime and criminals increasingly ignore national boundaries. Organized crime, terrorism, drug trafficking, and other types of crimes are committed in one or more countries by persons who move about the continents with relative ease. Despite the optimism of the television series *Star Trek* and its spin-offs, a "federation of planets" with a unified justice system seems unlikely for the foreseeable future. In fact, a "federation of countries" with a unified justice system is hard to imagine. More likely is an increased cooperation and coordination among countries as they try to combat international crime. To achieve that collaboration, citizens and justice officials of each country must understand the policies and philosophies of criminal justice procedures in the other countries. Without such understanding it will be difficult, even impossible, for officials to work with each other and for citizens to empathize with the procedures used to achieve justice in other countries.

343

Establishing the importance of appreciating the justice process of other countries is more easily accomplished than deciding just how that learning should occur and what aspects of the process should be covered. Obviously, the space allotted in one chapter of a introductory book is insufficient to delve into too great a depth. However, it is certainly sufficient to whet the appetite by showing, in general, the different ways that countries have chosen to structure their justice process. To that end, this chapter introduces four basic legal traditions (common, civil, socialist, and Islamic), then explains how those traditions have resulted in differing approaches to substantive and procedural law, and in contrasting procedures for policing, adjudicating, sentencing, and punishing.

LEGAL TRADITIONS

The concept of *legal tradition* refers to a culture's attitudes, values, and norms regarding the nature, role, and operation of law. It is a broad concept that implies a deeply rooted and historically based heritage. Legal traditions are not restricted to specific times or places. People living in different decades and in varying places can hold to a similar legal tradition.

Legal tradition should not be confused with the term *legal system*. If legal traditions are conceptual, legal systems are functional. When reference is made to a legal system our attention is being drawn to the specific organization and procedures a political entity sets forth to carry out the concepts of a legal tradition. An example may help show the difference between legal tradition and legal system.

The world's religions include Judaism, Christianity, and Islam. These are three main monotheistic religious "traditions." As traditions, each reflects attitudes, values, and norms about morality. However, within each tradition there have developed various "systems" to express each tradition's attitudes, values, and norms. We have, for example, Orthodox, Conservative, and Reform Jews; Catholic, Lutheran, and Baptist Christians; and Sunni or Shiite Muslims. There are some significant differences in the way Orthodox and Reform Jews express their Judaism, just as Catholics and Protestants, and Sunni and Shiites, have found different ways to portray the Christian and

Islam traditions. But, despite the different procedures within each religion, the groups under a religion have more in common with each other than they do with any of the groups from the other religions.

Just as a religious tradition gives rise to various systems to express that religion, legal traditions result in different systems to express the principles of a legal philosophy. The particular structure and procedures used in Canada, England, Australia, and the United States to enforce the law against offenders are quite different in many respects. However, these countries share what is known as the *common legal tradition*. Because of that heritage, the procedures, or legal system, in Canada has more in common with the Australian legal system than it does with the process in Germany or Italy, which share a *civil legal tradition*.

The distinction between legal tradition and legal system is important in this chapter. As you can imagine, it is not possible to review all the world's legal systems since that would require discussion of each country and, in some cases, each state or province within a country. Even discussion of the world's legal traditions is difficult since there is not agreement about the distinctive components of each tradition, or even about how many traditions exist today. For present purposes, we will consider four legal traditions and suggest a few ways to distinguish among them. In the context of discussing each legal tradition, one country will be offered as an example of that tradition. However, because of the difficulty inherent in trying to summarize and exemplify a topic like the law, it is important to remember that just as a description of United Methodist protocol is not necessarily accurate for all Christian denominations, a description, for example, of policing in Canada may not be true for policing in other countries following the common legal tradition. With that caution in mind, the quest begins with a look at the civil legal tradition and Germany as an example.

THE CIVIL LEGAL TRADITION

The oldest contemporary legal family is the civil legal tradition. Persons familiar with the American legal system often find this term confusing since *civil law* in United States jurisdictions refers to private wrongs (like contract disputes) in contrast to the *criminal law*, which handles social wrongs. But in its earliest meaning, civil law referred broadly to the law that people established for themselves — in contrast to the law of nature that was imposed upon them. The first versions of the civil laws were in the form of written codes, so when people outside the United States hear the term civil law, they are more likely to think of a written legal code rather than having a contract dispute or liable action come to mind.

The civil legal tradition originated in the written codes of Roman law and the written papal statements of the Roman Catholic church. While the Roman emperor used legal codes like the *Corpus Juris Civilis* (450 B.C.) to govern the secular world, the Roman Catholic church relied on papal decrees, especially from Pope Leo I (440-461) onward, to provide order to the sacred realm. By the ninth century, both Roman law and canon law had experienced their heyday, and other parts of Europe began influencing the specifics of civil law. But the principle of the civil legal tradition was well established by the time the Germans, French, and others were having their input — laws must be written down in a systematically arranged manner. That is, they must be codified. It is this codification that makes law binding because the written form means it was enacted by a recognized authority (for example, a monarch or a legislature) following formal procedures.

Because the primary source of law in the civil tradition is the written code, there is a potential problem of completeness. If the ruler or legislature tries to include in the written code all possible acts and the specifics of every case, the codes will be unreasonably long. That problem is countered by having the codes lay down general principles rather than specific solutions. The job of a civil law judge requires him or her to identify and apply the appropriate code principle for each particular case. For example, the German Penal Code briefly and concisely states the principle relevant to the crime of theft (Penal Code of the Federal Republic of Germany, 1987:190):

> Whoever takes moveable property not his own from another with the intention of unlawfully appropriating it to himself shall be punished by up to five years' imprisonment or by fine.

Theft occurs, very simply, when someone takes, without permission, another person's property. A German judge hearing a theft case must decide if the case is an example of the defendant taking someone else's property for the defendant's personal use. If the facts of the case reflect that situation, the defendant is guilty. Other legal traditions rely more on anticipating variations on the theme, and prepare laws that can be quite involved. Consider Colorado's (a common legal tradition jurisdiction) definition of theft (Colorado Revised Statutes, 1986:142):

> A person commits theft when he knowingly obtains or exercises control over anything of value of another without authorization, or by threat or deception, and:
> (a) Intends to deprive the other person permanently of the use or benefit of the thing of value; or
> (b) Knowingly uses, conceals, or abandons the thing of value in such manner as to deprive the other person permanently of its use or benefit; or
> (c) Uses, conceals, or abandons the thing of value intending that such use, conceal-

ment, or abandonment will deprive the other person permanently of its use and benefit; or

(d) Demands any consideration to which he is not legally entitled as a condition of restoring the thing or value to the other person.

Because common law, as seen in the next section, decides current cases on the basis of how similar cases were decided earlier, the law must refer to a variety of contingencies. It is not sufficient to simply state a general principle. But for now, let us continue with Germany as an example of one country's way to implement the civil law tradition. We do that by considering the police, courts, and corrections in Germany.

Germany as an Example of the Civil Legal Tradition

A number of different codifications of civil law followed the *Corpus Juris Civilis*, including the famous *Code Napoléon* (1804) which codified the civil law of France. During the first part of the nineteenth century, the idea of codification spread from France to other parts of Europe and in Latin America. Germany was among the countries finding favor with the idea of codification, but the Germans did not agree with basic principles used in developing the *Code Napoléon*. With significant deliberation and historical research, Germany finally succeeded in creating its version of a civil code (the German Civil Code of 1896), which became effective in 1900.

Germany's Policing

Both federal and state (*Länder*) level police agencies are found in contemporary Germany. The primary federal agencies are the Federal Office of Criminal Investigation (FOCI) and the Federal Border Police (FBP). Both operate out of the Federal Ministry of the Interior. The FOCI has a broad range of federal and international duties including the issuing of police reports and statistics and conducting research and development. The FOCI is also responsible for providing intelligence, identification, and technical analysis

services, and for holding advanced training courses in specialized areas of policing. The FBP are a fully motorized federal police with responsibility for protecting Germany's borders. FBP personnel receive the same training as state level police officers and they may transfer to a state police agency after serving at least seven years with the FBP (Fairchild, 1993; Kurian, 1989).

Day-to-day police operations are the responsibility of the state police in each of Germany's 16 *Länder*. Each state controls its own police force but the federal government acts as a liaison and coordinating agent. Despite the decentralization, there is considerable similarity in the police structure and operation in each state. Some of that similarity is the result of all police enforcing similar laws (*i.e.*, the federal laws), and the standard uniform (with different state sleeve patches) worn by police in each state.

The typical structure of state police has a three-part division (Kurian, 1989). The municipal police (*Schutzpolizei*) are the most visible since they wear uniforms and have a broad range of duties. They are the first to arrive on the scene and have initial responsibility for all aspects of enforcement and investigation. After the *Schutzpolizei* determine a crime has occurred, or have identified a suspect, the criminal police (*Kriminalpolizei*) are called in. These plain-clothes officers, who are similar to detectives in United States jurisdictions, have authority to search and seize and are responsible for developing a case and initiating charges against suspects. The third division is the Readiness or Stand-by Police (*Bereitschaftspolizei*), who comprise a paramilitary force acting only in units rather than as individual police officers. These officers provide support to the municipal police when needed for crowd control, emergency activities, and other civil control type situations.

Germany's Courts

The German national legislature determines, for the entire country, what behavior is criminal and what will be the accompanying punishment.

However, each German state is responsible for administering both the law and the punishment.

Germany's penal code places criminal offenses into one of two categories: felonies, which are punishable by imprisonment for at least one year, and misdemeanors, which are punishable by a shorter term or a fine (Kurian, 1989). The distinction is similar to that used in the United States, but German misdemeanors contain a broader range of offenses and include crimes like larceny, fraud, or negligent homicide, that would be considered felonies in many American jurisdictions.

A distinguishing feature of the civil legal tradition is a reliance on the inquisitorial rather than adversarial process for adjudication. The adversarial process, found especially in the common law tradition, assumes truth will arise from an open competition over who has the correct facts. The prosecution and defense propose their version of the "truth" and the judge or jury determines which side has the most accurate portrayal. Rather than a competition between opposing sides, the inquisitorial process is more like a continuing investigation. All parties in the case are expected to provide all relevant evidence to the court. The judge, not the attorneys for defense or prosecution, then calls and questions witnesses. As a result of this process, the civil legal tradition has a procedurally active judge and rather passive lawyers. This is nearly opposite the adversarial process, which has a procedurally passive judge and rather active advocates (Reichel, 1994).

The German states are responsible for administering federal law, so all trials are conducted at the state level. Federal courts exist only to handle appeals from the state courts. Fairchild (1993) describes three levels of criminal courts in the German states. At the bottom are the "county courts" that hear minor criminal cases. Above them are the "district courts" where major criminal cases are tried. As the uppermost state court, the "regional courts" hear appeals from the lower state courts and will also try some exceptional cases (e.g., treason). There are five "federal supreme courts" that operate as the court of last resort for appeals in criminal cases coming through the state courts. When the appeal is on a constitutional questions, the Federal Constitutional Court, decides the issue and returns the case to the lower court for final disposition.

Legal systems following the inquisitorial process seldom use a jury as American's know the term. Instead, participation from the public is in the form of lay judges. Persons are selected as lay judges from nominees provided by a community council. The lay judges are assigned to trials over a four year period but they only serve an average of one day per month. During the trial the lay judges serve along side a professional judge. Trials for the less serious crimes are heard by a panel of one professional judge and two lay judges. When the trial is for a more serious offense it will be heard by three professional judges and two lay judges. The verdict is by majority vote, so it is possible that the lay judges have a significant say in the outcome. However, since the professional judge or judges typically dominate the questioning and the deliberation, lay judges have to be especially assertive to have significant influence (Fairchild, 1993; Weigend, 1983).

Germany's Corrections

Germany's penal system is determined at the federal level but administered by the states. In addition to specifying the punishment for each crime, the federal government provides four main principles for the states to use to guide their penal philosophy: "The punishment should fit the crime, sentencing should be by the judge who tried the case, sanctions should not violate human dignity, and social justice should determine the execution of penal measures" (Kurian, 1989:144).

Imprisonment is certainly an available option, but there has been a move away from its use since 1970. Albrecht (1995) explains that between 1970 and 1994, there was a substantial shift from imprisonment to fines, probation, and various diversion programs. When offenders are given a prison sentence, it is likely to be in a prison classified as either *closed* or *open* and for a period of at least one month but no longer than 15 years. A life sentence is possible, but only for murder. Most of the prisons are large, old-fashioned, star-shaped buildings that pre-date World War II. The newer prisons are often built in pavilion style and are designed to hold 200 to 300 inmates. But it is really the prison alternatives that help set Germany apart from other countries, so we will concentrate attention on that aspect of German corrections.

Day fines are the primary non-custodial penalties used in Germany. Under this version of financial penalty, the fine's calculation is determined in two stages. First, the fine amount is linked to the severity of the crime. In Germany, the least serious crime can result in 5 day fine units and the most serious offense can bring 360 day fine units. In the second stage, the value of each day fine is determined according to the offender's net daily income. That value can vary from about $1.30 to $6,700 (2 DM to 10,000 DM). So, a person guilty of a relatively minor offense (*e.g.*, one at 12 day fine units) and a net daily income of $15, would be fined $180. A person committing a similar offense but having a net daily income of $45, would be fined $540. The fine amounts differ according to the offender's ability to pay, so each fine presumably has a similar economic impact on the offenders.

The German equivalent of probation is suspension of a prison term. Sentences of one year or less are expected to be suspended, and sentences of up to two years may be suspended if the offender presents low risk and the circumstances of the crime warrant suspension (Albrecht, 1995).

If a prison sentence is suspended, the offender may be required to abide by certain *conditions* (*e.g.*, community service, restitution) or *orders* (*e.g.*, report to the court, drug or alcohol treatment, surrendering of items the offender may possess). Supervision by a probation officer is not an automatic aspect of the suspended sentence. When supervision is required, it is stipulated as one of the orders.

Prisoners may be paroled after serving two-thirds of their sentence, or after serving one-half of a prison sentence as long as at least six months have been served. Early release from a life sen-

tence is possible as long as 15 years have been served (Teske and Albrecht, 1991). The period of parole is set at two to five years for non-life sentences and five years for parole on a life sentence. Since probation and parole are not administratively distinguished in Germany, offenders on parole may also be assigned to a probation officer for supervision. They are subject to the same conditions as are persons on probation and can also have their parole revoked.

THE COMMON LEGAL TRADITION

Because common law developed in England and impacted law's application in the British colonies, this legal tradition is the one most familiar to citizens of the United States . Today, the United States, Canada, Australia, New Zealand, India, and former British colonies in Africa, have legal systems counted among those of the common legal tradition. Exceptions include parts of those countries where France had great influence in the province's or state's history. So, Canada's province of Quebec and the state of Louisiana each have a strong civil law tradition despite being part of a common law country.

You will recall that the primary source of law in the civil legal tradition is the written code. For the common legal tradition, the primary source of law is custom. The distinction between codification and custom is confusing since it is possible, in fact likely, that common law is also expressed in written form. However, it is neither necessary nor sufficient that common law be written down for it to have legal authority. A brief review of the origin of common law will make this point more clearly.

In an attempt to return order to an increasingly disrupted kingdom, Henry II (1154-1189) issued the Constitutions of Clarendon (1164), which listed customs said to be the practice in England when the twelfth century had begun. The idea was that traditional, consistent, and reasonable ways of deciding disputes provided the appropriate source of law. Determining whether something was "customary" fell to members of the community who sat as a jury of peers. Judges were expected to follow legal custom by abiding by prior decisions in similar cases. In this manner, custom could be identified by reliance on the people and through reference to several cases. Importantly, however, the case was not referred to as the source of law, it merely provided proof that a legal principle (a custom) was once applied.

Eventually the practice of citing prior cases was done less to show custom and more as a way to reference authority. In this way common law developed a reliance on precedent or *stare decisis*, wherein courts are expected to abide by previously decided cases. Those cases were in written form, but they cannot be considered written law in the way the civil legal tradition views "written." The prior cases reflected custom, albeit custom in writing, rather than reflecting specific decisions by rulers or legislators. The criminal statutes found in common law countries today must be considered in the same way. When common law legislatures prepare written penal statutes or codes, they are not so much *making* written law (as do civil law legislatures) as they are *proposing* law. That is because final determination regarding the validity of a statute lies with the courts who will evaluate the legislature's work. In other words, civil law legislation stands on it own since the legislature is the source of law; but common law legislation is not authoritatively established until it passes examination of the courts since custom is the source of law.

Canada as an Example of the Common Legal Tradition

The German legal system provided an example of one way the civil legal tradition can be implemented. The other chapters of this book provide an extensive example of how United States jurisdictions administer a common legal tradition. To show both similarities and differences in how two countries in the same legal family set up a legal system, this chapter uses Canada as an example of the common law.

Canada's Policing

Canada has three level of law enforcement (federal, provincial, and municipal), with control and supervision decentralized to the government at each level. However, all criminal justice agencies in Canada operate under the national Criminal Code so police at each government level can enforce federal statutes. In addition to the Criminal Code, each municipality and province can enact their own laws; but the designation of crimes and their enforcement is essentially determined throughout Canada by the federal code.

The Royal Canadian Mounted Police (RCMP) is a federal agency responsible for enforcing federal statutes and executive orders, and for policing airports, government buildings, and remote geographical territories. It was formally established in 1920, but has precursors dating to 1845. The RCMP is headed by a commissioner who reports to the solicitor general of Canada.

The Mounties are the sole police agency for the Yukon and Northwest territories. Those territories alone comprise an area accounting for more than one-third of Canada, so it is not surprising that the RCMP make up more than one-fourth of all police personnel in Canada (Griffiths and Verdun-Jones, 1994). In addition to its federal policing duties, the RCMP serves as an information source for all police departments in Canada. Municipal and provincial investigation of economic crime (*e.g.*, money laundering) and organized crime receive assistance from the RCMP Economic Crime Branch and the National Crime Intelligence Branch. The services of the RCMP Crime Detection Laboratories, located across the country, are also available to the other police agencies.

Each of Canada's ten provinces has responsibility for enforcing the national Criminal Code in the province. However, a province can fulfill that obligation by contracting with the federal government to provide police services. Eight of the provinces have chosen the contract option and has the RCMP provide provincial policing. When operating as provincial police, the RCMP operate under the direction of the provincial attorney general, but under the administrative control of RCMP headquarters in Ottawa. The Mounties also enforce provincial laws when acting as the provincial police. The Quebec Police Force and the Ontario Provincial Police enforce the Criminal Code and provincial laws in their respective provinces.

Municipal police officers make up the largest body of police personnel in Canada. As Canada's "street cops," they provide the primary response to most crime. The municipal forces range in size from units of one or two officers to the over 6,000 members of the Montreal Urban Community Police. Like the provinces, municipalities can meet their policing obligation by contracting with the RCMP to act as local police. In 1992, 191 municipalities contracted with the RCMP and 397 municipalities had their own independent police force (Griffiths and Verdun-Jones, 1994).

Canada's Courts

The way Canada has classified an offense determines how the case flows through the system. Therefore, it is necessary to understand the classification before being able to follow a case through the courts. Also, it is important to note that the French influence in Quebec gives that province some unique aspects in its court structure and trial process. For that reason, the following description applies generally to the other nine provinces and the two federal territories.

Canada's Criminal Code places crimes into one of three categories. *Summary conviction offenses* are the least serious and result in only slight punishment. They include, for example, committing an indecent act, creating a public disturbance, soliciting prostitution, and driving a motor vehicle without the owner's consent. *Indictable offenses* are the most serious crimes and bring the harshest penalty. Typical indictable offenses are murder, possession of stolen goods, dangerous driving, and sexual assault. Falling between summary and indictable offenses are *hybrid offenses* like theft of an item valued less that $1,000 (Canadian), impaired driving, and some types of assault (Griffiths

and Verdun-Jones, 1994; Pease and Hukkila, 1990).

Determination of what category a defendant will be charged under is left to the public prosecutor, called the Crown Prosecutor. This responsibility gives the prosecutor significant discretionary power since the charge determines how quickly proceeding must begin, where and how the trial will be held, and the harshness of the eventual penalty. For example, summary conviction proceedings must begin within six months of the offense, but there is no time limit for the initiation of proceedings for an indictable offense. Also, summary conviction offense must be tried by a Provincial Court judge sitting alone, but indictable offenses may be tried in a number of courts depending on factors like the seriousness of the offense and the choice of the accused.

The prosecutor's power, and the impact of his or her decision, is especially obvious with the hybrid offenses. Since the hybrid offenses lie between summary conviction and indictable offenses, the prosecutor chooses which route through the system the case will follow. Because of the large number of such offenses (the Criminal Code has over 60 crimes classified as hybrid offenses), Canada's Parliament has giving the prosecutor significant procedural flexibility and an opportunity to exercise quite a bit of discretion (Griffiths and Verdun-Jones, 1994). Once the type of charge has been determined, the case goes to a provincial or territorial court. Canada actually has two separate court systems, the federal courts and the provincial courts. Since criminal cases begin at the province and territory level, our discussion begins there as well.

Canada's provinces and territories generally have a three-tiered court system going from provincial, and territorial courts at the lowest level, through superior courts (with name variation by province), to the courts of appeal at the highest level (Griffiths and Verdun-Jones, 1994). The provincial courts carry the greatest workload of any court level since all cases enter at this level. The majority will also be tried and finally disposed of in the provincial courts, but others (the most serious indictable offenses) will be sent to the superior court for trial.

Provincial courts may have separate divisions to handle family matters, cases of juvenile delinquency, traffic cases, and criminal cases. Most of the criminal cases are those that have been charged as summary conviction offenses. In general, such offenses may only be tried before a provincial court judge sitting without a jury. The accused person may appear in person at the trial, or may send their lawyer to represent them — unless the judge has issued a warrant requiring their attendance. The term "summary conviction" implies that casual and concise justice is dispensed. The appropriateness of the term was supported in a study of provincial courts in Toronto, which found that in the early 1970s a mere five minutes was the average time devoted to the accused person (Griffiths and Verdun-Jones, 1994).

Indictable offenses, and hybrid offenses charged as indictable, can be heard at either the superior or provincial court level. Griffiths and Verdun-Jones (1994) explain that the particular form and place of trial in superior court is determined by the category of indictable offense being charged. The most serious indictable offenses (*e.g.*, murder, treason, piracy) may only be tried by a judge of the Superior Court sitting with a jury, unless the judge and the attorney general consent to forego the jury. The least serious indictable offenses (*e.g.* theft, fraud, possession of stolen goods) may only be tried by a Provincial Court judge. If the charge is on an indictable offense not falling into either of those categories, the accused can choose the mode of trial. Robbery, dangerous driving, assault, and breaking and entering are examples of these "electable" offenses. The choices available to the accused are to have a trial by a Provincial Court judge, a Superior Court judge and jury, or a Superior Court judge. Failure to make a choice sends the case to a judge and jury.

At the federal court level, and standing as the country's court of last resort, is the Supreme Court of Canada. The Supreme Court justices are ap-

pointed by the federal government from lists prepared by the provinces. Also in the federal system is the Federal Court of Canada, which is divided into a Trial Division and a Court of Appeals. The Federal Court is not involved in the trial of criminal cases since those go from the provincial courts of appeal directly to the Supreme Court of Canada. Instead, the Federal Court deals with actions brought against the federal government and federal agencies (Griffiths and Verdun-Jones, 1994). For example, the Federal Court Trial Division might hear a case brought by a prisoner challenging a disciplinary practice of the federal agency in charge of correctional institutions.

Canada's Corrections

Corrections services in Canada are found primarily at the federal and provincial levels. Determination of which level an offender will go to is based on a "two-year rule." Offenders receiving a single sentence or series of sentences totaling 2 years or more fall under the jurisdiction of the federal corrections system. A sentence or sentences totaling less than 2 years is the responsibility of the provinces. An exception to the two-year rule is Newfoundland, where the province maintains jurisdiction over federal offenders.

Both the federal and provincial levels provide community-based and institutional correctional programs. Institutional programs at the federal level operate from prisons that are categorized as being maximum (11 in number), medium (19), or minimum (12) security level. Five other federal penitentiaries have a multi-level security designation (Pink-Murray Barristers & Solicitors, 1997). Federal prison facilities are administered by the Correctional Service of Canada under the direction of the Commissioner of Corrections. In addition to the prisons, the Correctional Service of Canada is also responsible for community correctional centers and forest work camps.

Women are imprisoned in facilities separate from those for men. Until 1995 there was just one such facility housing all federally sentenced women from throughout the country. That Penitentiary for Women, in Kingston, Ontario, was an extension of a men's prison built in 1934. Starting in 1995, the Correctional Service of Canada began building five small, regional federally operated facilities across the country. These new facilities will reduce the travel time for prisoner's family members and will give the women inmates better access to community services.

The primary community-based program at the federal level is parole. The National Parole Board (NPB) has parole authority over all federal offenders. However, only three of the provinces — British Columbia, Ontario, and Quebec — have established provincial parole boards, so the NPB also has authority over provincial offenders in the other five provinces. Generally, inmates are eligible for parole after serving one-third of their sentence or 7 years, whichever is shorter. The NPB reviews the cases of all inmates as they become eligible for parole and must conduct annual reviews on all cases not receiving parole until that inmate is either paroled or discharged. Griffiths and Verdun-Jones (1994) report that parole is not easily obtained by Canadian prisoners, with only about one-third of the federal offenders being granted parole. Upon receiving parole, the offender is supervised by a parole officer and must abide by conditions similar to those for parolees in United States jurisdictions. Violation of the parole conditions can result in the offender being returned to prison.

Provincial offenders in custody can be held in either *secure* or *open* facilities that are operated by the provinces or territories. However, the majority of provincial offenders are under some form of community supervision — the most frequent being probation (Griffiths and Verdun-Jones, 1994). As with parole, probation in Canada has many similarities with probation in the United States. Persons familiar with the organization and operation of one, would find it easy to understand the other. Other community-based programs at the province/territory level include community service, restitution, halfway house placement, and reconciliation programs.

THE SOCIALIST LEGAL TRADITION

The socialist legal tradition has clear historical links to civil law. In fact, some comparative legal theorists do not see the socialist legal tradition as a separate family. It is considered separate here because of its particular philosophical view of law's role and some resulting procedures in how the law is applied and enforced.

The legal system of the Union of Soviet Socialist Republics provided the philosophical and technical base for a socialist legal tradition. The "fall" of the USSR did not result in the collapse of the socialist legal tradition any more than the fall of the Roman Empire destroyed the civil legal tradition. So, to understand the socialist legal tradition today we must consider its initial application in the USSR.

One characteristic setting the socialist legal tradition apart for others is its view of law as artificial. The Romans and Western Continentals viewed law as binding because it was appropriately authorized and recorded. The English viewed law as binding because it recognized immemorial custom. The Russian people, even before the advent of the USSR, never came to see law as binding at all. For the Russian's law was an arbitrary work of an autocratic sovereign and a privilege of the bourgeoisie. Russian princes and czars not only created the law, they were above it. This point is important to understanding the role of law as perceived by Karl Marx and as implemented by Vladimir Lenin.

After the Bolshevik revolution (1917), Lenin, as the head of the new Soviet state, drew upon the traditional Russian view of law as artificial. A basic tenet of Marxism-Leninism was that under communism the need for law would wither away. Since law was artificial, that philosophy was neither surprising nor unreasonable to the Russian people. But until it had faded, law could play an important role in achieving the communist state.

Law would, in other words, be used to achieve other ends. Rather than being an absolute value that dictated how people and their government must behave, law would be a tool for accomplishing communist goals. As far as the Russian people were concerned, the idea that law was subordinate to policy was not much different than it being subordinate to the will of princes and czars. Law was, after all, artificial.

For the USSR, and today for the remaining socialist countries, the source of law is in the principles of the socialist revolution. Law does not stem from authorized codes, as in the civil legal tradition, nor in immemorial custom, as in the common legal tradition. Instead, law exists only to assure that the rights of the collectivized economy and the socialist state are placed above any rights of the individual. To carry out this role, socialist law has important economic and educational goals that can be seen in a description of the contemporary Chinese legal system.

China as an Example of the Socialist Legal Tradition

Political and economic changes beginning in 1989 had important impact on the legal systems in the former countries of the USSR and in other Central and Eastern European countries. Since an important aspect of that change was a growing appreciation for the rule of law, it seems appropriate to identify those countries as more closely affiliated today with the civil, rather than the socialist, legal tradition. But similar changes have not occurred in all socialist countries. Cuba, Vietnam, North Korea, and the People's Republic of China were less effected by challenges to traditional socialism and provide contemporary examples of the socialist legal tradition. China provides our specific example.

China's Policing

China's public security organs are responsible for investigating crime and for the arrest, detention, and interrogation of suspects. Public security agencies are found under several of China's ministries. For example, the ministries of railway transportation, forestry, transportation, air administration, and defense, each has their own public security agency. However, since the Ministry of Public Security oversees the agencies considered to comprise China's everyday police this discussion is restricted to that ministry.

The organizational structure of policing in China moves from the Central Government down though the Ministry of Public Security, to policing at the provincial (Bureau of Public Security), regional (Division of Public Security), and municipal (Department of Public Security) levels. It is the municipal level where Chinese policing looks most similar to police agencies in United States jurisdictions (Wang, 1996). The structure is more different when the municipal level is further subdivided into the *Pai Chu Shou*, or neighborhood police.

The bulk of everyday policing is handled by the *Pai Chu Shou* who deal with such activities as criminal investigation, peace keeping, residence registration, foot or bicycle patrol, and visiting offenders and their families. The "registration" duty is interesting since it is rather unique among the world's police. Every Chinese must register with the police and authorization is required before anyone can move out of an old residence and into a new one (Wang, 1996). In addition, all births and deaths are recorded at the police station. Finally, police officers responsible for census registration also supervise probationers and parolees. Chinese policing at this level also includes helping the lost find their homes, shopping for the elderly, removing garbage, and participating in conflict mediation sessions (Situ and Liu, 1996).

That description of *Pai Chu Shou* duties may sound like China is borrowing the Western notion of community policing. Actually, China was using a community policing model long before contemporary United States and Canada jurisdictions were viewing the idea as innovative. One of the reasons that community policing was popular early on in China is a result of socialism's reliance on the public for aspects of social control. This is not especially surprising since the very nature of socialist philosophy points to collectivism in all aspects of society's operation. In terms of policing, the public's involvement is with the Public Security Committees that are found in each urban neighborhood and rural village.

Public Security Committees range in size from 3 to 11 persons who have been elected to six month terms on the committee by their neighbors (Sheng and Zu-Yuan, 1993). As the need arises, the local police can mobilize the Public Security Committees to participate in crime prevention, but the committee members also have less organized responsibilities. Situ and Liu (1996) explain that the Public Security Committees duties include activities like informing the police about suspects in a crime, conducting surveillance of defendants prior to trial, patrol and safeguard the neighborhood, investigate minor offense like petty larceny and fist-fighting, and advising, educating, and even disciplining persons whose lifestyle may lead them to crime.

China's Courts

China's formal court system has four tiers. Going from the bottom up, they are the Basic People's Court, the Intermediate People's Court, the Higher People's Court, and finally the Supreme People's Court. The Basic People's Courts handle the majority of the ordinary criminal trials while the Intermediate People's Courts hear more serious criminal cases and appeals from the Basic People's Courts. Major criminal cases and appeals are heard by the Higher People's Courts, which operate at the province level and in some major cities. The Supreme People's Court serves primarily in an appellate capacity, but will also hear major criminal cases that have impact on the entire country (Situ and Liu, 1996).

The courts are essentially agencies of the central government (*i.e.*, the communist party) and as a result do not have judicial independence in the way Westerners think of the term. Court activities at each level are reviewed by a judicial committee. Members of the judicial committees are appointed by the people's congress at each level, and it is through the people's congress that the central government has its input and influence.

At the trial, those accused have the right to offer a defense, to argue the case, to explain their innocence, or to request leniency in punishment. While the defendant can provide self-defense, it is also possible to hire a lawyer or ask a close relative to defend his or her case. When cases are at trial with a public prosecutor, the court can appoint a lawyer to speak for the accused (Situ and Liu, 1996).

Like the situation in most civil law countries, China does not use a jury but instead has citizen input through representation of lay judges or *people's assessors*. Minor criminal cases are heard before a single judge, but more serious cases come before a panel of one to three professional judges and two to four people's assessors. The people's assessors are lay persons who have reached age 23 and are eligible to vote.

The main types of evidence presented at a trial in China are testimonies by witnesses, the defendant's confession, and hard evidence like the property stolen or weapons used. Situ and Liu note that defendant's have few due process rights during the trial. "The presumption of innocence, the exclusionary rule, protection against self-incrimination, the right to a jury trial, and protection against 'double jeopardy' are alien to the Chinese courts" (1996: 130).

Some types of cases, like ones involving state secrets, privacy, personal secrets, and juvenile delinquency, are tried in private. Most cases, however, are tried in public and the verdicts are announced in public.

In addition to its formal justice system, China is recognized as having an especially well-developed system of informal justice. In fact, the informal system is so integral that it sometimes operates along side the formal system. The Public Security Committees operate in this capacity at the policing level and the People's Mediation Committees (PMC) perform the informal role at the court level. China's constitution requires each urban neighborhood and each rural village to have a PMC. In addition, PMCs can be established at work places, schools, and other institutions.

Although the PMCs serve the socialist ideology very well, they have historical ties to Confucianism and the belief that moral education through mediation is the best way for communities to resolve conflict. The PMCs operate under the guidance of local governments and local people's courts. PMC members are elected by the people living or working in the PMC's jurisdiction. When a conflict arises, the parties can ask that a mediator get involved. But the PMC does not need to wait for an invitation. Because the mediators live in the community, they usually hear about problems early on and can respond quickly.

China's Corrections

China makes frequent use of the death penalty. Amnesty International recorded nearly 2,500 death sentences and almost 1,800 executions in China during 1994 (Amnesty International, 1995). Persons sentenced to death are placed in restraints until their sentence is carried out — sometimes within three days of the verdict (Human Rights Watch, 1993). Persons who are not executed, are typically placed in custody.

Custodial corrections in China is accomplished through more than 600 correctional institutions taking such forms as provincial and municipal prisons, reform-through-labor camps, and juvenile reformatories. The most serious offenders (usually ones with sentences of ten years or more) are assigned to prisons while the less serious one are sent to reform-through-labor camps (Chenguang, 1996). As the name suggests, all prisoners at these camps, when physically able to do so, must engage in productive labor for nine to ten hours a day. However, that distinction is not necessarily a good one for separating prisons from reform-through-labor camps since inmates in prisons also work. Since labor is one way to repay society for their crime, the prisoners receive only a small allowance for their work.

A key philosophy at the reform-through-labor camps is that education is a necessary ingredient for reforming the individual. The education provided to the prisoners is very political in nature and includes the study of laws and regulations and moral education in socialist ideology (e.g., positive attitudes toward work, acceptance of collectivism) and social ethics (Situ and Liu, 1996).

In addition to political education, Chinese corrections makes use of both rehabilitation and punishment strategies. Rehabilitation is seen in the reward system for good behavior. Prisoners are given opportunities to perform meritorious service as a way to atone for their crime. Good behavior is rewarded with oral commendations, material rewards, reduction in sentence length, and early release. Chenguang (1996) reports that between 1991 and 1994, twenty percent of the inmates in China received reduced terms of imprisonment as a result of their good behavior. On the other hand, inappropriate behavior or refusal to repent and reform will result in the termination of rehabilitation efforts or the application of additional punishment (Situ and Liu, 1996).

In its global report on prisons, the Human Rights Watch identified some of the less desirable aspects of imprisonment in China (Human Rights Watch, 1993). It is important to note that the report was also critical of some 18 other countries, including the United States and England, so we should not be too quick to take a "holier-than-thou" attitude. But, the comments about Chinese prisons are instructive since China has not always been forthcoming in relating information about its corrections process.

As described by the Human Rights Watch, the reform-through-labor camps may actually be factories, farms, or mines. Tasks at which the prisoners work can include breaking stone, fashioning tools, making toys and garments, sewing fishing nets, or assembling motor vehicles (Human Rights Watch, 1993). Although the prisoners are reportedly paid a small allowance, they are apparently charged for their food and there is some concern that the pay is not always sufficient to cover the cost of a meal. There are also reports that inmates are subjected to physical and psychological abuse by guards for petty infractions. Electric batons, although regulations restrict their use, are routinely employed to discipline prisoners through electric shock.

THE ISLAMIC LEGAL TRADITION

The Islamic legal tradition is unique among legal families in several respects. The first is its perception of law's source as being sacred rather than secular. The other legal traditions, especially civil and common, have religious links, but they remain distinct and separate from religion. The Islamic legal tradition, on the other hand, is completely reliant on religion.

Muslims, like Christians and Jews, believe in one God whom Muslims call Allah. Of Allah's messengers to the world, Muhammad (570?-632) is considered the most recent prophet by Muslims. The religion prescribed by Muhammad is Islam (Arabic for submission), and its followers are "those who submit to Allah" (Muslims).

Islamic law is called the *Shari'a*, the path to follow. Its primary ingredients are the *Qur'an* (Islam's holy book) and the *Sunna* (the statements and deeds of Muhammad). These two elements identify both crimes and punishments but they provide very little information regarding the legal process by which offenders are brought to justice.

Three categories of crime are distinguished in the *Shari'a*: hudud, quesas, and *ta'azir*. *Hudud*, which are offenses against God, require mandatory prosecution and must be punished in the manner prescribed in the *Qur'an* or the *Sunna*. The seven *hudud* crimes are adultery or fornication, defamation, drinking alcohol, theft, highway robbery, apostasy (the rejection of Islam by one professing Islamic faith), and rebellion or corruption of Islam. The punishment for *hudud* crimes include death by stoning for a married person committing adultery, hand amputation for theft, and whipping for persons using alcohol (Sanad, 1991).

Quesas crimes are less serious than *hudud* crimes and more serious than *ta'azir* crimes. They are similar to what other criminal codes call crimes against persons, and include acts like voluntary and involuntary homicide, assault, and battery. Punishment for these crimes can be either acts of retaliation by the victim or his family (*e.g.*, the eye for the eye, the nose for the nose) or financial compensation by the offender to the victim or his family.

The least serious of *Shari'a* crimes are the *ta'azir*. Included in this category are all offenses not identified as either *hudud* or *quesas* crimes. Examples of *ta'azir* crimes are petty theft, homosexuality, eating pork, neglect of prayers, and acts damaging to the public interest. A *Ta'azir* penalty can be execution but is more likely to be whipping, imprisonment, or a fine (Sanad, 1991).

In the *Shari'a* God identified the crimes and stipulated the penalty, but the law's application fell to humans. Not surprisingly, humans disagreed about how to apply God's law. Some Muslims took a strict interpretation and believed that every rule of law must be derived from the *Qur'an* or the *Sunna*. Others believed human reason and personal opinion could be used to elaborate the law. The latter camp suggested that as the centuries progressed from Muhammad's time, there were new behaviors or situations that had not been directly addressed in the early seventh century. Human reason, these Muslims believed, could be used to fill the gaps.

Because human reason could become human legislation, which is inappropriate since law comes from Allah and not from humans, it was important that the reasoning be subordinate to divine revelation. The result was a process known as *qiyas*, or reasoning by analogy. For example, Lippman *et al.* (1988) note that some judges have sentenced committers of sodomy (a behavior not mentioned in the *Qur'an* or Sunna) to the same penalty the *Qur'an* provides for adultery by reasoning that sodomy and adultery are similar offenses. The presence of *ta'azir* crimes also allows the *Shari'a* to keep pace with modern society by making criminal any act that might cause damage to the public interest or the public order. In this way, acts not specifically mentioned fourteen centuries ago (like traffic violations, embezzlement, or forgery) are still considered illegal by divine revelation rather than human legislation.

Saudi Arabia as an Example of the Islamic Legal Tradition

Like all religions, Islam has several branches and each has different ideas regarding both religious and legal issues. As a result, Islamic law is not uniformly applied throughout Islamic countries any more than civil, common, or socialist law is consistent across nations following those traditions. The *Shari'a* influences legal decision in parts of Africa, but countries of the Middle East are seen as offering the most clear examples of the Islamic legal tradition. Among those countries is Saudi Arabia, which can be considered the primary example of *Shari'a* in today's world.

Saudi Arabia's Policing

Each of Saudi Arabia's five regions has a police force, but policing in Saudi Arabia is clearly centralized since all police forces are controlled by the Director of Public Safety, who reports to the Minister of Interior. Included among these forces are the National Guard, the Frontier Force, the Coast Guard, and the Public Security Police. There is also a religious, or morals, police force (*mutawwiun*) organized by the authority of the king (Kurian, 1989). The *mutawwiun* rigorously enforce such religious rules as five daily prayers, modesty in female attire, and proscriptions against the use of alcohol.

The primary police force is the Public Security Police (PSP), which are the equivalent of a national police force. Alobied (1989) explains the PSP functions as falling into administrative, judicial, and social categories. Under its administrative functions, the PSP maintains the general order, handles emergency events, controls traffic, and participates in general policing duties. The PSP

judicial role includes crime investigation wherein the officer takes witness information, captures suspects, and provides information to police inspectors and to judges. The social function requires PSP officers to help people requesting service or needing emergency assistance.

Saudi Arabia's Courts

There is a dual court system in Saudi Arabia, with *Shari'a* courts handling criminal cases, family law, and some civil law. A separate system of administrative tribunals has jurisdiction over specific issues like traffic offenses and laws related to business and commerce. Our concern is with the *Shari'a* courts, which follow a three-tiered structure moving from the ordinary courts at the bottom, to the High Courts, then the Courts of Appeal (Reichel, 1994). The ordinary courts are presided over by a single Islamic judge (*qadi*). These courts are found in most every town and deal with minor domestic matters, misdemeanors, small claims, some *ta'azir* crimes, and *hudud* offenses of intoxication and defamation. *Hudud* and *qisas* offenses are heard in the High Courts, which also hear cases on appeal from the lower courts. A single judge hears the case unless a sentence of death, stoning, or amputation is required. A three-judge panel hears those cases.

While the structure of Saudi courts is not especially unique, some of the procedural law governing the trial process is. Sanad (1991) highlights the rules of evidence as being a particularly important distinguishing feature of Islamic law in general. Most Muslim scholars maintain that evidence in criminal cases must be restricted to confession and testimony. Regarding confession, it is not sufficient for the accused to simply admit to the charges. For a confession to be valid, the confessor must be a mature, mentally sound person who gives, with free will, a confession that is neither doubtful or vague (Reichel, 1994). Coerced confessions presumably are not acceptable or admissible, but Moore (1987) says flogging and long detention of suspects who refuse to confess occurs in Saudi Arabia.

For the second type of evidence, testimony, at least two witnesses should provide consistent testimony before a conviction on *hudud* and *qisas* crimes can be given. But just any witness is not acceptable. To be condoned the witness must be an adult male (one school accepts two females as equivalent to one male), known to have good memory, sound mind, and good character.

In addition to requirements about who can testify, there are rules regarding how many witnesses are required, and how the testimony is given. For a conviction on *hudud* and *qisas* offenses, at least two witness should provide consistent testimony about the accused's actions. In the case of adultery, four witnesses are required. Since there are seldom times when two devout male Muslims observe a burglary in process, or four such witnesses watch adultery taking place, the "evidence" in many criminal trials is incomplete. At this point the rules regarding how testimony is given come into play in the form of *oaths*.

According to Rosen (1989), witnesses under Islamic law are not sworn before testifying. In fact, there is even some understanding that less than truthful statements may be made in court as witnesses are speaking freely. However, if testimony reaches a point where neither side has adequately supported its claim, one party may challenge the other to take an oath. If the person challenged does so, he wins the case. Or, the person challenged can refer the oath back to the challenger who can secure victory by swearing to his own truthfulness. This process of challenging is not a haphazard one. The *qadi* plays a very important role since he decides which party will first challenge the other to take an oath. That decision is important since the first to swear wins the case. Rosen (1989) suggests the *qadi*, after observing the comments from witnesses and from the parties themselves, looks for the person most likely to know what is true about the case. That person is designated as the one first to be challenged to take the oath. Since false swearers will suffer the consequences of judgment day, devout Muslims take oaths very seriously and, presumably, truthfully.

Saudi Arabia's Corrections

The *Shari'a* requires seemingly harsh penalties for some crimes. Hand amputation for theft and beheading for adultery are examples that catch the attention of people in many western countries. These penalties are considered barbaric and violative of human rights by groups like Amnesty International, but Muslims claim that outsiders fail to understand the penalties in the context of Islamic society. For example, rather than being uncivilized, amputation and execution are seen by Muslims as ways to achieve justice and to spread an atmosphere of mercy, security, and harmony among the Muslim community.

Al-Sagheer (1994) explains that punishment has two main functions under the *Shari'a*. The first is deterrence, which requires a penalty to inflict enough pain that the offender refrains from offending again. The second function, protecting the community and correcting the offender, is designed to make the community safe and secure by reforming the criminal in addition to deterring him. These two functions are achieved through three types of worldly punishment:

(1) **Divine and discretionary punishment**, wherein the former is determined by Allah and is not subject to discussion and the latter is determined at the discretion of the judge.

(2) **Original and nonoriginal punishment**, with the former consisting of penalties provided for by law, and the latter including alternative (penalties replacing original ones), incidental (penalties associated with original ones), and supplementary (penalties imposed in addition to original ones) sanctions.

(3) **Corporal and physical punishment**, where the former affects the offender's body, liberty, or morale, and the latter affects the offender's financial resources by reducing them (Al-Sagheer, 1994).

Specific examples of each punishment type cannot be provided here, so we will concentrate on just two — the corporal punishment of imprisonment (deprivation of liberty) and the alternative sanction of *diyya*.

Saudi Arabia has a national penal system that operates both jails and prisons. Upon arrest, adults are placed in a police station jail for about one day, then they are transferred to a regional prison. The prisons house a mixed population of minor offenders, serious offenders, persons awaiting trial, and persons serving time (Murty, *et al.*, 1991). There is one central prison in each of Saudi Arabia's five regions. All five prisons would be considered to be medium security institutions by the standard used in United States jurisdictions. The inmates are housed in dormitory wards but some maximum security cells are available for administrative segregation and punishment purposes.

The alternative sanction of *diyya* must be understood in conjunction with the concepts of retaliation and mercy since Islamic *Shari'a* is simultaneously retributive and forgiving. On one hand, Muslims are directed by the *Qur'an* to retaliate with a life for a life, an eye for an eye, and generally wounds equal for equal (see the *Qur'an* 5:45). It is this philosophy of retaliation that supports such penalties as amputation and execution. The purpose of retaliation is not only deterrence, but also to eliminate grudges from the hearts of the victim and the victim's family. However, the requirement for retaliation is immediately tempered as the "life for a life" verse continues by noting that "if any one remits the retaliation by way of charity, it is an act of atonement for himself" (5:45). In other words, retaliation by the victim of a crime against the person (or the victim's family in the case of murder) is not only appropriate but required by Allah. However, if the victim or the victim's family can bring themselves to forgive the offender they will endear themselves to Allah.

When retaliation is waived by the victim or the victim's family, *diyya* is applied instead. Al-Sagheer defines *diyya* as "money paid to a harmed person or his heir in compensation for a felony committed against him" (1994: 85). When *diyya* replaces retaliation it is used to both deter the offender and to compensate the victim or his heirs. By waiving retaliation, an atmosphere of mercy and harmony among people is created.

The rules regarding who pays *diyya* and the amount paid are well established in Saudi Arabia. Al-Sagheer (1994) explains that the offender is expected to be the one who pays, but there are situations where *diyya* is paid by the offender's relatives or by the state treasury. For example, the offender pays if reconciliation is reached between the victim's blood heirs and the offender, or when the crime was committed by mistake. The offender's blood relatives are expected to pay *diyya* in such cases as intentional murder committed by a child or insane person, or cases of unintentional crimes against the person where the offender cannot afford to pay on his own. *Diyya* is paid from the state treasury when, for example, the offender has not been identified or when the crime was a mistake by an authorized doctor.

The amount of *diyya* differs by the harm done. Payment for the death of a Muslim male is the equivalent of 100 camels (50 camels for a Muslim female), while *diyya* for parts of the human body depend on whether the organ or limb consists of one (*e.g.*, a nose or tongue) or two (*e.g.*, arms and legs) parts. *Diyya* for loss of single parts, or both of two parts, is the equivalent of 100 camels, while loss of one of two parts is the equivalent of 50 camels.

The extent to which *diyya* is applied in Saudi Arabia for cases murder and other crimes against the person is difficult to determine. It obviously does not take the place of retaliation in all instances since Saudi Arabia continues to conduct amputations and hold executions. It may be, however, that *diyya* is more common when offender and victim are both Muslim since media reports of amputation and beheading are often about foreigners who have committed crimes in Saudi Arabia.

CHAPTER SUMMARY

This chapter provides an overview of the variety found in systems of social control. The goals have been to increase understanding of our own legal system by contrasting it with systems in other countries, and to prepare us for increased interaction with other countries on global crime and justice issues. This was accomplished by reviewing the four contemporary legal traditions: civil, common, socialist, and Islamic. To exemplify each legal tradition, a specific country's legal system was reviewed. From those reviews we found some similarities and differences in the structure and operation of police, courts, and corrections agencies in Germany (civil tradition), Canada (common tradition), China (socialist tradition), and Saudi Arabia (Islamic tradition).

✳ ✳ ✳ ✳ ✳

REFERENCES

Al-Sagheer, Mohamed Faleh
    1994   "Diyya Legislation in Islamic Shari'a and Its Application in the Kingdom of Saudi Arabia." Pages 80-91 in Uglješa Zvekić (ed.), *Alternatives to Imprisonment in Comparative Perspective*. Chicago: Nelson-Hall.
Albrecht, Hans-Jörg
    1995   "Sentencing and Punishment in Germany." Overcrowded Times, 6 (February): 1, 6-10.
Alobied, A.
    1989   "Police Functions and Organization in Saudi Arabia." Police Studies, 10: 80-84.
Amnesty International
    1995   "China: Death Penalty Figures." AI Index: ASA 17/17/95 London, United Kingdom: Amnesty International.
Chenguang, Ma
    1996   "Policy to Lower Recidivism." CJ International , 12 (July-August): 12.
Colorado Revised Statutes
    1986   Englewood, CO: Colorado District Attorneys Council.
Davidson, R., & Wang, Z.
    1996   "The Court System in the People's Republic of China with a Case Study of a Criminal Trial." Pages 139-153 in Obi N. Ignatius Ebbe (ed.) Comparative and International Criminal Justice Systems: Policing, Judiciary and Corrections . Boston: Butterworth-Heinemann.
Fairchild, Erika S.
    1993   Comparative Criminal Justice Systems . Belmont, CA: Wadsworth.
Fu, Hualing
    1990   "Police Reform and its Implication for Chinese Social Control." International Journal of Comparative and Applied Criminal Justice , 14: 41-48.
    1991   "Police Accountability: The Case of The People's Republic of China." Police Studies, 14: 140-150.

360

Griffiths, Curt T., and Simon N. Verdun-Jones
    1994   *Canadian Criminal Justice*. 2nd edition. Toronto, Canada: Harcourt Brace & Company, Canada.
Human Rights Watch
    1993   *The Human Rights Watch Global Report on Prisons*. New York: Human Rights Watch.
Kurian, George T.
    1989   *World Encyclopedia of Police Forces and Penal Systems*. New York: Facts on File.
Lippman, Matthew, Sean McConville, and Mordechai Yerushalmi
    1988   *Islamic Criminal Law and Procedure*. New York: Praeger.
Moore, Richter H., Jr.
    1987   "Courts, Law, Justice, and Criminal Trials in Saudi Arabia." *International Journal of Comparative and Applied Criminal Justice*, 11: 61-67.
Murty, Komanduri S., Julian B. Roebuck, and Mohammed A. Almolhem
    1991   "Profile of Adult Offenders in Dammam Central Prison, Saudi Arabia." *International Journal of Comparative and Applied Criminal Justice*, 15: 89-97.
Pease, Ken, and Kristiina Hukkila
    1990   "Criminal Justice Systems in Europe and North America." *HEUNI publication No. 17*. Helsinki, Finland: Helsinki Institute for Crime Prevention and Control.
Penal Code of the Federal Republic of Germany
    1987   Littleton, CO: Fred B. Rothman.
Pink-Murray Barristers & Solicitors
    1997   Internet information — web page. Halifax, Nova Scotia, February. [http://www.criminaldefence.com/library/punish/prisons.html].
Reichel, Philip L.
    1994   *Comparative Criminal Justice Systems: A Topical Approach*. Englewood Cliffs, NJ: Prentice Hall.
Rosen, Lawrence
    1989   *The Anthropology of Justice: Law as Culture in Islamic Society*. Cambridge, England: Cambridge University Press.
Sanad, Nagaty
    1991   *The Theory of Crime and Criminal Responsibility in Islamic Law: Shari'a*. Chicago, IL: Office of International Criminal Justice.
Sheng, Dai Yi, and Huang Zu-Yuan
    1993   "Organization and Functions of Public Security Agencies of the People's Republic of China." *EuroCriminology*, 5-6: 137-43.
Situ, Yingyi, and Weizheng Liu
    1996   "An Overview of the Chinese Criminal Justice System." Pages 125-37 in Obi N. Ignatius Ebbe (ed.), *Comparative and International Criminal Justice Systems: Policing, Judiciary and Corrections*. Boston: Butterworth-Heinemann.
Teske, Raymond and Hans-Jörg Albrecht
    1991   "An Overview of Probation Procedures and Statistics in the Federal Republic of Germany." Paper presented at Academy of Criminal Justice Sciences Annual Meeting. Nashville, TN, March.
Wang, Zheng
    1996   "The Police System in the People's Republic of China." Pages 155-67 in Obi N. Ignatius Ebbe (ed.), *Comparative and International Criminal Justice Systems: Policing, Judiciary and Corrections*. Boston: Butterworth-Heinemann.
Weigend, Thomas
    1983   "Sentencing in West Germany." *Maryland Law Review*, 42: 37-89.
Zhao, Guoling
    1991   "The People's Republic of China." Pages 429-454 in Dirk van Zyl Smit and Frieder Dünkel (eds.), *Imprisonment Today and Tomorrow*. Boston: Kluwer Law and Taxation Publishers.

EXAMINATIONS

FOR

CHAPTERS
2 - 16

Chapter Two

Name_____ Date_____ Section_____

TEST QUESTIONS

Multiple Choice

1. **Police involvement in a crime usually begins with:**
   a. A complaint from a victim or citizen.
   b. A police officer's observation of criminal activity.
   c. Information developed during surveillance or from an informant's tip.
   d. All of the above.

2. **A reason why the public is hesitant to report a crime to the police might include:**
   a. That, by law, only the victim can report a crime.
   b. The belief that the offender was unsuccessful in the perpetration of the crime.
   c. They are uncertain how to contact the police.
   d. None of the above.

3. **The single most important factor influencing a police officer's discretion to arrest an offender is:**
   a. Socioeconomic status of the offender.
   b. The presence of large crowds at the crime scene.
   c. The seriousness of the offense.
   d. The age of the offender.

4. **A suspect should be advised of their Miranda rights when:**
   a. He/she is in custody and being interrogated by the police.
   b. He/she is being asked any questions by the police.
   c. He/she is placed into a police lineup.
   d. None of the above.

5. **For the suspect's initial or first court appearance, they must be brought before a judge:**
   a. Prior to police questioning.
   b. Without unnecessary delay.
   c. Prior to detention in jail.
   d. Ten days after arrest.

6. **A popular type of bail-bond which includes payment of a fee to a bondsman for release from jail is known as a:**
   a. Property bond.
   b. Release on recognizance.
   c. Deposit bond.
   d. Surety bond.

7. **What is meant by the statement, "The prosecutor is said to have the broadest discretion within the criminal justice system?"**
   a. The prosecutor determines who the police arrest.
   b. The prosecutor determines which judge will hear felony cases.
   c. The prosecutor determines whether or not to file criminal charges against the suspect.
   d. None of the above

8. **A charging document typically containing the legal description of the crime committed, who allegedly committed it, and where and when it was committed, is known as the:**
   a. Legal brief.
   b. Information.
   c. Trial motion.
   d. Subpoena.

9. **At the arraignment hearing, an accused felon may plead:**
   a. Guilty.
   b. Nolo contendere.
   c. Not guilty.
   d. Any of the above

10. **One purpose of a pretrial hearing may include:**
    a. The court ruling on a motion to request a change of venue.
    b. The court ruling on a motion for a new trial.
    c. The court ruling on a motion for sentence reconsideration.
    d. The court ruling on a motion for a felony parole hearing.

11. **A speedy trial should be initiated within _____ days after arraignment.**
    a. 10
    b. 270 to 365
    c. 90 to 120
    d. None of the above

12. **Proof of guilt required at a criminal trial is:**
    a. Reasonable suspicion.
    b. Mere probable cause.
    c. By a preponderance of the evidence.
    d. Beyond a reasonable doubt.

13. **The screening process that attempts to eliminate potentially biased or unfair jurors is known as:**
    a. Trial de novo.
    b. Voir dire.
    c. Mala prohibita.
    d. Nunc pro tunc.

14. **The sentencing philosophy which embraces the concept of physically restraining and isolating offenders from society is known as:**
    a. Rehabilitation.
    b. Retribution.
    c. Incapacitation.
    d. Deterrence.

15. **In jurisdictions which have adopted a sentencing guidelines formula, two important focuses of the presentence investigation include:**
    a. The defendant's employment and marital history.
    b. The defendant's prior criminal record and severity of the current offense.
    c. The defendant's family and substance abuse history.
    d. The defendant's prior criminal record and their version of the crime.

16. **_____ is an alternative to incarceration which requires offenders to comply with certain court-ordered conditions.**
    a. Probation.
    b. Restoration.
    c. Compensation.
    d. Parole.

17. **_____ is used to reward an inmate who complies with prison regulations by providing them eligibility for early release.**
    a. Fixed time.
    b. Discretionary time.
    c. Mandatory time.
    d. Good time.

18. **Most parole boards are comprised of three to five members appointed by the _____.**
    a. Secretary of state.
    b. Attorney general of the state.
    c. Governor of the state.
    d. Chief justice of the state.

19. **Post-conviction appeals may be based on:**
    a. Police entrapment.
    b. Unethical conduct by a prosecutor.
    c. Illegal search and seizure.
    d. All of the above.

20. **The function of appellate courts is to:**
    a. Conduct new trials.
    b. Review the record of the lower court for legal errors.
    c. Determine the imposition of the death penalty after trial.
    d. None of the above

True/False

T F 1. As a result of research through victimization surveys, we know that over 70% of all crimes occurring are reported to the police.

T F 2. Preventive patrol remains one of the primary patrol techniques utilized by the police.

T F 3. Generally, police may make a warrantless arrest for a felony if there is sufficient probable cause and if no time is available to secure a warrant.

T F   4. During the booking process, the suspect is ordinarily fingerprinted and photographed.

T F   5. One of the primary purposes of the initial or first appearance in court is to determine a suspect's guilt or innocence.

T F   6. The right to court-appointed counsel applies only in felony cases.

T F   7. Diversion involves a contract with the prosecutor whereby an individual agrees to not again violate the law and to abide by other conditions in lieu of formal prosecution.

T F   8. During a preliminary hearing, the prosecution bears the burden of producing sufficient evidence that a crime was committed, it was committed by the suspect, and it was committed within the jurisdiction of the court.

T F   9. Plea bargaining is a process by which the defendant and judge agree upon an appropriate sentence.

T F   10. Pretrial hearings can reduce trial delays by resolving procedural questions raised by the defense.

T F   11. In the Supreme Court case of *Duncan v. Louisiana (1968)*, the court granted defendants an absolute right to jury trials in misdemeanor cases.

T F   12. At the trial, the primary role of the judge and jury is one of fact finding.

T F   13. Most jurisdictions require unanimous jury verdicts in criminal trials.

T F   14. The rehabilitative goal of sentencing seeks to prevent law-abiding citizens from turning to crime by the threat of punishment.

T F   15. A sentence with a range of 1-10 years in prison is an example of an indeterminate sentence.

T F   16. The Supreme Court case of *Gregg v. Georgia (1976)* ended capital punishment in the United States.

T F   17. Parole involves the release of an individual who has been confined in a correctional facility to the community under supervision.

T F   18. A pardon is the release of an inmate by executive order of a governor, which may be utilized to correct a mistake made by the criminal justice system.

T F   19. At any time, a defendant may move his or her appeal from the state to the federal court system.

T F   20. Defendants sentenced to probation are more likely to appeal their cases than those sentenced to prison.

Chapter Three

Name_____ Date_____ Section_____

Multiple Choice

1. **What is a set of statements about the real world called?**
   a. A concept.
   b. A theory.
   c. A proposition.
   d. A crime-specific analysis.
   e. All of the above.

2. **Most criminologists define crime as:**
   a. Law violating behavior.
   b. Deviant behavior.
   c. A status.
   d. Acts of force, fraud, or stealth.
   e. Serious chronic behavior.

3. **Which of the following is NOT a characteristic of control theories?**
   a. Deviance is taken for granted, conformity must be explained.
   b. Offenders and non-offenders are seen as essentially similar.
   c. The offender is poorly socialized.
   d. Criminal behavior is selfish and short-sighted.
   e. Factors which discourage crime are emphasized.

4. **Adventuresome, active, and physical persons are low in:**
   a. Self-control.
   b. Social control.
   c. Differential association.
   d. Anomie.
   e. Indirect control.

5. **Differences in crime rates are examined at which level of explanation?**
   a. Individual.
   b. Situational.
   c. Social psychological.
   d. Psychological.
   e. Macrosocial.

6. **Persons who are chronic offenders as youths are:**
   a. A very small percentage of the population.
   b. More likely to become involved in crime as adults.
   c. More likely to commit serious offenses.
   d. Likely to account for a majority of the police contacts in a birth cohort.
   e. All of the above.

7. Behavior which a group regards as unacceptable or that evokes a negative response is called:
   a. Criminal behavior.
   b. Delinquent behavior.
   c. Deviant behavior.
   d. Chronic behavior.
   e. Psychopathological behavior.

8. Whether they prefer control or learning theories, criminologists agree that _____ is important in the explanation of criminal behavior.
   a. Education.
   b. Learning.
   c. Deterrence.
   d. Rational choice.
   e. Socialization.

9. The basis of psychopathology may be:
   a. Psychological.
   b. Physiological.
   c. Genetic.
   d. Neurochemical.
   e. All of the above.

10. According to Hirschi and Gottfredson's self-control theory:
    a. Low self-control is established in adulthood.
    b. Persons vary throughout their lives in their levels of self-control.
    c. Self-control is taught through effective child rearing.
    d. Persons with self-control are likely to commit crimes.
    e. All of the above.

11. Sensitivity to the opinion of others is called:
    a. Attachment.
    b. Commitment.
    c. Social capital.
    d. Involvement.
    e. Self-control.

12. An excess of definitions favorable to law violations over definitions unfavorable to violations of the law is important in which theory?
    a. Social disorganization.
    b. Differential association.
    c. Anomie.
    d. Rational choice.
    e. All of the above.

13. "Birds of a feather flock together" describes the associations between offenders in which sort of theory?
    a. Differential association.
    b. Learning theories.
    c. Anomie theories.
    d. Control theories.
    e. All of the above.

14. **The criminal decision-making process is emphasized by:**
    a. Self-control theory.
    b. Anomie theory.
    c. Differential association.
    d. Rational choice theory.
    e. Social disorganization theory.

15. **The routine activities approach emphasizes:**
    a. Opportunities to commit crimes.
    b. Rational decision-making.
    c. Low self-control.
    d. Differential association.
    e. Anomie.

16. **Economic level, mobility, and heterogeneity affect:**
    a. Self-control.
    b. Social capital.
    c. Social learning.
    d. Social disorganization.
    e. Social control.

17. **In social learning theory, criminal behavior comes after:**
    a. Differential association.
    b. Definitions.
    c. Differential reinforcement.
    d. Neutralization.
    e. Ineffective child-rearing.

18. **"Early starters" are persons with:**
    a. Low self-control.
    b. Differential associations.
    c. Well-socialized children.
    d. Neurotransmitter deficiencies.
    e. Low intelligence.

19. **In institutional anomie theory, crime is caused by:**
    a. Social disorganization.
    b. Family values.
    c. The American Dream.
    d. Poor self-control.
    e. Differential association.

20. **Prosperity and technological innovations may cause crime, according to:**
    a. Learning theories.
    b. Self-control theory.
    c. The neurotransmitter hypothesis.
    d. The routine activity approach.
    e. Differential association theory.

True/False

T F 1. Most persons are criminals.

T F 2. Offenders tend to specialize in particular types of offenses.

T F 3. Learning theories emphasize factors which discourage crime.

T F 4. Control theories assume that everyone is motivated to commit crimes.

T F 5. Legal definitions of crime do not vary much from place to place.

T F 6. Major offenses are committed far more frequently than minor offenses.

T F 7. All criminal behavior is deviant behavior.

T F 8. According to labeling theorists, deviance is created by social groups.

T F 9. Gottfredson and Hirschi describe crimes as similar to smoking and skipping school.

T F 10. When someone is motivated to commit a crime, a crime will always occur.

T F 11. Control theorists believe that crime requires little skill or learning.

T F 12. Criminal punishments are formal controls.

T F 13. According to Sampson and Laub, employment and marriage can reduce criminality.

T F 14. The Classical School of Criminology emphasizes the psychopathology of criminal behavior.

T F 15. To learning theorists, conformity and crime are two sides of the same coin.

T F 16. According to Sutherland, criminal behavior is explained by general needs and values.

T F 17. According to Akers, "definitions" are attitudes.

T F 18. Delinquent acts are often committed in groups.

T F 19. According to anomie theory, Americans place too much emphasis on material wealth.

T F 20. Harm is the only way to judge the seriousness of an offense.

Chapter Four

Name_____ Date_____ Section_____

Multiple Choice

1. **Terms such as "police stress," "insanity," "judicial discretion," and "juvenile delinquency" are known as _____ in criminal justice research.**
   a. Abstract variables.
   b. Concepts.
   c. Independent variables.
   d. Propositions.
   e. None of the above.

2. **Theory in criminal justice:**
   a. Summarizes facts.
   b. Provides a conceptual scheme for research.
   c. Points to gaps in our knowledge.
   d. All of the above.
   e. None of the above.

3. **_____ reality refers to what we believe to be real and accurate since we have been told so by others, while _____ reality refers to that which we know due to our own personal experiences.**
   a. Experimental, Agreeable.
   b. Agreeable, Experimental.
   c. Agreement, Experiential.
   d. Perceptual, Objective.
   e. none of the above are correct.

4. **A type of experimental research strategy in which two or more independent variables are presented together in known as a _____ design.**
   a. Factorial.
   b. Replication.
   c. Causal.
   d. Complex.
   e. None of the above.

5. **Which of the following was (were) _not_ discussed as being one of the approaches used by researchers in criminal justice to collect data?**
   a. Survey research.
   b. Observational research.
   c. Experimental research.
   d. Pre-emptive research.
   e. All of the above were discussed.

373

6. **Research in criminal justice may be categorized by:**
   a. The goal of the research.
   b. The purpose of the research.
   c. The method of data collection.
   d. All of the above.
   e. Only a and c are correct.

7. **Which of the following is _not_ involved in systematic criminal justice research:**
   a. Formulating researchable problems.
   b. The collection of data and information.
   c. The analysis of data.
   d. The solution to the crime problem.
   e. All of the above are involved in this process.

8. **Research which seeks knowledge for the sake of knowledge is known as:**
   a. Exloratory research.
   b. Applied research.
   c. Pure research.
   d. Empirical research.
   e. Content research.

9. **Research which deals with the relational aspects of variables is known as:**
   a. Descriptive research.
   b. Exploratory research.
   c. Explanatory research.
   d. Conceptual research.
   e. None of the above.

10. **A correlation with a numerical value of zero indicates:**
    a. A perfect positive relationship between variables.
    b. A perfect negative relationship between variables.
    c. No relationship between variables.
    d. A positive regression analysis.
    e. An inverse relationship between variables.

11. **The term "scientific method" in criminal justice research implies:**
    a. The assignment of numbers to variables for operationalization.
    b. The analysis of statistics for drawing conclusions.
    c. A process of investigation for the acquistion of knowledge.
    d. All of the above.
    e. None of the above

12. **Exploratory studies may also be considered as:**
    a. Feasibility probes.
    b. Axioms on which theory is built.
    c. Research probes which do not employ concepts.
    d. All of the above are correct.
    e. None of the above are correct.

13. **The role of the researcher in observational researcher may be defined as follows:**
    a. Complete participant.
    b. Complete observer.
    c. Participant-as-observer.
    d. Observer-as-participant.
    e. All of the above.

14. _____ research is considered to be the most rigourous.
    a. Survey.
    b. Experimental.
    c. Observational.
    d. Pre-emptive.
    e. None of the above.

15. _____ statistics are those which summarize a collection of data, while _____ statistics are concerned with estimation and hypothesis testing.
    a. Correlational, Desriptive.
    b. Descriptive, Correlational.
    c. Inferential, Descriptive.
    d. Descriptive, Analytical.
    e. None of the above.

16. _____ statistics may be described as being univariate, bivariate, or multivariate.
    a. Inferential.
    b. Analytical.
    c. Descriptive.
    d. Correlational.
    e. None of the above.

True/False

T F 1. Criminological theories have established the truth about the causes of crime.

T F 2. Exploratory research deals mainly with describing criminal justice phenomena and situations.

T F 3. Descriptive statistics are designed to generalize sample data to more general populations.

T F 4. When conducting research, a researcher is obligated to abide by ethical principles at all times regardless of the circumstances.

T F 5. Theory and research should be considered to be mutually exclusive since each is directed to different aspects of scientific investigation.

T F 6. Victim surveys are the most accurate and reliable criminal justice data source.

T F 7. Qualitative research assigns numbers to the variables under study, then statistically analyzes important relationships.

T F 8. The ability to repeat or replicate a study increases our confidence in the findings, but does not contribute to growth in the body of scientific criminal justice knowledge.

T F 9. Theory in criminal justice functions to incorporate known empirical findings into a logically consistent framework.

T F 10. An inductive approach implies that we begin with developed theories which are then tested and validated by empirical research.

T F 11. After the criminal justice researcher formulates and specifies his/her problem, the data collection phase is relatively mechanical without encompassing any obstacles.

T F 12. Many of the decisions relating to data analysis are made early in the research process during the problem formulation stage.

T F 13. Establishing causality in the behavioral sciences is just as straightforward as it is with the hard sciences.

T F 14. Pure research in criminal justice is primarily concerned with the practical needs of the criminal justice system and the solution to the crime problem.

T F 15. In an experiment, subjects are systematically assigned to either a control group or an experimental group.

Chapter Five

Name_____ Date_____ Section_____

TEST QUESTIONS

Multiple Choice

1. **The four great influences which have shaped the development of law in Western Civilization are:**
   a. Greek philosophy, Roman Jurisprudence, Judeo-Christian religion and modern science.
   b. Greek philosophy, Roman Jurisprudence, Hindu religion, and the American Revolution.
   c. World War II, the civil rights movement, the assassination of President Kennedy, and the anti-Vietnam War protests.
   d. Greek philosophy, Roman organization, the Russian Revolution, and atomic energy

2. **The oldest and most general legal tradition found in Western Civilization is:**
   a. Common Law.
   b. Socialist Law.
   c. Moslem Law.
   d. Civil Law.

3. **In the course of the first twelve centuries, A.D.:**
   a. Greek Classical Philosophy, Roman Law and administrative practice, and Christian Doctrine fused.
   b. Greek Classical Philosophy negated Roman Law, then became the basis of Christian Doctrine.
   c. The Normans were successful in overrunning England, then established Civil Law in that country.
   d. The Normans brought Greek Classical Philosophy, Roman Law and administrative practice, and the Jural Postulates together.

4. **The revolt of the English nobility against the absolute power of the crown resulted in:**
   a. A written constitution.
   b. The establishment of a Supreme Court in England.
   c. The independence of the United States.
   d. The Magna Charta.

5. **The American and French Revolutions in the latter eighteenth century established:**
   a. The power of the mercantile class.
   b. The "Bill of Rights" in the United States and the "Rights of Man" in France.
   c. The "Bill of Rights" in France and the "Rights of Man" in the United States.
   d. The basis of a written constitution in both countries.

377

6. **The Americans introduced the first formal written constitution which was the result of:**
   a. A general election.
   b. A convention.
   c. Extensive research by legal scholars.
   d. Thomas Jefferson's common law education.

7. **The basic principle underlying the United States Constitution is:**
   a. The United States Constitution as the supreme written law.
   b. Supreme powers residing in the people.
   c. A federal government of delegated powers.
   d. The separation of power into three branches: the legislature,   the executive, and the judiciary.
   e. All of the above.

8. **The federal government in the United States was able to gain dominance over the various state governments because of:**
   a. The Civil War.
   b. The Fourteenth Amendment.
   c. The Sixteenth Amendment.
   d. The great depression.
   e. All of the above.

9. **Modern science has influenced the direction of law:**
   a. By establishing the psychiatrist as the ultimate authority on insanity.
   b. By confusing the trial judge, thus requiring the legislature to define their statutes more precisely.
   c. By introducing the computer as a research tool to locate law.
   d. By modifying the free will and self-responsibility concept of the civil and common law traditions.

10. **The belief that law is man made:**
   a. Rejects the theory of an outside law giver.
   b. Is explained by Justice Holmes' remark, "law is what the courts do."
   c. Neither "a" nor "b".
   d. Both "a" and "b".

11. **American legal history:**
   a. Dates from the landing of the Pilgrims at Plymouth Rock.
   b. Began with the death of Christ.
   c. Has moved through three stages: the Age of Discovery, the Age of Faith, and the Age of Anxiety.
   d. Can be found in all major libraries.
   e. All of the above.

12. **Alexis de Tocqueville believed American courts inevitably are asked to resolve important:**
   a. Eminent domain cases.
   b. Economic conflicts
   c. Political questions.
   d. Religious disputes.
   e. All of the above.

13. **Law can be found in:**
    a. Judicial decisions.
    b. Law textbooks and legal encyclopedias.
    c. Statute books.
    d. Legal periodicals.
    e. All of the above.

14. **Roscoe Pound feels all legal systems regardless of their legal tradition must rely on:**
    a. An underlying religious or moral belief.
    b. Certain jural postulates or principles.
    c. The consent of the governed.
    d. A strong police authority.

15. **The major objective of a constitution is to:**
    a. Notify the citizens of the power of the government.
    b. Establish the checks and balances system of government.
    c. Promote civics classes in local schools.
    d. Place limits on the government's authority.

16. **Unique to United States' constitutional government is:**
    a. The Congress's use of the committee system.
    b. The President's treaty-making powers.
    c. The Supreme Court's power of judicial review.
    d. Its unicameral form.

17. **The belief that law comes from outside the group is the basis for:**
    a. The Common Law.
    b. The natural law theories.
    c. The criminal code.
    d. Most American Law Institute Restatements of law.

18. **The two polar positions that have dominated philosophical speculation for centuries on what law is are:**
    a. Legal positivism versus natural law.
    b. The liberal versus conservative thinkers.
    c. The common versus civil tradition lawyers.
    d. Greek versus Germanic philosophers.

19. **The laws resulting from the legislative process are published in the form of:**
    a. Slip laws.
    b. Pocket parts.
    c. Citators.
    d. Loose leaf services.

20. **The complete opinions from United States Supreme Court cases are published in:**
    a. Statute books.
    b. Codes.
    c. Reporters.
    d. Encyclopedias.

True or False?

T F 1. Administrative law is an example of private law.

T F 2. Adjective law is another name for unwritten law.

T F 3. The goal of the communist version of Socialist Law is the elimination of law in an Utopian society.

T F 4. All states, except Louisiana, in the United States follow the common law tradition.

T F 5. The Civil Law tradition is based on an unwritten constitution.

T F 6. American Revolutionaries saw the Judge as an ally in gaining more freedom from the monarch.

T F 7. The Industrial Revolution in Europe brought changes in both the Civil and Common Law traditions.

T F 8. The development of the National Reporter System by West Publishing Company has greatly facilitated legal research.

T F 9. A volume of "annotated" statutes, in addition to the text of the statutes, will have cross references and case notes.

T F 10. A definition common to both natural and positive law is Justice Holmes' statement, "Law is what courts do."

T F 11. The President can issue proclamations and executive orders that have the force of law.

T F 12. In a general sense a constitution is a set of rules governing the affairs of an organized group.

T F 13. A constitutional convention is the way all constitutions come into existence.

T F 14. All state constitutions in the United States have been original creations with not much similarity to the federal constitution.

T F 15. The Age of Anxiety in American law dates from the Civil War and Reconstruction periods to World War I.

T F 16. Dominance of the judges was apparent during the frontier period prior to the Civil War — they created a legal system.

T F 17. Following World War I, law as a science became law as a social science.

T F 18. The Fourteenth Amendment to the Constitution created judges with lifetime appointments.

T F 19. The judges in a common law country such as the united States must defer to the legislature in all questions of ambiguity in the law.

T F 20. An adversarial justice system is inconsistent with political and economic systems emphasizing self-reliance and laissez faire.

Chapter Six

Name_____ Date_____ Section_____

Multiple Choice

1. **Which of the following is *not* a function of courts In American society:**
   a. Resolve disagreements among members of the community in civil cases.
   b. Enforce penal laws in criminal cases.
   c. Initiate cases against erring government officials.
   d. Declare any law passed by the legislature or any act of an executive official to be unconstitutional if it does not comport with the Constitution.

2. **The Crime Control model of criminal justice:**
   a. Is like an assembly line conveyor belt, down which moves an endless stream of cases.
   b. Looks like an obstacle course whereby successive stages are designed to present impediments to carrying the accused any further along in the criminal justice process.
   c. Considers crime as a government problem which must be prevented at all cost.
   d. Is the only model used in American society.

3. **The process whereby at a scheduled time and place after prior notice, the accused is called to court, informed of the charges against him and asked how he pleads is known as:**
   a. Preliminary examination.
   b. Arraignment.
   c. Initial appearance.
   d. Presentment.

4. **In jury trials, peremptory challenge means:**
   a. A challenge to a jury membership for which no reason need be stated.
   b. A challenge which can be used only in felony cases.
   c. A challenge which must be for causes specified by law.
   d. A challenge which can be used only by the defense, not by the prosecution.

5. **Which of the following statements is true:**
   a. All prison sentences must be served consecutively, meaning one after the other.
   b. An accused does not have a right to counsel during sentencing.
   c. The right to appeal is not a constitutional right, but all states, by statute, allow the accused to appeal a conviction.
   d. A writ of habeas corpus is filed by prisoners to improve conditions of incarceration.

6. **The power of a court to try and punish a person for an offense is known as:**
   a. Venue.
   b. Authority.
   c. Assignment.
   d. Jurisdiction.

381

7. **The term "dual court system" means:**
   a. That the United States has two courts systems — one for civil cases and another for criminal cases.
   b. That the United States has one court system for federal cases and another for state cases.
   c. That criminal cases may be tried in either state or federal courts.
   d. That in case of conflict, decisions of federal courts prevail over decisions of state courts.

8. **Which of the following statements is false:**
   a. The U.S. Supreme Court has one Chief Justice and eight associate justices.
   b. All U.S. Courts of Appeals hold office in Washington, DC.
   c. U.S. district court judges may be removed only by a process of impeachment.
   d. U.S. magistrate judges are not presidential appointees.

9. **Which of the following is *not* a myth about the power and function of judges:**
   a. That judges are well trained for what they do.
   b. That judges alone determine the punishment to be imposed on a guilty person.
   c. That judges wield vast power in the conduct of litigation.
   d. That courts can effectively control the conduct of the police.

10. **The chief law enforcement officer in a geographical territory is the:**
    a. Judge.
    b. Sheriff.
    c. Prosecutor.
    d. Jailer.

11. **The right to counsel is found in what amendment of the U.S. Constitution:**
    a. Fourth.
    b. Fifth.
    c. Sixth.
    d. Eighth.

12. **The privilege of the accused against self-incrimination means that:**
    a. He does not have to take the witness stand and that the prosecutor cannot ask questions which tend to incriminate him.
    b. Once on the witness stand, the accused cannot be asked questions which tend to incriminate him.
    c. The accused is protected from answering questions which may later subject him to civil liability.
    d. He cannot be compelled to appear without a lawyer in a grand jury proceeding.

13. **Bail:**
    a. Is defined as the security required by the state and given by the accused to ensure his appearance before the proper court at the scheduled time and place to respond to charges brought against him.
    b. Is allowed the accused in all criminal cases.
    c. Is not a right given in the U.S. Constitution.
    d. Is allowed only in misdemeanor cases.

14. **Which of the following states has banned plea bargaining:**
    a. Ohio.
    b. California.
    c. New York.
    d. Alaska.

15. **The term "percentage bail" refers to the practice whereby:**
    a. Bail bondsmen are allowed to charge the accused a certain percentage of the bail amount before they will post bail.
    b. The defendant deposits a percentage (usually 10% of the full bail) with the court for his release.
    c. If the defendant fails to appear in court, only a certain percentage of the bail amount is charged.
    d. The judge can charge only a certain percentage of a set amount for a defendant to be released pending trial.

16. **Which of the following statements is true:**
    a. A guilty plea that represents a voluntary and intelligent choice among alternatives available is not rendered invalid simply because it was made to avoid the possibility of the death penalty.
    b. A guilty plea is invalid even if strong evidence on the record supports findings of guilt if the accused continues to claim innocence.
    c. A prosecutor's promise does not have to be fulfilled for a plea to be valid, even if the defendant relied on it to a significant degree.
    d. The American Bar Association and the American Law Institute have both gone on record as in favor of abolishing plea bargaining.

17. **The term "voir dire" is used:**
    a. When sentencing a defendant.
    b. In jury selection.
    c. In application for bail.
    d. In plea bargaining.

18. **Which of the following is *not* one of the four traditional objectives of sentencing:**
    a. Rehabilitation.
    b. Restitution.
    c. Deterrence.
    d. Retribution.

19. **Which of the following statements is *not* true about alternative dispute resolution?**
    a. Alternative dispute resolution projects help divert minor criminal cases from over-burdened court systems.
    b. Arbitration is the preferred method of alternative dispute resolution in criminal cases.
    c. Participants are usually pleased with the outcomes of alternative dispute resolution hearings.
    d. Alternative dispute resolution allows for innovative solutions to minor criminal matters.

20. **Which of the following rights is *not* guaranteed in the United States Constitution?**
    a. Right to a fair and impartial trial.
    b. Right to confrontation of witnesses.
    c. Right to appeal a conviction.
    d. Right to protection against double jeopardy.

True/False

T F 1. Valid arrests can be made only with a warrant.

T F 2. In the adversary system of justice, the courts play a neutral role in the conflict among 'individuals and between individuals and the state.

T F 3. If a conviction is reversed by a higher court, a defendant can no longer be retried because that would violate the double jeopardy clause of the Constitution.

T F 4. It is constitutionally required that jury verdicts must be unanimous.

T F 5. The Constitution does not require a 12-member jury.

T F 6. Cases from state supreme courts are appealed directly to the U.S. Supreme Court and not to the other lower federal courts

T F 7. Under our system of justice, the loyalty of a defense lawyer is both to society and to his client.

T F 8. Plea bargaining has always been acknowledged by the United States Supreme Court as a legitimate part of the court process.

T F 9. An arrested person must be brought before a judge or magistrate, or commissioner "without unnecessary delay," meaning the delay must not be longer than 10 hours.

T F 10. The sentence is always imposed by the court, however, a number of states permit the jury to recommend or determine the punishment for certain offenses.

T F 11. Decisions of the United States Court of Appeals are not binding on state supreme courts.

T F 12. While the immediate function of every judicial decision is to settle the rights of the parties before the court, a secondary function is to forecast how subsequent, similar cases will be decided In the future.

T F 13. The basic rule is: If the penal provision used to prosecute an accused is a federal law, then the case is tried in federal court; conversely, if the penal law is invoked is a state law, the case is tried in a state court.

T F 14. The exclusionary rule holds that irrelevant evidence cannot be admitted In a criminal trial.

T F 15. The primary goal of victim-offender reconciliation projects is to punish the criminal offender.

T F 16. In most states, the prosecutor is an appointed official.

T F 17. In criminal cases, the government always presents its case before the defendant presents his or her case.

T F 18. The right to confront witnesses is guaranteed by the Fifth Amendment.

T F 19. Federal sentencing guidelines require a federal judge to sentence a criminal defendant within a narrow range of months or years.

T F 20. United States attorneys are appointed by federal district court judges.

Chapter Seven

Name_____ Date_____ Section_____

TEST QUESTIONS

Multiple Choice

1. To understand law enforcement in America today, it is important that we study _____ criminal justice history.
   a. French.
   b. Spanish.
   c. Dutch.
   d. English.
   e. Swedish.

2. There was a time when Christianity was the government as well as the church. Church law was enforced and judged by the church. The church requirements were harsh and there was serious abuse of power. It is important for police to know why there is an absolute need for:
   a. All religions to be reflected in our law.
   b. Christian prayer at all public events.
   c. Christian sanctuary from prosecution.
   d. Church protection for the accused.
   e. Separation of church and state.

3. The "police des mouers" was an early attempt to regulate and control _____ and keep the crime confined to designated parts of the community.
   a. Prostitution.
   b. Gambling.
   c. Illegal drugs.
   d. Illegal liquor.
   e. All of the above.

4. The most important single act in the history of English-American police history occurred in 1829 with the passage of the London Metropolitan Police Act. The individual who receives credit for this major accomplishment is:
   a. Patrick Colquhoum.
   b. Henry Fielding.
   c. Sir Robert Peel.
   d. Oliver Cromwell.
   e. Francis Tuckey.

5. With a few exceptions, police uniforms and the use of handguns became common:
   a. In Colonial times.
   b. After the War of 1812.
   c. Before the Civil War.
   d. After the Civil War.
   e. In the "Roaring 20s."

387

6. The early colonial history of America demonstrated evidence of White, Christian _____ especially directed toward _____.
   a. Love / the French.
   b. Violence / native Americans.
   c. Understanding / the Spanish.
   d. Sharing / the Irish.
   e. Kindness / non-Christians.

7. Day and night policing existed separately in early America until 1844 when _____ consolidated into one operation, and therefore lays claim to being the first twenty-four-hour police force in the U.S.
   a. New Haven.
   b. Boston.
   c. New York City.
   d. Chicago.
   e. Baltimore.

8. By attempting to control the desire of other people, the moralists in 1920 passed the Volstead Act and made America go dry. Our morality quickly and deeply eroded, all of which created and maintained a new menace in the form of:
   a. Large use of illegal drugs.
   b. Terrorism.
   c. Armed gangsterism.
   d. A flood of hate crime.
   e. Spouse and child abuse.

9. When the Bureau of Investigation was established in 1909, there was immediate fear of too much power in the hands of an ever-growing Federal government. Once initial suspicions were allayed that it would turn into some big, secretive, czarist police force it:
   a. Experienced little growth until the start of World Was II.
   b. Did precisely that.
   c. Experienced slow but steady growth.
   d. Grew very erratically.
   e. Did not get big, secretive, nor czarist.

10. After the American Revolution our leaders went too far with decentralization of power. In 1789 a Constitutional Convention created our second government. That Constitution provided no rights for the people against the use or abuse of police power. The "Bill of Rights" was added to the Constitution to protect Americans from:
    a. Foreign governments.
    b. Our federal government.
    c. Local, state, and federal government.
    d. a and b above.
    e. b and c above.

11. Although they did not have state-wide general police powers, the first state government to have a state military unit with limited police power was:
    a. Texas.
    b. Massachusetts.
    c. Arizona.
    d. New Mexico.
    e. California.

12. **The U.S. Supreme Court, in the 1960s, required local and state police to follow due-process of law and the Constitution of the land. The court spelled out procedures to be followed. Which of the following cases was responsible for this dramatic change?**
    a. Mapp v. Ohio.
    b. Escobedo v. Illinois.
    c. Miranda v. Arizona.
    d. All of the above.
    e. **a** and **c** above.

13. **Evidence indicates that _____ was the first professional detective in America.**
    a. Bill Tilghman.
    b. J. Edgar Hoover.
    c. Richard Sylvester.
    d. August Vollmer.
    e. Allan Pinkerton.

14. **Which of the following was a very ugly chapter in the U.S. history of justice and public safety?**
    a. The treatment of native Americans.
    b. Slavery.
    c. The arrest and treatment of Japanese Americans on the West coast during World War II.
    d. All of the above.
    e. **a** and **b** only.

15. **Many people made great contributions to police professionalism. One of the top leaders in this effort was the Chief of Police in Berkeley, California. He was:**
    a. August Vollmer.
    b. Richard Sylvester.
    c. O.W. Wilson.
    d. J. Edgar Hoover.
    e. George Wickersham.

16. **The turmoil of the 1960s had great impact on the vast majority of Americans and their understanding of the police, because of:**
    a. Radio.
    b. Extensive academic research on law enforcement.
    c. Higher levels of public education.
    d. Religion taking a public stand on the issues.
    e. Television.

17. **A point of interest in World War II was the enforcement of law, control of labor unions, and sabotage on our docks. During four years of war, there was no trouble on our docks because of an "understanding" with:**
    a. The U.S. Coast Guard.
    b. The Royal Canadian Police.
    c. A wartime Civilian Crime Control Commission.
    d. Private security.
    e. Organized crime.

18. **Major events took place in the 1960s that turned the criminal justice world upside down and placed it in the focus of public attention. Of the following list, which were *NOT* part of those events?**
    1. Race riots in many locations.
    2. The assassination of President Kennedy.
    3. The development of DNA identification.
    4. Three landmark Supreme Court cases.
    5. Vietnam.
    6. Widespread use of illegal drugs.
    a. 3 and 5.
    b. 3.
    c. 5.
    d. 5 and 6.
    e. 1 and 6.

19. **Police today are very different from what they were in the past. Society has changed and has forced the police to change. There are problems though. Of the following list, which problem areas are the police not well-prepared to deal with?**
    1. Religious and domestic terrorism.
    2. Nuclear terrorism.
    3. Chemical terrorism.
    4. Biological terrorism.
    5. Large scale hate crime.
    6. Cyberspace crime.
    a. All of the above.
    b. 1 and 5.
    c. 2, 3, and 4.
    d. 5 and 6.
    e. 6.

20. **There is no question that the challenge of crime in the future will require:**
    a. Hundreds and hundreds of additional police.
    b. A large number of police on foot patrol.
    c. Bigger and faster patrol cars.
    d. A reduction of citizen rights and greater censorship.
    e. Much more and better training and education.

True/False

T F 1. American law enforcement today is experiencing many problems. To understand those problems it is of paramount importance to know the historical development of policing not only in the United States but also in England.

T F 2. Although many Christian groups claim responsibility for English and American law and criminal justice, there is no evidence of their influence in our justice system until after the Civil War.

T F 3. Americans have expressed a fear of too much power in the hands of a centralized government. That fear is not found in English history. Our fear seems to be a direct result of the American Revolution and our struggle to free ourselves from the English "Big Brother."

T F 4. Under English rule, the thirteen colonies used both Anglo-Saxon and Norman concepts of law enforcement.

T F 5. Henry Fielding made many contributions to English law enforcement. His greatest accomplishment was the passage of the London Metropolitan Police Act, which resulted in the first London police agency in 1829.

T F 6. America is a violent nation. Our violent history is reflected in our treatment of native Americans, dating back to early colonization.

T F 7. The rebellion of the southern states, in 1861, resulted in America's most violent experience. The American Civil War contributed heavily to our reputation as a violent people.

T F 8. As America expanded westward, vigilante law was encouraged and often sponsored by the U.S. Marshal's Office because there just were not enough Marshals to cover all of the vast territory for which they were responsible.

T F 9. When the southern states opened fire on Fort Sumpter and started the Civil War, the U.S. Government had no organized intelligence service. Allan Pinkerton, the owner of a private security company, offered his service to the North. As a civilian, he gathered extensive intelligence information for the rest of the war.

T F 10. State police have developed into strong centralized bureaucracies in all fifty states.

T F 11. The Bill of Rights was added to the Constitution of the U.S. to protect citizens from our Federal government.

T F 12. In 1920, morally motivated people thought they could correct many of America's social and criminal problems by preventing others from drinking alcohol. In so doing, they unwittingly set the stage for one of our most criminal periods, the "Roaring 20s."

T F 13. The capture and imprisonment of John Dillinger in Chicago developed the FBI's first popular nickname, when Dillinger, surrounded by agents, yelled "Don't shoot, G-men!"

T F 14. The Wickersham Commission study of American Criminal Justice resulted in many sweeping changes in law enforcement and established high levels of police professionalism.

T F 15. Japanese "Nisei" who were born in America and therefore were U.S. citizens, were arrested by the thousands and put in undesirable concentration camps shortly after the start of World War II. These American citizens were given no rights nor protection under the law. They were held for almost four years and most lost everything. American justice did nothing to help them.

T F 16. The civil rights movement has had a great impact on American society, its law, and its police. The movement got its start in Montgomery, Alabama, when a young woman by the name of Rosa Parks was arrested for sitting in the White section of a city bus.

T F   17. The 1960s were a tumultuous period in American law enforcement. As a result of this era, almost no changes occurred in the daily operations of the average law enforcement agency.

T F   18. Landmark cases from the U.S. Supreme Court, such as Mapp, Escobedo, and Miranda, established due process rules for all law enforcement. These cases told local law enforcement that there are rules to follow, and that the police must follow them in their criminal justice efforts.

T F   19. One of many recommendations made in the Presidential report "The Challenge of Crime in a Free Society" was to educate all police officers to the level of a Bachelor's degree by 1984. Although most of the recommendations failed, this education requirement was accomplished.

T F   20. The FBI continues to be the only bright spot in American law enforcement. Today, they are almost without criticism. Both political parties have and continue to throw money and laurels at them.

Chapter Eight

TEST QUESTIONS

Multiple Choice

1. **The law enforcement agencies of the Untied States are best described as:**
   a. A single national organization.
   b. Numerous, semi-autonomous organizations which answer to the FBI.
   c. Numerous semi-autonomous organizations within each state which answer to the state police.
   d. Numerous, autonomous, fragmented law enforcement organizations with no centralized authority controlling all agencies.

2. **Which is a characteristic of the federal law enforcement agencies, i.e., FBI, BATF, U.S. Marshal Service, etc?**
   a. Federal law enforcement agencies outnumber local and state police agencies by 2 to 1.
   b. Federal law enforcement agencies perform general law enforcement activities with broad authority.
   c. All federal law enforcement agencies are large organizations.
   d. Federal agencies comprise only a small percent of the law enforcement agencies and have specialized responsibilities.

3. **Which of the following is a primary responsibility of the contemporary U.S. Marshals Service?**
   a. The execution of federal, state, county, and local arrest warrants.
   b. The transportation of federal prisoners as the need arises.
   c. The security of all federal, state, and country court facilities and personnel.
   d. The management of federal jails and correctional institutions.

4. **Which of the following activities is traditionally the responsibility of the Sheriff's Department?**
   a. Security of federal court facilities and personnel.
   b. Administration of the state prison and custody of its prisoners.
   c. Civil process related to serving the "orders" of the state court.
   d. Clearing center for the Uniform crime Reports.

5. **Which statement is mostly true?**
   a. A college-educated candidate for a local police department usually enter at the rank of sergeant.
   b. A college-educated candidate for a local police department usually enter at the rank of lieutenant.
   c. Federal law enforcement and local law enforcement agencies have the same minimum level of education required for the job.
   d. A college-educated candidate for a local police department usually enters the agency at the rank of patrol officer — the lowest rank in the hierarchy.

6. **While all of these may be the responsibility of the state police, which is the primary responsibility of most state police departments, i.e., upon which activity do they spend most of their time?**
   a. The management of state-wide criminal investigations.
   b. General patrol of interstate highways, freeways, and state routes.
   c. Investigation of local police departments in cases involving charges of corruption.
   d. Technical assistance and expertise to local police departments.

7. **The Posse Comitatus Act of 1878:**
   a. Prohibited military troops from using civilian law enforcement agencies to fight Indians.
   b. Prohibited the U.S. Marshals Service from employing outlaws.
   c. Prohibited the U.S. Marshals Service from using military troops for the purposes of civilian law enforcement.
   d. Prohibited sheriffs from using civilian posses to pursue escaped prisoners and outlaws.

8. **Which is not a responsibility of the FBI?**
   a. Responsibility for domestic intelligence matters related to espionage, sabotage, and subversive activities.
   b. Clearing house for Uniform Crime Reports.
   c. Investigate violations of federal law.
   d. National police organization to control local police agencies.

9. **The National Crime Information Center:**
   a. Is the nation's largest computerized data bank on criminal information.
   b. Contains information on wanted felons.
   c. Contains information on certain stolen items such as automobiles, boats, guns, and securities.
   d. All of the above.
   e. None of the above.

10. **Which federal law enforcement agency is not under the Department of the Treasury?**
    a. Secret Service.
    b. Federal Bureau of Investigation.
    c. United States Customs Service.
    d. Bureau of Alcohol, tobacco and Firearms.

11. **Traditionally sheriffs obtain their office by:**
    a. Appointment by the president.
    b. Appointment by the governor.
    c. Political appointment.
    d. Election.

12. **The two major types of activities performed by the urban police identified by the President's Commission on Law Enforcement are?**
    a. Traffic safety and fighting drug crimes.
    b. Mediate domestic disputes and juvenile crime fighting.
    c. Law enforcement and community service.
    d. Traffic safety and training.

13. **The primary responsibility of the Secret Service is:**
    a. To protect witnesses in the Witness Protection program.
    b. To investigate major felony crime committed on federal reservations.
    c. Investigate the illegal sale of firearms.
    d. To protect the President and other persons designated by Congress.

14. **Which agency is most likely to investigate the assault of a U.S. Postal worker on a city street while in the performance of his or her official duties?**
    a. Local police.
    b. FBI.
    c. U.S. Postal Investigation Service.
    d. U.S. Marshals Service.

15. **The election of the Sheriff:**
    a. Creates the advantage of citizen control of the office.
    b. Creates the disadvantage of possibility electing an unqualified law enforcement professional.
    c. Creates the disadvantage of mixing politics and law enforcement.
    d. All of the above.
    e. None of the above.

16. **Of the over 3,000 sheriff's departments only 12 sheriff departments have:**
    a. A computer.
    b. Less than 25 sworn officers.
    c. More than 1,000 sworn officers.
    d. Jail-related responsibilities.

17. **Approximately _____ percent of local police officers are females.**
    a. 8 to 9.
    b. 50.
    c. 60.
    d. No local police offices are females as females are excluded from local law enforcement.

18. **Approximately _____ percent of local police departments require a minimum education level of a bachelor's degree to become a police officer.**
    a. 1.
    b. 50.
    c. 80.
    d. 99.

19. **American local police officers can best be described as:**
    a. Specialists.
    b. Generalists.
    c. Just like their British counterparts.
    d. College educated.

20. **Which of the following is likely to disqualify a candidate for a job as police officer?**
    a. A misdemeanor conviction for domestic abuse which is over one year old.
    b. The use of illegal drugs within the last 12 months.
    c. Color blindness.
    d. All of the above.
    e. None of the above.

True/False

T F   1. The oldest federal law enforcement agency in the United States is the U.S. Marshals Service.

T F   2. The Federal Bureau of Investigation can investigate any crime, anywhere in the United Sates or its territories.

T F   3. The primary responsibility of the Secret Service is the protection of the President, presidential family members, the Vice President, and significant presidential candidates.

T F   4. The office of sheriff originated in England and was brought to America by early colonial settlers.

T F   5. The American urban police agencies are identical in administration and function to the British urban police agencies.

T F   6. The urban police officer develops a career emphasizing specialization in crime fighting abilities to the exclusion of all other abilities and services.

T F   7. The protection of federal witnesses whose testimony may endanger their lives is the responsibility of the FBI.

T F   8. The FBI operates a national crime laboratory which provides scientific and technical support to other police agencies.

T F   9. The assault of a mail carrier or the stealing of letters from a mail box is a state or local misdemeanor.

T F   10. The second-in-command in the Sheriff's Department is traditionally called the Undersheriff.

T F   11. A common title for the head of federal and state law enforcement agencies is Chief.

T F   12. Sheriff's departments tend to be small agencies with less than 25 sworn personnel.

T F   13. The chief of police of a municipal police agency obtains his or her position by election.

T F   14. Applicants with a bachelor's degree can enter most police departments at the rank of detective or lieutenant.

T F   15. Prerequisite knowledge, skills, and abilities for the position of police officer must be job related.

T F   16. The minimum age to become a police officer for most police departments is 18 years old.

T F   17. Most local police departments require that candidates for the position of police officer have a minimum of a bachelor's degree.

396

T F 18. In about one-half of the states a candidate can be disqualified for the job of police officer due to homosexuality activity.

T F 19. A good score on a general intelligence test is the primary qualification to become a police officer.

T F 20. Once a police recruit completes the police training academy he or she is sworn-in as a police officer and he or she receives no further training or evaluation.

Chapter Nine

Name_____ Date_____ Section_____

TEST QUESTIONS

Multiple Choice

1. **Which of the following is *generally not* a duty of the first officer on the scene:**
   a. Mark and package physical evidence.
   b. Arrest perpetrator if possible.
   c. Protect and preserve the crime scene.
   d. Perform first aid or call for medical assistance as necessary.
   e. Gather basic information about the crime from the victim and any witnesses.

2. **Which of the following is *not* a good example of information gathering:**
   a. Interviewing and interrogation.
   b. Applying for a search warrant.
   c. Fixed visual surveillance.
   d. Checking official records.

3. **A major trap into which an investigator can fall is:**
   a. Unwillingness to revise his theory of the crime.
   b. Searching the wrong address.
   c. Not getting the cooperation of a witness.
   d. Being spotted during a visual surveillance.

4. **The primary purpose of the jury is to:**
   a. Follow the judge's orders.
   b. Evaluate the performance of the attorneys.
   c. Find the defendant guilty if proved beyond a doubt.
   d. Evaluate the evidence presented in the case.

5. **In a case involving a charge of possession of drugs with intent to sell, which of the following best represents direct evidence:**
   a. Police agent testifies that he purchased drug from defendant.
   b. Laboratory identified material as a prohibited drug.
   c. Defendant admitted in court that he used this drug.
   d. Friends of defendant admitted in court that defendant had given them samples of the drug.

6. **Which of the following factors will guarantee the qualification of the criminalist as an expert in court:**
   a. Advanced education
   b. Years of experience.
   c. He has testified in other courts.
   d. He has testified in this court before.
   e. None of the above.

7. **Which of the following best represents a control sample of evidence:**
   a. Sample of blood from the suspect.
   b. Paint flakes from the point of entry in a burglary.
   c. Amphetamine sulfate obtained from a drug manufacturer.
   d. Bullet fired and recovered from suspect weapon.

8. **Which of the following procedures is *not* done before physical evidence is handled:**
   a. Photographing.
   b. Recording in notes.
   c. Diagram its position in sketch.
   d. Marking for identification.

9. **Which of the following is *not* of great importance in the processing of physical evidence:**
   a. Permission of property owner to search for evidence.
   b. Taking of photographs and notes before touching.
   c. Maintaining the integrity of the evidence.
   d. Maintaining the chain of possession.
   e. Proper marking for identification.

10. **Which of the following is the greatest danger faced by the expert witness in court:**
    a. Not receiving his expert witness fee.
    b. Objections raised by the defense attorney.
    c. Insufficient pretrial rehearsal.
    d. Not being qualified by the judge.
    e. Answering questions, as an expert, outside his field of expertise.

11. **Which of the following best represents physical evidence:**
    a. Testimony of the pathologist concerning the cause of death.
    b. Original copy of the search warrant.
    c. Bullet taken from body during autopsy.
    d. Sales receipt for firearm used in the crime.
    e. Sound of shot heard by witness.

12. **The primary goal of the criminalist in court is to:**
    a. Present evidence to convict the defendant.
    b. Follow the instructions of the prosecutor.
    c. Testify in a manner to impress the jury.
    d. Present honest opinions.

13. **For which of the following is the acronym IAFIS properly used:**
    a. Integrated Automated Fingerprint Identification System.
    b. Integrated Automated Firearms Identification System.
    c. International Association of Forensic Identification Specialists.
    d. International Applied Firearms Identification System.
    e. International Association of Fanatics Investigating Simpson.

14. **Which of the following statements concerning normal human blood is correct:**
    a. Type O has both anti-a and anti-b in the serum.
    b. Type A has anti-a in the serum.
    c. Type AB has no antibodies in the serum.
    d. All types contain anti-rabbit antibodies in the serum.

15. **Which of the following factors would be least likely to be determined in an autopsy:**
    a. Nature of the weapon used.
    b. Any apparent disease from which the victim suffered.
    c. Possible manufacturer of the gun used.
    d. Precise cause of death.

16. **Which of the following would be of *least* value in determining the distance from which a person had been shot:**
    a. Clothing burns from muzzle blast.
    b. Path of the bullet in the body.
    c. Nitrite deposits on the clothing.
    d. Powder particles on the clothing.

17. **Which of the following statements about field tests for blood is correct:**
    a. The reaction is positive only for human blood.
    b. Blood is the only substance that will give a positive reaction.
    c. A positive reaction is a confirmation that the substance is blood.
    d. The test need not be run directly on the original stain.

18. **Which of the following statements about DNA analysis is *incorrect*?**
    a. It is useful only on relatively fresh samples.
    b. It can be successfully used on mixed samples.
    c. The procedure may take some weeks to complete.
    d. It may be as useful in eliminating a suspect as in confirming his identity.

19. **Which of the following databases are *not* included in CODIS:**
    a. Missing persons records.
    b. Forensic records.
    c. Convicted offender records.
    d. Miscellaneous population records.

20. **Which of the following is an individual characteristic of a piece of glass:**
    a. Chemical composition.
    b. Density.
    c. Color.
    d. Rib mark patterns.
    e. Refractive index.

True/False

T   F   1. The primary goal of criminal investigation is to gather information that will convict the suspect(s).

T   F   2. Dead bodies should be removed from the scene as soon as possible so that bystanders do not get upset.

T   F   3. Loose ends in an investigation may be ignored if the prosecutor promises not to mention them.

T F 4. Most witness are more than eager to cooperate with a criminal investigator.

T F 5. Investigators must be completely honest with persons being interviewed or interrogated.

T F 6. All eyewitness testimony is direct evidence.

T F 7. The chain of custody of evidence is an important factor in determining the relevancy of the evidence.

T F 8. The results of analyses made by the criminalist are only opinions when presented in court.

T F 9. All latent fingerprints require some form of processing before they can be used for identification purposes.

T F 10. Autopsies can be performed adequately by an licensed physician.

T F 11. Autopsies should be performed on victims of auto accidents, even though the cause of death appears to be obvious.

T F 12. Items which are not found at a fire scene may be as significant as items which are found.

T F 13. Some rifled gun barrels have no individual characteristics.

T F 14. Bullet comparison is identical in principle to fingerprint comparison.

T F 15. The classic dermal nitrate test is one of the most reliable of criminalistic determinations.

T F 16. Because firearms barrels can change over time, there is no use in attempting to establish a data-base for identification purposes.

T F 17. The field tests for blood are effective on human blood only.

T F 18. The field tests for blood are useful as search techniques.

T F 19. The genetic-coding portion of DNA is the most useful for identifying a suspect.

T F 20. CODIS is a technique used by the National Security Agency to decode encrypted messages.

Chapter Ten

Name_____ Date_____ Section_____

Multiple Choice

1. **Vengeance, retribution, deterrence, and reform represent:**
   a. The historical purposes of corrections.
   b. Primitive approaches to corrections.
   c. Modern correctional philosophy.
   d. The predominant approaches in dealing with the offender during the reformation.

2. **Deterrence and reform are:**
   a. Polar opposites.
   b. Represent a different combination of treatment and punishment.
   c. Seldom conflict with each other.
   d. Are effective only in combination with each other.

3. **As societies became more technologically advanced and developed the ability to process large numbers of prisoners:**
   a. Prisoners were viewed as a useless resource.
   b. Banishment and corporal punishments become less palatable.
   c. Jails and prisons are no longer necessary.
   d. Prisoners were considered a liability to prison production and profit.

4. **In primitive societies the severest penalties were for:**
   a. Injuries to members of other tribes.
   b. Violation of the group's customs and codes.
   c. Injuries to tribal members.
   d. **b** and **c** above.

5. **The Classical School approach to corrections was primarily based on:**
   a. Freudian psychoanalysis.
   b. Judeo-Christian principles.
   c. Psychological hedonism.
   d. Communist ideals.

6. **In 1787 a group of Quakers developed a modern correctional system based on a philosophy that man has the ability to repent for wrongs committed and to reform. The First modern penitentiary based on this model was completed:**
   a. In 1725 in New York.
   b. In 1910 in Mississippi.
   c. In 1787 in Pennsylvania.
   d. None of the above.

7. **Jeremy Bentham:**
   a. Was an advocate of treatment versus punishment.
   b. Was an advocate of the classical school.
   c. Argued that punishment must be equal for all regardless of class status.
   d. Attempted to develop procedures for assigning punishments based on offense categories.
   e. **b, c** and **d** above.

8. **Treatment approaches in America prevailed in:**
   a. The 1920's.
   b. In the early 50's.
   c. At the turn of the century.
   d. In the 1970's and 1980's.

9. **Cessare Becarria is responsible for:**
   a. The transition from a focus on reform to punishment in modern America.
   b. Movement to a tougher, hard-line approach, in dealing with the offender population.
   c. Widespread use of the Guillotine in 18th century Europe.
   d. A change in focus from vengeance and punishment to prevention and reform in the mid 1700's.

10. **The purpose of imprisonment in the latter half of the 13th century England was to:**
    a. Provide for meditation and penitence.
    b. Insure that offenders were punished .
    c. Compel offenders to pay fines.
    d. None of the above.

11. **John Howard, an English businessman in 18th Century England, was concerned with:**
    a. The need to punish offenders more harshly.
    b. Implementation of ways to make sure offenders suffered sufficient pain and suffering.
    c. The poor conditions in English prisons and throughout Europe.
    d. All of the above.
    e. None of the above.

12. **The Auburn system:**
    a. Endorsed the silence system incorporated in the Pennsylvania system.
    b. Developed a system of solitary confinement in separate cells after 1821.
    c. Was highly regimented and required inmates to work together in groups during the day.
    d. Was more economical and efficient than the Pennsylvania System.
    e. All of the above.

13. **The Pennsylvania System did not survive due primarily to:**
    a. The prevailing philosophy of repentance and reformation.
    b. The ease of handling and caring for prisoners.
    c. The cost of confinement in individual cells and minimal contribution to the institution.
    d. The need for a system that would reduce the cost of operation.
    e. Both **c** and **d.**

14. **The Prison Industry system was designed to:**
    a. Reduce the cost of prison.
    b. To provide a means of keeping inmates under control.
    c. To create a system to compete with the private sectors.
    d. To insure reformation of inmates.

15. **The development of the first reformatory based on the "Irish System" was in:**
    a. Chicago, Illinois.
    b. Providence, Rhode Island.
    c. Hartford, Connecticut.
    d. Elmira, New York.
    e. None of the above.

16. **In addition to maximum security facilities, there developed other systems to include:**
    a. Medium security.
    b. Minimum security.
    c. Limited security.
    d. **a** and **b** above.

17. **Prison Camps (and prison farms) were developed in the 19th century in Southern states to:**
    a. Provide a more effective means of punishing inmates.
    b. To reduce the prison populations and minimize overall costs.
    c. Insure effective rehabilitation of inmates.
    d. To create an environment necessary to maximize deterrence and reform.
    e. None of the above.

18. **Correctional History has illustrated a movement from:**
    a. A more punitive and brutal approach to a less punitive, more humane approach.
    b. A desire to maim and torture to a desire to change and reform.
    c. An emphasis upon retribution and revenge to an emphasis upon prevention and deterrence.
    d. All of the above.
    e. None of the above.

19. **The History of Corrections has revealed that:**
    a. No progressive developments have taken place.
    b. We have not eliminated the desire for punishment in modern corrections.
    c. We are becoming increasingly focused on our ability to reform and rehabilitate.
    d. We have eliminated much of the corruption and abuses of the past.
    e. **b** and **d** above.

20. **History reveals that grand experiments and new philosophies:**
    a. Always create dramatic success in dealing with the offender population.
    b. Rarely had any positive influence on the handling of offender populations.
    c. Do not always create dramatic success in dealing with the criminal element.
    d. Have sometimes provided the stimulus for enlightened reform and positive change.
    e. **c** and **d** above

True/False

T F   1. Deterrence and reform were objectives employed in 17th century Europe.

T F 2. Punishment and treatment objectives seldom complement each other.

T F 3. Early English penalties were very mild and treatment oriented.

T F 4. The notion that inflicting pain on the offender had some intrinsic value was not widely recognized until the beginning of the 18th century.

T F 5. The doctrine that held that individuals weigh the pleasures and pains of individual actions and regulate behavior by selecting actions that bring the greatest pleasure and the least pain is referred to as Marxian.

T F 6. The "Positivist" (or Italian School) was based on the philosophy that crime is a natural phenomenon created by genetics or other forces.

T F 7. The Code of Hammurabi (1875 BC) urged an "eye for an eye" in order to satisfy the need for vengeance by, or on behalf of, the victim.

T F 8. The Enlightenment period was known for its lack of concern for humanity and focus on punishment.

T F 9. The extensive use of imprisonment as punishment did not occur until the 13th Century.

T F 10. John Howard proposed separation of young offenders from older, more calloused offenders.

T F 11. Meaningful Correctional reform began in the United States under the Direction of William Penn.

T F 12. The Pennsylvania System was premised on the belief that positive change in behavior was possible in a state of solitary confinement.

T F 13. Most prisons in the United States are now based on the Pennsylvania model.

T F 14. The Auburn System was run on the Congregate or Silent System.

T F 15. The Auburn System was premised on the notion of crime prevention through fear and punishment.

T F 16. The "Reformatory" was designed to serve inmates who were mostly violent and incorrigible.

T F 17. The Reformatory was based on the Irish System.

T F 18. The first Reformatory built in the United States was the accomplishment of Zebulon Brockway.

T F 19. Military Prisons were constituted by an act of Congress in 1795.

T F 20. Federal Prisons were designed to hold inmates who were not safe in state prisons.

Chapter Eleven

Name_____ Date_____ Section_____

TEST QUESTIONS

Multiple Choice

1. Which goal of the correctional process has not embraced public opinion or popular sentiment, relatively speaking, in the past two decades?
   a. Incapacitation.
   b. Retribution.
   c. Deterrence.
   d. Rehabilitation.

2. Which type of offender is typically more mainstream American, meaning employed, middle aged, living income and so on than their counterparts?
   a. Federal inmates.
   b. State inmates.
   c. Jail inmates.
   d. Mental institution detainees.

3. The Federal Bureau of Prisons houses approximately how many inmates?
   a. 15,000.
   b. 90,000.
   c. 145,000.
   d. 1,100,000.

4. The level system in the Federal Bureau of Prisons is an indicator of what about each facility?
   a. Inmate population.
   b. Security level.
   c. Type of offenders.
   d. Facility age.

5. The power to civilly commit persons incarcerated for sexually predatory crimes, immediately following completion of their prison sentence is:
   a. Legal and widespread among states.
   b. Legal and rarely done among states.
   c. Under consideration by the Supreme Court.
   d. Unconstitutional because of double jeopardy.

6. The effectiveness of boot camp, and boot camp-type programs on juvenile offenders is presently considered to be:
   a. Tremendous success.
   b. Moderate success.
   c. Too early and not enough data to tell.
   d. An abysmal failure.

7. **The prison, as a punishment, has experienced what type of growth since the late 1970's?**
    a. No growth.
    b. Decline.
    c. Large growth.
    d. Minimal growth.

8. **SUPERMAX in the United States is presently located in which city?**
    a. Alcatraz, CA.
    b. Lompoc, CA.
    c. Florence, CO.
    d. El Reno, OK.

9. **Relative to the Federal Bureau of Prisons, the state prison system in this country is:**
    a. Very large.
    b. Comparable in size.
    c. Much smaller.
    d. Fluctuating back and forth.

10. **The cost of housing an inmate in a state facility in the United States ranges between about what each year?**
    a. $16,000-$40,000.
    b. $ 9,500-$27,000.
    c. $21,000-$56,000.
    d. $34,000-$100,000.

11. **The range of options in community corrections divisions have been doing what during the past decade?**
    a. Declining sharply.
    b. Declining slowly.
    c. Remaining constant.
    d. Expanding.

12. **Community service as a form of community corrections involves:**
    a. Cash payments to victims.
    b. A program of supervised labor.
    c. Release from incarceration.
    d. Intensive supervision.

13. **Electronic monitoring is a popular option for state corrections officials because:**
    a. Eases overcrowding in prisons and jails.
    b. It is a very expensive initiative.
    c. Keeps drug offenders in the community.
    d. All of A, B & C.

14. **Overcrowding in the state prison system presently affects about how many of the fifty states?**
    a. 0.
    b. 25.
    c. 35.
    d. All 50.

15. **The CHEERS system is an example of a technological tool which does what?**
    a. Monitors electronic bracelets on inmates.
    b. Allows agency data bases to interact with each other.
    c. Allows corrections officials to determine if the offender is home at any given time.
    d. Provides a 10,000 volt shock to an offender with the touch of a button.

16. **Privatization of the American prison system can presently be categorized as what?**
    a. A large initiative.
    b. A relatively small but growing initiative.
    c. A large but declining initiative.
    d. Deemed unconstitutional.

17. **HIV infection in American prisons and jails presently consists of about how many known cases?**
    a. 1,000.
    b. 19,000.
    c. 28,000.
    d. 42,000.

18. **Three strike frequent felon laws are presently experiencing a:**
    a. Growth period.
    b. Period of decline.
    c. Rejection on constitutional grounds.
    d. Place in all fifty states.

19. **The chain gang concept, popular in the 1950's and 1960's in the South, is:**
    a. Unconstitutional today.
    b. Regaining popularity nationwide.
    c. Regaining popularity in the South.
    d. Considered barbaric and no longer in use.

20. **Treatment of juvenile offenders by the Court will likely continue to become what in the near future:**
    a. More treatment oriented.
    b. More punishment oriented
    c. More tolerant
    d. Less punishment oriented

True/False

T F   1. The Federal Bureau of Prisons is a larger system, from the standpoint of inmate population, than the state-level prison system in the United States.

T F   2. There are presently about eight times as many people on probation in the United States than are in prison.

T F   3. All fifty states operate a state-level prison system.

T F 4. Most jails in this country are administered by a county sheriff.

T F 5. Most persons incarcerated in American jails are African-American.

T F 6. The correctional office position is a relatively stress-free occupation.

T F 7. The use of computer technology in corrections is a growing trend.

T F 8. Prison privatization can be deemed an abandoned failure in 1990's corrections management.

T F 9. AIDS is a growing problem in American prisons from many perspectives.

T F 10. Three-strikes laws are increasingly unpopular with state legislatures.

Chapter Twelve

Name_____ Date_____ Section_____

Multiple Choice

1. **Juveniles are subject to the jurisdiction of a series of status offenses. These may include:**
   a. Truancy, and sexual promiscuity.
   b. Incorrigibility and ungovernability.
   c. Behavior endangering his/her own morals, health, or general welfare.
   d. **a** and **b**, but not **c**.
   e. **a**, **b**, and **c**.

2. **An official delinquent is someone:**
   a. Under the age of minority who has committed a delinquent act and has been arrested.
   b. Under the age of minority who has been wrongfully punished for a delinquent act they did not commit.
   c. Under the age of minority who has committed a delinquent act without being arrested.
   d. Over the age of minority who has committed a delinquent act and has been arrested, but not sent to an institution.

3. **In an attempt to develop an explanation for delinquency it would be most useful to:**
   a. Study the various theories which have been formulated and then decide which one is "right."
   b. Consider how much each of the various theories contributes to the explanation of delinquency.
   c. Decide that since none of the existing theories have caused juvenile delinquency to subside, they should not be considered seriously, other than to provide a basis for further research.
   d. Start anew without regard to the work of others on the subject; and therefore be free of the biases other researchers may have gotten hung up on which could be passed on through the study of their theories.

4. **Psychologists believe that early emotional deprivation is directly associated with later psychological disturbances and emotional problems. The family has the responsibility to:**
   a. Provide the child with love and security.
   b. Provide the child with protective shelter from outside pressures.
   c. Keep the child from adjusting to the social environment he is growing up in (if he/she is in an environment that has bad aspects).
   d. **a** and **b** only.
   e. **a**, **b**, and **c**.

5. **Except for the few crimes which are peculiar to women (prostitution, infanticide, abortion), crime and delinquency rates for males are greatly in excess of the rates for females:**
   a. For all ages.
   b. In every community in every nation.
   c. Throughout history for which organized statistics have been recorded.
   d. **a**, **b**, and **c**.
   e. **a** and **b** only.

6. **Which of the following is not a method of transferring a juvenile to a adult criminal court?**
   a. Judicial wavier.
   b. Prosecutorial discretion.
   c. Statutory Exclusion.
   d. None of the above.

7. **Many factors may contribute to the high delinquency rates of lower-class children. Factors described in this chapter include:**
   a. Biases of the police and courts.
   b. The severe disjunction between aspiration levels and expectations of many lower-class juveniles (goal-means discrepancy).
   c. The part of the city they are growing up in.
   d. **a**, **b**, and **c**.
   e. **a** and **b** only.

8. **With regards to the family environment perspective, factors which can lead to delinquent behavior include:**
   a. Faults in the roles played by members of the family.
   b. The nature of the interrelationships between family members.
   c. The social structure of the family.
   d. **a**, **b**, and **c**.
   e. **b** and **c** only.

9. **The differential association theory of delinquency causation focuses on:**
   a. Association of those of different races to see their point of view.
   b. Association with those of different social classes in an attempt to better understand them.
   c. Learning of attitudes and behaviors from those who are already delinquent or criminal.
   d. **a** and **b**.

10. **The consequences of being defined as delinquent is the focus of this theory:**
    a. Labeling.
    b. Containment.
    c. Lower class culture.
    d. Drift.

11. **In the late 1800's, criminal law reforms pertaining to juveniles were actively promoted by a group known today as:**
    a. The Children's Rights Committee.
    b. The President's Juvenile Rights Commission.
    c. Citizens for the Prevention of Cruelty to Children.
    d. The PTO.
    e. The Child Savers.

12. **Which of the following decisions of the Supreme Court have defined requirements of due process for juveniles:**
    a. Sheppard vs. United States, In Re Gault.
    b. Maxwell vs. United States, Sheppard vs. United States, in Re Winship.
    c. Kent vs. United States, In Re Gault; and In Re Winship.
    d. All of the above.
    e. None of the above.

13. **Juvenile law has provided for several hearings for juveniles. Which of the following is not included?**
    a. Detention hearing.
    b. Dispositional hearing.
    c. Inquisitorial hearing.
    d. Adjudicatory hearing.
    e. **a** and **c**.

14. **Diversion from the juvenile justice system is designed to prevent the negative consequences of criminal justice processes as they effect the individual. Diversion is aimed primarily at:**
    a. The repetitious offender.
    b. The offenders of the more serious crimes.
    c. The less serious delinquents.
    d. **a** and **b**.
    e. All of the above.

15. **The Youth Services Bureau administers a variety of services for youth. These include:**
    a. Counseling individual juveniles and providing placement in foster homes.
    b. Supplying special education and work assignments.
    c. Supplying direct aid for young men and women so they can better their material lives, decreasing their tendencies toward delinquency.
    d. **a** and **b**.
    e. **b** and **c**.

True/False

T F   1. Minors are subject only to the jurisdiction of the legal codes applying to adults.

T F   2. Each state has the authority to define what conduct constitutes delinquency.

T F   3. It is likely that at least 90% of all juveniles could be defined as unofficial delinquents.

T F   4. The term "parens patriae" means that the parents of a child must by held legally responsible for the actions of that child.

T F   5. Not until the early 1900's did the criminal court processes of the American justice system begin separating children from adults.

T F 6. There are no statutes or Supreme Court decisions defining the requirements of due process for juveniles.

T F 7. It is not possible (because of federal legislation) to process a juvenile through the adult criminal justice system even if he/she has violated a criminal law.

T F 8. Diversion is a judicial disposition which includes unconditional release.

T F 9. Prior to 1980, juveniles had no due process rights.

T F 10. The concept of the Youth Services Bureau, although as yet untried, promises to be a successful program once it gets started.

T F 11. There is a weak relationship between illegal drug ownership, drug abuse, and delinquency.

T F 12. The majority of homicide victims age 10-17 are killed by a friend or other acquaintance.

T F 13. Juvenile arrests rates for property remained relatively stable between 1980 and 1995.

T F 14. Between 1991 and 1995, increases in arrests for juvenile females were higher than for juvenile males for most offense categories.

T F 15. In 1995, about half of violent crimes committed by juveniles were committed by whites and about half were committed by blacks.

T F 16. The Juvenile Justice and Delinquency Prevention Act focused on federal mandates handed down to the states regarding the management of the delinquency problem.

T F 17. A juvenile can be held in detention until the adjudication hearing without benefit of a court hearing.

T F 18. It is the tradition of the juvenile court to provide juvenile court judges with specific sentences for each type of crime committed.

Chapter Thirteen

Name_____ Date_____ Section_____

TEST QUESTIONS

Multiple Choice

1. At the onset of the 1990s, there were _____ persons employed in private security, at a total cost of $_____ per year.
   a. 1.5 million / $52 million.
   b. 5.2 million / $15 million.
   c. 20 million / $152 billion.
   d. 5 million / $5.2 billion.

2. A milestone in the evolution of private security was in 1285 with the:
   a. Metropolitan Police Act.
   b. Creation of justices of the peace.
   c. Statute of Winchester.
   d. Courts of Assize.

3. During the Middle Ages, the _____ system was initiated.
   a. Watch and ward.
   b. Hue and cry.
   c. Bow Street Runners.
   d. Mutual pledge.

4. The _____ was the Statute of Winchester's method of restraining people who resisted watchmen in early England.
   a. Hue and cry.
   b. Tithing.
   c. Ball and cannon.
   d. Cat-o-nine-tails.

5. A long-standing controversy concerns the amount of _____ needed by private security personnel.
   a. Discretion.
   b. Formal education and training.
   c. Legislative support.
   d. Non-lethal weapons.

6. In-house security services are called _____, while _____ services are outside firms providing these services for a fee.
   a. Contract / proprietary.
   b. Proximidistal / cepholacaudal.
   c. Internal / external.
   d. Proprietary / contract.

7. **In 1851 the first contract private security organization in the U.S. was founded by:**
   a. Leslie Bow.
   b. Allan Pinkerton.
   c. Sir Winston Churchill.
   d. Hugh Mortimer.

8. **_____ was a significant catalyst in the growth of contract private security.**
   a. The Vietnam War.
   b. The Korean War.
   c. World War I.
   d. World War II.

9. **The security manager of today is likely to possess:**
   a. A master's degree and more than 25 years' experience.
   b. Less than 5 years' experience and an associate's degree.
   c. Three firearms at home and two at work.
   d. An associate's degree and 20 years' experience.

10. **The most effective security training programs consist of:**
    a. "Virtual reality" modules.
    b. Classroom lecture and hands-on training.
    c. Six trainers per trainee.
    d. Outdoor "shoot/don't shoot" ranges.

11. **A long-running debate concerning private security personnel is whether or not:**
    a. They should be armed.
    b. They should be uniformed.
    c. They should have marked vehicles.
    d. They should use batons.

12. **There are major concerns about public police officers:**
    a. Working without a backup security officer.
    b. Involved in secondary employment ("moonlighting").
    c. Using private security radios.
    d. Administering Miranda warnings to suspects for security personnel.

13. **An advanced method for identifying people is called:**
    a. Biometrics.
    b. Cloning.
    c. Urithroscopic ID.
    d. Image defusement.

14. **TQM stands for:**
    a. Tutum quo mandamus.
    b. Training quantum method.
    c. Totally qualified manager.
    d. Total quality management.

15. **The largest physical security market segment is:**
    a. Microchip technology.
    b. Satellite beaming technology.
    c. Inductive terminators.
    d. Electronic access control.

16. **Which of the following is not one of the three trends that are driving growth in private security?**
    a. Public concern about crime.
    b. The decline of morals among the crime-prone age cohort.
    c. Governmental reluctance to increase public safety spending.
    d. Technological advances in security products.

17. **The physical security industry can be divided into three broad segments, including all but which of the following?**
    a. Perimeter security.
    b. Interior security.
    c. Surreptitious monitoring.
    d. Access control.

18. **The four categories of perimeter security include microwave sensors, video motion detector systems, and:**
    a. Barrier sensors and buried sensors.
    b. LAN computers and rapid transit vehicles.
    c. Infrared and laser beams.
    d. Inchoate and radical lighting.

19. **A _____ test may be used to determine foreseeability (through similar prior criminal acts).**
    a. "Reasonable and prudent."
    b. "Three pronged litmus."
    c. "Totality of the circumstances."
    d. "Preponderance of evidence."

20. **An area that future security managers must master is:**
    a. Personnel administration.
    b. Laws of laser physics.
    c. Proportional allocations of technological devices.
    d. Cyberspace.

True/False

T F 1. A landowner can "contract away" culpability by hiring private security officers.

T F 2. Historically, security education has been offered mostly by private academies.

T F 3. Courts have held that security officers are not bound by *Mirand v. Arizona*.

T F 4. The most elaborate security system in ancient times was the Great Wall of China.

T F 5. Under England's "assize of arms," every male 15-60 years of age had to keep a weapon in his home for peacekeeping.

T F 6. Because of its high degree of effectiveness, England's watch and ward policing system remains in use today.

T F 7. Railroad companies were among the first companies to hire in-house, proprietary security officers.

T F 8. The logo of Pinkerton's National Detective Agency was an open eye, the motto, "We Never Sleep."

T F 9. The Wells Fargo armored car was unveiled in 1917.

T F 10. Studies have shown that private security personnel are often recruited among persons with minimal education and training.

T F 11. A RAND Corporation study found that nearly all private security officers have a high school diploma.

T F 12. Historically, security education has been offered mostly by private, 2-year colleges as an adjunct to their vocational-technical program.

T F 13. CPP stands for certified protection professional, and CST stands for certified security trainer.

T F 14. To date, no master's degree programs exist in security administration.

T F 15. Because no related federal, state, or local laws cover security training, security managers need not be too concerned with their personnel meeting training standards.

T F 16. Prior to Oregon's minimum training standards and licensing procedure for private security personnel of 1997, no such state training or certification requirements existed.

T F 17. Today about 10-20 percent of all security officers are armed.

T F 18. The relationship between public and private police, research indicates, is worse now than at any other time.

T F 19. There are now about two public police officers for every private security officer in the U.S.

T F 20. Typically, a security officer's liability is based on some form of negligence or failure to provide adequate security.

Chapter Fourteen

Name_____ Date_____ Section_____

TEST QUESTIONS

Multiple Choice

1. **Racial and ethnic classifications employed by government agencies are not neutral statistical devices. These classifications do which of the following?**
   a. Shape self-identification of Americans.
   b. Influence research and policy in the areas of race and ethnicity.
   c. Oversimplify the different racial/ethnic groups in America.
   d. All of the above.

2. **Which of the following best represents the current number of African-American men, aged 20-29, in prison/jail, probation, or parole on an average day?**
   a. One out of two.
   b. One out of three.
   c. One out of four.
   d. One out of ten.

3. **What is/are the main source of data on the level of crime in the United States?**
   a. Uniform Crime Reports.
   b. Self-report studies.
   c. National Crime Victimization Survey.
   d. All of the above.

4. **Which of the following is true during the national War on Drugs?**
   a. Drug-related arrest rates for African-Americans have increased much faster than those for whites.
   b. African-Americans are using drugs at a higher level than are whites.
   c. Whites make up about three-fourths of the prison sentences for drug possession.
   d. None of the above.

5. **The _____ show that African-Americans report a higher level of violent crime among those 12 years of age and older than do whites.**
   a. Uniform Crime Reports / Surveys.
   b. Self-report studies.
   c. National Crime Victimization.
   d. None of the above.

6. **Which of the following is/are true of America's African-American population?**
   a. A greater percentage of white children than African-American live below the poverty line.
   b. African-American middle class is becoming increasingly separated from very poor, "underclass" African-Americans.
   c. Most of the poor whites in America live in central cities.
   d. None of the above.

7. Today, African-Americans are about _____ as likely to be murdered as are whites.
   a. Twice.
   b. Three times.
   c. Seven times.
   d. Fifteen times.

8. Which of the following is/are true of intraracial crime in America?
   a. African-American offenders generally tend to choose white victims.
   b. White Americans generally tend to victimize Hispanics.
   c. Rape is consistently shown to be an inter-racial crime.
   d. The majority of victims of African-American robbers are whites.

9. Which of the following African-Americans was involved in a much-publicized and video-taped incident in which he was brutally beaten by several Los Angeles law enforcement authorities?
   a. Willie Smith.
   b. Rodney King.
   c. O.J. Simpson.
   d. John Singleton.

10. Many black Americans:
    a. Feel verbally and physically harassed by the police.
    b. Feel that police protection in black neighborhoods is insufficient.
    c. Feel response by police to 911 calls to be slower in black than in white neighbor-hoods.
    d. All of the above.

11. In a 1987 decision (*McCleskey V. Kemp*), the U.S. Supreme Court found that:
    a. Scientific research showing evidence of racial discrimination is not sufficient to challenge the constitutionality of the death penalty.
    b. The death penalty is applied disproportionately to African-American citizens.
    c. The delay of supplying counsel for black defendants is a basis for a constitutional challenge of the death penalty.
    d. The death penalty is constitutional when sufficient witnesses view the execution.

12. What is an explanation of the relative lack of research attention given to the Hispanic community and criminal justice?
    a. Hispanics are not recorded in the official data.
    b. Hispanic crime is frequently viewed as a mirror image of that of blacks.
    c. Self-report surveys show little Hispanic crime.
    d. None of the above.

13. This group, _____, has found its American communities unable to absorb the rapidly increasing number of immigrants from the home country. Consequently, many gangs have developed which are involved in heroin trafficking and money laundering in such cities as San Francisco, Los Angeles, Boston, Vancouver, and New York.
    a. The Japanese.
    b. The Vietnamese.
    c. The Chinese.
    d. The Cubans.

14. **The category "Hispanic" used by the U.S. Census Bureau includes Spanish-speaking groups:**
    a. Having Mexican heritage.
    b. From Puerto Rico or Cuba.
    c. From Central or South America.
    d. All of the above.

15. **Which of the following is the numerically largest Hispanic group in the United States?**
    a. Puerto Rican-Americans.
    b. Mexican-Americans.
    c. Cuban-Americans.
    d. Brazilian-Americans.

16. **Which of the following is/are true of Native Americans? Native Americans have:**
    a. Low life expectancy.
    b. High rates of illiteracy.
    c. High rates of unemployment.
    d. All of the above.

17. **Native Americans are over-represented (relative to their proportion in the population):**
    a. In federal prisons.
    b. In state prisons in the southeast states of Alabama, Georgia, Florida, North and South Carolina.
    c. In the nationwide death row total.
    d. None of the above.

18. **Which type of offenses account for the majority of those for which noncitizens are prosecuted in federal courts?**
    a. Weapons offenses.
    b. Household crimes.
    c. Drug and immigration offenses.
    d. Commercial robberies.

19. **For which of the following white ethnic groups has organized crime served as a vehicle for upward mobility on the way to the American Dream?**
    a. German-Americans.
    b. Irish-Americans.
    c. Belgian-Americans.
    d. Spanish-Americans.

20. **Blacks are over-represented (relative to their proportion in the population):**
    a. In arrests for violent crime.
    b. In prison populations.
    c. In overall arrests for all offenses.
    d. All of the above.

True/False

T   F   1. In American society, public concern with crime and fear of personal victimization is primarily focused on African-Americans.

T   F   2. Hispanics are currently America's largest minority group.

T   F   3. Someone classified as "Hispanic" by the United States Bureau of the Census may be white, black, or a Native American person.

T   F   4. Research and writing on the role of African-Americans in the criminal justice system has increased markedly in the last twenty years.

T   F   5. At every stage of the criminal justice system, blacks are represented in numbers roughly equivalent to their number in the population generally.

T   F   6. Studies which investigate reported self-reported offending by the respondent are usually known as "victimization surveys."

T   F   7. One objection to the findings of self-report surveys is that these surveys focus too much upon less serious forms of crime.

T   F   8. Historically, African-Americans have been disproportionately more likely to be murdered than whites.

T   F   9. Recently, most scholars have come to agree with the view that racism has been virtually eliminated from the American criminal justice system.

T   F 10. Victimization surveys indicate that, as in the case of black citizens, a large proportion of Hispanic offenders victimize other Hispanics.

T   F 11. Japanese-Americans consistently have higher crime rates than do Chinese-Americans.

T   F 12. Asian-Americans have lower arrest rates than whites, blacks, or Native Americans.

T   F 13. The classification of the American population into various racial/ethnic groups has little impact upon those groups.

T   F 14. During the 1980s, drug-related arrest rates for blacks increased much faster than they did for whites.

T   F 15. Most researchers believe that the differences between the race and crime estimates of the Uniform Crime Report and those of self-report surveys is a result of the self-report over-emphasis upon less serious forms of crime.

T F   16. The annual victimization rates of the National Crime Victimization Survey indicate a generally higher level of violent victimization among whites than blacks.

T F   17. Crimes against African-Americans are more likely to involve guns.

T F   18. Victimization data and police data show an overall pattern of increasing victimization of the American population since 1975.

T F   19. Gun-related lethal violence has started to grow disproportionately among very young blacks.

T F   20. Offenders murdering whites are more likely to be given the death penalty than those murdering blacks.

Chapter Fifteen

Name_____ Date_____ Section_____

TEST QUESTIONS

Multiple Choice

1. **The concern for personal safety can be traced to:**
   a. Our tribal ancestors.
   b. The middle ages.
   c. The last century.
   d. The 1970s.

2. **The idea of crime prevention as an important function can be traced to:**
   a. Henry Fielding.
   b. Sir Robert Peel.
   c. J. Edgar Hoover.
   d. Herbert Hoover.

3. **In the _____ presidential election crime was made an issue for the first time.**
   a. 1996.
   b. 1992.
   c. 1980.
   d. 1964.

4. **There are three elements present when a crime has been committed. Select the *incorrect* answer.**
   a. The individual wants to commit the crime.
   b. The opportunity to commit a crime is present.
   c. The individual has the ability to commit the crime.
   d. The police are present.

5. **The goal of crime prevention is to:**
   a. Decrease crime.
   b. Eliminate crime.
   c. Protect property.
   d. None of the above are correct.

6. **Crime prevention programs can involve attempts to _____. Select the *incorrect* answer.**
   a. Reduce crime.
   b. Fear of crime.
   c. Eliminate annoying offenses.
   d. Only eliminate major crimes.

7. **_____established a Crime Victims Fund.**
   a. Victims Crime Act of 1984.
   b. Victims-Assistance Law of 1997.

8. _____programs are instituted to reduce crime and fear of crime.
   a. Neighborhood Watch.
   b. Victim-Assistance.

9. _____implies a smaller geographical area.
   a. Neighborhood.
   b. Community.

10. **The purpose of media campaigns is:**
    a. To receive positive publicity for crime prevention programs.
    b. To make the public aware of crime prevention strategies and programs.

11. **At the local level_____ can provide specific crime information targeted for certain neighborhoods.**
    a. Crime prevention TV show.
    b. Crime newsletters.

12. **The term defensible space can be traced to a conference held in 1964 in:**
    a. New York.
    b. Wichita, Kansas.
    c. St. Louis, Missouri.
    d. Pittsburgh, Pennsylvania.

13. **Situational crime prevention refers to:**
    a. Eliminating all violent crimes.
    b. Eliminating all property crimes.
    c. Reducing opportunities for crime.
    d. None of the above.

14. **Throughout the 1950s and 1960s the criminal justice system placed emphasize on:**
    a. Victim Assistance.
    b. Offender rehabilitation.

15. **_____initiated the first ten prosecutor-based victim/witness assistance programs.**
    a. LEAA.
    b. MPA.
    c. AJ.
    d. COP.

16. **_____was passed which reinforces the use of victim impact statements and proposed that states adopt similar laws.**
    a. Victim Restitution Act of 1995.
    b. Crime Control Act of 1994.

17. **The _____ was significant in that it led to a dramatic increase in victims rights and victim/witness service programs.**
    a. 1950s.
    b. 1960s.
    c. 1970s.
    d. 1980s.

18. **Most of the victim assistance legislation activity has been influenced by individuals who have been:**
    a. Offenders.
    b. Suspects.
    c. Effected by crime.
    d. None of the above.

19. **_____ reported in their 1967 report that victims were the neglected subjects in the study of crime.**
    a. Walker Report.
    b. Victims Report.
    c. The Challenge of Crime in a Free Society.
    d. None of the above.

20. **A negative aspect of situational crime prevention is the concern about:**
    a. Displacement.
    b. Crime decreasing.

True/False

T F 1. Kenneth Ferraro believes that crime is decreasing.

T F 2. Crime prevention involves education, training, and public relations.

T F 3. The National Crime Prevention Institute describes crime prevention as any kind of effort aimed at controlling crime.

T F 4. Neither government nor the private sector have been involved in crime prevention.

T F 5. Crime prevention programs involve attempts to reduce crime.

T F 6. Crime prevention is nonexistent among police departments.

T F 7. Neighborhood Watch programs are instituted to reduce the fear of crime.

T F 8. The community has no role to play in crime prevention.

T F 9. The police do not need the assistance of the community to prevent crime.

T F 10. Effective crime prevention can be obtained without community involvement.

T F 11. The term community has multiple definitions depending upon an individuals perceptions.

T F 12. Crime prevention strategies function more efficiently when specific geographical areas are focused upon.

T F 13. Police departments do not know where violent crimes occurs.

T F 14. A neighborhoods crime problem begins with decay which further deepens the spiral of destruction.

T F 15. The media can play an influential role in crime prevention strategies.

T F 16. Jefferies coined the phase defensible space.

T F 17. According to defensible space inhabitants of public housing cannot control disorder.

T F 18. Crime prevention and community policing are not interrelated.

T F 19. Victims play a vital role assisting police officers and prosecutors in bringing criminals to justice.

T F 20. Crimes hit hardest among the poor and uneducated.

Chapter Sixteen

Name_____ Date_____ Section_____

TEST QUESTIONS

Multiple Choice

1. When concern is with how a culture's attitudes, values, and norms regard the nature, role, and operation of law, reference is being made to a:
   a. Legal system.
   b. Legal tradition.
   c. Legal ritual.
   d. Legal perspective.

2. When concern is with the specific organization and procedures a political entity sets forth to carry out the justice process, reference is being made to a:
   a. Legal system.
   b. Legal tradition.
   c. Legal ritual.
   d. Legal perspective.

3. Of the four major legal traditions, the _____ is the oldest, relies on codification, and has roots back to Roman law:
   a. Civil.
   b. Common.
   c. Socialist.
   d. Islamic.

4. The primary source of law in the civil legal tradition is:
   a. Custom.
   b. Principles of the socialist revolution.
   c. Written code.
   d. Divine revelation.

5. The primary responsibility for responding to crime in Germany lies with the _____.
   a. Federal police.
   b. Uniformed municipal police.
   c. Plain-clothes state police.
   d. Military police.

6. The belief that truth will arise from a free and open competition over who has the correct facts is most descriptive of:
   a. The adversarial process.
   b. The inquisitorial process.
   c. Private vengeance.
   d. None of the above.

7. The inquisitorial process relies on procedurally active _____ and rather passive
_____.
   a. Judges / Lawyers
   b. Lawyers / Judges
   c. Defense attorneys /Pprosecuting attorneys
   d. Witnesses / Jurors

8. The adversarial process relies on procedurally active _____ and rather passive
_____.
   a. Judges / Lawyers
   b. Lawyers / Judges
   c. Defense attorneys / Prosecuting attorneys
   d. Witnesses / Jurors

9. What two factors decide a German day fine?
   a. Victim's complaint and the value of any property lost.
   b. Offender's attitude and victim's wishes.
   c. Offender's age and number of prior offenses.
   d. Seriousness of offense and the offender's income level.

10. Since common law was "unwritten" law, where did judges look to decide if an act
was criminal or not?
   a. Immemorial custom.
   b. Oral histories.
   c. Church documents.
   d. A fifteenth century French code.

11. In Canada, the designation of acts as criminal is primarily done at the _____
level.
   a. Federal.
   b. Provincial.
   c. Municipal.
   d. None of the above.

12. Which of the following is *not* one of the three categories of crime under Canada's
criminal code?
   a. Summary conviction offenses.
   b. Indictable offenses.
   c. Felony offenses.
   d. Hybrid offenses.

13. John has received a 3 year sentence for burglary in Canada. Under whose jurisdiction will John be placed to serve that sentence?
   a. Federal government.
   b. Provincial government.
   c. Municipal government.
   d. None of the above.

14. The neighborhood police in China are responsible for:
   a. Patrolling neighborhoods.
   b. Crime investigation.
   c. Registration of people moving in and out of the neighborhood.
   d. All of the above.

15. **In China, "people's assessors" are:**
    a. Auxiliary police.
    b. Lay jurors.
    c. Defense attorneys.
    d. Witnesses paid by the communist party.

16. **Which of the following educational topics is most likely to be covered in a Chinese prison?**
    a. Mathematics.
    b. Religion.
    c. Auto mechanics.
    d. Benefits of collectivism.

17. **Which of the following is *not* a category of crime as identified in the Shari'a?**
    a. Hudud.
    b. Quesas.
    c. Hanafi.
    d. Ta'azir.

18. **In Saudi Arabia, adjudication lies primarily with:**
    a. A jury of peers (although they will all be male).
    b. A mixed bench of professional judges and lay people.
    c. A single judge.
    d. None of the above.

19. **In Islam, the book that is considered the word of God (Allah) is the:**
    a. Sunna.
    b. Qur'an.
    c. Giyas.
    d. Ijma.

20. **Why, under Islamic law, is it important which party in a dispute gets to challenge the other to take an oath?**
    a. The first person to swear automatically wins the case.
    b. The person who challenges the other does not have to present as many witnesses to support his claims.
    c. Lying under oath is not as serious if the person lying was first challenged by another person.
    d. The person who takes an oath cannot be punished by amputation.

True/False

T F   1. Although countries do not duplicate legal systems, it is possible for countries to share legal traditions.

T F   2. The civil legal tradition promotes the idea that crime exists only through legislation enacted by a legitimate authority.

T F   3. Canada is an example of a country following the civil legal tradition.

T F 4. For all crimes other than the most serious ones (e.g., murder and aggravated assault), German trials are held before a panel consisting entirely of lay judges.

T F 5. The Corpus Juris Civilis, codified the civil law of France.

T F 6. Rather than a competition between opposing sides, the inquisitorial adjudication process is more like a continuing investigation.

T F 7. Under common law, cases are decided by reference to specific codes prepared by the monarch or the legislature.

T F 8. The Constitutions of Clarendon was one of the earliest examples of the civil legal tradition's codification of law.

T F 9. A majority of Canada's ten provinces have chosen to contract with the federal government for police services and therefore have Mounties serving as provincial police.

T F 10. Adjudication in Chinese courts is entirely in the hands of a single judge.

T F 11. An important aspect of the socialist legal tradition, especially as it operates in China, is that the justice process be entirely formal.

T F 12. As a result of socialist principles, China has abandoned the death penalty as a penalty for criminal behavior.

T F 13. It is possible for Chinese prisoners to reduce their sentence length through good behavior.

T F 14. The Human Rights Watch reports that Chinese prisons are remarkably safe and secure places where inmates are protected from harm by guards and each other.

T F 15. The source of law under the Islamic legal tradition is action by the Caliph, or leader.

T F 16. The two main elements of Islamic law are the Qur'an and the Torah.

T F 17. Under Islamic law, it is a crime to eat pork or drink alcohol.

T F 18. Most Muslim scholars maintain that evidence in criminal cases must be restricted to confession of the accused or eyewitness testimony.

T F 19. Forgiveness is as important a concept in Islamic law as is retribution.

T F 20. In some Shari'a courts, the testimony of one female is considered to be worth that of two males.